Integrating Psychotherapy and Psychopharmacology

Integrating Psychotherapy and Psychopharmacology: A Handbook for Clinicians is a practical guide for the growing number of mental health practitioners searching for information on treatments that combine psychopharmacology, psychotherapy, and psychosocial rehabilitation. Research shows that combined approaches are among the most effective ways to treat an increasing number of psychiatric disorders. However, though these combined treatments are becoming the everyday practice of psychiatrists, psychologists, and other mental health professionals, identifying the right treatment plan can be notoriously difficult, and clinicians are often left scrambling to answer questions about how to design and customize their treatment strategies. In *Integrating Psychotherapy and Psychopharmacology*, readers will find these questions fully addressed and the answers explained, and they'll come away from the book with a toolbox full of strategies for helping their patients improve symptoms, achieve remission, and stay well using a combination of drug and psychological treatments.

Irismar Reis de Oliveira, MD, PhD, is a professor of psychiatry in the department of neurosciences and mental health at the Federal University of Bahia, Brazil. He is the creator of trial-based cognitive therapy and has trained therapists in Brazil and other countries in this model. Dr. de Oliveira also maintains a private practice and is the editor of *Standard and Innovative Strategies in Cognitive Behavior Therapy*.

Thomas Schwartz, MD, is a professor in the department of psychiatry at SUNY Upstate Medical University in Syracuse, New York, where he is also director of adult psychiatric clinical services, assistant director for psychiatric medical students, and director of the Depression and Anxiety Disorders Research Program. Dr. Schwartz also maintains a private practice and consults for the Indian Health Service, the Neuroscience Education Institute, pharmaceutical companies, and associated industries as well. He is the coeditor of *Depression: Treatment Strategies and Management*, 2nd edition.

Stephen M. Stahl, MD, PhD, is an adjunct professor of psychiatry at the University of California–San Diego, chairman of the Neuroscience Education Institute, and an honorary visiting senior fellow at the University of Cambridge. He is the author of over 450 articles and chapters; more than 1,200 scientific presentations and abstracts; and the author of many books, including the best-selling and award-winning *Stahl's Essential Psychopharmacology*, and *The Prescriber's Guide*, both now in their fourth editions, and the recently published series of clinical cases, *Case Studies: Stahl's Essential Psychopharmacology.*

Psychopharmacology and Psychotherapy in Clinical Practice
Bret A. Moore, PsyD, ABPP, Series Editor

Anxiety Disorders: A Guide for Integrating Psychopharmacology and Psychotherapy
by Stephen M. Stahl and Bret A. Moore

Integrating Psychotherapy and Psychopharmacology: A Handbook for Clinicians
by Irismar Reis de Oliveira, Thomas Schwartz, and Stephen M. Stahl

Integrating Psychotherapy and Psychopharmacology

A Handbook for Clinicians

Edited by
Irismar Reis de Oliveira, Thomas Schwartz, and
Stephen M. Stahl

Routledge
Taylor & Francis Group

NEW YORK AND LONDON

First published 2014
by Routledge
711 Third Avenue, New York, NY 10017

Simultaneously published in the UK
by Routledge
27 Church Road, Hove, East Sussex BN3 2FA

Library of Congress Cataloging-in-Publication Data

Integrating psychotherapy and psychopharmacology : a handbook for clinicians / edited by Irismar Reis de Oliveira, Thomas Schwartz and Stephen M. Stahl.
    pages cm
Includes bibliographical references and index.
1. Psychology, Pathological. 2. Mental illness—Treatment. 3. Psychotherapy.
4. Psychopharmacology. I. Oliveira, Irismar Reis de, editor of compilation. II. Schwartz, Thomas L., editor of compilation. III. Stahl, Stephen M., 1951– editor of compilation.
    RC454.I53 2014
    616.89′14—dc23
    2013021464

ISBN: 978-0-415-52997-6 (hbk)
ISBN: 978-0-415-83857-3 (pbk)
ISBN: 978-0-203-11732-3 (ebk)

Typeset in Minion
by Apex CoVantage, LLC

Printed and bound in the United States of America by Sheridan Books, Inc. (a Sheridan Group Company).

Contents

Figures

Tables

Contributors

Josué Bacaltchuk, Janssen Pharmaceutica, São Paulo, Brazil.

Christopher S. Brown, Department of Behavioral Health, Madigan Army Medical Center, Tacoma, Washington, USA.

Irismar Reis de Oliveira, Department of Neurosciences and Mental Health, Post Graduate Program, University Hospital, Federal University of Bahia, Brazil.

Mantosh J. Dewan, SUNY Upstate Medical University, Department of Psychiatry, Syracuse, New York, USA.

Karl Doghramji, Department of Psychiatry and Human Behavior, Department of Neurology, Department of Medicine, Thomas Jefferson University, Philadelphia, Pennsylvania, USA.

Manfred Döpfner, Department of Child and Adolescent Psychiatry and Psychotherapy, University Clinic, Cologne, Germany.

Wei Du, Department of Psychiatry, Drexel University College of Medicine, Philadelphia, Pennsylvania, USA.

Kauy M. Faria, Institute of Psychiatry, University of São Paulo Medical School, São Paulo, Brazil.

Edward S. Friedman, Department of Psychiatry, University of Pittsburgh School of Medicine, Pittsburgh, Pennsylvania, USA.

Roger P. Greenberg, SUNY Upstate Medical University, Department of Psychiatry, Syracuse, New York, USA.

John Greist, University of Wisconsin School of Medicine and Public Health and CEO of Healthcare Technology Systems, Madison, Wisconsin, USA.

Anıl Gündüz, Marmara University, School of Medicine, Istanbul, Turkey.

Phillipa J. Hay, Centre for Health Research, School of Medicine, University of Western Sydney, Sydney, and School of Medicine, James Cook University, Townsville, Australia.

S. Cory Harmon, Department of Behavioral Health, Madigan Army Medical Center, Tacoma, Washington, USA.

Aaron M. Koenig, Department of Psychiatry, University of Pittsburgh School of Medicine, Pittsburgh, Pennsylvania, USA.

Brian Johnson, SUNY Upstate Medical University, Department of Psychiatry, Syracuse, New York, USA.

Dimitri Markov, Thomas Jefferson University, Department of Psychiatry and Human Behavior, Philadelphia, Pennsylvania, USA.

Alice Medalia, Department of Psychiatry, Columbia University Medical Center, New York, New York, USA.

Bret A. Moore, University of Texas Health Science Center at San Antonio, San Antonio, Texas, USA.

Tais S. Moriyama, National Institute of Developmental Psychiatry for Children and Adolescents, INCT-CNPq, Porto Alegre, RS, Brazil, and Institute of Psychiatry, University of São Paulo Medical School, São Paulo, Brazil.

Lewis A. Opler, Department of Psychiatry, New York University School of Medicine, New York, New York, USA.

Mark G. Opler, Department of Psychiatry, New York University School of Medicine, New York, New York, USA.

Guilherme V. Polanczyk, National Institute of Developmental Psychiatry for Children and Adolescents, INCT-CNPq, Brazil, and Institute of Psychiatry, University of São Paulo Medical School, São Paulo, Brazil.

Luis A. Rohde, National Institute of Developmental Psychiatry for Children and Adolescents, INCT-CNPq, Porto Alegre, RS, Brazil.

Shilpa Sachdeva, SUNY Upstate Medical University, Department of Psychiatry, Syracuse, New York, USA.

Thomas L. Schwartz, SUNY Upstate Medical University, Department of Psychiatry, Syracuse, New York, USA.

David S. Shearer, Department of Family Medicine, Madigan Army Medical Center, Tacoma, Washington, USA.

Stephen M. Stahl, Department of Psychiatry, University of California, San Diego, San Diego, California, USA, and Cambridge University, Cambridge, UK.

Diane St. Fleur, SUNY Upstate Medical University, Department of Psychiatry, Syracuse, New York, USA.

Donna M. Sudak, Department of Psychiatry, Drexel University College of Medicine, Philadelphia, Pennsylvania, USA.

Mehmet Z. Sungur, Marmara University, School of Medicine, Istanbul, Turkey.

Fernanda S. Terzi, Institute of Psychiatry, University of São Paulo Medical School, São Paulo, Brazil.

Michael E. Thase, Perelman School of Medicine of the University of Pennsylvania and the Philadelphia Veterans Affairs Medical Center, Philadelphia, Pennsylvania, USA.

Stephen Touyz, School of Psychology and Discipline of Psychiatry, Executive Chair, Centre for Eating and Dieting Disorders, University of Sydney, Sydney, Australia.

Amy Wenzel, Department of Psychiatry, University of Pennsylvania School of Medicine, Philadelphia, Pennsylvania, USA.

Foreword

Both psychotherapy and medications are efficacious in the treatment of a wide range of psychiatric disorders, and the two are often combined. Neither is a panacea, but each monotherapy often has its uses, and the combination often improves on either one alone. In most instances, the empirically supported psychotherapies rival medications in the treatment of the nonpsychotic disorders; medication tends to work a little faster (by a matter of weeks) and to be a bit more robust (depending less on the skill of the therapist), whereas psychotherapy tends to have a broader effect and is often more enduring. For the psychotic disorders, medication treatment is usually primary, with psychotherapy playing an adjunctive role at best. The personality disorders are simply hard to treat with either.

It remains unclear how best to integrate psychotherapy and medications when the two are to be combined. That is the stated mission of this text. Schwartz and Sachdeva lead off with an integrative approach to combining psychotherapy and medications, and de Oliveira follows up with a description of a new cognitive behavioral approach called trial-based cognitive therapy (TBCT). Subsequent chapters focused on depression (Koenig, Friedman, and Thase), bipolar disorder (Sudak and Du), psychosis (Medalia, Opler, and Opler), anxiety disorders (Shearer, Brown, Harmon, and Moore), eating disorders (Hay, Bacaltchuk, and Touyz), ADHD (Moriyama et al.), insomnia (Doghramji and Markov), addiction (St. Fleur and Johnson), perinatal distress (Wenzel), sexual disorders (Sungur and Gündüz), computer applications (Greist), and psychosocial component in biological treatments (Greenberg and Dewan). All are marvelous.

The process is not always an easy one, as I will illustrate with respect to unipolar depression, the area that I know best. Both psychotherapy and medications are efficacious (in the sense that each is better than its absence) and both tend to be specific (in the sense of exceeding nonspecific controls) in the treatment of patients with more severe depressions, but it is not clear that either is as efficacious as the published literature makes it out to be or as specific as theory would suggest. The apparent efficacy of each monotherapy has been inflated by publication bias (Cuijper, Smit, Bohlmeijer, Hollon, and Andersson, 2010; Turner, Matthews, Linardatos, Tell, and Rosenthal, 2008), and neither exceeds nonspecific controls with patients with less severe depressions (Driessen, Cuijpers, Hollon, and Dekker, 2010). Both monotherapies clearly work (publication bias only inflates the apparent efficacy of each by about a third); they just do not work as well as the published literature would lead one to believe. Similarly, it is not that patients with less severe depressions do not benefit from treatment (most get better and more get better than would in its absence); it is just that when they do, they do so for nonspecific reasons related to simply coming in for treatment.

Combined treatment tends to improve on either monotherapy, but not by a lot. Each monotherapy tends to produce response rates of around 60% (with about half of those patients meeting criteria for remission) and combined treatment typically only boosts those rates by about 10%–15%. The two monotherapies clearly share overlapping processes or else the benefits of putting the two together would more nearly sum. What is more likely to be the case is that each monotherapy picks off patients that the other does not help; this is an instance of moderation that enhances the overall proportion of patients who are helped (Hollon et al., 2005). This is a pragmatic advantage for combined treatment.

The conventional wisdom is that combined treatment retains any advantage associated with either monotherapy. If medications work a little faster than psychotherapy, then combined treatment does as well. If psychotherapy has a broader effect on the quality of relationships, then combined treatment does that too. The one aspect of response that may not follow that general rule has to do with the long-term enduring effects produced by the cognitive and behavior therapies. Patients treated to remission with cognitive therapy or behavioral activation tend to be only about half as likely to relapse following treatment termination as patients treated to remission with medications (Hollon, Stewart, & Strunk, 2006). However, it is not clear that this holds when psychotherapy is combined with medications (Forand, DeRubeis, & Amsterdam, 2013). Combined treatment clearly undercuts the enduring effects of cognitive behavior therapy in the treatment of panic and the anxiety disorders and there are concerns that the same may be true for depression. Moreover, there are growing concerns that the antidepressant medications may suppress symptoms at the expense of worsening the course of the underlying disorder (Andrews, Kornstein, Halberstadt, Gardner, and Neale, 2011). What typically has been interpreted as an enduring effect for cognitive behavior therapy might turn out to be a long-term iatrogenic effect for psychotropic medications.

How this will all play out remains to be seen, but the pros and cons of combined treatment may turn out to be more difficult to discern than was previously thought. The chapters in this compilation should help the process along. They are bold, they are thoughtful, and they cut right to the heart of the clinical situation. This text should prove to be a most valuable addition to the clinical armamentarium.

Stephen Hollon

REFERENCES

Andrews, P. W., Kornstein, S. G., Halberstadt, L. J., Gardner, C. O., & Neale, M. C. (2011). Blue again: Perturbational effects of antidepressants suggest monoaminergic homeostasis in major depression. *Frontiers in Psychology, 2*, article 159.

Cuijpers, P., Smit, F., Bohlmeijer, E., Hollon, S. D., & Andersson, G. (2010). Is the efficacy of cognitive behaviour therapy and other psychological treatments for adult depression overestimated? A meta-analytic study of publication bias. *British Journal of Psychiatry, 196*, 173–178.

Driessen, E., Cuijpers, P., Hollon, S. D., & Dekker, J. J. M. (2010). Does pretreatment severity moderate the efficacy of psychological treatment of adult outpatient depression? A meta-analysis. *Journal of Consulting and Clinical Psychology, 78*, 668–680.

Forand, N. R., DeRubeis, R. J., & Amsterdam, J. A. (2013). Combining medication and psychotherapy in the treatment of major mental disorders. In M. J. Lambert (Ed.), *Garfield and Bergin's handbook of psychotherapy and behavior change* (6th ed., pp. 735–774). New York: Wiley.

Fournier, J. C., DeRubeis, R. J., Hollon, S. D., Dimidjian, S., Amsterdam, J. D., Shelton, R. C., & Fawcett, J. (2010). Antidepressant drug effects and depression severity: A patient-level meta-analysis. *Journal of the American Medical Association, 303*, 47–53.

Hollon, S. D., Jarrett, R. B., Nierenberg, A. A., Thase, M. E., Trivedi, M., & Rush, A. J. (2005). Psychotherapy and medication in the treatment of adult and geriatric depression: Which monotherapy or combined treatment? *Journal of Clinical Psychiatry, 66*, 455–468.

Hollon, S. D., Stewart, M. O., & Strunk, D. (2006). Cognitive behavior therapy has enduring effects in the treatment of depression and anxiety. *Annual Review of Psychology, 57*, 285–315.

Turner, E. H., Matthews, A. M., Linardatos, E., Tell, R. A., & Rosenthal, R. (2008). Selective publication of antidepressant trials and its influence on apparent efficacy. *NEJM, 358*, 252–260.

Preface

A paradigm shift is afoot today in mental health practices: namely, a resurgence of interest in evidence-based psychotherapies and in combining them with selected psychotropic medications. Traditionally, rivalries have grown up around "biological psychiatry" versus "psychotherapy" with turf wars between psychiatry and psychology, as well as lack of consensus as to which drug or which psychotherapy to use for a given disorder or patient. The idea that patients should be treated either by psychiatrist–psychopharmacologists or by psychologist–psychotherapists but not by both is rapidly falling out of favor and is seen as old fashioned and not very enlightened. Mental health training programs and psychiatry residencies throughout the United States, for example, are emphasizing psychotherapy training to a much greater extent than in past years. Research in psychotherapy is increasing exponentially, while the pace of innovation of new chemical entities is slowing. The realization is dawning that the best outcomes may be provided for many patients, and for many psychiatric disorders, by combining psychotherapy with psychopharmacology. Not only is this common sense with a great deal of face validity, but there is a growing evidence base for this, much of which is reviewed in this volume. There are even neurobiological underpinnings for combining psychotropic drugs with psychotherapies, which I have reviewed elsewhere (Stahl, 2011). The idea here is that if psychotropic drugs can alter downstream expression of genes, and so can learning experiences such as psychotherapy, then maybe drugs and psychotherapy can work together in combination to create an outcome, which is greater than the sum of its parts (Stahl, 2011). To the extent that there is evidence for this across a wide berth of psychiatric disorders, that evidence is reviewed in the chapters that follow.

Although "evidence-based medicine" has long been the standard for drug trials, for regulatory approvals of new drugs, and for treatment guidelines for selecting which drug for which patient, the efficacy of psychotherapies has begun to follow this approach as well, namely based upon randomized controlled trials. If "evidence-based psychotherapy" is somewhat in its adolescence, combination of psychopharmacology with psychotherapy is in its infancy, as the reader can determine from those sections reviewing the evidence base for combination treatment in the various chapters in this book. Here we have an up-to-date status report on the state of the art of drug treatment, psychotherapeutic treatment, and their combination, an evidence base that is rapidly changing, and which the reader will want to know as this is increasingly forming the basis of modern "best practices" in mental healthcare.

Specifically, this book includes a collection of internationally renowned investigators, clinicians, and authors, who review the vast waterfront of mental disorders, one by one, with chapters organized into three sections: evidence for the efficacy of psychotherapy, for psychopharmacology, and for their combination. I have had the pleasure to do a similar exercise covering the wide range of anxiety disorders in depth in another book in this series with Bret Moore (Stahl & Moore, 2012). Dr. Moore contributes with his coauthors a chapter on anxiety disorders here as well. This book, however, is broader in scope and covers many other disorders and conditions, as can be seen from the table of contents.

Just as there is no single drug for all patients, so there is no single psychotherapy for all patients. Here, not only are a number of classes of psychotropic agents reviewed, so are numerous specific, "manualized" (i.e., available in written manuals for standardization and training) psychotherapies. There is even a chapter on psychotherapy by computer. "Prescriptive" psychotherapies and evidence-based combinations of psychotherapies with drugs are the directions of current research and clinical practice. Hopefully, the reader will enjoy capturing this approach, which can be difficult to find, particularly in one place anywhere else in the literature. Applying the evidence and the lessons presented here may even help the clinician capture what is sometimes called the delightful synergy of "bad math," where the combination of best practices for psychotropic drug selection with the best practices for psychotherapy selection for an individual patient with a specific mental disorder leads to $1 + 1 = 10$ for effectiveness.

Stephen M. Stahl

REFERENCES

Stahl, S. M. (2011). Psychotherapy as an epigenetic "drug": Psychiatric therapeutics target symptoms linked to malfunctioning brain circuits with psychotherapy as well as with drugs. *Journal of Clinical Pharmacy and Therapeutics, 37,* 249–253.

Stahl, S. M., & Moore, B. A. (2012). *Anxiety disorders: A concise guide and casebook for psychopharmacology and psychotherapy integration.* New York: Routledge.

Series Editor Introduction

Psychopharmacology and Psychotherapy in Clinical Practice (PPCP) is one of Routledge's newest book series. Guided by the goal of informing students and practitioners on the latest clinical and translational research in psychopharmacology, psychotherapy, and the integration of the two, PPCP recruits the world's foremost experts in their respective fields. *Integrating Psychotherapy and Psychopharmacology* is the second of the series.

Editors Irismar Reis de Oliveira, MD, PhD; Thomas Schwartz, MD; and Stephen M. Stahl, MD, PhD, bring together a highly impressive group of psychiatrists and psychologists and deliver a groundbreaking work that explores the importance, practice, and intricacies of integrated treatment. These authors delve into the existing literature on combining medication and psychotherapy for a variety of disorders and present the findings in a comprehensive, but easily understandable, fashion. This is a unique accomplishment for a book of this scope and focus. The credentials of the editors are also of significance. Dr. de Oliveira is Professor of Psychiatry at Federal University of Bahia, Brazil, and developer of trial-based cognitive therapy (TBCT). TBCT is quickly gaining popularity among psychopharmacologists as an adjunct to pharmacotherapy. To date, the science supports its use. Thomas Schwartz is Professor of Psychiatry and Behavioral Sciences and Director of the Adult Psychiatry Clinic at SUNY Upstate Medical University. He has published numerous papers on combining psychotherapy and psychopharmacology in the amelioration of psychiatric disorders. Stephen M. Stahl is one of the most prominent psychiatrists and psychopharmacologists today. The author of over 450 articles and chapters and bestselling author of *Stahl's Essential Psychopharmacology* and *The Prescriber's Guide*, Dr. Stahl brings his vast knowledge and expertise to the book, which serves as its foundation.

As the editors aptly point out in the book's preface, a paradigm shift is occurring within the field of mental health. Familiarity with and use of evidence-based psychosocial interventions among psychopharmacologists is becoming the rule and not the exception. Psychologists and other mental health specialists who focus primarily on psychosocial treatments are gaining greater clarity on how medications can enhance the effectiveness of evidence-based psychotherapies.

Indeed, the interest in the benefits and best practices of integrated treatment is relatively new. However, much is being learned at a rapid pace. Spawned by recognized limitations in either modality as a standalone approach, it is my belief that integrated treatment will continue to gain attention within the academic and practice communities. *Integrating Psychotherapy and Psychopharmacology* is a great model volume to lead the way.

Bret A. Moore, PsyD, ABPP
Series Editor
Psychopharmacology and Psychotherapy in Clinical Practice

Integrating Psychotherapy and Psychopharmacology
Outcomes, Endophenotypes, and Theoretical Underpinnings Regarding Effectiveness

Thomas L. Schwartz and Shilpa Sachdeva

INTRODUCTION

This book strives to provide to the reader a compendium of information regarding specific psychiatric disorders and their amenability to be treated with integrated psychotherapy and psychopharmacology approaches. Evidence-based information will be provided, and in its absence, theoretical approaches and explanations will be given to explain why integration and simultaneous use of these two treatment modalities should make both biological and psychological sense to the practitioner and the patient. This introductory chapter will first review some typical integrative studies and their outcomes, where a specific psychotherapy technique and/or a specific psychopharmacological intervention were provided to patients with a defined psychiatric disorder. Clinical outcomes will be discussed briefly to set a tone for the following, psychiatric-disorder specific, chapters in this book where more in-depth analyses will be forthcoming. More important than reviewing initial hallmark outcomes, this chapter will briefly discuss endophenotypic neuroimaging findings regarding treatment integration and will finally attempt to theoretically explain why combining medications and psychotherapy makes sense from a neuroscience, or biological, perspective.

The chapters that follow will provide more in-depth information on key psychiatric disorders such as schizophrenia, depression, anxiety disorders, sleep, and substance use disorders. The final chapter will present itself as a foil to this introductory one, and the psychosocial aspects of prescribing psychopharmacological agents will be discussed and explained. In this way, the reader will have come full circle and will be able to appreciate the integrated treatment approach that this chapter will introduce called *psychopharmacopsychotherapy* (PPPT). PPPT should allow the prescribing clinician to engage in providing a greater amount of care, making intuitive sense, theoretical sense, and evidence-based sense from a biopsychosocial approach.

OUTCOME-BASED STUDIES ON INTEGRATED TREATMENT

Regarding major depressive disorder (MDD), one of the most commonly diagnosed and treated psychiatric disorders, there is likely the largest evidence base of completed studies regarding psychotherapy, psychopharmacology, and integrated treatment (PPPT) available. In deciding the course and type of treatment, numerous factors must be taken into account by the clinician, including pivotally, the severity of the depression (Thase et al., 1997). The greater the severity of MDD likely warrants more antidepressant medication utilization. Mild to moderate symptoms could easily be treated by psychotherapy and/or psychopharmacology independently. In fact, United Kingdom guidelines clearly denote that mild MDD should be treated with psychotherapy only, but combining treatments may be considered as severity increases (National Institute for Health and Clinical Excellence [NICE], 2009).

Some authors suggest strongly that depressed patients with personality disorders often have a decreased response to psychopharmacology alone compared to those without any Axis II symptomatology (Reich & Vasile, 1993; Thase, 1996). Specifically, it has been shown that patients with cluster A or cluster B personality pathology appear to have less satisfactory results to medication management than those with cluster C symptoms (Wilberg et al., 1998; Peselow, Sanfilipo, Fieve, & Gulbenkian, 1994). It also appears that MDD patients who have suffered trauma or abuse in childhood will preferentially respond to psychotherapy plus an antidepressant, while those without a trauma history appear to do well on an antidepressant alone (Nemeroff et al., 2003). As it is often the norm that clinicians treat comorbidity rather than single disorders, these integrated, combined approaches make intuitive sense (Schwartz & Rashid, 2007).

It is important to delineate up front that a majority of the following studies were conducted in patients with clear Axis I disorders and often with a relative lack of Axis I and Axis II comorbidity. Levels of psychiatric symptoms were often noted to be at a moderate degree, as subjects with severe depression may not be competent or capable of receiving informed consent or completing full study participation, and subjects with mild MDD symptoms may not have been ill enough to enter an experimental drug study for MDD.

We begin our MDD review with a key example: Keller et al. (2000) observed that the combined and integrated treatment of nefazodone (a serotonin agonist-reuptake inhibitor approved antidepressant) and cognitive behavioral analysis (CBASP) was significantly more efficacious than either treatment when used alone. This study was conducted with a stringent design and statistical analysis (Keller et al., 2000). It should be considered a hallmark study where integrated, evidence-based psychotherapy *and* pharmacotherapy, or psychopharmacopsychotherapy (PPPT) for short, together yielded a superior outcome result for subjects. This makes factual sense given this study's outcome and makes intuitive clinical sense that combining *two* active treatments should allow for better MDD response rates than *one* modality alone. Theoretically, understanding why PPPT works from a neuroscience and psychosocial point of view will be discussed later in this chapter and throughout the book.

To broaden the discussion regarding MDD, a trial by de Jonghe, Kool, van Aalst, Dekker, and Peen (2001) found that the combined PPPT (with psychodynamic supportive psychotherapy) was more effective than pharmacotherapy alone in their treatment. The psychotherapy here was short term, with sixteen 45-minute sessions, and the medication protocol included fluoxetine, amitriptyline, or moclobemide. At 24 weeks, the mean success rate in the pharmacotherapy alone versus combined medication plus psychotherapy group was 40.7% and 59.2%, respectively. This particular study was limited in that it did not have a psychotherapy-only arm, and patients were allowed to choose not to be involved in the pharmacotherapy-only treatment arm. A second de Jonghe et al. (2004) study used short-term psychodynamic supportive therapy alone or in combination with venlafaxine (SNRI), a selective serotonin norepinephrine reuptake inhibitor (SNRI), nortriptyline (TCA), or nortriptyline plus lithium. It found no distinction between psychotherapy alone compared to when PPPT was utilized in regards to objective Hamilton Rating Scale data. However, subjective patient responses on the Symptom Check List were significant for greater symptom improvement in the combined treatment group. This particular study was limited in that it did not have a psychopharmacology-only arm, and patients were allowed to choose not to be involved in the combination treatment arm due to fear of medication side effects.

A study conducted by Kool, Dekker, Duijsens, de Jonghe, and Puite (2003) observed that for MDD, a PPPT approach was more effective than pharmacotherapy alone. They also concluded that the combined therapy was more effective with patients with coexisting personality disorders. Bellino, Zizza, Rinaldi, and Bogetto (2006) studied MDD with comorbid borderline personality disorder (BPD) subjects and compared the combination of fluoxetine and interpersonal psychotherapy (IPT) with fluoxetine alone. Neither group showed a significant difference in MDD *remission* rates, although combination therapy showed significant positive differences in depressive symptoms, relationship satisfaction, and quality of life.

Regarding data in adolescents, the Treatment for Adolescents with Depression Study (TADS) observed that response rates to cognitive behavioral therapy (CBT) and fluoxetine PPPT were higher than with CBT alone or pharmacotherapy alone (Emslie et al., 2006).

The STAR*D (Sequenced Treatment Alternatives to Relieve Depression) trial and others suggest that psychotherapy used as augmentation of pharmacotherapy (psychotherapy added sequentially after incomplete antidepressant response) had a better impact on clinical symptoms of MDD than medication alone (Harley, Sprich, Safren, Jacob, & Fava, 2008; Thase et al., 2007). Furthermore, the REVAMP (Research Evaluating the Value of Augmenting Medication With Psychotherapy) trial evaluated MDD patients with incomplete antidepressant responses and placed subjects into one of several groups: (a) continued pharmacotherapy plus augmentation with cognitive behavioral analysis system of psychotherapy (CBASP), (b) continued pharmacotherapy and augmentation with brief supportive psychotherapy (BSP), and (c) continued optimized pharmacotherapy (MEDS) alone, and determined that neither augmentation psychotherapy modality nor continued psychopharmacology alone significantly improved MDD outcomes from a superiority point of view (Kocsis et al., 2009).

This equivocal finding is a segue to a disclaimer that the evidence base in MDD, and in other psychiatric disorders, clearly has both positive and negative findings. Sometimes comparing trials has an "apples and oranges" effect. The REVAMP trial was attempting to determine whether a strictly manualized CBASP would outperform a treatment as usual supportive psychotherapy condition. Studies in previous paragraphs utilized CBASP as combination treatment effectively. Other studies revealed success with psychodynamic psychotherapy. Therefore, validation and evaluation of the stringency of these studies warrants attention. The positive studies above and throughout this chapter are discussed initially to set the stage for a more theoretical discussion later in this chapter regarding the concept that psychotherapy plus pharmacotherapy makes biological and neuroscientific sense.

In regards to bipolar disorder, there is certainly less data and evidence base for combination treatment, or PPPT. Treatment guidelines often do not support using monotherapy, unipolar antidepressants as front line treatment as they are utilized in MDD (American Psychiatric Association, 2012). Oftentimes, mood stabilizing agents are used to treat both mania and depression. Finally, psychotherapy as a treatment for mania, alone or combined with a pharmacotherapy, is often fraught with ineffectiveness, as manic patients tend to lack insight regarding their behavior or even experience any motivation to change, since mania is an illness of denial. A review by Hollon and Ponniah evaluated bipolar disorder, cognitive behavioral therapy (CBT), and family-focused psychotherapy and found that these psychotherapies were effective adjunctives to medications for depressed phases only, and possibly useful for preventing future bipolar episodes of either pole as well. Psychoeducation has also been found to be effective in the prevention of mania/hypomania and possibly depression when added to consistent mood stabilization with psychopharmacology approaches (Hollon & Ponniah, 2010).

Another group determined that, in regards to bipolar disorder, supportive psychoeducation given to the individual patient statistically lowered the chances of mania, mixed features, and depression. Furthermore, when this type of therapy was applied to the patient's family and support system, it further reduced relapse into mania. Schmitz, Averill, Sayre, McCleary, Moeller, and Swann (2002) reviewed patients with bipolar disorder and comorbid substance misuse and randomly assigned 46 individuals to either 12 weeks medication monitoring alone or in combination with CBT, and found that the latter allowed for greater medication adherence based on patient self-report, as well as, consistent blood level maintenance of mood stabilizers. It is often assumed, and a well-noted clinical phenomenon, that when medication adherence increases, outcomes likely improve or are maintained longer. Lam et al. conducted studies with patients who were randomized to receive either "minimal psychiatric care" alone or with the addition of CBT for relapse prevention for 6 months. The patients in the experimental PPPT condition reported significantly greater compliance immediately after treatment and this extended to 18 and 24 months after CBT, although not at the 12-month assessment in longer-term assessments (Lam et al., 2003; Lam, Hayward, Watkins, Wright, & Sham, 2005). Many of these bipolar trials again focused on depression, not mania. Oftentimes, outcomes were measured in terms of medication adherence, which again, clinically should yield better maintenance of response and help in prophylaxis against relapse.

A more formal discussion regarding the treatment of anxiety disorder occurs later in this book and an in-depth review is well covered by Stahl and Moore (2013) in a separate publication. Here, as an introduction to integrated anxiety disorder treatment, panic disordered (PD) patients are the most often studied via CBT protocols, and it is considered a very effective standalone treatment. CBT can improve panic attacks, phobic avoidance, generalized anxiety, and anticipatory anxiety (Oei, Llamas, & Evans, 1997; Steketee & Shapiro, 1995). Oei et al. (1997) found that preexisting anxiety medication regimes did not affect long-term outcome of brief intensive group CBT in panic disorder (PD) with or without agoraphobia. Beurs, van Balkom, Lange, Koele, and van Dyke (1995) conducted a comparative outcome study and found that the PPPT fluvoxamine (SSRI) plus exposure in vivo demonstrated efficacy superior to that of any single modality treatment with double the effect size on self-reported agoraphobic avoidance.

There have been several other systematic evaluations by Sharp et al. (1996) and Marks et al. (1993) comparing CBT in combination with medications like fluvoxamine (SSRI) and alprazolam (benzodiazepine), and their findings suggest that both CBT and medications are effective individually, although the combination of both is more effective. SSRIs plus exposure and response prevention-based CBT are both established treatments for obsessive-compulsive disorder (OCD). CBT here may be an effective augmentation treatment strategy in treating OCD for patients who do not respond to SSRIs (Math & Janardhan, 2007). A small number of placebo-controlled trials have compared efficacy of medications and/or exposure and response prevention therapy (ERP), and it has been shown that ERP therapy combined with pharmacotherapy (a PPPT approach) to be superior to SSRIs alone in child and adult populations. In adults, Foa et al. (2005) conducted a randomized controlled trial to study clomipramine (TCA) alone, ERP alone, and their combination in 86 patients, and found that the PPPT approach was superior to clomipramine alone on all outcome measures. Simpson et al. (2008) conducted a randomized controlled trial in 108 patients to compare the effects of augmenting SSRIs with ERP or stress management training (another form of CBT) and found that ERP was superior to stress management training in reducing OCD symptoms and that augmentation to an SSRI with ERP was an effective strategy for reducing OCD symptoms. In the pediatric obsessive-compulsive disorder treatment study (POTS), sertraline (SSRI) was compared to ERP and combination PPPT. PPPT was superior at one of two sites (POTS team, 2004). Treatments for posttraumatic stress disorder (PTSD) broadly have been defined as biological or psychosocial in nature. Randomized clinical trials for adult PTSD have been conducted for various treatments, such as cognitive restructuring, imaginal exposure, in vivo exposure, and various combinations of these in a CBT context delivered in groups and individually (Bradley, Greene, Russ, Dutra, & Westen, 2005). The long-term effectiveness of medications in PTSD may be limited, as findings often suggest 30% complete remission after short-term treatment compared to 65%–79% with CBT (Foa et al., 1999). Rothbaum et al. (2006) studied whether a combination of sertraline (SSRI) with prolonged exposure therapy would result in greater improvement than continuation with sertraline alone in patients with chronic PTSD. They observed that sertraline itself led to a significant reduction in PTSD severity over 10 weeks of psychopharmacology-only treatment but was associated with no further reductions after 5 additional weeks of pharmacotherapy. In contrast, the other group who received combined modalities (PPPT) did exhibit further, continued reduction in PTSD symptom severity. Moreover, an augmentation effect was seen in patients with only partial medication response, allowing a greater chance of remission (Rothbaum et al., 2006).

Depressive and anxiety disorders seem amenable to combined psychotherapy plus pharmacotherapy, and there is clear evidence that an integrated approach often allows for more favorable outcomes in certain patient populations. Schizophrenia is one of the most chronic and debilitating psychiatric disorders, with typically less robust outcomes in regards to psychopharmacology or psychotherapy approaches. Long-term maintenance on antipsychotic medications has been considered to be the most important factor in preventing rehospitalization in these patients (Schooler et al., 1997). Mojtabai, Nicholson, and Carpenter (1998), in their comprehensive meta-analysis, found that psychosocial and psychotherapeutic treatments in patients with schizophrenia when combined with routine antipsychotic medication management produced better clinical outcomes. Gottdiener and Haslam (2003) conducted a different meta-analysis in which they studied psychodynamic psychotherapy, CBT and non-psychodynamic supportive therapies and observed that all three were associated with significant overall improvement in schizophrenia patients. Additionally, both psychodynamic and cognitive treatments produced similar effect sizes and, also, individual psychodynamic psychotherapy produced more significant improvements when used with medication management (PPPT). More specifically, cognitive remediation therapy has focused on improving cognitive and executive functioning deficits in schizophrenia. Several researchers have found specific improvements in cognitive abilities, and this has even been paired with evidence of increased neuronal plasticity and better preservation of brain tissue volume (Medalia & Choi, 2009; Fisher, Holland, Subramaniam, & Vinogradov, 2010). Even in this more chronic and theoretically more genetic and biologically oriented disorder, schizophrenia patients seem to respond to combined medication and psychotherapy approaches.

Attention-deficit hyperactivity disorder (ADHD) is quite different from schizophrenia, but it is also considered a highly neurodevelopmental disorder, often with childhood onset, which may persist into adulthood. Pharmacotherapy with stimulant medications has been the first-line treatment of ADHD since the 1950s. Stimulants are very effective as a monotherapy and are often heralded as one of the greatest psychopharmacological interventions when effect sizes are evaluated (Klassen, Miller, Raina, Lee, & Olsen, 1999; AHCPR, 1999; Johnson, Safranek, & Friemoth, 2005). However, stimulant use may not be sufficient by itself due to a variety of factors, such as noncompliance and high prevalence of comorbidities (Wilens, Biederman, & Spencer, 2002). A recent review of psychological treatments for ADHD in adults concluded that the most effective treatment may be CBT modified for use in ADHD specific symptoms (Vidal-Estrada, Bosch-Munso, Nogueira-Morais, Casas-Brugue, & Ramos-Quiroga, 2012).

In a study by Safren et al. (2005), 31 adults with residual ADHD symptoms and stable psychopharmacology treatment for ADHD were randomized to CBT augmentation or continuing medication alone. There were significantly more treatment responders among patients who received adjunctive CBT (56%) compared to those who received medications only (13%), supporting the hypothesis that CBT for adults with ADHD with residual symptoms may be a feasible and efficacious PPPT approach.

In another study by Rostain and Ramsay (2006), 43 subjects with ADHD received medication with or without CBT. Treatment outcomes were assessed by comparing measures of ADHD symptoms, social functioning, and also for comorbid symptoms, finding that combined PPPT integrated treatment was superior. Additionally, in an Irish study, a brief CBT group intervention was designed to treat adults with ADHD suffering from comorbid anxiety and depression and found that it may also be an effective intervention for residual symptoms (Bramham, Young, Bickerdike, Spain, McCartan, & Xenitidis, 2009). In another randomized, controlled 16-week, multisite trial in 303 adolescents with ADHD and substance use disorder, OROS-methylphenidate did not show greater efficacy than placebo for ADHD or for reduction in substance use in adolescents concurrently receiving individual CBT for co-occurring substance use disorder (Riggs et al., 2011). This final finding again should remind the reader that studies have limitations that must be considered and that researchers often study patients with a single psychiatric disorder. Investigating these highly comorbid states is often disappointing, in that outcomes for psychotherapy, medication management, or combined modalities is often fraught with negative or less impactful outcomes. The reader should also take away that integrating psychopharmacology and psychotherapy has been found in certain studies, across several psychiatric conditions, to be additive and helpful in facilitating improved outcomes even in some comorbid patients. It is unclear which modality should be started first, or if combination at the outset is more important. Neuroscientifically speaking, this may be important, as the authors will later discuss how both medications and psychotherapy may possibly restore dysfunctional neuroanatomic circuits to allow a greater reduction in psychiatric symptoms across disorders.

NEUROIMAGING STUDIES OF INTEGRATED TREATMENT APPROACHES

There exists a notion of how therapeutic effects of psychiatric treatments may act in psychiatric disorders where there may be symptom reduction by improvement in the efficiency of information processing in hypothetically malfunctioning brain neurocircuits (Stahl, 2012).

The pathology of most psychiatric disorders that consist of a myriad of heterogeneous symptoms likely cannot be explained by simple neurotransmitter imbalances. Treatment with a single agent improving these alleged imbalances likely is not the cure for most patients regardless of the disorder at hand. If this were the case, clinicians would need only one antidepressant, one anxiolytic, one mood stabilizer, and one antipsychotic. If it were this simple, then there would not have been a need for any new psychotropic drug development since the 1950s. Obviously, this is not the case.

Researchers, and clinicians in the near future, may be able to utilize genetic studies and neuroimaging techniques to provide themselves with more information regarding specific neuroanatomic brain areas and whether they are functioning optimally or ineffectively—thus allowing psychiatric symptoms to surface. These symptoms that the patient exhibits externally would be considered their *phenotype*. This type of nomenclature is needed in order for this section to progress. In the introductory segments of this chapter, outcome-based studies revealed that combining medications and psychotherapy (PPPT) may additively improve outcomes (symptoms or phenotypes) across psychiatric disorders. Why is this? Medications clearly are biological and effect changes upon biological entities such as neurotransmitters, transporters, enzymes, etc. Changes here may change the electrical state of different brain areas, thus improving or normalizing their respective functions, but what does psychotherapy do in the brain? Does psychotherapy allow some metaphysical psychological response to occur in our patients, or are there also correlated brain changes associated with psychotherapy that might better explain why combining both modalities are additive in nature, neurologically speaking? The remainder of this chapter will start with a general, hypothetical overview regarding the neuroscientific basis of integrating psychotherapy and pharmacotherapy and then will move toward specific neuroanatomical and physiological models to explain the clinical, phenotypical phenomena discussed in outcome studies referenced previously in this chapter.

Recent neurobiological evidence has helped in clarifying that learning and environmental experiences, such as psychotherapy, change brain circuits and function, as does psychopharmacology. Although our knowledge is still limited, initial findings have begun to give researchers a better understanding of how psychotherapy and psychopharmacology may affect the brain in similar, or different, ways. Either approach likely can alter brain structure and function, producing phenotypic symptom changes for patients. A study by Greenough, Black, and Wallace (1987) observed that rats raised in a social environment developed greater synapses in comparison with rats raised in isolation. Kandel (1998) conducted innovative experiments in sea snails, in which it was demonstrated that synaptic connections could be permanently changed or strengthened through regulation of gene expression connected with learning from the environment. He furthermore described evidence of new neural pathway development when new learning occurred, hence postulating that psychotherapy may cause changes in brain synapses as most forms of psychotherapy provide novel learning situations for patients. In these animal laboratory models, learning is a behavioral and a psychological process that creates new neuronal changes and connectivity in the absence of any pharmacotherapy agents.

As an overlap, long-lasting neuroanatomic changes can be produced by psychotherapy or pharmacotherapy via changing gene expression and protein formation in brain neural circuits, but also the environment itself (positive and negative life experiences) can produce epigenetic changes in gene expression to alter the strength of synaptic connections. For example, negative memories of childhood trauma may cause psychiatric symptoms by initiating unfavorable changes in circuits of the brain, and in turn good memories formed during psychotherapy may favorably alter the same brain circuits, or more likely create new ones that may be targeted by medications and, hence, produce relief from symptoms (Nestler, 2009; Sweatt, 2009; Baxter et al., 1992). Therefore, this section will attempt to focus upon neurological changes due to either psychopharmacology or psychotherapy, but the situation is further complicated by living environments and stress interactions at the level of the human genome. Kandel (1998) further commented on the plasticity and dynamic structure of the brain, correlating it with the psychotherapeutic process where representations of self and objects are observed to be variable over time. In this way, environmentally experienced activity may affect the development of dendrites, so their conformation to cognitive schemes may create mental representations that can be experienced as positive and resilient in nature, or as a risk for, and potential development of psychiatric symptoms (Gabbard, 2000).

Psychotherapy, particularly cognitive behavioral therapy (CBT), which is based upon learning new skills and coping tools, may produce alterations in neuronal pathways. These differences again would have to be mediated by changes in gene expression in the brain and ultimately alter strength and numbers that could facilitate a phenotypic change (externally exhibited symptoms).

To map out neural circuits and the neurocircuitry responsible for psychiatric symptom development, functional neuroimaging techniques and studies are most often utilized. Baseline functional neuroimaging in MDD has shown decreased activity in the dorsolateral prefrontal cortex (DLPFC), correlating with increased MDD symptom severity (Brody, Barsom, Bota, & Saxena, 2001a). Frewen, Dozois, and Lanius (2008) reviewed recent literature about neuroimaging in psychotherapy with the goal of linking psychotherapeutic intervention and mechanism of change to specific neural correlates. For example, they linked the skill training functions of CBT and interpersonal psychotherapy (IPT) that are designed to enhance coping, problem solving, and interpersonal functioning to improved or enhanced functioning of the DLPFC. In this study, patients exhibited observed, external, phenotypic symptoms of MDD, and imaging studies revealed the *endophenotype* of hypofunctioning DLPFC. This endophenotype may be considered a biomarker of MDD and could possibly aid in diagnosis, but in these studies it may serve as a measurement to determine whether the MDD brain can return to normal functioning (a normal endophenotype) after treatment. Dichter, Felder, Petty, Bizzell, Ernst, and Smoski (2009) used fMRI to study a group of patients with MDD and treated with behavioral activation, and they found that there were significant improvements in the patients after treatment with respect to increased responsiveness in the reward centers of the brain, particularly in the anticipation of rewards. In contrast to the DLPFC findings, these limbic findings are important because they link the cognitive aspects of MDD with those of drive, initiative, and perhaps even enjoyment. In another study, midbrain serotonin transporter (SERT) density increased after 12 months of psychodynamic psychotherapy for atypical depression (Lehto et al., 2008), suggesting that psychotherapy alone may be able to change serotonin functioning *and* neurocircuitry.

In reviewing anxiety disorders, Etkin and Wager (2007) found that untreated posttraumatic stress disorder (PTSD), or social anxiety disorder (SAD) both had greater activity in the amygdala and insula. Also, for PTSD, they described hypoactivation in the anterior cingulate cortex (ACC) and ventromedial prefrontal cortex (VMPFC), which might allow for phenotypic alterations in vigilance or emotional-contextual processing. PTSD-based emotional dysregulation may be one of the main clinical manifestations of this neuroanatomic finding. Existing treatment studies describe symptom recovery after normalization of regional blood flow to these previously affected areas. Absence of activation in the DLPFC, after CBT, in a study of patients with spider phobia by Paquette et al. (2003) provided strong support to the view that CBT reduces phobic avoidance neurologically. This is likely due to the hippocampal/ parahippocampal region involvement in deconditioning the DLPFC where hippocampal structures may be strengthened and allow for decreased cognitive misattributions and cata- strophic thinking at the level of the DLPFC (Gorman, Kent, Sullivan, & Koplan, 2000).

Regarding both anxiety and MDD, the amygdalae often play a critical role in the pro- duction of symptoms and act as a key center for processing sensory information from the environment and possibly being an initial site of molecular formation (long term potentia- tion (LTP)) of memories based upon patient–environment interactions (Stahl, 2008). It is postulated that when animals recover from depression or anxiety model conditions, they develop new synapses that inhibit those synapses formed during stress or trauma (Swe- att, 2009; Stahl, 2008). This, in turn, requires long-term potentiation (LTP) and glutamate neurotransmission at N-methyl-d-aspartate (NMDA) glutamate receptors. This research brings the reader back full circle, suggesting that a learning model is needed to recover from psychiatric symptoms. This may explain not only that psychotherapy may hypothetically change symptoms by altering learning-based neuronal circuits, but also how combination with medications that facilitate NMDA neurotransmission could potentially increase the efficacy of psychotherapy in changing neuronal circuits, and thus help in decreasing symp- toms (Stahl, 2012; Deveney, McHugh, Tolin, Pollack, & Otto, 2009). In fact, several smaller, investigational studies have suggested that increasing glutamate NMDA receptor efficiency and activity with glycine agonists may promote improved and faster responses after a few sessions of exposure based CBT.

So far, the authors have discussed functional neuroimaging changes after psychotherapy. However, some differences between psychopharmacology and psychotherapy were outlined in a randomized control trial of venlafaxine (an SNRI) versus CBT in MDD where both groups of responders had decreases in metabolism in DLPFC, a commonality between these two interventions. Subtle differences in responders to either medication or CBT were also seen in the basal ganglia and/or cingulate cortex (Kennedy et al., 2007). Martin, Martin, Rai, Richardson, & Royall (2001) had previously compared the effects of IPT and venlafaxine on regional cerebral blood flow (CBF) using SPECT, in a 6-week study of patients with MDD as well. Subjects in remission from venlafaxine and IPT observed that resting hypoperfu- sion of the prefrontal cortex renormalized after MDD remission, and there were increases in cerebral blood flow to right basal ganglia activity as well. Subjects in the IPT group alone differentially exhibited an increase in right posterior cingulate activity. A longer, 12-week study of similar design was conducted by Brody and colleagues (2001b), who used PET to examine patients who received IPT or paroxetine (SSRI). A decrease in dorsal and ventral prefrontal cortical metabolism with IPT treatment directly was reported here. In addition, the authors described an increase in metabolism in limbic and paralimbic regions (in this case, the right insula and left inferior temporal lobe) in both treatment groups compared to controls, although there was a decrease in DLPFC activation with paroxetine only. Continu- ing along this avenue of discussion, studies of MDD, CBT, and IPT were noted to promote similar changes in cortical-subcortical neurocircuitry (Roffman, Marci, Glick, Dougherty, & Rauch, 2005). This type of finding suggests that brain neuronal and neuroanatomic changes may occur from medication or psychotherapy modalities. There is clearly some overlap in these neurofunctional changes regardless of modality used, suggesting that integrated PPPT should allow for additive, curative central nervous system (CNS) effects to occur. There are also some clear differences in effects as well; certain brain functional changes do not overlap, making each modality a unique treatment.

Other studies also support that psychotherapy and psychopharmacology affect brain function in overlapping and also in unique ways, depending now upon the psychiatric disorder. Levin, Lazrove, & van der Kolk (1999) studied eye movement desensitization and reprocessing (EMDR) therapy in PTSD, and found increased CBF in ACC and in the left frontal lobe. Another study examined group CBT versus citalopram (SSRI) for treatment of SAD via PET, in which both groups exhibited a significant reduction of activity in limbic and paralimbic regions and no change in activity in VMPFC in the CBT group, in contrast to patients receiving only citalopram who exhibited activity reductions in this region after treatment. In addition, CBT groups showed decreased CBF in the periaqueductal gray (PAG) area, and the citalopram group exhibited thalamic reductions in CBF, potentially reflecting reductions in sensory input to the amygdala (Charney & Deutch, 1996). However, VMPFC components of these mechanisms remain unclear. It could be implied that CBT and citalopram therapy for SAD might dampen limbic response, albeit by different mechanisms—thus, adding to data supporting that combining treatment modalities may provide complimentary changes in brain function to alleviate SAD symptoms (Furmark et al., 2002). In OCD, it is often found that hyperactivity of the right caudate exists. Baxter et al. (1992) found that both fluoxetine (SSRI) and behavioral exposure and ERP produce similar decreases in cerebral metabolic rates in the head of the right caudate nucleus. Nakatani et al. (2003) studied behavioral therapy in treatment refractory OCD and found decreased cerebral blood flow in the right caudate after treatment as well.

Clinicians might consider the PPPT findings above, where some brain function changes overlap and others are unique (or complimentary), to be similar to rational polypharmacy approaches where psychopharmacologists combine different medications together to gain a greater theoretical effect (Topel, Zajecka, Goldstein, Siddiqui, & Schwartz, 2011). Take, for example, the treatment of initially resistant MDD where a patient is only partially better while taking an SSRI monotherapy. Most guidelines and clinical practitioners would not advocate combining two mechanistically similar SSRI antidepressants together. The first reason for this is the risk of serotonin toxicity adverse effects, but second is common sense, in that if the patient is not responding to a full-dosed SSRI using its specific mechanism of serotonin reuptake inhibition, why would a second, nearly identical SSRI work? Most clinicians would likely combine or augment with an agent that elevates monoamines other than serotonin. A common strategy here might be to add a norepinephrine–dopamine reuptake inhibitor (NDRI) such as bupropion. This way, there is little overlap, and only complimentary mechanisms of action impinging on the CNS to promote an antidepressant effect. Sometimes buspirone, a serotonin-1a receptor partial agonist is added to the initial SSRI monotherapy. This is another serotonergic approach, but it is not an SSRI mechanism and also might be considered complimentary and not wholly overlapping in mechanistic nature. Adding a psychotherapy simultaneously, or sequentially, may be like adding a partially overlapping *and* partially unique mechanism of action that all psychopharmacologists should find some comfort in understanding and utilizing in practice.

In summary, the authors have attempted now to convey in the first section of this chapter that clinical outcomes of combining medications and psychotherapy (psychopharmacopsychotherapy) may allow for additive clinical responses and improved phenotypic symptom reduction for a myriad of psychiatric conditions. In this second section, certain specific examples of functional neuorimaging (endophenotypes) have been discussed to document clear neuroanatomic and neurofunctioning changes that might occur with either psychotherapy or pharmacotherapy, or integrated PPPT. Both modalities affect brain function. In some cases there is overlap, and in others there are independent findings depending upon the disorder, drug, or psychotherapy utilized. The next, final section of this chapter will attempt to stream-line and theorize how PPPT might work in the generic brain across a myriad of psychiatric disorders. As research endeavors of psychiatric genetics and psychiatric neuroimaging con-tinue, several models will evolve with improving supportive evidence.

NEUROSCIENTIFIC MODELS OF PSYCHOPHARMACOPSYCHOTHERAPY

Consider psychotherapy as an epigenetic drug? A model proposed by Stahl (2012) would sug-gest that both pharmacotherapy and psychotherapy may converge upon similar neurocircuits to change brain functioning and alleviate psychiatric symptoms. The first two sections of this chapter revealed that combining, or integrating, psychotherapy and psychopharmacology approaches across a myriad of psychiatric disorders can increase effectiveness outcomes and that functional neuroimaging may reveal where in the brain it is likely that these treatments are imparting their effects. To better understand the findings in neuroimaging reviewed in the prior section of this chapter, and to understand how theorists may create neurobiological models, the reader must first understand the arbitrary testing methods set up to better delin-eate these neurocircuits. Researchers can utilize neuroimaging such as functional magnetic resonance imaging (fMRI) or positron emission scanning (PET) whereby they can measure the activity (hyper or hypo) of specific brain areas. These brain areas are connected by neu-rons, and these neurons have different receptors, transporters, and enzymes that may be fairly localized as well. These neuroanatomic connections create neurocircuits or neural networks. If there is an abnormality due to genetics, stressful environment, brain injury, etc., then a circuit may fire too much or too little, causing the specific neuroanatomic area to function excessively or in an underactive manner. This net change in activity, in either direction, likely can yield descriptive symptoms that the patient reports or exhibits. To test these specific circuits, researchers must come up with a *stress test* to make the specific neurocircuit work harder so it can be easily identified on imaging. This can then be compared amongst patients with psychiatric disorders and those without. Researchers can calculate the net differences in brain function, and if significant, then a possible neuroimaging endophenotype biomarker may be validated as pathognomonic for said disorder.

Some stress tests might include the n-back test, Stroop test, or fearful faces protocol. For the first, patients are asked to concentrate on storing memory, calculating, and recalling mathematical figures. This is a working memory and multitasking protocol that taxes the DLPFC. The second involves monitoring words that are printed in varying colors and using stored memory and language skills to report the color of the words that were typed, also for DLPFC multitasking. Why are these two important? Poor concentration, executive dysfunc-tion, and planning abilities may be noted in several DSM disorders. For example, poor atten-tion or concentration is specifically listed for ADHD, PTSD, GAD, MDD, mania, delirium, etc. (American Psychiatric Association, 2000). This would suggest that these phenotypic presentations may have similar underlying brain imaging (endophenotype) findings (i.e., hypoactive DPLFC), where utilizing a Stroop test while under fMRI condition might allow researchers to better diagnose active psychopathology, risk for future psychopathology, and also to determine what treatments may rectify the endophenotypic findings and lower phe-notypic psychiatric symptoms as an outcome measure. The fearful faces protocol determines how active limbic structures are, specifically the amygdalae, which accounts for fight-or-flight reactions in mammals. While in an imaging device, patients are shown a myriad of faces, some with neutral expressions, some with more intense emotions (fear, anxiety, irritability), and the extent to which the amygdalae become hyperactive is imaged and measured. This model does not measure cortical DLPFC function, but rather investigates the limbic system to determine whether it is too active (i.e., in depression or anxiety).

By utilizing some of these neuroimaging stress-testing protocols, investigators now may gain better insight as to how the brain is functioning in normal states, psychopathological states, and after treatment with either psychotherapy, pharmacotherapy, or psychopharma-cotherapy (PPPT). These types of studies may more concretely reveal why integration of both treatment modalities may allow for additive clinical outcomes similar to those addressed in the first section of this chapter. For example, the amygdala is likely a major brain center for initial processing of information from the environment and an initial site of molecular formation of memories (Stahl, 2008). The amygdalae keep track of personal experiences and help keep track of positive and rewarding experiences and negative or aversive ones. Synapses begin to form after real world experiences based upon fear or reward (Sweatt, 2009; Stahl, 2008). Animal models suggest that when subjects are placed into stressful environments, synapses form, and they potentially learn phobic avoidance for the aversive environment. These synapses are permanent and fire often to help the animal avoid the negative environmental cues and exposures. To train an animal to unlearn, or extinguish, its fear about a previously negative or aversive environment, new synapses are formed via long-term potentiation (LTP), allowing the animal to perceive that the environment is now neutral or even rewarding. In this way, new exposures allow new synapses, and summarily new learning occurs as the animal replaces painful memories with positive ones over time. Old memories (synaptic long-term potentiated synapses) are likely not truly replaced, but new memories and experiences (new synaptic LTP) begin to take precedence over the older ones and gain strength. This may be a fundamental working model of how psychotherapy works. Patients replace previous negative interpersonal experiences with positive ones where clinicians utilize terms such as *corrective emotional experiences, holding environments, containment of affect, cognitive restructuring of negative schema, interpersonal role modeling or transitioning*, etc. Perhaps, psychotherapy allows repeated exposure to neutral or positively rewarding situations and environments; new synapses are formed and neural networks are fired, which promote social affiliation instead of phobic avoidance and negative affect. Integrating medication management and psychotherapy strategies might converge (depending on the particular medication) at the level of the amygdalae, DLPFC, etc. The psychotherapy epigenetic environment may exert effects on new neuronal synapses and learning simultaneously, while pharmacologic agents act to mitigate neuroanatomic hyperfunctioning or hypofunctioning status of each specific brain area or circuitry. This may be the final common pathway whereby PPPT works to lower psychiatric symptom severity. With this working presupposition, creating a simple working neuroanatomic model of psychopharmacopsychotherapy is warranted. This model should draw together basic neuroanatomy and physiology, identifying CNS structures that are theoretically related to psychiatric symptom development, and next it should look to pilot studies that utilize psychiatric stress test models to determine if psychotherapy plus psychopharmacology is truly additive in the way that it might correct brain physiology and neurocircuitry firing to lower psychiatric symptoms.

A review by Liggan and Kay (1999) is informative and to some degree abstracted below. These authors paint a picture that psychotherapy is a modality that employs learning regardless of doctrine or dogma. Learning is a neurobiological process in the CNS, and symptom reduction, by way of psychotherapy can change brain function to alleviate symptoms. For discussion, it makes sense to begin with Hebb's rule. Hebb (1949) accurately postulated that the brain could store information (learning) only if neurons could modify their connectivity. This would require both the pre- and postsynaptic neurons to be actively engaged simultaneously during environmental stimulus or change. This is the model of LTP noted above. The greater the firing between two neurons, the greater likelihood that they will fire again, thus strengthening the connection. As neurons are multiply interconnected, neural networks are likely created, and each of these representative networks intertwines with other networks. If these networks begin to function excessively or erroneously and incorporate certain neuroanatomic brain regions into their firing patterns, then psychiatric symptoms may occur (Stein & Ludik, 1998). Neural networks may also be cortical maps. For example, if a patient witnesses a traumatic event, or multiple events, then the patient's factual sensory information neurons fire, amygdala neurons fire, VMPFC cortical neurons fire, and so on. These sequential firings create a cortical network and ultimately a map of firing neurons that represent the trauma. LTP or long-term depression (LTD) via corrective, safe experiences (i.e., psychotherapy), may change the character of the map or create a new map by using different firing patterns in the neuronal systems involved. LTP may create new synapses and new neural network maps of safe events (new learning), and LTD may help extinguish, or lower the likelihood, of older neural network firing of maps that represent trauma or aversive experiences.

The authors previously mentioned imaging findings in the DLPFC and in the amygdala for depressive and anxious states. There is ample evidence that these two brain regions relay information and signals back and forth (Bear, 1996). The rate-limiting apparatus creating plasticity and greater regional brain communication involves NMDA glutamate receptors and cortical activity. This way, rudimentary fight or flight, aggressivity or passivity, or not, information is transmitted from primitive limbic structures to the cortex, which is activated by way of NMDA receptor activation. Cortical association maps or neural networks are formed to create longer-standing memories based upon environmental experiences. A patient without psychiatric symptoms establishes good balance or tone between cortical and limbic CNS structures. A normal amount of cross talk (neuronal network firing) may provide checks and balances, which promotes behaviors that are related to resilient coping skills. As psychiatric symptoms develop, a specific neuronanatomic brain area may be stronger, or weaker, regarding neuronal network firing, and this imbalance may likely lead to the outward, phenotypic expression of psychiatric symptoms noted.

Based upon this, there are likely two neuranatomic memory systems that are supported by different neuroimaging findings (Squire et al., 1992). An *explicit* system uses higher cortical areas (temporal lobes) with much reliance upon hippocampal functioning to retain factual history about events. An *implicit* system is more primal, using the basal ganglia and limbic structures. The implicit system has models implicating aversive and fear conditioning neural circuitry (auditory thalamic areas projecting to the amygdala, auditory cortex, the amygdala, and the hypothalamus) (Kapp, Pasco, & Bixler, 1984). This system does not appear to be accessible for conscious memory recall like the explicit system, but rather promotes the learning of skills, drives, or preservation, and may be driven more by classical conditioning. The implicit system stores affective information and creates rules and prototypes for social engagement whereby future experiences are often weighed against these predefined representations. This system likely acts unconsciously, always scanning the environment and making predetermined judgments about social patterns and interactions, and it governs fairly fast behavioral and reflexive responses. This system is shaped from an early age, where the explicit system evolves in the later childhood years. The explicit, factual memory system is more conscious and accessible by the person at any given time. These theoretical memory constructs, on which many psychotherapy techniques hinge, likely map to more complex neuronal constructs (networks, neuroanatomic areas, etc.).

At one level, psychotherapy has direct access to explicit and factual memory, activating and utilizing higher cortical and hippocampal areas of the brain. Throughout therapy, implicit patterns are noticed, interpreted, or brought into awareness, and now both the explicit (cortical) and implicit (limbic) systems are brought to interact and affect behavior change. Medications may work in either system. It makes sense that psychological or psychotherapy approaches all are learning based and impact these two systems, but how might psychopharmacological approaches impact learning systems? Animal models suggest that altering neurotransmitter levels or availability (serotonin) can affect learning (Lavond, Kim, & Thompson, 1993). More often though, glutamate activity at NMDA receptors is discussed and implicated via LTP mechanisms, but serotonin, norepinephrine, and dopamine may also play an active role (Park, 1998). Interestingly, these are the most modulated monoamines, as the available psychopharmacotherapies mostly interact by raising or lowering monoamine levels or activity by way of transporter or enzyme inhibition, receptor antagonism, or agonism, etc. For example, and in regards to dopamine, in primate learning models, ascending dopamine pathways may be divided into *tonic* or *phasic* categories. Tonic dopamine pathway firing is felt to govern overall arousal and wakefulness, and to aid in attention and concentration. Phasic dopamine neuronal firing often occurs in situations where reward-based operant learning occurs. Drive and motivation may come as a result of this dopaminergic network firing. In primates, while learning a task, the phasic dopamine system is hyperactive. Effort by the animal in learning a new task will have a higher endogenous dopamine reward, making the animal work harder and learn more quickly. However, once a behavior is learned and mastered and its novelty wears off, phasic dopamine activity lowers. The dopamine phasic system allows for prediction error to occur in the animal. The animal can learn how accurate it is when dealing with new situations and to create a list of possible behaviors that may occur in that situation. Psychotherapy often allows patients to be given interpretations about their actions, or to be made aware or mindful of their actions, and next they are urged to change behaviors, or challenge their previous predictions (error prediction) and see if new ways of behaving will improve interpersonal rewards. There is also direct dopamine interaction with the glutamatergic NMDA learning apparatus here that is responsible for LTP. LTP occurs after patterns of neuronal firing are repeated and synaptic connectivity increases. LTD may be a method of lessening the firing of previously strengthened LTP synapses and neural networks. Evidence suggests that dopamine involvement in this neurocircuitry is weighted toward LTD. Perhaps as patients go through psychotherapy, where they try to change behaviors, beliefs, and attitudes that impair them via creating depression and anxiety symptoms, increasing dopaminergic tone by way of antidepressants may allow greater extinguishing of negative behaviors by lowering that behavior's associated neural network. This may directly link the neurochemistry of psychopharmacology to the neurochemistry of psychotherapy, which again may be neuroimaged (as discussed in previous sections) and studied. In fact, some neuroanatomical mapping has implicated the cortex, striatum, globus pallidus, subthalamic nucleus, and thalamus in this type of learning.

Serotonin likely contributes to learning pathways as well. Many more serotonergic psychotropics exist than dopaminergic ones. There are two proposed serotonin neural networks. The first is important in MDD, where the median raphe projects to the hippocampus, which is rich in serotonin-1a receptors. This pathway likely dictates how an animal will respond in aversive conditions. Lower activity here makes animals less resilient and more likely to respond with learned helplessness, a model of human MDD. In this pathway, serotonergic activity ultimately leads to downstream inhibitory actions in the hippocampus. The second path projects from the dorsal raphe to the hippocampus, but its terminus is deeper in the hippocampus and terminates upon serotonin-2a receptors. This system leads to downstream hippocampal activation. Antidepressants that act by blocking the serotonin transporter elevate available serotonin in synapses and have been shown to activate serotonin-1a receptors in the first circuit. In animal models, this is correlated to returning the animal's serotonergic circuitry to a nondepressed state. In this manner, nondepressed animals are stressed, depression ensues, and the animal is treated with an antidepressant. The serotonergic circuitry can be observed to change from a normal to abnormal and back to normal state in the paradigm outlined above. This is likely what occurred as well in the psychodynamic psychotherapy study mentioned previously (Lehto et al., 2008), where serotonin reuptake properties were altered similarly with psychotherapy. In this way, psychotherapy may facilitate both cortical and limbic structures to change neuronal networks or maps, and introducing psychotropics that manipulate neurotransmitters or receptors may facilitate neuronal plasticity as well, in an additive manner further allowing neural networks to adapt or change. The net effect could be external, phenotypic psychiatric symptom improvement.

In order to merge implicit/explicit learning theory and the neurobiological theories regarding PPPT, functional neuroimaging is helpful to review. Some functional imaging studies in the second section of the chapter described the endophenotypic effects of psychotherapy or medication management. For depression, psychotherapy and SSRI treatments both independently lowered right caudate activity, possibly indicating an impact in the implicit memory system (Baxter et al., 1992). For PTSD, EMDR psychotherapy increased DLPFC activity and lowered limbic activity, possibly showing the effect of EMDR impacting upon both explicit and implicit memory neuroanatomic systems. Linking brain regional activity changes to neurotransmitter changes was outlined also in a case prior to the Lehto et al. case. Viinamaki et al., in a more stringent case-control study, showed that psychodynamic psychotherapy in a mood disorder patient (Viinamaki, Kuikka, & Tiihonnen, 1998) allowed improved poor serotonin transporter activity in the PFC over the course of 1 year of psychotherapy, and this was correlated to symptom reduction. This link again shows that psychotherapy can affect brain function and may possibly allow for brain changes by creating different neurotransmitter activity. Clearly SSRI and SNRI facilitate serotonin reuptake directly. Adding one of these medications to psychotherapy should directly amplify the effects of psychodynamic psychotherapy in an additive or maximizing fashion. OCD also has neuroanatomic findings of altered brain function and volumetric changes that are linked in animal and human studies where data has shown that both psychotherapy and pharmacotherapy modalities affect brain neurochemical outcomes. Focusing on serotonin, tricyclic antidepressant (TCA) binding and serotonin platelet binding both increased when either treatment modality was utilized, again suggesting overlapping and additive CNS effects while treating anxiety disorders (Baer, 1996).

CONCLUSION: OPERATIONALIZING PPPT FOR THE CLINICIAN

In a rational polypharmacy treatment approach (Schwartz & Stahl, 2010), psychopharmacologists typically will not add an SSRI to another SSRI. As was previously discussed, clinicians might feel this is a redundant polypharmacy augmentation, and if (a) the serotonin transporters are already inhibited, (b) increasing synaptic serotonin has occurred, and (c) depression is not remitted, then adding a medication with a different serotonergic mechanism of action (serotonin-2a receptor antagonism, serotonin-1a receptor partial agonism) would be more complimentary in maximizing the impact on serotonergic neurocircuitry. In this instance, instead of augmenting with an atypical antipsychotic (5HT-2a receptor antagonism), a sedating antidepressant (trazodone with 5HT-2a receptor antagonism), or an anxiolytic (buspirone with 5HT-1a receptor partial agonism), an astute clinician might add psychodynamic psychotherapy which also affects serotonin functioning. This chapter has revealed at least two studies where this mode of psychotherapy clearly impacted serotonin levels and functioning and allowed for endophenotypic changes to be detected upon neuroimaging. Psychopharmacologists could easily view providing *their own* psychotherapy or referring out for psychotherapy as a serotonergic augmentation. Of course, psychotherapy should be held accountable to a given dose and duration, just like a pharmacological trial. IPT and CBT are often short term, with 12–20 consecutive weekly therapy sessions. This is akin to increasing an SNRI across its full dosing range. If that SNRI fails to create an antidepressant response, it is stopped and another medication is started. IPT and CBT have amassed many outcome studies (Butler, Chapman, Forman, & Beck, 2006; de Mello, de Jesus, Bacaltchuk, Verdeli, & Neugebauer, 2005), showing what an adequate trial consists of. If one of these short-term, directive psychotherapies fails, then its brain mechanism of action likely has not changed the neurocircuitry involved in the particular patient's depression. The particular mode of psychotherapy should be abandoned and another style of psychotherapy chosen. Perhaps, a switch to psychodynamic psychotherapy may be warranted if CBT or IPT fails. Similar to medications showing slightly different neurofunctioning effects, different psychotherapies may also affect different brain areas as well. Psychotherapies can be moved through just like a stringent dose and duration antidepressant trial can be conducted. In the opposite manner, a clinician conducting only psychotherapy, after a good trial, must be aware if the therapy is failing. In this case, again, a switch to a different form of psychotherapy, or a referral and introduction of an antidepressant is likely warranted.

If psychotherapy is felt to be a learning process whereby the explicit memory system is accessed in order to create new LTP and firing patterns and ultimately to affect changes in the implicit memory system secondarily, then many antidepressants could be viewed not as antidepressants, but as *cognitive or learning performance enhancers*. It was previously discussed that LTP and learning are not just glutamate dependent. Likely, dopamine input in the cortex and serotonergic input in the limbic structures may improve LTP, as well as synaptic and new neural network formation. Enhancing learning while engaged in psychotherapy could likely improve psychotherapeutic outcomes and symptom reduction. Psychotherapists could embrace any antidepressant as being an augmentation or performance-enhancing initiative when sequentially administered after psychotherapy fails to provide a full remission.

Finally, many psychopharmacologists feel that they are too busy, or choose not to provide psychotherapy services to their *medication management only patients*. More often, psychiatric clinicians are, more and more, hired by and working under the direction of hospitals, or subsidized clinics where the more costly psychiatrist is made to see four patients an hour, while a clinical social worker provides supportive eclectic long-term psychotherapy weekly. This leaves little, if any, time for psychotherapy in the psychiatric prescriber's office, let alone for active listening, or rapport building. Throughout this book, the editors urge the reader to pay particular attention to care models that describe how a prescribing psychopharmacologist may actually provide some active psychotherapy despite busy schedules and demands. By doing this, an *augmentation strategy* is always being provided when prescribing, even when a monotherapy only is being utilized.

If a psychopharmacologist cannot recall their training in psychotherapy, was never trained in formal outcome-based psychotherapies, or has no time to read and become proficient in some of the psychotherapies described throughout this book, there is hope. Psychopharmacologists could undergo a "vocational rehabilitation" in a few short steps that may return the core psychotherapy skills once effectively utilized in residency training to the forefront of daily clinical practice.

First, the psychopharmacologist must remind him- or herself that providing both psychotherapy and psychopharmacology to a patient simultaneously makes sense based upon the outcomes and neuroimaging data presented in this chapter. Almost all psychiatrists are trained in providing both modalities in one setting, but drift toward a *psychopharmacology model only* for the reasons noted above. A paper that should have gained more attention from prescribers, insurance companies, and government agencies was published by Dewan (1999), where an analysis was conducted to determine whether a psychiatrist providing both psychotherapy and psychopharmacology in one session (PPPT) was more costly than split therapy whereby the psychiatrist prescribes and other psychotherapists provide psychotherapy. This latter model is likely the most widely utilized in the United States and, given its propagation by major private and public insurance carriers, must be felt to be more effective, cost less to provide, or both. Dewan's study showed, by using insurance companies' cost data, that *brief* psychotherapy by a social worker was the least expensive treatment when used alone to treat a patient. When treatment required *both* psychotherapy and medication (PPPT), then combined treatment by a solo psychiatrist costs about the same or less than split treatment with a social worker psychotherapist, and it was usually less expensive than split treatment with a psychologist psychotherapist. This small paper was printed in a competitive, high-ranking journal and met with good reviews. However, it seems that this current split therapy practice has gone mostly unchanged. This third variable, cost, should also be on the psychopharmacologist's mind. One can prescribe and provide psychotherapy, which is clearly effective, changes brain function, and is cost effective in regards to the healthcare economy.

A second point revolves around the fact that it may be difficult to return to school, retrain, and learn new psychotherapy skills to provide to patients in the fast world of a psychopharmacology office. Psychopharmacologists must adhere to the old saying that "one is always doing psychotherapy," even in a 15- to 20-minute short visit. The key is to make those 20 minutes count. Patients should be seen as often as schedules and finances permit. This improves the doctor–patient relationship, partnership, and rapport. The final chapter of this book will provide the reader with ample evidence regarding how a prescriber may optimize his or her relationship with a patient, enhance response rates, placebo rates, adherence rates, etc.

A model of providing manualized psychopharmacopsychotherapy (M-PPPT) might be theorized, learned, and incorporated into clinical practice in the same amount of time that it takes to read this introductory chapter. M-PPPT's goal would be to develop a basic psychotherapy treatment for use by psychopharmacologists when employing a *medication management only model* for the treatment of MDD, or other psychiatric disorders. The psychopharmacologist must be aware and want to maintain the psychotherapeutic stance while in the daily practice providing psychopharmacology to patients. To be realistic, and honest, some psychopharmacologists are burned out, never liked training or providing psychotherapy, or find psychotherapy draining when compared to medication management sessions. Burned out psychopharmacologists may blame their employer or the insurance companies for enforcing the fast medication sessions and split model psychotherapy, but some psychopharmacologists use this as a rationalization because (a) they may not want to admit; (b) nor embrace psychotherapy as a technique either (1) due to philosophical stance, (2) the sometimes draining nature of psychotherapy, or (3) the learning curve of psychotherapy; or (c) the fact that it is often more lucrative to provide a higher volume of shorter medication management visits per day. M-PPPT interventions can be time limited and concise so that psychiatric symptom reduction may be achieved within the course of usual medication management only practices. Interventions have an easy learning curve so that these applications may be learned and utilized in practice immediately even if a stoic *medications only approach* is held to.

M-PPPT has a goal to increase the psychopharmacologist's awareness of the use of "common factors" felt to be universal to most employed psychotherapies (Greenberg, 2004). This simplistic approach often is initially taught in nurse practitioner or psychiatric residency training, or may be used later as a "vocational rehabilitation tool" for the veteran psychopharmacologist. Using a checklist approach, a psychopharmacology session may be broken down into sections, and both psychopharmacology and psychotherapy may be employed. It is recommended that at the time of outpatient admission and diagnosis that a few weekly medication *plus* psychotherapy sessions be used with gradual transitioning toward *psychopharmacology* sessions every few weeks per usual as symptoms reduce. Public domain rating scales are highly suggested. Rating scale use has been shown to improve outcomes (Zimmerman, Chelminski, Young, & Dalyrymple, 2011) in several psychiatric disorders and, more importantly, if conducted prior to the office visit, many psychiatric symptoms may be reviewed by the clinician in the first few minutes, allowing most of the session to be dedicated to psychoeducational informed consent and psychotherapeutic processes. A typical M-PPPT checklist might involve the following:

Psychopharmacology Components

   __Review previous note prior to session
   __Check rating scales prior to session
   __Ask about current positive or negative stressors
   __Lethality risk assessment
   __Review current pivotal target symptoms
   __Review medication list
   __Review side effects
   __Review medical problems
   __Check vitals
   __Provide informed consent
   __Positive and negative medication effects
   __Rationale for psychotherapy as adjunctive treatment

Psychotherapy

   __Provide psychoeducation about diagnosis and medication options
   __Provide > 3 core psychotherapy skills
      __motivation
      __empathy
      __openness
      __collaboration

__warmth
__positive regard
__sincerity
__corrective experience
__catharsis
__establish goals
__establish time limit
__establish patient effort needed

Documentation

__Compile note
__Contact collaterals
__Consult state mandated databases (For example NY's SafeAct or I-STOP Act)

This basic checklist is a manual. It covers the basic processes of a gold standard medication management visit, but at the same time, it works to motivate the psychopharmacologist to stay equally focused upon providing core psychotherapy techniques in session. As a simple checklist, it works to alert the psychopharmacologist and bring to awareness the need to work on basic psychotherapeutic approaches while in session. Implicitly, most psychopharmacologists initially trained and learned that providing psychotherapy is helpful to patients. At one time, these skills were likely intuitive and automatic (*implicit*). By using a simple checklist, current psychopharmacologists who are wed to a prescription writing only, hard-core, short visit, medication only approach might activate *explicit* memory systems, and via glutamatergic LTP, relearn and deploy these refreshed skills effectively. The dopaminergic pathways may increase drive and improve error prediction while learning M-PPPT; the serotonergic pathways may allow for better LDP away from the once aversive (cost, stress, job description, authority) psychotherapy model. The clinician's DLPFC may activate more upon PET scanning, and his or her amygdala may appear less active, and the clinician may emerge fairly quickly and competently a psychopharmacopsychotherapist again.

REFERENCES

Agency for Health Care Policy and Research (AHCPR). (1999). *Treatment of attention deficit/hyperactivity disorder.* Summary, Evidence Report/Technology Assessment: Number 11, AHCPR Publication No. 99-E017. Rockville, MD: Retrieved from http://www.ncbi.nlm.nih.gov/books/NBK11948/

American Psychiatric Association. (2000). *Diagnostic and statistical manual of mental disorders* (4th ed., text rev.) Washington, DC: American Psychiatric Press.

American Psychiatric Association. (2012). *Practice guidelines for treatment of patients with bipolar disorder* (2nd ed.). Retrieved from http://www.dbsanca.org/docs/APA_Bipolar_Guidelines.1783155.pdf

Baer, L. (1996). Behavior therapy: Endogenous serotonin therapy? *Journal of Clinical Psychiatry, 57,* 33–35.

Baxter, L. R., Schwartz, J. M., Bergman, K. S., Szuba, M. P., Guze, B. H., Mazziotta, J. C., & Phelps, M. E. (1992). Caudate glucose metabolic rate changes with both drug and behavior therapy for obsessive-compulsive disorder. *Archives of General Psychiatry, 49,* 681–689.

Bear, M. F. (1996). A synaptic basis for memory storage in the cerebral cortex. *Proceedings of the National Academy of Sciences of the USA, 93,* 13453–13459.

Bellino, S., Zizza, M., Rinaldi, C., & Bogetto, F. (2006). Combined treatment of major depression in patients with borderline personality disorder: A comparison with pharmacotherapy. *Canadian Journal of Psychiatry, 51,* 453–460.

Beurs, E., van Balkom, A., Lange, A., Koele, P., & van Dyke, R. (1995). Treatment of panic disorder with agoraphobia: Comparison of fluvoxamine, placebo, and psychological panic management combined with exposure and of exposure in vivo alone. *American Journal of Psychiatry, 152,* 683–691.

Bradley, R., Greene, J., Russ, E., Dutra, L., & Westen, D. (2005). A multidimensional meta-analysis of psychotherapy for PTSD. *American Journal of Psychiatry, 162,* 214–227.

Bramham, J., Young, S., Bickerdike, A., Spain, D., McCartan, D., & Xenitidis, K. (2009). Evaluation of group cognitive behavioral therapy for adults with ADHD. *Journal of Attention Disorders, 12,* 434–441.

Brody, A. L., Barsom, M. W., Bota, R. G., & Saxena, S. (2001b). Prefrontal-subcortical and limbic circuit mediation of major depressive disorder. *Seminars in Clinical Neuropsychiatry, 6,* 102–112.

Brody, A. L., Saxena, S., Stoesse, P., Gillies, L. A., Fairbanks, L. A., Alborzian, S. . . . Baxter, L. R. Jr. (2001a). Regional brain metabolic changes in patients with major depression treated with either paroxetine or interpersonal therapy: Preliminary findings. *Archives of General Psychiatry, 58,* 631–640.

Butler, A. C., Chapman, J. E., Forman, E. M., & Beck, A. T. (2006). The empirical status of cognitive behavioral therapy: A review of meta-analyses. *Clinical Psychology Review, 26,* 17–31.

Charney, D. S., & Deutch, A. (1996). A functional neuroanatomy of anxiety and fear: Implications for the pathophysiology and treatment of anxiety disorders. *Critical Reviews in Neurobiology, 10,* 419–446.

de Jonghe, F., Kool, S., van Aalst, G., Dekker, J., & Peen, J. (2001). Combining psychotherapy and antidepressants in the treatment of depression. *Journal of Affective Disorders, 64,* 217–229.

de Jonghe, F., Hendricksen, M., van Aalst, G., Kool, S., Peen, V., Van, R. . . . Dekker, J. (2004). Psychotherapy alone and combined with pharmacotherapy in the treatment of depression. *British Journal of Psychiatry, 185,* 37–45.

de Mello, M. F., de Jesus, M. J., Bacaltchuk, J., Verdeli, H., & Neugebauer, R. (2005). A systematic review of research findings on the efficacy of interpersonal therapy for depressive disorders. *European Archives of Psychiatry and Clinical Neurosciences, 255,* 75–82.

Deveney, C. M., McHugh, K., Tolin, D. F., Pollack, M. H., & Otto, M. (2009). Combining d-cycloserine and exposure based CBT for the anxiety disorders. *Clinical Neuropsychiatry, 6,* 75–82.

Dewan, M. J. (1999). Are psychiatrists cost-effective? An analysis of integrative versus split treatment. *American Journal of Psychiatry, 156,* 324–326.

Dichter, G. S., Felder, J. N., Petty, C., Bizzell, J., Ernst, M., & Smoski, M. J. (2009). The effects of psychotherapy on neural responses to rewards in major depression. *Biological Psychiatry, 66,* 886–897.

Emslie, G., Kratochvil, C., Vitiello, B., Silva, S., Mayes, T., McNulty, S. . . . March, J. (2006). Treatment for Adolescents with Depression Study (TADS): Safety results. *American Academy of Child and Adolescent Psychiatry, 45,* 1440–1455.

Etkin, A., & Wager, T. A. (2007). Functional neuroimaging of anxiety: A meta-analysis of emotional processing in PTSD, social anxiety disorder, and specific phobia. *American Journal of Psychiatry, 164,* 1476–1488.

Fisher, M., Holland, C., Subramaniam, K., & Vinogradov, S. (2010). Neuroplasticity-based cognitive training in schizophrenia: An interim report on the effects 6 months later. *Schizophrenia Bulletin, 36,* 869–879.

Foa, E. B., Dancu, C. V., Hembree, E. A., Jaycox, L. H., Meadows, E. A., & Street, G. P. (1999). A comparison of exposure therapy, stress inoculation training, and their combination for reducing posttraumatic stress disorder in female assault victims. *Journal of Consulting and Clinical Psychology, 67,* 194–200.

Foa, E. B., Liebowitz, M. R., Kozak, M. J., Davies, S., Campeas, R., Franklin, M. E. . . . Tu, X. (2005). Randomized, placebo-controlled trial of exposure and ritual prevention, clomipramine, and their combination in the treatment of obsessive-compulsive disorder. *American Journal of Psychiatry, 162,* 151–161.

Frewen, P. A., Dozois, D. J., & Lanius, R. A. (2008). Neuroimaging studies of psychological interventions for mood and anxiety disorders: Empirical and methodological review. *Clinical Psychology Review, 28,* 228–246.

Furmark, T., Tillfors, M., Marteinsdottir, I., Fischer, H., Pissiota, A., Långström, B., & Fredrikson, M. (2002). Common changes in cerebral blood flow in patients with social phobia treated with citalopram or cognitive behavioral therapy. *Archives of General Psychiatry, 59,* 425–433.

Gabbard, G. (2000). A neurobiologically informed perspective in psychotherapy. *British Journal of Psychiatry, 177,* 117–122.

Gorman, J. M., Kent, J. M., Sullivan, G. M., & Coplan, J. D. (2000). Neuroanatomical hypothesis of panic disorder, revised. *American Journal of Psychiatry, 157,* 493–505.

Gottdiener, W. H., & Haslam, N. A. (2003). A critique of the methods and conclusions in the patient outcome research team (PORT) report on psychological treatments for schizophrenia. *Journal of the American Academy of Psychoanalysis and Dynamic Psychiatry, 31,* 191–208.

Greenberg, R. P. (2004). Essential ingredients for successful psychotherapy: Effect of common factors. In M. J. Dewan, B. N. Steenbarger, & R. P. Greenberg (Eds.), *The art and science of brief psychotherapies: A practitioner's guide* (pp. 231–242). Washington, DC: American Psychiatric Publishing.

Greenough, W. T., Black, J. E., & Wallace, C. S. (1987). Experience and brain development. *Child Development, 58,* 539–559.

Harley, R., Sprich, S., Safren, S., Jacobo, M., & Fava, M. (2008). Adaptation of dialectical behavior therapy skills training group for treatment-resistant depression. *Journal of Nervous and Mental Disease, 196,* 136–143.

Hebb, D. O. (1949). *The organization of behavior.* New York: Wiley.

Hollon, S. D., & Ponniah, K. (2010) A review of empirically supported psychological therapies for mood disorders in adults. *Depression and Anxiety, 27,* 891–932.

Johnson, L. A., Safranek, S., & Friemoth, J. (2005). What is the most effective treatment for ADHD in children? *Journal of Family Practice, 54,* 166–168.

Kandel, E. R. (1998). A new intellectual framework for psychiatry. *American Journal of Psychiatry, 155,* 457–469.

Kapp, B. S., Pasco, J. P., & Bixler, M. A. (1984). The amygdale: A neuranatomical systems approach to its contributions to aversive conditioning. In N. Buttlers & L. R. Squire (Eds.), *Neuropsychology of memory* (pp. 473–488). New York: Guilford.

Keller, M. B., McCullough, J. P., Klein, D. N., Arnow, B., Dunner, D. L, Gelenberg, A. J. . . . Zajecka, J. (2000). A comparison of nefazodone, the cognitive behavioral analysis system of psychotherapy, and their combination for the treatment of chronic depression. *New England Journal of Medicine, 342,* 1462–1470.

Kennedy, S. H., Konarski, J. Z., Segal, Z. V., Lau, M. A., Bieling, P. J., McIntyre, R. S., & Mayberg, H. S. (2007). Differences in brain glucose metabolism between responders to CBT and venlafaxine in a 16-week randomized controlled trial. *American Journal of Psychiatry, 164,* 778–788.

Klassen, A., Miller, A., Raina, P., Lee, S. K., & Olsen, L. (1999). Attention deficit hyperactivity disorder in children and youth: A quantitative systematic review of the efficacy of different management strategies. *Canadian Journal of Psychiatry, 44,* 1007–1016.

Kocsis, J. H., Gelenberg, A. J., Rothbaum, B. O., Klein, D. N., Trivedi, M. H., Manber, R. . . . Thase, M. E. (2009). Cognitive behavioral analysis system of psychotherapy and brief supportive psychotherapy for augmentation of antidepressant nonresponse in chronic depression: The REVAMP Trial. *Archives of General Psychiatry, 66,* 1178–1188.

Kool, S., Dekker, J., Duijsens, I. J., de Jonghe, F., & Puite, B. (2003). Efficacy of combined therapy and pharmacotherapy for depressed patients with or without personality disorders. *Harvard Review of Psychiatry, 11,* 133–141.

Lam, D. H., Hayward, P., Watkins, E. R., Wright, K., & Sham, P. (2005). Relapse prevention in patients with bipolar disorder: Cognitive therapy outcome after 2 years. *American Journal of Psychiatry, 162,* 324–329.

Lam, D. H., Watkins, E. R., Hayward, P., Bright, J., Wright, K., Kerr, N. . . . Sham, P.(2003). A randomized controlled study of cognitive therapy for relapse prevention for bipolar affective disorder: Outcome of the first year. *Archives of General Psychiatry, 60,* 145–152.

Lavond, D., Kim, J. J., & Thompson, R. F. (1993). Mammalian brain substrates of aversive conditioning. *Annual Review of Psychology, 44,* 317–342.

Lehto, S. M., Tolmunen, T., Joensuu, M., Saarinen, P. I., Valkonen-Korhonen, M., Vanninen, R. . . . Lehtonen, J. (2008). Changes in midbrain serotonin transporter availability in atypically depressed subjects after one year of psychotherapy. Prog Neuropsychopharmacol. *Biological Psychiatry, 32,* 229–237.

Levin, P., Lazrove, S., & van der Kolk, B. (1999). What psychological testing and neuroimaging tell us about the treatment of posttraumatic stress disorder by eye movement desensitization and reprocessing. *Journal of Anxiety Disorders, 13,* 159–172.

Liggan, D. Y., & Kay, J. (1999). Some neurobiological aspects of psychotherapy: A review. *Journal of Psychotherapy Practice and Research, 8,* 103–114.

Marks, I., Swinson, R., Basoglu, M., Kuch, K., Noshirvani, H., O'Sullivan, G. . . . Sengun, S. (1993). Alprazolam and exposure alone and combined in panic disorder with agoraphobia: A controlled study in London and Toronto. *British Journal of Psychiatry, 162,* 776–787.

Martin, S. D., Martin, E., Rai, S. S., Richardson, M. A., & Royall, R. (2001). Brain blood flow changes in depressed patients treated with interpersonal psychotherapy or venlafaxine hydrochloride: Preliminary findings. *Archives of General Psychiatry, 58,* 641–648.

Math, S. B., & Janardhan, R. Y. C. (2007). Issues in the pharmacological treatment of obsessive-compulsive disorder. *International Journal of Clinical Practice, 61,* 1188–1197.

Medalia, A., & Choi, J. (2009). Cognitive remediation in schizophrenia. *Neuropsychology Review, 19,* 353–364.

Mojtabai, R., Nicholson, R. A., & Carpenter, B. N. (1998). Role of psychosocial treatments in management of schizophrenia: A meta-analytic review of controlled outcome studies. *Schizophrenia Bulletin, 24,* 569–587.

Nakatani, E., Nakgawa, A., Ohara, Y., Goto, S., Uozumi, N., Iwakiri, M. . . . Yamagami, T. (2003). Effects of behavior therapy on regional cerebral blood flow in obsessive-compulsive disorder. *Psychiatry Research, 124,* 113–120.

National Institute for Health and Clinical Excellence. (2009). Depression: The treatment and management of depression in adults. NICE Clinical guideline. Retrieved from http://www.nice.org.uk/nicemedia/live/12329/45888/45888.pdf

Nemeroff, C. B., Heim, C. M., Thase, M. E., Klein, D. N., Rush, A. J., Schatzberg, A. F. . . . Keller, M. B. (2003). Differential responses to psychotherapy versus pharmacotherapy in patients with chronic forms of major depression and childhood trauma. *Proceedings of the National Academy of Sciences, 100,* 14293–14296.

Nestler, E. J. (2009). Epigenetic mechanisms in psychiatry. *Biological Psychiatry, 65,* 189–190.

Oei, T. P., Llamas, M., & Evans, L. (1997). Does concurrent drug intake affect the long-term outcome of group cognitive behaviour therapy in panic disorder with or without agoraphobia? *Behaviour Research and Therapy, 35,* 851–857.

Paquette, V., Lévesque, J., Mensour, B., Leroux, J. M., Beaudoin, G., Bourgouin, P., & Beauregard, M. (2003). Change the mind and you change the brain: Effects of cognitive behavioral therapy on the neural correlates of spider phobia. *Neuroimage, 18,* 401–409.

Park, S. B. G. (1998). *Neural networks and psychopathology.* In D. J. Stein & J. Ludik (Eds.), *Neural Networks & Psychology* (pp. 68–79). Cambridge: Cambridge University Press.

Pediatric OCD Treatment Study (POTS) Team. (2004). Cognitive-behavior therapy, sertraline, and their combination for children and adolescents with obsessive-compulsive disorder: The Pediatric OCD Treatment Study (POTS) randomized controlled trial. *Journal of the American Medical Association, 292,* 1969–1976.

Peselow, E. D., Sanfilipo, M. P., Fieve, R. R., & Gulbenkian, G. (1994). Personality traits during depression and after clinical recovery. *British Journal of Psychiatry, 164,* 349–354.

Reich, J. H., & Vasile, R. G. (1993). Effect of personality disorders on the treatment outcome of Axis I conditions: An update. *Journal of Nervous and Mental Diseases, 181,* 475–484.

Riggs, P. D., Winhusen, T., Davies, R. D., Leimberger, J. D., Mikulich-Gilbertson, S., Klein, C. . . . Liu, D. (2011). Randomized controlled trial of osmotic-release methylphenidate with cognitive behavioral therapy in adolescents with attention-deficit/hyperactivity disorder and substance use disorders. *Journal of the American Academy of Child and Adolescent Psychiatry, 50,* 903–914.

Roffman, J. L., Marci, C. D., Glick, D. M., Dougherty, D. D., & Rauch, S. L. (2005). Neuroimaging and the functional neuroanatomy of psychotherapy. *Psychological Medicine, 35,* 1385–1398.

Rothbaum, B. O., Cahill, S. P., Foa, E. B., Davidson, J. R., Compton, J., Connor, K. M. . . . Hahn, C. G. (2006). Augmentation of sertraline with prolonged exposure in the treatment of posttraumatic stress disorder. *Journal of Traumatic Stress, 19,* 625–638.

Rostain, J. A., & Ramsay, J. R. (2006). A combined treatment approach for adults with ADHD: Results of an open study of 43 patients. *Journal of Attention Disorders, 10,* 150–159.

Safren, S. A., Otto, M. W., Sprich, S., Winett, C. L., Wilens, T. E., & Biederman, J. (2005). Cognitive behavioral therapy for ADHD in medication-treated adults with continued symptoms. *Behaviour Research and Therapy, 43,* 831–842.

Schmitz, J. M., Averill, P., Sayre, S., McCleary, P., Moeller, F. G., & Swann, A. (2002). Cognitive behavioral treatment of bipolar disorder and substance abuse: A preliminary randomized study. *Addictive Disorders and Their Treatment, 1,* 17–24.

Schooler, N. R., Keith, S. J., Severe, J. B., Matthews, S. M., Bellack, A. S., Glick, I. D. . . . Woerner, M. G. (1997). Relapse and rehospitalization during maintenance treatment of schizophrenia: The effects of dose reduction and family treatment. *Archives of General Psychiatry, 54,* 453–463.

Schwartz, T. L., & Rashid, A. (2007). Augmentation and combination pharmacotherapy trends in major depressive disorder: Results of a brief survey of psychiatrists. *P&T, 32,* 28–31.

Schwartz, T. L., & Stahl, S. M. (2010). Optimizing antidepressant management of depression: Current status and future perspectives. In J. F. Cryan & B. E. Leonard (Eds.), *Depression: From psychopathology to pharmacotherapy. Mod Trends Pharmacopsychiatry* (vol. 27, pp. 254–267). Basel: Karger.

Sharp, D., Power, K., Simpson, R., Swanson, V., Moodie, E., Anstee, J., & Ashford, J. (1996). Fluvoxamine, placebo, and cognitive behavior therapy used alone and in combination in the treatment of panic disorder and agoraphobia. *Journal of Anxiety Disorders, 10,* 219–242.

Simpson, H. B., Foa, E. B., Liebowitz, M. R., Ledley, D. R., Huppert, J. D., Cahill, S . . . Petkova, E. (2008). A randomized, controlled trial of cognitive behavioral therapy for augmenting pharmacotherapy in obsessive-compulsive disorder. *American Journal of Psychiatry, 165,* 621–630.

Squire, L. R., Ojemann, J. G., Miezin, F. M., Petersen, S. E., Videen, T. O., & Raichle, M. E. (1992). Activation of the hippocampus in normal humans: A functional anatomical study in normal humans. *Proceedings of the National Academy of Sciences, 89,* 1837–1841.

Stahl, S. M. (2008). *Stahl's essential psychopharmacology* (3rd ed.). New York: Cambridge University Press.

Stahl, S. M. (2010a). Psychiatric stress testing: Novel strategy for translational psychopharmacology. *Neuropsychopharmacology, 35,* 1413–1414.

Stahl, S. M. (2010b). Methylated spirits: Epigenetic hypotheses of psychiatric disorders. *CNS Spectrums, 15,* 220–230.

Stahl, S. M. (2012). Psychotherapy as an epigenetic 'drug': Psychiatric therapeutics target symptoms linked to malfunctioning brain circuits with psychotherapy as well as with drugs. *Journal of Clinical Pharmacy and Therapeutics, 37,* 249–253.

Stahl, S. M. (2013). *Stahl's essential psychopharmacology: Neuroscientific basis and practical applications* 4th ed.). Cambridge, UK: Cambridge University Press.

Stahl, S. M., & Moore, B. A. (2013). *Anxiety disorders: A guide for integrating psychopharmacology and psychotherapy (psychopharmacology and psychotherapy in clinical practice).* London: Routledge, Chapman & Hall.

Stein, D. J, & Ludik, J. (1998). *Neural networks & psychopathology.* Cambridge, UK: Cambridge University Press.

Steketee, G., & Shapiro, L. (1995). Exposure vs. cognitive restructuring in the treatment of panic disorder with agoraphobia. *Clinical Psychology Review, 15,* 317–346.

Sweatt, J. D. (2009). Experience dependent epigenetic modifications in the central nervous system. *Biological Psychiatry, 65,* 191–197.

Thase, M. E. (1996). The role of Axis II comorbidity in the management of patients with treatment-resistant depression. *Psychiatric Clinics of North America, 19,* 287–309.

Thase, M. E., Friedman, E. S., Biggs, M. M., Wisniewski, S. R., Trivedi, M. H., Luther, J. F. . . . Rush, J. (2007). Cognitive therapy versus medication in augmentation and switch strategies as second-step treatments: A STAR*D report. *American Journal of Psychiatry, 164,* 739–752.

Thase, M. E., Greenhouse, J. B., Frank, E., Reynolds, C. F., Pilkonis, P. A., Hurley, K. . . . Kupfer, D. J. (1997). Treatment of major depression with psychotherapy or psychotherapy-pharmacotherapy combinations. *Archives of General Psychiatry, 54,* 1009–1015.

Topel, M. E., Zajecka, J. M., Goldstein, C. N., Siddiqui, U. A., & Schwartz, T. L. (2011). Using what we have: Combining medications to achieve remission. *Clinical Neuropsychiatry, 8,* 4–27.

Vidal-Estrada, R., Bosch-Munso, R., Nogueira-Morais, M., Casas-Brugue, M., & Ramos-Quiroga, J. A. (2012). Psychological treatment of attention deficit hyperactivity disorder in adults: A systematic review. *Actas Españolas de Psiquiatría, 40,* 147–154.

Viinamaki, H., Kuikka, J., Tiihonnen, J. (1998). Changes in monamine transport density related to clinical treatment: A case controlled study. *Nordic Journal of Psychiatry, 55,* 39–44.

Wilberg, T., Friis, S., Karterud, S., Mehlum, L., Urnes, O., & Vaglum, P. (1998). Patterns of short-term course in patients treated in a day unit for personality disorders. *Comprehensive Psychiatry, 39,* 75–84.

Wilens, T. E., Biederman, J., & Spencer, T. J. (2002). Attention deficit/hyperactivity disorder across the lifespan. *Annual Review of Medicine, 53,* 113–131.

Zimmerman, M., Chelminski, I., Young, D., & Dalyrymple, K. (2011). Using outcome measures to promote better outcomes. *Clinical Neuropsychiatry, 8,* 28–36.

2

Trial-Based Cognitive Therapy (TBCT)
A New Cognitive-Behavior Therapy Approach

Irismar Reis de Oliveira

INTRODUCTION

Recent advances in neurobiology suggest that, similarly to drugs, psychotherapy changes brain circuits. Therapeutic effects of both drugs and psychotherapy are thought to occur in psychiatric disorders by improving the efficiency of information processing in malfunctioning brain circuits. As clinically effective treatments for psychiatric disorders, psychotherapy and psychopharmacology in combination can be therapeutically synergistic in several psychiatric conditions. Psychotherapy hypothetically induces epigenetic changes in brain circuits, enhancing the efficiency of information processing in malfunctioning neurons, and improving psychiatric symptoms, just like drugs (Stahl, 2012).

For cognitive therapy (CT) theorists, cognition occurs in three levels of information processing (Fig. 2.1). In the first and most superficial level are the automatic thoughts (ATs), defined as perceptions that occur rapidly in response to a situation; are not subjected to systematic, logical analysis; the person may be unaware of their presence or significance; and they also may or may not be distorted (Beck, 2012). The second or intermediate level of information processing comprises the underlying assumptions (UAs) or conditional beliefs, used to guide our behavior, emotional expression, and understanding of how the world operates. They are usually expressed as "if . . . , then . . . " statements (e.g., "If I go out alone, then I will be helpless") (Greenberger & Padesky, 1995). The third and deeper level of information processing, conceptualized as core beliefs (CBs), sometimes also called schemas, are global, rigid, and fundamental beliefs that people hold about themselves, the world, and/or the future, and that influence the types of ATs that people experience in specific situations (e.g., "I am incompetent" or "I am unlikable"). The goal of CT is to help patients uncover and restructure unhelpful and negative cognitions in the three levels (ATs, UAs, and CBs), reducing emotional distress and preventing relapse of psychiatric disorders (Wenzel, 2012).

CT is one of the therapeutic approaches within the larger group of cognitive behavioral therapies (CBT). It was developed in the 1960s by Aaron Beck at the University of Pennsylvania, as an active approach to treatment that helps patients to recognize and modify the ATs,

Cognitive Model

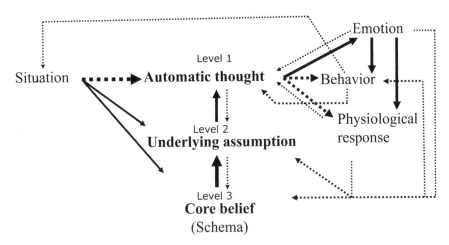

Figure 2.1 Interactions between cognitions and responses to cognitions (Copyright: Irismar Reis de Oliveira; http://trial-basedcognitivetherapy.com).

UAs, and unhelpful CBs that exacerbate emotional distress (Beck, 1976). Fig. 2.1 illustrates the interactions between different elements of the cognitive model and the reciprocal influences of each element over the others. The full arrows represent more direct effects, and the interrupted arrows represent possible indirect effects in the chain of elements triggered by a situation. The latter help explain why different situations provoke different reactions (interrupted arrow between *situation* and *automatic thought*) in different people or in the same people in different situations (de Oliveira, 2012a).

This chapter has three learning objectives: (a) introduce a new spinoff of CT called trial-based cognitive therapy (TBCT), designed as a more structured format of CT, easy to be learned by therapists and patients; (b) review studies of TBCT efficacy; and (c) discuss TBCT usefulness as a potential psychotherapy model to be combined with psychopharmacology in different psychiatric diagnoses.

Trial-Based Cognitive Therapy (TBCT)

TBCT is a new psychotherapeutic approach whose foundation is in CT and in the work of Franz Kafka, developed at the Department of Neurosciences and Mental Health at the Federal University of Bahia in Brazil (de Oliveira, 2011b). Its main techniques simulate court trials in which the patient role-plays the different characters in a tribunal. In trial-based thought record (TBTR), the main technique used in TBCT, an investigation or inquiry is undertaken by means of the downward arrow procedure (Burns, 1980), and the self-accusation/core belief (e.g., "I am a loser") is uncovered and restructured. This is done by having the patient role-play the different characters in a courtroom: After the inquiry (downward arrow), the prosecutor presents the evidence supporting the accusation/core belief, and the defense attorney presents the evidence not supporting the accusation/core belief. Subsequently, the jurors, role-played by the patient and by the therapist, evaluate the pleas and state the verdict. Although the use of a court metaphor is not new in psychotherapy (Freeman & DeWolf, 1992; Cromarty & Marks, 1995; Leahy, 2003), TBCT integrates the most important techniques of CBT and other modalities of psychotherapies (e.g., Gestalt [Perls, 1973], acceptance and commitment therapy [Hayes, Strosahl, & Wilson, 1999], compassion-focused therapy [Gilbert, 2010], metacognitive therapy [Wells, 2009]) in a manualized, transdiagnostic, case formulation-based approach (de Oliveira, in press).

Case Formulation

Case formulation, also known as case conceptualization, is a key element in therapy, and may be defined as a description of a patient's presenting problems, which uses theory to make explanatory inferences about causes and maintaining factors, as well as to inform interventions (Kuyken, Fothergill, Musa, & Chadwick, 2005). However, sharing its components with patients may be a complex and difficult task. As a highly individualized work, case conceptualization should be collaboratively built with the client, while educating him/her about the treatment model.

A conceptualization diagram (CD) is shown in Figs. 2.2 and 2.3. In the first level of information processing, a situation appraised by the patient as dangerous (*AT* box) elicits anxiety (*emotional reaction* box) that may paralyze him/her (*behavioral and physiological responses* box). Arrows returning to the *emotional reaction*, *AT*, and *situation* boxes inform the patient about the circular nature of these interactions (confirmatory bias) that prevent him/her from reappraising the situation and consequently changing the erroneous perceptions it triggered (de Oliveira, 2012a).

The CD might also be useful to make the patient understand that behaviors used in specific situations that elicit less anxiety and consequently yield a sense of immediate relief (e.g., avoidance) may progressively become a *safety behavior* (arrow directed from the *behavioral*

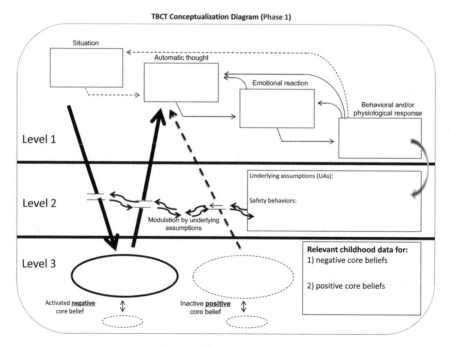

Figure 2.2 Conceptualization diagram showing an activated negative core belief (Copyright: Irismar Reis de Oliveira; http://trial-basedcognitivetherapy.com).

and physiological responses box from the first to the second level on the right side of the figure). This means that perceptions in the first level may progressively become *UAs* or *rules* that are now maintained by the *safety behaviors* (confirmatory bias) seen in the second level. Safety behaviors then assume a modulatory function. Under the influence of the UAs that support such behaviors, first-level appraisals, or ATs, may be repeatedly confirmed. Also, third-level (unconditional) *CBs* may be activated if UAs are challenged (for example, during exposure), or inactivated if UAs are not challenged (for example, by avoidance) (de Oliveira, 2012a).

Having sufficient practice in identifying and changing ATs by replacing them with more functional alternative appraisals, the patient may progressively notice changes in the other levels—for instance, activation of positive CBs. However, restructuring dysfunctional UAs and negative CBs are considered important steps for more durable results in therapy (Safran, Vallis, Segal, & Shaw, 1998).

Restructuring Dysfunctional ATs and Cognitive Distortions

ATs are rapid, evaluative thoughts that do not arise from deliberation or reasoning; as a result, the person is likely to accept them as true, without analysis (Beck, 2012). It is not uncommon for ATs to be distorted, resulting in dysfunctional emotional reactions and behaviors that, in turn, produce more cognitive errors that maintain a vicious circle (level 1 in Figs. 2.2 and 2.3) (de Oliveira, 2012a).

Table 2.1 includes 15 known cognitive distortions, their definitions and examples, as well as spaces for the patients to write down their own examples (Burns, 1980; Beck, 1976; Beck, 2012; Dryden, David, & Ellis, 2010; Leahy, 2003; Leahy, Tirch, & Napolitano, 2011). Teaching the patient to identify cognitive distortions is an important step to restructure such dysfunctional ATs. This may be done by means of the intrapersonal thought record (Intra-TR) described below (de Oliveira, 2012a).

Cognitive Distortions Questionnaire (CD-Quest)

The CD-Quest (see Appendix) was developed as an operational instrument, to be routinely used by patients to facilitate perceptions of the link between cognitive errors and their consequent emotional states, as well as dysfunctional behaviors. Also, it was designed to help therapists quantitatively assess and follow the clinical evolution of patients by means of its scores. It comprises 15 items that assess known cognitive distortions in two dimensions: frequency and intensity. The scores may range from 0 to 75, and the higher the score, the higher cognitive distorted thinking.

In the first study conducted by our group (de Oliveira et al., 2011), the initial psychometric properties of the CD-Quest in its Brazilian Portuguese version in a sample of university students were assessed. Medical and psychology students ($n = 184$; age $= 21.8 \pm 3.37$) were evaluated using the following instruments: CD-Quest, Beck Depression Inventory (BDI-II, Beck et al., 1996), Beck Anxiety Inventory (BAI, Beck et al., 1988), and the Automatic Thoughts Questionnaire (ATQ, Hollon & Kendall, 1980). These self-report instruments were applied collectively in classrooms. The CD-Quest showed good internal consistency (0.83–0.86) and concurrent validity with BDI (0.65), BAI (0.51), and ATQ (0.65). Furthermore, it was able to discriminate between groups possessing depressive (BDI $\geq$ 12) and anxious (BAI $\geq$ 11) indicators from those not possessing such indicators ($p < .001$). An exploratory factor analysis by means of principal components analysis with varimax rotation showed the presence of four

Table 2.1 Cognitive distortions, definitions, and examples.

Cognitive distortion	Definition	Examples	My examples
1. Dichotomous thinking (also called all-or-nothing, black and white, or polarized thinking)	I view a situation, a person or an event only in all-or-nothing terms, fitting them into only two extreme categories instead of on a continuum.	"I made a mistake, therefore I'm a failure." "I ate more than I planned, so I blew my diet completely."	
2. Fortune telling (also called catastrophizing)	I predict the future in negative terms and believe that what will happen will be so awful that I will not be able to stand it.	"I will fail, and this will be unbearable." "I'll be so upset that I won't be able to concentrate for the exam."	
3. Discounting or disqualifying the positive	I disqualify and discount positive experiences or events, insisting that they do not count.	"I passed the exam, but I was just lucky." "Going to college is not a big deal; anyone can do it."	
4. Emotional reasoning	I believe my emotions reflect reality, and I let them guide my attitudes and judgments.	"I feel she loves me, so it must be true." "I am terrified of airplanes, so flying must be dangerous."	
5. Labeling	I put a fixed, global label, usually negative, on myself or others.	"I'm a loser." "He's a rotten person." "She's a complete jerk."	
6. Magnification/ minimization	I evaluate myself, others, and situations, magnifying the negatives and/or minimizing the positives.	"I got a B. This proves how inferior I am." "I got an A. It doesn't mean I'm smart."	
7. Selective abstraction (also called mental filter and tunnel vision)	I pay attention to one or a few details and fail to see the whole picture.	"My boss said he liked my presentation, but since he corrected a slide, I know he did not mean it." "Even though the group said my work was good, one person pointed out an error, so I know I will be fired."	
8. Mind reading	I believe that I know the thoughts or intentions of others (or that they know my thoughts or intentions) without having sufficient evidence.	"He's thinking that I failed." "She thought I didn't know the project." "He knows I do not like to be touched this way."	
9. Overgeneralizing	I take isolated cases and generalize them widely by means of words such as "always," "never," "everyone."	"Every time I have a day off from work, it rains." "You only pay attention to me when you want sex."	
10. Personalizing	I assume that others' behaviors and external events concern (or are directed to) myself without considering other plausible explanations.	"I felt disrespected because the cashier did not say thank you to me" (not considering that the cashier did not say thank you to anyone). "My husband left me because I was a bad wife" (not considering that she was his fourth wife).	
11. Should statements (also "musts," "oughts," "have tos")	I tell myself that events, people's behaviors, and my own attitudes "should" be the way I expected them to be and not as they really are.	"I should have been a better mother." "He should have married Ann instead of Mary." "I shouldn't have made so many mistakes."	
12. Jumping to conclusions	I draw conclusions (negative or positive) from little or no confirmatory evidence.	"As soon as I saw him, I knew he had bad intentions." "He was looking at me, so I concluded immediately he thought I was responsible for the accident."	
13. Blaming (others or oneself)	I direct my attention to others as sources of my negative feelings and experiences, failing to consider my own responsibility; or, conversely, I take responsibility for others' behaviors and attitudes.	"My parents are the ones to blame for my unhappiness." "It is my fault that my son married a selfish and uncaring person."	
14. What if?	I keep asking myself questions such as "what if something happens?"	"What if my car crashes?" "What if I have a heart attack?" "What if my husband leaves me?"	
15. Unfair comparisons	I compare myself with others who seem to do better than I do and place myself in a disadvantageous position	"My father always preferred my elder brother because he is much smarter than I am." "I am a failure because she is more successful than I am."	

factors that together explained 56.6% of data variance. The factors consisted of the following types of cognitive distortions: (a) Factor I: dichotomous thinking, selective abstraction, personalizing, should statements, what if . . . , unfair comparisons; (b) Factor II: emotional reasoning, labeling, mind reading, jumping to conclusions; (c) Factor III: fortune telling, discounting positives, magnification/minimization; and (d) Factor IV: overgeneralizing, blaming. It was concluded that the CD-Quest was characterized by good psychometric properties, justifying the need for larger studies designed to determine its predictive validity, expand its construct validity, and measure the degree to which it is a useful measure of change achieved by patients in cognitive behavioral therapy.

Case Illustration (Mary-Ann)

Mary-Ann, aged 52, is a married teacher with a 9-year history of panic attacks; severe agoraphobia; phobias of closed spaces, planes, thunder, and crowds; and alcohol abuse. She stopped working and had been on sick leave for a year, after many previous interruptions due to frequent panic attacks at work. Her panics, agoraphobia, and alcohol intake increased progressively, making her more and more reclusive, as well as increasing the use of alcohol.

Fig. 2.3 illustrates Mary-Ann's CD, and Fig. 2.4 shows one of her Intra-TRs. Her ATs (e.g., "I'll pass out" during panics, and "I'll be out of breath if I enter closed rooms") probably resulted from her long-lasting activated CBs "I'm vulnerable" and "I'm helpless." Possible relevant aspects in her childhood that might have contributed to the development of negative CBs were her mother's extremely anxious and demanding attitudes and behaviors, with no demonstration of validation, affection, or encouragement when Mary-Ann was fearful and teary, while her father, besides frequently abusing alcohol, was absent and rarely

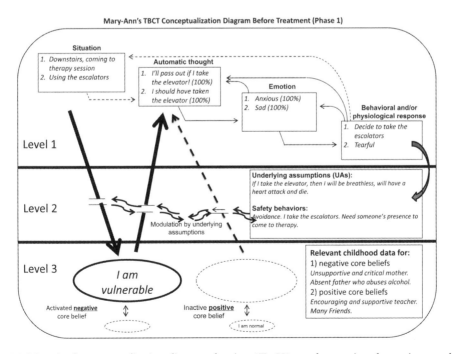

Figure 2.3 Mary-Ann's conceptualization diagram showing ATs, UAs, and an activated negative core belief (Copyright: Irismar Reis de Oliveira; http://trial-basedcognitivetherapy.com).

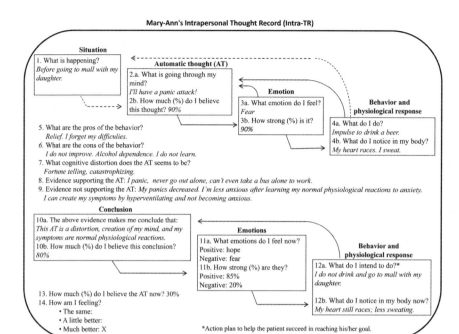

Figure 2.4 Mary-Ann's Intra-TR (Copyright: Irismar Reis de Oliveira; http://trial-basedcognitivetherapy.com).

Table 2.2 Questions to be answered by the patients when they fill in the Intra-TR.

Q1	What is happening?	Situation box
Q2a	What is going through my mind now?	Automatic thought box
Q2b	How much do I believe it?	
Q3a	What emotion do I feel?	Emotion box
Q3b	How strong is it?	
Q4a	What do I do?	Behavioral and physical response box
Q4b	What do I notice in my body?	
Q5	What are the pros of this behavior?	Advantages of the behavior
Q6	What are the cons of this behavior?	Disadvantages of the behavior
Q7	According to the cognitive distortions sheet, what distortion does this AT seem to be?	Cognitive distortion
Q8	Is there evidence that supports the AT?	Evidence supporting the AT
Q9	Is there evidence that does not support the AT?	Evidence not supporting the AT
Q10a	What does the above evidence make me conclude?	Conclusion box
Q10b	How much do I believe the conclusion?	
Q11a	What positive and negative emotions do I feel now?	New emotion box
Q11b	How strong are the emotions now?	
Q12a	What do I intend to do?	Action plan box
Q12b	What do I notice in my body now?	
Q13	How much do I believe the AT now?	Final evaluation of the AT
Q14	How am I now?	Final global evaluation

participative regarding the children's education and family issues. On the other hand, as a positive source of support, Mary-Ann's teacher was mindful, supportive, and encouraging during her entire elementary school years. Mary-Ann was spontaneous, caring with her peers, easily made friendships, and made durable and good friendships during her childhood and adolescence.

The catastrophic ATs, derived from CBs such as "I'm vulnerable," elicited great anxiety and fear, and were relieved, as well as maintained, by the activation of UAs (see level 2 of the CD in Fig. 2.3) and consequent safety behaviors (e.g., avoidance and alcohol use). Unfortunately, such compensatory strategies derived from UAs like "If I'm alone, I will have a stroke and may be invalid for the rest of my life," although producing immediate relief, backfired by activating and strengthening her negative UAs and CBs "I'm vulnerable" and "I'm dependent" (level 3 of the CD in Fig. 2.3) and generated great distress at every attempt to expose herself or go out alone.

Mary-Ann had 10 weekly sessions of TBCT, and also was prescribed escitalopram 10mg/ day. Sessions 1–5 helped her overcome panic attacks and agoraphobia. She had no more panic attacks after session 4, and resumed physical exercises, walking in the street and going to malls first with her daughter and then alone. Moving from another state to the therapist's city for treatment seems to have helped her abstain from alcohol by reducing drinking opportunities. Her worst fear, however, remained taking the elevator and being in closed spaces. In session 4, merely hearing the suggestion from the therapist that she could try to take the elevator in the therapist's presence made her cry and say that this was something unthinkable for her. However, in session 6, the therapist used the consensual role-play (CRP) technique to help her better understand and challenge her fear of elevators.

Intrapersonal Thought Record (Intra-TR)

The Intra-TR was developed to help patients in restructuring and modifying dysfunctional ATs (in session and as homework), and in reducing stress related to such ATs (Fig. 2.4). Its main strength is to include the same components as the first level of the CD, to which the patient was introduced in session 1, and is supposed to be familiar with. The patient is asked to respond to specific questions, reducing the vagueness when looking for alternative thoughts and feelings. When the patient memorizes the Intra-TR questions (Table 2.2), it is easier for him/her to respond to them in daily real life situations. Fig. 2.4 illustrates one of Mary-Ann's Intra-TRs filled in during session 3.

RESTRUCTURING UAS AND CHALLENGING SAFETY BEHAVIORS

Behavioral experiments are amongst the most powerful strategies for bringing about change in CBT (Bennett-Levy et al., 2004), providing a meeting ground for communication between knowledge derived from the rational mind and emotional mind (Padesky, 2004). Behavioral experiments are especially used to change UAs. These level 2 cognitions are expressed as conditional beliefs such as "If I go out alone, then I will have a heart attack and may die." Consequently, the sufferer usually avoids feared situations. In session 4 (see case illustration), Mary-Ann was helped to understand that exposing herself to feared situations (for example, going out alone to work) was necessary to overcome unpleasant emotions and behaviors.

Color-Coded Symptom Hierarchy (CCSH)

A strategy that may help patients to increase the chances of doing behavioral experiments is providing a hierarchy of symptoms to which they are supposed to be exposed in order to obtain symptom remission (de Oliveira, 2012a). After collecting a detailed list of symptoms (Table 2.3), such as OCD or social phobia symptoms, in which the patient scores each one according to the CCSH shown in Fig. 2.5, the therapist informs him/her that there will be no focus on blue symptoms, but s/he will choose two or three green symptoms to practice exposure as homework during the week. In general, the therapist uses CRP (see below) to help patients accept to exposing themselves to yellow symptoms, usually during therapy sessions. These are symptoms patients resist confronting when they are alone, and CRP seems to make this challenge acceptable, at least in the therapist's presence, but sometimes also as homework. The therapist explains that the patient will NEVER need to challenge red (the most feared) symptoms. This information tends to make the patient more willing to comply with the technique because there is no pressure to confront the most anxiety-provoking items. So, if the therapist decides to use CRP for red symptoms, s/he explains that the intent is not to convince the patient to go through with exposure but to understand what is going on—e.g., why the patient is fearful or ambivalent (de Oliveira, 2102a).

Therapist and patient keep track of individual and global symptom scores weekly. The patients notice that the scores continue to decrease (both those to which s/he exposed him/ herself and those which s/he did not). Patients are very surprised to realize that even red symptom scores decrease, making exposure acceptable because they gradually become yellow or green. Showing the patient a global score chart (Fig. 2.6) helps him/her track weekly progress and notice scores change.

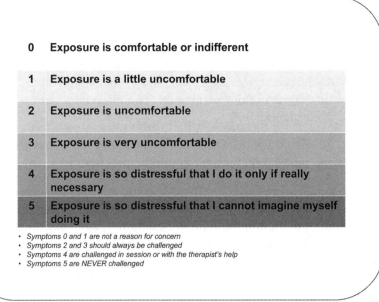

Figure 2.5 Color-coded symptom hierarchy (CCSH) card to facilitate exposure implementation (Copyright: Irismar Reis de Oliveira; http://trial-basedcognitivetherapy.com).

Table 2.3 Mary-Ann's symptom scores (0–5) assessed according to the color-coded symptom hierarchy (CCSH) card in Fig. 2.5.

Session	01	02	03	04	05	06	07	08	09	10	11	12	13	14	15	16	17	18	19	20
Date	/	/	/	/	/	/	/	/	/	/	/	/	/	/	/	/	/	/	/	/
Go out alone (known places)	5	5	5	4	4	3	3	2	1	0										
Go out alone (unknown places)	5	5	5	5	5	4	4	3	3	2										
Come alone to therapy (from downstairs)	3	3	2	2	1	0	0	0	0	0										
Come alone to therapy (from the other side of the avenue)	4	4	3	3	2	1	0	0	0	0										
Enter a closed elevator (few people)	5	5	5	5	5	4	4	4	2	1										
Enter a closed elevator (crowded)	5	5	5	5	5	5	4	4	3	2										
Enter a panoramic elevator (few people)	5	5	5	5	5	4	3	2	1	0										
Enter a panoramic elevator (crowded)	5	5	5	5	5	5	4	3	2	1										
Lock restroom (no one at home)	5	4	4	3	2	1	1	1	0	0										
Lock restroom (husband at home)	4	4	3	2	2	1	0	0	0	0										
Resume work	5	5	5	5	5	5	4	4	3	2										
TOTAL SCORE (sum of individual items)	*51*	*50*	*47*	*44*	*41*	*33*	*27*	*22*	*15*	*9*										
Number of exposures you do not allow yourself to do (reds and yellows)	*10*	*10*	*8*	*7*	*7*	*6*	*5*	*2*	*0*	*0*										

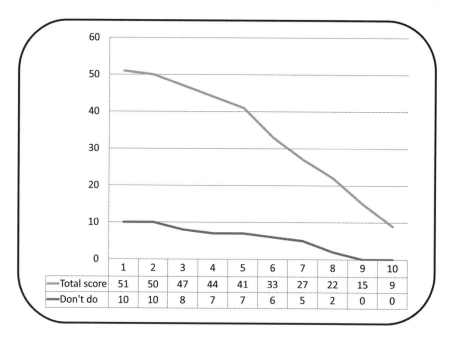

Figure 2.6 Mary-Ann's chart showing weekly progress (total score and the number of things she wasn't able to do), based on the CCSH.

Consensual Role-Play (CRP)

The CRP is a seven-step method to help patients deal with ambivalence and help them make decisions, increasing the chance of the patient in confronting situations made difficult by UAs and repeatedly reinforced safety behaviors (de Oliveira, 2012a). CRP typically takes 30–40 minutes, and can be repeated as often as necessary regarding particular decisions. The therapist tells the patient that what s/he learns is more important than the decision itself, thus freeing the patient to ventilate concerns and not try to please the therapist.

Technique Description

Fig. 2.7 illustrates, from steps 1 through 7 (de Oliveira, 2012a), how the patient is:

Step 1: encouraged to list the cons/disadvantages and pros/advantages of implementing the desired/necessary, but unpleasant/feared, action/behavior.

Step 2: helped to make the dissonance (ambivalence) between "reason" and "emotion" explicit (Padesky, 2004), by assigning percentage weights to advantages and disadvantages of implementing the action according to reason and emotion. The therapist informs the patient that one should not assume that reason is better than emotion or vice versa, and that the goal is to reach a consensus between them. Although in anxiety disorders, the goal is to stimulate the patient to empower a rational stance over emotion (e.g., fear), there are circumstances for which the goal is to make patients express and liberate emotion. If patients cannot separate reason from emotion (e.g., in alexithymia), the therapist asks them to distinguish between the internal voices that say "go" and "don't go" (e.g., "Do you sometimes notice an internal voice that says, 'You should meet your friends at the pub' speaking to another voice that says, 'You know that if you go you will resume drinking?'").

Step 3: encouraged to use the empty-chair approach (Carstenson, 1955) to reach a consensus between "the rational self" (chair 1) and "the emotional self" (chair 2) in a ± 15-minute dialogue, making emotion speak to reason and vice versa.

Step 4: requested to review with the therapist what was learned from steps 1 through 3.

Step 5: asked to use a third chair as the "consensus self" (chair 3) and reassess the percentage weights of advantages versus disadvantages in order to reach a consensus between his/her rational and emotional selves.

Step 6: asked if s/he is ready to implement the unpleasant/feared action/behavior.

Step 7: helped, if the answer is "yes," to design an action plan to raise the chances of success in implementing the behavior, so s/he can organize what to do, anticipate obstacles, find solutions, and follow up the outcomes; or, if the answer is "no," to design an action plan to help him/her gather information and decide later.

Case Illustration (Mary-Ann, Continued)

In session 6, after collecting disadvantages and advantages of taking the elevator (Fig. 2.7), Mary-Ann gave a 70% weight to advantages of taking the elevator (versus 30% for disadvantages) according to reason, but 95% weight to disadvantages (versus 5% for advantages) according to emotion (step 2). By means of the empty-chair approach (Greenberg, 2011), the therapist asked Mary-Ann to reach a consensus between "reason" and "emotion" in a ± 15-minute dialogue (step 3) during which she switched from one chair to the other as "Mary-Ann Reason" (the one who said, "You can take the elevator") and "Mary-Ann Emotion," (the one who said, "No, you can't take the elevator"). After this step, the therapist asked Mary-Ann

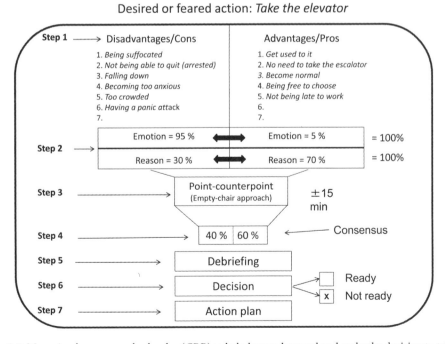

Figure 2.7 Mary-Ann's consensual role-play (CRP) to help her understand and make the decision to take the elevator (Copyright: Irismar Reis de Oliveira; http://trial-basedcognitivetherapy.com).

to sit in the consensus chair and assess the weight of advantages versus disadvantages, coming to a consensus between rational and emotional perspectives. Mary-Ann was able to give a 60% weight for the advantages of taking the elevator versus 40% weight for the disadvantages (step 4). Next (step 5), after a debriefing of what Mary-Ann learned from steps 1–4, the therapist asked her if she was ready to make a decision (step 6). She said she wasn't ready to take the elevator, and the decision was that she would not do that, so the therapist proposed an action plan to help her gather information that might enable her to decide another time (Fig 2.8). If she had made the decision to take the elevator as a behavior experiment (homework), the therapist would have helped her organize an action plan to increase the chances of success (step 7).

In session 7, CRP was also used, and she said she was not ready to enter an elevator. However, in session 8, though anxious, Mary-Ann spent 40 minutes in an elevator with the therapist. Most of session 9 was also dedicated to exposure to the elevator. In session 10, she stated that elevators seemed to be an issue no more, and asked the therapist to help her resist alcohol, as she would soon return to her city, where not using alcohol was a challenge. Another CRP was implemented to help her decide to abstain for 2 more months, after which she would decide whether she wanted to stop drinking permanently or not. Treatment was concluded, and she returned to her city.

Since then, after 6 months, Mary-Ann resumed work, had no more panic attacks, and was able to go out alone and exercise. As she lives in a small village, she had no more opportunities to take elevators but could be in closed spaces without much anxiety. Although she did not stop drinking, she reduced the frequency of alcohol use to parties and occasional weekends.

Action Plan: *Take the elevator*

Proposed actions:
    a. *searching for elevator risks on the Internet*
    b. *beginning with panoramic elevators in the mall with my daughter and then by myself*
    c. *continue other exposures (going out alone, locking myself in a room alone home) that make me feel stronger*
    d.

Possible obstacles to actions:
    a. *I do not have access to the Internet where I am staying*
    b. *not sure if there is an elevator with panoramic view there*
    c. *none*
    d.

Solutions to obstacles:
    a. *call my friend Rita and ask her to do the search*
    b. *if not panoramic view, ask my daughter to take me to another mall a little farther*
    c. *no problem*
    d.

Follow-up:
    a. *Rita sent me an Internet search informing that the risk of having an elevator accident was much lower than riding a car*
    b. *I didn't go to the mall because my daughter wasn't available*
    c. *No problem*
    d.

Figure 2.8 Mary-Ann's action plan (step 7 of CRP) to help her gather information to make the decision to take the elevator in the future (Copyright: Irismar Reis de Oliveira; http://trial-basedcognitivetherapy.com).

RESTRUCTURING NEGATIVE[1] CORE BELIEFS (CBS)

The activation of certain underlying negative CBs may carry out a primary role in the manifestation of cognitive, affective, and behavioral symptoms. Besides aiding the patient to identify and modify dysfunctional thoughts and emotions, helping the patient to restructure dysfunctional CBs is fundamental in order for therapeutic results to be consistent and long lasting (de Oliveira, 2012b; Wenzel, 2012). One difficulty in restructuring more superficial levels of cognition is that, frequently, the more functional alternative thoughts that are generated to challenge the dysfunctional ATs are disqualified by thoughts (also automatic) of the type "yes, but . . ." derived from the activated negative CBs (de Oliveira, 2007). I present here a novel approach to changing beliefs, namely, the trial-based thought record (TBTR; de Oliveira, 2008; de Oliveira, 2011d) or, in short, "the trial."

Trial-Based Thought Record (TBTR) or "the Trial"[2]

Although the defense attorney technique has been traditionally used in cognitive therapy (Freeman & DeWolf, 1992; Cromarty & Marks, 1995; Leahy, 2003), the trial technique (de Oliveira, 2008) was designed to deal with "yes, but . . ." ATs elicited by activated negative CBs (de Oliveira, 2007), having received this name for two reasons: On the one hand, it involves a simulation of a law trial, and, on the other hand, it was inspired from the work of the same name, *The Trial*, by the Czech writer, Franz Kafka (Kafka, 1925/1998). In this book, the character, Joseph K., for unrevealed reasons, is arrested by law officials, and ultimately condemned and executed without ever being allowed to know for which crime he was accused (de Oliveira, 2011b).

Starting with the idea that Kafka was perhaps proposing self-accusation as a universal principle (De-Oliveira, 2011b, 2011c, 2012b), which is often implicit and out of awareness, and, therefore, does not allow for an adequate defense, this technique hypothesizes that self-accusation could be understood as a manifestation of a negative CB, when activated. Therefore, the rationale for developing the trial technique would be to foster awareness on the patients' part of negative CBs regarding themselves (self-accusations). In this way, unlike what happens to Joseph K. in Kafka's novel, the idea is to stimulate patients to develop more positive and helpful CBs throughout the therapy.

Also, as being overwhelmed by intense emotional reactions and not knowing how to cope with their intensity, is one of the most troubling experiences for patients (Leahy et al., 2011), since its original format, the trial has evolved as a technique designed to help patients understand and deal with the overwhelming emotional burden produced by the activation of negative CBs.

The trial incorporates in a structured format and sequence several techniques already used in cognitive therapy and other approaches: empty-chair (Carstenson, 1955), downward arrow (Beck, 1976; Burns, 1980), examining the evidence (Beck, 2012; Greenberger & Padesky, 1995), defense attorney (Freeman & DeWolf, 1992; Cromarty & Marks, 1995; Leahy et al., 2011), thought reversal (Freeman & DeWolf, 1992), upward arrow (De-Oliveira, 2011a; Leahy, 2003), developing a more positive schema (Leahy, 2003), positive self-statement logs (Beck, 2012), and writing letters (Pennebaker & Beall, 1986) (See Table 2.4).

Illustration of the trial-based thought record in a patient with OCD.

Please briefly describe the situation: In session, Dr. de Oliveira asks me to remove the student card from my wallet.

1. Investigation to uncover core belief	2. Prosecutor's plea	3. Defense attorney's plea	4. Prosecutor's second plea	5. Defense attorney's second plea	6. Meaning of the defense attorney's plea	7. Juror's verdict
What was going through your mind before you started to feel this way? Ask yourself what these thoughts meant about yourself, supposing they were true. The answer *"If these thoughts were true, it means I am ..."* is the uncovered **self-accusation** (core belief).	State all the evidence you have that **supports** the accusation/core belief that you have identified in column 1.	State all the evidence you have that **does not support** the accusation/core belief that you have identified in column 1.	State that question, discount, or disqualify each piece of positive evidence in column 3, usually expressed as "yes, but ..." thoughts.	Read each thought of column 4 **first**, and **then** copy down each corresponding evidence in column 3, connecting them with the conjunction BUT.	State the meaning you attach to each sentence in column 5.	Enumerate a list of cognitive distortions and make a succinct report, considering who made fewer distortions.
Downward arrow technique: *She's not succeeding in studying.* *She's too anxious.* *She will not finish her master's degree course.*	1. *She's lost control of her whole life.* 2. *She can't absorb information quickly.* 3. *She's slow at reasoning.* 4. *She doesn't do well when interacting with people and controlling her environment.*	1. *She doesn't check her driver's license, and she hasn't lost control.* 2. *Her OCD score fell today.* 3. *She can remember some techniques without having to reread the book.* 4. *She's completing the evidence chart.*	*BUT:* 1. *She checks on other items.* 2. *She's not cured.* 3. *She can't remember them all.* 4. *She still believes she's imperfect.*	*BUT:* 1. *... she doesn't check her driver's license and hasn't lost control.* 2. *... her OCD score fell today;* 3. *... she can remember some of the techniques without having to reread the book.* 4. *... she's completing the evidence chart.*	**It means that:** 1. *She can stop herself from checking; therefore, she's capable.* 2. *She can cure herself; therefore, she will be fine.* 3. *She can learn; therefore, she has no reason to be concerned.* 4. *She sees the other side of her imperfection (that she is normal); therefore, she will be fine.*	**Prosecutor** **Defense** 1. Overgeneralizing 1. *True* 2. Mind reading 2. *True* 3. Dichotomous thinking 3. *True* 4. Discounting positives 4. *True* **Prosecutor** **Defense** 1. Discounting positives 1. *True* 2. Discounting positives 2. *True* 3. Discounting positives 3. *True* 4. Discounting positives 4. *True* **Verdict:** *innocent*
If the thoughts above were true, what would they mean about you? → **I am:** *imperfect* **I feel:** *anxious*						
Now, how much (%) do you believe you are *imperfect*? **Initial:** *100%* **Final:** *40%*	Now, how much (%) do you believe you are *imperfect*? *100%*	Now, how much (%) do you believe you are *imperfect*? *80%*	Now, how much (%) do you believe you are *imperfect*? *90%*	Now, how much (%) do you believe you are *imperfect*? *70%*		Now, how much (%) do you believe you are *imperfect*? *55%*
What emotion does this belief make you feel? *Anxiety* How strong (%) is it? **Initial:** *100%* **Final:** *40%*	How strong (%) is your anxiety now? *100%*	How strong (%) is your anxiety now? *80%*	How strong (%) is your anxiety now? *90%*	How strong (%) is your anxiety now? *70%*		How strong (%) is your anxiety now? *55%*

Technique Description

Step 1—inquiry (Table 2.4, *column 1*). Initially, the patient is asked to present an uncomfortable situation or problem. The therapist asks what goes through the patient's mind when he/she notices a strong feeling or emotion. This phase of the technique is designed to pursue the ATs linked to the current emotional state, and is recorded in column 1. To uncover which is the activated negative core belief (or one to be activated) responsible for the ATs and the current emotional state, the therapist uses the downward arrow approach (Burns, 1980; de Oliveira, 2011a). For example, the therapist asks what the ATs that were just expressed mean about the patient, assuming they are true. The answer, normally expressed as "I am . . ." phrases, corresponds to the activated negative CB. In the example in Table 2.4, the patient expressed the belief "I am imperfect." The therapist then explains that the procedure (the trial) begins in a similar way to an investigation or inquiry with the aim of discovering the validity of the accusation (in this case, self-accusation) that corresponds to the negative CB. The therapist then asks how much the patient finds this belief to be true and what emotions are felt. The percentages indicating the credit that the patient gives to the negative CB and the corresponding emotional response intensity are recorded in the lower part of column 1, in the space where one reads "Initial." The space where one reads "Final" will be filled in when the session is over, after the conclusion of the task called "Preparation for the appeal." Here (see step 7 below) one assesses how much the patient believes the negative CB (e.g., "I'm imperfect"), after its deactivation and the activation of the positive CB (e.g., "I'm normal").

Step 2—prosecutor's plea (Table 2.4, *column 2*). Columns 2 and 3 of the trial have been designed to help the patient put together information that supports (column 2) and also information that does not support (column 3) the negative CB. Column 2 corresponds to the prosecutor's first plea, where the patient is stimulated to identify all the evidence that supports the negative CB, taken as self-accusation. What is normally seen is that the patient tends to produce more ATs, generally cognitive distortions, instead of evidence. I therefore suggest that the therapist not correct the patient, because later on, during the jury evaluation (column 7), the patient will be guided to take this aspect into consideration, noticing that the prosecutor tends to produce predominantly cognitive distortions. The information gathered and recorded in column 2 has the objective of making evident the internal arguments that the patient uses to support negative CBs.

Step 3—defense attorney's first plea (Table 2.4, *column 3*). In column 3, the patient is actively stimulated to identify all the evidence that does not support the negative CB. If the therapist perceives that the patient is bringing opinions more than evidence, s/he can subtly suggest that the patient give fact-based examples. Although patients generally improve after the conclusion of column 3 (percentage reduction corresponding to how much they deem the negative CB to be true, and the intensity of the emotional response), some do not improve or improve very little because of a lack of credibility of the alternatives brought to challenge the dysfunctional ATs.

Step 4—prosecutor's second plea (Table 2.4, *column 4*). Column 4 is devoted to the thoughts such as "yes, but . . ." that the patient uses to disqualify or minimize the evidence or rational thoughts brought by the defense in column 4, causing them to have less credit. As the example in column 4 illustrates, by using the conjunction "but," the therapist actively stimulates the expression of other dysfunctional ATs, which maintain the negative emotional reactions and dysfunctional behaviors. The mood of the patient tends to return to the level s/he presented in column 2, during the first manifestation of the prosecutor. The therapist can then use such oscillations to show the patient how his/her mood depends on how s/he perceives the situation, positively (defense attorney's perspective) or negatively (prosecutor's perspective).

Step 5—defense attorney's second plea (Table 2.4, *columns 5 and 6*). Columns 5 and 6 are the central aspects of this technique. The patient is conducted to invert the propositions of columns 3 and 4, once again connecting them with the conjunction "but." This is done by asking the patient to read each sentence in column 4, followed by the conjunction "but," and then copying down each corresponding sentence of column 3 in column 5. For instance, Ida read, "She checks on other items" (column 4), added "but," and copied down the sentence "she's not checking on her driving license and has not lost control," obtaining: "She checks on other items, but she's not checking on her driving license and has not lost control." After reading the resulting reversed sentence, the patient is stimulated to record the new meaning, now positive, brought about by this strategy, being asked by the therapist to go further by means of the adverb "therefore." Ida's corresponding conclusion registered in column 6 was: "It means that she can stop herself from checking; therefore, she's capable." After concluding all the items, the usual result of this strategy is the change of perspective of the situation to a more positive and realistic one, causing the patient to reduce the force of the dysfunctional ATs.

Step 6—jury's verdict (Table 2.4, *column 7*). Column 7 contains the analytical part of the trial, presented under the form of a jury deliberation. Taking the juror's perspective, the main question to be considered is: Who had the least cognitive distortions? Here, in almost the totality of cases, the patients acquit themselves of the accusation, represented by the negative CB, after they identify the cognitive distortions made by the prosecutor and notice that the defense attorney makes no cognitive distortions.

The credit the patient attributes to the negative CB and the intensity of the corresponding emotion are evaluated at the end of each character's performance, being recorded in the lower part of all the columns. Such percentages demonstrate the oscillation of the patient's emotions when his/her attention is focused on negative perceptions (prosecutor) or positive ones (defense attorney).

Finally, the trial is used to activate (or even develop) new positive CBs through the above-mentioned upward arrow technique (de Oliveira, 2007; de Oliveira, 2011a), in contrast with the downward arrow (Burns, 1980) used in column 1. For this, the therapist asks: "Supposing the defense attorney is right, what does this say about you?" In the example of Table 2.4, the patient brings up the new positive CB "I am normal."

Step 7—preparation for the appeal (Tables 2.5 *and* 2.6). Table 2.5 is the homework record that the patient will be asked to fill in, being encouraged to gather on a daily basis, during the week, the elements that support the positive CB. The homework is assigned as a preparation for the appeal requested by the prosecutor when the patient acquits him/herself of the accusation, or, rarely, requested by the defense, when the patient does not consider him/herself innocent at the end of the trial. Also, the patient indicates daily how much he or she finds the new CB to be true.

Table 2.6 was adapted to fit in two or more positive CBs, when several trials and appeals have been carried out. Notice that the time taken by the patient to do homework will be the same, regardless of how many positive CBs s/he might be nurturing in the diary. A fact, a piece of evidence or element that supports a new positive belief may support others, and in this way the patients always keep watch over the activity of the previously restructured negative CBs that, frequently, become active again if they are left outside the attention span. Therefore, this form allows patients to strengthen several new positive CBs simultaneously (de Oliveira, 2012b). The fundamental aspect at this stage is that the patient take time outside the session to pay attention to the facts and events that support the positive CBs, and this implies that the defense attorney be chosen as an ally.

Another homework assignment, after the patient is considered not guilty of the accusation(s), is writing an assertive letter to the prosecutor, explaining why s/he will no longer submit him/herself to the prosecutor's demands. Although writing letters is a therapeutic strategy used in different psychotherapy models (Pennebaker, 2012), in TBCT, this technique is also derived from the work of Franz Kafka, *Letter to My Father* (Kafka, 2008). Kafka's father never received this letter, but writing it seems to have been important for Kafka (Murray, 2004).

Research Carried Out

In the first article describing the trial (de Oliveira, 2008), a modified version of the seven-column dysfunctional thought record (DTR; Greenberger & Padesky, 1995) was proposed to change negative CBs by way of combining a strategy involving sentence reversion (Freeman & DeWolf, 1992) and the analogy to a law trial (Cromarty & Marks, 1995; Leahy, 2003). The patients ($n = 30$) took part in a jury simulation and showed changes in their attachment to negative CBs as well as in the intensity of corresponding emotions after each step during a session (investigation, prosecutor's allegation, defense attorney's allegation, prosecutor's reply, defense's rejoinder, and jury's verdict). The results of this work showed significant mean reductions between the percentage figures after the investigation (taken as baseline), the defense attorney's allegation ($p < 0.001$) and the jury's verdict, from the beliefs ($p < 0.001$), as well as from the intensity of emotions ($p < 0.001$). Significant differences were also observed between the first and second defense allegations ($p = 0.009$), and between the second defense allegation and the jury's verdict with respect to the CBs ($p = 0.005$) and to the emotions ($p = 0.02$). The conclusion was that the trial could, at least temporarily, help the patients in a constructive way to reduce the attachment to negative CBs and the corresponding emotions (de Oliveira, 2008).

In a randomized clinical study (de Oliveira, 2012), the trial was studied in 36 patients with social anxiety disorder (SAD), in which the experimental group was treated with the trial ($n = 17$), and the contrast group ($n = 19$) was treated with a conventional model of CT that included the seven-column DTR (Greenberger & Padesky, 1995), associated with the positive data log (PDL; Beck, 2012). Both groups received psychoeducation regarding the cognitive model and types of cognitive distortions, and discussed with the therapist the individualized case conceptualization diagram. The objective of both treatments was to restructure the CBs in order to reduce the symptoms of social phobia. Exposure was not actively stimulated in either of the groups. When a mixed ANOVA was carried out, significant reductions were observed ($p < 0.001$) in both approaches on scores in the Liebowitz Social Anxiety Scale (LSAS; Liebowitz, 1987), the fear of negative evaluation scale (FNE; Watson & Friend, 1969), and in the Beck Anxiety Inventory (BAI; Beck, Epstein, Brown, & Steer, 1988). Nevertheless, the one-way ANCOVA, taking the baseline data as covariables, showed that the trial was significantly more effective than the contrast group in reducing the FNE ($p = 0.01$), and social avoidance and distress ($p = 0.03$). The data on quality of life of this study (Powell et al., 2013) showed that the trial was significantly better at posttreatment (bodily pain, social functioning, and emotional role) and at follow-up (emotional role) relative to the contrast group. Also, a significant treatment effect on the emotional role domain at 12-month follow-up denoted a sustained effect of the trial relative to conventional CT, suggesting that this study provides preliminary evidence that this approach is at least as effective as CT, specifically when the standard seven-column DTR and the PDL are used, in improving several domains of quality of life in SAD.

In a trans-diagnostic replication (de Oliveira et al., 2012) of the preliminary study (de Oliveira, 2008), 166 patients were submitted to the trial to assess their adherence to their negative CBs and corresponding emotions, the trial first use being assessed. Significant reductions existed in percent values after the first and second defense attorney pleas, as well as after the jury's verdict and initial preparation for the appeal (p < 0.001), relative to the investigation phase. Significant differences also emerged between the defense attorney's first and second pleas and between the defense attorney's second plea and the jury's verdict, as well as preparation for the appeal (p < 0.001). There was no significant difference between percentages presented by patients submitted to the trial used in the empty-chair format relative to the conventional (static) format. Similarly, there was no difference between outcomes, regardless of therapists' level of exposure (experience) to the trial. It was concluded that this approach might help patients reduce attachment to negative CBs and corresponding emotions, confirming the results of the preliminary study (de Oliveira, 2008). The sample size of this study was recently extended to 259 patients (de Oliveira, Duran, & Velasquez, 2012), confirming its findings regarding CBs and emotion change, but further indicating that the empty-chair format may be more efficacious than the conventional static format in reducing the intensity of corresponding emotions, and that significantly more patients treated with the empty-chair format concluded all the steps of the technique.

Case Illustration (Ida)

Ida (see also de Oliveira, 2011d), married, in her 30s, diagnosed with borderline personality disorder and obsessive-compulsive disorder (OCD), initially also presenting with a major depressive episode, had been anxious, angry, and aggressive for 3 years. She had difficulty dealing with subordinates (she was a manager in a company) and went on sick leave. Her depression worsened. Ida could not resume work and stopped her master's degree studies. She mutilated herself and made suicide attempts due to depressive symptoms and a severe anxiety that did not reduce with different antidepressants, used alone and in combination, and high doses of benzodiazepines.

Her benzodiazepines were tapered and replaced with quetiapine, 400 mg/day, while she had weekly cognitive restructuring of beliefs such as "I'm a failure, incompetent, inadequate" by examining evidence for and against them. Though her anxiety decreased, external events reactivated her beliefs, and she mutilated herself again.

Six months before the session yielding the trial session demonstrated below, Ida started repeatedly verifying her purse, daily, for hours, checking 13 items by touching and reading each word in the documents and cards. Intensive exposure, ritual prevention, and cognitive restructuring therapy (two to three weekly sessions to a total of 18 sessions) stopped her checking within 2 months. The trial illustrated in Table 2.4 was a successful attempt to restructure the CB "I'm imperfect," while Table 2.5 shows her homework diary.

Trial Demonstration Session[3]

Table 2.4 summarizes the use of the trial in one of Ida's sessions during which the therapist asked her to remove the student card from her purse, after allowing her to check the documents only for 5 minutes, instead of the 1 hour she needed. Ida was unable to do it because of her high anxiety level. The dialogue below is a transcription of a session, modified to keep Ida's confidentiality and to make the text more didactic.

Step 1—inquiry (Table 2.4, column 1)

THERAPIST (T): Ida, we've already seen from the conceptualization diagram that these ATs are activated by negative UAs and CBs. For instance, if you remove the student card from your purse, what do you think will happen?

PATIENT (P): I'll feel too anxious and will not stand it.

T: This is your UA. Anyhow, you are already very anxious. Not allowing yourself to continue checking the documents, what does it mean about you?

P: It means that I'm imperfect, and the idea that I'm imperfect is unbearable for me.

T: Can you identify this as a CB, activated by this exposure in which you not only are not allowing yourself to check, but are also trying to remove the student card to keep it away from you? To what extent to you believe this CB "I'm imperfect" now?

P: I believe it 100%.

T: I'd like to propose to you that we consider this belief you have just uncovered as a kind of self-accusation and put this CB "I am imperfect" on trial. Believing it 100%, what does it make you feel?

P: Anxious.

T: How strong is your anxiety now?

P: 100%.

Step 2 – prosecutor's first plea (Table 2.4, column 2)

T: Perhaps it would be important for us to activate your internal prosecutor, so that she can put forward the arguments that she has to show that this accusation is really correct: "I am imperfect." I'd like to ask you to sit in this chair and bring the arguments you have, as a prosecutor, that you are imperfect. Would you please imagine yourself sitting in the chair in front of you and refer to yourself as Ida or "she"?

P: Yes, of course. She has lost control of her whole life.

T: Yes.

P: She's unable to absorb information quickly. She's slow at reasoning.

T: "She's unable to absorb information quickly." And you also said that she's slow at reasoning. . . .

P: Yes, she's slow at reasoning. She's not succeeding in acting with perfection with respect to interacting with people and controlling her environment. . . .

T: And all these things indicate that she is imperfect. . . .

P: Yes, she is imperfect. Yesterday she realized that all the techniques in that book on cognitive therapy you suggested that she read, she wanted to remember them all, but there were some that she couldn't remember, she had to reread it. . . .

T: She wanted to remember all the techniques . . . ? There are more than 80 techniques in that book! And she wanted to remember all the techniques?

P: Yes, without needing to reread them.

T: And she couldn't, is that it?

P: Yes.

T: And this is an argument you have that she is imperfect. That is, "She was unable to remember all the techniques from the book, without having to reread it."

P: I have another argument to prove that she is imperfect: she's not able to study these days . . . because she can't do two things at the same time (dedicate herself to the treatment exercises and study as well). In her head, she can only do one thing at a time, and she used to being able to do several things at the same time.

T: OK. Can you go to that chair in front of you and be Ida? So, having listened to what has been put forward here by your internal prosecutor: You lost control of your whole life, you are unable to absorb information quickly, you are slow at reasoning, you are not succeeding in acting with perfection with respect to interacting with people and controlling your environment, you were unable to remember all the techniques from the book without having to reread it, and you have not been able to study these days because you can't do two things at the same time. When you hear these arguments from the prosecutor, how much do you believe you are imperfect?

P: 100%.

T: And how intense is your anxiety?

P: 100%.

T: I suppose these seem to be the arguments that are sustaining this self-accusation "I am imperfect."

P: Right.

Step 3—defense attorney's first plea (Table 2.4, *column 3*)

T: I'd like to ask you to sit in this other chair now and be a defense attorney. As a defense attorney, do you think these accusations against Ida are fair?

P: No.

T: And why isn't the accusation fair?

P: Because . . . Oh, God! Let me see.

T: You are not obliged to answer all the pleas brought by the prosecutor. You may answer them, but you may also put forward other things.

P: She's not checking on her driver's license and hasn't lost control.

T: What else?

P: The OCD score decreased today.

T: OK. Good. "The OCD score decreased today," right?

P: Yes. We checked and it had decreased between Wednesday and today. A third piece of evidence is that she can remember some of the techniques without needing to reread the book.

T: OK, without needing to reread . . . the book . . .

P: Yesterday, a friend of hers commented in front of her husband that Ida knew a lot about computer service management. She used to work with Ida.

T: What else? What more do you have as arguments, facts, or pieces of evidence to be put forward to defend Ida?

P: Oh, I have one more argument: She's filling out the beliefs chart.

T: OK. She had stopped for a while, hadn't she?

P: Yes, but she went back to filling it out as usual.

T: So, she's filling out the evidence chart.

P: Right.

T: OK. Now we have sufficient arguments for the defense, don't we?

P: Yes.

T: Would you please go back to the defendant's chair? Listen to what the defense attorney said about you: "You are not checking on your driver's license, you haven't lost control, the OCD score decreased today, you can remember some techniques without having to reread the book, yesterday a friend of yours commented in front of her husband that you knew a lot about computer service management, and you are filling out the evidence chart." In view of these pieces of evidence that have been put forward by your internal defense attorney, to what extent do you believe that you are imperfect?

P: 80%.

T: So, it has decreased to 80%. And the anxiety?

P: It has decreased to 80% too.

T: They go together. Do you know the next step?

Step 4—prosecutor's second plea (Table 2.4, *column 4)*

P: It is the prosecutor. The right to response, right?

T: Exactly. So, can you come back to the prosecutor's chair? What does the prosecutor do now?

P: This is easy. She disqualifies the arguments of the defense attorney.

T: This is easy because it is automatic, and it is like this. The defense attorney said: "She's not checking on her driver's license and has not lost control," but . . .

P: . . . she checks on other items.

T: OK. "The OCD score decreased today," but . . .

P: . . . she's not cured.

T: "She can remember some techniques without rereading the book," but . . .

P: . . . she can't remember them all.

T: "Yesterday, a friend of hers commented in front of her husband that she knew a lot about computer service management," but . . .

P: . . . this is meaningless since she's on sick leave.

T: "She's filling out the evidence chart," but . . .

P: . . . her belief in her imperfection is active.

T: Can you go back to Ida's chair? The prosecutor has just said: You check on other items, you are not cured, you can't remember all the techniques, knowing a lot about computer service management is meaningless because you are on sick leave, and your belief in your imperfection is active. To what extent do you believe you are imperfect, after hearing these arguments?

P: 90%.

T: It has gone up to 90%, and what happened to your anxiety?

P: 90%.

T: They go together.

Step 5—defense attorney's second plea (Table 2.4, *columns 5 and 6*)

T: Now, let's see what we can do with this. You can imagine that the defense attorney has the right to speak again. . . .

P: Exactly.

T: I would like you to come to this chair now. As you seem to have no more arguments as a defense attorney, I'd like to give you good news. You don't need them. All you have to do is use the same strategy used by the prosecutor—that is, use the conjunction "but." Can you read the first prosecutor's plea? I'll tell you what to do afterwards.

P: "She checks on other items."

T: Please, add the conjunction "but" and just copy what you said before as a defense attorney.

P: " . . . she's not checking on her driving license and has not lost control."

T: Can you read the whole sentence, please, including both the prosecutor and the defense attorney's pleas?

P: She checks on other items, but she's not checking on her driving license and has not lost control.

T: What does it mean about Ida?

P: This means that she's able to stop checking on the items.

T: Would you add the word "therefore" after this and conclude what this means about Ida?

P: Therefore . . . therefore, she's capable.

T: Please, do the same for all the items—that is, read what the prosecutor said, add the conjunction "but," copy what you said before, and conclude with the meaning of the new sentence.

P: She's not cured, but her OCD score decreased today. This means that she will be cured.

T: Therefore . . .

P: . . . she will be fine.

T: Right. Please, go on.

P: She doesn't remember all the techniques, but she can remember some of the techniques without rereading the book. This means that she's able to learn; therefore, she has no reason to be concerned about that.

T: OK.

P: It's meaningless because she's on sick leave, but yesterday a friend of hers commented in front of her husband that she knew a lot about computer service management. It means that, since she has the knowledge, she can go back to being a good manager; therefore, she will be fine.

T: Yes.

P: Her belief in her imperfection is active, but she has filled out the evidence chart. It means that she is succeeding in seeing the other side of her imperfection; therefore, she's a normal person.

T: OK. Please, go back to the defendant's chair. Listen carefully what the defense attorney said about you: You're not checking on your driver's license, and you have not lost control. It means that you're able to stop checking on the items; therefore, you're capable; your OCD score decreased today. It means that you will be cured; therefore, you will be fine; you can remember some of the techniques without rereading the book. It means that you're able to learn; therefore, you have no reason to be concerned about that; yesterday, a friend of yours commented in front of her husband that you knew a lot about computer service management. It means that, since you have the knowledge, you can go back to being a good manager; therefore, you will be fine; you have filled out the evidence chart. It means that you're succeeding in seeing the other side of your imperfection; therefore, you're a normal person.

P: Right.

T: As you listen to these arguments put forward by your internal defense attorney, to what extent do you believe you are imperfect?

P: It has decreased to 70%.

T: And what happened to your anxiety?

P: 70%.

Step 6—jury's verdict (Table 2.4, *column 7*)

T: OK. This is important because we are now going into another phase, which is the phase of the jury. So, we are actually going to be acting as members of the jury. As jurors, it is extremely important that we be objective and impartial. Please, let's go to the jurors' chairs. We are the only ones admitted to this room, as juror number 1 (you) and juror number 2 (me). The judge, the prosecutor, the defense attorney, and Ida should wait until we decide the verdict, right? Don't forget: No one but the jurors is allowed to enter this room. Ida is not allowed to enter this room.[4]

P: Right.

T: Please, here you have the most important jury's document: the distortions sheet. You know it well. So then, let's go to the prosecutor's pleas: "She has lost control of her whole life." Do you see any distortion here?

P: Yes, this is overgeneralization. The prosecutor here, in this case, is committing the distortion of overgeneralization. Ida lost control, but there was no way of exerting control because she did not have the knowledge to do this. It is not of her "whole life." So, here the prosecutor is overgeneralizing.

T: "She does not absorb information quickly." What do you say?

P: The prosecutor is discounting . . . because there are moments when she can read quickly.

T: "She has slow reasoning."

P: I think that the prosecutor is also discounting here.

T: "She's not succeeding in acting with perfection with respect to interacting with people and controlling her environment."

P: Here, to a certain extent, I think that the prosecutor is mind reading what people think about Ida. . . . Yes, I think it is mind reading.

T: "She can't remember all the techniques."

P: That is an actual fact! I did not remember all the techniques.

T: Would you please tell me why you say that? Ida is not allowed to enter this room and you have just said "I." Would you please tell her to leave this room?

P: You are right. Let me rephrase that: "She can't remember all the techniques." Anyhow, I think it is an actual fact; she can't remember all the techniques.

T: OK, but do you think she would be able to learn absolutely everything? Is this something you perceive to be possible? Do you think that people learn all the techniques and remember absolutely everything?

P: I don't think so. But before, she used to read a whole book and absorb a good part of it—practically the whole book. Now she can't. So, actually, the prosecutor is not doing any distortion. It is a piece of evidence.

T: Does it mean she is imperfect because of this?

P: No. In actual fact, the cost of learning everything is very high.

T: Very high, indeed. "She's not managing to study these days."

P: This is not true. She is studying a few hours every day. This is not what she thinks she should, but she's studying. This is all-or-nothing.

T: "She can't do two things at the same time, and she used to be able to do various things."

P: Actually, this is a real piece of evidence too. The prosecutor in this case is not committing any distortion. She can't do these things at the same time.

T: She's not managing now, at this moment. But what is her objective right now, what is her priority?

P: It's her treatment. So she's really trying to dedicate herself to the therapy.

T: Let's go to the defense attorney pleas: "She's not checking her driver's license and has not lost control."

P: This is not a distortion. This is true.

T: "The OCD score decreased today."

P: This is not a distortion either because Ida saw it.

T: "She can manage to remember some techniques without rereading the book."

P: This is also true.

T: "Yesterday, a friend of hers commented in front of her husband that she knew a lot about computer service management."

P: This is also real evidence; her friend made a comment.

T: "She's filling out the evidence chart."

P: This is also real evidence; the chart is here, and Ida fills it out daily.

T: What happened during the prosecutor's right to response?

P: In the prosecutor's right to response, she rebutted all the arguments, all the pieces of evidence (that are real) put forward by the defense attorney. She discounted all the evidence brought by the defense attorney.

T: Can we consider discounting for all these items?

P: Yes.

T: And what happened during the defense attorney's right to response? Can we say that the defense attorney used the same arguments we considered as true, and that she just added meanings to them? Please, take a look. What do you see here?

P: They are all true.

T: In other words, the defense attorney committed no cognitive distortions.

P: The prosecutor made several cognitive distortions. She was not fair, really. The defense attorney was fairer, more consistent in her arguments, because they were based on evidence. . . .

T: Exactly. Would you say that this is more balanced? Please, take a look at the prosecutor's and the defense attorney's columns. What verdict should we take to the judge?

P: Not guilty.

T: I'll go back to the judge's chair and you will announce the verdict, right?

P: OK.

T: Have the jurors reached a verdict?

P: Yes, your honor.

T: And what is it?

P: Your honor, the verdict is not guilty, based on the fact that the prosecutor made many distortions and the defense attorney didn't make any distortion.

P: Would you please go to the defendant's chair?

T: You have just learned the sentence: not guilty. How much do you believe now you are imperfect?

P: 55%.

T: And the anxiety?

P: It has also decreased to 55%.

Step 7—preparation for the appeal (Tables 2.5 and 2.6)

T: Ida, the court is now closed. Let's go back to our therapeutic setting. I would like to ask you a question: If this is true (what was said by the defense attorney and what was confirmed by the jury), what does it mean about you?

P: It means I am not imperfect. It means I'm normal.

T: And what is the importance of learning these things, Ida?

P: Dr. Oliveira, this is very important because I saw that I don't need to be perfect: I need to be normal, right? So . . . I have proof today that I am capable of being normal. With this, I really can pick up the student card and put it inside a book (I don't even need to keep it close to me). I can put it here in the notebook.

T: What is your level of suffering now, for example, when you are doing this?

P: Much lower. . . .

T: Would you say then that your belief "I am imperfect" in a certain way is less active now . . . ?

P: It is much less active now. The trial proved to me that I don't need to be perfect, but rather, normal; and the prosecutor was very unfair, insistent and overbearing today. . . .

T: And you even answered some of the prosecutor's demands—for example, "She can't re-member all the techniques in the book." Would you say that a normal person needs to remember everything all the time?

P: No, it is not necessary.

T: Would you say, then, that your expectation level diminished a bit?

P: Exactly, it decreased, because it is actually my high expectation level that leads to a level of suffering for perfection. I think it takes too much out of me. I can do it, but the price is very high.

T: Actually what we aim for here is that you be able to work continuously with the defense attorney because the prosecutor is always demanding a rehearing, isn't she?

P: Yes.

T: That's why it is important for you to work daily on the evidence chart together with the defense attorney.

P: Exactly.

T: If we had to start this here today, do you have at least one or two pieces of evidence that prove that you are normal?

P: I am happy here! The student card . . . One piece of evidence is that today I only looked once at the driver's license, and that means that I succeeded in conquering the driver's license.

T: You did. Anything else?

P: Now I have managed to conquer the student card.

T: OK. I am going to leave another item for you to finish this evening. And I would really like you to always register here in the parentheses, each time you finish, to what extent you believe this new belief: "I'm normal." To what extent do you believe this now, Ida?

P: 60%.

T: And how much do you believe this belief you are imperfect?

P: 40%.

T: How is your anxiety level?

P: 40%.

T: Great! I have something else to propose to you, but before I would like to ask you whom do you choose as your ally from now on, the prosecutor or the defense attorney?

P: The defense attorney for sure!

T: So, would you like to remember what the defense attorney concluded about you today?

P: Of course.

T: Please, take a look at this record we have just filled out during the trial. I will ask you to copy down all the pleas of the defense attorney from the third and sixth columns. However, instead of using "she," please, copy them in the first person. Please, write it down in the evidence-based meaning card. [The therapist gives a card to Ida.] Would you please start copying the sentence 1 in column 3?

P: [Copying] 1. I don't check my driver's license, and I haven't lost control.

T: I will ask you to add the expression "It means that," and copy the sentence you wrote in column 6.

Table 2.5 Ida's appeal preparation—one-belief form (Copyright: Irismar Reis de Oliveira; http://trial-basedcognitivetherapy.com).

Please, write down here, daily, at least one piece of evidence supporting the new core belief in the space between parentheses. Also, please, write how much (%) you believe the new core belief in the space between parentheses.

Positive core belief: I am *normal*.

Date: 21/Oct/2011 (60%)
1. I succeeded in removing the driver's license from the purse.
2. I also managed to remove the student card from the purse.
3. I came back to my city by bus.

Date: 22/Oct/11 (60%)
1. I didn't check the driver's license.
2. I studied for 4 hours.
3. I called my friend Mary.

Date: 23/Oct/11 (65%)
1. I got my notebook repaired.
2. My husband asked me for (and received) advice regarding his work.
3. I studied for 4 hours.

Date: 24/Oct/11 (55%)
1. I studied for 2 hours.
2. I visited my parents.
3. I didn't check the driver's license.

Date: 25/Oct/11 (50%)
1. I studied for 2 hours.
2. I read a chapter on worry.
3.

Date: 26/Oct/11 (55%)
1. I studied for 5 hours.
2. I was invited to be a witness in a wedding.
3. I watched a movie.

Date: 27/Oct/11 (60%)
1. I studied for 4 hours.
2. I exercised.
3. I went to the supermarket.

Date: 28/Oct/11 (65%)
1. I called my friend Jennifer.
2. I studied for 2 hours.
3. I went to church.

Date: 29/Oct/11 (70%)
1. I was less anxious today.
2. I haven't had a crisis for a week.
3. I studied for 4 hours.

Date: 30/Oct/11 (70%)
1. I studied for 5 hours.
2. I visited my parents.
3. I sent e-mails.

Date: 31/Oct/11 (65%)
1. My cousin Mary visited me.
2. I made a search on the Internet.
3. I sent a birthday card.

Date: 01/Nov/11 (60%)
1. I exercised.
2. I called my friend Donna.
3. I read an article.

Date: 02/Nov/11 (70%)
1. I studied for 3 hours.
2. I went to the mall.
3. I entered a store and succeeded in not buying anything.

Date: 03/Nov/11 (75%)
1. I sent e-mails.
2. I studied for 2 hours.
3. I made a summary and remembered the subjects I studied.

Date: 04/Nov/11 (75%)
1. I sent a chapter of my thesis to my adviser.
2. I didn't check the driver's license.
3. I called my mother-in-law.

Date: 05/Nov/11 (60%)
1. I replied my supervisor's e-mail.
2. I made the changes suggested by my adviser.
3. I exercised.

Table 2.6 Ida's appeal preparation—two or more–belief form (Copyright: Irismar Reis de Oliveira; http://trial-basedcogitivetherapy.com).

Please, write down here, daily, at least one piece of evidence supporting each new core belief in the space between parentheses.

I am: *capable*	**I am:** *assertive*	**I am:** *normal*	**I am:** *lovable*
Date: 08/Nov/2012 (40%)	(45%)	(60%)	(40%)
1. I sent comments to my adviser today.	1. I sent comments to my adviser today.	1. I sent comments to my adviser today.	1. My husband called me to ask how I was.
2. I revised a chapter of my thesis.	2.	2. I revised a chapter of my thesis.	2.
3.	3.	3. I woke up feeling well.	3.
Date: 09/Nov/2012 (45%)	(45%)	(60%)	(50%)
1. I read a new paper for my thesis.	1.	1.	1. I received a caring e-mail from a friend.
2. I told my mother I would not have lunch with her today.	2. I told my mother I would not have lunch with her today.	2. I told my mother I would not have lunch with her today.	2.
3. I did exposure.	3. I did exposure.	3.	3.
Date: 10/Nov/2012 (55 %)	(50%)	(65%)	(50%)
1. My adviser liked the comments I sent him.	1.	1.	1.
2. I received a visit from an aunt.	2.	2. I received a visit from an aunt.	2. I received a visit from an aunt.
3.	3.	3.	3.
Date: 11/Nov/2012 (55%)	(55%)	(65%)	(55%)
1. I made a search on the Internet about dissertation models.	1. I told my parents that I was tired and should go to bed early.	1.	1. My mother bought candies for me.
2.	2.	2.	2. My parents visited me today.
3.	3.	3.	3.

Evidence-Based Meaning Card
(What the Evidence Means About Me)

> # *I am normal*
>
> 1. *I don't check my driver's license and I haven't lost control. It means that I can stop myself checking, therefore, I'm capable.*
> 2. *My OCD score fell today. It means that I can cure myself, therefore, I will be fine.*
> 3. *I can remember some techniques without having to reread the book. It means that I can learn, therefore, I have no reason to be concerned.*
> 4. *I'm completing the evidence chart. It means that I see the other side of my imperfection (that is, that I'm normal), therefore, I will be fine.*

Figure 2.9 Ida's Evidence-based meaning card, derived from the defense attorney's pleas, copied by the patient from columns 3 and 6 of the TBTR in Table 2.4, in the first person, to help her remember the conclusions she reached role-playing the defense attorney (Copyright: Irismar Reis de Oliveira; http://trial-basedcognitivetherapy.com).

P: It means that I can stop myself from checking; therefore, I'm capable.

T: Fine. Would you please complete the card with the other sentences? After that, I will ask you to read all the sentences to me. Also, this is something I will ask you to read whenever you feel distressed. Please, always carry this card with you (Fig. 2.9). We call it an *evidence-based meaning card* because the defense attorney used evidence instead of the distortions used by the prosecutor.

Summary of the Session

T: [After Ida completed the evidence-based meaning card and read all the sentences] Ida, how would you summarize this work that we have been doing here today?

P: I think that we are continuing with that work of taking the items and working with them … This has been improving, and we saw from the chart that with this discipline of taking the item and not checking on it, we are going to beat the OCD (and not the contrary; it will then no longer control me), and this gives me a very strong feeling of relief, of hope, of diminished anxiety. I was having difficulty (at that moment when we took an item out of my purse) in putting it away and not looking at it anymore, but the trial showed me that I can do it, because I managed to prove that I am normal, that I don't need to be perfect. And we found the accused not guilty; consequently, it was easier for me to put the item away and not look at it any more. That was very positive.

T: And how much do you expect that this will help you today; in other words, to what extent do you believe that you will really succeed in not looking at the item you have just taken out of your purse?

P: I believe 90%. Perhaps I will have to look at it when I take it out of here; then I will have to police myself not to spend too much time looking at it and put it in another place where I won't look. I managed to do it with the driver's license, and I am going to succeed with the student card too.

T: Anything else you would like to add?

P: No.

T: That's fine, then, Ida. I think you did an excellent job here, didn't you?

P: Yes, very good. The work has gone very well this week.

Guidelines to the Use of the Trial

Here are some of the rules therapists should follow in order to make the TBTR work optimally (de Oliveira, 2012b):

1. Make sure that sentences are relatively short so that the patient has no problem when reversing them (long sentences are difficult to understand by the patient after sentence reversal);
2. Make sure that the defense attorney's arguments in column 3 (Table 2.4) are not exclusively limited to responding to the prosecutor's plea in column 2; stimulate the patient to explore different aspects and areas of his/her life (other than the accusation);
3. When the trial is conducted in more than one session, do not stop it just after the prosecutor's plea; always try to stop the trial after the defense attorney's plea (columns 3, 5, and 6);
4. If the patient considers him/herself guilty—an extremely rare outcome, when the technique is used properly—this is not a problem; the defense attorney should ask for an appeal so that the trial can be repeated in the following session as an appeal; in this case, it is essential that homework be that the patient gather evidence that confirms the positive CB (choosing the defense attorney as an ally);
5. If the patient decides (another extremely rare case, meaning that he or she might have misunderstood the purpose of the technique) that s/he will continue working with the prosecutor instead of the defense attorney for homework assignment, interrupt the trial and ask him/her for advantages and disadvantages of such a decision;
6. When the prosecutor interrupts the defense attorney's plea with "yes, but . . ." thoughts, tell the patient that the prosecutor should wait for his/her turn. You may turn to the empty prosecutor's chair and tell him/her that s/he must wait for his/her turn to speak. Also, if the patient tends to use the defense arguments when playing the role of the prosecutor, s/he should be praised for thinking positively, but, in any case, must return to the prosecutor's plea);
7. Sometimes the negative CB is so activated that the patient, acting as the defense attorney or a juror, not only does not succeed in generating evidence in favor of the accused, but uses "yes, but" thoughts. In this case, ask him/her: Who is speaking now? If the patient recognizes the prosecutor acting, gently ask him/her to speak in the defense attorney's perspective, reminding him/her that this is the defense attorney's turn;
8. Sometimes, the patient has no evidence or argument as a prosecutor against the defense attorney's plea after the therapist reads the sentence and says "but. . . ." In this case, draw a line and, when inverting the sentences, just copy the sentence and ask the patient what it means about the accused;

9. Finally, in some severe Axis I disorders and in some personality disorder patients, even when the defense attorney is repeatedly successful in acquitting the patient, self-accusation returns (negative CB easily activated); in this case, the trial-based metacognitive awareness (TBMA or trial II, where the patient sues the prosecutor, accusing him/her of incompetence [never won a lawsuit], abuse [pursues the patient everywhere], and harassment [humiliates the patient]) is used, with more durable results. This is a step of the therapy when the patient is informed and trained in taking some perspective (metacognition). The prosecutor has much less or no more credibility for him/her at this stage (de Oliveira, 2011c).

COMBINING TBCT AND PSYCHOPHARMACOLOGY

TBCT is a modality of CBT and, as such, may be used in combination with medications. There is abundant evidence in the literature demonstrating the efficacy of CBT alone or in combination with pharmacotherapy for many psychiatric disorders. This is shown in detail in specific chapters in this book.

Here, I demonstrate how TBCT may be used by psychopharmacologists to help reluctant patients adhere to medications—or, sometimes, reduce or stop them, when necessary—and to use this approach to challenge ATs, UAs, and CBs that often undermine the patients' compliance to prescribed medications.

Case Illustration (Martha)

Martha is a 45-year-old single female dentist who presented for consultation because of her difficulty dealing with several specific phobias (e.g., thunder, heights, planes, crowds) and low mood. Her main complaints involved a long-lasting fear of planes and, more recently, sadness, lack of energy, fatigue, somnolence, and difficulty concentrating. She presented three low-mood episodes in the past 5 years, but had never complied with the antidepressants prescribed by her psychiatrist because of worries regarding side effects. Her attendance to consultations was erratic and dependent on symptom intensity. She had recently started a new relationship with Paul, who lived in a different state. Although Paul had visited her fortnightly, she was unable to travel to visit him as well, and engaged in self-deprecation because of that. Martha's ATs ("Paul will leave me," "There is no hope"), UAs ("If I take the plane, it will crash, or at least I will lose control and go crazy up there"), and CBs ("I'm weak," "I'm a failure," "I'm not good enough") grew 1 month previously to consultation because Paul told her he would not be able to keep visiting her as frequently as before. She accepted the psychiatrist's proposal to help her deal with the fear of traveling and reluctance to take an SSRI by using a time-limited course of weekly TBCT sessions. After introducing the cognitive model by means of the CD, and educating her on the cognitive distortions (Table 2.1 and appendix), the psychiatrist was able to help her challenge the ATs by means of the Intra-TR, the UAs with the CCSH and CRP (the latter was first used to help her decide to take the SSRI and then to take the plane to visit Paul), and restructure the negative CBs using trials I and II. Her mood symptoms remitted by session 5. Besides traveling by plane 3 months after starting therapy (session 8), Martha was complying with the SSRI 6 months after treatment termination.

Discussion

It is not possible to know for sure what helped this patient the most: psychotherapy, psychopharmacology, or the combination of both. Combining TBCT and an SSRI may have helped Martha achieve remission and allow for the optimization of the therapy itself. That is, TBCT may have helped the patient to make the decision to comply with the medication, and the medication may have improved her mood and anxious symptoms, generating a possibly synergistic virtuous cycle.

As discussed by Wenzel in Chapter 11, in this book, pharmacotherapy may relieve patients of bothersome symptoms that have the potential to interfere with making good use of psychotherapy (e.g., fatigue, sleep disturbance), and the resolution of these symptoms can help patients assume readiness for psychotherapy. On the other hand, psychotherapy may help patients identify and address self-defeating attitudes and behaviors that hinder compliance with prescribed medications. Thus, pharmacotherapy and psychotherapy are likely to exert bidirectional influences on one another in the mechanism by which each modality exerts its effects, as well as in the issues that are discussed at the time of the appointments.

There is a debate regarding whether combination therapy should ideally be delivered as split treatment (more than one professional) or provided by a single psychiatrist (Koenig, Friedman, & Thase, Chapter 3 in this book). When provided as a split treatment, it is not infrequent that collaboration does not occur between the prescriber and the therapist, and the difficult-to-treat patients may continue "difficult to treat" (Greenberg & Dewan, Chapter 14 in this book). TBCT is a case-formulation, evidence-based approach that might be easily learned by new therapists (e.g., psychopharmacologists) and patients alike because of its very structured presentation format and easy-to-remember techniques. TBCT's techniques can be used flexibly by psychiatrists, according to the patients' needs. In the above example, they were also used to help the patient comply with the prescribed medication.

CONCLUSION

The present chapter introduces TBCT, a new psychotherapy approach whose foundation is in cognitive therapy but also incorporates elements of several other evidence-based psychotherapy models. It illustrates how to teach the cognitive model to the patients by means of a CD. The CD-Quest and the Intra-TR help patients identify and challenge negative ATs. The CCSH and the CRP, strategies shaped to help patients make decisions involving the confrontation of safety behaviors, facilitate the modification of dysfunctional UAs. The TBTR (trial I) is used by the therapist to help the patient identify and change negative CBs, preparing him/her for more in-depth cognitive and emotional work with trial II, in which metacognitive, acceptance, and compassion training is further developed. Finally, TBCT may be used by clinicians in a combined psychotherapy–psychopharmacology treatment format.

NOTES

1. TBTR is also called "trial I" because two other techniques used in TBCT, not included in this chapter, are referred to as "trial II" and "trial III." Here, TBTR will be referred to as "the trial."
2. This is a transcription of one of Ida's sessions during the OCD work phase. The filling in of the corresponding forms "the trial" and "preparation for the appeal" are in Tables 2.4 and 2.5, respectively.
3. To Herbert Deinert (1964), Kafka's parable "Before the Law" (and its context, the chapter "In the Cathedral") is the central piece of Kafka's novel *The Trial.*

REFERENCES

Beck, A. T. (1976). *Cognitive therapy and the emotional disorders.* New York: International Universities Press.

Beck, A. T., Epstein, N., Brown, G., & Steer, R. A. (1988). An inventory for measuring clinical anxiety: Psychometric properties. *Journal of Consulting and Clinical Psychology, 56,* 893–897.

Beck, A. T., Steer, R. A., Ball, R., & Ranieri, W. (1996). Comparison of Beck Depression Inventories -IA and -II in psychiatric outpatients. *Journal of Personality Assessment, 67,* 588–597.

Beck, J. S. (2012). *Cognitive behavior therapy: Basics and beyond* (2nd ed.). New York: Guilford Press.

Bennett-Levy, J, Westbrook, D., Fennel, M., Cooper, M., Rouf, K., & Hackmann, A. (2004). Behavioural experiments: Historical and conceptual underpinnings. In J. Bennett-Levy, G. Butler, M. Fennel, A. Hackmann, M. Mueller, & D. Westrook (Eds.), *Oxford guide to behavioural experiments in cognitive therapy* (pp. 1–20). Oxford, UK: Oxford University Press.

Burns, D. D. (1980). *Feeling good: The new mood therapy.* New York: Signet.

Carstenson, B. (1955). The auxiliary chair technique—a case study. *Group Psychotherapy, 8,* 50–56.

Cromarty, P., & Marks, I. (1995). Does rational role-play enhance the outcome of exposure therapy in dysmorphophobia? A case study. *British Journal of Psychiatry, 167,* 399–402.

Deinert, R. (1964). Kafka's parable "Before the law." *The Germanic Review.* Retrieved from https://courses.cit.cornell.edu/hd11/BeforeTheLaw.html

de Oliveira, I. R. (2007). Sentence-reversion-based thought record (SRBTR): A new strategy to deal with "yes, but . . ." dysfunctional thoughts in cognitive therapy. *European Review of Applied Psychology, 57,* 17–22.

de Oliveira, I. R. (2008). Trial-based thought record (TBTR): Preliminary data on a strategy to deal with core beliefs by combining sentence reversion and the use of an analogy to a trial. *Revista Brasileira de Psiquiatria (RBP Psychiatry), 30,* 12–18.

de Oliveira, I. R. (2011a). Downward/upward arrow. *Common language for psychotherapy procedures.* Retrieved from www.commonlanguagepsychotherapy.org

de Oliveira, I. R. (2011b). Kafka's trial dilemma: Proposal of a practical solution to Joseph K.'s unknown accusation. *Medical Hypotheses, 77,* 5–6.

de Oliveira, I. R. (2011c). Trial-based cognitive therapy. *Common language for psychotherapy procedures.* Retrieved from www.commonlanguagepsychotherapy.org

de Oliveira, I. R. (2011d). Trial-based thought record. *Common language for psychotherapy procedures.* Retrieved from www.commonlanguagepsychotherapy.org

de Oliveira, I. R. (2012a). Assessing and restructuring dysfunctional cognitions. In I. R. de Oliveira (Ed.), *Standard and innovative strategies in cognitive behavior therapy.* Rijeka, Croatia: InTech. Retrieved from www.intechopen.com

de Oliveira, I. R. (2012b). Use of the trial-based thought record to change negative core beliefs. In I. R. de Oliveira (Ed.), *Standard and innovative strategies in cognitive behavior therapy.* Rijeka, Croatia: InTech. Retrieved from www.intechopen.com

de Oliveira, I. R. (in press). *Trial-based cognitive therapy: Clinician's manual.*

de Oliveira, I. R., Duran, E. P., & Velasquez, M. (2012, October 18–21). *A transdiagnostic observation of the efficacy of the trial-based thought record in changing negative core beliefs and reducing self-criticism.* Poster presented at NEI Global Psychopharmacology Congress, San Diego, CA.

de Oliveira, I. R., Hemmany, C., Powell, V. B., Bonfim, T. D., Duranll, E. P., Novais, N., Cesnik J. A. (2012). *CNS Spectrums, 17,* 16–23.

de Oliveira, I. R., Osório, F. L., Sudak, D., Abreu, J. N., Crippa, J. A. S., Powell, Wenzel, A. (2011, November 10–13). *Initial psychometric properties of the cognitive distortions questionnaire (CD-Quest).* Paper presented at the 45th Annual Meeting of the Association for Behavioral and Cognitive Therapies (ABCT), Toronto, Canada.

de Oliveira, I. R, Powell, V. B., Wenzel, A., Seixas, C., Almeida, C., Grangeon, M. C., Sudak, D. (2012). Controlled study of the efficacy of the trial-based thought record (TBTR), a new cognitive therapy strategy to change core beliefs, in social phobia. *Journal of Clinical Pharmacy and Therapeutics, 37,* 328–334.

Dryden, W., David, D. & Ellis, A. (2010). Rational emotive behavior therapy. In K. S. Dobson (Ed.), *Handbook of cognitive behavioral therapies* (pp. 226–276). New York: Guilford Press.

Freeman, A., & DeWolf, R. (1992). *The 10 dumbest mistakes smart people make and how to avoid them.* New York: HarperPerennial.

Gilbert, P. (2010). *Compassion focused therapy.* New York: Routledge.

Greenberg, L. S. (2011). Two-chair technique. *Common language for psychotherapy procedures.* Retrieved from www.commonlanguagepsychotherapy.org

Greenberger, D., & Padesky, C. A. (1995). *Mind over mood.* New York: Guilford Press.

Hayes, S. C., Strosahl, K. D., & Wilson, K. G. (1999). *Acceptance and commitment therapy: An experiential approach to behavior change.* New York: Guilford Press.

Hollon, S. D., & Kendall, P. C. (1980). Cognitive self-statements in depression: Development of an automatic thoughts questionnaire. *Cognitive Therapy and Research, 4,* 383–395.

Kafka, F. (1925/1998). *The trial.* New York: Schocken.

Kafka, F. (2008). *Letter to my father*. NC: Howard Colyer (Original work published as *Brief an den Vater*, 1953). Lulu, North Carolina.

Kuyken, W., Fothergill, C. D., Musa, M., & Chadwick, P. (2005). The reliability and quality of cognitive case formulation. *Behaviour Research and Therapy, 43*, 1187–1201.

Leahy, R. L. (2003). *Cognitive therapy techniques: A practitioner's guide*. New York: Guilford Press.

Leahy, R. L., Tirch, D., & Napolitano, L. A. (2011). *Emotion regulation in psychotherapy*. New York: Guilford Press.

Liebowitz, M. R. (1987). Social phobia. *Modern Problems in Pharmacopsychiatry, 22*, 141–173.

Murray, N. (2004). *Kafka: A biography*. New Haven: Yale University Press.

Padesky, C. (2004). Behavioural experiments: At the crossroads. In J. Bennett-Levy, G. Butler, M. Fennel, A. Hackmann, M. Mueller, & D. Westrook (Eds.), *Oxford guide to behavioural experiments in cognitive therapy* (pp. 433–438). Oxford, UK: Oxford University Press.

Pennebaker, J. W. (2012). Expressive writing therapy. *Common language for psychotherapy procedures*. Retrieved from www.commonlanguagepsychotherapy.org

Pennebaker, J. W., & Beall, S. K. (1986). Confronting a traumatic event: Toward an understanding of inhibition and disease. *Journal of Abnormal Psychology, 95*, 274–281.

Perls, F. (1973). *The gestalt approach and eyewitness therapy*. Palo Alto, CA: Science and Behavior Books.

Powell, V. B., de Oliveira, I. R. O. H., Seixas, C., Almeida, C., Grangeon, M. C., Caldas, M., . . . de Oliveira, I. R. (2013). Changing core beliefs with trial-based therapy may improve quality of life in social phobia: A randomized study. *Revista Brasileira de Psiquiatria (RBP Psychiatry), 35*, 1–5.

Safran, J. D., Vallis, T. M., Segal, Z. V., & Shaw, B. F. (1998). Assessing core cognitive processes in cognitive therapy. In J. D. Safran (Ed.), *Widening the scope of cognitive therapy: The therapeutic relationship, emotion, and the process of change*. Northvale, NJ: Jason Aronson.

Stahl, S. M. (2012). Psychotherapy as an epigenetic 'drug': Psychiatric therapeutics target symptoms linked to malfunctioning brain circuits with psychotherapy as well as with drugs. *Journal of Clinical Pharmacy and Therapeutics, 37*, 249–253.

Watson, D., & Friend, R. (1969). Measurement of social-evaluative anxiety. *Journal of Consulting and Clinical Psychology, 33*, 448–457.

Wells, A. (2009). *Metacognitive therapy for anxiety and depression*. New York: Guilford Press.

Wenzel, A. (2012). Modification of core beliefs in cognitive therapy. In I. R. de Oliveira (Ed.), *Standard and innovative strategies in cognitive behavior therapy*. Rijeka, Croatia: InTech. Retrieved from www.intechopen.com

Appendix

Cognitive Distortions Questionnaire (CD-Quest)

Irismar Reis de Oliveira, MD, PhD

All of us have thousands of thoughts a day. These thoughts are words, sentences, and images that pop into our heads as we are doing things. Many of these thoughts are accurate, but many are distorted. This is why they are called cognitive errors or cognitive distortions.

For example, Paul is a competent journalist who had his 10-page work assessed by John, the editor of an important local newspaper. John amended one paragraph and made a few other suggestions of minor importance. Although John approved Paul's text, Paul became anxious and found himself thinking: "This work is not good at all. If it were good, John wouldn't have made any corrections."

For Paul, either the work is good or it is bad. This kind of thinking error is sometimes called dichotomous thinking. As this thought returned to Paul's mind several times from Friday to Sunday (3 days), and Paul believed it at least 75%, he made a circle around number 4 in the fourth column of the grid below.

1. **Dichotomous thinking (also called all-or-nothing, black-and-white, or polarized thinking):** I view a situation, a person or an event in "either–or" terms, fitting them into only two extreme categories instead of on a continuum.
   EXAMPLES: "I made a mistake; therefore my performance was a failure"; "I ate more than I planned, so I blew my diet completely."
   Paul's example: *This work is not good at all. If it were good, John wouldn't have made any corrections.*

Frequency: Intensity:	No (It did not occur)	Occasional (1–2 days during the past week)	Much of the time (3–5 days during the past week)	Almost all of time (6–7 days during the past week)
I believed it …	0			
A little (up to 30%)		1	2	3
Much (31% to 70%)		2	3	4
Very much (more than 70%)		3	4	5

Please, turn the page and assess your own thinking style.

Cognitive Distortions Questionnaire (CD-Quest)

Irismar Reis de Oliveira, MD, PhD

Name: ....

Date: ....

Please, make a circle around the number corresponding to each option below, indicating cognitive errors or distortions that you have made during this past week. When assessing each cognitive distortion, please, indicate how much you believed it in the exact moment it occurred (not how much you believe it now), and how often it occurred during this past week.

DURING THIS PAST WEEK, I FOUND MYSELF THINKING THIS WAY:

1. **Dichotomous thinking (also called all-or-nothing, black-and-white, or polarized thinking):** I view a situation, a person or an event in "either–or" terms, fitting them into only two extreme categories instead of on a continuum.
   EXAMPLES: "I made a mistake; therefore my performance was a failure"; "I ate more than I planned, so I blew my diet completely."

Frequency: Intensity:	No (It did not occur)	Occasional (1–2 days during the past week)	Much of the time (3–5 days during the past week)	Almost all of the time (6–7 days during the past week)
I believed it . . .	0			
A little (up to 30%)		1	2	3
Much (31% to 70%)		2	3	4
Very much (more than 70%)		3	4	5

2. **Fortune telling (also called catastrophizing):** I predict the future in negative terms and believe that what will happen will be so awful that I will not be able to stand it.
   EXAMPLES: "I will fail and this will be unbearable"; "I'll be so upset that I won't be able to concentrate for the exam."

Frequency: Intensity:	No (It did not occur)	Occasional (1–2 days during the past week)	Much of the time (3–5 days during the past week)	Almost all of the time (6–7 days during the past week)
I believed it . . .	0			
A little (up to 30%)		1	2	3
Much (31% to 70%)		2	3	4
Very much (more than 70%)		3	4	5

3. **Discounting the positive:** I disqualify positive experiences or events, insisting that they do not count.
   EXAMPLES: "I passed the exam, but I was just lucky"; "Going to college is not a big deal; anyone can do it."

Frequency: Intensity:	No (It did not occur)	Occasional (1–2 days during the past week)	Much of the time (3–5 days during the past week)	Almost all of the time (6–7 days during the past week)
I believed it . . .	0			
A little (up to 30%)		1	2	3
Much (31% to 70%)		2	3	4
Very much (more than 70%)		3	4	5

4. **Emotional reasoning:** I believe my emotions reflect reality and let them guide my attitudes and judgments.
   EXAMPLES: "I feel she loves me, so it must be true"; "I am terrified of airplanes, so flying must be dangerous"; "My feelings tell me I should not believe him."

Frequency: Intensity:	No (It did not occur)	Occasional (1–2 days during the past week)	Much of the time (3–5 days during the past week)	Almost all of the time (6–7 days during the past week)
I believed it . . .	0			
A little (up to 30%)		1	2	3
Much (31% to 70%)		2	3	4
Very much (more than 70%)		3	4	5

5. **Labeling:** I put a fixed, global label, usually negative, on myself or others.
   EXAMPLES: "I'm a loser"; "He's a rotten person"; "She's a complete jerk."

Frequency: Intensity:	No (It did not occur)	Occasional (1–2 days during the past week)	Much of the time (3–5 days during the past week)	Almost all of the time (6–7 days during the past week)
I believed it ...	0			
A little (up to 30%)		1	2	3
Much (31% to 70%)		2	3	4
Very much (more than 70%)		3	4	5

6. **Magnification/minimization:** I evaluate myself, others, and situations, placing greater importance on the negatives, and/or placing much less importance on the positives.
   EXAMPLES: "I got a B. This proves how bad my performance was"; "I got an A. It means the test was too easy."

Frequency: Intensity:	No (It did not occur)	Occasional (1–2 days during the past week)	Much of the time (3–5 days during the past week)	Almost all of the time (6–7 days during the past week)
I believed it ...	0			
A little (up to 30%)		1	2	3
Much (31% to 70%)		2	3	4
Very much (more than 70%)		3	4	5

7. **Selective abstraction (also called mental filter and tunnel vision):** I pay attention to one or a few details and fail to see the whole picture.
   EXAMPLES: "Michael pointed out an error in my work. So, I can be fired" (not considering Michael's overall positive feedback); "I can't forget that a small peace of information I gave during my presentation was wrong" (not considering its success and the audience's great applause).

Frequency: Intensity:	No (It did not occur)	Occasional (1–2 days during the past week)	Much of the time (3–5 days during the past week)	Almost all of the time (6–7 days during the past week)
I believed it ...	0			
A little (up to 30%)		1	2	3
Much (31% to 70%)		2	3	4
Very much (more than 70%)		3	4	5

8. **Mind reading:** I believe that I know the thoughts or intentions of others (or that they know my thoughts or intentions) without having sufficient evidence.

EXAMPLES: "He's thinking that I failed"; "She thought I didn't know the project"; "He knows I do not like to be touched this way."

Frequency: Intensity:	No (It did not occur)	Occasional (1–2 days during the past week)	Much of the time (3–5 days during the past week)	Almost all of the time (6–7 days during the past week)
I believed it ...	0			
A little (up to 30%)		1	2	3
Much (31% to 70%)		2	3	4
Very much (more than 70%)		3	4	5

9. **Overgeneralization:** I take isolated negative cases and generalize them, transforming them in a never-ending pattern, by repeatedly using words such as "always," "never," "ever," "whole," "entire," etc.

EXAMPLES: "It was raining this morning, which means it will rain during the whole weekend"; "What a bad luck! I missed the plane, so this will interfere in my entire vacation"; "My headache will never stop."

Frequency: Intensity:	No (It did not occur)	Occasional (1–2 days during the past week)	Much of the time (3–5 days during the past week)	Almost all of the time (6–7 days during the past week)
I believed it ...	0			
A little (up to 30%)		1	2	3
Much (31% to 70%)		2	3	4
Very much (more than 70%)		3	4	5

10. **Personalization:** I assume that others' behaviors and external events concern (or are directed to) myself without considering other plausible explanations.

EXAMPLES: "I thought I was disrespected because the cashier did not say thank you to me" (not considering that the cashier did not say thank you to anyone); "My husband left me because I was a bad wife" (not considering that she was his fourth wife).

Frequency: Intensity:	No (It did not occur)	Occasional (1–2 days during the past week)	Much of the time (3–5 days during the past week)	Almost all of the time (6–7 days during the past week)
I believed it ...	0			
A little (up to 30%)		1	2	3
Much (31% to 70%)		2	3	4
Very much (more than 70%)		3	4	5

11. **Should statements (also "musts," "oughts," "have tos"):** I tell myself that events, people's behaviors, and my own attitudes "should" be the way I expected them to be and not as they really are.
    EXAMPLES: "I should have been a better mother"; "He should have married Ann instead of Mary"; "I shouldn't have made so many mistakes."

Frequency: Intensity:	No (It did not occur)	Occasional (1–2 days during the past week)	Much of the time (3–5 days during the past week)	Almost all of the time (6–7 days during the past week)
I believed it ...	0			
A little (up to 30%)		1	2	3
Much (31% to 70%)		2	3	4
Very much (more than 70%)		3	4	5

12. **Jumping to conclusions (also called arbitrary inference):** I draw conclusions (negative or positive) from little or no confirmatory evidence.
    EXAMPLES: "As soon as I saw him I knew he would do a lousy work"; "He looked at me in a way that I immediately knew he was responsible for the accident."

Frequency: Intensity:	No (It did not occur)	Occasional (1–2 days during the past week)	Much of the time (3–5 days during the past week)	Almost all of the time (6–7 days during the past week)
I believed it ...	0			
A little (up to 30%)		1	2	3
Much (31% to 70%)		2	3	4
Very much (more than 70%)		3	4	5

13. **Blaming (others or oneself):** I direct my attention to others as sources of my negative feelings and experiences, failing to consider my own responsibility; or, conversely, I take responsibility for others' behaviors and attitudes.
    EXAMPLES: "My parents should be blamed for my unhappiness."; "It is my fault that my son married a selfish and uncaring person."

Frequency: Intensity:	No (It did not occur)	Occasional (1–2 days during the past week)	Much of the time (3–5 days during the past week)	Almost all of the time (6–7 days during the past week)
I believed it …	0			
A little (up to 30%)		1	2	3
Much (31% to 70%)		2	3	4
Very much (more than 70%)		3	4	5

14. **What if?:** I keep asking myself questions such as "What if something happens?"
    EXAMPLES: "What if my car crashes?" "What if I have a heart attack?" "What if my husband leaves me?"

Frequency: Intensity:	No (It did not occur)	Occasional (1–2 days during the past week)	Much of the time (3–5 days during the past week)	Almost all of the time (6–7 days during the past week)
I believed it…	0			
A little (up to 30%)		1	2	3
Much (31% to 70%)		2	3	4
Very much (more than 70%)		3	4	5

15. **Unfair comparisons:** I compare myself with others who seem to do better than I do and place myself in a disadvantageous position.
    EXAMPLES: "My father always preferred my elder brother because he is much smarter than I am"; "I can't stand that she is more successful than I am."

Frequency: Intensity:	No (It did not occur)	Occasional (1–2 days during the past week)	Much of the time (3–5 days during the past week)	Almost all of the time (6–7 days during the past week)
I believed it …	0			
A little (up to 30%)		1	2	3
Much (31% to 70%)		2	3	4
Very much (more than 70%)		3	4	5

Integrating Psychopharmacology and Psychotherapy in Mood Disorders
Major Depression

Aaron M. Koenig, Edward S. Friedman, and Michael E. Thase

INTRODUCTION

Depression is one of the world's greatest public health concerns (Murray & Lopez, 1996), and in industrialized nations it is the leading cause of disability (Kessler et al., 2006). Theoretical and clinical approaches to the treatment of depression have changed greatly since the psychoanalytic models that dominated the psychiatric landscape in the mid-twentieth century. Seminal developments in the 1950s and 1960s included recognition that several distinctly different types of medication had antidepressant effects, which ultimately shaped the influential monoamine hypotheses of depression and helped to redefine treatment for decades to come. Concurrently, the pioneering work of Beck (cognitive therapy), Klerman and Weisman (interpersonal psychotherapy), and others led to the introduction of several time-limited, operationalized forms of psychotherapy specifically developed to treat depression. As our understanding of the etiology, pathophysiology, and risk factors for depression have grown, additional pharmacological and psychosocial therapies have continued to be introduced.

Comprehensive psychiatric treatment across a broad spectrum of psychiatric illnesses has come to encompass both psychotherapeutic and pharmacologic interventions, often referred to as "combined" treatment. Combined treatment can be offered simultaneously (at the same time) or additively, which can be further delineated by the order of implementation (psychotherapy first augmented by medication, or pharmacological treatment supplemented by therapy). Combined treatment can also be "split" (provided by two or more providers) or "integrated" (same psychiatrist providing both), with the former approach being more common as a result of modern-day cost and supply issues.

Much of the existing literature that discusses the benefits and limitations of combined treatment is based on clinical opinion or theoretical speculation, and lacks a strong empirical basis. However, a growing number of clinical trials over the past two decades have demonstrated that combined treatments may be superior, in certain circumstances, to either type of intervention used independently. Even with this evidence, pharmacotherapy is still the most common treatment modality for many psychiatric disorders, particularly the mood disorders, as insurance providers often place limits on the number of sessions of psychotherapy due to cost concerns. To reverse this trend, a larger empirical evidence base demonstrating the utility and necessity of combined treatment will be necessary. This chapter is designed to provide a framework to help the psychiatric practitioner understand the benefits and limitations of combination treatment in the management of adult patients with depression.

Historical Perspective

Following the introduction of the first effective antidepressant medications, acceptance of medication as standalone or additive treatment (in addition to psychotherapy) was not widely accepted by the psychoanalytic community that then dominated the field of psychiatry. Freudian theory posited that "suppression of symptoms" through pharmacotherapy would interfere with access to psychic conflict, thereby preventing resolution of the underlying dynamic causes of a clinical disorder. This disdain for pharmacotherapy was especially true in the management of "neurotic" conditions such as depression, though there was some recognition of the value of medications in certain populations with more pernicious and disabling conditions such as schizophrenia. In patients with schizophrenia, for example, medications helped to target unpredictable behavior and disorganized thinking, both of which would interfere with the conduct of psychotherapy. During the 1960s and 1970s, behavior therapists similarly argued that pharmacological relief of symptoms would interfere with the learning of new behaviors or result in state-dependent learning. The use of psychotropic medications thus was seen by behaviorists as a "last resort" for the most severe and refractory cases. Many patients also remained hesitant to take medications, perhaps regarding this intervention as an affirmation of failure or weakness, or as being more stigmatizing than psychotherapy.

Paykel's *Handbook of Affective Disorders,* originally published in 1982 (Paykel, 1982), was one of the first textbooks to include a chapter on combining medications and psychotherapy. The chapter, written from the perspective of psychotherapists confronting the growing dominance of psychopharmacology at that time, noted the paucity of evidence for combining psychotherapy and medications. It enumerated possible negative effects of drug therapy on psychotherapy, including the beliefs that introducing medications might engender transference reactions within the therapeutic process, undercut defenses, alter patient expectation, and ultimately reduce the efficacy of therapy. The authors also speculated on benefits of medication, including the possibility that medications might stabilize ego functions and thus enable better psychotherapy participation.

In the setting of increasing evidence from RCTs that both pharmacotherapy and targeted forms of psychotherapy were efficacious as monotherapies, the use of combined treatment began to gain wider acceptance during the 1990s (Friedman, 1997). The American Psychiatric Association's (1993) practice guidelines for major depressive disorder at the time, based on systematic review of the literature and expert consensus, recommended specific situations that would justify the use of combined treatment, including when either treatment alone was only partially effective, when the clinical circumstances suggested two discrete targets of therapy (such as symptom reduction addressed by medication and social/occupational problems addressed by psychotherapy), or when the prior course of illness was chronic. By the middle of the decade, consumers were rating combination therapy highly (Seligman, 1995)—particularly in comparison to pharmacotherapy alone as provided by primary care physicians—despite limited empirical validation (Friedman, 1997).

During recent years, the evidence base for combining psychotherapy and pharmacotherapy has continued to grow. With regards to healthcare trends, the pendulum has swung to the opposite position. Pharmacotherapy is now the most common treatment modality for mood disorders, primarily due to the fact that insurance providers are increasingly limiting the duration and scope of psychotherapy, but also due to an increase in general patient acceptance of pharmacotherapeutic interventions. At the center of this trend has been the issue of cost, since it is generally more costly to treat an episode of depression with the combination of psychotherapy and pharmacotherapy, rather than pharmacotherapy alone. Thus, the routine prescription of combined treatment, without evidence of clear benefits, can sometimes not be justified or warranted.

INTERPRETING THE LITERATURE

Measuring the Efficacy of Antidepressants and Psychotherapy

Before embarking on a discussion of particular treatment strategies, it may be useful to briefly examine the methods used to assess the efficacy of treatments. For over 40 years, the randomized controlled trial (RCT) has been the gold standard modality for evaluating medical therapies. The major strengths of RCTs are that random assignment helps to ensure that treatment groups are comparable, the use of standardized protocols helps to ensure that an experiment is replicable, and the inclusion of one or more comparison groups provides the context for assessing the impact of an intervention. For pharmacotherapy studies, a double-blind placebo control group is the standard means to determine treatment efficacy—the outcome of the placebo control group reflects the impact of all factors except those directly resulting from the pharmacologic effects of the medication. There is not an ideal analogue for a placebo in studies of psychosocial interventions. For example, a "pseudotherapy" condition does not really function as a placebo if the clinician providing the intervention knows it is a "dud." As a result, investigators sometimes use a waiting list or assessment-only control group in early studies and a three-arm design (with psychotherapy, active drug, and placebo) for more advanced studies. The major inherent limitation of RCTs is that the study protocol—with inclusion and exclusion criteria that may rule out a large majority of depressed people seeking treatment—limits generalizability to the patients seen in everyday clinical practice. For this reason, two types of RCTs are now recommended: an initial series of highly controlled studies to establish whether or not the treatment works (i.e., *efficacy* research designs, which emphasize the internal validity of the experiment), followed by larger, more inclusive studies conducted in "real world" settings (i.e., *effectiveness* research designs, which emphasize generalizability).

The impact of an acute intervention for depression should be apparent within a few months, and thus studies of the initial phase of treatment typically last between 4 to 12 weeks for pharmacotherapy and between 8 to 16 weeks for psychotherapy. The traditional outcome of interest is termed "response," which has been defined as at least a 50% reduction in symptom burden (Frank et al., 1991). Many individuals who experience at least a 50% reduction in symptom intensity will no longer meet criteria for a major depressive episode and will also perceive qualitative improvement. A number of reliable and valid assessment scales are available to quantify symptom burden, including older standards such as the Hamilton Rating Scale for Depression (HAM-D) (Hamilton, 1960), the Montgomery Asberg Depression Rating Scale (MADRS) (Montgomery & Asberg, 1979), and the Beck Depression Inventory (BDI) (Beck et al., 1961), as well as newer measures such as the depression subscale of the Patient Health Questionnaire (PHQ9) (Kroenke, Spitzer, & Williams, 2001) and the Inventory of Depressive Symptomatology (IDS) (Rush et al., 1986). Clinician-administered rating scales are rarely used in day-to-day practice, and in this setting self-administered scales such as the BDI and PHQ are ideal. An abbreviated, self-reported version of the IDS, known as the QIDS-SR (Rush et al., 2003), has the additional advantage of being in the public domain, which means that it can be administered without cost.

Recently, investigators and clinicians have been using the more restrictive term "remission" to describe treatment success (Keller, 2003; Thase, Sloan, & Kornstein, 2002). Remission describes a virtually complete relief of depressive symptoms, such that the person who has remitted would have a level of symptom burden essentially indistinguishable from someone who has never been depressed (Frank et al., 1991; Rush et al., 2006). Remission can be thought of as the "gateway" to recovery (or a period of sustained remission, lasting at least 2 months or longer). Remission is also a necessary, though not sufficient, state for resolution of the psychosocial and vocational impairments that are often associated with a depressive episode. In practice, however, it may take months or even years for normalization of functional status (Mintz et al., 1992). The construct of remission is now well-validated, and responders who do not remit have been shown to have a higher risk for subsequent relapse (Judd et al., 1998; Paykel et al., 1995; Thase et al., 1992) and poorer social and vocational functioning (Miller et al., 1998). Specific symptom severity scores to define remission have been validated for each of the commonly used rating scales (e.g., a HAM-D score of < 7, a MADRS score of < 10, or a QIDS-SR score of < 5) (Rush et al., 2003; Zimmerman, Posternak, & Chelminksi, 2004). The major advantage of using remission—rather than response—to define a successful outcome in research studies is that a larger amount of improvement is required, which increases certainty that the patients who are said to have benefited from an intervention have truly experienced a positive outcome.

Over the past few years, there has been some controversy regarding the effectiveness of antidepressants (see, for example, Kirsch et al., 2002; Turner et al., 2008). Results of the early clinical trials of antidepressants in the 1960s shaped the expectation that an effective medication could be expected to deliver a response rate of approximately 67%, as compared to a placebo response rate of around 33%. The advantage for the active drug in this scenario was large, whether expressed as an absolute value (a 34% "rate difference"), a relative benefit (100% or twofold advantage), an odds ratio (OR = 4.1), or as the Number Needed to Treat for benefit (NNT = 2). The effect of treatment can also be described by computing standardized difference scores or effect sizes (abbreviated as d) on measures such as the HAM-D or MADRS, which are most commonly calculated by dividing the difference score between the active treatment and placebo by the pooled standard deviation (Cohen, 1977). In the scenario described above, a 33% advantage in response rate corresponds to a roughly 6-point difference on the HAM-D. As the standard deviation of the HAM-D at posttreatment is usually about 10 points, d would equal about 0.6.

It is not difficult to detect large effects in RCTs, and, in the studies conducted in the 1960s and 1970s, investigators only needed to enroll about 30 to 50 patients per arm in order to have an acceptable level of statistical power (or at least an 80% chance of obtaining a statistically significant finding). The situation in recent years has been different, however, as there is now strong evidence that effect sizes observed in placebo-controlled studies of antidepressants have grown progressively smaller across the past few decades. In fact, average drug versus placebo differences in response rates more typically range from 10% to 15% in contemporary studies, with NNT values ranging from 7 to 10, and effect sizes on the order of $d = 0.3$ or 0.4. Differences of this magnitude are judged to be moderate or even small effects, and are on the margin of what can be considered to be clinically significant (Cipriani et al., 2006).

In an era in which such modest drug–placebo differences are the norm, investigators must plan to enroll much larger samples in order to maintain acceptable statistical power. Indeed, a study would need to be quite large—on the order of 300 patients per arm—to have adequate statistical power to detect a 10% difference in response rates (Thase, 2002). As few studies enroll more than 150 patients per arm, it should come as no surprise that about one half of contemporary studies fail to detect significant differences between placebo and antidepressants with proven efficacy. Statisticians refer to this type of outcome as a Type 2 error (or failure to confirm a statistically significant difference because of inadequate power), with the high rate of Type 2 errors being emblematic of a loss of "signal detection" or decreased "assay sensitivity." Although there are a number of reasons for this trend, a steady increase in the average placebo response rate over the past 30 years accounts for at least part of the problem (Walsh et al., 2002). As the chemical composition of placebo has not changed, the growing placebo response rate likely reflects both higher expectations of benefit by study subjects, as well as changes in the population of depressed people who enroll in clinical trials (with a shift to less severely or pervasively ill study participants).

This difficulty in signal detection also extends to comparisons between active antidepressant medications or between psychotherapy and an antidepressant. Specifically, the drug versus placebo difference may be thought of as the upward boundary of signal detection, and it is proportionally more difficult to discern a difference between two effective therapies than it is to find an effect between an active therapy and a placebo (Thase, 2002). Thus, unless adequately powered to find modest between-group differences, comparative studies are essentially destined to find that there are "no significant differences" between two therapies. It is even more difficult to test "non-inferiority" (or to confirm with a high degree of certainty that two treatments have equivalent effects), as non-inferiority studies typically need to enroll at least three times as many subjects as a study designed to determine whether treatment A is superior to treatment B. The field has thus been stymied by the inability to differentiate between therapies that are truly comparable and those that may have modest, but still clinically meaningful differences.

Measuring Combined Antidepressant and Psychotherapy Efficacy

It has long been assumed that psychotherapy and pharmacotherapy have additive or even synergistic effects in the treatment of depression (American Psychiatric Association [APA], 1993). In this regard, an additive effect refers to two treatments, together, resulting in better outcomes than would be expected from either treatment alone, with a synergistic effect describing an outcome that amounts to a response beyond what is expected from the summation of the monotherapies. After several decades of research on this topic, two conclusions can be drawn: Psychotherapy and pharmacotherapy have, at best, only partially additive effects, and there is no solid evidence that combining these treatments actually results in synergistic effects. However, to better understand these realities, we must first examine how combination treatment trials are performed.

Most studies that examine the efficacy of depression treatments involve relatively short-term trials (Frank et al., 1991), and, given the heterogeneity of major depressive disorder, the sample compositions of particular studies can vary remarkably with respect to the proportion of participants with severe, chronic, recurrent, comorbid, or treatment-resistant depressive episodes. Thus, a study that samples a relatively acute, milder, and less complicated patient population is unlikely to yield the same results as a trial of a more severe and complex group of patients.

Another problem stems from overestimation of the likely effects of treatment. Specifically, it is now known that so-called "nonspecific effects" of treatment are generally larger than the specific effects of particular antidepressants and psychotherapeutic modalities in modern clinical trials (Thase, 2002). After taking into account the magnitude of placebo-expectancy effects, the specific effects of treatment are relatively modest (with Cohen's d effect size values ranging between 0.2 and 0.5), which means that studies need to be relatively large in order to have the statistical power to reliably detect between-group differences (Thase, 2002). For example, although it is true that most early studies comparing cognitive therapy (CT) and pharmacotherapy, singly and in combination, indicated that combining these modalities did not result in statistically significant additive effects (Friedman, 1997), it is also true that these studies only had the power to detect relatively large additive effects. Whereas most studies comparing psychotherapy and pharmacotherapy, singly and in combination, have had 30 or fewer patients in each arm of the experiment, a study designed to reliably detect a small additive effect would need to enroll more than 250 patients in each treatment condition (Kraemer & Thiemann, 1987). To our knowledge, only one such large, adequately powered study has ever been conducted (Keller et al., 2000). It is also true that a small overall additive effect in a study of a heterogeneous group of patients may conceal a mixture of outcomes, ranging from no additive effect among the less severe or less complicated patients to a large effect in particular subgroups (Friedman et al., 2006; Jindal & Thase, 2003; Pampallona et al., 2004; Hollon et al., 2005).

The varying ideologies of different schools of psychotherapy, each with competing concepts of etiology, diagnosis, and treatment of mental illness, have also complicated the evaluation of the efficacy of combining treatments. Each psychotherapeutic orientation faces unique challenges when pharmacotherapy is incorporated into the treatment approach. In addition, clinicians invariably bring their own theoretical bias to the treatment setting, which can influence the therapeutic process during combination treatment. Some practitioners are oriented, by preference or training, to provide a specific form of psychotherapy, such as psychoanalysis, cognitive behavioral therapy (CBT), or interpersonal therapy (IPT). To these clinicians, psychotherapy is seen as the primary treatment modality, with pharmacological agents being used adjunctively. For psychoanalysts, challenges include maintaining their theoretical orientation while simultaneously evaluating for psychiatric disorders that may benefit from adjunctive medication, relative inexperience with medications, and lack of role models for combined treatment. In CBT, the focus of combined treatment is the synergistic use of each modality to maximize the overall effects of the intervention. For example, a CBT therapist might focus on a patient's negative thoughts and dysfunctional beliefs about taking a medication, with the goal of improving compliance. This may further improve cognitive distortions, which in turn can lead to improvement in the patient's ability to utilize therapy techniques and achieve desired behavioral outcomes. For a pharmacologically oriented psychiatrist, psychotherapy may be seen as a modality that augments the benefit of a medication. Although there may be disagreements about which approach is the most clinically efficacious, most psychiatrists agree that optimally, the combination of modalities should be complementary and improve overall patient care.

Another critical factor to consider in evaluating combined treatment efficacy is patient expectation. Conversations with friends and relatives who have been in treatment, stories in the media, portrayals of psychiatric treatments in the movies, and direct consumer advertising by drug companies all shape expectations and attitudes. In addition, a patient's unconscious conflict about the treatment and its related outcome may influence response. For example, patients may not respond to therapy if they think that medication "corrected" their problem, nor may they respond to medication if the idea of "talk therapy" is more psychologically tolerable to them. These factors may manifest in the clinical setting as therapy or medication noncompliance, repeated emergence of intolerable side effects, or defensive and negative attachment to treatment that prevents clinical improvement.

Moving Toward a Biological Understanding

Dualistic theories separating mind and brain are being replaced with more integrated models, with Kandel proposing a new framework to conceptualize mind–brain interactions. This framework includes the principles that all mental processes derive from the brain; genes and their protein products determine neuronal connections and functioning; learning can produce alterations in gene expression; and altered gene expression changes neuronal connections that contribute to maintaining maladaptive behaviors. Viewed from this perspective, psychotherapy and pharmacotherapy produce long-term symptom change by altering gene expression and structurally changing the brain.

Neuroimaging, as well as other neurobiological techniques, has been used to study similarities and differences between the actions of psychotherapy and pharmacotherapy on brain pathways in depression. Investigators have analyzed patients treated with SSRIs and CBT, and have shown that CBT is associated with characteristic metabolic changes in the frontal cortex, cingulate, and hippocampus, as opposed to the characteristic changes in the prefrontal cortex, hippocampus, and subgenual cingulate regions that result from treatment with an SSRI. Some interpret these findings to indicate that CBT and medications have different primary anatomical targets of action, with cortical "top-down" effects characterizing psychotherapeutic impact and subcortical "bottom-up" factors accounting for the effects of medication. This imaging data lends support to the theory that combination treatment may be synergistic in its benefits, with each modality affecting a different anatomical pathway of the brain.

Other imaging studies using PET and fMRI have examined differences in brain regional activation in depressed and anxious subjects relative to controls, and in patients before and after treatment. Ressler and Mayberg (2007) note that the brain regions most reproducibly found to be dysregulated in common emotional disorders are the prefrontal cortex (PFC) and subgenual cingulate cortex (Cg25), which seem to be involved in emotional experience and processing, as well as the subcortical hippocampus and amygdala, which are involved in emotional memory formation and retrieval. Cg25 is involved in the production of sad emotions and in antidepressant response, and is also activated during transient sadness. After recovery from depression, its activity remains decreased compared to baseline. Overactivation of the amygdala has been observed in depression (Ressler & Mayberg, 2007), and studies that implicate Cg25 have found significant amygdala decreases with response to CBT treatment for social phobia. As the field of functional neuroimaging evolves over the coming decades, the additional data that will be generated will invariably help to inform a more precise understanding of the efficacy of these interventions in the real-world clinical setting.

EVIDENCE BASE

Antidepressant Medications and Modern Psychotherapies

Antidepressants are effective for treating the full spectrum of depressive disorders, from dysthymic disorder and acute major depressive episodes to more classical episodes of melancholia

(A.P.A., 2010; Bauer et al., 2007; Thase & Kupfer, 1996). Although once mostly prescribed by psychiatrists, the widespread availability of safer classes of antidepressant medications, as well as changes in healthcare delivery, have resulted in a large increase in the number of depressed individuals who receive treatment from primary care providers. (Bauer et al., 2007; Depression Guideline Panel, 1993) Of course, depressive episodes may also be treated effectively with focused forms of psychotherapy, such as CBT or IPT. For individuals presenting with a nonpsychotic major depressive episode of mild to moderate severity, the initial choice of therapy often depends on the preference of the patient and the discipline of the provider. Psychologists and social workers are more likely to recommend psychotherapy or counseling before considering a trial of medication, while primary care physicians are more likely to prescribe antidepressant medication instead of referring out for therapy. Psychiatrists will usually prescribe medication, although they may combine it with psychotherapy.

The so-called "depression-focused psychotherapies" currently dominate the psychotherapeutic landscape, and have done so since the early 1980s. Cognitive therapy (CT), first introduced by Beck, Rush, Shaw, and Emery (1979), is the best-studied psychological treatment for major depression, followed by interpersonal therapy (IPT), which retains a reasonable evidence base, and behavioral therapy (BT), with a more limited evidence base. These newer therapies have emerged at a time when there has been a growing interest in the field for documenting treatment efficacy. The development of manuals to specify therapeutic methods and guide learning has enhanced their reproducibility and has also permitted independent assessment of fidelity and adherence to treatment protocols. The developers of these newer therapies have also been ready and willing to conduct controlled clinical trials demonstrating the efficacy of their interventions, leading to a large volume of efficacy research, as well as studies of relative efficacy in comparison with pharmacological treatments. In contrast, many of the leaders of the psychodynamic tradition have not placed a high value on this type of research. The apparent unwillingness of dynamically oriented academicians to conduct such studies has ultimately undermined their power base within academic psychiatry, where a premium is placed on level of research funding and number of high-impact publications in scholarly journals.

Combining Psychotherapy and Antidepressant Medications

Given that both a wide range of antidepressant medications and depression-focused psychotherapies have been found efficacious in the treatment of depression, it is logical that efforts have been made to combine the two. The rationale for this strategy includes the hopes that combined treatment might increase the overall degree of symptom relief, increase the breadth of response (with both symptom relief and improvement in social functioning), and also increase the patient's adherence to treatment (since receiving psychotherapy increases the likelihood that a patient will start and comply with necessary antidepressant treatment) (Hollon et al., 2005). A positive effect in any of these areas might justify the decision to use combined treatment. The difficulty in making this decision, however, lies in the uncertainty that remains with respect to which patients are most likely to benefit from a combined treatment strategy.

CBT Plus Medication Management

Many of the early studies that examined the combination of antidepressant medication and CBT found no advantage for this combination when compared with either treatment as monotherapy (Murphy et al., 1984; Hollon et al., 1992). Subsequent meta- and mega-analyses (Conte et al., 1986; Thase et al., 1997), addressing the problem of small sample sizes in earlier studies, concluded that combination treatment did provide an advantage over either monotherapy. This was especially true for more severely depressed and more chronic patients (Friedman et al., 2004; Pampallona et al., 2004). Friedman and Thase (2007) concluded that adding CT to pharmacotherapy increased the likelihood of response in depressed patients, showing a clinically meaningful effect that was at least as large as the average difference between antidepressant and placebo in contemporary RCTs. A large study by Keller and colleagues (N = 681), using nefazodone as the medication and the Cognitive Behavioral Analysis System of Psychotherapy (CBASP) as the talk therapy, demonstrated that the combination of nefazodone and CBASP was significantly superior to either treatment alone in a large sample of chronically depressed patients (Keller et al., 2000). The difference in response rate between the combined treatment group and either monotherapy group was > 25% for study completers. This difference is quite impressive and, as a result, the study rekindled interest in combining medication and psychotherapy to produce more favorable outcomes.

The cognitive-biological model provides a theoretical basis for combining pharmacotherapy and psychotherapy (Wright & Thase, 1992). This model takes a systems approach, appreciating that multiple influences—including cognitive, behavioral, interpersonal, social, cultural, and biological—contribute to the development and expression of a psychiatric disorder. In theory, efficacy of combination treatment may result from targeting different vulnerability factors. From this perspective, interventions designed to improve a problem in one system may also contribute to improvement in others, in mutually reinforcing ways. For example, a cognitive intervention to ensure medication compliance intervenes on the cognitive and biological systems in a synergistic manner: A positive behavioral outcome results in improved medication compliance, which leads to a greater degree of biological stabilization of the illness, thus making it more likely that the patient will continue to take their medications in the future.

As mentioned previously, one recent and compelling area of research supporting such a model comes from state-of-the-art functional imaging studies. Drevets (2003) examined patients with mood disorders and identified a region in the subgenual prefrontal cortex that was 40% decreased in volume in patients with depression. Mayberg (2003) also identified this region as a common target of pharmacotherapy, since it is the area in the brain with the highest concentration of serotonin. When investigators (Goldapple et al., 2004) analyzed patients treated with either an SSRI medication (paroxetine) or CBT, they found that CBT was associated with characteristic metabolic changes in the frontal cortex, cingulate, and hippocampal regions of the brain, as opposed to the characteristic changes in the prefrontal cortex, hippocampus, and subgenual cingulate regions that result from treatment with an SSRI. These exciting data help to support the theoretical position that combination treatment may be synergistic in its benefit, with each modality affecting a different brain region.

These intriguing discoveries also accompany new work examining the role of genomics in helping to determine which treatments are most beneficial to specific groups of patients. For example, Lesch and colleagues (1996) reported on an insertion–deletion polymorphism of the serotonin transporter gene that affects transcriptional activity and accounts for differences in serotonin transporter density among individuals. Of the 27 variants of this gene, one polymorphism in the promoter region has a long and short allele variation; the latter allele is less functional than the former allele. Caspi and colleagues (2003) studied the genetic profile in 1,057 consecutive births in New Zealand over 26 years, and at age 26, 17% of the members of this cohort reported a major depressive episode. While neither life stress nor 5-HTT transporter genotype predicted depression onset, subjects with the short form of the allele demonstrated increased depressive episodes in the context of greater stressful life events, whereas those with the long form of the allele had lower rates of depression in the context of steady levels of life stress. In a study that combined neurobiological and genomic observations, Pezawas and colleagues (2005) identified the cingulate–amygdala pathway as the structural and functional site for the differences produced by these polymorphisms. They suggest that variation in this system may provide a susceptibility mechanism for depression, with individuals who express this genetic vulnerability demonstrating biased information processing of emotionally laden stimuli. Other studies have also correlated this polymorphic variation with antidepressant response (Kugaya et al., 2004; Yu et al., 2002). This genomic and functional brain imaging data suggests that CBT-biologic interactions may reveal more specific and measurable benefits of combination treatment strategies.

Wright and Thase (1992) have elaborated on several assumptions that derive from the cognitive-biologic model and may be used to inform treatment. First, cognitive processes modulate the effects of the external environment on CNS components involved in emotion and behavior. For example, stressful life events can modulate neurotransmitter function, activation of CNS pathways, and neuroendocrine tone. Second, dysfunctional cognitions are the product of both psychological and physiological influences. Third, biological treatments can alter cognitions. Fourth, cognitive and behavioral interventions can modulate biological processes. Fifth, environmental, cognitive, behavioral, emotional, and biological processes should be conceptualized as components of a whole system. As a consequence of these assumptions, a clinician combining CBT and pharmacotherapy might attempt to integrate these components into a comprehensive case conceptualization, in order to enhance the efficacy of their intervention.

Similar to this framework, McCullough's Cognitive Behavioral Analysis System of Psychotherapy (CBASP) was developed to address problems encountered in the treatment of patients with chronic forms of depression, including dysthymia (McCullough, 2000). CBASP (and CBT adapted for treatment resistant and chronic depression) are usually provided in the context of optimized pharmacotherapy. Traditional CBT, when modified for treatment-resistant and chronic depression, addresses prolonged hopelessness and helplessness, persistent anhedonia and anergia, strongly entrenched dysfunctional beliefs, repeated interpersonal ineffectiveness, and the importance of maintaining pharmacotherapy (Antonuccio et al., 1984; Cole, Brittlebank, & Scott, 1994; Thase & Howland, 1994; Fava et al., 1997; Wright, Basco, & Thase, 2006). McCullough conceptualizes chronic depression as the product of dysfunctional cognitions of helplessness, hopelessness, and failure that are linked to a detached and maladaptive interpersonal style, which is ultimately reinforced by habitually poor social problem solving. Crucially, the patient's history of medication failure reinforces his belief in the inevitability of a prolonged course of illness. Such perceptual distortions lead to behaviors that are incompatible with a patient's desired outcomes (such as giving up on medication adherence, which reduces the likelihood of achieving or sustaining a prolonged remission of symptoms). CBASP helps such patients reestablish interpersonal connections and learn new and adaptive coping styles, ultimately leading to a better chance for recovery. Keller and colleagues (2000) compared CBASP to the serotonin–norepinephrine reuptake inhibitor nefazodone, used alone and in combination. They found that each monotherapy yielded a response rate of 55%, while the combination produced an 85% response rate at the end of 12 weeks of treatment. This study, most notably, supported the use of combination treatment in the difficult to treat depressed population. More recently, however, an NIMH-sponsored study of CBASP augmentation in chronic depression did not replicate the Keller et al. study results (Trivedi et al., 2008).

IPT Plus Medication Management

The efficacy of IPT has been studied in a number of RCTs involving outpatients with nonpsychotic MDD, and there is now reasonably broad empirical support for the use of IPT in the treatment of MDD. Overall, these effects are similar in magnitude to acute phase antidepressant pharmacotherapy, although the time course of symptom reduction appears to be slower. IPT may be less effective for patients with prominent anxiety, certain types of personality pathology, and more pronounced interpersonal difficulties. Such patients may do better if treated with the combination of IPT and pharmacotherapy.

Combined treatment has demonstrated additive benefit compared with either IPT or amitriptyline alone (Weissman, 1979; DiMascio et al., 1979). Two other trials have also examined the combination of IPT and pharmacotherapy (Blom et al., 2007; Schramm et al., 2007). In the first trial, in which 193 outpatients with mild to moderate MDD were randomized for up to 16 weeks to receive IPT alone, nefazodone alone, IPT plus placebo, or IPT plus nefazodone, no significant treatment differences were found on the primary dependent measure, the HAM-D. On the MADRS, the combination of medication with psychotherapy was more effective in reducing depressive symptoms compared with medication alone, although the differences between the combination and either IPT alone or IPT plus placebo were not statistically significant. It should be noted that the lack of a placebo control group in this study limits interpretation of the findings, as it is possible that the outcome of the nefazodone-alone condition would not have surpassed a placebo-only condition.

A second controlled trial of IPT tested the benefit of an intensive, hospital-based therapy program in 124 inpatients with MDD (Schramm et al., 2007). A total of 124 depressed inpatients were randomized to receive either 5 weeks of treatment as usual (antidepressant pharmacotherapy and milieu therapy) or treatment enhanced by individual and group IPT sessions. For patients treated with adjunctive IPT, intent-to-treat analyses revealed that adjunctive treatment provided a significantly greater reduction of depressive symptoms at week 5 as compared with the treatment-as-usual group. Response rates were 70% for the group that received adjunctive IPT, compared with 51% for the treatment-as-usual comparison group. Although not statistically significant, a smaller trend in remission rates was also evident (49% versus 34%). A secondary analysis indicated that the advantage provided by adjunctive IPT was largely accounted for by superior outcomes in the subset of patients with chronic depressive syndromes (Schramm et al., 2008).

In addition to these RCTs, further evidence of the potential utility of combining IPT and pharmacotherapy is found in a meta-analysis of individual patient data conducted by Thase et al. (1997). This report compared the outcomes of nearly 600 patients treated with the combination of imipramine or nortriptyline and IPT versus those of patients treated with either IPT or CBT alone. Results indicated a modest advantage for combined treatment overall, with a significant interaction between pretreatment severity and treatment outcome. Specifically, the advantage of combined treatment over psychotherapy alone was relatively small (roughly 10% difference in remission rates) among the patients with milder depression, but large (roughly 30%) among the subset of patients with more severe, recurrent depression.

As both IPT and CBT have been shown to be effective acute phase therapies, direct comparisons of these interventions are also of particular interest. Markowitz et al. (1998) randomly assigned 110 HIV-seropositive men with depressive disorders to one of four treatment conditions: IPT, CBT, or supportive psychotherapy with or without imipramine monotherapy. At the end of the 17-week protocol, IPT and supportive therapy with active imipramine were equally effective. On most analyses, IPT was also more effective than CBT. The authors speculated that IPT may be a better fit than CBT for the real-world concerns of depressed HIV-seropositive patients.

Results of several studies have also suggested that IPT alone may be less useful for particular groups of depressed patients. The first potential indicator of poorer response to IPT is a high level of anxiety, which was identified in three different trials conducted by a group at the University of Pittsburgh (Brown et al., 1996; Feske et al., 1998; Frank et al., 2000). The second, a perhaps conceptually related indicator, is complicated bereavement. In a small study of older patients with "bereavement-related depression," Reynolds et al. (1999) found that IPT plus pill placebo was significantly less effective than treatment with nortriptyline alone, with the group receiving IPT showing no better response than the group that received pill placebo alone. The combination of IPT and nortriptyline did not enhance outcomes compared with pharmacotherapy alone, but the group receiving combined therapy did have a lower dropout rate.

A third potential indicator of poor response to IPT monotherapy is subsyndromal minor depression or dysthymia. In one of the largest studies of psychotherapy of depression ever undertaken, Browne and colleagues (2002) evaluated the outcomes of 707 primary care adult outpatients with chronic dysthymic disorder, with or without a history of MDD. Patients were randomly assigned to IPT alone, sertraline alone, or the two strategies in combination. Results indicated that the patients who received sertraline had significantly better outcomes, with response rates among completers at month 6 of 47% (IPT alone), 60% (sertraline alone), and 58% (combination). Similar results were found in a study by Markowitz and colleagues (2005), which was conducted in 94 outpatients with dysthymic disorder. In this trial, IPT and sertraline were again compared, both alone and in combination with pharmacotherapy, with a fourth arm, brief supportive psychotherapy (BSP), also included to control for the potential nonspecific effects of therapeutic support. They found that patients who received sertraline—whether alone or in combination with IPT—improved significantly more than those who received IPT or BSP alone.

A fourth potential indicator, medical complexity, is suggested by the results of the Cardiac Randomized Evaluation of Antidepressant and Psychotherapy Efficacy (CREATE) study (Lesperance et al., 2007). This 12-week RCT enrolled 284 patients from nine academic centers, and used a 2 x 2 factorial design to randomly assign patients to receive 12 weekly sessions of IPT plus clinical management or clinical management only, in combination with either citalopram or pill placebo. Whereas citalopram was found to be superior to placebo in terms of symptom reduction and remission rates, IPT was no more effective than clinical management, whether it was combined with citalopram or placebo.

Psychodynamic Psychotherapy Plus Medication Management

Psychoanalysis serves as the foundation for long-term and short-term therapies for a wide range of mental disorders, and is the origin of many "common factor" concepts such as the therapeutic alliance (Gabbard, 2004a, 2004b; Groves, 1996). A voluminous and rich theoretical and clinical literature attests to the effectiveness of psychoanalysis and psychodynamic psychotherapy for MDD (Coynes 1986; Busch, Rudden & Shapiro, 2004). There are also a limited, but growing number of studies that examine the combination of psychodynamic modalities with antidepressant medications.

A series of studies conducted in the Netherlands examined a manual-based model of brief dynamic psychotherapy (BDP) in outpatients with MDD (de Jonghe et al., 2001, 2004; Dekker et al., 2005). In the first trial (de Jonghe et al., 2001), 167 outpatients with mild to moderate forms of MDD were randomized to receive 6 months of treatment with either 16 sessions of BDP plus antidepressant medications or antidepressants alone. The antidepressant protocol was flexible, and permitted three steps across 6 months of randomized treatment: fluoxetine, followed by amitriptyline and the MAOI moclobemide, if necessary. In terms of both acceptability of treatment and outcome, the investigators found significant differences that favored combined treatment over pharmacotherapy alone. Response rates after 6 months of treatment were 59% for patients who received combined therapy and 41% for patients who received only pharmacotherapy. A second report (Kool et al., 2003) from this trial indicated that the advantage of combined treatment was largely explained by the outcomes of patients with comorbid personality disorders, who tended to respond poorly to pharmacotherapy alone. The added benefit of combined treatment was small among the subset of patients who did not have personality problems.

A second study by this group examined whether combination therapy demonstrated advantages over BDP alone (de Jonghe et al., 2004). Using a similar 6-month protocol, 191 patients with mild to moderate MDD were randomized to receive either BDP alone or BDP in combination with antidepressant pharmacotherapy. The pharmacotherapy protocol in the study was updated to include four steps: the SNRI venlafaxine, an SSRI, nortriptyline, and nortriptyline plus lithium. Fewer significant differences were evident in this study, though the combined therapy group was found to have more improvement on the patient self-reported measure of depressive symptoms. Results of these trials were pooled with those of a third smaller study (Dekker et al., 2005) to conduct a meta-analysis of individual patient data comparing the three strategies (dynamic psychotherapy alone, pharmacotherapy alone, and combined treatment) (de Maat et al., 2008). In this pooled data set, combined therapy was found to be superior to pharmacotherapy alone in terms of ratings by patients, therapists, and independent evaluators. Combined treatment was superior to psychodynamic psychotherapy alone on only the patient-reported outcome measure. There was also a strong trend on the independent observer-rated HAM-D, but little difference on the therapist-rated variable. A fourth study by this group (Dekker et al., 2008) focused on the speed of response to treatment with BDP versus pharmacotherapy. A total of 141 outpatients with MDD were randomized to the two modalities, with results favoring pharmacotherapy at the week 4 assessment but showing no difference at week 8. Although the evidence base is less robust than for CBT or IPT, these findings do suggest that BDP is an effective intervention, both alone and in combination with antidepressants.

From a more practical perspective, a randomized controlled trial was performed by Burnand and colleagues to investigate the cost effectiveness of combined treatment with clomipramine and psychodynamic psychotherapy (versus clomipramine alone) for major depressive disorder (Burnand et al., 2002). Seventy-four patients were assigned to 10 weeks of outpatient treatment with one of two treatment arms, and marked improvement was noted in both groups. Combined treatment, however, was associated with less treatment failure and better work adjustment at 10 weeks, as well as better global functioning and lower hospitalization rates at discharge. A cost savings of more than $2,000 per patient in the combined treatment group, derived from lower rates of hospitalization and fewer lost work days, exceeded the expenditures related to providing psychotherapy. The authors concluded that their findings supported the cost effectiveness of providing supplemental psychodynamic psychotherapy for patients with MDD on antidepressant medication.

Clinical Models of Combining Medications and Psychotherapy in Depression

According to current APA Practice Guidelines, the combination of psychotherapy and antidepressant medication is indicated as an initial treatment for moderately or severely depressed patients with psychosocial issues, interpersonal problems, or comorbid Axis II disorders. In addition, patients who have a history of trauma, partial response to one treatment modality, or a history of medication nonadherence may also benefit from combined treatment. In the real-world clinical setting, any number of clinicians may be involved in the treatment of such patients. Typically, the number of treatment providers can range from one to three clinicians. In one-person therapy, the psychiatrist provides individual psychotherapy as well as medication treatment. Multiperson therapy usually involves one therapist (who may be a psychiatrist, psychologist, clinical counselor, or social worker) conducting psychotherapy, while the other clinician, a medical doctor (usually a psychiatrist) prescribes medications. Additional therapists may oversee couples, marriage, or family therapy. There are benefits and drawbacks to the delivery of care under these different models, which we will now attempt to highlight.

Split Treatment

The term "split treatment" describes a situation in which medications are prescribed by a physician or nurse practitioner, and therapy is conducted by a nonmedical mental health professional. Positive aspects of this strategy include a greater choice of clinicians, the ability to bypass the problem of a shortage of psychiatrists to provide both treatments, and the opportunity to instill a "team" approach that promotes adherence to a treatment plan. Drawbacks may include a lack of communication among the practitioners, as well as potential legal risks. For example, does the patient understand confidentiality of, and between, their providers, or who is responsible during an emergency? These issues highlight the need for regular exchanges of information between clinicians, and are particularly important with patients who may split transference between two providers—one provider may be seen as "giving and nurturing," while the other may be seen as "withholding and aloof." Similarly, countertransference issues, such as one clinician identifying with the patient's idealized or devalued image of the other provider, can interfere with therapy. These issues must be addressed, and each co-provider must be compatible and respectful of the other, so that the split treatment program can succeed.

In some situations, a therapist may have concerns about the quality of the medications being used, or may suggest that a regimen needs to be reconsidered. For example, a patient may be experiencing significant side effects from his medications, or may demonstrate a lack of sufficient clinical improvement. If it is deemed in the patient's interest for the therapist to question the medication regimen or the prescriber's skill, these misgivings should be initially shared with the prescribing physician, not the patient. Even nuanced observations about the appropriateness of a medication regimen may raise unnecessary doubt about the quality of pharmacologic care. This may undermine a potentially effective treatment regimen, and may also destroy a patient's trust in the physician. It is important for clinicians of all backgrounds to recognize that drug selection and use are not based solely on diagnosis, but also on an understanding of the patient's history and clinical circumstances. If a therapist, after a good-faith effort to understand the methods and course of treatment, still has misgivings about the intervention, he should inform his counterpart that a second opinion might be useful. This should then be suggested to the patient without raising undue alarm. Communication between treating clinicians should occur as frequently as needed, but unfortunately there is no standard for how frequent this should be. We will now follow with a case example, highlighting an ideal implementation of the split-treatment model.

Barbara is a 65-year-old female who has been employed as a receptionist for the past 15 years. Her husband, Donald, passed away last year from a sudden heart attack. Barbara was devastated by the loss of her husband, and immediately reached out to her church ministry, seeking emotional support. She participated in weekly group counseling sessions, as well as periodic individual sessions, for several months after her husband's death. Despite these efforts, Barbara's feelings of sadness and loss continued to worsen. She noted ongoing difficulty adjusting to life without Donald, and at times felt hopeless and without a desire to "go on." Given the severity of her symptoms, Barbara's pastor referred her to a licensed social worker, Phil, for individual therapy. Barbara met with Phil for an intake appointment, and they agreed to engage in a 12- to 16-week course of IPT, focused on Barbara's feelings of loss and grief. Barbara and Phil established a strong therapeutic alliance, and completed nine weekly sessions of IPT. Despite noticing some improvement, Barbara continued to endorse feelings of sadness, anhedonia, as well as difficulty sleeping. She also, at times, failed to take her medications prescribed for diabetes, hypertension, and neuropathy. Given her ongoing symptomatology, as well as her medical comorbidities, Phil referred Barbara for a consultation with Dr. Pritchard, a psychiatrist with whom Phil has worked for a number of years. After obtaining a release of information from Barbara, Phil contacted Dr. Pritchard, and the two discussed the patient's case and ongoing symptoms. Together, they agreed that the introduction of an antidepressant might be helpful, and Dr. Pritchard suggested this to Barbara during their initial appointment. Barbara agreed with the plan, and was started on daily citalopram, which was titrated to a therapeutic dose (40 mg/day) over several weeks. After 2 months, Barbara reported a significant improvement in her mood, interest in her surroundings, and sleep pattern. She became more engaged in social activities, attending weekly sewing groups at her church, as well as signing up for a pottery class at a local community center. She completed a 16-session course of IPT with Phil, and continues to take citalopram, with a plan to follow up with Dr. Pritchard again in 2 months.

Integrated Treatment: CBT and Pharmacotherapy

CBT and pharmacotherapy share many features that facilitate an integrated treatment approach. Both treatments are empirically based and pragmatic, with structure and psychoeducation playing a critical role in their implementation. The need for adherence to a therapeutic plan is also critical to the success of both modalities. Key methods for integrating CBT with pharmacotherapy in the treatment of depression are discussed below.

In research studies, CBT and pharmacotherapy are typically opposed to one another, in order to examine the relative efficacy of each intervention. Separate clinicians deliver the two treatments, and defined protocols must be followed in order to reduce variation in therapy methodology. To our knowledge, there are no studies of combined therapy in which the same psychopharmacotherapist delivers both interventions, or in which a pharmacotherapist works as part of an integrated team with a nonprescribing cognitive therapist, with both clinicians using a flexible, patient-centered approach. Furthermore, pharmacotherapy protocols in controlled comparative studies are handicapped by the requirement that patients remain on an initial medication for 12 to 16 weeks, regardless of their level of response. In real-world practice, however, a medication switch or augmentation strategy could be implemented over this same time frame, allowing the combined model to benefit from the strengths of each treatment, as well as the flexibility to customize methods to meet the particular needs of a patient (Wright & Thase, 1992; Wright, 2004).

For example, CBT might be implemented to target anhedonia, concomitant anxiety, or procrastination in a patient with an anxious depression complicated by socially isolating avoidance behaviors. Pharmacotherapy can be tailored to the individual, and—though the first treatment may not be effective—following a reasonable medication algorithm, a realistic appraisal of positive medication effects on individual depressive symptoms can promote a process of gradual improvement. Simultaneously, the therapist can help the patient examine his or her belief that "because my last med trial didn't help, no med will ever help," therein helping to modify unrealistic expectations of an immediate and complete response to a single intervention. For patients with severe, complex, or high-risk depression, pharmacotherapy can be augmented with CBT to help modify thoughts of helplessness and hopelessness, as well as introduce alternative behaviors in response to suicidal ideation before the onset of a medication's effect. Examples of pharmacotherapy strategies that can influence a patient's ability to use CBT include: (a) selecting medications that improve concentration, sleep, energy, or other functions needed to obtain full benefit from psychotherapy; (b) minimizing side effects that might interfere with implementation of CBT; and (c) being wary of negative interactions, such as potentially interfering with the effects of CBT through simultaneous use of high-potency benzodiazepines (Marks et al., 1993).

Since pharmacotherapists and cognitive therapists both utilize structuring techniques and psychoeducation, a pharmacotherapy session can typically be implemented using standard CBT techniques such as setting an agenda, checking symptomatic status, targeting specific problems for intervention (in particular, therapy-blocking behaviors that lead to medication noncompliance), maintaining a collaborative empirical position, and using feedback to promote patient understanding. Psychoeducational materials such as readings, videos, and computer-assisted learning can also be employed to convey information about medications and CBT. For example, clinicians trained in both CBT and pharmacotherapy might present a brief overview of how medications and therapy work as partners in treatment, and then offer more specific education on pharmacotherapy strategies and side effects. Following this, they could present the CBT model, demonstrating ways to record and modify automatic thoughts, identify dysfunctional attitudes and beliefs, initiate alternative behaviors, and monitor for relapse.

A straightforward, albeit secondary mechanism by which CBT may help to improve the outcome of pharmacotherapy is through improved medication adherence. Typical CBT interventions to improve adherence include eliciting and modifying maladaptive cognitions about treatment (such as "If I take a drug, it means that I'm weak," "I'm always the one who gets side effects," or "Doctors who prescribe medications don't really want to listen to you"). Furthermore, behavioral methods such as using reminder systems, pairing medication taking with routine activities, and developing specific plans to overcome identified barriers to adherence may be helpful in promoting follow-through with the treatment plan. We will now follow with another case example, highlighting some of the benefits of an integrated treatment approach.

John is a 38-year-old male who teaches history at a local high school. He presented to a university-based mental health clinic with complaints of low mood, episodes of crying, difficulty concentrating, decreased energy, and inability to complete work tasks on time. Five years earlier, John had experienced similar symptoms, and was diagnosed with depression by his PCP. He was treated with Prozac for a year, during which time his symptoms improved and he chose to discontinue the medication. Recently, over a 2-month period, John noticed increasing conflicts with his new principal, difficulty "staying on top" of his grading, and a greater number of hours spent in bed each evening. His wife also noticed that John appeared "sadder and more irritable" than usual. John was seen by a psychiatrist at the clinic, who diagnosed a recurrent depressive episode, and suggested treatment with a time-limited course of psychotherapy (CBT), an antidepressant, or a combination of the two. Having never engaged in "talk therapy" before, John expressed interest in trying CBT, and attended twice-weekly CBT sessions over the following 4 weeks. Despite noticing an improvement in his productivity at work, and being able to "catch up" on his grading, he continued to report difficulty concentrating and feelings of sadness, and his wife complained of continued irritability. John's psychiatrist suggested the addition of an antidepressant, to which John agreed, and Prozac was restarted. Over the next 6 weeks, John's symptoms improved dramatically—he began to feel "happier," was able to "enjoy things" that he hadn't enjoyed for a while, and was noted to be getting along better with his wife. His newly learned coping strategies, introduced during therapy, helped to further reduce his depressive symptoms. Over the next 2 years, he maintained these gains, including normalization of his daily functioning, promotion to Assistant Chair of the history department, and better relations with his wife. He continued on daily Prozac, and also participated in occasional "booster" CBT sessions, once every few months as needed during particularly stressful times of the year.

CONCLUSIONS

The proximal goal of combining psychotherapeutic and pharmacologic treatments for MDD is to help the patient achieve a complete and sustained remission, ultimately maximizing the chance of recovery from the disorder and improving long-term prognosis. In making decisions about combination therapy, clinicians can best serve their patients by using a comprehensive treatment model, individualizing treatment plans, and when combined treatment is initiated, integrating psychotherapy and pharmacology through session structure and psychoeducation. Although psychotherapy and pharmacotherapy alone may be suitable treatments for many, more severely and/or more chronically depressed patients will likely benefit from a strategy that combines antidepressant medication with a psychotherapeutic modality, such as IPT, CBT, or BDP. However, more research is needed to accurately identify patient characteristics that predict which patients will benefit most from a combined treatment approach.

With that said, researchers and clinicians should also stay apprised of recent outcome data suggesting that psychotherapy, used alone, may be effective in treating certain forms of depression. Controlled studies show that up to 70% of patients with mild to moderate depression, dysthymia, panic disorder, social phobia, generalized anxiety disorder, and primary insomnia achieve adequate response to psychotherapy alone. There is little reason to expose such patients to medication side effects, or the higher relapse rates that have been shown to correlate with pharmacotherapy discontinuation (as compared to psychotherapy). Clinicians must also be cognizant of patient differences in type and severity of symptoms, patient acceptance and/or preference, past psychiatric illness course, and treatment history when deciding whether or not to employ a combined strategy. The patient needs to be educated about the risks and benefits of alternate treatments, including integrated therapy (by the same provider) and each monotherapy respectively. If the patient's ability to understand treatment options is compromised by their condition, involvement of appropriate healthcare proxies or family members becomes important.

Whether combination therapy is delivered as split treatment or provided by a single psychiatrist—an ideal that is impractical because there are not enough psychiatrists to adequately address current public health need—it is not always necessary or cost effective to offer every patient combined treatment. And as we have seen at times, there is only limited evidence supporting the use of combined treatment. An outstanding goal remains to develop methods of identifying subgroups of depressed patients who are most likely to benefit from medication alone, therapy alone, or the two in combination. While this call for research has been made over the past few decades, the practical question of "which treatment to use, and when" remains unanswered. Until definitive prospective data are available in studies with adequate power and diverse samples, or new technology is available (such as imaging techniques discussed above) we suggest focusing on variables that are associated with lower response rates to pharmacotherapy alone (such as chronicity, inpatient status, and other indicators of marked severity) and monitoring the response of each patient using symptom severity measures, in order to identify those patients who may require a swift change from monotherapy to combination treatment.

REFERENCES

American Psychiatric Association. (1993). Practice guideline for major depressive disorder in adults. *American Journal of Psychiatry, 150,* 1–26.

American Psychiatric Association (A.P.A.). (2010). Practice guideline for the treatment of patients with major depressive disorder (3rd ed.). *American Journal of Psychiatry,* DOI: 10.1176/appi.books.9780890423387.654001.

Antonuccio D. O., Atkins, W. T., Chatham, P. M., Monagin, J. A, Tearnan, B. H., & Ziegler, B. L. (1984). An exploratory study: The psychoeducational group treatment of drug-refractory unipolar depression. *Journal of Behavior Therapy and Experimental Psychiatry, 15,* 309–313.

Bauer, M., Bschor, T., Pfennig, A., Whybrow, P. C., Angst, J., Versiani, M., et al. (2007). World Federation of Societies of Biological Psychiatry guidelines for biological treatment of unipolar depressive disorders in primary care. *World Journal of Biological Psychiatry, 8,* 67–104.

Beck, A. T., Rush, A. J., Shaw, B. F., & Emery, G. (1979). *Cognitive therapy of depression.* New York: Guilford Press.

Beck, A. T., Ward, C. H., Mendelson, M., Mock, J., & Erbaugh, J. (1961). An inventory for measuring depression. *Archives of General Psychiatry, 4,* 561–571.

Blom, M. B. J., Jonker, K., Dusseldorp, E., Spinhoven, P., Hoencamp, E., Haffmans, J., & van Dyck, R. (2007). Combination treatment for acute depression is superior only when psychotherapy is added to medication. *Psychotherapy and Psychosomatics, 76,* 289–297.

Brown, C., Schulberg, H. C., Madonia, M. J., Shear, M. K., Houck, P. R. (1996). Treatment outcomes for primary care patients with major depression and lifetime anxiety disorders. *American Journal of Psychiatry, 153,* 1293–1300.

Browne, G., Steiner, M., Roberts, J., Gafni, A., Byrne, C., Dunn, E., et al. (2002). Sertraline and/or interpersonal psychotherapy for patients with dysthymic disorder in primary care: 6-month comparison with longitudinal 2-year follow-up of effectiveness and costs. *Journal of Affective Disorders, 68,* 317–330.

Burnand Y., Antonio A., Kolatte E., Venturini A., Rosset, N. (2002). Psychodynamic psychotherapy and clomipramine in the treatment of major depression, *Psychiatric Services, 53,* 585–590.

Busch, F. N., Rudden, M., & Shapiro, T. (2004). *Psychodynamic treatment of depression.* Washington, DC: American Psychiatric Publishing, Inc.

Caspi, A., Sugden, K., Moffitt, T. E., Taylor, A., Crai, I. W., Harrington, H., et al. (2003). Influence of life stress on depression: Moderation by a polymorphism in the 5-HTT gene. *Science, 301,* 386–389.

Cipriani, A., Barbui C., Brambilla, P., Furukawa, T. A., Hotopf, M., & Geddes, J. R. (2006). Are all antidepressants really the same? The case of fluoxetine: A systematic review. *Journal of Clinical Psychiatry, 67,* 850–864.

Cohen, J. (1977). *Statistical power analysis for the behavioral sciences.* New York: Academic Press.

Cole, A. J., Brittlebank, A. D., & Scott, J. (1994). *The role of cognitive therapy in refractory depression.* Chichester, UK: Wiley.

Conte, H. R., Plutchik, R., Wild, K. V., & Karasu, T. B. (1986). Combined psychotherapy and pharmacotherapy for depression. *Archives of General Psychiatry, 43,* 471–479.

Coynes, J. C. (Ed.). (1986). *Essential papers on depression.* New York: University Press.

de Jonghe, F., Hendricksen, M., van Aalst, G., Kool, S., Peen, V., Van, R., et al. (2004). Psychotherapy alone and combined with pharmacotherapy in the treatment of depression. *British Journal of Psychiatry, 185,* 37–45.

de Jonghe, F., Kool, S., Van Aalst, G., Dekker, J., & Peen, J. (2001). Combining psychotherapy and antidepressants in the treatment of depression. *Journal of Affective Disorders, 64,* 217–229.

de Maat, S., Dekker, J., Schoevers, R., van Aalst, G., Gijsbers-van Wijk, C., Hendriksen, M., et al. (2008). Short psychodynamic supportive psychotherapy, antidepressants, and their combination in the treatment of major depression: A mega-analysis based on three randomized clinical trials. *Depression and Anxiety, 25,* 565–574.

Dekker, J., Molenaa, P. J., Kool, S., Van Aalst, G., Peen, J., & de Jonghe, F. (2005). Dose-effect relations in time-limited combined psycho-pharmacological treatment for depression. *Psychological Medicine, 35,* 47–58.

Dekker, J. J., Koelen, J. A., Van, H. L., Schoevers, R. A., Peen, J., Hendriksen, M., et al. (2008). Speed of action: The relative efficacy of short psychodynamic supportive psychotherapy and pharmacotherapy in the first 8 weeks of a treatment algorithm for depression. *Journal of Affective Disorders, 109,* 183–188.

Depression Guideline Panel. (1993). *Depression in Primary Care, Vol. 2: Treatment of Major Depression.* Clinical Practice Guideline Number 5. Rockville, MD: U.S. Department of Health and Human Services, Agency for Health Care Policy and Research.

DiMascio, A., Weissman, M. M., Prusoff, B. A., Neu, C., Zwilling, M., & Klerman, G. L. (1979). Differential symptom reduction by drugs and psychotherapy in acute depression. *Archives of General Psychiatry, 36,* 1450–1456.

Drevets, W. C. (2003). Neuroimaging abnormalities in the amygdale in mood disorders. *Annals of the New York Academy of Sciences, 985,* 420–444.

Fava, G. A., Savron, G., Grand, S., & Rafanelli, C. (1997). Cognitive behavioral management of drug-resistant major depressive disorder. *Journal of Clinical Psychiatry, 58,* 278–282.

Feske, U., Frank, E., Kupfer, D. J., Shear, M. K., & Weaver, E. (1998). Anxiety as a predictor of response to interpersonal psychotherapy for recurrent major depression: An exploratory investigation. *Depression and Anxiety, 8,* 135–141.

Frank, E., Prien, R. F., Jarrett, R. B., Keller, M. B., Kupfer, D. J., Lavori, P.W., et al. (1991). Conceptualization and rationale for consensus definitions of terms in major depressive disorder. Remission, recovery, relapse, and recurrence. *Archives of General Psychiatry, 48,* 851–855.

Frank, E., Shear, M. K., Rucci, P., Cyranowski, J. M., Endicott, J., Fagiolini, A., et al. (2000). Influence of panic-agoraphobic spectrum symptoms on treatment response in patients with recurrent major depression. *American Journal of Psychiatry, 157,* 1101–1107.

Friedman, E. S. (1997). Combined therapy for depression. *Journal of Practical Psychiatry and Behavioral Health, 3,* 211–222.

Friedman, E. S., & Thase, M. E. (2007). Combining cognitive therapy and medication treatment. In G.O. Gabbard (Ed.), *Textbook of psychotherapeutic treatments* (pp. 263–285). Washington, DC: American Psychiatric Press.

Friedman, E. S., Wright, J. H., Jarrett, R. B., & Thase, M. E. (2006). Combining cognitive behavior therapy and medication for mood disorders. *Psychiatric Annals, 36,* 321–328.

Friedman, M. A., Detweiler-Bedell, J. B., Leventhal, H. E., Home, R., Keitner, G. I., & Miller, I.W. (2004). Combined psychotherapy and pharmacotherapy for the treatment of major depressive disorder. *Clinical Psychology Science and Practice, 11,* 47–68.

Gabbard, G. O. (2004a). *Long-term psychodynamic psychotherapy: A basic text.* Washington, DC: American Psychiatric Publishing.

Gabbard, G. O. (2004b). *Psychodynamic psychiatry in clinical practice* (3rd ed.). Washington, DC: American Psychiatric Press.

Goldapple, K., Segal, Z., Carson, C., Lau, M., Bieling, P., Kennedy, S., & Mayberg, H. (2004). Modulation of cortical-limbic pathways in major depression: Treatment-specific effects of cognitive behavior therapy. *Archives of General Psychiatry, 61,* 34–42.

Groves, J. E. (Ed.). (1996). Essential papers on short-term dynamic therapy. New York: New York University Press.

Hamilton, M. (1960). A rating scale for depression. *Journal of Neurology, Neurosurgery and Psychiatry, 23,* 56–62.

Hollon, S. D., Jarrett, R. B., Nierenberg, A. A., Thase, M. E., Trived, M., & Rush, A. J. (2005). Psychotherapy and medication in the treatment of adult and geriatric depression: Which monotherapy or combined treatment? *Journal of Clinical Psychiatry, 66,* 455–468.

Hollon, S. D., DeRubeis, R. J., Evans, M. D., Wiemer, M. J., Garvey, M. J., Grove, W. M., & Tuason, V. B. (1992). Cognitive-therapy and pharmacotherapy for depression: Singly and in combination. *Archives of General Psychiatry, 49,* 774–781.

Jindal, R. D., & Thase, M. E. (2003). Integrating psychotherapy and pharmacotherapy to improve outcomes among patients with mood disorders. *Psychiatric Services 54,* 1484–1490.

Judd, L. L., Akiskal, H. S., Maser, J. D., Zeller, P. J., Endicott, J., Coryell, W., et al. (1998). A prospective 12-year study of subsyndromal and syndromal depressive symptoms in unipolar major depressive disorders. *Archives of General Psychiatry, 55,* 694–700.

Keller, M. B. (2003). Key considerations in choosing an antidepressant. *Postgraduate Medicine 114,* 10–18.

Keller, M. B., McCullough, J. P., Klein, D. N., Arnow, B., Dunner, D. L., Gelenberg, A. J., et al. (2000). A comparison of nefazodone, the cognitive behavioral-analysis system of psychotherapy, and their combination for the treatment of chronic depression. *New England Journal of Medicine, 342,* 1462–1470.

Kessler, R. C., Akiskal, H. S., Ames, M., Birnbaum, H., Greenberg, P., Hirschfeld, R. M., et al. (2006). Prevalence and effects of mood disorders on work performance in a nationally representative sample of U.S. workers. *American Journal of Psychiatry, 163,* 1561–1568.

Kirsch, I., Moore, T. J., Scoboria, A., & Nicholls, S. S. (2002). The emperor's new drugs: An analysis of antidepressant medication data submitted to the U.S. Food and Drug Administration. *Prevention and Treatment, 5,* 1.

Kool, S., Dekker, J., Duijsens, I. J., de Jonghe, F., & Puite, B. (2003). Efficacy of combined therapy and pharmacotherapy for depressed patients with or without personality disorders. *Harvard Review of Psychiatry, 11,* 133–141.

Kraemer, H. C., & Thiemann, S. (1987). *How many subjects? Statistical Power Analysis I Research.* Newbury Park, CA: Sage.

Kroenke, K., Spitzer, R. L., & Williams, J. B. (2001). The PHQ-9: Validity of a brief depression severity measure. *Journal of General Internal Medicine, 16,* 606–613.

Kugaya, A., Sanacora, G., Staley, J. K., Malison, R. T., Bozkurt, A., Khan, S., et al. (2004). Brain serotonin transporter availability predicts response to selective serotonin reuptake inhibitors. *Biological Psychiatry, 56,* 497–502.

Lesch, K. P., Bengel, D., Heils, A., Sabol, S. Z., Greenberg, B. D., Petri, S., et al. (1996). Association of anxiety-related traits with a polymorphism in the serotonin receptor gene regulatory system. *Science, 274,* 1527–1531.

Lesperance, F., Frasure-Smith, N., Koszycki, D., Laliberté, M. A., van Zyl, L. T., Baker, B., et al. (2007). Effects of citalopram and interpersonal psychotherapy on depression in patients with coronary artery disease—The Canadian Cardiac Randomized Evaluation of Antidepressant and Psychotherapy Efficacy (CREATE) trial. *JAMA, 297,* 367–379.

Markowitz, J. C., Kocsis, J. H., Bleiberg, K. L., Christos, P. J., & Sacks, M. (2005). A comparative trial of psychotherapy and pharmacotherapy for "pure" dysthymic patients. *Journal of Affective Disorders, 89,* 167–175.

Markowitz, J. C., Kocsis, J. H., Fishman, B., Spielman, L. A., Jacobsberg, L. B., Frances, A. J., et al. (1998). Treatment of depressive symptoms in human immunodeficiency virus-positive patients. *Archives of General Psychiatry, 55,* 452–457.

Marks, I. M., Swinson, R. P., Basoglu, M., Kuch, K., Noshirvani, H., O'Sullivan, G., et al. (1993). Alprazolam and exposure alone and combined in panic disorder with agoraphobia: A controlled study in London and Toronto. *British Journal of Psychiatry, 162,* 776–787.

Mayberg, H. S. (2003). Modulating dysfunctional limbic-cortical circuits in depression: Towards development of brain-based algorithms for diagnosis and optimized treatment. *British Medical Bulletin, 65,* 193–207.

McCullough, J. P. (2000). *Cognitive behavioral analysis system of psychotherapy: Treatment of chronic depression.* New York: Guilford Press.

Miller, I. W., Keitner, G. I., Schatzberg, A. F., Klein, D. N., Thase, M. E., Rush, A. J., et al. (1998). The treatment of chronic depression, part 3: Psychosocial functioning before and after treatment with sertraline and imipramine. *Journal of Clinical Psychiatry, 59,* 608–619.

Mintz J., Mintz, L. I., Arruda M. J., & Hwang, S. S. (1992). Treatments of depression and the functional capacity to work. *Archives of General Psychiatry, 49,* 761–768.

Montgomery, S. A., & Åsberg, M. (1979). A new depression scale designed to be sensitive to change. *British Journal of Psychiatry, 134,* 382–389.

Murphy, G. E., Simons, A.D., Wetzel, R. D., & Lustman, P. J. (1984). Cognitive therapy and pharmacotherapy: Singly and together in the treatment of depression. *Archives of General Psychiatry, 41,* 33–41.

Murray, C. J. L., & Lopez, A. D. (1996). Evidence-based health policy—lessons from the Global Burden of Disease Study. *Science, 274,* 740–741.

Pampallona, S., Bollini, P., Tiabaldi, G., Kupelnick, B., & Munizza, C. (2004). Combined pharmacotherapy and psychological treatment for depression: A systematic review. *Archives of General Psychiatry, 61,* 714–719.

Paykel, E. S. (1982). *Handbook of affective disorders.* New York, NY: Guilford Press.

Paykel, E. S., Ramana, R., Cooper, Z., Hayhurst, H., Kerr, J., & Barocka, A. (1995). Residual symptoms after partial remission: An important outcome in depression. *Psychological Medicine, 25,* 1171–1180.

Pezawas, L., Meyer-Lindenberg, A., Drabant, E. M., Verchinski, B. A., Munoz, K. E., Kolachana, B. S., et al. (2005). 5-HTTLPR polymorphism impacts human cingulated-amygdala interactions: A genetic susceptibility mechanism for depression. *Nature Neuroscience, 8,* 828–834.

Ressler, K. J., & Mayberg, H. S. (2007). Targeting abnormal neural circuits in mood and anxiety disorders: From the laboratory to the clinic. *Nature Neuroscience, 10,* 1116–1124.

Reynolds, C. F., III., Miller, M. D., Pasternak, R. E., Frank, E., Perel, J. M., Cornes, C., et al. (1999). Treatment of bereavement-related major depressive episodes in later life: A controlled study of acute and continuation treatment with nortriptyline and interpersonal psychotherapy. *American Journal of Psychiatry, 156,* 202–208.

Rush, A. J., Giles, D. E., Schlesser, M. A., Fulton, C. L., Weissenburger, J., & Burns, C. (1986). The Inventory for Depressive Symptomatology (IDS): Preliminary findings. *Psychiatry Research, 18,* 65–87.

Rush, A. J., Kraemer, H. C., Sackeim, H. A., Fava, M., Trivedi, M. H., Frank, E., et al. (2006). Report by the ACNP Task Force on response and remission in major depressive disorder. *Neuropsychopharmacology, 31,* 1841–1853.

Rush, A. J., Trivedi, M. H., Ibrahim, H. M., Carmody, T. J., Arnow, B., Klein, D. N., et al. (2003). The 16-Item Quick Inventory of Depressive Symptomatology (QIDS), clinician rating (QIDS-C), and self-report (QIDS-SR): A psychometric evaluation in patients with chronic major depression. *Biological Psychiatry, 54,* 573–583.

Schramm, E., Schneider, D., Zobel, I., van Calker, D., Dykierek, P., Kech, S., et al. (2008). Efficacy of interpersonal psychotherapy plus pharmacotherapy in chronically depressed inpatients. *Journal of Affective Disorders, 109,* 65–73.

Schramm, E., van Calker, D., Dykierek, P., Lieb, K., Kech, S., Zobel, I., et al. (2007). An intensive treatment program of interpersonal psychotherapy plus pharmacotherapy for depressed inpatients: Acute and long-term results. *American Journal of Psychiatry, 164,* 768–777.

Seligman, M. (1995). The effectiveness of psychotherapy: The Consumer Reports study. *American Psychologist, 50,* 965–974.

Thase, M. E. (2002). Comparing the methods used to compare antidepressants. *Psychopharmacology Bulletin, 36*(suppl. 1), 4–17.

Thase, M. E., & Howland, R. H. (1994). Refractory depression: Relevance of psychosocial factors and therapies. *Psychiatric Annals, 24,* 232–240.

Thase, M. E., Greenhouse, J. B., Frank, E., Reynolds, C. F., III, Pilkonis, P. A., Hurley, K., et al. (1997). Treatment of major depression with psychotherapy-pharmacotherapy combinations. *Archives of General Psychiatry, 54,* 1009–1015.

Thase, M. E., & Kupfer, D. J. (1996). Recent developments in the pharmacotherapy of mood disorders. *Journal of Consulting and Clinical Psychology, 64,* 646–659.

Thase, M. E., Simons, A. D., McGeary, J., Cahalane, J. F., Hughes, C., Harden, T., & Friedman, E. (1992). Relapse after cognitive behavior therapy of depression: Potential implications for longer courses of treatment? *American Journal of Psychiatry, 149,* 1046–1052.

Thase, M. E., Sloan, D. M., & Kornstein, S. (2002). Remission as the critical outcome of depression treatment. *Psychopharmacology Bulletin, 36,* 12–25.

Trivedi, M. H., Kocsis, J. H., Thase, M. E., Morris, D. W., Wisniewski, S. R., Leon, A. C., et al. (2008). REVAMP—Research Evaluating the Value of Augmenting Medication with Psychotherapy: Rationale and design. *Psychopharmacology Bulletin, 41,* 5–33.

Turner, E. H., Matthews, A. M., Linardatos, E., Tell, R. A., & Rosenthal, R. (2008). Selective publication of antidepressant trials and its influence on apparent efficacy. *New England Journal of Medicine, 358,* 252–260.

Walsh, B. T., Seidman, S. N., Sysko, R., & Gould, M. (2002). Placebo response in studies of major depression: Variable, substantial, and growing. *JAMA, 287,* 1840–1847.

Weissman, M. M. (1979). The psychological treatment of depression: Research evidence for the efficacy of psychotherapy alone, in comparison and in combination with pharmacotherapy. *Archives of General Psychiatry, 36,* 1261–1269.

Wright, J., Basco, M. R., & Thase, M. E. (2006). *Learning cognitive-behavior therapy: An illustrated guide.* Washington, DC: American Psychiatric Press, Inc.

Wright, J. H. (2004). Combined cognitive therapy and pharmacotherapy. In R. Leahy (Ed.), *Contemporary cognitive therapy* (pp. 341–366). New York: Guilford Press.

Wright, J. H., & Thase, M. E. (1992). Cognitive and biological theories: A synthesis. *Psychiatric Annals, 22,* 451–458.

Yu, Y. W., Tsai, S. J., Chen, T. J., Lin, C. H., & Hong, C. J. (2002). Association study of the serotonin transporter promoter polymorphism and symptomology and antidepressant response in major depressive disorders. *Molecular Psychiatry, 7,* 1115–1119.

Zimmerman, M., Posternak, M. A., & Chelminski, I. (2004). Implications of using different cut-offs on symptom severity scales to define remission from depression. *International Clinical Psychopharmacology, 19,* 215–220.

4

Integrating Psychopharmacology and Psychotherapy in Mood Disorders
Bipolar Disorder

Donna M. Sudak and Wei Du

INTRODUCTION

Bipolar disorder, once considered an easily treatable illness, is a severe, recurrent mental illness that often poorly responds to treatment. Bipolar patients spend nearly 50% of their lives with symptoms (Judd et al., 2002). Because the illness frequently begins in adolescence or early adulthood, it has dual consequences—the burden of the illness and the ravaging effects on normal development. Patients with bipolar disorder must accept that they have a chronic illness, which requires long-term pharmacological treatment. Childbearing and career choices are also impacted by the diagnosis.

Bipolar disorder commonly co-occurs with anxiety disorders, substance abuse, or dependence and medical disorders (Feldman, Gwizdowski, Fischer, Yang, & Suppes, 2012), which complicates treatment. Additionally, suicide is a frequent complication of the illness. Of patients with bipolar disorder, 15%–20% die by suicide (Baldessarini, Pompili, & Tondo, 2006). Suicidal risk and rates are similar in both Bipolar I and Bipolar II patients, and mixed states and more depressive episodes increase the risk (Undurraga, Baldessarini, Valenti, Pacchiarotti, & Vieta, 2012).

In addition to pharmacological management, psychotherapeutic treatments have been found to be extremely beneficial adjuncts to treatment. This chapter will provide a review of psychological and pharmacological treatment strategies and a guide to conceptualization and treatment planning for individual patients.

General Description of the Disorder

The essential features of bipolar disorder are distinct episodes of mood dysregulation, accompanied by symptoms that are cognitive, behavioral, and vegetative, and which have severe interpersonal consequences. Inter-episode recovery occurs, but its length varies. At least one episode of mania or hypomania must occur to make the diagnosis. The distinction between Bipolar I and Bipolar II is the presence of mania or hypomania, respectively. The DSM IV-TR criteria are listed in Table 4.1.

Table 4.1 DSM-IV criteria for bipolar disorder.

DSM IV-TR, *Diagnostic and Statistical Manual of Mental Disorders,* fourth edition, text revision (DSM IV-TR).

DSM IV-TR Criteria for a Manic Episode

A distinct period of persistently elevated, expansive, or irritable mood, lasting throughout at least 4 days, that is clearly different from the usual nondepressed mood.

During the period of mood disturbance, three (or more) of the following symptoms have persisted (four if the mood is only irritable) and have been present to a significant degree:

- Inflated self-esteem or grandiosity
- Decreased need for sleep (e.g., feels rested after only 3 hours of sleep)
- More talkative than usual or pressure to keep talking
- Flight of ideas or subjective experience that thoughts are racing
- Distractibility (i.e., attention too easily drawn to unimportant or irrelevant external stimuli)
- Increase in goal-directed activity (socially, at work or school, or sexually) or psychomotor agitation
- Excessive involvement in pleasurable activities that have a high potential for painful consequences (e.g., unrestrained buying sprees, sexual indiscretions, or foolish business investments)

The symptoms do not meet criteria for a mixed episode.

The episode is severe enough to cause marked impairment in social or occupational functioning, or necessitates hospitalization, and/or there are psychotic features.

The symptoms are not due to the direct physiologic effects of a substance (e.g., a drug of abuse, medication, or other treatment) or a general medical condition (e.g., hyperthyroidism).

Adapted from American Psychiatric Association: Diagnostic and Statistical Manual of Mental Disorders, 4th ed, text rev. Washington, DC, American Psychiatric Association, 2000.

DSM IV-TR Criteria for a Mixed Episode

The criteria are met both for a manic episode and for a major depressive episode (except for duration) nearly every day for at least 1 week.

The mood disturbance is sufficiently severe to cause marked impairment in occupational functioning or in usual social activities or relationships with others or to necessitate hospitalization to prevent harm to self or others, or the mood disturbance has psychotic features.

The symptoms are not due to the direct physiologic effects of a substance (e.g., a drug of abuse, medication, or other treatment) or a general medical condition (e.g., hyperthyroidism).

DSM IV-TR Criteria for Bipolar Type I Disorder Not Otherwise Specified

Criteria, except for duration, are currently (or most recently) met for a manic, a hypomanic, a mixed, or a major depressive episode.

There has previously been at least one manic episode or mixed episode.

The mood symptoms cause clinically significant distress or impairment in social, occupational, or other important areas of functioning.

The mood symptoms in the first two criteria are not better accounted for as schizoaffective disorder and are not superimposed on schizophrenia, schizophreniform disorder, delusional disorder, or psychotic disorder not otherwise specified.

The mood symptoms in the first two criteria are not due to the direct physiologic effects of a substance (e.g., a drug of abuse, medication, or other treatment) or a general medical condition (e.g., hyperthyroidism).

DSM IV-TR Criteria for Bipolar Type II Disorder

Presence (or history) of one or more major depressive episodes.
Presence (or history) of at least one hypomanic episode.
There has never been a manic episode or a mixed episode.

DSM IV-TR Criteria for Bipolar Type I Disorder

Presence (or history) of one or more major depressive episodes.
Presence (or history) of at least one manic episode.

The mood symptoms in the first two criteria are not better accounted for as schizoaffective disorder and are not superimposed on schizophrenia, schizophreniform disorder, delusional disorder, or psychotic disorder not otherwise specified.

Bipolar disorder has a lifetime prevalence of approximately 5% in adults in the United States, if all forms of the disorder are included (Merikangas et al., 2011). Although the central feature of mood dysregulation is present in all forms of the disorder, the condition is heterogeneous—the clinical course varies from patient to patient in terms of numbers of episodes, triggers for episodes, perpetuating and protective factors, and typical symptoms. Each of these elements has implications for treatment selection.

Recurrence of bipolar disorder is common. In the STEP-BD study, 58.4% of patients had a history of recurrence, often within 2 years of initial recovery (Perlis et al., 2006). Despite the dramatic presentation when patients are manic, depressive recurrence is far more common (Alda, Hajek, Calkin, & O'Donovan, 2009). Similar to major depression, residual symptoms at initial recovery are the most likely predictive factors for future recurrence (Perlis et al., 2006). Sub-syndromal depression exists 30% to 50% of the time in Bipolar Type I patients (Huxley & Baldessarini, 2007). This is a significant source of morbidity in such patients. It also may influence the mortality from suicide.

Manic episodes produce dramatic changes in cognition and future functioning. Fifty percent of patients are not recovered 12 months after an episode, and only 25% fully recover (Keck et al., 1998). Those individuals with psychosis and an index episode that is manic have the worst prognosis. Delays in diagnosis are common, even though there has been an explosion in the diagnosis in youth (Liebenluft, 2011). The average patient spends 10 years from the time of first presentation until he/she is accurately diagnosed (Kupfer, Frank, Grochocinski, & Cluss, 2002). Fifty to sixty percent of bipolar patients develop the disorder in adolescence (Perlis et al., 2004), and these individuals have higher rates of psychosis, comorbid psychiatric conditions, and hospitalization (Axelson et al., 2006), with 44% making at least one suicide attempt in one series (Lewinsohn, Klein, & Seeley, 1995). In adolescence and young adulthood, the complexity of social and academic demands, the desire for peer group acceptance, and the limited ability to have perspective frequently exacerbates the illness by limiting the acceptance of the diagnosis. Additionally, when the disorder presents earlier in life, it is more common to be in the rapid-cycling form and less amenable to treatment (Birmaher et al., 2006).

Cognitive impairment is common in both phases of the illness. Manic patients often have significant problems recalling behavior during an episode. Both phases of the illness have characteristic impairments of insight, judgment, concentration, and memory.

PHARMACOTHERAPY

Pharmacotherapy is the cornerstone of treatment for bipolar disorder. Acute episodes of mania, mixed states, or depression in bipolar disorder require timely and effective pharmacological interventions, often in conjunction with other treatment modalities such as acute inpatient hospitalization, to stabilize patients and mitigate high-risk complications.

This section will focus on the evidence for pharmacotherapeutic approaches in different phases of bipolar disorder in adults. The data from pediatric trials are briefly discussed. When appropriate, recommendations from the most current evidence-based treatment guidelines are also emphasized.

Acute Manic Episodes

Acute manic episodes (used interchangeably with acute mania) are the hallmark of bipolar disorder and are often associated with psychotic symptoms and significant psychosocial impairment. Pharmacotherapy is critical for a rapid stabilization of acutely manic patients.

Monotherapy with lithium, valproate (the salt form of valproic acid), or second-generation antipsychotics (SGAs) is recommended as the first-line treatment for acute mania (VA/DoD, Affairs, & Defense, 2010; Malhi et al., 2012; Yatham et al., 2005; Goodwin, 2009). Lithium and valproate are thought to act through a number of neurotransmitters, second messenger systems, and other molecular targets (Gould, Quiroz, Singh, Zarate, & Manji, 2004). SGAs interact with differential affinities with a series of dopamine and serotonin receptors.

The evidence supporting the first-line use of lithium and valproate is substantial, as summarized by Sachs, Dupuy, and Wittmann (2011). Bowden et al. (1994) conducted the first randomized controlled trial demonstrating the acute anti-manic efficacy of lithium. This well-designed study further validated the findings from earlier clinical trials and countered criticism of suboptimal methodology. Subsequently, lithium has been frequently used as a comparator or in adjunctive trials testing the efficacy of SGAs in acute mania, further extending evidence for its efficacy. For example, lithium was found to be superior to placebo in pivotal studies examining the anti-manic efficacy of quetiapine (Bowden et al., 2005).

The efficacy of valproate monotherapy in acute mania has been demonstrated in several randomized controlled trials (Emrich, von Zerssen, Kissling, Moller, & Windorfer, 1980; Pope, McElroy, Keck, & Hudson, 1991; Bowden et al., 1994; Bowden et al., 2006). Valproate appears to be well tolerated and can be administered in a loading dose for rapid stabilization (Hirschfeld, Baker, Wozniak, Tracy, & Sommerville, 2003; Hirshfeld, Allen, McEvoy, Keck, & Russell, 1999). Allen et al. (2006) further suggested that maintaining plasma level of valproate between 75 and 100 mg/L is necessary to achieve an adequate anti-manic effect.

Aripiprazole, asenapine, olanzapine, quetiapine, risperidone, and ziprasidone have been demonstrated as efficacious as monotherapy for acute mania in multiple randomized controlled trials. Aripiprazole was efficacious for acute mania in three randomized controlled trials (Keck et al., 2003; Keck, Orsulak, & Cutler, 2009; Sachs, Sanchez, & Marcus, 2006). Olanzapine was shown to be superior to placebo in two short-term trials and one 12-week trial (Tohen et al., 1999; Tohen et al., 2000; Tohen et al., 2006; Tohen et al., 2009). Vieta et al. (2008b) reported the efficacy of olanzapine in a large naturalistic study (EMBLEM). Metabolic syndrome is a significant clinical concern with olanzapine, which may have impacted its use. There are several controlled trials supporting the anti-manic efficacy of quetiapine (Sachs et al., 2004; Bowden et al., 2005; McIntyre, Brecher, Paulsson, Hizar, & Mullen, 2005;

Cutler et al., 2008). Overall, quetiapine is well tolerated, with somnolence and weight gain being the major adverse events. Risperidone monotherapy is also significantly more efficacious than placebo in mania (Hirschfeld et al., 2004; Khanna et al., 2005; Smulevich et al., 2005). Risperidone is known to cause prolactin elevation, extrapyramidal symptoms, and weight gain. Paliperidone, an active derivative of risperidone, did show a positive anti-manic effect in one randomized controlled trial (Vieta et al., 2010b). Ziprasidone is effective in acute mania, as shown in three randomized controlled trials (Keck et al., 2003; Potkin, Keck, Segal, Ice, & English, 2005; Vieta et al., 2010a). Among the three newly approved SGAs (iloperidone, asenapine, and lurasidone), only asenapine is currently indicated for acute mania. In two 3-week trials, asenapine monotherapy was significantly more effective than placebo (Chwieduk & Scott, 2011). The role of clozapine in acute mania is unclear; there are no randomized controlled trials at present. However, it may be considered as a third-line choice in patients who have failed adequate trials of multiple agents or in patients with refractory mania (Yatham et al., 2005; VA/DoD, Affairs, & Defense, 2010). Close monitoring of serious adverse reactions including agranulocytosis is mandatory when patients are started on clozapine.

Although monotherapy with lithium, valproate, and SGAs is clearly efficacious, there are limited studies that evaluate the direct comparative efficacy of mood stabilizing agents including lithium and valproate, and SGA monotherapy in acute mania. A recent meta-analysis was completed using 1,631 patients in nine studies in which lithium or valproate was compared against one of the following SGAs: risperidone, olanzapine, ziprasidone, aripiprazole, and quetiapine (Tarr, Glue, & Herbison, 2011). The authors concluded that SGAs may have a potential advantage over lithium or valproate in the treatment of acute mania. In addition, SGAs seem to have a faster onset based on the change of clinical rating scores. Cipriani et al. (2011) conducted a more comprehensive meta-analysis based on 68 randomized controlled trials (16,073 patients) to assess the comparative efficacy of anti-manic medications in acute mania. Lamotrigine, gabapentin, topiramate, haloperidol, and asenapine were included in this analysis. This analysis showed that haloperidol, risperidone, and olanzapine outperformed all other drugs in efficacy. SGAs have better tolerability than haloperidol and other mood stabilizing agents. This finding of haloperidol's superior efficacy is significant since the first-generation antipsychotics are no longer commonly used for bipolar disorder due to their acute and long-term tolerability issues (akathesia, extrapyramidal symptoms, and tardive dyskinesia). Ironically, chlorpromazine, was the first antipsychotic approved for bipolar disorder by the FDA.

In patients who do not respond or who partially respond to monotherapy with first-line medications, carbamazepine or its derivative, oxcarbazepine may be considered as second-line choices (Goodwin, 2009; Yatham et al., 2005; VA/DoD, Affairs, & Defense, 2010). The mechanism of action of carbamazepine remains unclear (Gould, Quiroz, Singh, Zarate, & Manji, 2004). Consistent with the findings in the early studies of limited methodological rigor, two randomized controlled trials showed that carbamazepine (in extended release formulation) was superior to placebo (Weisler et al., 2005; Weisler et al., 2006). Furthermore, carbamazepine's efficacy is very similar to that of lithium and valproate in the treatment of acute mania (Kusumakar et al., 1997). The main factor limiting the utility of carbamazepine is its potential to cause significant drug–drug interactions due to potent CYP450 induction (Nasrallah, Ketter, & Kalali, 2006). Oxcarbazepine, a keto derivative of carbamazepine, is reported not to cause autoinduction of CYP450 (Baruzzi, Albani, & Riva, 1994), and thus a lower risk of drug–drug interactions. Several guidelines recommend oxcarbazepine as a second- or third-line anti-manic agent (VA/DoD, Affairs, & Defense, 2010; Yatham et al., 2005). However, current evidence remains weak in support of its anti-manic efficacy; one negative study was reported in children, and there have been no randomized controlled trials done in adults (Popova, Leighton, Bernadbarre, Bernardo, & Vieta, 2007; Wagner et al., 2006; Vasudev et al., 2011).

Patients who failed to respond to monotherapy as described above often require a combination therapy. As a recommended first-line treatment for severe mania with or without psychotic features, combination therapy employing lithium, valproate, and SGAs seems to improve the overall disease outcome as evidenced by a 20% increase in the responder rate compared with monotherapy (Yatham et al., 2005). The evidence is strongest for combining lithium or valproate with risperidone, quetiapine, or aripiprazole (Malhi et al., 2012; Vieta et al., 2008c). The combination of olanzapine with lithium or valproate is also efficacious (Tohen et al., 2002). Evidence of using ziprasidone combination with lithium or valproate appears to be the weakest among all. Asenapine adjunctive treatment with lithium or valproate is superior to placebo (Chwieduk & Scott, 2011). Paliperidone adjunctive therapy with lithium or valproate is not superior to lithium or valproate monotherapy (Berwaerts et al., 2011).

The combination of lithium with valproate or carbamazepine has also been demonstrated to be efficacious and safe in uncontrolled trials (Reischies, Hartikainen, & Berghofer, 2002; Small, Klapper, & Marhenke, 1995). Such combinations can be useful in patients who do not respond or who are intolerant to the combination of treatments detailed above.

Benzodiazepines are frequently used in addition to the medications detailed above, in managing acute manic episodes, especially in patients with aggressive or assaultive behaviors. However, there are no well-controlled studies to support benzodiazepine monotherapy as a mood stabilizing agent. Furthermore, the long-term use of benzodiazepines is highly discouraged because of the concerns about physical dependence and misuse. It is known that substance abuse is highly prevalent and often causes destabilization in bipolar patients, resulting in poor treatment responses (Stedman, Pettinati, Brown, Calabrese, & Raines, 2010).

Although valproate and carbamazepine are efficacious in acute mania, there is no convincing evidence for the anti-manic effect of other anticonvulsants. In fact, the evidence is conclusive that gabapentin and topiramate are ineffective in randomized controlled trials (Pande, Crockatt, Janney, Werth, & Tsaroucha, 2000; Rosa, Fountoulakis, Siamouli, Gonda, & Vieta, 2011; Kushner, Khan, Lane, & Olson, 2006). Lamotrigine monotherapy in acute mania is not supported by current limited data despite its efficacy in long-term maintenance treatment of bipolar disorder. However, gabapentin may be effective in the treatment of comorbid anxiety in such patients (Rakofsky & Dunlop, 2011), and topiramate may be useful in mitigating the risk of weight gain due to the SGAs, as suggested by a recent 8-week open-label study using topiramate to augment olanzapine (Wozniak et al., 2009).

Acute Depressive Episodes

As stated in the introduction, depressive episodes of bipolar disorder are the most frequent type of mood disturbance in the illness (Judd et al., 2002). Functional impairment, decrease in quality of life, and suicide are the major concerns associated with recurrent depressive symptoms.

Only quetiapine and the combination of olanzapine/fluoxetine are currently approved by the FDA for bipolar depression. Quetiapine's efficacy has been consistently demonstrated in five 8-week, randomized controlled trials (Weisler, Calabrese, & Thase, 2008; Young et al., 2010; Suppes et al., 2010; McElroy, Weisler, & Chang, 2010). In EMBOLDEN I and II trials, two different dose regimens of quetiapine were compared to either lithium/placebo (Young et al., 2010) or paroxetine/placebo (McElroy, Weisler, & Chang, 2010). Both doses of quetiapine showed a significant effect on depressive symptoms compared to lithium, paroxetine, or placebo. Furthermore, there is evidence to support a lower risk of a switch to mania with quetiapine (Suppes et al., 2010). Tohen et al. (2003) showed that the olanzapine/fluoxetine combination was superior to olanzapine monotherapy and placebo in the registration trial. Lamotrigine has been shown to be efficacious for bipolar depression in two well-designed studies, and response rates with lamotrigine were significantly higher than placebo (van der Loos, Mulder, & Hartong, 2009; Calabrese, Bowden, & Sachs, 2003). Thus, lamotrigine along with quetiapine and olanzapine are recommended as first- or second-line agents (for olanzapine due to adverse effects; VA/DoD, Affairs, & Defense, 2010) for the treatment of bipolar depression.

Lithium has been commonly considered as a first-line agent in bipolar depression by several guidelines (VA/DoD Affairs, & Defense, 2010). However, the evidence to support this practice remains limited. In EMBOLDEN I trial, lithium did not separate from placebo (Young et al., 2010).

The clinical trials evaluating the efficacy of several other mood stabilizing agents and SGAs for bipolar depression did not produce positive results. For example, aripiprazole and ziprasidone failed to show efficacy for bipolar depression in a 7-week trial (Thase, Jonas, & Khan, 2008) and two randomized controlled outpatient trials (Lombardo, Sachs, Kolluri, Kremer, & Yang, 2012) respectively. The data of lamotrigine monotherapy for bipolar depression are ambiguous (Bauer, Ritter, Grunze, & Pfenning, 2012).

Similar to acute mania, combination therapy is commonly prescribed for bipolar depression, especially in patients treated with long-term maintenance therapy who develop a breakthrough depressive episode. Various combinations have been proposed: mood stabilizing agents plus SGAs, mood stabilizing agents plus anticonvulsants, SGAs plus antidepressants, and mood stabilizing agents plus antidepressants. However, the strength of current evidence is at best modest for most combination regimens (Malhi et al., 2009; Yatham et al., 2005). Addition of lamotrigine to lithium was more effective than placebo in reducing depressive symptoms in a multicenter, double-blind, placebo-controlled trial (van der Loos, Mulder, & Hartong, 2009). Lithium plus valproate combination was well tolerated, and as effective as lithium or valproate plus an SSRI in a small controlled trial (Young, Joffe, & Robb, 2000).

However, the role of antidepressants as monotherapy or combination therapy remains unclear. Monotherapy with antidepressants, especially in the initial phase, continues to be prevalent in clinical practice (Baldassano & Hosey, 2011). In a recent review by Bauer et al. (2012), five randomized, controlled studies were identified in which monotherapy with imipramine, fluoxetine, paroxetine, tranylcypromine, and venlafaxine were evaluated in bipolar depression. The authors summarize that antidepressants are an option for short-term use, but whether they should be used as monotherapy or combination with mood stabilizing agents remains controversial.

Except for studies of the fixed dose combination of olanzapine and fluoxetine that is approved for bipolar depression, there have been few adequately designed trials evaluating the effect of adjunctive therapy of antidepressants. STEP-BD (Sachs et al., 2007) failed to show benefits of paroxetine and bupropion as adjuncts to mood stabilizing agents (lithium, valproate, carbamazepine, or SGAs). Leverich et al. (2006) also reported that the addition of bupropion, venlafaxine, or sertraline to a mood stabilizing agent resulted in no significant difference in bipolar depression. This study is limited by the lack of a placebo group in the trial. An early meta-analysis suggested that antidepressants were efficacious and safe in bipolar depression (Gijsman, Geddes, Rendell, Nolen, & Goodwin, 2004), whereas a most recent systematic review and meta-analysis with additional studies found that antidepressants were not statistically superior to placebo or other standard treatment for bipolar depressants (Sidor & MacQueen, 2011). Nemeroff et al. (2001) conducted an important double-blind randomized study comparing adjunctive imipramine and paroxetine in patients with bipolar depression. Imipramine and paroxetine were effective only in the patients with lithium level below 0.8 meq/L. This result suggests that adding antidepressants may be beneficial for patients who have difficulty tolerating a lithium dose increase. Despite the controversy, antidepressants may be reserved as second- or third-line agents for refractory bipolar depression.

The risk of medication-induced mania (affective switch) is another possibility that complicates the use of antidepressants in bipolar depression. A number of studies have shown that some antidepressants can cause switching to mania or hypomania, therefore worsening the course of the illness (Post et al., 2006). Tricyclic antidepressants (TCAs), MAOIs, and venlafaxine (an SNRI) are more likely to cause the switch (Malhi et al., 2012; Post et al., 2006). Despite a lack of clear efficacious evidence in acute bipolar depression, bupropion and SSRIs have lower switch rates compared to TCAs and SNRIs (Sidor & MacQueen, 2011).

Mixed Episodes and Rapid Cycling

Mixed episodes or states are associated with elevated suicidal risk, higher comorbidity with substance abuse and personality disorders, and poorer response to treatments (McElroy et al., 1995). Rapid cycling, defined as four or more episodes of acute mania within a year, occurs in 15% of patients with bipolar disorder and more often in women than in men. Similar to mixed episodes, rapid cycling is also associated with higher rates of comorbidity, poorer treatment response, and an elevated suicidal risk (Tondo, Hennen, & Baldessarini, 2003). Among all factors that may contribute to rapid cycling, hypothyroidism, antidepressants, and substance abuse are well documented (Schneck, 2006).

Since there are no clinical studies conducted specifically in patients with mixed episodes, current evidence and treatment recommendations are based on the subgroup analysis of clinical trials of acute episodes in which patients with mixed episodes have been included. Thus, the overall strength of the evidence for the pharmacological treatment of mixed episodes is limited.

Most of the SGAs are efficacious for mixed episodes; olanzapine and quetiapine XR have the best evidence as monotherapy (McIntyre & Yoon, 2012). There is insufficient evidence to suggest that the combination therapy with valproate or lithium and SGAs is more efficacious than monotherapy. Most importantly, lithium is not recommended by most of the treatment guidelines as a first-line agent in mixed episodes due to its inconsistent efficacy in this particular population. Valproate and carbamazepine are effective for mixed episodes (Swann, Bowden, & Morris, 1997; Yatham et al., 2005; Weisler et al., 2005; Weisler et al., 2006).

Similar to mixed episodes, studies regarding rapid cycling are very limited. A meta-analysis of earlier studies revealed that lithium was at least partially effective in patients with rapid cycling (Kupka, Luckenbaugh, Post, Leverich, & Nolen, 2003). Lithium plus carbamazepine appears to work better for patients with rapid-cycling features (Denicoff et al., 1997). Valproate may be as effective as lithium in rapid cyclers (Calabrese et al., 2005). A subgroup analysis of several randomized controlled trials involving olanzapine, quetiapine, and aripiprazole supports their efficacy in rapid cycling (McIntyre & Yoon, 2012).

Maintenance Treatment

Long-term prophylaxis is critical in the management of bipolar disorder. Patients who have achieved stabilization from an acute episode of depression, hypomania, or mania should be continued on the effective medications used in the acute phase treatment unless intolerable adverse effects occur. Recurrence rates are estimated at 60%–80% after the discontinuation of lithium therapy (Yatham et al., 2005). Treatment guidelines strongly recommend that patients who are stabilized with medications during an acute manic episode should continue for at least 6 months with the effective agents and probably be prescribed lifelong prophylaxis (VA/DoD, Affairs & Defense, 2010).

Lithium has long been considered the gold standard of maintenance therapy, especially for prophylaxis regarding the recurrence of mania (Prien, Point, Caffey, & Klet, 1973; Malhi et al., 2009). Olanzapine, quetiapine, aripiprazole, and risperidone long-acting injectable (risperidone LAI) are approved by the FDA for maintenance therapy with slightly different side effect profiles. Olanzapine and quetiapine are effective in delaying relapse in both mania and depression (Tohen et al., 2006; Malhi et al., 2009) whereas aripiprazole and risperidone LAI are only effective in delaying relapse of mania (Keck, Calabrese, & McQuade, 2006; Quiroz, Yatham, Palumbo, Karcher, & Kusumaker, 2010). Clozapine is often reserved for either monotherapy or combination therapy in the refractory bipolar disorder, but there are no randomized controlled trials with clozapine in this population. Some case reports support clozapine's efficacy (Frye, Ketter, Altshuler, & Denicoff, 1998). In an 18-month study, lamotrigine was demonstrated to be effective in delaying relapse to both mania and depression (Bowden, Calabrese, & Sachs, 2003; Calabrese, Bowden, & Sachs, 2003). Currently there is only one randomized clinical maintenance trial in which valproate did not separate from placebo (Bowden, Calabrese, & McElroy, 2000), but most clinicians continue to use valproate in long-term maintenance treatment. Studies assessing carbamazepine's (or oxcarbazepine) prophylactic efficacy are scarce (Gitlin & Frye, 2012). There are some indications that carbamazepine may be more effective for certain subpopulations of bipolar disorder such as patients with psychotic delusions (Greil, Ludwig-Mayerhofer, & Erazo, 1997; Kleindienst & Greil, 2000). Oxcarbazepine did not separate from placebo in a combination study with lithium (Vieta, Cruz, & Garcia-Campayo, 2008).

Pharmacotherapy in Pediatric Bipolar Disorder

Compared with the evidence in adult population, data to support the overall efficacy of mood stabilizing agents and SGAs in pediatric bipolar disorder are still very limited. Liu et al. (2011) completed a comprehensive review and meta-analysis involving 29 open-label and 17 double-blind trials of various mood stabilizing agents and SGAs in the pediatric population. Risperidone, aripiprazole, olanzapine, quetiapine, and ziprasidone are efficacious as monotherapy in pediatric bipolar disorder. Open-label and double-blind studies also support the effectiveness of valproate; but double-blind studies with lithium or carbamazepine are lacking (Liu et al., 2011). Correll et al.'s (2010) comparative analysis of nine pediatric bipolar trials showed that SGAs had a larger effect size than traditional mood stabilizing agents only in youth. The analysis suggests that SGAs may offer greater benefits than traditional mood stabilizing agents.

Evidence Basis for Combined Biological and Psychological Treatment of Bipolar Disorder

There is no evidence for psychosocial treatments for bipolar disorder as a "standalone" treatment for bipolar disorder (Lam, Burbeck, Wright, & Pilling, 2009). It is widely acknowledged that treatment of bipolar disorder requires pharmacological management in the acute phase, and continuing pharmacological treatment to prevent further episodes, but that the outcomes obtained from pharmacological treatment, both in the acute phase of the illness and in preventing relapse, are far from ideal (Hlastala et al., 1997; Gellar et al., 2002; Gitlin, Swendsen, Heller, & Hanimen, 1995). There is a compelling rationale for the use of psychotherapeutic interventions in bipolar patients. Medical treatment alone is insufficient in newly diagnosed patients who need substantial help with adherence to treatment and acceptance of the diagnosis, with the treatment of residual and subthreshold symptoms, and with the repair of psychosocial crises caused by behavior during acute episodes and restoration of good psychosocial functioning. This is a disorder where combined treatment is truly the preferred strategy. Psychosocial treatments can only be applied when patients can learn and remember—generally, in the absence of severe psychotic and behavioral symptoms. The amount of material presented must be titrated to the patient's needs.

Particular attention must be paid to the need to grieve for particular aspects of the patient's life that must be modified. When patients have family members with the disorder, they may have distorted perceptions of what it could mean for them. Additionally, many individuals are diagnosed after they have had their own children and must come to terms with the meaning of this regarding potential heritability and the effects of the disorder on parenting. Advocacy and managing stigma are a necessity.

Multiple sizable randomized controlled trials indicate that combined treatment works to increase the breadth of recovery (Miklowitz et al., 2007; Frank et al., 2008), the speed of recovery (Miklowitz et al., 2007), decrease the frequency and increase the time to relapse (Lam, Hayward, Watkins, Wright, & Sham, 2005; Frank et al., 2008; Miklowitz et al., 2007; Colom et al., 2003a), and increase the acceptability and adherence to medication treatment (Cochran, 1984). These studies will be detailed in the sections that describe the available treatments. Lam et al.'s meta-analysis (2009) found that augmenting medication with complex psychoeducation, family-focused treatment, cognitive behavioral therapy, or interpersonal social rhythm therapy significantly improves patients' function and symptoms, and delays or prevents relapse compared to controls. This review considered some heterogeneous studies—patients were treated in groups and individually and were at different stages of the disorder.

One issue in comparing studies of psychosocial treatments is that there is such heterogeneity of studies and measures—although the majority of studies indicate positive benefits of the psychosocial treatments available. Despite this, the diversity of patients, variability of exclusion criteria, difference in severity and symptoms, lack of description, and control about number of lifetime episodes make most of these studies difficult to compare (Schottle, Huber, Bock, & Meyer, 2001). STEP-BD is an exception, and did not indicate a difference between the treatments tested (Miklowitz et al., 2007).

Adherence is a major concern—although it is not the only reason patients improve with psychosocial treatments, it is certainly benefitted by them. Thirty percent of bipolar patients take 70% or less of their medication (Scott & Pope, 2002), and rates of nonadherence range from 40% to 60% in multiple studies (Colom, Vieta, Tacchi, Sanchez-Moreno, & Scott, 2005). Reviews of the psychological treatments detailed in this chapter indicate that adherence benefits from each of the approaches (Sajatovic, Davies, & Hrouda, 2004), but that adherence does not entirely account for patient improvement.

Cognitive Behavioral Therapy (CBT)

There are several treatment manuals available for the implementation of CBT in bipolar disorder, (Basco & Rush, 2005; Lam, Hayward & Bright, 1999; Newman, Leahy, Beck, Reilly-Harrington, Gyulai, 2001; Reilly-Harrington & Knauz, 2005; Scott et al., 2006), but the most tested protocols are those of Scott (Scott et al., 2006) and Lam (Lam et al., 2005). Modifications of CBT have been developed for children (Pavuluri et al., 2004). The key elements of treatment with CBT include education about CBT and the illness, the use of cognitive and behavioral approaches to the symptoms of depression and mania, and the use of cognitive and behavioral strategies to increase adherence and prevent relapse.

Scott and colleagues (Scott et al., 2006) found that CBT improved symptoms 6 months after treatment compared to the control group and that relapse rates were 60% less in the treatment group for 18 months compared to controls. Lam et al. (2005) studied a group of bipolar patients over 30 months after recovering 12 to 20 sessions of CBT. The patients' time to relapse increased significantly, and patients spent 110 fewer days in episodes than the control group. Mood, social functioning, and goal attainment improved. For the most part, the treatment effect occurred in the first year. Although CBT as studied is a time-limited treatment, giving the chronic nature of bipolar disorder and the shifting needs of patients over a lifetime, booster sessions are most likely needed in the "real world." The basic model for treatment with CBT involves patient education, targeting the cognitive, behavioral, and affective disturbances with cognitive behavioral strategies and avoidance of functional decrements and psychosocial crises. The goal is to maximize adherence, stop the progression of episodes and repair developmental/skill deficits, and prevent relapse.

Family-Focused Treatment (FFT)

Family-focused treatment, as developed by Miklowitz and Goldstein (1997), is the most intensively studied family psychotherapeutic intervention, although there are studies of other forms of family interventions, including for use during hospitalization (Clarkin et al., 1990) and for couples (Clarkin, Carpenter, Hull, Wilner, & Glick, 1998) that have been shown to be efficacious in preventing relapse and rehospitalization. The latter two interventions have common features of psychoeducation, identifying stressors and improving communication and coping, and enhancing adherence.

FFT developed from research on expressed emotion; that is, in families with a high degree of criticism, hostility, and emotional overinvolvement, psychiatric patients have notoriously poor outcomes (Butzlaff & Hooley, 1998). There are aspects of FFT that attend to psychoeducation, relapse prevention, identification of prodromal symptoms, and planning for relapse, in addition to adherence work. However, the distinguishing characteristic of FFT is the work that occurs to enhance communication and solve problems between family members.

Miklowitz and Goldstein's (1997) FFT is comprised of three components: psychoeducation, communication-enhancement, and skills training. The treatment developed by observing that high degrees of expressed emotion in family members of bipolar patients predicted higher levels of relapse and symptom severity in a 9- to 12-month follow-up period. It is designed to be a time-limited intervention, generally 21 sessions over 9 months.

Clinical trials with large groups of patients have shown effectiveness of FFT in decreasing the percentage of patients who relapse and increasing the time to relapse (Miklowitz et al., 2008). In a small study (46 patients), FFT helped decrease patients' symptoms when administered solely to caregivers (Perlick et al., 2010). Twelve to fifteen sessions of FFT administered to caregivers decreased recurrence in afflicted family members and decreased the depression frequently present in family members. One reason this finding may have considerable importance is that only one third of patients with bipolar disorder are reported to use outpatient mental health services in any 12-month period (Wang et al., 2005).

Multiple studies of FFT in adults and youth have shown the treatment is helpful (Morris, Miklowitz, & Waxmonsley, 2007), and draw attention to the need for intervention early in the life of bipolar patients. Fifty to sixty percent of patients have an onset of bipolar disorder before critical developmental skills are acquired that would allow for independent living (Perlis et al., 2004). These include skills to consolidate identity, form relationships, succeed academically, manage care for oneself, and become independent and autonomous. Problem solving, social skills, and self-management skills are often substantially lacking in patients with bipolar disorder. In addition, burdens on families with bipolar members are significant—emotional, financial, and practical issues are substantial costs. Family members may also have preconceived ideas about the meaning of the illness either culturally or because other afflicted family members exist.

Interpersonal Social Rhythm Therapy (IPSRT)

The concept that anchors IPSRT is that circadian rhythms are central to the development of mood problems, and that when events occur that disrupt them (stressful or not), the effects on sleep, appetite, energy, and alertness that occur can cause vulnerable individuals to develop mood instability and episodes of mania, hypomania, and depression. In addition, there is a focus on nonadherence (Frank, 2007). The therapy is grounded by a personal conceptualization for each mood episode regarding the interaction between social supports, temperament, coping strategies, the flexibility of the patient's biological clock, and stressful life events. IPSRT helps patients to accept that even medications might be insufficient in certain circumstances.

In addition to attention to circadian rhythm disruption, IPSRT works to help patients focus on interpersonal events that lead to the development of mood problems and helps patients repair interpersonal deficits that put them at risk for future problems. It also attends to the existential issues faced by patients, such as integrating the concept of having a chronic illness and grieving losses (Frank, 2007).

Treatment with IPSRT in the acute phase has been found to be more effective than intensive clinical management in terms of patients having significant increases in the time until the next episode, whether or not they receive maintenance IPSRT. Particular patient characteristics that meant that patients were highly responsive to IPSRT include the absence of a history of lifetime anxiety disorders and overall good medical health. The acutely ill depressed patient and the patient just recovering from mania or mixed episodes are most responsive to IPSRT (Frank, 2005). Two multisite randomized controlled trials show that IPSRT produces faster recovery from depression, fewer suicide attempts (Rucci et al., 2002), longer interepisode recovery (Frank et al., 2005), and improved psychosocial, and occupational functioning (Frank et al., 2005; Frank et al., 2008). IPSRT has also been adapted for adolescents, with promising results in a pilot study (Hlastala, Kotler, McClellan, & McCauley, 2010).

Psychoeducation

The central feature of psychoeducational approaches to bipolar disorder is that awareness of the mood state and prodromal symptoms, and a well-defined plan to implement at the time of the prodrome is the cornerstone of managing the disorder. Individual psychoeducation has been shown to be effective in the prevention of manic episodes and in increasing the time between manic episodes (Perry, Tarrier, Morriss, McCarthy, & Limb, 1999). Group psychoeducation has significant efficacy in patients who receive the intervention when the mood symptoms are in remission, with fewer relapses, increased time to relapse and fewer and shorter hospitalizations (Colom et al., 2003a). Additionally, the educational approach is more effective than what would be accounted for by better medication adherence alone (Colom et al., 2003b). There is an emphasis on doing exercises to underscore prodromal symptoms and to teach lifestyle modifications to enhance regularity as a key part of maintaining stability.

A "hybrid" strategy that has been tested within the Veterans Administration System is the Life Goals Program developed by Bauer and McBride (1996), and studied by Bauer (Bauer et al., 2006), and Simon (Simon, Ludman, Bauer, Unützer, & Operskalski, 2006). These treatment protocols involve coordinating evidence-based pharmacotherapy, enhanced adherence with nursing support, monitoring and targeting prodromal symptoms, and five sessions of group psychoeducation, followed by a group that uses behavioral and interpersonal strategies to target goal attainment. Treatment with this program has been shown in randomized controlled trials to decrease manic episodes over 2 years (Simon et al., 2006), and to decrease the length of manic episodes (Bauer et al., 2006; Simon et al., 2006) in addition to increasing quality of life and social functioning (Bauer et al., 2006). Depressive episodes were not, however, impacted by treatment.

Effective psychotherapies for bipolar patients share many common traits (Lam et al., 2009). They each regard the disorder from a stress-diathesis model, focus on psychoeducation and obtaining the best possible adherence to medication, and teach patients self-monitoring skills. Patients are encouraged to make necessary modifications to their lifestyles by using every tool available, and anticipatory guidance and problem solving facilitate relapse prevention. Each specific psychotherapy takes a different approach to interpersonal relationships, skill training, and cognitive modification.

The choice between the psychosocial treatments available is not as clear for clinicians and patients, and few matching studies exist. Common sense would indicate that patient conceptualization would be the most effective way to determine which treatment might be the best fit. There are also some known characteristics of the treatments that may help with decision making.

Miklowitz's review of the evidence for the use of psychotherapeutic approaches in bipolar disorder specifies particular characteristics that guide patient selection, since 17 of 18 randomized controlled trials show that all successful psychotherapy treatments decrease relapse and numbers of episodes for between 12 and 30 months after treatment (Miklowitz, 2008). Types of episodes, state of recovery, and psychosocial supports are all determining factors. CBT and FFT work best for depressive symptomatology, and are less effective when the patient is manic. CBT and group psychoeducation work best when instituted when the patient is recovered. FFT and IPSRT are most effective when implemented early in the resolution of an acute manic or during an acute depressive episode. Patients with prominent manic symptoms may benefit more from approaches that enhance social and interpersonal stability and regular structure of circadian rhythms, or from psychoeducation paired with systems of care. Adolescent patients with involved family members may benefit most from FFT.

STEP-BD compared adjunctive psychotherapy for bipolar depression (not treatment effects on relapse prevention or decreased number of episodes) and found no significant difference between FFT, IPSRT, or CBT. All of the active treatments produced faster recovery than medication, with no differences between groups, and all treatments had a beneficial effect on patients psychosocial functioning. All treatments were more effective than a three-month psychoeducational intervention (Miklowitz et al., 2007).

A recent randomized controlled trial of bipolar patients with subsyndromal symptoms that compared 20 sessions of CBT with six sessions of group psychoeducation produced equivalent outcomes on 18 month follow-up because of the increased number of sessions and the need for specialized therapy training. The delivery costs, however, were quite different, with CBT being six times more expensive. The authors recommended a "stepped care" approach as a rational way to deploy resources for bipolar patients, with targeted therapy employed for particular symptoms (Parikh et al., 2013). Thoughtful analysis also must account for the costs of treatment when making decisions about patient care.

REFERENCES

Alda, M., Hajek, T., Calkin, C., & O'Donovan, C. (2009). Treatment of bipolar disorder: New perspectives. *Annals of Medicine, 41*(3), 186–196.

Allen, M., Hirschfeld, R., Wozniak, P., Baker, J., & Bowden, C. (2006). Linear relationship of valproate serum concentration to response and optimal serum levels for acute mania. *American Journal of Psychiatry, 163,* 272–275.

American Psychiatric Association (2000). *Diagnostic and Statistical Manual of Mental Disorders* (4th ed., text revision [DSM IV-TR]). Washington, DC: American Psychiatric Association.

Axelson, D. A., Birmaher, B., Strober, M., Gill, M. K., Valeri, S., Chiappetta, L., . . . Keller, M. (2006). Phenomenology of children and adolescents with bipolar spectrum disorders. *Archives of General Psychiatry, 63,* 1139–1148.

Baldassano, C., & Hosey, A. (2011). Bipolar depression: An evidence-based approach. *Current Psychiatric Reports, 13,* 483–487.

Baldessarini, R. J., Pompili, M., & Tondo, L. (2006). Suicide in bipolar disorder: Risks and management. *CNS Spectrums, 11,* 465–471.

Baruzzi, A., Albani, F., & Riva, R. (1994). Oxcarbazepine—Pharmacokinetic interactions and their clinical relevance. *Epilepsia, 35*(Suppl. 3), 14–19.

Basco, M. R., & Rush, A. J. (2005). *Cognitive behavioral therapy for bipolar disorder.* New York: Guilford.

Bauer, M. S., & McBride, L. (1996). *Structured group psychotherapy for bipolar disorder: The Life Goals Program.* New York: Springer.

Bauer, M. S., McBride, L., Williford, W. O., Glick, H., Kinosian, B., Altshuler, L., . . . Cooperative Studies Program 430 Study Team. (2006). Collaborative care for bipolar disorder: part I. Intervention and implementation in a randomized effectiveness trial. *Psychiatric Services, 57,* 927–936.

Bauer, M., Ritter, P., Grunze, H., & Pfenning, A. (2012). Treatment options for acute depression in bipolar disorder. *Bipolar Disorders, 14*(Suppl. 2), 37–50.

Berwaerts, J., Lane, R., Nuamah, I. F., Lim, P., Remmerie, B., & Hough, D. W. (2011). Paliperidone extended-release as adjunctive therapy to lithium or valproate in the treatment of acute mania: A randomized, placebo-controlled study. *Journal of Affective Disorder, 129,* 252–260.

Birmaher, B., Axelson, D., Strober, M., Gill, M. K., Valeri, S., Chiappetta, L., . . . Keller, M. (2006). Clinical course of children and adolescents with bipolar spectrum disorders. *Archives of General Psychiatry, 63,* 175–183.

Bowden, C. L., Brugger, A. M., Swann, A. C., Calabrese, J. R., Janicak, P. G., Petty, F., . . . Frazer, R. N. (1994). Efficacy of divalproex vs lithium and placebo in the treatment of mania. *JAMA, 271,* 918–924.

Bowden, C., Calabrese, J., & McElroy, S. (2000). A randomized, placebo-controlled 12-month trial of divalproex and lithium in treatment of outpatients with bipolar I disorder. *Archives of General Psychiatry, 57,* 481–489.

Bowden, C., Calabrese, J., & Sachs, G. (2003). A placebo-controlled 18-month trial of lamotrigine and lithium maintenance treatment in recently manic or hypomanic patients with bipolar I disorder. *Archives of General Psychiatry, 60,* 392–400.

Bowden, C., Grunze, H., Mullen, J., Brecher, M., Paulsson, B., Jones, M., . . . Svensson, K. (2005). A randomized, double-blind, placebo-controlled efficacy and safety study of quetiapine or lithium as monotherapy for mania in bipolar disorder. *Journal of Clinical Psychiatry, 66,* 111–121.

Bowden, C., Swann, A., Calabrese, J., Rubenfaer, L., Wozniak, P., & Collins, M. E. (2006). A randomized, placebo-controlled, multicenter study of divalproex sodium extended release in the treatment of acute mania. *Journal of Clinical Psychiatry, 67,* 1501–1510.

Butzlaff, R. L., & Hosley, J. M. (1998). Expressed emotion and psychiatric relapse: A meta-analysis. *Archives of General Psychiatry, 55,* 542–552.

Calabrese, J., Bowden, C., & Sachs, G. (2003). A placebo-controlled 18-month trial of lamotrigine and lithium maintenance treatment in recently depressed patients with bipolar I disorder. *Journal of Clinical Psychiatry, 64,* 1013–1024.

Calabrese, J., Shelton, M., Rapport, D., Youngstrom, E., Jackson, K., Bilali, S., . . . Findling, R. L. (2005). A 20-month, double-blind, maintenance trial of lithium versus divalproex in rapid-cycling bipolar disorder. *American Journal of Psychiatry, 162,* 2152–2161.

Chwieduk, C., & Scott, L. (2011). Asenapine: A review of its use in the management of mania in adults with bipolar I disorder. *CNS Drugs, 25,* 251–267.

Cipriani, A., Barbui, C., Salanti, G., Rendell, J., Brown, R., Stockton, S., . . . Geddes, J. R. (2011). Comparative efficacy and acceptability of antimanic drugs in acute mania: A multiple-treatments meta-analysis. *Lancet, 378,* 1306–1315.

Clarkin, J. F., Carpenter, D., Hull, J., Wilner, P., & Glick, I. (1998). Effects of psychoeducational intervention for married patients with bipolar disorder and their spouses. *Psychiatric Services, 49,* 531–533.

Clarkin, J. F., Glick, I. D., Haas, G. L., Spencer, J. H., Lewis, A. B., Peyser, J., . . . Lestelle, V. (1990). A randomized clinical trial of inpatient family intervention. V. Results for affective disorders. *Journal of Affective Disorders, 18,* 17–28.

Cochran, S. D. (1984). Preventing medical noncompliance in the outpatient treatment of bipolar affective disorders. *Journal of Consulting and Clinical Psychology, 52,* 873–878.

Colom, F., Vieta, E., Martinez-Aran, A., Reinares, M., Goikolea, J. M., Benabarre, A., . . . Corominas, J. (2003a). A randomized trial on the efficacy of group psychoeducation in the prophylaxis of recurrences in bipolar patients whose disease is in remission. *Archives of General Psychiatry, 60,* 402–407.

Colom, F., Vieta, E., Reinares, M., Martínez-Arán, A., Torrent, C., Goikolea, J. M., & Gastó C. (2003b). Psychoeducation efficacy in bipolar disorders: Beyond compliance enhancement. *Journal of Clinical Psychiatry, 64,* 1101–1105.

Colom, F., Vieta, E., Tacchi, M. J., Sanchez-Moreno, J., & Scott, J. (2005). Identifying and improving non-adherence in bipolar disorders. *Bipolar Disorders, 7,* 24.

Correll, C., Sheridan, E., & DelBello, M. (2010). Antipsychotic and mood stabilizer efficacy and tolerability in pediatric and adult patients with bipolar I mania: A comparative analysis of acute, randomized, placebo-controlled trials. *Bipolar Disorders, 12,* 116–141.

Cutler, A., Datto, C., Nordenhem, A., Dettore, B., Acevedo, L., & Darko, D. (2008). Effectiveness of extended release formulation of quetiapine as monotherapy for the treatment of acute bipolar mania. *International Journal of Neuropsychopharmacology, 11*(Suppl 1), 184.

Denicoff, K., Smith-Jackson, E., Disney, E., Ali, S., Leverich, G., & Post, R. (1997). Comparative prophylactic efficacy of lithium, carbamazepine, and the combination in bipolar disorder. *Journal of Clinical Psychiatry, 58,* 470–478.

Emrich, H., von Zerssen, D., Kissling, W., Moller, H., & Windorfer, A. (1980). Effect of sodium valproate on mania. The GABA hypothesis of affective disorders. *Archiv fur Psychiatrie und Nervenkrankheiten, 229,* 1–16.

Feldman, N. S., Gwizdowski, I. S., Fischer, E. G., Yang, H., & Suppes, T. (2012). Co-occurrence of serious or undiagnosed medical conditions with bipolar disorder preventing clinical trial randomization: A case series. *Journal of Clinical Psychiatry, 73,* 874–877.

Frank, E. (2005). *Treating bipolar disorder: A clinician's guide to interpersonal and social rhythm therapy.* New York: Guilford.

Frank, E. (2007). Interpersonal and social rhythm therapy: A means of improving depression and preventing relapse in bipolar disorder. *Journal of Clinical Psychology: In session, 63,* 463–473.

Frank, E., Kupfer, D. J., Thase, M. E., Mallinger, A. G., Swartz, H. A., Fagiolini, A. M., . . . Monk, T. (2005). Two-year outcomes for IPSRT in individuals with bipolar 1 disorder. *Archives of General Psychiatry, 62,* 996–1004.

Frank, E., Soreca, I., Swartz, H. A., Fogolini, A. Z., Mallinger, A. G., Thase, M. E., . . . Kupfer, D. J. (2008). The role of interpersonal and social rhythm therapy in improving occupational functioning in patients with bipolar I disorder. *American Journal of Psychiatry, 165,* 1559–1565.

Frye, M., Ketter, T., Altshuler, L., & Denicoff, K. (1998). Clozapine in bipolar disorder: Treatment implications for other atypical antipsychotics. *Journal of Affective Disorders, 48,* 91–104.

Geller, B., Craney, J. L., & Bolhofner, K. (2002). Two-year prospective follow-up of children with a pre-pubestral and early adolescent bipolar disorder phenotype. *American Journal of Psychiatry, 159,* 927–933.

Gijsman, H., Geddes, J., Rendell, J., Nolen, W., & Goodwin, G. (2004). Antidepressants for bipolar depression: A systematic review of randomized, controlled trials. *American Journal of Psychiatry, 161,* 1537–1547.

Gitlin, M., & Frye, M. (2012). Maintenance therapies in bipolar disorders. *Bipolar Disorders, 14*(Suppl. 2), 51–65.

Gitlin, M. J., Swendsen, J., Heller, T. L., & Hanimen, C. (1995). Relapse and impairment in bipolar disorder. *American Journal of Psychiatry, 152,* 1635–1640.

Goodwin, G. (2009). Evidence-based guidelines for treating bipolar disorder: Revised second edition—recommendations from the British Association for Psychopharmacology. *Journal of Psychopharmacology, 23,* 346–388.

Gould, T., Quiroz, J., Singh, J., Zarate, C., & Manji, H. (2004). Emerging experimental therapeutics for bipolar disorder: Insights from the molecular and cellular actions of current mood stabilizers. *Molecular Psychiatry, 9,* 734–755.

Greil, W., Ludwig-Mayerhofer, W., & Erazo, N. (1997). Lithium versus carbamazepine in the maintenance treatment in prophylaxis of bipolar disorders—a randomized study. *Journal of Affective Disorders, 43,* 151–161.

Hirschfeld, R., Allen, M., McEvoy, J., Keck, P., & Russell, J. (1999). Safety and tolerability of oral loading divalproex sodium in acutely manic bipolar patients. *Journal of Clinical Psychiatry, 60,* 815–818.

Hirschfeld, R., Baker, J., Wozniak, P., Tracy, K., & Sommerville, K. (2003). The safety and early efficacy of oral-loaded divalpreoex versus standard-titration divalproex, lithium, olanzapine, and placebo in the treatment of acute mania associated with bipolar disorder. *Journal of Clinical Psychiatry, 64,* 841–846.

Hirschfeld, R., Keck, P., Kramer, M., Karcher, K., Canuso, C., Eerdekens, M., & Grossman, F. (2004). Rapid antimanic effect of risperidone monotherapy: A 3-week multicenter, double-blind, placebo-controlled trial. *American Journal of Psychiatry, 161,* 1057–1065.

Hlastala, S. A., Frank, E., Mallinger, A. G., Thase, M. E., Ritenour, A.M., & Kupfer, D. J. (1997). Bipolar depression: An underestimated treatment challenge. *Depression and Anxiety, 5,* 73–83.

Hlastala, S. A., Kotler, J. S., McClellan, J. H., & McCauley, E. A. (2010). Interpersonal and social rhythm therapy for adolescents with bipolar disorder: Treatment development and results from an open trial. *Depression and Anxiety, 27,* 457–464.

Huxley, N., & Baldessarini, R. J. (2007). Disability and its treatment in bipolar disorder. *Bipolar Disorders, 9,* 183–196.

Judd, L. L., Akiskal, H. S., Schettler, P. J., Endicott, J., Maser, J., Solomon, D. A., . . . Keller, M. B. (2002). The long-term natural history of the weekly symptomatic status of bipolar I disorder. *Archives of General Psychiatry, 59,* 530–537.

Keck, P., Calabrese, J., & McQuade, R. (2006). A randomized, double-blind, placebo-controlled 26-week trial of aripiprazole in recently manic patients with bipolar I disorder. *Journal of Clinical Psychiatry, 64,* 626–637.

Keck, P., Marcus, R., Tourkodimitris, S., Ali, M., Liebeskind, A., Saha, A., . . . Aripiprazole Study Group. (2003). A placebo-controlled, double-blind study of the efficacy and safety of aripiprazole in patients with acute bipolar mania. *American Journal of Psychiatry, 160,* 1651–1658.

Keck, P. E., McElroy, S. L., Stratkowski, S. M., West, S. A., Sax, K. N., Hawkins, . . . Haggard, P. (1998). Twelve-month outcome of patients with bipolar disorder following hospitalization for a manic or mixed episode. *American Journal of Psychiatry, 155,* 646–652.

Keck, P., Orsulak, P., & Cutler, A. (2009). Aripirazole monotherapy in the treatment of acute bipolar I mania: A randomized, double-blind, placebo- and lithium-controlled study. *Journal of Affective Disorders, 112,* 36–49.

Keck, P., Versiani, M., Potkin, S., West, S., Giller, E., & Ice, K. (2003). Ziprasidone in the treatment of acute bipolar mania: A three-week, placebo-controlled, double-blind, randomized trial. *American Journal of Psychiatry, 160,* 741–748.

Khanna, S., Vieta, E., Lyons, B., Grossman, F., Eerdekens, M., & Kramer, M. (2005). Risperidone in the treatment of acute mania: Double-blind, placebo-controlled study. *British Journal of Psychiatry, 187,* 229–234.

Kleindienst, N., & Greil, W. (2000). Differential efficacy of lithium and carbamazepine in the prophylaxis of bipolar disorder: Results of the MAP study. *Neuropsychopharmacology, 42*(Suppl. 1), 2–10.

Kupfer, D. J., Frank, E., Grochocinski, V. J., & Cluss, P. A. (2002). Demographic and clinical characteristics of individuals in a bipolar case registry. *Journal of Clinical Psychiatry, 63,* 120–125.

Kupka, R., Luckenbaugh, D., Post, R., Leverich, G., & Nolen, W. (2003). Rapid and non-rapid cycling bipolar disorder: A meta-analysis of clinical studies. *Journal of Clinical Psychiatry, 64,* 1483–1494.

Kushner, S., Khan, A., Lane, R., & Olson, W. (2006). Topimarate monotherapy in the management ofacute mania: Results of four double-blind placebo-controlled trials. *Bipolar Disorders, 8,* 15–27.

Kusumakar, V., Yatham, L., Haslam, D., Parikh, S., Matte, R., Silverstone, P., & Sharma, V. (1997). Treatment of mania, mixed state, and rapid cycling. *Canadian Journal of Psychiatry, 42*(Suppl. 2), 79–86.

Lam, D. H., Burbeck, R., Wright, K., & Pilling, S. (2009). Psychological therapies in bipolar disorder: The effect of illness history on relapse prevention—a systematic review. *Bipolar Disorders, 11,* 474–482.

Lam, D. H., Hayward, P., & Bright, J. (1999). *Cognitive therapy for bipolar disorder: A therapist's guide to concepts, methods, and practice.* New York: John Wiley and Sons.

Lam, D. H., Hayward, P., Watkins, E. R., Wright, K., & Sham, P. (2005). Relapse prevention in patients with bipolar disorder: Cognitive therapy outcome after two years. *American Journal of Psychiatry, 162,* 324–329.

Leibenluft, E. (2011). Severe mood dysregulation, irritability, and the diagnostic boundaries of bipolar disorder in youths. *American Journal of Psychiatry, 168,* 129–142.

Lewinsohn, P. M., Klein, D. N., & Seeley, J. R. (1995). Bipolar disorder in community sample of older adolescents and prevalence, phenomenology, comorbidity, and course. *Journal of the American Academy of Child and Adolescent Psychiatry, 34,* 454–463.

Leverich, G., Altshuler, L., Frye, M., Suppes, T., McElroy, S. K., Kupka, R., . . . Post, R. M. (2006). Risk of switch in mood polarity to hypomania or mania in patients with bipolar depression during acute and continuation trials of venlafaxine, sertraline, and bupropion as adjuncts to mood stabilizers. *American Journal of Psychiatry, 163,* 232–239.

Liu, H., Potter, M., Woodworth, K., Yorks, A., Petty, C., Wozniak, J., . . . Biederman, J. (2011). Pharmacologic treatments for pediatric bipolar disorder: A review and meta-analysis. *Journal of the American Academy of Child and Adolescent Psychiatry, 50,* 749–762.

Lombardo, I., Sachs, G., Kolluri, S., Kremer, C., & Yang, R. (2012). Two 6-week, randomized, double-blind, placebo-controlled studies of ziprasidone in outpatients with bipolar I depression: Did baseline characteristics impact trial outcome? *Journal of Clinical Psychopharmacology, 32,* 470–478.

Malhi, G., Adams, D., Lampe, L., Paton, M., O'Connor, N., Newton, L., . . . Berk, M. (2009). Clinical practice recommendations for bipolar disorder. *Acta Psychiatry of Scandinavica, 119*(Suppl. 439), 27–46.

Malhi, G., Bargh, D., McIntyre, R., Gitlin, M., Frye, M., Bauer, M., & Berk, M. (2012). Balance efficacy, safety, and tolerability recommendations for the clinical management of bipolar disorder. *Bipolar Disorders, 14*(Suppl. 2), 1–21.

McElroy, S., Strakowski, S., Keck, P., Tugrul, K., West, S., & Lonczak, H. (1995). Differences and similarities in mixed and pure mania. *Comprehensive Psychiatry, 36,* 187–194.

McElroy, S., Weisler, R., & Chang, W. (2010). A double-blind, placebo-controlled study of quetiapine and paroxetine as monotherapy in adults with bipolar depression (EMBOLDEN II). *Journal of Clinical Psychiatry, 71,* 163–174.

McIntyre, R., Brecher, M., Paulsson, B., Hizar, K., & Mullen, J. (2005). Quetiapine or haloperidol as monotherapy for bipolar mania—a 12-week, double-blind, randomized, parallel, placebo-controlled trial. *European Neuropsychopharmacology, 15,* 573–585.

McIntyre, R., & Yoon, J. (2012). Efficacy of antimanic treatments in mixed states. *Bipolar Disorders, 14*(Suppl. 2), 22–36.

Merikangas, K. R., Jin, R., He, J. P., Kessler, R. C., Lee, S., Sampson, N. A., . . . Zarkov, Z. (2011). Prevalence and correlates of bipolar spectrum disorder in the world mental health survey initiative. *Archives of General Psychiatry, 68,* 241–251.

Miklowitz, D. J. (2008). Adjunctive psychotherapy for bipolar disorder: State of the evidence. *American Journal of Psychiatry, 165,* 1408–1419.

Miklowitz, D. J., Axelson, D. A., Birmaker, B., George, E. L., Taylor, D. O., Schneck, C. D., . . . Brent, D. A. (2008). Family-focused treatment of adolescents with bipolar disorder: Results of a 2-year randomized trial. *Archives of General Psychiatry, 65,* 1053–1061.

Miklowitz, D. J., & Goldstein, M. J. (1997). *Bipolar disorder: A family focused treatment approach.* New York: Guilford Press.

Miklowitz, D. J., Otto, M. W., Frank, E., Reilly-Harrington, N. A., Kogan, J. N., Sachs, G. S., . . . Wisniewski, S. R. (2007). Intensive psychosocial intervention enhances functioning in patients with bipolar depression: Results from a 9-month randomized controlled trial. *American Journal of Psychiatry, 104,* 1348–1355.

Miklowitz, D. J., Otto, M. W., Frank, E., Reilly-Harrington, N. A., Wisniewski, S. R., Kogan, J. N., . . . Sachs, G. S. (2007). Psychological treatments for bipolar depression: A one-year randomized trial from the STEP-BD. *Archives of General Psychiatry, 64,* 419–427.

Morris, C. D., Miklowitz, D. J., & Waxmonsley, J. A. (2007). Family focused treatment for bipolar disorder in adults and youth. *Journal of Clinical Psychology: In Session, 63,* 443–445.

Nasrallah, H., Ketter, T., & Kalali, A. (2006). Carbamazepine and valproate for the treatment of bipolar disorder: A review of the literature. *Journal of Affective Disorders, 95,* 69–78.

Nemeroff, C., Evans, D., Gyulai, L., Sachs, G., Bowden, C., Gergel, I., . . . Pitts, C. D. (2001). Double-blind, placebo-controlled comparison of imipramine and paroxetine in the treatment of bipolar depression. *American Journal of Psychiatry, 158,* 906–912.

Newman, C. F., Leahy, R. L., Beck, A. T., Reilly-Harrington, N., & Gyulai, L. (2001). *Bipolar disorder: A cognitive therapy approach.* Washington, DC: American Psychological Press.

Pande, A., Crockatt, J., Janney, C., Werth, J., & Tsaroucha, G. G. (2000). Gabapentin in bipolar disorder: A placebo-controlled trial of adjunctive therapy. *Bipolar Disorders, 2,* 249–255.

Parikh, S. V., Zaretsky, A., Beaulieu, S., Yatham, L. N., Young, L. T., Patelis-Siotis, I., . . . Streiner, D. L. (2012). A randomized controlled trial of psychoeducation or cognitive behavioral therapy in bipolar disorder: A Canadian network for mood and anxiety treatments (CANMAT) study [CME]. *Journal of Clinical Psychiatry, 73,* 803–810.

Pavuluri, M. N., Graczyk, P. A., Henry, D. B., Carbray, J. A., Heidenreich, J., & Miklowitz, D. J. (2004). Child and family-focused cognitive behavioral therapy for pediatric bipolar disorder: Development and preliminary results. *Journal of the American Academy of Child and Adolescent Psychiatry, 43,* 528–537.

Perlick, D. A., Miklowitz, D. J., Lopez, N., Chow, J., Kalvin, C., Adzhiashilli, V., & Aronson, A. (2010). Family-focused treatment for caregivers of patients with bipolar disorder. *Bipolar Disorder, 12,* 627–637.

Perlis, R. H., Miyahara, S., Marangell, L. B., Wisniewski, S. R., Ostacher, M., DelBello, M.P., . . . STEP-BD Investigators. (2004). Long-term implications of early onset in bipolar disorder: Data from the first 1000 participants in the Systematic Treatment Enhancement Program for Bipolar Disorder (STEP-BD). *Biological Psychiatry, 55,* 875–881.

Perlis, R. H., Ostacher, M. L., Patel, J. K., Marangell, L. B., Zhang, H., Wisniewski, S. R., . . . Thase, M. E. (2006). Predictors of recurrence in bipolar disorder: Primary outcomes from the (STEP-BD) systematic treatment enhancement program for bipolar disorder. *American Journal of Psychiatry, 163,* 217–224.

Perry, A., Tarrier, N., Morriss, R., McCarthy, E., & Limb, K. (1999). Randomised controlled trial of efficacy of teaching patients with bipolar disorder to identify early symptoms of relapse and obtain treatment. *British Medical Journal, 318,* 149–153.

Pope, H., McElroy, S., Keck, P., & Hudson, J. (1991). Valproate in the treatment of acute mania. A placebo-controlled study. *Archives of General Psychiatry, 48,* 62–68.

Popova, E., Leighton, C., Bernadbarre, A., Bernardo, M., & Vieta, E. (2007). Oxcarbazepine in the treatment of bipolar and schizoaffective disorders. *Expert Review of Neurotherapeutics, 7,* 617–626.

Post, R., Altshuler, L., Leverich, G., Frye, M., Nolen, W., Kupka, R., . . . Mintz, J. (2006). Mood switch in bipolar depression: Comparison of adjunctive venlafaxine, bupropion and sertraline. *British Journal of Psychiatry, 189,* 124–131.

Potkin, S., Keck, P., Segal, S., Ice, K., & English, P. (2005). Ziprasidone in acute bipolar mania: A 21-day randomized, double-blind, placebo-controlled replication trial. *Journal of Clinical Psychiatry, 25,* 301–310.

Prien, R., Point, P., Caffey, E., & Klet, C. (1973). Prophylactic efficacy of lithium carbonate in manic-depressive illness. *Archives of General Psychiatry, 28,* 337–341.

Quiroz, J., Yatham, L., Palumbo, J., Karcher, K. K., & Kusumaker, V. (2010). Risperidone long-acting injectable monotherapy in the maintenance treatment of bipolar disorder. *Biological Psychiatry, 68,* 156–162.

Rakofsky, J., & Dunlop, B. (2011). Treating nonspecific anxiety and anxiety disorders in patients with bipolar disorder: A review. *Journal of Clinical Psychiatry, 72,* 81–90.

Reilly-Harrington, N., & Knauz, R. D. (2005). Cognitive-behavior therapy for rapid cycling bipolar disorder. *Cognitive and Behavioral Practice, 12,* 66–75.

Reischies, F., Hartikainen, J., & Berghofer, A. (2002). Initial lithium and valproate combination therapy in acute mania. *Neuropsychobiology, 46*(Suppl. 1), 22–27.

Rosa, A., Fountoulakis, K., Siamouli, M., Gonda, X., & Vieta, E. (2011). Anticonvulsant treatment of mania a class effect? Data from randomized clinical trials. *CNS Neuroscience & Therapeutics, 17,* 167–177.

Rucci, P., Frank, E., Kostelnik, B., Fagiolini, A., Mallinger, A. G., Swartz, H. A., . . . Kupfer, D. J. (2002). Suicide attempts in patients with bipolar I disorder during acute and maintenance phases of intensive treatment with pharmacotherapy and adjunctive psychotherapy. *American Journal of Psychiatry, 159,* 1160–1164.

Sachs, G., Chengappa, K., Suppes, T., Mullen, J., Brecher, M., Devine, N., & Sweitzer, D. (2004). Quetiapine with lithium or divalproex for the treatment of bipolar mania: A randomized, double-blind, placebo-controlled study. *Bipolar Disorders, 6,* 213–223.

Sachs, G., Dupuy, J., & Wittmann, C. (2011). The pharmacologic treatment of bipolar disorder. *Journal of Clinical Psychiatry, 72,* 704–715.

Sachs, G. S., Nierenberg, A. A., Calabrese, J. R., Marangell, L. B., Wisniewski, S. R., Gyulai, L., . . . Thase, M. E. (2007). Effectiveness of adjunctive antidepressant treatment for bipolar depression. *New England Journal of Medicine, 356,* 1711–1722.

Sachs, G., Sanchez, R., & Marcus, R. (2006). Aripiprazole in the treatment of acute manic or mixed episodes in patients with bipolar I disorder: A 3-week placebo-controlled study. *Journal of Psychopharmacology, 20,* 536–546.

Sajatovic, M., Davies, M., & Hrouda, D. R. (2004). Enhancement of treatment adherence among patients with bipolar disorder. *Psychiatric Services, 55,* 264–269.

Schneck, C. (2006). Treatment of rapid-cycling bipolar disorder. *Journal of Clinical Psychiatry, 67,* 22–27.

Schottle, D., Huber, C. G., Bock, T., & Meyer, T. D. (2011). Psychotherapy for bipolar disorder: A review of the most recent studies. *Current Opinion in Psychiatry, 24,* 549–555.

Scott, J., Paykel, E., Morriss, R., Bentall, R., Kinderman, P., Johnson, T., . . . Hayhurst, H. (2006). Cognitive behavioral therapy for severe and recurrent bipolar disorders: Randomized controlled trial. *British Journal of Psychiatry, 188,* 313–320.

Scott, J., & Pope, M. (2002). Self-reported adherence to treatment with mood stabilizers, plasma levels and psychiatric hospitalization. *American Journal of Psychiatry, 159,* 1927–1929.

Sidor, M., & MacQueen, G. (2011). Antidepressants for the acute treatment of bipolar depression: A systematic review and meta-analysis. *Journal of Clinical Psychiatry, 72,* 156–167.

Simon, G. E., Ludman, E. J., Bauer, M. S., Unützer, J., & Operskalski, B. (2006). Long-term effectiveness and cost of a systematic care program for bipolar disorder. *Archives of General Psychiatry, 63,* 500–508.

Small, J., Klapper, M., & Marhenke, J. (1995). Lithium combined with carbamazepine or haloperidol in the treatment of mania. *Psychopharmacology Bulletin, 31,* 265–272.

Smulevich, A., Khanna, S., Eerdekens, M., Karcher, K., Kramer, M., & Grossman, F. (2005). Acute and continuation risperidone monotherapy in bipolar mania: A 3-week placebo-controlled trial followed by a 9-week double-blind trial of risperidone and haloperidol. *European Neuropsychopharmacology, 15,* 75–84.

Stedman, M., Pettinati, H., Brown, E. K., Calabrese, J., & Raines, S. (2010). A double-blind, placebo-controlled study with quetiapine as adjunct therapy with lithium or divalproex in bipolar I patients with coexisting alcohol dependence. *Alcoholism: Clinical and Experimental Research, 34,* 1822–1831.

Suppes, T., Datto, C., Minkwitz, M., Nordenhem, A., Walker, C., & Darko, D. (2010). Effectiveness of the extended release formulation of quetiapine as monotherapy for the treatment of acute bipolar depression. *Journal of Affective Disorders, 121,* 106–115.

Swann, A., Bowden, C., & Morris, D. (1997). Depression during mania. Treatment response to lithium or divalproex. *Archives of General Psychiatry, 54,* 37–42.

Tarr, G., Glue, P., & Herbison, P. (2011). Comparative efficacy and acceptability of mood stabilizer and second generation antipsychotic monotherapy for acute mania—A systematic review and meta-analysis. *Journal of Affective Disorders, 134,* 14–19.

Thase, M., Jonas, A., & Khan, A. (2008). Aripiprazole monotherapy in nonpsychotic bipolar I depression: Results of 2 randomized, placebo-controlled studies. *Journal of Clinical Psychiatry, 28,* 13–20.

Tohen, M., Calabrese, J., Sachs, G. S., Banov, M. D, Detke, H. C., Risser, R., . . . Bowden, C. L. (2006). Randomized, placebo-controlled trial of olanzapineas mintanence in patients with bipolar I disorder responding to active treatment with olanzapine. *American Journal of Psychiatry, 163,* 247–256.

Tohen, M., Chengappa, K., Suppes, T., Zarate, C., Calabrese, J., Bowden, C., . . . Breier, A. (2002). Efficacy of olanzapine in combination with valproate or lithium in the treatment of mania in patients partially nonresponsive to valproate or lithium monotherapy. *Archives of General Psychiatry, 59,* 62–69.

Tohen, M., Jacobs, T., Grundy, S., McElroy, S., Banov, M., Janicak, P., . . . Breier, A. (2000). Efficacy of olanzapine in acute bipolar mania: A double-blind, placebo-controlled study. The Olanzapine HGGW Study Group. *Archives of General Psychiatry, 57,* 841–849.

Tohen, M., Sanger, T., McElroy, S., Tollefson, G., Chengappa, K., Daniel, D., . . . Toma, V. (1999). Olanzapine versus placebo in the treatment of acute mania. Olanzapine HIGEH Study Group. *American Journal of Psychiatry, 156,* 702–709.

Tohen, M., Vieta, E., Calabrese, J., Ketter, T., Sachs, G., Bowden, C., . . . Breier, A. (2003). Efficacy of olanzapine and olanzapine-fluoxetine combination in the treatment of bipolar I depression. *Archives of General Psychiatry, 60,* 1079–1088.

Tohen, M., Vieta, E., Goodwin, G., Sun, B., Amsterdam, J., Banov, M., . . . Bowden, C. (2009). Olanzapine versus divalproex versus placebo in the treatment of mild to moderate mania: A randomized, 12-week, double-blind study. *Journal of Clinical Psychiatry, 67,* 1776–1789.

Tondo, L., Hennen, J., & Baldessarini, R. (2003). Rapid-cycling bipolar disorder: Effects of long-term treatments. *Acta Psychiatrica Scandinavica, 108,* 4–14.

Undurraga, J., Baldessarini, R. J., Valenti, M., Pacchiarotti, I., & Vieta, E. (2012). Suicidal risk factors in bipolar I and II disorder patients. *Journal of Clinical Psychiatry, 73,* 778–782.

VA/DoD. (2010). *VA/DoD clinical practice guideline for management of bipolar disorder in adults.* Retrieved from http://www.healthquality.va.gov/Management_of_Bi.asp

van der Loos, M., Mulder, P., & Hartong, E. (2009). Efficacy and safety of lamotrigine as add-on treatment to lithium in bipolar depression: A multicenter, double-blind, placebo-controlled trial. *Journal of Clinical Psychiatry, 70,* 223–231.

Vasudev, A., Macritchie, K., Vasudev, K., Watson, S., Geddes, J., Young, A. H. (2011). Oxcarbazepine for acute affective episodes in bipolar disorder. *Cochrane Database Systemic Review, 7*(12), CD004857.

Vieta, E., Cruz, N., & Garcia-Campayo, J. (2008a). A double-blind randomized, placebo-controlled prophylactic trial of oxcarbazepine as adjunctive treatment to lithium in the long term treatment of bipolar I and II disorder. *International Journal of Neuropsychopharmacology, 11,* 445–452.

Vieta, E., Panicali, F., Goetz, I., Reed, C., Comes, M., & Tohen, M. (2008b). Olanzapine monotherapy and olanzapine combination therapy in the treatment of mania: 12-week results from the European Mania in Bipolar Longitudinal Evaluation of Medication (EMBLEM) observational study. *Journal of Affective Disorders, 106,* 63–72.

Vieta, E., Ramey, T., Keller, D., English, P. A., Loebel, A. D., & Miceli, J. (2010a). Ziprasidone in the treatment of acute mania: A 12-week, placebo-controlled, haloperidol-referenced study. *Journal of Psychopharmacology, 24,* 547–558.

Vieta, E., T'joen, C., McQuade, R., Carson, W., Marcus, R., Sanchez, R., . . . Nameche, L. (2008c). Efficacy of adjunctive aripiprazole to either valproate or lithium in bipolar mania patients partially nonresponsive to valproate/lithium monotherapy: A placebo-controlled study. *American Journal of Psychiatry, 165,* 1316–1325.

Vieta, F., Nuamah, I., Lim, P., Yuen, E., Palumbo, J., Hough, D., & Berwaerts, J. (2010b). A randomized placebo- and active-controlled study of paliperidone extended release for the treatment of acute manic and mixed episodes of bipolar I disorder. *Bipolar Disorders, 12,* 230–243.

Wagner, K., Kowatch, R., Emslie, G., Findling, R., Wilens, T., McCague, K., . . . Linden, D. (2006). A double-blind, randomized, placebo-controlled trial of oxcarbazepine in the treatment of bipolar disorder in children and adolescents. *American Journal of Psychiatry, 163,* 1179–1186.

Wang, P. S., Kane, M., Olfson, M., Pincus, H. A., Wells, K. B., & Kessler, R. C. (2005). Twelve-month use of mental health services in the United States. *Archives of General Psychiatry, 62,* 629–640.

Weisler, R., Calabrese, J., & Thase, M. (2008). Efficacy of quetiapine monotherapy for the treatment of depressive episodes in bipolar I disorder: A post hoc analysis of combined results from 2 double-blind, randomized, placebo-controlled studies. *Journal of Clinical Psychiatry, 69,* 769–782.

Weisler, R., Hirschfeld, R., Cutler, A., Gazda, T., Ketter, T., Keck, P., . . . SPD417 Study Group. (2006). Extended-release carbamazepine capsules as monotherapy in bipolar disorder: Pooled results from two randomised, double-blind, placebo-controlled trials. *CNS Drugs, 20,* 219–231.

Weisler, R., Keck, P., Swann, A., Cutler, A., Ketter, T., Kalali, A., & Group, S. S. (2005). Extended-release carbamazepine capsules as monotherapy for acute mania in bipolar disorder: A multicenter, randomized, double-blind, placebo-controlled trial. *Journal of Clinical Psychiatry, 66,* 323–330.

Wozniak, J., Mick, E., Waxmonsky, J., Kotarski, M., Hantsoo, L., & Biederman, J. (2009). Comparison of open-label, 8-week trials of olanzapine monotherapy and topiramate augmentation of olanzapine for the treatment of pediatric bipolar disorder. *Journal of Child and Adolescent Psychopharmacology, 19,* 539–545.

Yatham, L., Kennedy, S., O'Donovan, C., Parikh, S., MacQueen, G., McIntyre, R., . . . Gorman, C. P. (2005). Canadian Network for the Mood and Anxiety Treatments (CANMAT) guidelines for the management of patients with bipolar disorder: Consensus and controversies. *Bipolar Disorders, 7*(Suppl. 3), 5–69.

Young, A., McElroy, S., Bauer, M., Philips, N., Chang, W., Olausson, B., . . . EMBOLDEN I (Trial 001) Investigators. (2010). A double-blind, placebo-controlled study of quetiapine and lithium monotherapy in adults in the acute phase of bipolar depression (EMBOLDEN I). *Journal of Clinical Psychiatry, 71,* 150–162.

Young, L., Joffe, R., & Robb, J. (2000). Double-blind comparison of addition of a second mood stabilizer versus an antidepressant to an initial mood stabilizer for treatment of patients with bipolar depression. *American Journal of Psychiatry, 157,* 124–126.

5

Integrating Psychopharmacology and Cognitive Remediation to Treat Cognitive Dysfunction in the Psychotic Disorders

Alice Medalia, Lewis A. Opler, and Mark G. Opler

INTRODUCTION

Schizophrenia is a complex neuropsychiatric syndrome with both neurodevelopmental and neurodegenerative features. While it is challenging to determine the rates of schizophrenia in a given population, global estimates are approximately 0.5%–1% (Bromet & Fennig, 1999; Harrison, 1997; Lewis & Lieberman, 2000; Thaker & Carpenter, 2001). The causes of schizophrenia are gradually being elucidated, and substantial evidence now exists for several environmental risk factors, including advanced paternal age (Malaspina et al., 2002), prenatal nutritional deprivation (Susser et al., 1996), and *in utero* exposure to infection (Brown, 2011). Genetic and familial factors have also been implicated and suggest that gene–gene as well as gene–environment interactions may occur during pathogenesis.

Different etiologies may be linked to differences in treatment response, symptom presentation, and age of onset in different populations of patients with schizophrenia (Opler et al., 2013; Rosenfield et al., 2010). Symptomatic onset is commonly defined by the emergence of psychosis during early adulthood. Patients who are later diagnosed with schizophrenia exhibit a wide variety of changes during early development, including social withdrawal, decreased functioning, and cognitive impairment. Many of these changes can be seen prior to the onset of psychosis, during a prodromal period lasting several weeks to years (Corcoran, Malaspina, & Hercher, 2005).

Perspectives on what constitute essential symptoms of the disease have evolved over time. The "core" symptoms of schizophrenia are often grouped into five factors, including positive, negative, dysphoric mood, activation/hostility, and autistic preoccupation (White, Harvey, Opler, & Lindenmayer, 1997). There is substantial diversity in the pathophysiology of the symptoms within these groups. In this review, we will discuss a separate dimension of schizophrenia, specifically patterns of cognitive dysfunction that are a universal feature of the disorder.

Cognitive Dysfunction in Schizophrenia

Cognition refers to thinking skills, the intellectual skills that allow you to perceive, acquire, understand, and respond to information. This includes the abilities to pay attention, remember, process information, solve problems, organize and reorganize information, communicate, and act upon information (Medalia & Revheim, 2002). Cognitive impairment is a core symptom of schizophrenia that is evident in the prodrome, at first episode of psychosis, and is persistent but stable, throughout the course of illness (Hoff, Svetina, Shields, Steward, & DeLisi, 2005). Relative to the general population, 70%–80% of people with schizophrenia show cognitive impairments, while close to 100% have cognitive deficits relative to their own premorbid ability level. The magnitude of cognitive deficits is in the range of one to two standard deviations below the mean for healthy individuals as measured by standardized tests of cognition (Green, Kern, & Heaton, 2004). Cognitive functioning has been shown to predict whether a person with schizophrenia will be able to meet functional goals (Green, 1996), and thus it is recognized as an important symptom to target in treatment. The cognitive symptoms most frequently cited as impacting functional outcome in people with schizophrenia include: speed of processing, memory, attention, reasoning, and tact/social cognition. Impairment in these domains is related to symptom and medication management, participation in psychosocial rehabilitation programs, and to skills integral to community integration, including functioning in social, vocational, and educational domains. Cognitive deficits add significantly to illness burden and thus over the last 20 years have increasingly been the focus of developing pharmacologic and behavioral interventions such as cognitive remediation (CR). The following sections provide an overview of the research on these emerging therapeutic interventions.

PHARMACOLOGICAL TREATMENT OF COGNITIVE SYMPTOMS IN SCHIZOPHRENIA

While preliminary evidence suggests that pharmacological agents alone can improve cognition in schizophrenia, there needs to be more research. To "jump start" the process to find behavioral and pharmacological treatments that impact not only cognition but functional outcome as well, NIMH sponsored meetings on the Measurement and Treatment Research to Improve Cognition in Schizophrenia. Among the important accomplishments of MATRICS are the development of the MATRICS Consensus Cognitive Battery or MCCB (Marder & Fenton, 2004) and the identification of the following promising neurochemical targets: D1-dopamine receptors in the prefrontal cortex (PFC); serotonin receptors in the PFC and anterior cingulate cortex; the glutamatergic excitatory synapse; the acetylcholine nicotinic and muscarinic acetylcholine receptors; and the brain gamma-aminobutyric acid (GABA) system (Tamminga, 2006).

In this section we review randomized controlled clinical trials as well as open clinical studies and case reports involving the neurochemical targets suggested by the MATRICS group. We also discuss some other agents showing promise.

D1-Dopamine Mediated Processes

Extensive work on the role for D1-dopamine receptors in the PFC in cognitive functioning in humans and in nonhuman primates has created great interest in the potential role of D1 agonists on cognition in schizophrenia (Arnsten, Cai, Murphy, & Goldman-Rakic, 1994; Goldman-Rakic, Muly, & Williams, 2000).

Randomized Controlled Trials (RCTs) of D1-Dopamine Mediated Processes

Barch and Carter (2005) found that compared to placebo, patients with schizophrenia receiving 0.25 mg/kg of D-amphetamine while maintained on haloperidol or fluphenazine demonstrated improved performance on working memory, language production, and Stroop tasks; given blockade of D2 receptors by ongoing neuroleptic treatment, results were interpreted as being due to stimulation of D1-dopamine receptors in the PFC.

George et al. (2007) were unable to demonstrate that a single 20 mg subcutaneous dose of the dopamine D1 agonist dihydrexidine (DAR-0100) improved cognition; additional studies are ongoing given that a single dose may be insufficient.

Serotonin Receptor Agonists and Antagonists

Meltzer and Massey (2011) underscore that the prototypical antipsychotic clozapine, as well as aripiprazole, asenapine, iloperidone, lurasidone, olanzapine, quetiapine, risperidone, and ziprasidone, produce blockade of serotonin 5-HT2A receptors and directly or indirectly stimulate 5-HT1A receptors; they further suggest that 5-HT6 and 5HT7 receptor antagonism may contribute to beneficial effects of these antipsychotics on cognition and in particular suggest that 5-HT7 antagonism may be the basis for procognitive effects of amisulpride, which has no effect on other 5-HT receptors.

Randomized Controlled Trials of Serotonin Receptor Agonists and Antagonists

Sumiyoshi et al. (2001a) randomly assigned 26 patients with schizophrenia to adjunctive treatment with either 30 mg/day of tandospirone, a 5-HT1A agonist, or placebo and demonstrated improvement in executive function and verbal memory after 6 weeks in the tandospirone group. In a separate study, Sumiyoshi et al. (2007) assigned 73 patients receiving atypical antipsychotics to receive either buspirone, 30 mg/day, or placebo. Significant improvement in the buspirone group was found on the Digit Symbol Substitution Test, a measure of attention and motor performance.

Akhondzadeh et al. (2009) conducted a 12-week, double-blind placebo-controlled trial of the 5-HT3 antagonist ondansetron, adding either ondansetron (8 mg/day) or placebo to risperidone in 30 stable patients. Administration of ondansetron significantly improved visual reproduction, visual paired associate and figural memory subtests of the Wechsler Memory Scale–Revised.

An Open Study of the Serotonin Receptor Agonist Tandospirone

Sumiyoshi et al. (2001b) administered tandospirone, 30 mg/day, to 11 outpatients already stabilized on haloperidol and biperiden. The Wechsler Memory Scale–Revised (WMS–R) was administered at baseline and 4 weeks after addition of tandospirone. Eleven age-matched patients with schizophrenia not given tandospirone were also tested at baseline and after a 4-week interval, but assignment was neither random nor blind. Tandospirone add-on caused significant improvement in the Verbal but not the Visual Memory score of the WMS–R.

Acetylchoinesterase Inhibitors, Nicotinic Receptors, and Muscarinic Receptors

In the 1970s, it was found that Alzheimer's disease was caused, at least in part, by degeneration of cholinergic neurons arising in the nucleus basalis of Meynert. Subsequently, acetylcholinesterase inhibitors (rivastigmine, donepezil, and galantamine) were approved to treat cognition in persons with Alzheimer's disease. Several studies have looked at cholinergic agonists and anticholinesterase inhibitors as potential cognitive enhancers in persons with schizophrenia.

Randomized Controlled Trials of Acetylcholinesterase Inhibitors, Nicotinic Receptors, and Muscarinic Receptors

Lee, Lee, and Kim (2007a) enrolled 24 patients with schizophrenia stabilized on haloperidol and randomly assigned subjects to receive either donepezil (5 mg/day) or placebo for 12 weeks. While the donepezil group compared to the placebo group showed only a trend on MMSE scores at week 12 (p = 0.56), verbal recognition and verbal recall memory improved significantly (p < 0.05).

Most RCTs find donepezil comparable to placebo. These include studies by Freudenreich et al. (2005) in which donepezil or placebo was added for 8 weeks to ongoing AP treatment in 36 community-treated outpatients with schizophrenia and, while well tolerated, neither donepezil or placebo led to changes in any measures of cognition or psychopathology; and a study by Kohler et al. (2007) in which donepezil or placebo was added to APs for 16 weeks without any treatment effects on any cognitive functions or clinical symptoms.

Similarly, despite one open trial suggesting promise for rivastigmine (Lenzi, Maltinti, Poggi, Fabrizio & Colil, 2003), Sharma, Reed, Aasem, & Kumari (2006) did not find improvement in cognition with adjunctive rivastigmine compared to placebo in a randomized, placebo-controlled, double-blind, 24-week study. Using a randomized crossover design, Chouinard et al. (2007) found no improvement in any cognitive variables at 3 months or at 6 months when rivastigmine was added to antipsychotics in patients with schizophrenia and cognitive deficits.

In contrast to donezepil and rivastigmine, galantamine has been shown in several RCTs to improve cognition in schizophrenia. Schubert, Young, and Hicks (2006) randomized 16 patients with schizophrenia or schizoaffective disorder stabilized on risperidone to receive either galantamine (n = 8) or placebo (n = 8). The Repeatable Battery for Assessment of Neuropsychological Status (RBANS) showed that patients receiving galantamine experienced an overall improvement in cognitive performance, with the RBANS Total scale score demonstrating statistical significant in the galantamine group as compared to the placebo group; additionally the RBANS Attention and Delayed Memory subscale performance was robustly improved in patients receiving galantamine, normalizing cognitive performance in these domains.

Lee, Lee, and Kim (2007b) conducted a 12-week double-blind, placebo-controlled trial of galantamine as adjunctive treatment to 24 patients with schizophrenia stabilized on conventional antipsychotics for at least 3 months at the time of enrollment. The score for recognition on the Rey Complex Figure Test improved significantly in patients receiving galantamine. Still to be addressed is whether galantamine trials have been somewhat more successful than donepezil and rivastigmine trials because galantamine, in addition to being an anticholinesterase inhibitor, modulates the nicotinic cholinergic receptors leading to an increase in acetylcholine release (Woodruff-Pak, Vogel, & Wenk, 2001).

Barr et al. (2008) conducted a randomized, double-blind, placebo-controlled, crossover study of the effects of nicotine on attention in nonsmokers with schizophrenia (n = 28) and healthy controls (n = 32). Subjects received either a 14 mg transdermal nicotine or identical placebo path, and a cognitive battery was conducted before and 3 hours after patch application. Nicotine significantly improved the performance of the Continuous Performance Test Identical Pats (CPT-IP) Version I in both schizophrenics and healthy controls. In addition, nicotine reduced commission errors on the CPT-IP while improving performance on a Card Stroop task to a greater extent in persons with schizophrenia.

Zhang et al. (2012) demonstrated that the alpha-7 nicotinic receptor agonist tropisetron improved both immediate and delayed memory. Shekhar et al. (2008) administered either the muscarinic receptor agonist xanomeline or placebo to 20 subjects with schizophrenia in a double-blind, placebo-controlled, 4-week trial examining efficacy on both symptoms and cognitive function using a battery of neuropsychological tests. On the cognitive battery, xanomeline led to clinically significant improvements in verbal learning, short-term memory, list learning, story recall, delayed memory, and digit span tests.

An Open Study of Rivastigmine and a Case Report of Donepezil

Lenzi et al. (2003) added rivastigmine to ongoing antipsychotic therapy in 16 clinically stable subject with schizophrenia for 12 months, starting at 3 mg/day and escalating monthly to a maximum of 12 mg/day. Significant improvements were seen in cognitive function and learning and memory, with trends for improvement in attention. Howard, Thornton, Altman, and Honer (2002) report the case of a 54-year-old woman with schizophrenia and cognitive impairment being treated with quetiapine whose memory improved following the addition of donepezil.

The NMDA-Glutamate System

The clinical observations that would later lead to the glutamate hypofunction hypothesis of schizophrenia were made 50 years ago by Luby and colleagues (Luby, Gottlieb, Cohen, Rosenbaum, & Domino, 1962; Domino & Luby, 2012), who proposed that phencyclidine (PCP) caused a transient psychosis in normal volunteers more like schizophrenia than that caused by lysergic acid diethylamide. Work by Javitt and colleagues (Javitt, Jotkowitz, Sircar, & Zukin, 1987; Javitt & Zukin, 1989) demonstrated that PCP binding blocked the influx of calcium through excitatory channels gated by NMDA-glutamate receptors (NMDARs). Subsequently, Javitt and Zukin (1991) proposed that phencylidine psychosis, by creating hypoglutamatergia, caused a psychosis more like schizophrenia than that caused by amphetamine in that, in addition to positive symptoms, PCP psychosis is characterized by negative and cognitive symptoms as well.

Randomized Controlled Trials (RCTs) of Agents Impacting the NMDA-Glutamate System

Adding N-acetylcysteine, a precursor of glutathione, to maintenance antipsychotic regimens has been shown to decrease symptom severity (Berk et al., 2008) and auditory sensory processing (Lavoie et al., 2008) in patients with schizophrenia.

Goff et al. (2008) randomized 38 outpatients with schizophrenia in a double-blind, parallel-group, 8-week add-on trial of once-weekly d-cycloserine, 50 mg, or placebo, while continuing ongoing treatment with any antipsychotic except clozapine. As an exploratory analysis of memory consolidation, the Logical Memory Test (LMT), modified to measure recall after 7 days, was administered at baseline and after a single weekly dose of d-cycloserine, and found that delayed thematic recall was significantly improved with a single dose of d-cycloserine as compared to placebo.

Mezler, Geneste, Gault, & Marek (2010) have preliminary reports suggesting efficacy without metabolic side effects of LY-2140023, a prodrug that becomes a glutamate receptor agonists, but clinical trials are ongoing.

An Open Study of D-Serine

Kantrowitz et al. (2010) openly administered 30, 60, or 120 mg/kg/day of D-serine to 42 antipsychotic-stabilized patients with schizophrenia or schizoaffective disorder and measured outcome using the PANSS and MATRICS. While significant improvement in PANSS total, positive, negative, and general psychopathology scores were seen on all three doses, on MATRICS, only nonsignificant improvement was found at 30 mg/kg/day, but highly significant improvement was found in patients receiving 60 mg/kg and 120 mg. Plasma levels of D-serine were obtained and correlated with improved symptomatic and neuropsychological function.

The GABA System

Randomized Controlled Trials (RCTs) of Agents Affecting the GABA System

Menzies et al. (2007) randomly assigned eleven patients with chronic schizophrenia to receive either 2 mg of oral lorazepam and a 0.9-mg intravenous flumazenil bolus followed by a flumazenil infusion of 0.0102 mg/minute compared with oral and intravenous placebo. Both groups were tested on a working memory task by personnel blind to assignment. Lorazepam impaired working memory performance, and flumazenil enhanced it.

Lewis et al. (2008) conducted a trial of the GABA agonist MK-0777 on cognition. Fifteen male patients were randomly assigned to receive either MK-0777 (increased to 16 mg/day by the end of week 2) or placebo for 4 weeks in a double-blind, placebo-controlled, parallel group design. Compared with placebo, the group receiving MK-0777 demonstrated improved performance on the N-Back, AX Continuous Performance Test, and Preparing to Overcome Prepotency tests.

Buchanan et al. (2011) enrolled 60 persons with schizophrenia in a 4-week, multicenter, double-blind, placebo-controlled randomized clinical trial. Participants were randomized to: MK-0777 3 mg b.i.d. (n = 18); MK-0777 8 mg b.i.d. (n = 21); or placebo (n = 21). Cognition was assessed with the MATRICS, AX-Continuous Performance Test, and N-Back. There were no significant group differences on the primary outcome measure, the MATRICS Consensus Cognitive Battery composite score, while secondary analyses suggested that participants randomized to placebo performed significantly better on visual memory and reasoning/problem-solving tests than participants assigned to either MK-0777 dose. Despite negative findings, the authors conclude that a more potent partial agonist with greater intrinsic activity at the GABA(A) alpha-2 site might be needed and that the GABA(A) receptor remains a promising target.

Other Agents

Randomized controlled trials of other agents. While randomized controlled trials (Keefe et al., 2007a) suggest that both first- and second-generation antipsychotics improve cognition, both Keefe et al. (2007b) and Goldberg et al. (2007) caution that the improvement may be due to practice effects.

Based on reports that dehydroepiandrosterone (DHEA) was helpful with symptoms and medication side effects, Ritsner, Gibel, Ratner, Tsinovoy, & Strous (2006) randomized 55 patients with schizophrenia to receive either DHEA (200 mg/day) for 6 weeks followed by placebo for 6 weeks or to receive placebo for 6 weeks followed by placebo for 6 weeks. While no benefit was found for side effects and quality-of-life scores, 6 weeks of DHEA but not of placebo was associated with a significant improvement in total PANSS scores and in cognitive functions of visual sustained attention and visual and movements skills.

Norepinephrine via its action at alpha-2a noradrenergic receptors has been shown to improve memory in nonhuman primates (Arnsten, Cai, & Goldman-Rakic, 1988), leading to the hypothesis that alpha-2a noradrenergic receptor agonists might improve cognitive functions in schizophrenia. Friedman et al. (2001) randomized subjects with DSM-IV schizophrenia and receiving haloperidol, fluphenazine, thiothixene, triluoperazine, or risperidone to additionally receive either 2 mg of guanfacine daily or placebo for 4 weeks; 38 subjects completed the clinical trial (guanfacine n = 19; placebo n = 19). Primary analyses did not find clinically significant differences in change scores on any of the cognitive tests. Given that D1 antagonism of typical neuroleptics may have countered possible benefits of guanfacine, post hoc exploratory nonparametric statistics was performed on the 11 patients who were receiving risperidone and revealed differences favoring guanfacine on spatial working memory and continuous performance (CPT) test performance. Friedman et al. (2001) report this as a negative study but also as one that suggests that further research on guanfacine added to risperidone is warranted.

Ritsner et al. (2010) in an 8-week, double-blind, randomized, placebo-controlled trial compared 30 mg/day of pregnenolone (PREG), 200 mg/day of PREG, 400 mg/day of dehydroepiandrosterone, and placebo as adjunctive treatment in 58 schizophrenia and schizoaffective disorder patients. Only subjects randomized to 30 mg/day of pregnenolone demonstrated clinically significant improvement in attention and working memory performance, as well as on positive symptom scores and extrapyramidal side effects.

Levkovitz et al. (2010) recruited and randomly assigned 54 early-phase schizophrenia patients to receive in a 2:1 ratio minocycline 200 mg/day or placebo within 2 weeks of being initiated on an atypical antipsychotic (risperidone, olanzapine, quetiapine, or clozapine). Clinical, cognitive, and functional assessments were conducted at baseline and after 6 months. Minocycline had a beneficial effect on executive function (working memory, cognitive shifting, and cognitive planning).

Cho et al. (2011) conducted an 8-week, double-blind clinical trial, randomly assigning 21 stable outpatients with schizophrenia and stabilized with risperidone to received added mirtazapine or placebo. The mirtazapine group, in addition to showing an improvement in negative symptoms, demonstrated a statistically significant improvement in vocabulary and immediate memory.

Prasad et al. (2012) using a double-blind, placebo-controlled design, randomized subjects with schizophrenia who had been exposed to herpes simplex virus, type 1 (HSV1) to either add-on valacyclovir (n = 12) or placebo (n = 12) to stable doses of APs for 18 weeks. A computerized neurocognitive battery was administered at baseline and follow-up. While symptom severity and side effects, evaluated using standardized scales and a study-specific semistructured checklist, did not improve, the valacyclovir group showed statistically significant improvement in verbal memory, working memory, and visual object learning compared with the placebo group. Both replication in this subgroup as well as in patients not exposed to HSV1 is needed, but this intriguing study provides evidence that supplemental valacyclovir may alleviate impairment in cognition but not psychotic symptoms in persons with schizophrenia with a history of exposure to HSV1.

Strengths/Benefits and Weaknesses/Limitations of Using Pharmacotherapy as the Sole Approach

Pharmacotherapy is never used alone; even a session addressing medication management involves a doctor–patient relationship. In the 1970s, Klerman carried out landmark studies showing that while antidepressants were the first line treatment of major depressive disorder, both cognitive behavioral and interpersonal psychotherapy (IPT) added significant value (Weissman, 2006). What evolved into IPT was initially Klerman's manualization of what occurs in a supportive psychotherapy session exploring stressors while focused on medication management; he did not expect what came to be IPT to significantly affect depression. This "control" turned out to have a positive effect on depression as well as synergizing with antidepressants (Weissman, 2006).

In contrast to these landmark studies on antidepressants and psychotherapy, while we are cautiously optimistic that psychotherapy and medication will work together, evidence supporting cognitive remediation (CR) is further along than that supporting pharmacotherapy alone for cognition in schizophrenia, and definitive studies regarding CR and medication are either in progress or require replication. We speculate, in part based on clinical experience, that CR and some medications when combined will lead to greater improvement in cognition than either alone. Given the growing appreciation of the devastating effects of cognitive impairment, as well as preliminary results from a few ongoing studies, cautious optimism regarding the benefits to patients with schizophrenia that will come from combined pharmacotherapy and CR is warranted.

More rigorous designs, larger studies, and replication are needed, but the work ahead is imperative given the need to treat cognitive symptoms of schizophrenia if our patients are to achieve remission and full recovery.

COGNITIVE REMEDIATION

The two central tenets underlying all treatments defined as cognitive remediation (CR) for people with schizophrenia are that cognition can be rehabilitated through behavioral learning-based interventions and that through targeting specific areas of dysfunction, improvements in cognitive performance are translated to produce changes in real-world functions. These tenets are reflected in the definition of CR as a behavioral-based intervention targeting cognitive deficits (e.g., attention, memory, executive function, social cognition, or metacognition) using scientific principles of learning with the ultimate goal of improving functional outcomes. Specific methods of treating cognition in schizophrenia are founded upon neuropsychology, our understanding of how people learn, and experience treating cognition in neurologically impaired populations. Cognitive remediation for schizophrenia is, first and foremost, predicated upon evidence that people with schizophrenia are capable of learning, and this is reflected both behaviorally and in *neuroplasticity*—the process whereby neurons in the brain adjust their activity in response to new situations or changes in the environment. A growing literature on the neuropsychological and cognitive neuroscience bases of learning supports the concept of neuroplasticity in the brains of people with schizophrenia, despite the underlying neuropathology. Thus, through cognitive exercises, neuroanatomical connections may be strengthened and/or repaired, yielding changes in neuropsychological abilities. Exercises are designed to restore those cognitive skills that have been adversely affected by illness processes. Empirical evidence for this therapeutic mechanism in schizophrenia patients is suggested by data showing that patients receiving CR demonstrate changes in neural activity (Hooker et al., 2012) and a decelerated loss of and, in some cases, increase in gray matter volume, associated with improved cognition (Eack et al., 2010). The physiology of neuroplasticity informs CR practices. For example, findings indicate that poor plasticity is related to poor consolidation during learning, but that, through repeated practice, neural plastic problems may be overcome to allow for learning to occur (Nemeth & Janacsek, 2011) and enable use of adaptive cognitive skills in real-world contexts (Spaulding, Sullivan, & Poland, 2003). Thus, by harnessing the plastic ability of the brain to overcome preexisting neurophysical limitations, CR is able to improve cognitive functioning and facilitate transfer of cognitive skill to daily living skills.

Restorative approaches to CR target basic neuro- and sociocognitive skills, such as information processing in the visual and/or auditory domains, as well as discrete cognitive skills, ranging from simple attention and memory to facial affect identification, to theory of mind and complex problem-solving skills. Typically, drill-and-practice exercises are employed, most often using a computerized cognitive training program, although paper-and-pencil or verbal tasks may be used as well. At present, there are multiple computer-based programs marketed for cognitive remediation for neuropsychiatric disorders. While there have been no head-to-head comparisons of computer based programs, those that engage learners and capitalize on motivational properties of cognitive tasks yield more favorable outcomes (Medalia & Choi, 2010). Restorative approaches targeting basic neurocognitive skills are commonly paired with cognitive, social-cognitive, and social-behavioral exercises, and/or metacognitive (cognition concerning one's own cognition) exercises to contextualize cognitive processes, aid abstraction, and assist individuals to develop strategies for completing cognitive tasks (Hogarty & Flesher, 1999; Medalia, Revheim, & Herlands, 2009; Wykes & Reeder, 2005). Given that cognitive deficits in the schizophrenia population are heterogeneous, broad approaches that target multiple domains and levels of cognitive impairment will likely provide the most benefit to the largest number of patients (Wykes & Huddy, 2009).

Empirical Evidence for the Effectiveness of CR

Impact on Neurocognitive Symptoms

Recent meta-analyses of CR for the neuro-cognitive symptoms of schizophrenia have studied over 2,100 patients (McGurk, Twamley, Sitzer, McHugo, & Mueser, 2007a; Wykes, Huddy, Cellard, McGurk, & Czobor, 2011). Meta-analytic reviews describing schizophrenia samples have characterized the average CR research participant as in their mid 30s and mostly (67%) men, with 12 years of education, mild to moderate psychiatric symptoms, and receiving psychiatric treatment on either an inpatient or outpatient basis. In a clinical research setting, CR is delivered, on average, for a total of 32 hours, 2 to 3 times per week over the course of 17 weeks. CR approaches studied include the sole use of restorative drill-and-practice exercises or a hybrid mix of drill and practice with strategy intervention. Drill and practice entails repetitive trials of an exercise that largely engages one cognitive function—for example, remembering the dinner orders of three restaurant patrons (verbal memory). Strategy interventions are characterized by discussion between clinician and client about techniques to enhance learning—for example, how to use chunking (the appetizers, main courses, desserts) to remember more information. Older CR clinical trials most often delivered the treatment to individuals, although group-based interventions are increasingly being studied as a more cost effective solution. Treatments target on average about three of the following cognitive domains: attention, executive function, working memory, verbal learning and memory, and processing speed (McGurk et al., 2007a; Wykes et al., 2011). Cognitive remediation for schizophrenia has a low medium effect size for improving overall cognition (ES = 0.41–0.45) and daily functioning (ES = 0.36), with a small effect on improving psychiatric symptoms (ES = 0.28) (McGurk et al., 2007a). Effect sizes for specific domains of cognition are small to medium (ES range: 0.25–0.65) with impact on verbal learning and memory typically larger than for other domains. The persistence of effect has been measured in at least 11 studies, showing on average that after 8 months, there continues to be a moderate effect (ES = 0.43) for cognitive improvement (Wykes et al., 2011).

In the most recent meta-analysis of 40 randomized controlled trials (Wykes et al., 2011), greater effect sizes were seen when studies excluded diagnoses other than schizophrenia and schizoaffective disorder, and subjects had less symptom severity. High versus low chlorpromazine equivalence (data only available in 13 studies), subject age, therapy duration, or trial methodology did not impact effect on neuro-cognition or functional outcome. Importantly, when CR was paired with other psychosocial interventions, and strategy instruction was paired with drill and practice, the impact on functional outcome was significantly greater.

Impact on Social Cognitive Symptoms

A 2012 meta-analysis of CR for the social-cognitive symptoms of schizophrenia reviewed 19 studies consisting of 692 subjects, the majority of whom had schizophrenia or schizoaffective disorder (Kurtz & Richardson, 2012). The average research participant was in his mid 30s and male (69%), with 12 years of education, mild to moderate psychiatric symptoms, an average of 13 years illness duration, and receiving psychiatric treatment on either an inpatient or outpatient basis. In a clinical research setting, there is a large range in the way CR for social cognition is delivered: 1–93 hours of treatment delivered over 1–62 weeks. About one third of the studies used a restorative approach to focus primarily on training facial affect perception, whereas 47% (9 of the 19 studies) trained 2–4 domains of social cognition. The domains of social cognition that are targeted with the interventions include facial affect identification and discrimination, social cue perception, theory of mind, and attributional style. The greatest effect sizes for social cognition remediation was found on facial affect perception with a moderate large effect of 0.71 for affect identification, which was significantly moderated by illness duration, and a large effect of 1.01 for affect discrimination. No effect was seen on attributional style, which concerns how intentions are interpreted, or social cue perception, which concerns identification of the nature of social interactions. A moderate effect of 0.46 was seen for theory of mind, and this effect was positively moderated by longer illness duration.

Cognitive remediation for social cognition in schizophrenia has a medium effect size for improving overall psychiatric symptoms (ES = 0.68) but no effect on positive or negative symptoms, suggesting that the overall improvement stemmed from impact on anxiety and mood symptoms. The effects of social cognitive CR on measures of observer-rated community and institutional functioning were large (ES = 0.78) with evidence of a better response in younger, better-educated patients, and patients who are hospitalized and treated with high doses of antipsychotics.

Strengths/Benefits and Weaknesses/Limitations of Using CR as the Sole Approach

While the moderate effect sizes of CR on both cognitive and functional outcomes support its use as an evidence-based treatment, an ongoing challenge for the field is to identify treatment techniques that produce largest cognitive change for each participant, and enhance transfer of cognitive gains to improvement in daily functioning. Thus, the challenge is not only to boost the positive group findings, but also to address the substantial individual differences in response to cognitive remediation interventions. Within this context, the question arises: Is CR as a standalone treatment most effective at promoting change in cognition and functional outcome, or should it be paired with other interventions in order to boost the moderate effect sizes obtained when it is used as the sole treatment? Is it possible to use our knowledge of neuroplasticity, motivation, and learning to engineer better standalone CR interventions that are scalable and personalized? If other interventions are to be used, what are they?

To some extent these questions can be addressed through our understanding of the factors associated with a positive response to CR. Studies that specifically examined predictors of response to CR (Medalia & Richardson, 2005; Fiszdon, Choi, Bryson, & Bell, 2006; Kurtz, Seltzer, Fujimoto, Shagan, & Wexler, 2009; Twamley, Burton, & Vella, 2011) in addition to recent meta-analytic studies (McGurk et al., 2007a; Wykes et al., 2011; Kurtz & Richardson, 2012) that have looked at moderators of effect size for cognitive and functional outcomes, indicate that patient and treatment variables intertwine to produce a positive response. Patient variables that predict response to CR include baseline cognitive profile—and in particular, degree of attention deficit, intrinsic motivation to learn, psychiatric symptom severity, and ability to generalize what is learned. On the treatment side, there is evidence that treatments that supplement drill and practice with strategy instruction, pair CR with other psychiatric rehabilitation programs, provide sufficient treatment intensity, and use better-trained clinicians yield larger effects. Taken together, these findings are consistent with theories of learning and highlight the two-step process of first tuning the cognitive skill and then facilitating generalization to promote functional change.

Currently, there is tremendous interest in harnessing technological innovations in computer software to create training conditions thought to optimize changes in neural activity underlying cognitive learning in schizophrenia (Vinogradov, Fisher, & de Villers-Sidani, 2012). The goal is to create a new generation of restorative computer-based CR exercises that incorporate precisely defined learning events, repeated over thousands of trials, using a standardized series of cognitive exercises that employ implicit learning to improve task performance. Driving these efforts is the belief that if "brain fitness" exercises are properly designed, they could be used as standalone CR, a therapeutic device that would be regulated by the FDA and administered—perhaps remotely—with little need for professional intervention. This effort to articulate and translate neural principles into the design of computerized cognitive training is an emerging field and awaits more evidence that it is effective at improving cognitive skills independent of those trained, or facilitating functional improvement (Murthy et al., 2012; D'Souza et al., 2013).

Alternatively, adjunctive pharmacotherapy might offer promise to surpass the glass ceiling of moderate effect sizes for cognitive enhancement via standalone CR. We know that the most attention impaired and most symptomatic patients have a poorer response to CR. If medications were effective at reducing the attention deficit and symptoms, perhaps response to CR could be enhanced, at least in terms of boosting cognition. Medication also has the advantage of being more scalable than the highly intensive, standalone "brain-fitness" programs, which require many hours of training.

The challenge of enhancing generalization to functional outcome may, on the other hand, require a different approach. When patients make task-specific cognitive gains from repeated drill-and-practice memory training trials, the intent is for the changes to translate to everyday or novel undertakings such as remembering appointments or employment tasks. However, this level of generalization does not always occur (Fiszdon, Choi, Bryson, & Bell, 2006; Kurtz, Seltzer, Fujimoto, Shagan, & Wexler, 2009). The core issue here is that there is considerable variability in the extent to which individuals, regardless of whether they have psychosis, are able to generalize what they learn, and in people with compromised brain function such as schizophrenia, there is often a generalization deficiency, so acquired information may lie stagnant within a single task or domain (Bellack, Weinhardt, Gold, & Gearon, 2001). Therefore, generalization, which is an automatic process in healthy individuals, requires specific, targeted interventions in individuals with schizophrenia.

To achieve better outcomes, many cognitive remediation programs supplement training tasks by conducting therapy sessions, either separate or integrated into the remediation curriculum, that seemingly facilitate the transfer of cognitive gains toward more functional abilities. When the sessions are integrated into CR, it is called a "bridging" technique to facilitate generalization. When the therapy is not integrated, it is called "pairing" or "embedding" CR in a larger psychiatric rehabilitation context. The meta-analytic studies provide strong support for pairing CR within a broader psychiatric rehabilitation context (McGurk et al., 2007a; Wykes et al., 2011). By integrating CR with other behavioral interventions, effect sizes for functional gain move to the large range, whereas standalone programs have significantly lower, small effects on functional outcome. CR has been embedded within the context of a variety of evidence-based programs such as work therapy, supported employment, and functional skills training with positive effects for both neuro-cognitive and functional outcomes, that exceed the effects of providing either CR or the skills training alone (Bowie, McGurk, Mausbach, Patterson, & Harvey, 2012). These data support the synergistic effect of combining CR with psychosocial skills training in order to enhance cognitive skills and promote generalization to measures of community function.

COMBINATION OF PHARMACOLOGICAL AND PSYCHOSOCIAL TREATMENT

A new and promising area of research concerns the combination of pharmacotherapy and cognitive remediation to enhance cognition. While the efficacy of each treatment alone is limited, perhaps together they can synergistically produce larger effect sizes, with more people responding. The rationale for combing treatments is based on our understanding of cognition, neuroplasticity, and the factors associated with successful skills training. Cognitive functions can be conceptualized as existing on a hierarchy, with some cognitive skills relatively circumscribed and basic, and others being complex and multidimensional. Auditory working memory is, for example, a more circumscribed skill than problem solving, which requires working memory, planning, goal setting, prioritization, and reasoning. When treating cognition, treatment can proceed by first targeting the "lower" or more basic discrete cognitive skills, and then moving to target the more complex skills. This approach, which is called "bottom up," assumes that the basic skills must be tuned before more complex skills can work efficiently. At present, cognitive training exercises are used to enhance the more basic cognitive skills, but pharmacotherapy holds out the promise of a more efficient treatment.

If pharmacotherapy targeted the basic cognitive skills, cognitive remediation could then focus on the more complex skills, in essence promoting generalization of cognitive benefit by teaching and training how to use the pharmacologically enhanced basic cognitive skills to perform the multidimensional cognitive tasks.

Research on the mechanisms underlying neuroplasticity also informs a combined treatment approach. There is reason to believe that no matter how effective a pharmacologic agent is, if the cognitive skill is not utilized, then the impact on neuroplasticity and functional outcome will be minimal. This argument, which derives from evidence that neuroplasticity is associated with an active engagement of cognition in novel situations, recognizes cognition as malleable to the extent it is exercised (Valenzuela et al., 2012). Given this, we can expect that if persons with schizophrenia are given medication to improve working memory and attention, but remain relatively homebound and isolated, they will not be exposed to new situations where they can use their skills, will not interact in novel cognitively demanding situations, and will not improve their cognitive and daily functioning. Following this line of reasoning, by combining pharmacotherapy with CR that targets basic and/or complex processes, the neuro chemically enhanced cognitive skills will be exercised in a novel interactive environment and thus more likely to improve.

Finally, our understanding of the factors associated with successful skills training provides a rationale for combining treatments. Psychosocial skills training requires many of the cognitive functions (e.g., attention, learning) that are impaired in schizophrenia. There have been studies showing that cognitive remediation can enhance cognition and therefore skills training (Bell, Zito, Greig, & Wexler, 2008; McGurk, Mueser, Feldman, Wolfe, & Pascaris, 2007b; Bowie et al., 2012), indicating the advantage of pairing a cognitive intervention with skills training. The cognitive remediation improves the attention and memory needed to maximize the benefit from the skills training. However, cognitive remediation takes time. Another possibility is to enhance learning pharmacologically instead of with cognitive remediation, and to pair the pharmacological intervention with a behavioral treatment, thus promoting pharmacologically the learning that is necessary to benefit from skills training.

Combined treatment studies raise questions about the relative efficacy of each treatment alone, compared to the combination of treatments and to placebo. A four-cell design is necessary to answer this: (a) drug and cognitive remediation, (b) drug and control cognitive remediation, (c) placebo drug and cognitive remediation training, or (d) placebo drug and control cognitive remediation. Control cognitive remediation is achieved by having people work on generic computer games that activate attention but are nonspecific in terms of requiring other cognitive skills, and/or by having people repetitively work on the same level of difficulty of a remediation task, so that by never progressing to more challenge, there is no remediation value. Large sample sizes are needed to achieve adequate power to detect differences in the four-cell design. Some researchers have chosen two-cell designs to instead focus on the benefit of adding drug/placebo to everyone receiving a psychosocial intervention and stabilized on antipsychotics, or adding cognitive remediation/control to everyone receiving a given drug.

Review of RCTs

There are two published RCTs involving combined pharmacotherapy and psychosocial treatment (Gottlieb et al., 2011; D'Souza et al., 2013). Gottleib et al. (2011) tested the hypothesis that a dose of d-cycloserine could potentiate beneficial effects of two CBT lessons on delusional severity by promoting consolidation of the learned exercise material. In a double-blind cross-over design, 21 outpatients with schizophrenia or schizoaffective disorder and moderately severe delusions were randomized to receive a single dose of either d-cycloserine 50 mg or placebo in a counterbalanced order on 2 consecutive weeks 1 hour prior to a CBT intervention involving training in the generation of alternative beliefs. Using assessments of symptom change from baseline to 7 days following the first study drug administration and 7 days following the second study drug administration, the authors found no significant d-cycloserine treatment effect on delusional distress or severity. However, there was an unexpected order effect, whereby subjects who received d-cycloserine first had significantly reduced delusional severity, distress, and belief conviction compared to subjects who received placebo first. Noting research with animal models in which d-cycloserine enhances learning only when accompanying the first exposure to training, the authors speculated that d-cycloserine should be administered immediately prior to an initial skills training session to exploit the facilitation of "new learning," whereas subsequent (multiple) skills training sessions may reinforce learning, even if unaccompanied by d-cycloserine.

D'Souza et al. (2013) reported a study that evaluated the feasibility, safety, tolerability, and efficacy of 12 weeks of D-Serine combined with CR, in the treatment of cognitive deficits in schizophrenia subjects at two academic sites in India and the United States. In a randomized, partial double-blind, placebo-controlled, parallel-group design, 104 schizophrenia subjects (U.S. site = 22, India site = 82) were randomized to: (a) D-Serine (30 mg/kg) + CR, (b) D-Serine + control CRT, (c) CR + placebo D-Serine, and (d) Placebo + control CR. A "device" type CR that required five sessions per week on the computer was used. Completion rates were 84% and 100% in the Indian and U.S. samples, respectively. On various outcome measures of safety and tolerability, the interventions were well tolerated. D-Serine and CRT did not show any significant effect on the Global Cognitive Index, although both interventions showed differential site effects on individual test performance. CR resulted in a significant improvement in verbal working memory, and a trend toward improvement in attention/vigilance. This is the first study to demonstrate the feasibility, safety, and tolerability of combination pharmacotherapy and CRT in a multicenter international clinical trial. These preliminary findings provide support for future studies using higher doses of D-Serine that have been shown to be efficacious or other pharmacotherapies, along with different cognitive remediation strategies that are more personalized and that target a range of cognitive skills.

There is one unpublished, completed study that combined Atomoxetine with cognitive remediation. Tamminga (2012) examined the relative benefits of administering to schizophrenia patients treated with the stable, second-generation antipsychotic drug (APD-2): (a) the drug Atomoxetine and cognitive remediation training, (b) the drug Atomoxetine and remediation control training, (c) placebo and cognitive remediation training, or (d) placebo and remediation control training. Atomoxetine or matching placebo was administered at a dose of 40 mg b.i.d. (80 mg/day) or the placebo equivalent. The remediation sequence lasted for 60–90 minutes and was administered three times weekly for 12 weeks; the remediation control was administered on the same schedule and for the same duration. Psychiatric rating scales were completed at baseline, 1, 2, 3, 4, 5, and 6 months, whereas the neuropsychological battery was completed at baseline and at 3 and 6 months. The researchers collected fMRI BOLD data with the N-back task before and after the remediation. Results are pending.

Strengths and Benefits of Using a Combined Approach

Given the growing appreciation of the devastating effects of cognitive impairment and the sound rationale for combining pharmacotherapy and CR, this is a promising new area of research. However, it is also a challenging area in which to conduct research. The large sample sizes required to examine interaction effects, and extended timeline and personnel to accommodate the CR component, add to protocol complexity. Attrition in CR studies is on average less than 10%, and 90% of studies do not provide payment for CR sessions. When medication is added to CR, the study timeline and complexity of the rating requirements increases significantly, as does attrition. This might lead some investigators to start paying subjects to attend CR, a practice that might in fact diminish cognitive outcomes (Medalia & Saperstein, 2012) and certainly limit scalability, since community clinics do not pay subjects to attend treatment programs. By pegging payment to the assessment visits, the potential negative impact on motivation and learning, as well as scalability, can be avoided, while keeping compensation consistent with the obligations required. Another consideration is that just as investigators face choices in the type of pharmacologic agent they choose to study, so do they face choices in the variant of CR they use. Large multisite trials face issues of treatment fidelity and scalability of therapist training, which can make the device like interventions appealing, though support for their efficacy is still pending (Murthy et al., 2011). It is promising that eclectic CR approaches that utilize therapists and incorporate skills training have been successfully used in small multisite trials (Bowie et al., 2012).

Importantly, the choice of CR approach needs to take into consideration whether the goal is to practice the cognitive skill being chemically treated, or to enhance generalization to higher-order skills and everyday functioning. The transfer of cognitive gains to everyday life entails a process called generalization, and appears to require time and opportunities to practice new skill sets and for others to adapt to these changes. Furthermore, a variety of other person-related and environmental factors can also limit the extent to which cognitive abilities transfer to everyday life. Performance anxiety, self-competency beliefs, intrinsic motivation, and an autonomy-supportive environment have all been identified as factors that are significantly associated with improvement in functional performance (Medalia & Saperstein, 2011). While pharmacotherapy may enhance the capacity for a given cognitive skill, a CR approach that addresses these factors may facilitate the translation from capacity to competency in real-life situations. Thus, pairing pharmacotherapy with CR may assure the greatest amount of neuroplasticity and clinical benefit.

REFERENCES

Akhondzadeh, S., Mohammadi, N., Noroozian, M., Karamghadiri, N., Ghoreishi, A., Jamshidi, A. H., & Forghani, S. (2009). Added ondansetron for stable schizophrenia: A double blind, placebo controlled trial. *Schizophrenia Research, 107*, 206–212.

Arnsten, A. F., Cai, J. X., & Goldman-Rakic, P. S. (1988). The alpha-2 adrenergic agonist guanfacine improves memory in aged monkeys without sedative or hypotensive side effects: Evidence for alpha-2 receptor subtypes. *The Journal of Neuroscience, 8*, 4287–4297.

Arnsten, A. F., Cai, J. X., Murphy, B. L., & Goldman-Rakic, P. S. (1994). Dopamine D1 receptor mechanisms in the cognitive performance of young adult and aged monkey. *Psychopharmacology, 116*, 143–151.

Barch, D. M., & Carter, C. S. (2005). Amphetamine improves cognitive function in medicated individuals with schizophrenia and in healthy volunteers. *Schizophrenia Research, 77*, 43–58.

Barr, R. S., Culhave, M. A., Jubelt, L. E., Mufti, R. S., Dyer, M. A., Weiss, A. P., et al. (2008). The effects of transdermal nicotine on cognition in nonsmokers with schizophrenia and nonpsychiatric controls. *Neuropsychopharmacology, 33*, 480–490.

Bell, M. D., Zito, W., Greig, T., & Wexler, B. E. (2008). Neurocognitive enhancement therapy with vocational services: Work outcomes at two-year follow-up. *Schizophrenia Research, 105*, 18–29.

Bellack, A. S., Weinhardt, L. S., Gold, J. M., & Gearon, J. S. (2001). Generalization of training effects in schizophrenia. *Schizophrenia Research, 48*, 255–262.

Berk, M., Copolov, D., Dean, O., Lu, K., Jeavons, S., Schapkaitz, I., et al. (2008). N-acetyl cysteine as a glutathione precursor for schizophrenia—a double-blind, randomized, placebo-controlled trial. *Biological Psychiatry, 64,* 361–368.

Bowie, C. R., McGurk, S. R., Mausbach, B., Patterson, T. L., & Harvey, P. D. (2012). Combined cognitive remediation and functional skills training for schizophrenia: Effects on cognition, functional competence, and real-world behavior. *American Journal of Psychiatry, 169,* 710–718.

Bromet, E. J., & Fennig, S. (1999). Epidemiology and natural history of schizophrenia. *Biological Psychiatry, 46,* 871–881.

Brown, A. S. (2011). Exposure to prenatal infection and risk of schizophrenia. *Frontiers in Psychiatry, 2,* 63.

Buchanan, R. W., Keefe, R. S., Lieberman, J. A., Barch, D. M., Csernansky, J. G., Goff, D. C., et al. (2011). A randomized clinical trial of MK-0777 for the treatment of cognitive impairments in people with schizophrenia. *Biological Psychiatry, 69,* 442–449.

Cho, S. J., Yook, K., Kim, B., Choi, T. K., Lee, K. S., Kim, Y. W., et al. (2011). Mirtazapine augmentation enhances cognitive and reduces negative symptoms in schizophrenia patients treated with risperidone: A randomized controlled trial. *Progress in Neuropsychopharmacology and Biological Psychiatry, 35,* 208–211.

Chouinard, S., Stip, E., Poulin, J., Melun, J. P., Godbout, R., Guuillem, F., & Cohen, H. (2007). Rivastigmine treatment as an add-on to antipsychotics in patients with schizophrenia and cognitive deficits. *Current Medical Research & Opinion, 23,* 575–583.

Corcoran, C., Malaspina, D., & Hercher, L. (2005). Prodromal interventions for schizophrenia vulnerability: The risks of being "at risk." *Schizophrenia Research, 73,* 173–184.

Domino, E. F., & Luby, E. D. (2012). Phencyclidine/schizophrenia: One view toward the past, the other to the future. *Schizophrenia Bulletin, 38,* 914–919.

D'Souza, D. C., Radhakrishnan, R., Perry, E., Bhakta, S., Singh, N. M., Yadav, R., et al. (2013). Feasibility, safety, and efficacy of the combination of D-serine and computerized cognitive retraining in schizophrenia: an international collaborative pilot study. *Neuropsychopharmacology, 38*(3):492–503.

Eack, S. M., Hogarty, G. E., Cho, R. Y., Prasad, K. M., Greenwald, D. P., Hogarty, S. S., & Keshavan, M. S. (2010). Neuroprotective effects of cognitive enhancement therapy against gray matter loss in early schizophrenia: Results from a 2-year randomized controlled trial. *Archives of General Psychiatry, 67,* 674–682.

Fiszdon, J. M., Choi, J., Bryson, G. J., & Bell, M. D. (2006). Impact of intellectual status on response to cognitive task training in patients with schizophrenia. *Schizophrenia Research, 87,* 261–269.

Freudenreich, O., Herz, L., Deckersbach, T., Evins, A. E., Henderson, D. C., Cather, C., & Goff, D. C. (2005). Added donepezil for stable schizophrenia: A double-blind, placebo-controlled trial. *Psychopharmacology, 181,* 358–363.

Friedman, J. I., Adler, D. N., Temporini, H. D., Kemether, E., Harvey, P. D., White, L., et al. (2001). Guanfacine treatment of cognitive impairment in schizophrenia. *Neuropsychopharmacology, 25,* 402–409.

George, M. S., Molnar, C. E., Grenesko, E. L., Anderson, B., Mu, Q., Johnson, K., et al. (2007). A single 20 mg dose of dihydrexidine (DAR-0100), a full dopamine D1 agonist, is safe and tolerated in patients with schizophrenia. *Schizophrenia Research, 93,* 42–50.

Goff, D. C., Cather, C., Gottlieb, J. D., Evins, A. E., Walsh, J., Raeke, L., et al. (2008). Once-weekly D-cycloserine effects on negative symptoms and cognition in schizophrenia: An exploratory study. *Schizophrenia Research, 106,* 320–327.

Goldberg, T. E., Goldman R. S., Burdick, K. E., Malhotra, A. K., Lencz, T., Patel, R. C., et al. (2007). Cognitive improvement after treatment with second-generation antipsychotic medications in first-episode schizophrenia: Is it a practice effect? *Archives of General Psychiatry, 64,* 1115–1122.

Goldman-Rakic, P. S., Muly, E. C., & Williams, G. V. (2000). D1 receptors in prefrontal cells and circuits. *Brain Research Brain Research Reviews, 31,* 295–301.

Gottlieb, J. D., Cather, C., Shanahan, M., Creedon, T., Macklin, E. A., & Goff, D. C. (2011). D-cycloserine facilitation of cognitive behavioral therapy for delusions in schizophrenia. *Schizophrenia Research, 131,* 69–74.

Green, M. F. (1996). What are the functional consequences of neurocognitive deficits in schizophrenia? *American Journal of Psychiatry, 153,* 321–330.

Green, M. F., Kern, R. S., & Heaton, R. K. (2004). Longitudinal studies of cognition and functional outcome in schizophrenia: Implications for MATRICS. *Schizophrenia Research, 72,* 41–51.

Harrison, P. J. (1997). Schizophrenia: A disorder of neurodevelopment? *Current Opinion in Neurobiology, 7,* 285–289.

Hoff, A. L., Svetina, C., Shields, G., Steward, J., & DeLisi, L. E. (2005). Ten year longitudinal study of neuropsychological functioning subsequent to a first episode of schizophrenia. *Schizophrenia Research, 78,* 27–34.

Hogarty, G. E., & Flesher, S. (1999). Practice principles of cognitive enhancement therapy for schizophrenia. *Schizophrenia Bulletin, 25,* 693–708.

Hooker, C. I., Bruce, L., Fisher, M., Verosky, S. C., Miyakawa, A., & Vinograd, S. (2012). Neural activity during emotion recognition after combined cognitive plus social cognitive training in schizophrenia. *Schizophrenia Research, 139,* 53–59.

Howard, A. K., Thornton, A. E., Altman, S., & Honer, W. G. (2002). Donepezil for memory dysfunction in schizophrenia. *Journal of Psychopharmacology, 16,* 267–270.

Javitt, D. C., Jotkowitz, A., Sircar, R., & Zukin, S. R. (1987). Non-competitive regulation of phencyclidine/sigma-receptors by the N-methyl-D-aspartate receptor antagonist D-(-)-2-amino-5-phosphonovaleric acid. *Neuroscience Letters, 78,* 193–198.

Javitt, D. C., & Zukin, S. R. (1989). Interaction of [3H]MK-801 with multiple states of the N-methyl-D-aspartate receptor complex of rat brain. *Proceedings of the National Academy of Sciences USA, 86,* 740–744.

Javitt, D. C., & Zukin, S. R. (1991). Recent advances in the phencyclidine model of schizophrenia. *American Journal of Psychiatry, 148,* 1301–1308.

Kantrowitz, J. T., Malhotra A. K., Cornblatt, B., Silpo, G., Balla, A., Suckow, R. F., et al. (2010). High dose D-serine in the treatment of schizophrenia. *Schizophrenia Research, 121,* 125–130.

Keefe, R. S., Bilder, R. M., Davis, S. M., Harvey, P. D., Palmer, B. W., Gold, J. M., et al. (2007a). Neurocognitive effects of antipsychotic medications in patients with chronic schizophrenia in the CATIE trial. *Archives of General Psychiatry, 64,* 633–647.

Keefe, R. S., Sweeney, J. A., Hongbin, G., Hamer, R. M., Perkins, D. O., McEvoy, J. P, & Lieberman, J. A. (2007b). Effects of olanzapine, quetiapine, and risperidone on neurocognitive function in early psychosis: A randomized double-blind 52-week comparison. *American Journal of Psychiatry, 164,* 1061–1071.

Kohler, C. G., Martin, E. A., Kujawski, E., Bilker, W., Gur, R. E., & Gur, R. C. (2007). No effect of donepezil on neurocognition and social cognition in young persons with stable schizophrenia. *Cognitive Neuropsychiatry, 12,* 412–442.

Kurtz, M. M., & Richardson, C. L. (2012). Social cognitive training for schizophrenia: A meta-analytic investigation of controlled research. *Schizophrenia Bulletin, 38,* 1092–1104.

Kurtz, M. M., Seltzer, J. C., Fujimoto, M., Shagan, D. S., & Wexler, B. E. (2009). Predictors of change in life skills in schizophrenia after cognitive remediation. *Schizophrenia Research, 107,* 267–274.

Lavoie, S., Murray, M. M., Deppen, P., Knyazeva, M. G., Berk, M., Boulat, O., et al. (2008). Glutathione precursor, n-acetyl-cysteine, improves mismatch negativity in schizophrenia patients. *Neuropsychopharmacology, 33,* 2187–2219.

Lee, B. J., Lee, J. G., & Kim, Y. H. (2007). A 12-week, double-blind, placebo-controlled trial of donepezil as an adjunct to haloperidol for treating cognitive impairments in patients with chronic schizophrenia. *Journal of Psychopharmacology, 21,* 421–427.

Lee, S. W., Lee, J. G., Lee, B. J., & Kim, Y. H. (2007). A 12-week, double-blind, placebo-controlled trial of galantamine adjunctive treatment to conventional antipsychotics for the cognitive impairments in chronic schizophrenia. *International Clinical Psychopharmacology, 22,* 63–68.

Lenzi, A., Maltinti, E., Poggi, E., Fabrizio, L., & Colil, E. (2003). Effects of rivastigmine on cognitive function and quality of life in patients with schizophrenia. *Clinical Neuropharmacology, 26,* 317–321.

Levkovitz, Y., Medlovich, S., Riskes, S., Braw, Y., Levkovitch-Verbin, H., Gal, G., et al. (2010). A double-blind, randomized study of minocycline for the treatment of negative and cognitive symptoms in early-phase schizophrenia. *Journal of Clinical Psychiatry, 71,* 138–149.

Lewis, D. A., Cho, R. Y., Carter, C. S., Eklund, K., Forster, S., Kelly, M. A., & Montrose, D. (2008). Subunit-selective modulation of GABA type A neurotransmission and cognition in schizophrenia. *American Journal of Psychiatry, 165,* 1585–1593.

Lewis, D. A., & Lieberman, J. A. (2000). Catching up on schizophrenia: Natural history and neurobiology. *Neuron, 28,* 325–334.

Luby, E. D., Gottlieb, J. S., Cohen, B. D., Rosenbaum, G., & Domino, E. F. (1962). Model pychoses and schizophrenia. *American Journal of Psychiatry, 119,* 61–67.

Malaspina, D., Brown, A., Goetz, D., Alia-Klein, N., Harkavy-Friedman, J., Harlap, S., & Fennig, S. (2002). Schizophrenia risk and paternal age: A potential role for de novo mutations in schizophrenia vulnerability genes. *CNS Spectrums, 7,* 26–29.

Marder, S. R., & Fenton, W. (2004). Measurement and treatment research to improve cognition in schizophrenia: NIMH MATRICS initiative to support the development of agents for improving cognition in schizophrenia. *Schizophrenia Research, 72,* 5–9.

McGurk, S. R., Mueser, K. T., Feldman, K., Wolfe, R., & Pascaris, A. (2007b). Cognitive training for supported employment: 2–3 year outcomes of a randomized controlled trial. *American Journal of Psychiatry, 164,* 437–441.

McGurk, S. R., Twamley, E. W., Sitzer, D. I., McHugo, G. J., & Mueser, K. T. (2007a). A meta-analysis of cognitive remediation in schizophrenia. *American Journal of Psychiatry, 164,* 1791–1802.

Medalia, A., & Choi, J. (2010). Motivational enhancements in schizophrenia. In V. Roder & A. Medalia (Eds.), *Understanding and treating neuro- and social cognition in schizophrenia patients* (pp. 1–15). Basel, Switzerland: Karger.

Medalia, A., & Revheim, N. (2002). *Dealing with cognitive dysfunction associated with psychiatric disabilities: A handbook for families and friends of individuals with psychiatric disorders.* Albany, NY: New York State Office of Mental Health.

Medalia, A., Revheim, N., & Herlands, T. (2009). *Cognitive remediation for psychological disorders.* New York: Oxford University Press, Inc.

Medalia, A., & Richardson, R. (2005). What predicts a good response to cognitive remediation interventions? *Schizophrenia Bulletin, 31,* 942–953.

Medalia, A., & Saperstein, A. (2011). The role of motivation for treatment success in schizophrenia. *Schizophrenia Bulletin, 37*(Suppl 2), S122–S128.

Meltzer, H. Y., & Massey, B. W. (2011). The role of serotonin receptors in the action of atypical antipsychotic drugs. *Current Opinion Pharmacology, 11,* 59–67.

Menzies, L., Ooi, C., Kamath, S., Suckling, J., McKenna, P., Fletcher, P., et al. (2007). Effects of gamma-aminobutyric acid-modulating drugs on working memory and brain function in patients with schizophrenia. *Archives of General Psychiatry, 64,* 156–167.

Mezler, M., Geneste, H., Gault, L., & Marek, G. J. (2010). LY2140023, a prodrug of the group II Metabotropic glutamate receptor agonist LY-404039 for the potential treatment of schizophrenia. *Current Opinion Investigational Drugs, 11,* 833–845.

Murthy, N. V., Mahnckem, H., Wexler, B. E., Maruff, P., Inamadar, A., Zucchetto, M., et al. (2012). Computerized cognitive remediation training for schizophrenia: An open label, multi-site, multinational methodology study. *Schizophrenia Research, 139,* 87–91.

Nemeth, D., & Janacsek, K. (2011). The dynamics of implicit skill consolidation in young and elderly adults. *Journal of Gerontology Series B: Psychology Sciences and Social Sciences, 66,* 15–22.

Opler, M., Malaspina, D., Gopal, S., Nuamah, I., Savitz, A. J., Singh, J., & Hough, D. (2013). Effect of parental age on treatment response in adolescents with schizophrenia. *Schizophrenia Research,* doi:pii: S0920-9964(13)00528-8. 10.1016/j.schres.2013.10.001. PMID: 24144440

Prasad, K. M., Eack, S. M., Keshavan, J. S., Yoken, R. H., Iyengar, S., & Nimgaonkar, V. L. (2012). Antiherpes virus-specific treatment and cognition in schizophrenia: A test-of-concept randomized double-blind placebo-controlled trial. *Schizophrenia Bulletin, 39*(4), 857–866.

Ritsner, M. S., Gibel, A., Ratner Y., Tsinovoy, G., & Strous, R. (2006). Improvement of sustained attention and visual and movement skills, but not clinical symptoms, after dehydroepiandrosterone augmentation schizophrenia: A randomized, double-blind, placebo-controlled, crossover trial. *Journal of Clinical Psychopharmacology, 26,* 495–499.

Ritsner, M. S., Gibel, A., Shleifer, T., Boguslavsky, I. Zayed, A., Maayan, R., et al. (2010). Pregnenolone and dehydroepiandrosterone as an adjunctive treatment in schizophrenia and schizoaffective disorder: An 8-week, double-blind, randomized, controlled, 2-center, parallel-group trial. *Journal of Clinical Psychiatry, 7,* 1351–1362.

Rosenfield, P. J., Kleinhaus, K., Opler, M., Perrin, M., Learned, N., Goetz, R., et al. (2010). Later paternal age and sex differences in schizophrenia symptoms. *Schizophrenia Research, 116,* 191–195.

Schubert, M. H., Young, K. A., & Hicks, P. B. (2006). Galantamine improves cognition in schizophrenic patients stabilized on risperidone. *Biological Psychiatry, 60,* 530–533.

Sharma, T., Reed, C., Aasem, I., & Kumari, V. (2006). Cognitive effects of adjunctive 24-weeks rivastigmine treatment to antipsychotics in schizophrenia: A randomized, placebo-controlled, double-blind investigation. *Schizophrenia Research, 85,* 73–83.

Shekhar, A., Potter, W. Z., Lightfoot, J., Lienemann, J., Dube, S., Mallinckrodt, C., et al. (2008). Selective muscarinic receptor agonist xanomeline as a novel treatment approach to schizophrenia. *American Journal of Psychiatry, 165,* 1033–1039.

Spaulding, W. D., Sullivan, M., & Poland, J. (2003). *Treatment and rehabilitation of severe mental illness.* New York: Guilford Press.

Sumiyoshi, T., Matsui, M., Nohara, S., Yamashita, I., Kurachi, M., Sumiyoshi, C., et al. (2001a). Enhancement of cognitive performance in schizophrenia by addition of tandospirone to neuroleptic treatment. *American Journal of Psychiatry, 158,* 1722–1725.

Sumiyoshi, T., Matsui, M., Yamashita, I., Nohara, S., Kurachi, M., Uehara, T., et al. (2001b). The effect of tandospirone, a serotonin(1A) agonist, on memory function in schizophrenia. *Biological Psychiatry, 49,* 861–868.

Sumiyoshi, T., Park, S., Jayathilake, K., Roy, A., Ertugrul, A., & Meltzer, H. Y. (2007). Effect of buspirone, a serotonin1A agonist, on cognitive function in schizophrenia: A randomized, double-blind, placebo-controlled study. *Schizophrenia Research, 95,* 158–168.

Susser, E., Neugebauer, R., Hoek, H. W., Brown, A. S., Lin, S., Labovitz, D., & Gorman, J. M. (1996). Schizophrenia after prenatal famine. Further evidence. *Archives of General Psychiatry, 53,* 25–31.

Tamminga, C. A. (2006). The neurobiology of cognition in schizophrenia. *Journal of Clinical Psychiatry, 67,* 9–13.

Tamminga, C. A. (2012). Treating cognition in schizophrenia with atomoxetine and cognitive remediation. Retrieved from http://clinicaltrials.gov/ct2/show/study/NCT00628394

Thaker, G. K., & Carpenter, W. T. (2001) Advances in schizophrenia. *Nature Medicine, 7,* 667–671.

Twamley, E. W., Burton, C. Z., & Vella, L. (2011). Compensatory cognitive training for psychosis: Who benefits? Who stays in treatment? *Schizophrenia Bulletin, 37*(Suppl 2), S55–S62.

Valenzuela, M. J., Matthews, F. E., Brayne, C., Ince, P. Halliday, G., Kril, J. J., et al. (2012). Multiple biological pathways link cognitive lifestyle to protection from dementia. *Biological Psychiatry, 71,* 783.

Vinogradov, S., Fisher, M., & de Villers-Sidani, E. (2012). Cognitive training for impaired neural systems in neuropsychiatric illness. *Neuropsychopharmacology, 37,* 43–76.

Weissman, M. M. (2006). A brief history of interpersonal psychotherapy. *Psychiatric Annals, 36,* 553–557.

White, L., Harvey, P. D., Opler, L. A., & Lindenmayer, J. P. (1997). Empirical assessment of the factorial structure of clinical symptoms in schizophrenia. A multisite, multimodel evaluation of the factorial structure of the positive and negative syndrome scale. The PANSS Study Group. *Psychopathology, 30,* 263–274.

Woodruff-Pak, D. S., Vogel, R. W., & Wenk, G. L. (2001). Galantamine: Effect on nicotinic receptor binding, acetylcholinesterase inhibition, and learning. *Proceedings of the National Academy of Science, 98,* 2089–2094.

Wykes, T., & Huddy, V. (2009). Cognitive remediation for schizophrenia: It is even more complicated. *Current Opinions in Psychiatry, 22,* 161–167.

Wykes, T., Huddy, V., Cellard, C., McGurk, S. R., & Czobor, P. (2011). A meta-analysis of cognitive remediation for schizophrenia: Methodology and effect sizes. *American Journal of Psychiatry, 168,* 472–485.

Wykes, T., & Reeder, C. (2005). *Cognitive remediation therapy for schizophrenia: Theory and practice.* London: Brunner Routledge.

Zhang, X. Y., Liu, L., Hong, X., Chen, C. D., Xiu, M. H., Yang, F. D., et al. (2012). Short-term tropisetron treatment and cognitive and p50 auditory gating deficits in schizophrenia. *American Journal of Psychiatry, 169,* 974–981.

Integrating Psychopharmacology and Psychotherapy in Anxiety Disorders*

David S. Shearer, Christopher S. Brown, S. Cory Harmon, and Bret A. Moore

INTRODUCTION

The following chapter synthesizes research on the use of various treatment modalities for anxiety disorders, including psychotherapy, pharmacotherapy, and the combination of the two. The latter modality is of particular interest given the widespread usage of this treatment strategy in clinical practice and the paucity of research documenting its efficacy (Olfson, Marcus, Wan, & Geissler, 2004). Combined treatment makes rational sense, and perhaps for this reason it has not been examined empirically to the same extent as psychotherapy and pharmacotherapy individually.

Olafson et al. (2004) compared data from the 1987 National Medical Expenditure Survey (NMES) and 1999 Medical Expenditure Panel Survey (MEPS) to describe trends in outpatient anxiety disorder treatment. They found an increase in the use of combined psychotherapy/pharmacotherapy from 29% of the 1987 sample to 32% of the 1999 sample. During that time period, the use of anxiolytics decreased, while the use of antidepressants increased (although neither trend reached statistical significance). The authors note that "[a]lthough combination treatment is supported by treatment guidelines and expert opinion, there is currently little experimental evidence concerning this clinical practice" (p. 1171). Earlier reports estimated an even higher amount of combined treatment in this population. Wardle (1990) estimated that 55%–95% of patients presenting for psychotherapeutic anxiety treatment were taking some form of medication for anxiolytic effect. With the prevalence of this treatment approach in mind, we now review psychotherapeutic, pharmacologic, and combined treatment approaches for anxiety disorders.

GENERALIZED ANXIETY DISORDER

Generalized anxiety disorder (GAD) is relatively common; data from the U.S. National Comorbidity Study Replication yielded a 12-month prevalence of 3.1% (Kessler, Chiu, Demler, & Walters; 2005b) and a lifetime prevalence of 5.7% (Kessler, Berglund, Demler, Jim, Merkangas, & Walters; 2005a). The hallmark symptoms of GAD are pervasive and excessive worry about multiple events or activities (e.g., health, relationships, work). The worry is judged to be uncontrollable, and occurs conjointly with three or more of the following symptoms: muscle tension, restlessness/feeling keyed up, concentration difficulties, irritability, being easily fatigued, and sleep disturbance. GAD is diagnosed when the worry occurs more days than not, for a period of at least 6 months, and causes significant distress or impairment in functioning. GAD is not diagnosed when the worry focus is a feature of another Axis I disorder (e.g., worry about having a panic attack, as in panic disorder). GAD is frequently comorbid with other anxiety, mood, and substance-related disorders. As opposed to everyday worry, GAD worry is pervasive, longer lasting, is perceived to be less controllable, often occurs without an identifiable trigger, more often has accompanying physical symptoms, is more distressing, and significantly interferes with functioning (APA, 2000).

Psychological Treatment

The American Psychological Association (2012) notes strong research support for the use of cognitive behavioral therapy (CBT) in treating GAD. Techniques in common usage include cognitive therapy related to the process and value of worrying, practicing effective problem solving, relaxation training, planning time for both worrying and pleasurable/activating activities, in vivo exposure, imaginal exposure, and systematic desensitization (APA, 2012; Gould, Otto, Pollack, & Yap, 1997). Emerging therapies showing initial promise include acceptance- and mindfulness-based therapies. One trend that has emerged from research on GAD is a conceptualization of the disorder as "basic anxiety," implying that its treatments may also be useful for other anxiety disorders (Rapee, 1991).

CBT approaches of various types have been shown to produce robust treatment gains, which are often maintained over periods of a year or longer, and with relatively low dropout rates (Borkovec, Newman, Pincus, & Lytle, 2002; Borkovec & Ruscio, 2001; Butler, Fennell, Robson, & Gelder, 1991; Covin, Ouimet, Seeds, & Dozois, 2008; Gorman, 2003). Treatment appears most effective when delivered individually to younger adults (Covin et al., 2008). However, variability in study outcomes has caused debate, leading some to draw more cautious conclusions about the magnitude of treatment effects or their maintenance over extended periods of time (Durham & Allan, 1993; Westen & Morrison, 2001). Interpersonally focused therapy may be a useful addition to standard CBT due to the negative effect of interpersonal problems on remission and maintenance of treatment gains (Borkovec et al., 2002).

CBT is an effective sole treatment for GAD. Its effects appear equivalent to those of commonly prescribed medications, and in many cases, treatment strategy decisions may be based primarily on patient preference and access to care (Mitte, 2005b). A variety of therapy techniques have demonstrated effectiveness, and they are widely taught within mental health training programs. Some literature suggests that the best candidates for this form of GAD treatment are younger patients who present to treatment from nonpsychiatric settings, such as through referral from a primary care provider (Covin et al., 2008; Durham & Allan, 1993).

Pharmacologic Treatment

Several pharmacologic agents are U.S. Food and Drug Administration (FDA) approved in the treatment of GAD: alprazolam, duloxetine, escitalopram, paroxetine, and venlafaxine. The general consensus is that selective serotonin reuptake inhibitors (SSRIs), dual serotonin and norepinepherine reuptake inhibitors (SNRIs), and nonsedating tricyclic antidepressants

(TCAs) are the first-line pharmacologic agents for GAD (e.g., Ballenger et al., 2001; Davidson et al., 2010). A disadvantage of pharmacologic treatment versus CBT is that the long-term efficacy of pharmacologic agents may be reduced after discontinuation of the medication (e.g., Gould, Otto, Pollack, & Yap, 1997). Benzodiazapines (BZDs) have been found efficacious in the treatment of GAD and may be particularly relevant for short-term treatment given their rapid onset (Goodman, 2004; Hidalgo, Tupler, & Davidson, 2007; Mitte, Noack, Steil, & Hautzinger, 2005). However, the side effect profile of BZDs, and the evidence that they do not effectively treat the depression that is commonly comorbid with GAD, may make this class of medication less appealing than the SSRIs and SNRIs for long-term treatment (Gorman, 2003). More recent meta-analyses support the use of antidepressants as first-line treatment for GAD. For example, Schmitt and colleagues found imipramine, venlafaxine, and paroxetine superior to placebo in the treatment of GAD in an analysis that spanned research through 2002 (Schmitt, Gazalle, Lima, Cunha, Souza, & Kapczinski, 2004). Hidalgo et al. (2007) reported in their meta-analysis that a calcium channel blocker (pregabalin) and an antihistamine (hydroxyzine) had the greatest effect sizes for the treatment of GAD followed by an SNRI (venlafaxine XR), benzodiazepines, and SSRIs. Interestingly, Hidalgo and colleagues found in their review of studies that buspirone (a serotonin 1A partial agonist) was not a highly effective treatment for GAD. This evidence suggests that prescribers may wish to consider hydroxyzine or pregabalin as well as SSRIs and SNRIs. Ballenger and colleagues (2001) note that hydroxyzine may be best used for acute symptoms, as it may not treat common comorbid disorders of GAD (as do the SSRIs/SNRIs) and due to its sedating effects.

Combined Treatment

Some earlier research has suggested a potential benefit of combining medication with psychological treatment for GAD. Lader and Bond (1998) found evidence that buspirone combined with psychological treatment may be advantageous. In their meta-analysis of research comparing pharmacological to psychological treatments for anxiety disorders, Bandelow and colleagues determined there is insufficient data on combined treatment strategies to draw definitive conclusions about outcomes for GAD (Bandelow, Seidler-Brandler, Becker, Wedekind, & Ruther, 2007). A more recent meta-analysis evaluated combined psychological and pharmacological treatment for anxiety disorders (Hoffman, Sawyer, Korte, & Smits, 2009). Medications in this meta-analysis included benzodiazepines, SSRIs, buspirone, a TCA, and a reversible monoamine oxidase inhibitor (MAOI). The authors report that "... medication may be a useful strategy for enhancing acute phase CBT outcomes, especially for panic disorder and generalized anxiety disorder" (p. 167). This is reminiscent of the Power et al. (1990) finding that combined treatment with medication (diazepam) and CBT was advantageous in the early treatment phase for GAD (Power et al., 1990). Therefore, the most gains in combination therapy for GAD may occur in the early phases of treatment. This would potentially include the use of BZDs during the acute stages of combined treatment (Hearon & Otto, 2012) and for short-term treatment purposes as well (e.g., Mitte et al., 2005).

SPECIFIC PHOBIA

Specific phobia is the most common of all the anxiety disorders, with a lifetime prevalence of 12.5% (Kessler et al., 2005a) and a 12-month prevalence of 8.7% (Kessler et al., 2005b). Specific phobia is characterized by an irrational fear of an object or situation (e.g., spiders, closed spaces) that the person realizes is unreasonable. Exposure to the feared object results in avoidance or else is endured with intense anxiety or dread (e.g., "white knuckling" through a plane ride). In children, recognizing that the fear is unreasonable is not required to make the diagnosis. Specific phobia is only diagnosed if the avoidance or anxiety causes significant impairment in functioning or if the individual experiences substantial distress about having the phobia. There are five phobia subtypes: animal, natural environment, blood–injection–injury, situational, and other. LeBeau et al. (2010) report the following lifetime prevalence estimates: animal (3.3%–7%), natural environment (e.g., heights, storms; 8.9%–11.6%), blood–injection–injury (3.2%–4.5%), situational (e.g., flying, elevators; 5.2%–8.4%), and other (e.g., fear of choking, vomiting). Women are approximately twice as likely as men to have a specific phobia, and onset typically occurs in childhood or early adolescence (APA, 2000). Despite strong support for the efficacy of treatment, many individuals with phobias do not seek care (Antony & Barlow, 2002).

Psychological Treatment

The American Psychological Association (2012) notes strong research support for the use exposure therapy with specific phobia. The most effective type of exposure (e.g., in vivo, imaginal, virtual reality, systematic desensitization) often depends upon the specific feared stimulus. Exposure therapy, which is effective with a variety of anxiety disorders, stands out as nearly universally recommended for treating specific phobias, although it must be implemented with care (Grös & Antony, 2006; Wolitzky-Taylor, Horowitz, Powers, & Telch, 2008). In vivo exposure may be the most effective variant, although it can be the most challenging for patients (Choy, Fyer, & Lipsitz, 2007; Wolitzky-Taylor et al., 2008). Virtual reality exposure has been studied more with phobias than with other anxiety disorders, in particular for situations that are difficult or impractical to encounter in vivo (e.g., multiple airline flights, looking over the edge of tall buildings; Krijn, Emmelkamp, Olafsson, & Biemond, 2004; Parsons & Rizzo, 2008; Powers & Emmelkamp, 2008). There is limited but positive support for a one-session, 3-hour treatment modality combining hierarchical exposure, modeling, cognitive therapy, and behavioral reinforcement (Zlomke & Davis, 2008). The technique of applied muscle tension is used only with the blood–injection–injury subtype to counteract fainting.

Exposure-based psychotherapy is a clear first-line treatment for most specific phobias due to its large effect and high success rate. As with panic disorder, anxiolytic medication may prove counterproductive due to reinforcement of avoidant behavior and slower habituation to stimuli. However, some patients may be unwilling or unable to commit to the challenging exposure exercises of psychotherapy, or may have phobias that they encounter infrequently enough (e.g., only flying once every few years) to justify use of anxiolytics as a primary treatment strategy.

Pharmacologic Treatment

The general consensus among experts is that pharmacologic monotherapy for specific phobias is generally not indicated (Choy et al., 2007; Craske, Antony, & Barlow, 2006; Fyer, 1987; Grös & Antony, 2006). While some have suggested there may be some short-term utility of medication, particularly BZDs (e.g., Choy et al., 2007; Hayward & Wardle, 1997; Whitehead, Blackwell, & Robinson, 1978), others have described BZDs to be of limited or no utility in the treatment of specific phobia (Bernadt, Silverstone, & Singleton, 1980; Sartory, 1983; Thom, Sartory, &

Johren, 2000). At this time, medication monotherapy may be best used as a secondary strategy for patients unable or unwilling to access behavioral therapy (BT) or CBT treatment.

Grös and Anthony (2006) have commented on the lack of research investigating antidepressant use for specific phobia. There is some limited evidence suggesting that SSRIs may be effective; Abene and Hamilton (1998) provide two case reports of fluoxetine treatment for depression having the unintended effect of resolving a comorbid fear of flying that predated the onset of depression in both cases. Benjamin, Ben-Zion, Karbofsky, and Dannon (2000) report the results of a pilot study comparing paroxetine to placebo for patients meeting specific phobia criteria. They found that paroxetine (up to 20 mg once daily) was superior to placebo in this small-scale pilot study. Overall, more research is needed to investigate the utility of SSRIs in the treatment of specific phobias.

In most cases, medication alone appears to be at best of limited efficacy, and in some cases ineffective, as compared to the robust response reported for behavioral and cognitive therapies for specific phobia (Wolitzky-Taylor et al., 2008). In addition, psychological treatment of specific phobias may result in longer-term gains than medication only regimens (e.g., Thom et al., 2000).

Combination Treatment

Reviews written regarding the use of pharmacologic treatment combined with psychotherapy have generally concluded that BT or cognitive therapy (CT) alone is either more, or equally as effective, as the combination of BT or CT and medication in the treatment of specific phobia (Choy, Fyer, & Lipsitz, 2007; Grös & Antony, 2006; Hoffman, Pollack, & Otto, 2006; Sartory, 1983). Overall, leaders in the field have generally been cautious or discouraging with regard to the use of medication (e.g., Antony & Barlow, 2002; Craske et al., 2006; Gamble et al., 2010; Harvey & Rapee, 2002; Hoffman et al., 2006; McGlynn & Vopat, 1994; Otto, Basden, Leyro, McHugh, & Hoffman, 2007; Roy-Byrne & Cowley, 2007). The few randomized trials conducted in this area tend to support this conclusion (Marks, Viswanathan, Lipsedge, & Gardner, 1972; Whitehead et al., 1978; Wilhelm & Roth, 1997; Zitrin, Klein, & Woerner, 1978; Zitrin, Klein, Woerner, & Ross, 1983).

A recent development in the combined (medication plus psychotherapy) treatment of specific phobias involves the use of d-cycloserine (DCS), a partial agonist at the glycine recognition site on the glutamatergic N-methyl-D-aspartate (NMDA) receptor. DCS may facilitate memory consolidation of extinction that occurs during cognitive and behavior treatments for specific phobia (Hoffman et al., 2006). DCS is being investigated as an adjunct to enhance behavioral and cognitive treatments for specific phobias (Norberg, Krystal, & Tolin, 2008). Ressler et al. (2004) conducted a randomized, double-blind study of adults with acrophobia to compare exposure treatment results when combined with either DCS or placebo. They concluded that DCS reduces anxiety by enhancing the learning process that occurs during exposure. Hoffman et al. (2006) found similar results in a study evaluating the use of DCS with exposure therapy for social anxiety disorder. Norberg et al. (2008) conducted a meta-analysis of the research on facilitation of fear extinction and exposure therapy with d-cycloserine. They searched published studies between 1998 and 2007. Effect sizes for DCS were "large" across all samples analyzed. The authors concluded that DCS enhances fear extinction/exposure therapy in persons with anxiety disorders. The patients in the two studies that did not support the use of DCS in combination with exposure therapy were noted to have nonclinical levels fear, perhaps accounting for this disparity (Guastella, Dadds, Lovibond, Mitchell, & Richardson, 2007; Guastella, Lovibond, Dadds, Mitchell, & Richardson, 2007).

In sum, the combination of pharmacologic treatments with CBT for specific phobia has not yielded significantly positive effects as compared with CBT alone. While promising, the use of DCS in conjunction with exposure/extinction therapy has not been evaluated comprehensively enough to recommend as a treatment at this time.

SOCIAL PHOBIA

Social phobia (also termed social anxiety disorder) is a commonly occurring disorder; lifetime prevalence in the United States is estimated at 12.1% (Kessler et al., 2005a) and 12-month prevalence at 6.8% (Kessler et al., 2005b). Social phobia is characterized by persistent and impairing fear in social or performance situations, which results in anxiety and avoidance of the situation. Frequently feared situations are parties, public speaking, interactions with authority figures, and meeting new people. In adults, the fear is recognized as excessive or unreasonable, but this feature may be absent in children. While fear of embarrassment is common in social situations, the anxiety and avoidance must significantly interfere with functioning or the individual must be significantly distressed about having the phobia in order for the diagnosis to be warranted.

Socially phobic individuals fear embarrassment in social or performance situations and are concerned they will be judged negatively by others. Physiologic responses such as increased heart rate, nausea, sweating, tremors, muscle tension, gastrointestinal disturbance, and/or blushing are common, and in severe cases, phobic individuals may have a panic attack. Social phobia can be self-perpetuating in that fear in social situations may result in anxiety symptoms, which then may have an actual effect on performance, leading to increased embarrassment, more anticipatory anxiety, and so on (APA, 2000).

Psychological Treatment

The American Psychological Association (2012) reports strong research support for CT and BT for social phobia. Specific techniques include cognitive restructuring related to social rejection and failure, exposure to anxiety-provoking social situations to the point of habituation, behavioral experiments, applied relaxation, and social skills training. There is evidence for the effectiveness of a broad array of CBT techniques (Rodebaugh, Holaway, & Heimberg, 2004), with the greatest evidence for exposure therapy (Gould, Buckminster, Pollack, Otto, & Yap, 1997; Heimberg, 2001; Taylor, 1996). Some studies indicate that CT may often be an unnecessary addition to exposure (Gould et al., 1997), or that it may be effective because it contains elements of exposure (Taylor, 1996). Group treatment appears equally effective as compared to individual treatment and may be more cost effective (Gould et al., 1997; Heimberg, 2001). Although there is some evidence for the effectiveness of social skills training, this does not necessarily indicate that skill deficits are inherent to the disorder (Rowa & Antony, 2005). Promising innovations with limited research to date include virtual reality exposure therapy, interpersonal therapy, mindfulness-based therapy, and novel stimulus exposure (Parsons & Rizzo, 2008; Rowa & Antony, 2005).

Psychotherapy alone can be an effective treatment for social phobia, and the cost effectiveness of group treatment may also come with the benefit of additional exposure to social situations. As is the case with other anxiety disorders, challenging exercises may be unpalatable for some patients, and therapy can represent a significant commitment of time and effort.

Pharmacologic Treatment

While research on treatment of social phobia with pharmacologic agents combined with psychological treatments has been limited, there has been an abundance of research evaluating the efficacy of pharmacologic monotherapy for social phobia. Multiple meta-analytic reviews have established the efficacy and tolerability of SSRIs in the treatment of social phobia (Federoff & Taylor, 2001; Gould, Buckminster, Pollack, Otto, & Yap, 1997; Hedges, Brown, Shwalb, Godfrey, & Larcher, 2007; Ipser, Kairiki, & Stein, 2008; Stein, Ipser, & van Balkom, 2009b). There is evidence that SNRIs may be equally effective to SSRIs in the treatment of social phobia (Ipser et al., 2008; Roy-Byrne & Cowley, 2007). The FDA has approved several medications for the treatment of social phobia including the SSRIs fluvoxamine, paroxetine, and sertraline, and the SNRI venlafaxine. Both MAOIs and reversible inhibitors of monoamine A (RIMAs) have demonstrated efficacy in treating this disorder as well (e.g., Gould et al., 1997; Sareen & Stein, 2000; Stein et al., 2009b). However, MAOIs and RIMAs may be less effective than SSRIs (Stein et al., 2009b) and/or may have side effects or dietary restrictions that make them a less tolerable or desirable treatment option (Gould et al., 1997; Ipser et al., 2008). Similarly, high-potency benzodiazepines (e.g., alprazolam and clonazepam) have been found to be a beneficial treatment for social phobia (Federoff & Taylor, 2001; Roy-Byrne & Cowley, 2007), but utility may be attenuated by risk of dependence and side effects (Gould et al., 1997; Ipser et al., 2008). Some earlier reviews suggest that beta-blockers might be useful for treating performance-related anxiety, but perhaps not generalized social anxiety (Gould et al., 1997; Sareen & Stein, 2000). A more recent meta-analysis by Ipser and colleagues (2008) suggests that beta-blockers lack efficacy in the treatment of performance-related anxiety as well. In their comprehensive review of pharmacologic treatments for anxiety disorders, Roy-Byrne and Cowley (2007) report that there is some limited evidence for the use of other medications including gabapentin, pregabalin, topirimate, and bupropion. More research is needed to clarify the role and efficacy of these medications in the treatment of social anxiety.

Combined Treatment

Results of studies evaluating the utility of combining pharmacotherapy with psychological treatment for social phobia have been mixed and mostly disappointing. Randomized controlled trials (RCTs) evaluating the combination of fluoxetine with CBT have not shown an advantage to combination treatment over monotherapies (Clark et al., 2003; Davidson et al., 2004). Blomhoff and colleagues found that in a general medicine practice environment, sertraline plus CBT was an efficient and effective treatment for social phobia (Blomhoff et al., 2001). In an RCT evaluating the combination of moclobemide (RIMA) with either psychological management or CBT versus CBT plus placebo, the researchers found some advantage early in treatment for the combined group on outcome measures (Prasko et al., 2006). However, upon 6-month follow-up, there was no advantage of combined treatment, and best outcomes were for CBT groups. In an RCT investigating the treatment of social phobia with phenelzine (an irreversible MAOI), group CBT, and their combination, results showed that the combination of phenelzine and group CBT were "superior to either treatment alone and to placebo on dimensional measures as well as rates of response and remission" (p. 287; Blanco et al., 2010). However, the potential side effects of irreversible MAOIs such as hypertensive crisis, insomnia, and weight gain, in addition to the dietary restrictions, may make this class of medication less attractive as a first-line treatment. More studies of combined treatment for social phobia are clearly needed.

OBSESSIVE-COMPULSIVE DISORDER

Obsessive-compulsive disorder (OCD) is an uncommon relative to other anxiety disorders; lifetime prevalence is estimated at 1.6% (Kessler et al., 2005a), and 12-month prevalence is estimated at 1.0% (Kessler et al., 2005b). The essential feature of OCD is time-consuming (i.e., more than 1 hour per day), markedly distressing, and/or significantly impairing obsessions or compulsions that are recognized at some point by the individual as unreasonable or excessive. Obsessions are recurrent and persisting thoughts, images, or impulses that are intrusive and distressing and are recognized by the individual as being self-generated. The obsessions cause significant anxiety, and the individual seeks to neutralize them with an alternate thought or action (e.g., compulsion) or tries to ignore or suppress the content. Compulsions are repetitive behaviors or mental actions that the individual feels compelled to perform in response to the obsession to reduce anxiety or prevent a feared negative consequence. Compulsions are excessive and/or are not realistically connected to the event they are designed to neutralize. Common compulsions are counting, silently repeating words over and over, checking, and hand washing. OCD is associated with significant impairment in quality of life with most individuals exhibiting fluctuations in illness severity depending on stress level (APA, 2000).

Psychological Treatment

The American Psychological Association (2012) notes strong research support for the use of exposure with response prevention (ERP) and CT, and modest support for acceptance and commitment therapy. The American Psychiatric Association (APA, 2007) reports strongest research support for ERP, with a lesser degree of support for CT. Any variant of CBT is superior to nonspecific psychotherapy, with much of the difference in CBT studies due to variation in baseline symptom severity (Gava et al., 2009). ERP is most effective if exercises are supervised by the therapist, response prevention is complete, and in vivo and imaginal exposure are both utilized (Abramowitz, 1996). Exposure-based therapy has a significant impact on overall symptom severity and on anxiety, but it does not have a significant effect on the depressed mood that is sometimes associated with OCD (Cox, Swinson, Morrison, & Lee, 1993). Although BT and CBT significantly help the average patient, it is also typical for some moderate symptoms to persist (Eddy, Dutra, Bradley, & Westen, 2004).

Psychotherapy alone has been found to be an effective treatment for OCD, although there is clearer evidence than with some anxiety disorders for the benefits of combined treatment (APA, 2007), especially given the common persistence of some symptoms even in cases of successful therapy. One significant factor influencing the choice to pursue therapy is the availability of a therapist proficient in ERP, which can be a challenging technique to implement effectively (Kobak, Greist, Jefferson, Katzelnick, & Henk, 1998).

Pharmacologic Treatment

Pharmacologic monotherapy recommendations for OCD have mostly centered on clomipramine, a tricyclic antidepressant (TCA), and the SSRIs. Clomipramine is a potent serotinergic drug, and its metabolite has noradrenergic reuptake inhibition properties. RCTs and subsequent reviews and meta-analyses have consistently demonstrated the superiority of clomipramine to placebo, and sometimes a slight advantage of clomipramine over SSRIs (e.g., Ackerman & Greenland, 2002; Abramowitz, 1997; Christensen, Hadzi-Pavlovic, Andrews, & Mattick, 1987; The Clomipramine Collaborative Study Group, 1991; Cox, Swinson, Morrison, & Lee, 1993; Freeman, Trimble, Deakin, Stokes, & Ashford, 1994; Mundo, Maina, & Uslenghi, 2000; Piccinelli, Pini, Bellantuono, &Wilkinson, 1995; Pigott et al., 1990). In choosing between an SSRI and clomipramine, the provider must weigh the risk/benefit profile. The potential treatment advantage of clomipramine (Ackerman & Greenland, 2002) must be balanced against the greater risk of lethality in overdose for clomipramine versus the SSRIs as a class. In addition to risk of lethal overdose, clomipramine may have more problematic side effects that could lead to early discontinuation of treatment. As a result, an SSRI may be a best first choice over clomipramine (e.g., Jefferson et al., 1995; Kobak et al., 1998). Of note, SSRIs are the first-line recommendation in the American Psychiatric Association practice guidelines for treatment of OCD (APA, 2007). Clomipramine, fluoxetine, fluvoxamine, paroxetine, and sertraline are FDA-approved for OCD.

There is little support, too few or inadequate studies, unacceptable side effects, or unclear results for the recommendation of the use of MAOIs, other TCAs (nortriptyline, imipramine), buspirone, atypical antipsychotics, or BZDs as monotherapy to treat OCD at this time (e.g., Foa, Steketee, Kozak, & Dugger, 1987; Hollander, Kaplan, & Stahl, 2003; Jenike, Baer, Minichiello, Rauch, & Buttolph, 1997; McDougle et al., 1995; Thoren, Asber, Cronholm, Jornestedt, & Traskman, 1980; Vallejo, Olivares, Marcos, Bulbena, & Menchon, 1992).

Combined Treatment

Randomized controlled studies of combined behavioral therapy (e.g., exposure therapy) and pharmacotherapy have centered around two medications: clomipramine and fluvoxamine (Cottraux et al., 1990; Foa et al., 2005; Marks, Stern, Mawson, Cobb, & McDonald, 1980). Foa and colleagues (2005) report that clomipramine is an effective monotherapy for OCD. However, they go on to conclude that exposure and ritual prevention (a type of behavior therapy) as a monotherapy may be superior to either clomipramine alone, or by extension, other serotonin reuptake inhibitors (SRIs). In an early study, Marks et al. (1980) concluded that in vivo exposure was the treatment of choice for OCD, but noted that clomipramine is useful for compulsive ritualizers when they also present with depressed mood.

DCS has been investigated as adjunctive treatment to facilitate behavioral therapy for OCD (Storch et al., 2007; Wilhelm et al., 2008). Storch et al. found no significant support for the use of DCS as an adjunctive treatment for OCD. Wilhelm et al. (2008) found some initial support that DCS augmentation may accelerate and potentiate behavior therapy for OCD, at least in the initial stages of treatment.

An earlier meta-analysis compared the use of SRIs (clomipramine, fluoxetine, and fluvoxamine) to BT, CT, and the combination of these therapies in the treatment of OCD (van Balkom et al., 1994). This meta-analytic review spanned outcome studies between 1970 and 1993 and concluded the following: SRIs, BT, and combined BT + SRI treatments were superior to placebo; patients rated BT as superior to SRIs and combined treatment superior to SRIs alone; assessor ratings showed no difference between these three treatments (SRI, BT, or SRI + BT) (van Balkom et al., 1994). Another meta-analysis was conducted that evaluated psychotherapy, pharmacotherapy, and a combination of these therapies in the treatment of OCD (Eddy, Dutra, Bradley, & Westen, 2004). This study spanned published articles between 1980 and 2001 and included three psychotherapies (CT, ERP, CBT) and 14 different pharmaco-therapies. Of the psychotherapies, the more behaviorally based therapies were more effective than the more cognitively based therapies. Overall, effect sizes for combined pharmacotherapy and psychotherapy were found to be "... higher than those reported for psychotherapy alone, suggesting that combined pharmacotherapy and psychotherapy may be the most effective intervention for patients with OCD" (p. 1023). The authors go on to caution that this is a tentative conclusion due to the small number of studies available for combined treatment. A meta-analysis conducted by Hoffman, Sawyer, Korte, and Smits (2009) affirms Eddy and col-leagues' findings that combined CBT with pharmacotherapy is more effective than CBT alone in the acute treatment of OCD, but perhaps not over the long term. Together this research provides evidence that combined treatment may be an effective treatment strategy for OCD.

POSTTRAUMATIC STRESS DISORDER

Posttraumatic stress disorder (PTSD) is defined by reexperiencing, avoidance, numbing, and hyperarousal following exposure to a traumatic event in which death or serious injury oc-curred or was threatened, and which resulted in intense fear, helplessness, or horror. The symptoms are distressing or impair functioning (APA, 2000). Lifetime and 12-month preva-lence estimates for PTSD in the U.S. general population are 6.8% (Kessler et al., 2005a) and 3.5% (Kessler et al., 2005b), respectively.

Reexperiencing may take the form of intrusive memories, flashbacks, or nightmares. Some individuals experience intense distress or psychological reactivity when confronted with re-minders of the event. The event is so distressing that individuals seek to avoid reminders (e.g., thoughts, emotions, conversations, activities, places, people) associated with the event and may also forget important details of the trauma. Individuals may feel detached from others, exhibit a restricted range of emotion, lose interest in activities, and may believe there is no need to plan for the future, as though life has been foreshortened. Hyperarousal may include sleeplessness, irritability, concentration difficulties, being easily startled, and overly vigilant to surroundings. PTSD can occur in both adults and children, with symptom onset typically occurring within 3 months of the trauma. Social support, family history, personality, and childhood experiences may mediate the development of the disorder.

Psychological Treatment

The American Psychological Association (2012) notes strong research support for the use of pro-longed exposure (PET), cognitive processing therapy (CPT), present-centered therapy (PCT), seeking safety (with comorbid substance disorder), and, more controversially, eye movement desensitization retraining (EMDR). Further, it notes modest support for stress inoculation train-ing (SIT), and notes that psychological debriefing has no support and is potentially harmful.

The American Psychiatric Association (APA, 2004; Benedek, Friedman, Zatzick, & Ursano, 2009) notes the strongest research support for exposure-based psychotherapies, with addi-tional support noted for other CBT techniques and to a lesser extent psychodynamic therapy. Psychotherapies with high levels of research support tend to include elements of narration, cognitive restructuring, in vivo exposure, stress inoculation or relaxation, and psychoeduca-tion (Foa & Meadows, 1997). Overall, although modern psychotherapies for PTSD (espe-cially those with exposure components) are highly effective and show initial results with good maintenance, many patients continue to experience significant residual symptoms, and for chronic PTSD a rehabilitative rather than curative model may be most appropriate (Bradley, Greene, Russ, Dutra, & Westen, 2005; Shalev, Bonne, & Eth, 1996).

Early research on virtual reality exposure suggests that it holds promise, especially for cuing memories of scenarios that are difficult to replicate otherwise (e.g., plane crash, combat; Krijn et al., 2004). Simple narrative interventions may be administered effectively by lay people in situations lacking professional treatment (Foa & Meadows, 1997). Single-session debriefings immediately after potentially traumatic events do not improve natural recovery and may be actively harmful (American Psychological Association, 2012; van Emmerik, Kamphuis, Hulsbosch, & Emmelkamp, 2002).

Particularly, focused research attention has been paid to military/veteran populations with combat/deployment trauma, and the Department of Veterans Affairs and Department of Defense (2010) have collaborated on clinical practice guidelines. The guidelines note significant benefit with trauma-focused therapy (including exposure and/or cognitive therapy) and stress inoculation therapy; some benefit with psychoeducation, imagery rehearsal, psychodynamic therapy, hypnosis, relaxation training, group therapy, and family therapy; and unknown benefit with Internet-based CBT, ACT, and dialectical behavior therapy.

Several psychotherapeutic approaches to PTSD enjoy extensive research support and are considered first-line treatments without adjunctive pharmacotherapy. However, the chronic nature of symptoms, variety of potentially traumatic events, and often-complex environmental influences involved with PTSD mean that many patients will not achieve adequate improvement with therapy alone. Many individuals with this disorder may be reluctant to seek any treatment because of stigma and/or genuine systemic/environmental consequences (Yehuda, 2002). Addressing psychiatric comorbidity, substance abuse, and physical injury may complicate treatment, and cultural considerations must always be considered (Hoge, 2011; VA & DoD, 2010).

Psychopharmacologic Treatment

There is clear evidence that pharmacological treatments for PTSD are effective, and the SSRIs are generally considered to be the first-line pharmacologic treatment for this disorder (Albucher & Liberzon, 2002; Benedek, Friedman, Zatzick, & Ursano, 2009; Golier, Legge, & Yehuda, 2007; Hageman, Andersen & Jorgensen, 2001; Stein, Ipser, & Seedat, 2009a; Stein, Seedat, van der Linden, & Zungu-Dirwayi, 2000; Yehuda, 2002). The FDA has approved two SSRIs for the treatment of PTSD: sertraline and paroxetine. It is possible that the SNRI venlafaxine may have some benefit, and there is some case evidence supporting this (e.g., Hammer & Frueh, 1998), but the abundant evidence for SSRIs continues to make them the first-line choice. Interestingly, there is evidence that suggests the SSRIs may be less effective for the subset of patients with combat-related PTSD (Benedek et al., 2009). Nevertheless, Hoge (2011) concludes that both the SSRIs and SNRIs both have a role in the treatment of patients with combat-related PTSD. Both the TCAs and MAOIs have shown benefit in the treatment of this disorder (Albucher & Liberzon, 2002; Golier et al., 2007; Yehuda, 2002), but may be considered second- and third-line therapies, respectively, due to issues related to safety and tolerability (Hageman et al., 2001).

An exciting development in this area has been the finding that the alpha-adrenergic antagonist, prazosin, can be an effective augmentation treatment for trauma-related nightmares and sleep problems (Raskind et al., 2003; Raskind et al., 2007; Taylor et al., 2008). Prazosin may be used to augment existing pharmacotherapy, which would include SSRIs and other antidepressants (Benedek et al., 2009).

BZDs are generally not recommended in the treatment of PTSD due to a variety of factors that include questions about efficacy (e.g., Braun, Greenberg, Dasberg, & Lerer, 1990; Golier et al., 2007). In relationship to the treatment of combat-related PTSD, Hoge (2011) discourages the use of BZDs due to evidence that they may impair recovery or interfere with extinction of fear conditioning. Similar concerns have been put forward by others (e.g., Yehuda, 2002).

The use of atypical antipsychotics (e.g., risperidone, quetiapine) as an adjunctive treatment to SSRIs or SNRIs for PTSD has come into question recently (Hoge, 2011). Several reviewers reported that initial data showed a potential benefit of this class of medications as adjunctive treatments for PTSD, especially for partial responders (Benedek et al., 2009; Golier et al., 2007). However, a recent RCT investigating the use of adjunctive risperidone in a veteran population found no significant additive benefits over placebo (Krystal et al., 2011). Further research is needed to clarify whether these medications have a role in the treatment of PTSD, especially given the potential for serious side effects.

Overall, we can conclude that antidepressant medications, especially serotinergic agents, are effective in the short- and long-term treatment of PTSD. Prazosin appears to be an effective augmenting agent to address the nightmares and sleep problems frequently seen with PTSD.

Combination Treatment

Combining psychological and pharmacologic therapies in the treatment of PTSD is frequently seen in clinical practice and has been recommended by some experts (e.g., Ballenger et al., 2000; Shalev, Bonne, & Eth, 1996). However, the authors of a review of pharmacological enhancement of behavioral therapy for PTSD report that the ". . . majority of studies combining antidepressant and other anti-anxiety medication with behavioral therapies have not been successful or have been mixed at best" (p. 294; Choi, Rothbaum, Gerardi, & Ressler, 2009). In their recent meta-analysis of combined pharmacotherapy and psychological treatment for PTSD, Hetrick and colleagues determine there is not enough evidence available to conclude that combined therapy is any more or less effective than either treatment alone (Hetrick, Purcell, Garner, & Parslow, 2010). Results of individual RCTs have been mixed. Rothbaum and associates found evidence that partial responders to an SSRI (sertraline) improved somewhat with the addition of CBT, but there was no comparison between combined treatment and CBT alone (Rothbaum et al., 2006). In a small pilot study, adding CBT to sertraline resulted in substantial gains over sertraline alone (Otto et al., 2003). On the other hand, another RCT found no additive benefit in augmenting CBT with a different SSRI (paroxetine CR) over placebo (Simon et al., 2008). Some have made the intriguing and intuitively appealing suggesting that D-cycloserine (DCS) may provide enhancement of fear extinction for patients with PTSD. Whether DCS might be reliably beneficial in the treatment of PTSD remains to be seen.

In sum, despite common clinical practice and the rational conclusion that two effective therapies might be improved in combination, evidence is still too limited to produce a clear conclusion regarding the potential benefit of combining psychological with psychopharmacological treatment.

AGORAPHOBIA WITHOUT HISTORY OF PANIC

Agoraphobia occurs in multiple disorders, and appropriate diagnosis depends on accompanying symptoms. Agoraphobia without history of panic disorder centers on the fear of panic-like symptoms (as opposed to fearing a full panic attack, as in panic disorder) occurring where it would be difficult or embarrassing to exit or where help is perceived to be unlikely or unavailable. Panic-like symptoms are any of 13 panic attack symptoms (e.g., palpitations, chest pain, etc.) or may be other feared physical symptoms (e.g., loss of bladder control). Common feared situations include traveling on buses or trains, venturing outside alone, and being in a crowd or standing in line. Agoraphobic individuals typically avoid feared situations or enlist a companion to join them. When impossible, the event may be endured, albeit with significant distress. Lifetime prevalence is estimated at 1.4% of the U.S. general population (Kessler et al., 2005a); 12-month prevalence is 0.8% (Kessler et al., 2005b). Agoraphobia without history of panic may frequently be misdiagnosed; a specific phobia or social phobia diagnosis should be carefully ruled out (APA, 2000).

Psychological, Pharmacological, and Combination Treatment

Almost no research has been conducted on the treatment of agoraphobia without history of panic disorder, especially when compared to the plentiful research on treating panic disorder with and without agoraphobia. There are at least two studies examining psychotherapeutic treatment. Techniques studied included direct exposure (e.g., reinforcement, extinction, in vivo exposure), indirect exposure (e.g., imaginal exposure, systematic desensitization), and other techniques (e.g., behavior scheduling, problem solving; Jansson & Öst, 1982). Direct exposure techniques appear to have the greatest impact on agoraphobic avoidance, with gains made posttreatment and maintained at 6-month follow-up (Jansson & Öst, 1982; Trull, Nietzel, & Main, 1988). Research on combined psychotherapy and pharmacotherapy for agoraphobia without history of panic disorder is virtually nonexistent; this paucity of information makes it difficult to draw definitive conclusions. Housebound agoraphobic patients can have difficulty accessing in-person care, and the future growth of telehealth services holds promise for increasing their access to behavioral treatment.

PANIC DISORDER WITH AND WITHOUT AGORAPHOBIA

Recurrent, unexpected panic attacks are the hallmark feature of panic disorder, which affects approximately 4.7% of U.S. adults in their lifetime (Kessler et al., 2005a) and 2.7% within a 12-month period (Kessler et al., 2005b). Panic attacks consist of the sudden development of at least four of the following symptoms that peak within 10 minutes: rapid heart rate, sweating, trembling, perceived shortness of breath, choking sensation, chest pain, nausea, dizziness, derealization/depersonalization, fear of loss of control/going crazy, fear of dying, numbness/tingling, and chills or hot flashes. Panic disorder is only diagnosed if panic attack criteria are met and the individual then experiences at least 1 month of worry or behavioral change related to the attack. To merit a diagnosis of panic disorder, at least two panic attacks must be perceived as occurring "out of the blue." Panic attacks with known situational triggers also commonly co-occur in individuals diagnosed with panic disorder. Panic attack frequency and constancy varies widely; some individuals experience regular panic attacks (e.g., daily for a week) and then no attacks for months, while others may experience more moderate frequency (e.g., once per week) over many weeks. Worry about having additional panic attacks may result in agoraphobic behavior.

Psychological Treatment

The American Psychological Association (2012) notes strong research support for the use of CBT techniques including in vivo exposure to avoided situations, interoceptive exposure to bodily sensations, CT, and relaxation training. It notes modest research support for applied relaxation and psychodynamic therapy, with the latter described as controversial. The American Psychiatric Association (APA, 2009) clinical practice guideline recommends CBT as an effective treatment provided it is available and the patient is willing. CBT has been found to have a comparatively low dropout rate and to be deliverable in group format to increase cost effectiveness (Gould, Otto, & Pollack, 1995).

There is much research comparing the relative effectiveness of various CBT techniques. Exposure techniques are consistently found to be centrally important to impacting both panic and agoraphobia, and are better applied in a graded fashion than through flooding (Bakker, van Balkom, Spinhoven, Blaauw, & van Dyck, 1998; Clum, Clum, & Surls, 1993; Cox, Endler, Lee, & Swinson, 1992). CT appears to have little additive impact on anxiety, but is useful for associated depression that is less responsive to exposure (Mitte, 2005a). Some research indicates that CBT techniques for panic may be applied effectively in a self-management/ self-help format (Barlow, Ellard, Hainsworth, Jones, & Fisher, 2005). Virtual reality exposure is emerging as a potentially useful addition to CBT treatment for this disorder (Powers & Emmelkamp, 2008).

Psychotherapy alone is effective as a first-line treatment for this disorder, with exposure-focused CBT techniques recommended as a primary tool. Exposure therapy, and in particular interoceptive exposure, relies upon the bodily experience of anxiety symptoms, and concurrent use of anxiolytic medication may suppress such sensations and lead to difficulty attaining habituation. In some cases, the use of such medication may also constitute an avoidance behavior that perpetuates the disorder (Ahmed, Westra, & Stewart, 2008; Barlow, Craske, Cerny, & Klosko, 1989; Spiegel & Bruce, 1997). However, as with many anxiety disorders, exposure-based techniques may be challenging or unpalatable for certain patients, especially if applied incorrectly. If they are implemented, the patient should first clearly understand the rationale and commit to regular exercises.

Pharmacologic Treatment

SSRIs have become predominantly the first-line pharmacologic treatment for panic disorder with and without agoraphobia due to efficacy, low side effect profile, absence of tolerance/ withdrawal, efficacy in treating comorbid depression, and lack of dietary restrictions (Bakker, van Balkom, & Stein, 2005; Roy-Byrne & Cowley, 2007). Three SSRIs are FDA-approved for the treatment of panic disorder: fluoxetine, paroxetine, and sertraline. An SNRI, venlafaxine, has been shown to be effective in treating uncomplicated panic (Bradweijn, Stein, Salinas, Emlien, & Whitaker, 2005), and there is some evidence that treatment response to venlafaxine may be similar to that of the SSRIs (Pollack et al., 2007). Some have found that TCAs (especially imipramine) and SSRIs are equally effective in treating panic disorder (Mitte, 2005a; Bakker et al., 2005; Bakker, Van Balkom, & Spinhoven, 2002). However, the side effect profile and tolerability of TCAs is not as advantageous as that for SSRIs (Bakker et al., 2002; Roy-Byrne & Cowley, 2007).

High-potency BZDs, such as alprazolam, have been found to be as effective as SSRIs and TCAs in the treatment of panic disorder (e.g., Mitte, 2005a). Despite this efficacy, experts in the field caution that BZDs may best be considered a second-line or adjunct treatment for panic disorder due to problems with risk of tolerance and withdrawal, absence of efficacy for depressive symptoms, and a more problematic side effect profile (Bakker et al., 2005; Michelson & Marchione, 1991; Mitte, 2005a). Further, there is some evidence that use of BZDs may result in a loss of treatment gains after discontinuation, especially when compared to CBT alone (Marks et al., 1993). Given the rapid relief and efficacy of high-potency BZDs for panic disorder, some recommend that this medication be used to provide rapid relief from symptoms and/or in those patients who do not respond to other treatments (Roy-Byrne & Cowley, 2007).

MAOIs have some research supporting efficacy with panic disorder, but their significant side effect profile and dietary restrictions decrease their utility (Liebowitz, Gorman, Fyer, & Klein, 1985; Sheehan, Ballenger, & Jacobsen, 1980). Beta-blockers have not proven to be superior to placebo and are not recommended (Michelson & Marchione, 1991). Despite evidence that a variety of pharmacologic agents can be effective for panic disorder, some 20% to 40% of these patients are nonresponders to pharmacologic treatment for panic disorder (Slaap & denBoer, 2001).

Combined Treatment

Several meta-analyses have been conducted investigating the combination of psychopharmacology and CBT interventions for panic disorder with and without agoraphobia (Furukawa, Watanabe, & Churchill, 2007; Gould, Otto, & Pollack, 1995; Mitte, 2005a; Van Balkom et al., 1997). Some have suggested a slight superiority of combination treatment versus either CBT or pharmacotherapy alone (Furukawa et al., 2007; Mitte, 2005a; Van Balkom et al., 1997). This combination of psychopharmacologic and CBT interventions may be advantageous earlier in treatment (Barlow et al., 2000; Van Balkom et al., 1997). However, when longer-term outcomes are considered, CBT is often at least as (if not more) effective, especially after medication has been discontinued (e.g., Barlow, Gorman, Shear, & Woods, 2000; Marks et al., 1993; Mitte, 2005a). In an early meta-analysis, investigators found that CBT treatment was more advantageous than either pharmacotherapy or combined treatment alone, was more cost effective, and resulted in less attrition from treatment (Gould et al., 1995). In a review, McHugh, Smits, and Otto (2009) conclude that combined treatments show only a "limited benefit over monotherapies" (p. 600). In an RCT study of imipramine and CBT, Barlow et al. (2000) found monotherapies and combined treatments to be more effective than placebo in the acute phase. However, ultimately, CBT was better tolerated and had longer lasting effects. Watanabe, Churchill, and Furukawa (2009) concluded that there are too few studies of combined CBT with BZDs to make any definitive statements regarding this treatment approach. However, in an RCT study of combined alprazolam plus CBT, the authors found minimal gains during treatment that ultimately resulted in treatment gain losses after taper of the alprazolam during follow-up. Relapse was common for these participants after cessation of the alprazoalm (Marks et al., 1993). Alternatively, Marks and colleagues found significant effect sizes and maintenance of treatment gains with exposure treatment alone, suggesting that CBT monotherapy was preferred to use of a BZD alone or in combination. In an investigation of buspirone, an RCT found that CBT plus buspirone was no better than CBT plus placebo for panic (Cottraux et al., 1995). Findings regarding the use of DCS as an adjunctive treatment to exposure therapy for panic have been mixed with some positive results (Otto et al., 2010) and some negative (Siegmund, Goefels, & Finck, 2011). In sum, it does not appear that combined treatment for panic confers substantial additional benefit in the treatment of panic disorder in adults over that of psychological or pharmacological monotherapy, and that BZD use may interfere with outcome in some cases (Aaronson, Katzman, & Gorman, 2007). More research is needed in this area before conclusive decisions can be made regarding the use of combination therapies for panic with or without agoraphobia.

CONCLUSION

This chapter reviewed the current state of research on the use of psychological, pharmacological, and combined therapies to treat individual anxiety disorders. Overall, there is a great deal of support for psychotherapeutic interventions, a similarly large amount of supporting evidence for the use of pharmacologic agents for many of the anxiety disorders, and more mixed conclusions, or insufficient data, regarding the use of combined treatment strategies. This last finding is particularly interesting given the frequent clinical practice of combining psychological and pharmacological treatments for anxiety disorders in general.

There is relatively stronger evidence supporting the use of a combined strategy for several anxiety disorders. Patients with GAD may respond well, especially in the early stages of psychotherapy, to the addition of pharmacotherapy. Combined strategies may be an effective approach for the treatment of OCD as well. Surprisingly, while monotherapies for PTSD enjoy solid support, the evidence in favor of the combination of the two is still too limited to draw clear conclusions. However, adjunctive use of prazosin with psychotherapy seems warranted given that nightmares may not resolve adequately with CBT strategies alone. It is notable that the adjunctive use of atypical antipsychotics with SSRIs for PTSD has not received clear support despite early positive indications. There is caution about the use of pharmacologic treatments in general with specific phobia; the data supports a robust response to psychotherapeutic interventions as compared to that of pharmacologic monotherapy or combined therapy. Panic disorder and social phobia both respond well to either pharmacologic or psychotherapy monotherapy with no significant advantage of combined treatment. There is insufficient data to draw conclusions about combined treatment of agoraphobia with or without panic disorder. In sum, clinicians treating anxiety disorders have powerful treatment tools in either psychotherapy or pharmacotherapy alone, but can have less confidence in the utility of combining the two for some disorders, especially specific phobia, social phobia, panic disorder, and agoraphobia.

NOTE

* The views expressed are those of the author(s) and do not reflect the official policy of the Department of the Army, the Department of Defense, or the U.S. Government.

REFERENCES

Aaronson, C. J., Katzman, G.P., & Gorman, J. M. (2007). *Combination pharmacotherapy and psychotherapy for the treatment of major depressive and anxiety disorders.* In P. E. Nathan & J. M. Gorman (Eds.), *A guide to treatments that work,* (pp. 681–710). New York: Oxford University Press.
Abene, M. V., & Hamilton, J. D. (1998). Resolution of fear of flying with fluoxetine treatment. *Journal of Anxiety Disorders, 12,* 599–603.
Abramowitz, J. S. (1996). Variants of exposure and response prevention in the treatment of obsessive-compulsive disorder: A meta-analysis. *Behavior Therapy, 27,* 583–600.

Abramowitz, J. S. (1997). Effectiveness of psychological and pharmacological treatments for obsessive-compulsive disorder: A quantitative review. *Journal of Consulting and Clinical Psychology, 65,* 44–52.

Ackerman, D. L., & Greenland, S. (2002). Multivariate meta-analysis of controlled drug studies for obsessive-compulsive disorder. *Journal of Clinical Psychopharmacology, 22,* 309–317.

Ahmed, M., Westra, H. A., & Stewart, S. H. (2008). A self-help handout for benzodiazepine discontinuation using cognitive behavioral therapy. *Cognitive and Behavioral Practice, 15,* 317–324.

Albucher, R. C., & Liberzon, I. (2002). Psychopharmacological treatment in PTSD: A critical review. *Journal of Psychiatric Research, 36,* 355–367.

American Psychiatric Association. (2000). *Diagnostic and Statistical Manual of Mental Disorders* (4th ed., text revision). Washington DC: American Psychiatric Association.

American Psychiatric Association. (2004). *Practice guideline for the treatment of patients with acute stress disorder and post-traumatic stress disorder.* Arlington, VA: American Psychiatric Association.

American Psychiatric Association. (2007). *Practice guideline for the treatment of patients with obsessive-compulsive disorder.* Arlington, VA: American Psychiatric Association.

American Psychiatric Association. (2009). *Practice guideline for the treatment of patients with panic disorder* (2nd ed.). Arlington, VA: American Psychiatric Association.

American Psychological Association, Division 12: Society of Clinical Psychology. (2012). *Website on research-supported psychological treatments.* Retrieved from http://www.div12.org/PsychologicalTreatments/index.html

Antony, M. M., & Barlow, D. H. (2002). Specific phobias. In D. H. Barlow (Ed.), *Anxiety and its disorders* (2nd ed., pp. 380–417). New York: Guilford.

Bakker, A., van Balkom, A. J. L. M., & Spinhoven, P. (2002). SSRIs vs. TCAs in the treatment of panic disorder: A meta-analysis. *Acta Psychiatrica Scandinavica, 106,* 163–167.

Bakker, A., van Balkom, A. J. L. M., Spinhoven, P., Blaauw, B. M. J. W., & van Dyck, R. (1998). Follow-up on the treatment of panic disorder with or without agoraphobia: A quantitative review. *Journal of Nervous and Mental Disease, 186,* 414–419.

Bakker, A., van Balkom, A. J. L. M., & Stein, D. J. (2005). Evidence-based pharmacotherapy of panic disorder. *International Journal of Neuropsychopharmacology, 8,* 473–482.

Ballenger, J. C., Davidson, J. R. T., Lecrubier, Y., Nutt, D. J., Borkovec, T. D., Rickels, K., Stein, D.J., & Wittchen, H. (2001). Consensus statement on generalized anxiety disorder from the international consensus group on depression and anxiety. *Journal of Clinical Psychiatry, 62* (Suppl. 11), 53–58.

Ballenger, J. C., Davidson, J. R. T., Lecrubier, Y., Nutt, D. J., Foa, E. B., Kessler, R. C., McFarlane, A. C., & Shalev, A. Y. (2000). Consensus statement on posttraumatic stress disorder from the international consensus group on depression and anxiety. *Journal of Clinical Psychiatry, 61*(Suppl. 5), 60–66.

Bandelow, B., Seidler-Brandler, U., Becker, A., Wedekind, D., & Ruther, E. (2007). Meta-analysis of randomized controlled comparisons of psychopharmacological and psychological treatments of anxiety disorders. *The World Journal of Biological Psychiatry, 8,* 175–187.

Barlow, D. H., Craske, M. G., Cerny, J. A., & Klosko, J. S. (1989). Behavioral treatment of panic disorder. *Behavior Therapy, 20,* 261–282.

Barlow, J. H., Ellard, D. R., Hainsworth, J. M., Jones, F. R., & Fisher, A. A. (2005). A review of self-management interventions for panic disorders, phobias and obsessive-compulsive disorders. *Acta Psychiatrica Scandinavica, 111,* 272–285.

Barlow, D. H., Gorman, J. M., Shear, M. K., & Woods, S. W. (2000). Cognitive behavioral therapy, imipramine, and their combination for panic disorder. *JAMA, 283,* 2529–2536.

Benedek, D. M., Friedman, M. J., Zatzick, D., & Ursano, R. J. (2009, March). Guideline watch: Practice guideline for the treatment of patients with acute stress disorder and posttraumatic stress disorder. *Focus: The Journal of Lifelong Learning in Psychiatry, 7,* 204–213.

Benjamin, J., Ben-Zion, I. Z., Karbofsky, E., & Dannon, P. (2000). Double-blind placebo-controlled pilot study of paroxetine for specific phobia. *Psychopharmacology, 149,* 194–196.

Bernadt, M. W., Silverstone, T., & Singleton, W. (1980). Behavioral and subjective effects of beta-adrenergic blockade in phobic subjects. *British Journal of Psychiatry, 137,* 452–457.

Blanco, C., Heimberg, R. G., Schneier, F. R., Fresco, D. M., Chen, H., Turk, C. L., . . . Liebowitz, M. R. (2010). A placebo controlled trial of phenelzine, cognitive behavioral group therapy and their combination for social anxiety disorder. *Archives of General Psychiatry, 67,* 286–295.

Blomhoff, S., Haug, T. T., Hellstrom, K., Holme, I., Humble, M., Madsbu, H. P., & Wold, J. E. (2001). Randomised controlled general practice trial of sertraline, exposure therapy and combined treatment in generalized social phobia. *British Journal of Psychiatry, 179,* 23–30.

Borkovec, T. D., Newman, M. G., Pincus, A. L., & Lytle, R. (2002). A component analysis of cognitive behavioral therapy for generalized anxiety disorder and the role of interpersonal problems. *Journal of Consulting and Clinical Psychology, 70,* 288–298.

Borkovec, T. D., & Ruscio, A. M. (2001). Psychotherapy for generalized anxiety disorder. *Journal of Clinical Psychiatry, 26*(Suppl. 11), 37–42.

Bradley, R., Greene, J., Russ, E., Dutra, L., & Westen, D. (2005). A multidimensional meta-analysis of psychotherapy for PTSD. *American Journal of Psychiatry, 162,* 214–227.

Bradweijn, J., Stein, A. A., Salinas, E., Emlien, G., & Whitaker, T. (2005). Venlafaxine extended release capsules in panic disorder. *British Journal of Psychiatry, 187*, 352–359.

Braun, P., Greenberg, D., Dasberg, H., Lerer, B. (1990). Core symptoms of PTSD unimproved by alprazolam treatment. *Journal of Clinical Psychiatry, 51*, 236–238.

Butler, G., Fennell, M., Robson, P., & Gelder, M. (1991). Comparison of behavior therapy and cognitive behavior therapy in the treatment of generalized anxiety disorder. *Journal of Consulting and Clinical Psychology, 59*, 167–175.

Choi, D. C., Rothbaum, B. O., Gerardi, M., & Ressler, K. J. (2009). Pharmacological enhancement of behavioral therapy: Focus on posttraumatic stress disorder. In M. B. Stein & T. Steckler (Eds.), *Behavioral neurobiology of anxiety and its treatment, current topics in behavioral neurosciences*. Heidelberg: Springer.

Choy, Y., Fyer, A. J., & Lipsitz, J. D. (2007). Treatment of specific phobia in adults. *Clinical Psychology Review, 27*, 266–286.

Christensen, H., Hadzi-Pavlovic, D., Andrews, G., & Mattick, R. (1987). Behavior therapy and tricyclic medication in the treatment of obsessive-compulsive disorder: A quantitative review. *Journal of Consulting and Clinical Psychology, 55*, 701–711.

Clark, D. M., Ehlers, A., McManus, F., Hackmann, A., Fenell, M., Campbell, H., . . . Louis, B. (2003). Cognitive therapy versus fluoxetine in generalized social phobia: A randomized placebo controlled trial. *Journal of Consulting and Clinical Psychology, 71*, 1058–1067.

The Clomipramine Collaborative Study Group: Clomipramine in the treatment of patients with obsessive-compulsive disorder. (1991). *Archives of General Psychiatry, 48*, 730–738.

Clum, G. A., Clum. G. A., & Surls, R. (1993). A meta-analysis of treatments for panic disorder. *Journal of Consulting and Clinical Psychology, 61*, 317–326.

Cottraux, J., Mollard, E., Bouvard, M., Marks, I., Sluys, M., Nury, A. M., Douge, R., & Ciaidella, P. (1990). A controlled study of fluvoxamine and exposure in obsessive-compulsive disorder. *International Clinical Psychopharmacology, 5*, 17–30.

Cottraux, J., Note, I., Cungi, C., Legeron, P., Heim, F., Chneiweiss, L., Bernard, G., & Bouvard, M. (1995). A controlled study of cognitive behavior therapy with buspirone or placeboin panic disorder with agoraphobia. *British Journal of Psychiatry, 167*, 635–641.

Covin, R., Ouimet, A. J., Seeds, P. M., & Dozois, D. J. A. (2008). A meta-analysis of CBT for pathological worry among clients with GAD. *Journal of Anxiety Disorders, 22*, 108–116.

Cox, B. J., Endler, N. S., Lee, P. S., & Swinson, R. P. (1992). A meta-analysis of treatments for panic disorder with agoraphobia: Imipramine, alprazolam, and in vivo exposure. *Journal of Behavior Therapy and Experimental Psychiatry, 23*, 175–182.

Cox, B. J., Swinson, R. P., Morrison, B., & Lee, P. S. (1993). Clomipramine, fluoxetine, and behavior therapy in the treatment of obsessive-compulsive disorder: A meta-analysis. *Journal of Behavior Therapy and Experimental Psychiatry, 24*, 149–153.

Craske, M. G., Antony, M. M., & Barlow, D. H. (2006). *Mastering you fears and phobias: Therapist guide* (2nd ed.). New York: Oxford University Press.

Davidson, J. R. T., Foa, E. B., Huppert, J. D., Keefe, F. J., Franklin, M. E., Compton, J. S., . . . Gadde, K. M. (2004). Fluoxetine, comprehensive cognitive behavioral therapy, and placebo in generalized social phobia. *Archives of General Psychiatry, 61*, 1005–1013.

Davidson, J. R., Zhang, W., Connor, K. M., Ji, J., Jobson, K., Lecrubier, Y., . . . Versiani, M. (2010). A psychopharmacological treatment algorithm for generalized anxiety disorder (GAD). *Journal of Psychopharmacology, 24*, 3–26.

Department of Veterans Affairs & Department of Defense (2010). *VA/DoD Clinical practice guidelines for management of post-traumatic stress, Version 2.0*. Washington, DC: Department of Veterans Affairs.

Durham, R. C., & Allan, T. (1993). Psychological treatment of generalized anxiety disorder: A review of the clinical significance of results in outcome studies since 1980. *British Journal of Psychiatry, 163*, 19–26.

Eddy, K. T., Dutra, L., Bradley, R., & Westen, D. (2004). A multidimensional meta-analysis of psychotherapy and pharmacotherapy for obsessive-compulsive disorder. *Clinical Psychology Review, 24*, 1011–1030.

Federoff, I. C., & Taylor, S. (2001). Psychological and pharmacological treatments of social phobia: A meta-analysis. *Journal of Clinical Psychopharmacology, 21*, 311–324.

Foa, E. B., Liebowitz, M. R., Kozak, M. J., . . . Tu, X. (2005). Randomized, placebo controlled trial of exposure and ritual prevention, clomipramine, and their combination in the treatment of obsessive-compulsive disorder. *American Journal of Psychiatry, 162*, 151–161.

Foa, E. B., & Meadows, E. A. (1997). Psychosocial treatments for posttraumatic stress disorder: A critical review. *Annual Review of Psychology, 48*, 449–480.

Foa, E. B., Steketee, G., Kozak, M. J., & Dugger, D. (1987). Effects of imipramine on depression and obsessive-compulsive symptoms. *Psychiatry Research, 21*, 123–136.

Freeman, C. P., Trimble. M. R., Deakin, J. F., Stokes, T. M., & Ashford, J. J. (1994). Fluvoxamine versus clomipramine in the treatment of obsessive-compulsive disorder: A multi-center, randomized, double-blind, parallel group comparison. *Journal of Clinical Psychiatry, 55*, 301–305.

Furukawa, T. A., Watanabe, N., & Churchill, R. (2007). Combined psychotherapy plus antidepressants for panic disorder with or without agoraphobia. *Cochrane. Database. Syst. Rev.*, CD004364.

Fyer, A. J. (1987). Simple phobia. *Modern Problems in Pharmacopsychiatry, 22*, 174–192.

Gamble, A. L., Harvey, A. G., & Rapee, R. M. (2010). Specific phobia. In D. J. Stein, E. Hollander, & B. O. Rothbaum (Eds.), *Textbook of anxiety disorders* (2nd ed., pp. 525–546). Arlington, VA: American Psychiatric Publishing.

Gava, I., Barbui, C., Aguglia, E., Carlino, D., Churchill, R., De Vanna, M., & McGuise, H. (2009). *Psychological treatments versus treatment as usual for obsessive-compulsive disorder (OCD)*. New York: Wiley.

Golier, J. A., Legge, J., & Yehuda, R. (2007). Pharmacological treatment of posttraumatic stress disorder. In P.E Nathan & J. M. Gorman (Eds), *A guide to treatments that work*, (pp. 475–512). New York: Oxford University Pres.

Goodman, W. K. (2004). Selecting pharmacotherapy for generalized anxiety disorder. *Journal of Clinical Psychiatry, 65*, 8–13.

Gorman, J. M. (2003). Treating generalized anxiety disorder. *Journal of Clinical Psychiatry, 64*(Suppl. 2), 24–29.

Gould, R. A., Buckminster, S., Pollack, M. H., Otto, M. W., & Yap, L. (1997). Cognitive behavioral and pharmacological treatment for social phobia: A meta-analysis. *Clinical Psychology: Science and Practice, 4*, 291–306.

Gould, R. A., Otto, M. W., & Pollack, M. H. (1995). A meta-analysis of treatment outcome for panic disorder. *Clinical Psychology Review, 15*, 819–844.

Gould, R. A., Otto, M. W., Pollack, M. H., & Yap, L. (1997). Cognitive behavioral and pharmacological treatment of generalized anxiety disorder: A preliminary meta-analysis. *Behavior Therapy, 28*, 285–305.

Grös, D. F., & Antony, M. M. (2006). The assessment and treatment of specific phobias: A review. *Current Psychiatry Reports, 8*, 298–303.

Guastella, A. J., Dadds, M. R., Lovibond, P. F., Mitchell, P., & Richardson, R. (2007). A randomized controlled trial of the effect of D-cycloserine on exposure therapy for spider fear. *Journal of Psychiatric Research, 41*, 466–471.

Guastella, A. J., Lovibond, P. F., Dadds, M. R., Mitchell, P., & Richardson, R. (2007). A randomized controlled trial of the effect of D-cycloserine on extinction and fear conditioning in humans. *Behaviour Research and Therapy, 45*, 663–672.

Hammer, M. B., & Frueh, B. C. (1998). Response to venlafaxine in a previously antidepressant treatment-resistant combat veteran with posttraumatic stress disorder. *International Clinical Psychopharmacology, 13*, 233–234.

Hageman, I., Andersen, H. S., Jorgensen, M. B. (2001). Post-traumatic stress disorder: A review of psychobiology and pharmacotherapy. *Acta Psychiatrica Scandinavica, 104*, 411–422.

Harvey, A., & Rapee, R. (2002). Specific phobia. In D. J. Stein & E. Hollander (Eds.), *Textbook of anxiety disorders*, (pp. 343–355). Washington DC: American Psychiatric Publishing, Inc.

Hayward, P., & Wardle, J. (1997). The use of medication in the treatment of phobias. In G. C. L. Davey (Ed.), *Phobias: A handbook of theory, research and treatment*, (pp. 281–298). New York: Wiley.

Hearon, B. A, & Otto, M. W. (2011). The biology and efficacy of combination strategies for anxiety disorders. In S. G. Hoffman (Ed.), *Psychobiological approaches for anxiety disorders: treatment combination strategies* (Wiley Series in Clinical Psychology). Manchester, UK: Wiley-Blackwell.

Hedges, D. W., Brown, B. L., Shwalb, D. A., Godfrey, K., & Larcher, A. M. (2007). The efficacy of selective serotonin reuptake inhibitors in adult social anxiety disorders: A meta-analysis of double blind, placebo controlled trials. *Journal of Psychopharmacology, 21*, 102–111.

Heimberg, R. G. (2001). Current status of psychotherapeutic interventions for social phobia. *Journal of Clinical Psychiatry, 62*(Suppl. 1), 36–42.

Hetrick, S. E., Purcell, R., Garner, B., & Parslow, R. (2010). Combined pharmacotherapy and psychological therapies for post traumatic stress disorders (PTSD) (Review). *The Cochrane Collaboration.*

Hidalgo, R. B., Tupler, L. A., & Davidson, J. R. T. (2007). An effect-size analysis of pharmacologic treatments for generalized anxiety disorder. *Journal of Psychopharmacology, 21*, 864–872.

Hoffman, S .G., Pollack, M. H., & Otto, M. W. (2006). Augmentation treatment of psychotherapy for anxiety disorders with D-cycloserine. *CNS Drug Reviews, 12*, 208–217.

Hoffman, S. G., Sawyer, M. A., Korte, K. J., & Smits, J. A. J. (2009). Is it beneficial to add pharmacotherapy to CBT when treating anxiety disorders? A meta-analytic review. *International Journal of Cognitive Therapy, 2*, 160–175.

Hoge, C. W. (2011). Interventions for war-related posttraumatic stress disorder: Meeting veterans where they are. *Journal of the American Medicine Association, 306*, 549–551.

Hollander, E., Kaplan, A., & Stahl, S. M. (2003). A double blind, placebo controlled trial of clonazepam in obsessive-compulsive disorder. *World Journal of Biological Psychiatry, 4*, 30–34.

Ipser, J. C., Kariuki, C., & Stein, D. J. (2008). Pharmacotherapy for social anxiety disorder: A systematic review. Expert Rev. *Neurotherapeutics, 8*, 235–257.

Jansson, L., & Öst, L. G. (1982). Behavioral treatments for agoraphobia: An evaluative review. *Clinical Psychology Review, 2*, 311–336.

Jefferson, J. W., Altemus, M., Jenike, M. A., Pigott, T. A., Stein, D. J., & Greist, J. H. (1995). Algorithm for the treatment of obsessive-compulsive disorder (OCD). *Psychopharmacology 31*, 487–490.

Jenike, M. A., Baer, L., Minichiello, W. E., Rauch, S. L., & Buttolph, M. L. (1997). Placebo controlled trial of fluoxetine and phenelzine for obsessive-compulsive disorder. *American Journal of Psychiatry, 154*, 1261–1264.

Kessler, R. C., Berglund, P., Demler, O., Jin, R., Merikangas, K. R., & Walters, E. E. (2005a). Lifetime prevalence and age-of-onset distributions of *DSM-IV* disorders in the National Comorbidity Survey Replication. *Archives of General Psychiatry, 62*, 593–602.

Kessler, R. C., Chiu, W. T., Demler, O., & Walters, E. E. (2005b). Prevalence, severity, and comorbidity of 12-month *DSM-IV* disorders in the National Comorbidity Survey Replication. *Archives of General Psychiatry, 62*, 617–627.

Kobak, K. A., Greist, J. H., Jefferson, J. W., Katzelnick, D. J., & Henk, H. J. (1998). Behavioral versus pharmacological treatments of obsessive-compulsive disorder: A meta-analysis. *Psychopharmacology, 136*, 205–216.

Krijn, M., Emmelkamp, P. M. G., Olafsson, R. P., & Biemond, R. (2004). Virtual reality exposure therapy of anxiety disorders: A review. *Clinical Psychological Review, 24*, 259–281.

Krystal, J. H., Rosenheck, R. A., Cramer, J. A Vessicchio, J. C., Jones, K. M., Vertrees, J. E., Stock C., et al. (2011). Adjunctive risperidone treatment for antidepressant-resistant symptoms of chronic military service-related PTSD: A trial. *JAMA, 306*, 493–502.

Lader, M. H., & Bond, A. J. (1998). Interaction of pharmacological and psychological treatments of anxiety. *British Journal of Psychiatry, 173*(Suppl. 34), 42–48.

LeBeau, R. T., Glen, D., Liao, B., Wittchen, H. U., Beesdo-Baum, K., Ollendick, T., & Craske, M. G. (2010). Specific phobia: A review of DSM-IV specific phobia and preliminary recommendations for DSM-V. *Depression and Anxiety, 27*, 148–167.

Liebowitz, M. R., Gorman, J. M, Fyer, A. J, & Klein, D. F. (1985). Social phobia: Review of a neglected anxiety disorder. *Archives of General Psychiatry, 42*, 729–736.

Marks, I. M., Stern, R. S., Mawson, D., Cobb, J., & McDonald, R. (1980). Clomipramine and exposure for obsessive-compulsive rituals. *British Journal of Psychiatry, 136*, 1–25.

Marks, I. M, Swinson, R. P., Basoglu, M., Kuch, K., Noshirvani, H., O'Sullivan, G., . . . Wickwire, K. (1993). Alprazolam and exposure alone and combined in panic disorder with agoraphobia: A controlled study in London and Toronto. *British Journal of Psychiatry, 162*, 776–787.

Marks, I. M., Viswanathan, R., Lipsedge, M. S., & Gardner, R. (1972). Enhanced relief of phobias by flooding during waning diazepam effect. *British Journal of Psychiatry, 121*, 493–505.

McDougle, C. J., Barr, L. C., Goodman, W. K., Pelton, G. H., Aronson, S. C., Anand, A., & Price, L. H. (1995). Lack of efficacy of clozapine monotherapy in refractory obsessive- compulsive disorder. *American Journal of Psychiatry, 152*, 1812–1814.

McGlynn, F. D., & Vopat, T. (1994). Simple phobia. In C. G. Last & M. Hersen (Eds.), *Adult behavior therapy casebook* (pp. 139–152). New York: Plenum.

McHugh, R. K., Smits, J. A. J., & Otto, M. W. (2009). Empirically supported treatment for panic disorder. *Psychiatric Clinics of North America, 32*, 593–610.

Michelson, L. K., & Marchione, K. (1991). Behavioral, cognitive, and pharmacological treatments of panic disorder with agoraphobia: Critique and synthesis. *Journal of Consulting and Clinical Psychology, 59*, 100–114.

Mitte, K. (2005a). A meta-analysis of the efficacy of psycho- and pharmacotherapy in panic disorder with and without agoraphobia. *Journal of Affective Disorders, 88*, 27–45.

Mitte, K. (2005b). Meta-analysis of cognitive behavioral treatments for generalized anxiety disorder: A comparison with pharmacotherapy. *Psychological Bulletin, 131*, 785–795.

Mitte, K., Noack, P., Steil, R., & Hautzinger, M. (2005). A meta-analytic review of the efficacy of drug treatment in generalized anxiety disorder. *Journal of Clinical Psychopharmacology, 25*, 141–150.

Mundo, E., Maina, G., & Uslenghi, C. (2000). Multicentre, double-blind, comparison of fluvoxamine and clomipramine in the treatment of obsessive-compulsive disorder. *International Clinical Psychopharmacology, 15*, 69–76.

Norberg, M. M., Krystal, J. H., & Tolin, D. F. (2008). A meta-analysis of D-cycloserine and the facilitation of fear extinction and exposure therapy. *Biological Psychiatry, 63*, 1118–1126.

Olfson, M., Marcus, S. C., Wan, G. J., & Geissler, E. C. (2004). National trends in the outpatient treatment of anxiety disorders. *Journal of Clinical Psychiatry, 65*, 1166–1173.

Otto, M. W., Basden, S. L., Leyro, T. M., McHugh, R. K., & Hofmann, S. G. (2007). Clinical perspectives on the combination of D-cycloserine and cognitive behavioral therapy for the treatment of anxiety disorders. *CNS Spectrums, 21*, 51–61.

Otto, M. W., Hinton, D., Korbly, N. B., Chea, A., Ba, P., Gershuny, B. S., & Pollack, M. H. (2003). Treatment of pharmacotherapy-refractory posttraumatic stress disorder among Cambodian refugees: A pilot study of combination treatment with cognitive-behavior therapy vs. sertraline alone. *Behavioral Research and Therapy, 41*, 1271–1276.

Otto, M. W., Tolin, D. F., Simon, N. M., Pearlson, G. D., Basden, S., Neunier, S. A., . . . Pollack, M. H. (2010). Efficacy of D-Cycloserine for enhancing response to cognitive-behavior therapy for panic disorders. *Biological Psychiatry, 67*, 365–370.

Parsons, T. D., & Rizzo, A. A. (2008). Affective outcomes of virtual reality exposure therapy for anxiety and specific phobias: A meta-analysis. *Journal of Behavior Therapy and Experimental Psychiatry, 39*, 250–261.

Piccinelli, M., Pini, S., Bellantuono, C., & Wilkinson, G. (1995). Efficacy of drug treatment in obsessive-compulsive disorder: A meta-analytic review. *British Journal of Psychiatry, 166*, 424–443.

Pigott, T. A., Pato, M. T., Bernstein, S. E., Grover, G. N., Hill, J. L., Tolliver, T. J., & Murphy, D. L. (1990). Controlled comparisons of clomipramine and fluoxetine in the treatment of obsessive-compulsive disorder: Behavioral and biological results. *Archives of General Psychiatry, 47*, 926–932.

Pollack, M., Mangano, R., Entsuah, R., Tzanis, E., Simon, N. M., & Zhang, Y. (2007). A randomized controlled trial of venlafaxine ER and paroxetine in the treatment of outpatients with panic disorder. *Psychopharmacology, 194*, 233–242.

Power, K. G., Simpson, R. J., Swanson, V., Wallace, L. A., Fesitner, A. T. C., & Sharp, D. (1990). A controlled comparison of cognitive behavior therapy, diazepam, and placebo, alone and in combination, for the treatment of generalized anxiety disorder. *Journal of Anxiety Disorders, 4*, 267–292.

Powers, M. B., & Emmelkamp, P. M. G. (2008). Virtual reality exposure therapy for anxiety disorders: A meta-analysis. *Journal of Anxiety Disorders, 22,* 561–569.

Prasko, J., Dockery, C., Horacek, J., Houbova, P., Kosova, J., Klaschka, J., . . . Hoschl, C. (2006). Moclobemide and cognitive behavioral therapy in the treatment of social phobia: A six month controlled study and 24 months follow up. *Neuroendocrinology Letters, 27,* 473–481.

Rapee, R. M. (1991). Generalized anxiety disorder: A review of clinical features and theoretical concepts. *Clinical Psychology Review, 11,* 419–440.

Raskind, M. A., Peskind, E. R., Hoff, D. J., Hart, K. L., Holmes, H. A., Warren, D., . . . McFall, M. E. (2007). A parallel group placebo controlled study of prazosin for trauma nightmares and sleep disturbance in combat veterans with posttraumatic stress disorder. *Biological Psychiatry, 61,* 928–934.

Raskind, M. A., Peskind, E. R., Kanter, E. D., Petrie, E. C., Radant, A., Thompson, C. E., . . . McFall, M. E. (2003). Reduction of nightmares and other PTSD symptoms in combat veterans by prazosin: A placebo-controlled study. *American Journal of Psychiatry, 160,* 371–373.

Ressler, K. J., Rothbaum, B. O., Tannenbaum, L., Anderson, P., Graap, K., Zimand, E., . . . Davis, M. (2004). Cognitive enhancers as adjuncts to psychotherapy: Use of D-cycloserine in phobic individuals to facilitate extinction of fear. *Archives of General Psychiatry, 61,* 1136–1144.

Rodebaugh, T. L., Holaway, R. M., & Heimberg, R. G. (2004). The treatment of social anxiety disorder. *Clinical Psychology Review, 24,* 883–908.

Rothbaum, B. O., Cahill, S. P, Foa, E. B., Davidson, J. R., Compton, J., Connor, K. M., . . . Hahn, C. G. (2006). Augmentation of sertraline with prolonged exposure in the treatment of posttraumatic stress disorder. *Journal of Traumatic Stress, 19,* 625–638.

Rowa, K., & Antony, M. M. (2005). Psychological treatments for social phobia. *Canadian Journal of Psychiatry, 50,* 308–316.

Roy-Byrne, P. P., & Cowley, D. S. (2007). Pharmacological treatments for panic disorder, generalized anxiety disorder, specific phobia, and social anxiety disorder. In P. E Nathan & J. M. Gorman (Eds.), *A guide to treatments that work,* (pp. 395–430). New York: Oxford University Press.

Sareen, J., & Stein, M. (2000). A review of the epidemiology and approaches to the treatment of social anxiety disorder. *Drugs, 59,* 494–509.

Sartory, G. (1983). Benzodiazepines and behavioural treatment of phobic anxiety. *Behavioural Psychotherapy, 11,* 204–217.

Schmitt, R., Gazalle, F. K., de Lima, M. S., Cunha, A., Souza, J., & Kapczinski, F. (2004). The efficacy of antidepressants for generalized anxiety disorder: A systematic review and meta-analysis. *Revista Brasileira de Psiquiatria, 27,* 18–24.

Shalev, A., Bonne, O., & Eth, S. (1996). Treatment of posttraumatic stress disorder: A review. *Psychosomatic Medicine, 58,* 165–182.

Sheehan, D. V., Ballenger, J. C., & Jacobsen, G. (1980). Treatment of endogenous anxiety with phobic hysterical and hypochondriacal symptoms. *Archives of General Psychiatry, 37,* 51–59.

Siegmund, A., Golfels, F., Finck, C., Halisch, A., Räth, D., Plag, J., & Ströhle, A. (2011). D-Cycloserine does not improve but might slightly speed up the outcome of in vivo exposure therapy in patients with severe agoraphobia and panic disorder in a randomized double blind clinical trial. *Journal of Psychiatric Research, 45,* 1042–1047.

Simon, N. M., Connor, K. M., Lang, A., J., Rauch, S., Krulewicz, S., LeBeau, R. T., . . . Pollack, M. H. (2008). Paroxetine CR augmentation for posttraumatic stress disorder refractory to prolonged exposure therapy. *Journal of Clinical Psychiatry, 69,* 400–405.

Slaap, B. R., & den Boer, J. A. (2001). The prediction of nonresponse to pharmacotherapy in panic disorder: A review. *Depression and Anxiety, 14,* 112–122.

Spiegel, D. A., & Bruce T. J. (1997). Benzodiazepines and exposure-based cognitive behavior therapies for panic disorder: Conclusions from combined treatment trials. *American Journal of Psychiatry, 154,* 773–781.

Stein, D. J., Ipser, J. C., & Seedat, S. (2009a). Pharmacotherapy for posttraumatic stress disorder (PTSD) (Review). *The Cochrane Library,* 2009(1).

Stein, D. J., Ipser, J. C., & van Balkom, A. J. (2009b). Pharmacotherapy for social anxiety disorder (Review). *The Cochrane Library,* 2009(1).

Stein, D. J., Seedat, S., van der Linden, G. J. H, & Zungu-Dirwayi, N. (2000). Selective serotonin reuptake inhibitors in the treatment of post-traumatic stress disorder: A meta analysis of randomized controlled trials. *International Journal of Psychopharmacology, 15*(Suppl 2), S31–S39.

Storch, E. A., Merlo, L. J., Bengtson, M., Murphy, T. K, Lewis, M. H., Yang, M. C., . . . Goodman W. K. (2007). D-cycloserine does not enhance exposure response prevention therapy in obsessive-compulsive disorder. *International Clinical Psychopharmacology, 22,* 230–237.

Taylor, S. (1996). Meta-analysis of cognitive behavioral treatments for social phobia. *Journal of Behavior Therapy and Experimental Psychiatry, 27,* 1–9.

Taylor, F. B., Martin, P., Thompson, C., Williams, J., Mellman, T. A., Gross, C., . . . Raskind, M. A. (2008). Prazosin effects on objective sleep measures and clinical symptoms in civilian trauma posttraumatic stress disorder: A placebo controlled study. *Biological Psychiatry, 63,* 629–632.

Thom, A., Sartory, G., & Jöhren, P. (2000). Comparison between one-session psychological treatment and benzodiazepine in dental phobia. *Journal of Consulting and Clinical Psychology, 68,* 378–387.

Thoren, P., Asberg, M., Cronholm, B., Jornestedt, L., & Traskman, L. (1980). Clomipramine treatment of obsessive-compulsive disorder, I: A controlled clinical trial. *Archives of General Psychiatry, 37,* 1281–1285.

Trull, T. J., Nietzel, M. T., & Main, A. (1988). The use of meta-analysis to assess the clinical significance of behavior therapy for agoraphobia. *Behavior Therapy, 19,* 527–538.

Vallejo, J., Olivares, J., Marcos, T., Bulbena, A., & Menchon, J. M. (1992). Clomipramine versus phenelzine in obsessive-compulsive disorder: A controlled clinical trial. *British Journal of Psychiatry, 161,* 665–670.

Van Balkom, A. J. L. M., Bakker, A., Spinhoven, P., Blaauw, B. M. J. W, Smeenk, S., & Ruesink, B. (1997). A meta-analysis of the treatment of panic disorder with or without agoraphobia: A comparison of psychopharmacological, cognitive behavioral, and combination treatments. *The Journal of Nervous and Mental Disease, 185,* 510–516.

Van Balkom, A. J. L. M., van Oppen, P., Vermeulen, A. W. A., van Dyck, R., Nauta, M. C. E., & Vorst, H. C. M. (1994). A meta-analysis of the treatment of obsessive-compulsive disorder: A comparison of antidepressants, behavior, and cognitive therapy. *Clinical Psychology Review, 14,* 359–381.

van Emmerik, A. A. P., Kamphuis, J. H., Hulsbosch, A. M., & Emmelkamp, P. M. G. (2002). Single session debriefing after psychological trauma: A meta-analysis. *The Lancet, 360,* 766–771.

Wardle, J. (1990). Behaviour therapy and benzodiazepines: Allies or antagonists? *British Journal of Psychiatry, 156,* 163–168.

Watanabe, N., Churchill, R., & Furukawa, T. A. (2009). Combined psychotherapy plus benzodiazepines for panic disorder. *Cochrane Database.* Syst. Rev, DC005335.

Westen, D., & Morrison, K. (2001). A multidimensional meta-analysis of treatments for depression, panic, and generalized anxiety disorder: An empirical examination of the status of empirically supported therapies. *Journal of Consulting and Clinical Psychology, 69,* 875–899.

Whitehead, W. E., Blackwell, B., & Robinson, A. (1978). Effects of diazepam on phobic avoidance behavior and phobic anxiety. *Biological Psychiatry, 13,* 59–64.

Wilhelm, S., Buhlmann, U., Tolin, D. F., Meunier, S. A., Pearlson, G. D., Reese, H. E., . . . Rauch, S. L. (2008). Augmentation of behavioral therapy with d-cycloserine for obsessive-compulsive disorder. *American Journal of Psychiatry, 165,* 335–341.

Wilhelm, F. H., & Roth, W. T. (1997). Clinical characteristics of flight phobia. *Journal of Anxiety Disorders, 11,* 241–261.

Wolitzky-Taylor, K. B., Horowitz, J. D., Powers, M. B., & Telch, M. H. (2008). Psychological approaches in the treatment of specific phobias: A meta-analysis. *Clinical Psychology Review, 28,* 1021–1037.

Yehuda, R. (2002). Post-traumatic stress disorder. *New England Journal of Medicine, 246,* 108–114.

Zitrin, C. M., Klein, D. F., & Woerner, M. G. (1978). Behavior therapy, supportive psychotherapy, imipramine, and phobias. *Archives of General Psychiatry, 35,* 307–316.

Zitrin, C. M., Klein, D. F., Woerner, M. G., & Ross, D. C. (1983). Treatment of phobias: I. Comparison of imipramine hydrochloride and placebo. *Archives of General Psychiatry, 40,* 125–138.

Zlomke, K., & Davis, T. E. (2008). One-session treatment of specific phobias: A detailed description and review of treatment efficacy. *Behavior Therapy, 39,* 207–223.

Integrating Psychopharmacology and Psychotherapy in Eating Disorders

Phillipa J. Hay, Josué Bacaltchuk, and Stephen Touyz

INTRODUCTION

This chapter focuses on the integrated use of psychopharmacology and psychotherapy as applied to the treatment of patients with anorexia nervosa (AN), bulimia nervosa (BN), binge-eating disorder (BED), and eating disorder not otherwise specified (EDNOS).

General Description of the Disorder

Prevalence and Diagnostic Features

In a nationally representative study of EDs in the United States in 2001–2003, the lifetime prevalence of AN was 0.9% in women and 0.3% in men; BN was 1.5% in women and 0.5% in men; and BED was 3.5% in women and 2.0% in men (Hudson, Hiripi, Pope, & Kessler, 2007). In the *Diagnostic and Statistical Manual of Mental Disorders* fifth edition (DSM-5; APA, 2000) AN is characterized by a relentless pursuit of thinness, resulting in weight loss or failure to gain weight during growth, a refusal to maintain a normal body weight, and a fear of gaining weight or becoming fat or persistent behaviors to avoid weight gain. In the fifth revision (APA, 2013) an earlier (APA, 2000) the criterion amenorrhoea was removed, and fat phobia was also be removed as an essential criteria. BN diagnostic criteria (APA, 2013) comprise the presence of regular episodes of binge eating (uncontrolled overeating of large amounts of food) followed by extreme weight control compensatory behaviors and an intense preoccupation with weight and shape issues as an expression of self-worth. BED is characterized by recurrent episodes of binge eating with associated distress and an absence of regular use of the compensatory behaviors found in BN. In the DSM-5 other specified eating disorders include patients who appear to have a mixed disorder—for example, regular purging following eating normal-sized food portions or a disorder in which binge eating or purging behaviors are below specified frequency or duration criteria.

General Clinical Considerations

EDs cause notable distress, medical morbidity, and increased mortality (Arcelus, Mitchell, Wales, & Nielsen, 2011). People with AN are by definition in a starvation state. In community surveys (e.g., Hudson et al., 2007), over 40% of patients with BED are obese, and high rates of psychiatric comorbidity, particularly anxiety disorders and depression, also occur. AN age of onset is usually in early to mid-adolescence. In BN and BED, the onset is in later adolescence and young adulthood. With treatment, around 40% of patients with AN will make a good 5-year recovery, 40% remain symptomatic but with limited disability, and 20% of patients suffer chronic disability. Outcomes are notably better early in the illness course and in children and adolescents (Steinhausen, 2002). Outcomes are also better in BN and EDNOS, but only up to 50% of those with BN make a full recovery (Steinhausen & Weber, 2009), and EDs frequently go undiagnosed and untreated (Hart et al., 2011). Treatment needs to address medical, social, and psychological dimensions.

Literature for this chapter was sourced from systematic reviews by the authors (search dates up to 2011) and a Medline search using terms "Bulimia," "Treatment," "Humans," 2009–2012. Treatment efficacy is reported on the basis of randomized controlled trials (RCTs) and meta-analyses of RCTs.

PHARMACOLOGICAL TREATMENT

Review of Clinical Trials

Antipsychotic Medication

The only ED for which there has been tested efficacy for antipsychotics is AN, where they are thought to act by targeting dopaminergic and/or serotonergic dysfunction (Kaye, 2008). Findings were mixed and adverse effects problematic in the first trials of first-generation antipsychotics. However, there have been promising trials of the second-generation antipsychotics. Olanzapine, a 5HT2/D2 receptor antagonist, has been tested in four RCTs. In the first nonblind RCT, olanzapine (mean dose 10 mg/d) was compared to chlorpromazine (50 mg/day) added to standard care in 15 AN patients (Mondraty et al., 2005). In this trial, olanzapine showed greater efficacy than chlorpromazine in reducing ED ruminations. Brambilla et al. (2007) compared low-dose olanzapine to placebo as an adjunctive treatment with cognitive-behavior psychotherapy in 30 AN outpatients. Olanzapine was associated with increased weight gain, and reduced depressive symptoms and aggressiveness, but only for patients of the binge–purge type. Bissada, Tasca, Barber, and Bradwejn (2008) compared olanzapine combined with a day-hospital treatment for 10 weeks to placebo in 34 AN participants. There was significantly reduced time to achieving target weight and increased proportion (87.5% versus 55.6%) of patients achieved weight restoration to BMI > 18.5. Whilst completion rates were high (82%), 55% of eligible patients declined to be randomized, indicating a potential problem of low acceptance of olanzapine by people with AN possibly due to olanzapine's well-known effects on weight gain. A small (n = 23) later RCT of olanzapine by Attia et al. (2011) found no end-of-treatment differences in depression, body shape concerns, ED symptoms, or other psychological symptoms. There was a greater improvement in BMI with olanzapine of unclear clinical relevance.

There is one RCT of amisulpride, a D2 and D3 receptor antagonist at higher doses with presynaptic antagonism at lower doses. In this RCT, low (50 mg/day) dose amisulpride was compared to fluoxetine (mean dose 28 mg/day) and to clomipramine (mean dose 57.69 mg/day) in 35 inpatients with AN. Excepting higher weight gain (with amisulpride), there were no other differences between groups (Ruggiero et al., 2001).

There are two RCTs of quetiapine. Court et al. (2010) tested quetiapine (mean dose 322.5 mg/day) plus treatment as usual (TAU) versus TAU over 12 weeks in 33 (21 completers) AN patients followed for 1 year. With the exception of a marginal reduction in ineffectiveness and interoceptive awareness favoring quetiapine, there were no differences found in weight gain, ED, or other symptoms. More recently, Powers, Klabunde, and Kaye (2012) compared nine participants receiving placebo to six receiving quetiapine (mean dose 177.7 mg/day SD = 90.8) in an 8-week trial. There were no between-group differences in any outcomes including weight. The authors commented on the difficulty in recruiting participants from an initial 207 screened. This largely seemed to be because they did not wish to take medication, and especially medication that might result in weight gain.

In sum, there are few and small RCTs of antipsychotics and very few of those that may be less sedating and less likely to cause severe weight gain feared by patients. Antipsychotics do not consistently promote weight gain, and potential long-term deleterious effects of antipsychotics in EDs have not been determined yet (Hay & Claudino, 2012). At present there is no specific indication for their use, although they are used in clinical practice as adjunctive to refeeding programs in AN (Powers, Klabunde, & Kaye, 2012).

Antidepressants and Like Medications

Antidepressants are used in EDs both for specific effects on mood but also appetite regulation and satiety. Their use in AN has been argued on the basis of shared inheritance with depression, most notably serotonin, and concurrent depressive and obsessional psychopathology (Kaye, 2008). Seven RCTs have been conducted of antidepressants in the acute phase of AN, and two in relapse prevention after weight gain. The former were summarized in a systematic review by Claudino et al. (2006). Only four placebo-controlled RCTs were identified, three of the tricyclic antidepressants (TCA) amitriptyline and clomipramine, and one of the selective serotonin reuptake inhibitor (SSRI) fluoxetine. No meta-analyses were possible. Only one RCT reported a significant effect of drug (amitriptyline or cyproheptadine) versus placebo in time to achieve weight gain. RCTs were of variable quality, allocation concealment not reported in four, and doses of antidepressants were potentially subtherapeutic in two. The body of evidence does not support antidepressant use in AN, and tricyclic drugs carry noted cardiovascular risk. A body of work summarized in Kaye (2008) supports the view that there is a poor response to antidepressants because of adverse effects of starvation in the 5-HT1A receptor and in extracellular 5-HT concentrations.

There are two double-blind RCTs that have tested fluoxetine in the post–weight restoration phase in AN (Kaye et al. 2001; Walsh et al. 2006). Kaye et al. (2001) (n = 35) found significantly more patients on fluoxetine had reduced relapse rates during 1-year follow-up after hospital discharge as compared to a placebo control group. Attrition was very high in the placebo group (84% versus 37% in the treatment group), and for most, the decision to terminate the study was based on symptoms indicating a relapse. Walsh et al. (2006), in a larger trial of 93 patients, did not find adding fluoxetine to CBT helped prevent relapse. Finally, Halmi et al. (2005), in a trial of 122 patients, reported an unacceptably high rate of attrition (73%) in participants randomized to a fluoxetine (60 mg/day) arm compared to CBT arm (57% attrition) or combination arm (59%). Thus, antidepressant use is supported neither in the acute nor maintenance phases of AN treatment. RCTs of selective noradrenergic and other antidepressant classes are needed in both the acute and relapse prevention phases of AN treatment.

The efficacy of antidepressant treatment in BN is, in contrast, much better studied. This is particularly so for high-dose fluoxetine 60 mg/day (Fluoxetine BN Collaborative Study Group, 1992; Goldstein, Wilson, Ascroft, & al-Banna, 1999). In addition, the action in BN appears to be independent of effects on mood and seems to be due to augmentation of satiety mechanisms and reduced binge eating (Goldstein, Wilson, Ascroft, & al-Banna, 1999; Walsh et al., 2000). There have been several systematic reviews and meta-analyses supporting a range of classes of agents, in reducing binge eating and vomiting and improving mood and anxiety symptoms (see Table 7.1). Specific SSRIs evaluated include fluoxetine, citalopram, sertraline, and fluvoxamine.

However, there are a number of caveats in the use of antidepressants as a sole treatment for BN. For example, Bacaltchuk and Hay (2003) found pooled abstinence rates were less than 20% when antidepressants were used without any concurrent psychosocial intervention. Moreover, Agras et al. (1992) found that one third of the 25% of patients who were abstinent at the end of treatment relapsed over time. In contrast, a small number of relapse prevention studies have reported the efficacy of continued pharmacotherapy (Fichter, Kruger, Rief, Holland, & Dohne, 1996; Romano Halmi, Sarkar, Koke, & Lee, 2002). However, these findings should be considered with caution due to high attrition (around 90% at 1 year follow-up in Romano et al. [2002]). Attrition is also high in most trials (around 40%)

Table 7.1 Selected findings from meta-analyses of randomized controlled trials of antidepressant or topiramate versus placebo or no treatment control in bulimia nervosa and binge eating disorder (AD = antidepressants, MAOI = monoaminooxidase inhibitor).

Review	Medications	Effect size
Bulimia nervosa:		
Bacaltchuk & Hay, 2003	Tricyclics: 3 trials	Binge abstinence: 0.86 95% CI 07;1.07
	MAOI: 2 trials	Binge abstinence: 0.81 95% CI 0.68;0.96
	Fluoxetine: 3 trials	Binge abstinence: 0.90 95% CI 0.8;1.02
	Other ADs: 10 trials	Binge abstinence: 0.89 95% CI 0.84;0.9
NICE, 2004	MAOI: 1 trial	Binge abstinence: 0.77 95% CI 0.62;0.95
	Tricyclics/SSRI: 6 trials	Binge abstinence: 0.88 95% CI 0.83;0.94
Arbaizar, et al., 2008	Topiramate: 2 trials	Binging/week: −4.4 SD1.3 *vs* −1.7 SD2.2
		Body weight: −2.8 SD1.6 *vs* −0.03 SD0.35
Binge eating disorder:		
NICE, 2004	SSRIs: 3 trials	Binge abstinence: 0.77 95% CI 0.63;0.93
	Topiramate: 1 trial	Binge abstinence: 0.56 95% CI 0.34;0.92
Stefano et al., 2008	SSRIs: 7 trials	Binge abstinence: 0.77 95% CI 0.65;0.92
	Imipramine:	Body weight: 0.03 95% CI −0.49;0.55 NS
Reas & Grilo, 2008	SSRIs: 7 trials	Binge abstinence: 0.81 95% CI 0.70;0.94
	Atomoxetine: 1 trial	Binge abstinence: 0.43 95% CI 0.21;0.89
	Anticonvulsant: 3 trials	Binge abstinence: 0.63 95% CI 0.51;0.78
	Sibutramine: 2 trials	Binge abstinence: 0.80 95% CI 0.69;0.94
	All 13 trials	Binge abstinence: 0.74 95% CI 0.66,0.84
	8 trials	Body weight: −3.42 95% CI −4.25;−2.58
Arbaizar et al., 2008	Topiramate: 3 trials	Binging/week: −5.2SD0.3 *vs* −3.7SD 0.4
		Body weight: −6.4 SD0.6 *vs* −1.0 SD0.2
Vocks et al., 2010	Psychotherapy: 5 trials	Binge eating: 0.82 95% CI 0.41;1.22
	Structured self-help: 4 trials	Binge eating: 0.84 95% CI 0.37;1.30
	Pharmacotherapy: 6 trials	Binge eating: 0.52 95% CI 0.15;0.89

of single pharmacological treatments. It is unclear how much of this is due to adverse effects of medication or patient preference for psychological therapies. Attrition is least for SSRIs, possibly because of their short-term perceived effects on reduction in appetite and weight.

In practice guidelines fluoxetine at 60 mg/day is the only medication with a strong recommendation in BN (Aigner, Treasure, Kaye, Kasper, & World Federation of Societies of Biological Psychiatry, 2011; APA, 2006). Early response of > 60% reduction in binge eating in the first 3 weeks of treatment is associated with a favorable outcome in a secondary analysis of two studies by Sysko, Sha, Wang, Duan, and Walsh (2010). With regards to other SSRIs, there are three very small RCTs of citalopram (Milano, Petrella, & Capasso, 2005a), sertraline (Milano, Petrella, Sabatino, & Capasso, 2004), and fluvoxamine (Milano, Siano, Petrella, Sabatino, & Capasso, 2005b) from the same research group. All three RCTs support their efficacy. A small (n = 27) single-blind trial comparing fluoxetine and citalopram found no differences in outcomes and high attrition (Leombruni et al., 2006). A later study (Giaquinto, Capasso, Petrella, & Milano, 2006) compared the three SSRIs in these trials and reported that fluvoxamine or fluoxetine were associated with a greater reduction in binge eating and purging when compared to 100 mg daily of sertraline (100 mg daily). Finally, it is likely there is publication bias (Balcaltchuk & Hay, 2003) in favor of positive trials of SSRIs, and a large (n = 300) negative trial of fluvoxamine 150–300 mg remains published only in secondary reports.

Antidepressants that act on the noradrenergic system have been less studied. There have been small open trials of reboxetine, a selective noradrenaline reuptake inhibitor, and milnacipran, a selective serotonin and noradrenaline reuptake inhibitor, reporting positive findings but no RCTs. Bupropion is an antidepressant that blocks reuptake of noradrenaline and dopamine. It reduced binge eating and purging episodes compared to placebo in a RCT of 55 BN participants (Horne et al., 1988). However, the same trial also reported an unacceptably high rate (7%) of generalized tonic-clonic seizures.

Antidepressants may also have a role in the treatment of BED. There have been several RCTs of SSRIs or other antidepressants for BED. These have evaluated imipramine, fluvoxamine, sertraline, fluoxetine, escitalopram, and citalopram (Hay & Claudino, 2012). Most have been small (n = 85 or fewer) and of short duration (mean duration of 10 weeks, all less than 20 weeks) with a high placebo response reported (Jacobs-Pilipski et al., 2007). Two meta-analyses (see Table 7.1) have found significantly reduced binge eating remission rates with fewer effects on mood and mixed effects on body weight. Malhotra, King, Welge, Brusman-Lovins, and McElroy (2002) and Bernardi and Pallanti (2010) have reported positive outcomes in BED for venlafaxine and duloxetine (both selective serotonin and noradrenaline reuptake inhibitors) in preliminary open trials. There has been one RCT of 40 obese patients with BED where atomoxetine was associated with greater improvement in binge eating behaviors and weight loss and was reasonably tolerated (McElroy et al., 2007a). Sibutramine is a selective serotonin and noradrenaline inhibitor that is used in weight loss. In BED, the meta-analysis of Reas and Grilo (2008) found sibutramine was associated with significantly reduced binge eating and weight loss compared to placebo. However, adverse cardiovascular events in obese people have led to its withdrawal from markets in the United States, Europe, and other countries.

Mood Stabilizing Agents

Mood intolerance and emotional impulsivity is a known feature of EDs, particularly but not limited to BN. Up until recently, mood stabilizing agents such as lithium and anticonvulsant drugs have received little attention. A very small (n = 16) early placebo-controlled RCT of lithium treatment in acute phase AN was supportive of greater weight gain in the active group (Gross et al., 1981). However, this study was never followed by more substantive trials and has been largely forgotten. More recently, an anticonvulsant, topiramate, has been assessed in EDs for its putative anti-impulsivity and weight-losing effects (McElroy et al., 2007b). Hoopes et al.'s (2003) RCT found that participants with BN treated with topiramate had significantly greater reductions in mean weekly binge and/or purge days than those on placebo (44.8% versus 10.7% for placebo), as well as greater weight loss with topiramate (1.8 kg, compared to the placebo group mean increase of 0.2 kg). A second study by Nickel et al. (2005) reported topiramate (250 mg/day) over a 10-week period significantly reduced binge/purge frequency and weight and improved health-related quality of life compared to a placebo condition in 60 participants. Caveats were the adverse effects of cognitive impairment and neurological symptoms such as paresthesia. Its teratogenic potential may also be problematic.

Topiramate has also been trialed in two double-blind placebo-controlled RCTs in obese patients with BED. The first enrolled 61 subjects for 14 weeks of treatment (median dose 213 mg/day) (McElroy et al., 2003). The second larger multicenter trial (McElroy et al., 2007b) enrolled 394 patients for 16 weeks and used a median dose of 300 mg/day. In both RCTs, topiramate reduced binge frequency, increased binge remission and weight loss, and improved psychological comorbidity. High attrition and adverse effects were problematic, however.

Zonisamide, another anticonvulsant, has been tested against placebo in a RCT of 60 obese women with BED (McElroy et al., 2006). Mean endpoint dose of zonisamide was 436 mg/day over 16 weeks. Although more effective than placebo like topiramate, zonisamide had considerable side effects and was poorly tolerated. Attrition was high (50%) in the drug-treated group. A meta-analysis (Reas & Grilo, 2008) of these trials has reported large effects for binge remission and weight loss (see Table 7.1).

Anxiolytic and Other Agents

Anxiolytic drugs such as benzodiazepines are little studied in EDs, and use is limited in AN. One small study of 14 patients (9 with AN) has tested d-cycloserine, a glutamate partial agonist (Steinglass et al., 2007). Results were mixed, and food intake was not enhanced.

The postulate that ED behaviors (specially binge eating) are "addictive-like" led to studies of the opiate antagonist naltrexone. Results of trials of naltrexone in bulimic disorders have been mixed (Mitchell et al., 1989; Marrazzi et al., 1995), and there are no RCTs of naloxone. There is interest in baclofen (a centrally acting c-amino-butyric acid B [GABA-B] receptor agonist) and mermantine (a low-to-moderate-affinity noncompetitive NMDA receptor antagonist) but no RCTs. Finally, in this group, there has been a single positive RCT (Faris et al., 2000) of ondansetron for BN, but more trials are needed.

Anti-Obesity Agents

Anti-obesity agents are of interest in aiding weight reduction and attenuating binge eating in patients with BED and weight disorder. Sibutramine, a selective serotonin and noradrenaline inhibitor, has been discussed above. Other trials have been adjunct to behavioral or psychological approaches. Two RCTs have tested orlistat, a lipase inhibitor, against placebo in combination with a mildly reduced-calorie diet (89 obese patients with BED) or combined with CBT-based guided self-help manual for 12 weeks (50 patients). After 24 weeks, patients taking orlistat showed greater mean weight loss (–7.4% versus –2.3%), as well as a greater reduction of ED symptoms, compared to those taking placebo (Golay et al., 2005). Grilo, Masheb, & Salant (2005b) reported better results in the orlistat group for both binge remission (64% versus 36%) and clinically significant weight loss (> 5% from baseline weight: 36% versus 8%).

Strengths/Benefits and Weaknesses/Limitations of Using Pharmacotherapy as Sole Approach

In sum, drug treatments in EDs have weak to moderate evidence for efficacy. There is some evidence for antidepressants, particularly high-dose fluoxetine in BN, and anticonvulsants (e.g., topiramate) or anti-obesity agents (e.g., orlistat) for BED. Low-dose antipsychotic medication or other anxiolytic agents may be clinically useful as adjunct treatment in the early phases of treating AN where emotional arousal is high and food and weight obsessive ruminations most intense. Drug therapies such as topiramate and anti-obesity medication may aid weight loss in obese or overweight patients with BED, but their use is limited by potentially serious adverse effects. It is also noted that placebo response is relatively high in BED.

No pharmacotherapy is recommended as first-line treatment or sole treatment for an ED. If psychotherapy is not available or accessible, then antidepressants may be a useful interim or alternate treatment for BN. However, it is unlikely that some form of psychological therapy is unavailable, albeit in a guided or pure self-help format (see below). As described above, AN is a complex disorder, and treatment is multidimensional and multidisciplinary. Patient preference is also for psychological approaches, which may explain the relative poorer efficacy and higher attrition in drug versus psychotherapy trials for other EDs. For example, a recent meta-analysis (see Table 7.1) of comparative effect sizes for treatments of BED combined results of 38 studies of RCTs and uncontrolled studies and pooled all types of pharmacotherapy, as well as psychotherapies in computing comparative effect sizes (Vocks et al., 2010). The paper found larger effect sizes for psychotherapy, although the pooling of a range of forms of both psychotherapy and pharmacotherapy was problematic. The role of medication as adjunct to psychotherapy is discussed below.

PSYCHOSOCIAL TREATMENT

Review of Clinical Trials and Strengths/Benefits and Weaknesses/Limitations of Using Psychotherapy as Sole Approach

Psychotherapies are treatments of choice for AN, BN, and BED. The best evidence for psychotherapies is CBT in adults with BN and family-based treatment (FBT) in children and adolescents with AN. Other approaches such as interpersonal therapy (IPT), dynamic psychotherapies, and dialectical behavior therapy also have some evidence of efficacy.

Family-Based Therapy (FBT)

In children and adolescents with AN, the recommended approach is family therapy. The most studied family therapy approach is manualized Maudsley FBT (Lock & Fitzpatrick, 2010). There have been extensive trials of FBT and other forms of family therapy in adolescents and children with AN or BN. These have included inpatient and outpatient trials and trials post–weight restoration, as well as acute phase AN. RCTs have been supportive of family therapy when compared to individual therapies in adolescents but less consistent for adults with AN and adolescents with BN (Lock et al. 2010; Godart et al. 2012).

Cognitive-Behavior Therapy (CBT)

Forms of cognitive therapy (CT) and CBT have been trialed in AN RCTs with mixed results (Hay et al., 2003). In marked contrast, CBT as developed by Fairburn (2008) for BN (CBT-BN) and variations of CBT-BN have been tested in many RCTs of participants with BN and BED with comorbid obesity. CBT has been compared to wait list control groups, other psychotherapies, behavioral weight loss therapy, and pharmacological therapies. It has been evaluated in group, guided self-help (Wilson & Zandberg, 2012), and other forms of delivery. Several systematic reviews of BN RCTs have consistently found CBT to be well supported, and it is regarded as "first-line" therapy (Hay et al., 2009; NICE, 2004).

CBT for BN has been compared favorably to pharmacotherapy, most notably antidepressant therapies, and attrition rates are notably higher in antidepressant control groups. Imipramine and desipramine, respectively, were compared to CBT-BN in two RCTs (Mitchell et al., 1990; Agras et al., 1992). In the first RCT, group-based CBT-BN had higher binge-eating remission compared to imipramine. Results of the second RCT were inconclusive (see Table 7.2). Goldbloom et al. (1997) compared CBT-BN plus fluoxetine with fluoxetine alone and CBT-BN alone. Mitchell et al. (2001) compared pure self-help CBT plus fluoxetine with fluoxetine alone; and Jacobi, Dahme, and Dittman (2002) have compared CBT to fluoxetine and combined therapy. No significant differences have been found in outcomes when fluoxetine is compared with CBT, or combined CBT and fluoxetine, or when fluoxetine was combined with CBT versus CBT alone or nutritional counseling. CBT has been found effective as well for BED (Hay et al., 2009). With regards to medication, effects of CBT in reducing BED symptoms have not been enhanced when combined with desipramine (Agras et al., 1994) or fluoxetine (Devlin et al 2005; Grilo et al., 2005a). However, as shown in Table 7.2, CBT has been found to be enhanced when combined with topiramate (Claudino et al., 2007).

A further development of CBT is the extended form, CBT-E, which includes modules addressing predisposing and (more relevant to severe and enduring AN) perpetuating or maintaining factors for all EDs. The "transdiagnostic" CBT-E for BN has been tested in a RCT of normal or above normal weight participants where it was compared to CBT, and an advantage was found for CBT-E for those with more complex presentations and comorbidities (Fairburn et al., 2009).

Other Therapies

A small number of other psychotherapies have been used and evaluated in RCTs for EDs. These include focal psychoanalytic psychotherapy (FPT), cognitive analytic therapy (CAT), and SSCM, and readiness and motivation therapy (Lock & Fitzpatrick, 2010; Geller, Brown, & Srikameswaran, 2011). Overall, the number and quality of trials of psychotherapies in AN are insufficient to support any therapy, with the probable exception of FBT, with a good level of evidence (Lock & Fitzpatrick, 2010). Mindfulness alone or as practiced as part of dialectical behavioral therapy or other therapies also shows promise in open prospective trials of people with EDs, as reported in a systematic review by Wanden-Berghe, Sanz-Valero, and

Table 7.2 Randomized controlled trials for bulimia nervosa (BN) or binge eating disorder (BED) comparing cognitive-behavior therapy (CBT) combined with either antidepressant drug or psychotherapy alone: Outcomes at end of therapy and follow-up.

Study and quality	Intervention(s)	Outcome at end R_X	Follow-up
Mitchell et al., 1990 BN, n = 171, 27% DO, RB moderate	1. CBT & imipramine 2. CBT & placebo 3. Imipramine 4. Placebo	Group CBT superior to drug therapy & placebo on all ED measures & mood	Keel et al. (2002) NS active R_X except placebo worse social adjustment (p < 0.05)
Agras et al., 1992 BN, n = 71, 14% DO RB low	1/2. Desipramine 16/24 wks 3. CBT 4/5. CBT & 16/24 wks drug	CBT & combined superior to 16-week drug, NS differences 1 & 2	At 32 weeks, 24-week combined superior to single R_X (p < 0.005)
Leitenberg et al., 1994 BN, n = 21, 33% DO RB moderate	1. CBT & ERP 20 wks 2. Desipramine 3. Combined	Purging abstinence: CBT 71%, drug 0%, Both 57%	6 months significant reductions both CBT arms but not sole drug
Agras et al., 1994 BED n = 109, 22% DO, RB moderate	1. BWLT 2. CBT & BWLT 3. CBT & BWLT & desipramine	At 12 wks CBT superior to BWLT for binging but not weight loss	1-year NS binge abstinence 1:14% 2:28% 3:32% NS weight
Beumont et al., 1997 BN n = 67, 27% DO RB moderate	1. Fluoxetine 60 mg 2. Placebo both with NC over 8 weeks	NS differences except restraint, weight concerns, & weight lower with drug	20 weeks NS difference between groups higher relapse in drug
Goldbloom et al., 1997 BN, n = 76, 43% DO, RB mod.	1. Fluoxetine 60 mg 2. CBT-BN 16 weeks 3. Combined	Binge abstinence NS: 17% fluoxetine, 43% CBT, 25% combined (completers)	No report
Walsh et al., 1997 BN n = 120, 34% DO, RB low	1/2. CBT & drug placebo 3/4. Supportive R_X & drug/placebo 5. Desipramine/fluoxet	CBT superior binge abstinence 67%, placebo 38%, Supportive R_X & Drug/placebo 29%, drug alone 35%	No report
Mitchell et al., 2001 BN, n = 91, RB moderate	1. Fluoxetine 2. Placebo 3. Pure SH & placebo 4. PSH & drug	Vomiting less with drug & SH, binge abstinence NS but greater with PSH	No report
Ricca et al., 2001 BED n = 108, 23% DO RB moderate	1. CBT 2/3. CBT & fluoxatine/fluvoxamine 4/5. fluoxet/fluvox	All CBT groups significant reduction binging but not drug groups	R_X ceased over 4 wks, CBT groups retained advantage
Jacobi et al., 2002 BN, n = 89, 61% DO, RB moderate	1. CBT 20 sessions 2. Fluoxetine 60 mg 3. Combined	Binge abstinence NS: 5/19 CBT, 2/16 drug, 3/18 combined	1 year, binge abstinence: 4/10 CBT 1/8 drug, 1/9 both
Molinari, et al. 2005 BED, n = 65, 8% DO, RB high	All diet & NC 1. CBT 2. Fluoxetine 3. Combined	Less binging with CBT & greater weight loss in both CBT groups (p = 0.001)	No report

(Continued)

Table 7.2 Continued

Study and quality	Intervention(s)	Outcome at end R_X	Follow-up
Walsh, atl., 2004 BN/EDNOS, n = 91, 69% DO RB moderate	1. CBT-Guided SH (GSH) 2. Fluoxetine 3. Placebo & GSH 4. Placebo alone	Binge abstinence NS: 12.2% GSH, 9.5% fluoxetine/placebo	No report
Grilo et al., 2005a BED n = 108, 20% DO RB low	1. Fluoxetine 60 mg 2. Placebo 3. CBT & drug 4. CBT & placebo All 16 weeks	Binge abstinence: 22% fluoxetine, 26% placebo 50% combined 61% CBT with placebo p < 0.01	No report CBT also greater weight loss at end R_X
Devlin et al., 2005 BED, n = 116, 36% DO RB moderate	All group BWLT 1. Fluoxetine 2. Placebo 3. Fluox & CBT 4. Placebo & CBT	Binge abstinence: 62% CBT, vs. 33% no CBT, p < 0.001, 52% fluoxetine vs. 41% placebo NS	2-year maintenance phase
Claudino et al., 2007 BED, n = 37, 23% DO, RB low	1.Topiramate 2. Placebo Both with CBT	Weight loss more with drug p < 0.05 Binge abstinence 84% drug 61% placebo p = 0.03	No report

NS = not significant, NC = nutritional counseling, included in this table as provided similar behavioral and psychoeducational management to CBT, R_X = treatment, DO = dropout, RB = risk of bias on base of adequate allocation concealment, blinding, and use of intention-to-treat approach in analyses, wks = weeks, BWLT = behavioral weight loss therapy, SH = self-help.

Wanden-Berghe (2011). Other therapies with demonstrated efficacy in RCTs of BN and BED include IPT and dialectical behavior therapy (reviewed in Hay et al., 2009). In RCTs, behavior weight loss therapies (BWLT) have been found to reduce binge eating and aid weight loss in overweight people with BED, but effects may not be sustained over time (Hay et al., 2009).

Combination of Pharmacological and Psychosocial Treatment: Strengths and Benefits of Using a Combined Approach

In AN, all drugs have been tested with the presumption that they are used as adjunct to nutritional and psychological programs. Results are inconclusive for both antipsychotic and antidepressant use. In BN (see Table 7.2), there have been several RCTs comparing antidepressants in combination with CBT with inconsistent results. When pooled in meta-analyses (e.g., NICE, 2004), findings suggest that (a) drug-alone treatments are less efficacious in reducing binge-eating rates than when combined with CBT, and (b) attrition in the antidepressant arms of such trials is high. However, combined drug (particularly topiramate) and CBT may enhance the efficacy of CBT or other psychotherapy alone. RCTs in BED of combined antidepressants or other medications with CBT have suggested little advantage over CBT alone in reducing binge eating (Agras et al., 1994; Devlin et al., 2005; Grilo et al., 2005a). However, there may be positive effects for increased weight loss and reduced binge eating beyond the effects of psychotherapy (Agras et al., 1994) or drug alone (Ricca et al., 2001). In a placebo RCT of 31 people with obesity and binge eating, those treated for 8 weeks with imipramine maintained weight loss and reduced binge eating better than those treated with placebo in a 24-week follow-up phase where nutritional counseling and behavioral management was provided (Laederach-Hofmann et al., 1999). There has also been a positive RCT of topiramate combined with CBT (Claudino et al., 2007), but adverse effects were more common with topiramate. Finally, where psychotherapy is not available, antidepressants, particularly fluoxetine at 60 mg/day, may serve as an evidence-based alternative with or without self-help CBT in bulimic disorders (e.g., Mitchell et al., 2001).

RECOMMENDATIONS FOR FUTURE STUDIES/RESEARCH

While the evidence base for treatments in other EDs, especially BN, is more robust than in AN, it is striking that there have been no new trials of antidepressants in recent years. This is despite mixed findings that require further study into the efficacy of combined antidepressants and efficacious psychotherapies such as CBT-E. The benefits of fluoxetine, the only U.S. FDA-approved treatment for BN, remain unclear in the longer term. It is also unclear whether benefits of pharmacotherapy on weight gain for AN and weight loss for BED are sustained over time. The use of both adjunct antipsychotics and antidepressants in EDs may be greater than evidence would suggest appropriate, and more definitive RCTs of treatments that test common clinical practice are required.

REFERENCES

Agras, W. S., Rossiter, E. M., Arnow, B., Schneider, J. A., Telch, C. F., Raeburn, S. D., et al. (1992). Pharmacologic and cognitive behavioral treatment for bulimia nervosa: A controlled comparison. *American Journal of Psychiatry, 149,* 82–87.

Agras, S. W., Telch, C. F., Arnow, B., Eldregde, K., Wilfley, D. E., Raeburn, S. D., et al. (1994). Weight loss, cognitive behavioral, and desipramine treatments in binge eating disorder—An addictive design. *Behavioural Therapy, 25,* 225–238.

Aigner, M., Treasure, J., Kaye, W., Kasper, S., & The World Federation of Societies of Biological Psychiatry [WFSBP] Task Force on Eating Disorders (2011). *The World Journal of Biological Psychiatry, 12,* 400–443.

American Psychiatric Association. (2000). *Diagnostic and statistical manual of mental disorders (DSM-IV-TR).* (4th ed., text revision). Washington, DC: American Psychiatric Association.

American Psychiatric Association. (2006). Practice guidelines for the treatment of patients with eating disorders. In *Practice guidelines for the treatment of psychiatric disorders* (3rd ed., pp. 1097–1222). Arlington, VA: American Psychiatric Association.

American Psychiatric Association. (2013). *Diagnostic and Statistical Manual of Mental Disorders—5 (DSM-5)* Arlington, VA: American Psychiatric Association. Arcelus, J., Mitchell, A., Wales, J., & Nielsen, S. (2011). Mortality in eating disorders: A meta-analysis. *Archives of General Psychiatry, 68,* 179–183.

Attia, E., Kaplan A. S., Walsh, B. T., Gershkovich, M., Yilmaz, Z., Musante, D., & Wang, Y. (2011). Olanzapine *versus* placebo for out-patients with anorexia nervosa. *Psychological Medicine, 41,* 2177–2182.

Arbaizar, B., Gómez-Acebo, I., Llorca, J. (2008). Efficacy of topiramate in bulimia nervosa and binge-eating disorder: A systematic review. *General Hospital Psychiatry 30,* 471–475.

Bacaltchuk, J., & Hay, P. J. (2003). Antidepressants versus placebo for people with bulimia nervosa. *Cochrane Database of Systematic Reviews, 4,* Art. No.: CD003391. doi: 10.1002/14651858.CD003391

Bernardi, S., & Pallanti, S. (2010). Successful duloxetine treatment of a binge eating disorder: A case report. *Journal of Psychopharmacology, 24,* 1269–1272.

Beumont, P. J., Russell, J. D., Touyz, S. W., Buckley, C., Lowinger, K., Talbot, P., & Johnson, G. F. (1997). Intensive nutritional counselling in bulimia nervosa: A role for supplementation with fluoxetine? *Australian and New Zealand Journal of Psychiatry, 31,* 514–524.

Bissada, H., Tasca, G. A., Barber, A. M., & Bradwejn, J. (2008). Olanzapine in the treatment of low body weight and obsessive thinking in women with anorexia nervosa: A randomized, double-blind, placebo-controlled trial. *American Journal of Psychiatry, 165,* 1281–1288.

Brambilla, F., Garcia, C. S., Fassino, S., Daga, G. A., Favaro, A., Santonastaso, P., et al. (2007). Olanzapine therapy in anorexia nervosa: Psychobiological effects. *International Clinical Psychopharmacology, 22,* 197–204.

Claudino, A. M., de Oliveira, I. R., Appolinario, J. C., Cordás, T. A., Duchesne, M., Sichieri, R., & Bacaltchuk, J. (2007). Randomized, double-blind, placebo-controlled trial of topiramate plus cognitive-behavior therapy in binge eating disorder. *Journal of Clinical Psychiatry, 68,* 1324–1332.

Claudino, A., Hay, P., Lima, M. S., Bacaltchuk, J., Schmidt, U., & Treasure, J. (2006). Antidepressants for anorexia nervosa. *Cochrane Database of Systematic Reviews, 25*(1), CD004365.

Court, A., Mulder, C., Kerr, M., Yuen, H. P., Boasman, M., Goldstone, S., . . . Berger, G. (2010). Investigating the effectiveness, safety and tolerability of quetiapine in the treatment of anorexia nervosa in young people: A pilot study. *Journal of Psychiatric Research, 44*, 1027–1034.

Devlin, M. J., Goldfein, J. A., Jiang, H., Raizman, P. S., Wolk, S., Mayer, L., et al. (2005). Cognitive behavioral therapy and fluoxetine as adjunct to group behavioral therapy for binge eating disorder. *Obesity Research, 13*, 1077–1088.

Fairburn, C. G. (2008). *Cognitive behavior therapy for eating disorders.* New York: Guilford Press.

Fairburn, C. G., Cooper, Z., Doll, H. A., O'Connor, M. E., Bohn, K., Hawker, D. M., et al. (2009). Transdiagnostic cognitive behavioral therapy for patients with eating disorders: A two-site trial with 60-week follow-up. *American Journal of Psychiatry, 166*, 311–319.

Faris, P. L., Suck Won Kim, S. W., Meller, W. H., Goodale, R. L. Oakman, S. A., Hofbauer, R., et al. (2000). Effect of decreasing afferent vagal activity with ondansetron on symptoms of bulimia nervosa: A randomised, double-blind trial. *Lancet, 355*, 792–797.

Fichter, M. M., Kruger, R., Rief, W., Holland, R., & Dohne, J. (1996). Fluvoxamine in prevention of relapse in bulimia nervosa: Effects on eating specific psychopathology. *Journal of Clinical Psychopharmacology, 16*, 9–18.

Fluoxetine Bulimia Nervosa Collaborative Study Group. (1992). Fluoxetine in the treatment of bulimia nervosa: A multicenter, placebo-controlled, double-blind trial. *Archives of General Psychiatry, 49*, 139–147.

Giaquinto, K., Capasso, A., Petrella, C., & Milano, W. (2006). Comparative study between three different SSRIs in the treatment of bulimia nervosa. *Pharmacology Online, 1*, 11–14.

Geller, J., Brown, K. E., & Srikameswaran, S. (2011). The efficacy of a brief motivational intervention for individuals with eating disorders: A randomized control trial. *International Journal of Eating Disorders, 44*, 497–505.

Godart, N., Berrthoz, S., Curt, F., Perdereau, F., Rein, Z., Wallier, J., et al. (2012). A randomized controlled trial of adjunctive family therapy and treatment as usual following inpatient treatment for anorexia nervosa adolescents. *Plos ONE, 7*, 1–9.

Golay, A., Laurent-Jaccard, A., Habicht, F., Gachoud, J. P., Chabloz, M., Kammer, A., & Schutz, Y. (2005). Effect of orlistat in obese patients with binge eating disorder. *Obesity Research, 3*, 1701–1708.

Goldbloom, D. S., Olmsted, M., Davis, R., Clewes, J., Heinmaa, M., Rockert, W., & Shaw, B. (1997). A randomized controlled trial of fluoxetine and cognitive behavioural therapy for bulimia nervosa: Short-term outcome. *Behavior Research and Therapy, 35*, 803–811.

Goldstein, D. J., Wilson, M. G., Ascroft, R. C., & al-Banna, M. (1999). Effectiveness of fluoxetine therapy in bulimia nervosa regardless of co-morbid depression. *International Journal of Eating Disorders, 25*, 19–27.

Grilo, M. C., Masheb, R. M., & Salant, S. L. (2005b). Cognitive behavioral therapy guided self-help and orlistat for the treatment of binge eating disorder: A randomized, double-blind, placebo-controlled trial. *Biological Psychiatry, 57*, 1193–1201.

Grilo, C. M., Masheb, R. M., & Wilson, G. T. (2005a). Efficacy of cognitive behavioural therapy and fluoxetine for the treatment of binge eating disorder: A randomised double-blind placebo-controlled comparison. *Biological Psychiatry, 57*, 301–309.

Gross, H. A., Ebert, M. H., Faden, V. B., Goldberg, S. C., Nee, L. E., & Kaye, W. H. (1981). A double-blind controlled trial of lithium carbonate primary anorexia nervosa. *Journal of Clinical Psychopharmacology, 1*, 376–381.

Halmi, K, A., Agras, W. S., Crow, S., Mitchell, J., Wilson, G. T., Bryson, S. W., & Kraemer, H. C. (2005). Predictors of treatment acceptance and completion in anorexia nervosa. Implications for future study designs. *Archives of General Psychiatry, 62*, 776–781.

Hart, L. M., Granillo, M. T., Jorm, A. F., & Paxton, S. J. (2011). Unmet need for treatment in the eating disorders: A systematic review of eating disorder specific treatment seeking among community cases. *Clinical Psychology Review, 31*, 727–735.

Hay, P. J., Bacaltchuk, J., Byrnes, R. T., Claudino, A. M., Ekmejian, A. A., & Yong, P. Y. (2003). Individual psychotherapy in the outpatient treatment of adults with anorexia nervosa. *Cochrane Database of Systematic Reviews, 4*, CD003909. (Updated to 2008). doi: 10.1002/14651858.CD003909

Hay, P. J., Bacaltchuk, J., Kashyap, P., & Stefano, S. (2009). Psychotherapy for bulimia nervosa and binge eating. *Cochrane Database of Systematic Reviews, 3*, CD000562. (Updated to 2007).

Hay, P. J., & Claudino, A. M. (2012). Clinical psychopharmacology of eating disorders: A research update. *The International Journal of Neuropsychopharmacology, 15*, 209–222.

Hoopes, S. P., Reimherr, F. W., Hedges, D. W., Rosenthal, N. R., Kamin, M., Karim, R., et al. (2003). Treatment of bulimia nervosa with topiramate in a randomized, double-blind, placebo-controlled trial, part 1: Improvement in binge and purge measures. *Journal of Clinical Psychiatry, 64*, 1335–1341.

Horne, R. L., Ferguson, J. M., Pope, H. G., Jr., Hudson, J. I., Lineberry, C. G., Ascher, J., & Cato, A. (1988). Treatment of bulimia with bupropion: A multicenter controlled trial. *Journal of Clinical Psychiatry, 49*, 262–266.

Hudson, J. I., Hiripi, E., Pope, H. G., & Kessler, R. C. (2007). The prevalence and correlates of eating disorders in the National Comorbidity Survey Replication. *Biological Psychiatry, 61*, 348–358.

Jacobi, C., Dahme, B., & Dittman, R. (2002). Cognitive-behavioural, fluoxetine and combined treatment for bulimia nervosa: Short- and long-term results. *European Eating Disorders Review, 10*, 179–198.

Jacobs-Pilipski, M. J., Wilfley, D. E., Crow, S., & Walsh, B. T., Lilenfeld, L. R., West, D. S., et al. (2007). Placebo response in binge eating disorder. *International Journal of Eating Disorders, 40*, 204–211.

Kaye, W. H. (2008). Neurobiology of anorexia and bulimia nervosa. *Physiology and Behavior, 94,* 121–135.

Kaye, W. H., Nagata, T., Weltzin, T. E., Hsu, L. K., & Sokol, M. S. (2001). Double-blind placebo-controlled administration of fluoxetine in restricting- and purging-type anorexia nervosa. *Biological Psychiatry, 49,* 644–652.

Keel, P. K., Mitchell, J. E., Davis, T. L., & Crow, S. J. (2002). Long-term impact of treatment in women diagnosed with bulimia nervosa. *International Journal of Eating Disorders, 31,* 151–158.

Laederach-Hofmann, K., Graf, C., Horber, F., Lippuner, K., Lederer, S., Michel, R., & Schneider, M. (1999). Imipramine and diet counseling with psychological support in the treatment of obese binge eaters: A randomized, placebo-controlled double-blind study. *International Journal of Eating Disorders, 26,* 231–244.

Leitenberg, H., Rosen, J. C., Wolf, J., Vara, L. S., Detzer, M. J., & Srebnik, D. (1994). Comparison of cognitive-behavior therapy and desipramine in the treatment of bulimia nervosa. *Behavior Research and Therapy, 32,* 37–45.

Leombruni, P., Amianto, F., Delsedime, N., Gramaglia, C., Bbate-Daga, G., & Fassino, S. (2006). Citalopram versus fluox-etine for the treatment of patients with bulimia nervosa. *Advances in Therapy, 23,* 481–484.

Lock, J. D., & Fitzpatrick, K. K. (2010, 11 April). Anorexia nervosa. *British Medical Journal Clinical Evidence.* http://bestpractice.bmj.com.ezproxy.uws.edu.au/best-practice/evidence/1011.html

Lock, J., Le Grange, D., Agras, W. S., Moye, A., Bryson, S. W., & Jo, B. (2010). Randomized clinical trial comparing family-based treatment with adolescent-focused individual therapy for adolescents with anorexia nervosa. *Archives of General Psychiatry, 67,* 1025–1032.

Malhotra, S., King, K. H., Welge, J. A., Brusman-Lovins, L., & McElroy, S. L. (2002). Venlafaxine treatment of binge-eating disorder associated with obesity: A series of 35 patients. *Journal of Clinical Psychiatry, 63,* 802–826.

Marrazzi, M. A., Bacon, J. P., & Kinzie, J. (1995). Naltrexone use in the treatment of anorexia nervosa and bulimia nervosa. *International Journal of Clinical Psychopharmacology, 10,* 163–172.

McElroy, S. L., Arnold, L. M., Shapira, N. A., Keck, P. E., Rosenthal, N. R., Karim, M. R., Kamin, M., & Hudson, J. I. (2003). Topiramate in the treatment of binge-eating disorder associated with obesity: A randomized, placebo-controlled trial. *American Journal of Psychiatry, 160,* 255–261.

McElroy, S. L., Guerdjikova, A., Kotwal, R., Welge, J. A., Nelson, E. B., Lake, K. A., et al. (2007a). Atomoxetine in the treatment of binge-eating disorder: A randomized placebo-controlled trial. *Journal of Clinical Psychiatry, 68,* 390–398.

McElroy, S. L., Hudson, J. I., Capece, J. A., Beyers, K., Fisher, A. C., & Rosenthal, N. R. & Topiramate Binge Eating Disorder Research Group (2007b). Topiramate for the treatment of binge eating disorder associated with obesity: A placebo-controlled study. *Biological Psychiatry, 61,* 1039–1048.

McElroy, S. L., Kotwal, R., Guerdjikova, A. I., Welge, J. A., Nelson, E. B., Lake, K. A., et al. (2006). Zonisamide in the treatment of binge eating disorder with obesity: A randomized controlled trial. *Journal of Clinical Psychiatry, 67,* 1897–1906. Erratum in: *Journal of Clinical Psychiatry* (2007), 68, 172.

Milano, W., Petrella, C., & Capasso, A. (2005a). Treatment of bulimia nervosa with citalopram: A randomized controlled trial. *Biomedical Research, 16,* 85–87.

Milano, W., Petrella, C., Sabatino, C., & Capasso, A. (2004). Treatment of bulimia nervosa with sertraline: A randomized controlled trial. *Advances in Therapy, 21,* 232–237.

Milano, W., Siano, C., Petrella, C., Sabatino, C., & Capasso, A. (2005b). Treatment of bulimia nervosa with fluvoxamine: A randomized controlled trial. *Advances in Therapy, 23,* 278–283.

Mitchell, J. E., Christenson, G., Jennings, J., Huber, M., Thomas, B., Pomeroy, C., & Morley, J. (1989). A placebo-controlled, double-blind crossover study of naltrexone hydrochloride in outpatients with normal weight bulimia. *Journal of Clinical Psychopharmacology, 9,* 94–97.

Mitchell, J. E., Fletcher, L., Hanson, K., Mussell, M. P., Seim, H., Crosby, R., & Al-Banna, M. (2001). The relative efficacy of fluoxetine and manual-based self-help in the treatment of outpatients with bulimia nervosa. *Journal of Clinical Psychopharmacology, 21,* 298–304.

Mitchell, J. E., Pyle, R. L., Eckert, E. D., Hatsukami, D., Pomeroty, C., & Zimmerman, R. (1990). A comparison study of antidepressants and structured intensive group psychotherapy in the treatment of bulimia nervosa. *Archives of General Psychiatry, 47,* 149–157.

Molinari, E., Baruffi, M., Croci, M., Marchi, S., & Petroni, M. L. (2005) Binge eating disorder in obesity: Comparison of different therapeutic strategies. *Eating and Weight Disorders,* 10, 154–161.

Mondraty, N., Birmingham, C. L., Touyz, S., Sundakov, V., Chapman, L., & Beaumont, P. (2005). Randomized controlled trial of olanzapine in the treatment of cognitions in anorexia nervosa. *Australasian Psychiatry, 13,* 72–75.

National Institute for Clinical Excellence (NICE). (2004). *Eating disorders: Core interventions in the treatment and management of anorexia nervosa, bulimia nervosa and related disorders.* Clinical Guideline Number 9. London: NICE.

Nickel, C., Tritt, K., Muehlbacher, M., Pedrosa, G. F., Mitterlehner, F. O., Kaplan, P., et al. (2005). Topiramate treatment in bulimia nervosa patients: A randomized, double-blind placebo-controlled trial. *International Journal of Eating Disorders, 38,* 295–300.

Powers, P. S., Klabunde, M., & Kaye, W. (2012). Double-blind placebo-controlled trial of quetiapine in anorexia nervosa. *European Eating Disorders Review, 20,* 331–334.

Reas, D. L., & Grilo, C. M. (2008). Review and meta-analysis of pharmacotherapy for binge-eating disorder. *Obesity, 16,* 2024–2028.

Ricca, V., Mannucci, E., Mezzani, B., Moretti, S., Di Bernardo, M., Bertelli, M., et al. (2001). Fluoxetine and fluvoxamine combined with individual cognitive-behaviour therapy in binge eating disorder: A one-year follow-up study. *Psychotherapy and Psychosomatics, 70,* 298–306.

Romano, S. J., Halmi, K. A., Sarkar, N. P., Koke, S. C., & Lee, J. S. (2002). A placebo-controlled study of fluoxetine in continued treatment of bulimia nervosa after successful acute fluoxetine treatment. *American Journal of Psychiatry, 159,* 96–102.

Ruggiero, G. M., Laini, V., Mauri, M. C., Ferrari, V. M. S., Clemente, A., Mantero, M., et al. (2001). A single blind comparison of amisulpride, fluoxetine and clomipramine in the treatment of restricting anorectics. *Progress in Neuro-Psychopharmacology & Biological Psychiatry, 25,* 1049–1059.

Stefano, S. C., Bacaltchuk, J., Blay, S. L., & Appolinário, J. C. (2008). Antidepressants in short-term treatment of binge eating disorder: Systematic review and meta-analysis. *Eating Behaviours, 9,* 129–136.

Steinglass, J., Sysko, R., Schebendach, J., Broft, A., Strober, M., & Walsh, B. T. (2007). The application of exposure therapy and d-cycloserine to the treatment of anorexia nervosa: A preliminary trial. *Journal of Psychiatric Practice, 13,* 238–245.

Steinhausen, H. C. (2002). The outcome of anorexia nervosa in the 20th century. *American Journal of Psychiatry, 159,* 1284–1293.

Steinhausen, H. C., & Weber, S. (2009). The outcome of bulimia nervosa: Findings from one-quarter century of research. *American Journal of Psychiatry, 166,* 1331–1341.

Sysko, R., Sha, N., Wang, Y., Duan, N., & Walsh, B. T. (2010). Early response to antidepressant treatment in bulimia nervosa. *Psychological Medicine, 40,* 999–1005.

Vocks, S., Tuschen-Caffier, B., Pietrowsky, R., Rustenbach, S. J., Kersting, A., & Herpertz, S. (2010). Meta-analysis of the effectiveness of psychological and pharmacological treatments for binge eating disorder. *International Journal of Eating Disorders, 43,* 205–217.

Walsh, B. T., Agras, W. S., Devlin, M. J., Fairburn, C. G., Wilson, G. T., Kahn, C. M. A., & Chally, M. K. (2000). Fluoxetine for bulimia nervosa following poor response to psychotherapy. *American Journal of Psychiatry, 157,* 523–531.

Walsh, B. T., Fairburn, C. G., Mickley, D., Sysko, R., & Parides, M. K. (2004).Treatment of bulimia nervosa in a primary care setting. *American Journal of Psychiatry, 161,* 556–561.

Walsh T., Kaplan, A. S., Attia, E., Olmsted, M., Parides, M., Carter, J. C., et al. (2006). Fluoxetine after weight restoration in anorexia nervosa. *Journal of the American Medical Association, 295,* 2605–2612.

Walsh, B. T., Wilson, G. T., Loeb, K. L., Devlin, M. J., Pike, K. M., Roose, S. P., et al. (1997). Medication and psychotherapy in the treatment of bulimia nervosa. *American Journal of Psychiatry, 154,* 523–531.

Wanden-Berghe, R. G., Sanz-Valero, J., & Wanden-Berghe, C. (2011). The application of mindfulness to eating disorders treatment: A systematic review. *Eating Disorders, 19,* 34–48.

Wilson, G. T., & Zandberg, L. J. (2012). Cognitive behavioral guided self-help for eating disorders: Effectiveness and scalability. *Clinical Psychology Review, 32,* 343–357.

Integrating Psychopharmacology and Psychotherapy to Treat Children with ADHD

Tais S. Moriyama, Guilherme V. Polanczyk, Fernanda S. Terzi, Kauy M. Faria, Manfred Döpfner, and Luis A. Rohde

INTRODUCTION

Attention deficit hyperactivity disorder (ADHD) is one of the most common mental disorders in childhood. It is estimated that approximately 5% of children and adolescents are affected worldwide (Polanczyk, de Lima, Horta, Biederman, & Rohde, 2007) and that most of them will present with symptoms and associated functional deficit in adult life (Faraone, Biederman, & Mick, 2006). The impact of ADHD can be devastating; the disorder pervades different areas of functioning, and symptoms are associated with lower academic achievements (Mannuzza, Klein, Bessler, Malloy, & Hynes, 1997), marital problems, difficulties with offspring (Barkley & Fischer, 2010), lower employment status and unemployment (Mannuzza et al., 1997; Stein, 2008), more frequent involvement in traffic accidents (Barkley & Cox, 2007), and increased risk for other psychiatric disorders (Mannuzza, Klein, Bessler, Malloy, & LaPadula, 1998). Because of its pervasive impact, therapeutic interventions should target not only symptoms but also other aspects of psychosocial functioning. Treatment guidelines such as those from the National Institute of Health and Clinical Excellence (NICE, 2008), American Academy of Pediatrics (AAP, 2011), American Academy of Child and Adolescent Psychiatry (AACAP; Pliszka, 2007), European Guideline (Taylor et al., 2004), and Global Consensus (Remschmidt, 2005) recommend psychopharmacological and psychosocial interventions, isolated or in combination according to specific clinical configuration, as first-line treatment for ADHD. This review addresses specifically the issue of what evidence supports the efficacy and effectiveness of pharmacological, psychosocial, or combined treatment for children with ADHD. Our aim is to comprehensively review the literature, providing clinicians with empirically based information on this topic. Fortunately, an extensive amount of studies have already examined the efficacy of different treatment strategies for ADHD.

The first report of an intervention for inattention and hyperactivity is from 1937, when Benzedrine was prescribed to calm down hyperactive children and make them more able to concentrate (Clements & Peters, 1962). To date, 17 meta-analyses have been published (Bjornstad & Montgomery, 2005; Cheng, Chen, Ko, & Ng, 2007; Connor, Fletcher, & Swanson, 1999; Fabiano et al., 2009; Faraone, 2009; Faraone & Biederman, 2002; Faraone, Biederman, & Roe,

2002; Faraone, Biederman, Spencer, & Aleardi, 2006; Faraone & Buitelaar, 2010; Hanwella, Senanayake, & de Silva, 2011; Hazell et al., 2011; Klassen, Miller, Raina, Lee, & Olsen, 1999; Majewicz-Hefley & Carlson, 2007; Schachter, Pham, King, Langford, & Moher, 2001; Storebo et al., 2011; Van der Oord, Prins, Oosterlaan, & Emmelkamp, 2008; Zwi, Jones, Thorgaard, York, & Dennis, 2011), reporting the findings of hundreds of clinical trials testing interventions for ADHD (see Tables 8.1, 8.2, and 8.3 for an overview of those 17 meta-analyses). Due to the large amount of data, the information about efficacy presented here has been based on the best level of evidence available (i.e., when possible meta-analytic data is described, when pooled estimation is not available or updated, we have described individual results from clinical trials). Before discussing ADHD treatment, we briefly present some updated information about ADHD prevalence, clinical presentation, and diagnostic criteria.

ATTENTION DEFICIT HYPERACTIVITY DISORDER

Epidemiology

Reported prevalence of ADHD in children and adolescents varies across different studies depending on the methodology used. A pooled estimation based on 102 epidemiological studies resulted in a rate of 5.29% for children and adolescents, with the disorder more common among school-age children (prevalence of around 6%) than among adolescents (3%) (Polanczyk et al., 2007).

Diagnosis

ADHD is characterized by symptoms of *inattention*, *hyperactivity*, and/or *impulsivity*, starting early in childhood and to a degree that is above what is expected for the child's developmental stage.

Inattention refers to difficulty initiating, remaining engaged in, and completing a task. Common behavioral manifestations of inattention are difficulty in following instructions, planning and organizing tasks, listening and understanding when spoken to, keeping track of objects, and remaining aware of appointments and deadlines. *Hyperactivity* is characterized by excess activity and constant feelings of restlessness. Patients report being uncomfortable when still, which causes them to be in constant motion and increases non-goal-directed activity; they are frequently standing, walking, talking, or simply moving without purpose in inappropriate contexts. *Impulsivity* refers to difficulty in delaying or inhibiting an action in disregard of its consequences. It is associated with the urgency for immediate gratification, even when postponement could lead to advantage. Impulsive behaviors can be expressed as difficulty in waiting one's turn or for the appropriate time (especially for pleasurable or desired activities) and a tendency to act without thinking, such as giving the first answer that comes to mind irrespective of its accuracy.

The diagnosis of ADHD is exclusively grounded on clinical information, and no subsidiary exam is required. The two most used classification systems—DSM-IV (American Psychiatric Association, 1994) and ICD-10 (World Health Organization, 1993)—pose very similar criteria. One of the main differences between them is that ICD-10 requires that symptoms be present in both the two dimensions (attention and hyperactivity/impulsivity), whereas DSM-IV classifies symptoms under only one of the two dimensions (attention or hyperactivity/impulsivity) and requires that symptoms be evident in at least one of them. Both classificatory systems require at least six out of nine symptoms of inattention or at least six out of nine symptoms of hyperactivity/impulsivity for the diagnosis of ADHD, and symptoms must persist for at least 6 months to a degree that is maladaptive and inconsistent with the developmental stage. It is good clinical practice (and a requirement of both DSM and ICD) to verify whether symptoms pervade in more than one environment—for example, home and school. Disruptive behaviors that are exclusive to one environment may reflect inadequacy of the environment itself rather than problems with the individual. DSM-IV allows three possible diagnoses (subtypes): combined type ADHD (if criteria for inattention and hyperactivity/impulsivity are met); predominantly inattentive subtype (criteria for attention deficit are met, but criteria for hyperactivity/impulsivity are not met); and predominantly hyperactive-impulsive (if criteria for hyperactivity/impulsivity are met, but criteria for inattention are not met). According to ICD-10, it is possible to make the following diagnosis: disturbance of activity and attention (general criteria for hyperkinetic disorder are met, but not for conduct disorder); hyperkinetic conduct disorder (criteria for conduct disorder is also met); other hyperkinetic disorders; hyperkinetic disorder; unspecified.

One important thing to keep in mind for the clinical evaluation of patients is the fact that ADHD symptoms may vary significantly depending on age. Hyperactivity in preschoolers, for example, will be presented as running and climbing, while older children will report difficulty in remaining seated; adolescents will fidget, and adults might report inner feelings of restlessness without perceivable hyperactivity. Additionally, the symptoms may only be perceived when the deficient abilities are demanded; this is especially true for attention deficits. Underreporting of symptoms is not rare; ADHD patients might develop compensatory skills for their deficits that can make symptoms assessment difficult. The disorder and its symptoms can also be interpreted as personality traits; inattention is frequently considered to be laziness or lack of commitment to intellectual performance, while impulsiveness is judged as spontaneity, audaciousness, or lack of empathetic moral concern. It is very important, though, to carefully examine the presence of symptoms and the individual developmental stage when diagnosing ADHD.

PHARMACOTHERAPY FOR ADHD

Pharmacological treatment of ADHD can be divided into two classes of drugs: stimulants and nonstimulants. Stimulant medications have been used for decades and are the most extensively studied drugs (see Table 8.1 for an overview of meta-analysis of clinical trials testing stimulants for the treatment of ADHD; Table 8.2 for the comparison of stimulants with nonstimulants; and Table 8.3 for the comparison of stimulants with psychosocial treatments). Most commonly used stimulants are methylphenidate, mixed amphetamine salts, and amphetamine derivatives. Stimulant drugs are similar to each other in terms of their mechanism of action, efficacy, and side effects. The term "nonstimulant," however, is a very generic word and does not describe a group encompassing drugs with common characteristics; "nonstimulant" drugs differ from each other with respect to their mechanisms of action and pharmacological class. They include a variety of drugs such as antidepressants (imipramine and bupropion), alfa-2 agonists (clonidine, guanfacine), and others (modafinil and atomoxetine) (see Table 8.1 for meta-analysis reporting the ES of nonstimulants for ADHD and Table 8.2 for an overview of meta-analysis comparing nonstimulants to stimulants). Nevertheless, most meta-analyses grouped all nonstimulants and computed a single pooled effect size (ES) for all drugs. This information has reduced clinical value since available data shows that the efficacy of different nonstimulants is considerably varied.

Table 8.1 Meta-analyses reporting ES of stimulants and nonstimulants for ADHD.

First author, year	N of studies included (participants)	Age range (% of boys)	Selection criteria	Intervention	Duration of trials included	Sources of search	Studies included quality	Pooled effect size (ES) for ADHD symptoms reduction with respective confidence interval and other relevant results about efficacy
Schachter, 2001 (Schachter et al., 2001)	62 (2,897)	2.4–18 y (mean 8.7) (88.1% boys)	1) Placebo-controlled RCT; 2) Involving short-act methylphenidate; 3) Age below 18y; 4) Primary diagnosis of ADD in a systematic reproducible way.	Methylphenidate	2–28 (mean 3.3 weeks)	Biological Abstracts, CINAHL, Cochrane Library, Current Contents, Dissertation Abstracts, EMBASE, ERIC, Medline, PsycINFO, HEALTHSTAR (1981–1999)	Low	ES 0.78 (0.64–0.91) for teachers' report ES 0.54 (0.40–0.67) rated by parents Strong indication of publication bias Overall doses used were very low
Faraone, 2002 (Faraone & Biederman, 2002)	6(384)	Not described (Child to adults)	1) Placebo-controlled design, blind rating of outcomes; 2) Presentation of means and SD for drug and placebo; 3) Use of structured methods of assessment; 4) At least 2 weeks of follow-up.	MAS	Not described	Current Content, EMBASE, PSYCHLIT, PsycINFO, PubMed (date for search not provided)	Studies quality was not systematically assessed	ES 1.0 (0.9–1.1) Significant heterogeneity Indication of publication bias, Corrected ES 0.84 (0.67–1.0)
Faraone, 2002 (Faraone et al., 2002)	4(188)	5–17 y (not provided)	1) Blinded ratings of outcome; 2) Presentation of means and SD; 3) Use of structured method for the assessment of symptoms.	MAS vs. Methylphenidate SR	3–6 weeks	PubMed	Studies quality was not systematically assessed	ES 0.25 (0.12–0.39) for the comparison of Adderall vs. methylphenidate favoring the first. Funnel plot suggestive of publication bias, corrected ES 0.12 (z = 2.0; p = 0.04).

Study	N (subjects)	Sample characteristics	Drug comparison	Follow-up	Databases searched	Studies quality	Results
Faraone, 2010 (Faraone & Buitelaar, 2010)	23 (not computed)	Mean age varied from 9 to 15 years (Proportion of male varied from 60%–100%)	Amphetamines vs. Methylphenidate	Not described	CINAHL, Cochrane Library, EMBASE, ERIC, E-psyche, Medline, PREMEDLINE, PubMed, Social Sciences Abstracts (1979–ending date not provided)	Studies quality was not systematically assessed	Significant differences favoring amphetamine over methylphenidate: ES 1.03 vs. 0.77. ES greater for children vs. adolescents, teacher and physician ratings vs. parent rating; ES were negatively correlated with study length. Significant publication bias for studies of methylphenidate but smaller than that for amphetamine although the last was not significant. Significant heterogeneity for amphetamines studies but not for methylphenidate
		1) Children and adolescents; 2) Published in English after 1979; 3) Randomized, double-blind, placebo-controlled; 4) Diagnosis according to DSM-II, DSM-III, DMS-IIIR, DSM-IV; 5) At least 2 weeks of follow-up 6) Presented means and SDs (drug and placebo).					
Connor, 2001 (Connor et al., 1999)	11 (150)	8–15y (mean 10.6y) (Proportion of male not reported)	Clonidine	3–51 (mean 7 weeks)	Current Contents (1996–1999), Medline (1980–1999), PsycINFO (1984–1999), Non-peer-reviewed research sources	3 studies weaker than average and 8 stronger than average.	ES 0.58 (0.27–0.89; extracted from 6 studies with better methodology and homogeneous results) 0.75 for parent-rated symptoms and 0.56 for teacher-rated symptoms.
		1) Numeric data; 2) Outcome directly related to ADHD features; 3) More than 1 subject; 4) Mean sample age bellow 18y.					

(Continued)

Table 8.1 Continued

First author, year	N of studies included (participants)	Age range (% of boys)	Selection criteria	Intervention	Duration of trials included	Sources of search	Studies included quality	Pooled effect size (ES) for ADHD symptoms reduction with respective confidence interval and other relevant results about efficacy
Cheng, 2007 (Cheng, et al., 2007)	9 (1,828) 1,615 ADHD+/ ODD-213 ADHD+/ ODD+	Not described (only studies with children and adolescents were included)	1) Randomized placebo-controlled clinical trials; 2) ADHD any subtype; 3) Atomoxetine was compared to placebo; 4) Children and adolescents; 5) Outcome was the rating scale ADHD-RS-IV; 6) Adverse events, withdrawals or dropouts reported.	Atomoxetine	Not described	Cochrane Central Register of Controlled Trial (CENTRAL 2006 Issue3), Medline, PsycINFO, PubMed (1985–2006)	Overall good	For ADHD without comorbidity with ODD: 0.64 (0.52–0.76) for overall symptoms, 0.56 (0.46–0.66) for inattention and 0.55 (0.37–0.73) for hyperactivity/impulsivity. Significant heterogeneity (I^2 67%) for hyperactivity/impulsivity. For ADHD in comorbidity with ODD: 0.69 (0.44–0.95) for total scores, 0.69 (0.44–0.94) for inattention, 0.59 (0.34–0.85) for hyperactivity/impulsivity. Significant heterogeneity for almost all outcomes. NNT for both condition (with and without ODD) very similar and around 3.4. Evidence of publication bias according to Egger's test, but not when Begg's test was used.

ADHD = attention deficit hyperactivity disorder; ADHD-RS-IV = Attention Deficit Hyperactivity Disorder Rating Scale IV; CI = confidence interval; DSM-II, DSM-III, DSM-IIIR, DSM-IV = *Diagnostic and Statistical Manual of Mental Disorders* Second, Third, Third revised, or Fourth edition, respectively; ES = effect size; LOCF= last observation carried forward; MAS = mixed amphetamine salts; NNT = number needed to treat; ODD = oppositional defiant disorder; SD = standard deviation; vs.= versus; SR = standard release; y = years.

Table 8.2 Meta-analyses comparing stimulants with nonstimulants for ADHD.

First author, year	N of studies included (participants)	Age range (% of boys)	Selection criteria	Intervention	Duration of trials included	Sources of search	Studies included quality	Pooled effect size (ES) for ADHD symptoms reduction with respective confidence interval and other relevant results about efficacy
Faraone, 2006 (Faraone, Biederman, Spencer et al., 2006)	29 (not described)	Mean age 9–15y; (64%–100% for 28 studies and one study included only girls)	1) Randomized double-blind, placebo-controlled clinical trials; 2) DSM-IIIR or DSM-IV ADHD; 3) 2 weeks or more; 4) Presented means and SDs; 5) 20 or more subjects in drug or placebo group; Excluded if: 1) Less than 20 subjects per group; 2) Explored appropriate dose for future work; 3) Sample recruitment based on comorbid condition; 4) Outcome rated in laboratory environment.	Short-acting stimulants vs. Long-acting stimulants vs. Nonstimulants (Atomoxetine, Bupropion, Modafinil)	Not described	CINAHL, Cochrane Library, ERIC, E-psyche, Medline, Ovid, PREMEDLINE, PubMed, Social Sciences Abstracts; Presentations APA and AACAP meetings. (1979– ending date not provided)	Studies quality was not systematically assessed	ES of nonstimulants found to be significantly less than those for immediate-release stimulants ($F_{(1,27)} = 28.4$, $p < 0.0001$) or long acting stimulants ($F_{(1,27)} = 14.1$, $p = 0.0008$. No difference between the two classes of stimulants ($F_{(1,27)} = 2.4$, $p = 0.14$. Difference between stimulants and nonstimulants remained significant even after adjustments for confounders ($F_{(1,27)} = 11.3$, $p = 0.05$. No evidence of publication bias. No evidence of heterogeneity except for long-acting stimulants.

(Continued)

Table 8.2 Continued

First author, year	N of studies included (participants)	Age range (% of boys)	Selection criteria	Intervention	Duration of trials included	Sources of search	Studies included quality	Pooled effect size (ES) for ADHD symptoms reduction with respective confidence interval and other relevant results about efficacy
Faraone, 2009 (Faraone, 2009)	32 (not described)	Mean age 8–15 years (60%–100% male, with the exception of one trial that included only girls)	1) Randomized, double-blind, placebo-controlled methodology; 2) DSM-III, DSM-IIIR, or DSM-IV ADHD; 3) 6–18 years of age; 3) 2 weeks or more; 4) Presented means and SDs; Exclusion: 1) Less than 20 subjects per group; 2) Explored appropriate dose for future work; 3) Sample recruitment based on comorbid condition.	Short-acting stimulants vs. Long-acting stimulants vs. Nonstimulants (Atomoxetine, Modafinil, Bupropion, Paroxetine, Guanfacine)	Not described	CINAHL, Cochrane Database, E-psyche, ERIC, Medline, Ovid, PREMEDLINE, PubMed, Social Sciences Abstracts, APA and AACAP meetings. (1979–ending date not provided)	Studies quality was not systematically assessed	ES for short-acting stimulants 0.99 (0.88–1.1); ES long-acting stimulants 0.95 (0.85–1.1); nonstimulants 0.57 (0.53–0.62). ES for atomoxetine 0.63 (0.57–0.69; ES Bupropion 0.22 (−0.11–0.55); Modafinil 0.52 (0.45–0.58); Clonidine 0.03 (−0.48–0.53), Guanfacine ES 0.8 (0.53–1.07). ES of nonstimulants were significantly less than those for short- and long-acting stimulants (F[1,31] = 25; p < 0.0001 and F[1,31] = 15; p = 0.001 respectively) No evidence of publication bias. Significant heterogeneity for long-acting stimulants with 68% of variability resulting from variability (p < 0.0001). Nonsignificant heterogeneity for short-acting stimulants and nonstimulants with low I^2.

Study	N (studies)	Age (%)	Inclusion criteria	Comparison	Duration	Databases searched	Quality assessment	Results
Hazell, 2010 (Hazell et al., 2011)	7 (1,368)	10.2y (81.6%)	1) Randomized, controlled trials (open label also included); 2) Duration of 6 weeks; 3) Assessment of ADHD Rating Scale-IV-Parent Version; rated by investigators after interview with parents; 5) Atomoxetine compared to methylphenidate 6) Age 6–18y.	Atomoxetine vs. Methylphenidate	Results were based on 6 weeks evaluation	ClinicalTrials.gov, EMBASE, Lilly Product Literature Database, Medline, PsycINFO. (Up to August 2008)	All studies of atomoxetine included were funded by Eli Lilly, atomoxetine manufacturer	Non-inferiority analysis based on proportion of respondents (≥ 40% reduction from baseline). After 6 weeks 53.5% (46.7–60.4%) of patients taking atomoxetine responded, and 54.4% (47.6–61.1%) of those taking methylphenidate. Non-inferiority of atomoxetine to methylphenidate (absolute difference –0.9% (–9.2–7.5%)). Dose of methylphenidate was overall low for all studies (0.41 to 0.52 mg/Kg/day).
Hanwella, 2011 (Hanwella et al., 2011)	9 (2,762)	6–16y (77.6%)	1) Randomized, controlled trials (open label also included); 2) Diagnosis of ADHD according the DSM-IV; 3) Atomoxetine compared to methylphenidate.	Atomoxetine vs. Methylphenidate	3–10 weeks	Cochrane Central Register of Controlled Trials and Cochrane Database of Systematic Reviews, PubMed, references of articles. (January 1995–December 2010)	Studies evaluated using Detsky Quality Scale for Randomized Trials; all had a score of 12 or higher	No significant standardized mean difference between atomoxetine and methylphenidate (0.09 (0.08–0.26) (Z = 1.06, p = 0.29)). Long-acting methylphenidate was superior to atomoxetine but not short-acting methylphenidate. Significant heterogeneity between studies (p = 0.002, I^2 = 67%) Publication bias not assessed.

AACAP = American Academy of Child and Adolescent Psychiatry; ADHD = attention deficit hyperactivity disorder; APA = American Psychiatric Association; CI = confidence interval; DSM-IV = *Diagnostic and Statistical Manual for Mental Disorders*; ER = extended release; ES = effect size; FDA = Food and Drug Administration; LA-St (long-acting stimulants); N-St = nonstimulants; RR = relative risk; SA-St = short-acting stimulant; SD = standard deviation; vs. = versus; y = years

Table 8.3 Meta-analyses reporting effect size of psychosocial interventions for ADHD.

First author, year	N of studies included (participants)	Age range (% of boys)	Selection criteria	Intervention
Klassen, 1999 (Klassen et al., 1999)	26 (999)	Studies included patients from 2–17, mean age not provided (69–100%)	1) Randomized controlled clinical trials; 2) Published 1981 or later; 3) DSM-II diagnostic criteria; 4) Age 0–18y; 5) ADD, ADD-H, or ADHD made in explicit reproducible way; 6) At least 1 week of stimulants for pharmacotherapy and a whole course of psychotherapy for behavioral intervention; 7) Parents or teachers rating scales as an outcome; 8) Data presentation suitable for meta-analysis.	Stimulants vs. psychosocial intervention (behavioral parents training, CBT) vs. combination
Bjornstad, 2005 (Bjornstad & Montgomery, 2005)	2 (one study with 146 participants of interest for this analysis and another with 16)	MTA 7–9.9y Not described for the other study	1) Randomized controlled trials; 2) Intervention behavioral family therapy, cognitive behavioral family therapy, or functional family therapy not combined with medication; 3) Children and adolescents; 4) Diagnosis of ADHD or ADD according to DSM-III or DSM-IV.	Behavioral-based family therapy
Majewicz-Hefley, 2007 (Majewicz-Hefley & Carlson, 2007)	8 (not described, participants in the combined treatment group varied from 18 to 136)	Mean age 7.3–8.5y (not described)	1) English language; 2) Diagnosis of ADHD; 3) Combination of pharmacological and psychosocial treatment; 4) Necessary information to calculate ES; 5) Outcomes in inattention, or hyperactivity, or impulsivity, or social skills academics.	Combination of pharmacotherapy and psychosocial treatment

Duration of trials included	Sources of search	Studies included quality	Pooled effect size (ES) for ADHD symptoms reduction with respective confidence interval and other relevant results about efficacy
Pharmacological treatment 7–28 weeks Psychosocial interventions follow-up 10 weeks–24 months	CIJE (1981–1997), Current Contents (1985–1997), EMBASE (1988–1997), First Search (Article First) (1990–1997), Healthstar (1981–1997), Medline (1981–1997), PsychoINFO (1981–1997), reference list from book chapters and reviews published in main journals.	Majority (17) had reasonable good methodology. All drug studies used crossover design. Only 2 drug studies but all involving psychotherapy used between groups design.	Daily doses of stimulants were overall low. ES for stimulants vs. placebo 1.03 (0.84–1.21) according to teachers' ratings and 0.86 (0.58–1.14) for parents' ratings; ES for psychosocial vs. control or comparison 0.40 (0.48–1.28) according to teachers and 0.49 (0.29–1.27) for parents' rating; ES for combination vs. control or comparison 3.78 (0.51–8.06) according to teachers' ratings and 7.35 (2.4–12.29) according to parents' ratings; ES for combination vs. medication 1.29 (0.72–3.29) for teachers' rating and 0.46 (–2.94–3.86) according to parents' ratings; ES for combination vs. psychosocial 2.01 (0.16–4.17) according to teachers' rating, 5.91 (3.19–8.63) for parents' rating.
MTA 14 months Not described for the other study	Biosis, CINAHL, Cochrane Central Register of Controlled Trials (The Cochrane Library Issue 3, 2004), Dissertation Abstracts, MEDLINE, PsycINFO, Sociofile, hand searches of relevant journals and bibliographies, contact to experts in the field. (available years until April 2004)	Only studies with adequate methodology were included.	Pooled estimation was not possible. ESs provided were computed for each of the studies in separate. Study 1 (NIMH MTA) ES for parents'-rated inattention –0.09 (–0.025–0.07); parents'-rated hyperactivity –0.11 (–0.29–0.07); teachers'-rated inattention –0.01 (–0.21–0.19), teachers'-rated hyperactivity –0.15 (–0.35–0.05) Study 2 ES –0.15 (–0.35–0.05) for teacher-rated hyperactivity.
2–24 months	PsycINFO, reference lists of articles (1900–2004, although authors report search starting date as the year 1900, to our knowledge PsycINFO indexes publication only from 1967 forward)	Studies quality was not systematically assessed.	ES for inattention 1.27 (0.83–1.72); hyperactivity 1.27 (0.79–1.75); impulsivity 0.91 (0.56–1.25). ES for social skills 0.9 (0.5–1.3). ES for academic functioning 0.19 (0.02–0.37). (Outliers were excluded from analysis when its presence led to significant heterogeneity.)

(Continued)

Table 8.3 (continuation) Meta-analyses of trials testing psychosocial interventions for ADHD.

First author, year	N of studies included (participants)	Age range (% of boys)	Selection criteria	Intervention
Van der Oord, 2008 (Van der Oord et al., 2008)	24 (not described)	Mean age 7.6–11.8y (not described)	1) Randomized controlled design; 2) Parent or teacher scales as outcome measures; 3) Primary diagnosis of ADHD; 4) When applicable, the medication treatment used short-acting methylphenidate; 5) When applicable, the psychosocial treatment was clearly described as behavioral or cognitive behavioral; 6) Treatment conducted in a clinical (outpatient) setting; 7) Age between 6 and 12 years old; 8) Data reported allowed calculation of pre- to posttreatment ES; 9) Reported outcomes in terms of either ADHD symptoms, ODD/CD symptoms, social behavior, or academic functioning; 10) Methylphenidate dose was administered individually at a fixed dose, or an optimally titrated dose, rather than at varying doses.	Behavioral or cognitive behavioral intervention vs. methylphenidate vs. combination
Fabiano, 2009 (Fabiano et al., 2009)	174 (101 are single-subject studies) Number of participants per group based on study design: 539 between-groups; 1,077 pre-post; 386 within-subject; 101 single-subject	Mean age 7.1–8.9y (74.5–84.5% male) Mean age computed for groups based on design	1) Diagnosis of ADHD or behavioral description compatible with ADHD, for studies including other externalizing problems at least 50% of participants with comorbid ADHD; 2) IQ ≥ 80; 3) age < 18 years or mean age above 5 years; 4) Disorder not better accounted by a organic cause; 5) For between-groups design at least 1 group treated with behavior therapy strict principles; 6) Necessary information to calculate ES; 7) Primarily treatment outcomes studies.	Behavioral-based interventions

Duration of trials included	Sources of search	Studies included quality	Pooled effect size (ES) for ADHD symptoms reduction with respective confidence interval and other relevant results about efficacy
Methylphenidate 2–104 weeks; Psychosocial intervention 9.5–164 hours	ISI Web of Science, PubMed, PsycINFO, references lists of other articles. (January 1985–September 2006)	Studies quality was not systematically assessed.	ES for methylphenidate 1.53 (1.23–1.82) according to parents' rating; 1.83 (1.43–2.12) rated by teachers. ES for psychosocial intervention 0.87 (0.73–1.01) according to parents' rating; 0.75 (0.49–1.01) for teachers' rating. ES for combination 1.89 (1.39–2.40) for parents and 1.77 (1.08–2.46) for teachers' ratings.
			ES for methylphenidate alone or in combination did not differ significantly from each other, but both were significantly superior to psychosocial interventions.
			Significant heterogeneity for almost all outcomes and treatments.
			ES for academic functioning was low for all treatments 0.19 (0.03–0.36) for psychosocial; 0.33 (−0.14–0.81) for methylphenidate; 0.35 (−0.02–0.71) for the combination of both. Social behavior outcomes showed comparable moderate mean weighted ES for all treatments.
			Behavioral interventions were superior to cognitive behavioral interventions according to parents'-rated ADHD symptoms.
			No significant correlation between duration of psychosocial treatment and ES.
Mean number of sessions varied from 7–40 Mean computed for groups based on study design and type of intervention	PsycINFO, references list of articles, serial search of tables of content of journals from 1968 to 2006 (9 journals were systematically searched), dissertation identified using PsycINFO and ProQuest dissertation database, experts in the field were contacted.	Not systematically assessed.	Weighted ES 0.74 (0.52–0.95) for between-groups design; 0.63 (0.54–0.71); unweighted ES for within-subject design 2.64 (1.03–4.24); 3.78 (2.82–4.74).
			Large difference in effect size depending on the type of measure; laboratory observation of child behavior yielded an average effect size of 1.05, whereas child behavior in the same setting was 0.19.

(Continued)

Table 8.3 (continuation) Meta-analyses of trials testing psychosocial interventions for ADHD.

First author, year	N of studies included (participants)	Age range (% of boys)	Selection criteria	Intervention
Zwi, 2011 (Zwi et al., 2011)	5 (284)	Mean age 4–13y (36% male)	1) Randomized or quasi randomized design; 2) Parents' training compared to no-treatment or waiting list or treatment as usual; 3) ADHD was the main focus; 4) 5–18 years; 5) ADHD or hyperkinetic disorder according to DSM-II, DSM-IV or ICD-10; diagnosis by a specialist using operationalized diagnostic criteria; 6) At least 1 outcome related to the child's behavior. **Exclusion** 1) Combined intervention delivered to the child.	Parents' training (behavioral or cognitive behavioral based) vs. treatment as usual
Storebø, 2011 (Storebø et al., 2011)	11 (747)	5–12 years (four trials girls to boys 1:3 or 1:4; in three 1:2; in three 1:7–1:20)	1) Randomized trials; 2) Intervention included social skills training; 3) 5–18 years; 4) Diagnosis of ADHD according to DSM-III, DSM-IIIR, DSM-IV, or hyperkinetic disorder from ICD-10 or based on cut-off scores on validated rating scales.	Social skills training (based on behavioral/ cognitive behavioral model)

ADD = attention deficit disorder; ADHD = attention deficit hyperactivity disorder; Biosis = biological abstracts; CD = conduct disorder; CIJE = current index to journal in education; DSM-III, DMS-IIIR, DSM-IV = *Diagnostic and Statistical Manual of Mental Disorders* Third, Third revised, or Fourth edition, respectively; ES = effect size; ICD-10 = *International Classification of Diseases* 10th edition;

Duration of trials included	Sources of search	Studies included quality	Pooled effect size (ES) for ADHD symptoms reduction with respective confidence interval and other relevant results about efficacy
8 weeks to 5 months	CENTRAL (2010, Issue 3); CINAHL, Dissertation Abstracts International; EMBASE; metaRegister of Controlled Trials; MEDLIE; PsycINFO; experts in the field were contacted. (all available years until September 2010)	Risk of bias unclear or high for most studies.	Quantitative data for this pooled estimation was based on 3 studies for children externalizing symptom outcome, 2 for internalizing symptoms, and 2 for outcomes referring to parents. ES for externalizing symptoms improvement 0.32 (0.18–0.83) nonsignificant, significant heterogeneity. ES for internalizing symptoms 0.48 (0.13–0.84) significant, $I^2 = 9\%$.
8–10 weeks (8 trials) up to 2 years	AMED, CENTRAL (2011, Issue 1), CINAHL, EMBASE, ERIC, MEDILINE, MetaRegister of Controlled Trials (October 2010). PsycINFO, Social Abstracts. Online conference abstracts. Contact with 176 experts on the field. (all available years until March–June 2011)	Low quality (high risk for bias due to systematic errors in most trials)	Nonsignificant effect of treatment for most outcomes; ES for teachers'-rated social skills 0.16 (–0.04–0.36); ES for parent-rated social skills 0.22 (0.04–0.4); ES for participant-rated social skills 0.21 (–0.09–0.51); ES teacher-rated ADHD symptoms –0.02 (–0.19–0.16); ES parents-rated ADHD symptoms –0.49 (–0.79–0.19); Combined use of medication, presence of comorbidity, and combined parents' training did not influenced treatment ES.

IQ = intelligence quotient; NIMH MTA = The National Institute of Mental Health Multimodal Treatment Study of ADHD; ODD = oppositional defiant disorder; Sociofile = Sociological Abstracts; vs. = versus; y = years

Stimulant Medications for the Treatment of ADHD

Data supporting the efficacy of stimulants for ADHD is very robust. Meta-analyses conducted so far consistently show stimulants to significantly decrease ADHD symptoms in the short term. Most meta-analyses report large ESs independently on stimulant drugs used (see Tables 8.1 and 8.2). There are three different meta-analyses that computed ESs of methylphenidate for ADHD. A meta-analysis published in 2001 covering literature until 1999 found the lowest but still moderate ESs of 0.78 for teachers' ratings and 0.54 for parent-rated ADHD symptoms (Schachter et al., 2001). However, the studies included used very low doses of methylphenidate, which may explain the discrepancy with more recent results of 0.77 for children and adolescents aged 9–15 (Faraone, Biederman, Spencer et al., 2006), and 1.53 for children aged 7–11 according to parent ratings and 1.83 for teachers' ratings (Van der Oord et al., 2008). ESs found for methylphenidate tend to be slightly lower than that of amphetamine derivatives (ES 1.03 versus 0.77) (Faraone & Buitelaar, 2010), but the real clinical significance of this finding is controversial, since both classes present large ES (i.e., higher than 0.8). When the ES for different stimulants are pooled together, the ES found is very similar to that for each individual drug—1.03 for overall ADHD symptoms (Klassen et al., 1999). Most studies compute ES based on the comparison with placebo and use ADHD rating scales scores reduction as a main outcome. Proportion of respondents is not commonly used as an outcome for meta-analysis. A meta-analysis showing non-inferiority of atomoxetine to methylphenidate found methylphenidate to promote symptom relief of at least 40% to 54.5% of patients after 6 weeks of treatment. Nevertheless, the studies included in this estimation used very low doses of methylphenidate, and this number might have been underestimated (Hazell et al., 2011). Long- and short-acting drugs seem not to differ in terms of their efficacy. Faraone et al. found no significant difference for the ES of short- and long-acting formulation for children and adolescents in two meta-analyses (Faraone, 2009; Faraone, Biederman, Spencer et al., 2006)—similar ES of 0.99 and 0.95 for youths taking short- and long-acting formulation, respectively.

Nonstimulant Medications

Nonstimulant medications are considered second line treatments for ADHD. Nevertheless, they have an important role in the case of treatment failure with stimulants, intolerance, or contra-indication and may be an option in specific cases of comorbidity (e.g., atomoxetine for ADHD comorbid with anxiety disorders [Geller et al., 2007]). Evidence of effectiveness is good for atomoxetine, extended-release guanfacine, and extended-release clonidine. Other drugs like bupropion, modafinil, and imipramine have also shown some positive results for the treatment of ADHD but with more limited evidence.

Among nonstimulants, atomoxetine is certainly the drug whose effect is most strongly supported by empirical evidence. A meta-analysis based on a systematic review of randomized placebo-controlled clinical trials available until 2006 found the ES of atomoxetine to be 0.64 for children with ADHD (Cheng et al., 2007). Although this meta-analysis is based on the result of only nine clinical trials, the studies included were overall of good quality, and more than 1,800 patients were included in total, providing strong evidence for the accuracy of the estimated ES. Furthermore, a more recent meta-analysis published in 2009 found very similar results with an ES of 0.63 (Faraone, 2009). The direct comparison of atomoxetine and stimulants was also assessed using pooled estimations. A study of non-inferiority of atomoxetine using the proportion of respondent as a main outcome showed that 53.5% of children taking atomoxetine responded after 6 weeks of treatment, but this study used very peculiar inclusion criteria that led to the exclusive inclusion of clinical trials funded by Eli Lilly, atomoxetine manufacturer (Hazell et al., 2011). Another meta-analysis with adequate methodology also found no standardized mean differences between atomoxetine and methylphenidate as a group. When methylphenidate was separated into two groups (long- and short-acting stimulants), long- but not short-acting stimulants were found to be superior to atomoxetine (Hanwella et al., 2011).

Clonidine and guanfacine are alpha-2 agonists. Clonidine is a low-cost alternative that—although not as effective as stimulants or atomoxetine—might be a reasonable option for low-income populations. The efficacy of clonidine for ADHD has been tested in some clinical trials with poor methodology. A meta-analysis of available studies until 1999 revealed an overall medium effect size of 0.58 for the six studies with better methodology (including a total of 84 patients) (Connor et al., 1999). A more recent meta-analysis using more restricted inclusion criteria found an insignificant ES of 0.03, but this estimation was based on a single study that fulfilled criteria to be included in the meta-analysis (Faraone, 2009). After this meta-analysis, other relevant trials were published. A randomized controlled study with adequate sample size demonstrated the superiority of extended-release clonidine to placebo (Jain, Segal, Kollins, & Khayrallah, 2011); and another well-conducted randomized trial demonstrated extended-release clonidine to be superior to placebo as an adjunctive drug in combination with stimulants (Kollins et al., 2011). Extended-release guanfacine has also been shown to be superior to placebo for the treatment of ADHD with a pooled ES calculated of 0.8 (0.53–1.07) based on two studies also published after the abovementioned meta-analysis (Biederman et al., 2008; Sallee et al., 2009). Clonidine was also found to be superior to carbamazepine (Nair & Mahadevan, 2009). The superiority of clonidine to carbamazepine is worth reporting because clonidine is a low-cost alternative for the treatment of ADHD in economically deprived populations where, because of its sedative effect, carbamazepine has frequently been used in an attempt to calm down hyperactive children.

Modafinil is a nonstimulant medication used for the treatment of narcolepsy. The efficacy of modafinil for ADHD has been tested in clinical trials, and the only meta-analysis reporting a pooled estimation for its efficacy found an ES of 0.52 against placebo (Faraone, 2009).

Bupropion is also an alternative, but the only pooled estimation available found an effect size of 0.22 (−0.11–0.55) (Faraone, 2009). This estimation, however, was based on a very limited number of studies (subjects) (Faraone, 2009).

Desipramine and paroxetine have also been tested for ADHD. Although pooled estimation is not available for tricyclic antidepressants, there are a considerable number of trials demonstrating their efficacy (Spencer et al., 1996). Nevertheless, it is reasonable to consider tricyclic antidepressants only after failure of two or three stimulants and atomoxetine, since it is associated with significant side effects and is less effective than stimulant medications (AAP, 2011).

Strengths/Benefits and Weaknesses/Limitations of Using Pharmacotherapy as Sole Approach

Pharmacological treatment for ADHD is relatively accessible for the population and is associated with a robust and prompt decrease of ADHD symptoms for a considerable proportion of patients. Nevertheless, side effects are a source of concern, and scarce data exist on

the long-term effect of pharmacological treatments. Meta-analyses are consistent in reporting side effects to be unequivocally associated with stimulants when compared to placebo.
The most commonly reported side effect is decreased appetite (30%), followed by insomnia
(17%) (Schachter et al., 2001), but other, less-specific side effects are also common such as
headache, irritability, agitation, nervousness, and tremors. Stimulants can also exacerbate
psychotic (Cherland & Fitzpatrick, 1999) and manic symptoms (Ross, 2006), and should be
used with some additional caution for epileptic children because of its theoretical potential
to induce seizures (Kattimani & Mahadevan, 2011). Side effects are relatively common with
stimulants: Four children treated with methylphenidate are needed for one to present with
decreased appetite, and seven for insomnia (Schachter et al., 2001). Atomoxetine is also associated with a range of side effects but reported number needed to harm (NNHs) tends to
be higher: 8.8 for appetite loss, 19.4 for somnolence, 22.5 for abdominal pain (Cheng et al.,
2007) (data for insomnia not presented). Although NNHs reported for atomoxetine seem to
be better than those for stimulants, a meta-analysis comparing different drugs on the proportion of patients presenting side effects found no significant differences between atomoxetine
and stimulants with regard to insomnia and appetite loss (Peterson, McDonagh, & Fu, 2008).
Another well-known adverse event associated with stimulants and atomoxetine is growth
deceleration (Faraone, Biederman, Morley, & Spencer, 2008; Kratochvil et al., 2006). Both
stimulants and atomoxetine are associated with modest but significant delays in height and
weight gain (Faraone et al., 2008; Kratochvil et al., 2006). However, height and weight are
easy to monitor and, once growth deceleration is detected, it can be managed. Stimulants and
atomoxetine can also increase blood pressure and heart rate, but the risk for serious cardiac
events among children taking stimulants is not different from that of the general population
(Elia & Vetter, 2010; Stiefel & Besag, 2010), and discontinuation due to cardiac side effects
is rarely reported in clinical trials (Peterson et al., 2008). Side effects were also present in
the majority of trials testing alpha-2 agonists; for clonidine, sedation is the most commonly
reported symptom, followed by irritability, sleep disturbance, blood pressure drop, hypotension, dry month, and dizziness (Connor et al., 1999). Guanfacine is more selective than clonidine, causing a similar pattern of side effects but in lower frequencies (Biederman et al., 2008;
Sallee et al., 2009). Even though adverse events are relatively common, stimulants and atomoxetine are well tolerated and estimated dropout rates due to adverse events are low: 9% for
amphetamines in Castells et al.'s meta-analysis (Castells, Ramos-Quiroga, Bosch, Nogueira, &
Casas, 2011) and 4% for atomoxetine according to a review combining data from different
clinical trials sponsored by Eli Lilly company (Kratochvil et al., 2006).

Apart from side effects, another source of concern is the long-term adherence and effectiveness of pharmacological treatments. The vast majority of studies are limited in follow-
up time, and studies lasting more than 4 weeks are exceptional. A meta-regression showed
length of study duration to be inversely associated with ES (Faraone & Buitelaar, 2010), which
suggests that ESs computed by short-time trials may not be equivalent to ESs computed
by long-term trials. Castells and colleagues' meta-analysis found that although the power
of amphetamine for the treatment of ADHD is relatively high (pooled ES 0.72), amphetamines do not improve treatment retention rates when compared to placebo (Castells et al.,
2011). The clinical significance of this data, however, is difficult to interpret because of the
short duration of trials included (mean 8 weeks). Sustained-release preparations are thought
to increase adherence because of their better posology, but unfortunately very few meta-
analyses studied the issue of adherence. Retention in treatment has only been analyzed as an
outcome for ES estimation in one meta-analysis. However, authors did not compare long- to

short-acting drugs. They have compared different amphetamine derivatives (mixed amphetamine salts [MAS], lisdexamphetamine, and dextroamphetamine) (Castells et al., 2011). All amphetamine derivatives and amphetamines as a group were found to significantly and considerably decrease ADHD symptoms (ES for dexamphetamine 0.6, ES for lisdexamphetamine extracted from a single study 0.8; ES for MAS 0.73) (Castells et al., 2011), but only MAS increased retention to treatment (Castells et al., 2011). Because long-term follow-ups are not available for most clinical trials (an exception is the NIMH Collaborative Multisite Multimodal Treatment Study of Children with Attention-Deficit/Hyperactivity Disorder— MTA study), most data about treatment persistence comes from retrospective analysis of healthcare providers' datasets, a source susceptible to a diversity of bias. Those studies have consistently found higher rates of persistence with long-acting versus short-acting stimulants (Lawson, Johnsrud, Hodgkins, Sasane, & Crismon, 2012; Marcus, Wan, Kemner, & Olfson, 2005; Palli, Kamble, Chen, & Aparasu, 2012), but overall persistence rates are very poor for both formulations; more than 50% of patients are no longer using stimulants after 90 days, and treatment maintenance for more than 180 days is exceptional (Lawson et al., 2012; Marcus et al., 2005; Winterstein et al., 2008).

Although pharmacotherapy seems to be clearly beneficial for ADHD and a vast amount of clinical trials have already tested the effect of different drugs, available evidence is restricted by the fact that the great majority of trials included predominantly boys with ADHD combined type, had short follow-up times and were conducted in specialty clinics or university-based hospitals (see Tables 8.1, 8.2, and 8.3 for details). Furthermore, especially for newer drugs, a considerable part of the evidence comes from manufacturer-funded trials (59% in Peterson and colleagues' meta-analysis for adult ADHD [Peterson et al., 2008]), and trials reporting effectiveness rather than just efficacy are almost inexistent (e.g., an outcome frequently evaluated is symptom reduction, but academic, occupational, and social functioning are rarely assessed [Peterson et al., 2008]). One of the few meta-analyses that computed data on efficacy and effectiveness separately found methylphenidate to robustly reduce ADHD symptoms (ES of 1.53 and 1.83 according to parents and teachers, respectively), but the impact of the drug on academic performance was much lower, with an ES of 0.33 (Van der Oord et al., 2008).

PSYCHOSOCIAL INTERVENTIONS FOR ADHD

Behavioral and cognitive behavioral therapies are the most empirically tested psychosocial interventions for ADHD. Parent training and school-based interventions are the most used treatment modalities, but child-focused interventions—for example, social skills training— are also implemented in different settings. Behavioral therapy relies on principles of operant conditioning and other learning theories. The therapist collects detailed information about behaviors that lead to behavior problems with the intention of identifying trigger situations generating these behaviors and possible reinforcements to its reoccurrence. After a complete analysis, a detailed plan is proposed on how to deal with the child to avoid trigger situations or reinforcement of the unwanted behaviors (Antshel & Barkley, 2008). The main aim is to extinguish unwanted behaviors. Additionally, children can be trained to develop strategies on planning and execution of tasks that require attention and organization. In clinical trials, interventions tend to be less personally tailored, and manualized sessions are the rule. Many different manuals for behavior therapy in ADHD are available (Bauermeister, So, Jensen, Krispin, & El Din, 2006). Cognitive principals are also used for helping children to develop cognitive strategies for self-monitoring, self-control, and planning. It is a common clinical practice to target ADHD core symptoms with pharmacotherapy while psychosocial interventions are prescribed for the associated functioning deficits like academic and social problems. However, clinical trials do demonstrate that behavioral interventions are also capable of reducing core symptoms of ADHD.

Few meta-analyses have examined the use of psychosocial interventions for ADHD, but they report very divergent results. Klassen et al. (1999) systematically reviewed the literature of randomized clinical trials published between 1981 and 1997. Authors found that behavioral parental training and cognitive behavioral therapy did not reduce ADHD symptoms. ES for psychosocial versus control or comparison was 0.40 (−1.28–0.48) according to teachers and 0.49 (−1.27–0.29) for parent rating (Klassen et al., 1999). Similar results were found by other authors for behavioral-based family therapy (ES computed separately for each of the only two studies to fulfill inclusion criteria was between −0.15 and −0.01 for all outcomes examined [Bjornstad & Montgomery, 2005]). For parental training, either behavior- or cognitive-behavior–oriented intervention results are also similar (nonsignificant ES for externalizing symptoms improvement of 0.32 [0.18–0.83]) (Zwi et al., 2011). The same happens for social skills training based on behavior or cognitive-behavior principals—ES for teachers social skills ratings = 0.16 (−0.04–0.36); ES for parent social skills ratings = 0.22 (0.04–0.4); ES for participant's social skills ratings = 0.21 (−0.09–0.51); ES for teacher ratings of ADHD symptoms = −0.02 (−0.19–0.16); and ES for parent ratings of ADHD symptoms = −0.49 (−0.79–0.19) (Storebo et al., 2011). On the other hand, a more recent meta-analysis including only studies with randomized controlled design found a large ES ranging from 0.75 to 0.87, depending on the rater (parents or teachers) (Van der Oord et al., 2008). Psychosocial treatments included in this meta-analysis were behavioral or cognitive behavioral interventions, and a discrete superiority for behavior over cognitive behavior interventions was found (Van der Oord et al., 2008). Fabiano and colleagues also found moderate ES for psychosocial intervention in studies using between group designs (0.74; CI = 0.52–0.95) and large ES (2.64; CI = 1.03–4.24) for investigations using within subject designs (Fabiano et al., 2009). This meta-analysis, however, included single case studies, and in total 101 of the 174 subjects included were from single-subject reports (Fabiano et al., 2009). Single-subject designs are common in evaluating behavioral interventions, and a large amount of information pertaining to these interventions was generated by studies using this design. Nevertheless, this study design can lead to overestimation of the intervention ES due to selection bias, lack of comparison group, and blindness.

In summary, the efficacy of psychosocial treatments for ADHD is not well established based on randomized clinical trials that use ADHD symptoms as the main outcome. However, meta-analyses covering a broader range of trials with less stringent patient inclusion criteria and a broader range of outcome parameters show moderate to high effect sizes of behavioral interventions. One important aspect to consider is that the main objective of psychosocial treatments might not be specifically to decrease symptoms but to improve overall functioning. It is difficult to compute pooled estimation for these outcomes since procedures to evaluate psychosocial functioning are not as standardized as those for symptoms. Furthermore, the majority of clinical trials do not report the impact of interventions on psychosocial functioning but target academic performance as a measure of functioning. According to the Fabiano et al. meta-analysis, neither pharmacotherapy nor psychotherapy have shown a positive impact on academic achievements—ES of 0.19 (0.03–0.36) for psychosocial treatment and 0.33 (−0.14–0.81) for methylphenidate (Van der Oord et al., 2008). The same meta-analysis, however, found comparable moderate ES for social behavior outcomes for both treatments.

Strengths/Benefits and Weaknesses/Limitations of Using Psychosocial Interventions as Sole Approach

The use of psychotherapy for ADHD, in particular for preschool children, is common clinical practice. Guidelines recommend behavioral therapy (parent training or school-based intervention) as a first-line treatment for preschoolers and in children with less severe ADHD symptoms, and suggest that pharmacotherapy should be implemented in moderate to severe cases or after failure of psychosocial interventions (NICE, 2008; AAP, 2011). Another issue to be considered regarding the use of psychosocial interventions for ADHD is the necessity for specialized professionals to conduct or supervise the sessions. This can limit its use in certain contexts where it is difficult to find professionals trained in behavior or cognitive-behavior therapy.

COMBINATION OF PHARMACOTHERAPY AND PSYCHOTHERAPY FOR ADHD

The efficacy of combining psychotherapy with pharmacotherapy for ADHD has been examined in three different meta-analyses, and results are very homogenous across them. Klassen and colleagues (Klassen et al., 1999) found the combination of psychosocial and pharmacological treatment to have a large ES when compared to the control condition—ES = 3.78 (0.51–8.04) according to teacher ratings and ES = 7.35 (2.4–12.29) according to parent's ratings. Nevertheless ES for most studies was estimated based on within-group comparison, and the lack of an active control condition might be responsible for part of the large effect found. In addition, combined interventions seem to be superior to psychosocial intervention alone (ES = 2.01, CI = 0.16–4.17, according to teachers' ratings, and ES = 5.91; CI = 3.19–8.63, for parents). Nevertheless, a combination intervention did not offer an advantage over medication alone, according to teachers' ratings—ES = 1.28 (–0.72–3.29)—and according to parents' ratings—ES = 0.46 (–2.94–3.86) (Klassen et al., 1999). In another meta-analysis comparing methylphenidate to psychosocial and combined treatment, very similar results were reported. The ES for combination did not differ significantly from methylphenidate alone, and both were significantly superior to psychosocial interventions (Van der Oord et al., 2008). A third meta-analysis computing the effect of combined treatment also found a large ES (1.27 for inattention, 1.27 for hyperactivity, 0.91 for impulsivity), but other treatment strategies were not evaluated (Majewicz-Hefley & Carlson, 2007). Taken altogether, these data suggest that the combination of psychotherapy and pharmacological can significantly reduce ADHD symptoms, but apparently there is no additive effect when the two modalities are combined.

Strengths/Benefits and Weaknesses/Limitations of Using a Combination of Pharmacotherapy and Psychotherapy

The combination of pharmacological and psychosocial interventions for the treatment of ADHD in children and adolescents has been proposed as a solution to treat severe cases of ADHD or to address not only symptom reduction but also associated functional deficits (Döpfner, 2010). Combining psychotherapy with drug treatment, however, increases the economic cost and time expended with treatment. Thus, clinicians should be cautious and offer such intense treatment schemes only when clearly justifiable or desired by patients and families. The fact that meta-analytic data failed to prove the superiority of combined treatment over pharmacological treatment alone does not mean that this association is not helpful for certain patients. As previously discussed, meta-analyses have to rely on available studies and, although a large number of trials have already been published, there is still much to be covered before final conclusions can be made. Studies using stepwise care approaches and smart designs are able to demonstrate additional effects of psychotherapy in cases in which pharmacotherapy has little or no effect (Döpfner et al., 2004). Moreover, long-term outcomes may be different from short-term results. MTA is one of the very few long-term clinical trials for ADHD. This multisite randomized clinical trial enrolled 579 children with ADHD combined type, who were allocated in four arms for 14 months: medication management, behavior therapy, combination of both, or usual community care. After the first 14 months, the MTA became an uncontrolled naturalistic study, and children were followed for up to 8 years. The active phase endpoint (14 months) clearly showed superiority of pharmacotherapy over behavioral therapy and community care for ADHD symptom relief, and small gains with combination (compared to medication alone) were only visible in overall functioning and comorbid symptoms (MTA, 1999). Nevertheless, group differences were not sustained long term. Almost all the differences found at 14 months vanished after 2 years and were clearly no longer present at the 8-year follow-up (Abikoff, Hechtman, Klein, Gallagher et al., 2004; Abikoff, Hechtman, Klein, Weiss et al., 2004; Molina et al., 2009). At the time of this last follow-up, ADHD patients were functioning below controls independent of treatment group (Molina et al., 2009), and participants still taking medication performed no better than those who dropped medication (Abikoff, Hechtman, Klein, Gallagher et al., 2004; Molina et al., 2009). Children with the best functioning at the 8-year follow-up were those with better initial response and who sustained gains over the first 2 years of treatment (Molina et al., 2009). The study's main conclusion may be that long-term prognosis of ADHD depends more on individual characteristics than on treatment choice per se. This information, together with the other data described in this review, reinforce the need for individually tailored treatment plans with frequent reevaluation of treatment gains over symptoms and functioning.

RECOMMENDATIONS FOR FUTURE STUDIES/RESEARCH

Although a large amount of data already exists on the efficacy of different treatments for ADHD, a lot more has to be done to clarify clinically relevant questions. The vast majority of trials available included predominantly male patients with ADHD combined type, and had very limited time to follow up. Studies comparing psychosocial, pharmacological, and combined treatment are rare, limiting conclusions about differences between interventions, since outcome measurements are heterogeneous across studies. Additionally, psychosocial interventions can be very diverse, and computing together data from different studies might be the same as "putting together oranges and apples." In this context, given the limited available studies, perhaps meta-analysis is not the best tool for assessing the level of evidence for psychosocial intervention. Comprehensive systematic reviews with critical revisions of the studies are still a good alternative to orient clinical practice with regard to the use of psychotherapy for ADHD. Finally, it is important to note the scarcity of studies assessing functional outcomes when the efficacy of ADHD interventions is evaluated. The field needs to move beyond assessments based only on symptomatic scales.

REFERENCES

Abikoff, H., Hechtman, L., Klein, R. G., Gallagher, R., Fleiss, K., Etcovitch, J., . . . Pollack, S. (2004). Social functioning in children with ADHD treated with long-term methylphenidate and multimodal psychosocial treatment. *Journal of the American Academy of Child and Adolescent Psychiatry, 43,* 820–829.

Abikoff, H., Hechtman, L., Klein, R. G., Weiss, G., Fleiss, K., Etcovitch, J., . . . Pollack, S. (2004). Symptomatic improvement in children with ADHD treated with long-term methylphenidate and multimodal psychosocial treatment. *Journal of the American Academy of Child and Adolescent Psychiatry, 43,* 802–811.

American Academy of Pediatrics (AAP). (2011). ADHD: Clinical practice guideline for the diagnosis, evaluation, and treatment of attention-deficit/hyperactivity disorder in children and adolescents. *Pediatrics, 128,* 1007–1022.

American Psychiatric Association (APA). (1994). *Diagnostic and Statistical Manual of Mental Disorders* (4th ed.). Washington, DC: American Psychiatric Press.

Antshel, K. M., & Barkley, R. (2008). Psychosocial interventions in attention deficit hyperactivity disorder. *Child and Adolescent Psychiatric Clinics of North America, 17,* 421–437.

Barkley, R. A., & Cox, D. (2007). A review of driving risks and impairments associated with attention-deficit/hyperactivity disorder and the effects of stimulant medication on driving performance. *Journal of Safety Research, 38,* 113–128.

Barkley, R. A., & Fischer, M. (2010). The unique contribution of emotional impulsiveness to impairment in major life activities in hyperactive children as adults. *Journal of the American Academy of Child and Adolescent Psychiatry, 49,* 503–513.

Bauermeister, J. J., So, C. Y., Jensen, P. S., Krispin, O., & El Din, A. S. (2006). Development of adaptable and flexible treatment manuals for externalizing and internalizing disorders in children and adolescents. *Revista Brasileira de Psiquiatria, 28,* 67–71.

Biederman, J., Melmed, R. D., Patel, A., McBurnett, K., Konow, J., Lyne, A., & Scherer, N. (2008). A randomized, double-blind, placebo-controlled study of guanfacine extended release in children and adolescents with attention-deficit/hyperactivity disorder. *Pediatrics, 121,* e73–84.

Bjornstad, G., & Montgomery, P. (2005). Family therapy for attention-deficit disorder or attention-deficit/hyperactivity disorder in children and adolescents. *Cochrane Database of Systematic Reviews, 2,* CD005042.

Castells, X., Ramos-Quiroga, J. A., Bosch, R., Nogueira, M., & Casas, M. (2011). Amphetamines for attention deficit hyperactivity disorder (ADHD) in adults. *Cochrane Database of Systematic Reviews, 6,* CD007813.

Cheng, J. Y., Chen, R. Y., Ko, J. S., & Ng, E. M. (2007). Efficacy and safety of atomoxetine for attention-deficit/hyperactivity disorder in children and adolescents-meta-analysis and meta-regression analysis. *Psychopharmacology, 194,* 197–209.

Cherland, E., & Fitzpatrick, R. (1999). Psychotic side effects of psychostimulants: A 5-year review. *Canadian Journal of Psychiatry, 44,* 811–813.

Clements, S. D., & Peters, J. E. (1962). Minimal brain dysfunctions in the school-age child. Diagnosis and treatment. *Archives of General Psychiatry, 6,* 185–197.

Connor, D. F., Fletcher, K. E., & Swanson, J. M. (1999). A meta-analysis of clonidine for symptoms of attention-deficit hyperactivity disorder. *Journal of the American Academy of Child and Adolescent Psychiatry, 38,* 1551–1559.

Döpfner, M. (2010). Psychosocial and other non-pharmacological treatments. In T. Banaschewski, D. Coghill, M. Danckaerts, M. Döpfner, L. A. Rohde, J. A. Sergeant, E. J. S. Sonuga-Barke, E. Taylor, & A. Zuddas (Eds.), *ADHD and hyperkinetic disorder* (pp. 77–90). Oxford: Oxford University Press.

Döpfner, M., Breuer, D., Schurmann, S., Metternich, T. W., Rademacher, C., & Lehmkuhl, G. (2004). Effectiveness of an adaptive multimodal treatment in children with attention-deficit hyperactivity disorder—global outcome. *European Child & Adolescent Psychiatry, 13*(Suppl. 1), 117–129.

Elia, J., & Vetter, V. L. (2010). Cardiovascular effects of medications for the treatment of attention-deficit hyperactivity disorder: What is known and how should it influence prescribing in children? *Paediatric Drugs, 12,* 165–175.

Fabiano, G. A., Pelham, W. E., Jr., Coles, E. K., Gnagy, E. M., Chronis-Tuscano, A., & O'Connor, B. C. (2009). A meta-analysis of behavioral treatments for attention-deficit/hyperactivity disorder. *Clinical Psychology Review, 29,* 129–140.

Faraone, S. V. (2009). Using meta-analysis to compare the efficacy of medications for attention-deficit/hyperactivity disorder in youths. *P & T: A Peer-Reviewed Journal for Formulary Management, 34,* 678–694.

Faraone, S. V., & Biederman, J. (2002). Efficacy of Adderall for attention-deficit/hyperactivity disorder: A meta-analysis. *Journal of Attention Disorders, 6,* 69–75.

Faraone, S. V., Biederman, J., & Mick, E. (2006). The age-dependent decline of attention deficit hyperactivity disorder: A meta-analysis of follow-up studies. *Psychological Medicine, 36,* 159–165.

Faraone, S. V., Biederman, J., Morley, C. P., & Spencer, T. J. (2008). Effect of stimulants on height and weight: A review of the literature. *Journal of the American Academy of Child and Adolescent Psychiatry, 47,* 994–1009.

Faraone, S. V., Biederman, J., & Roe, C. (2002). Comparative efficacy of Adderall and methylphenidate in attention-deficit/hyperactivity disorder: a meta-analysis. *Journal of Clinical Psychopharmacology, 22,* 468–473.

Faraone, S. V., Biederman, J., Spencer, T. J., & Aleardi, M. (2006). Comparing the efficacy of medications for ADHD using meta-analysis. *Medscape General Medicine, 8,* 4.

Faraone, S. V., & Buitelaar, J. (2010). Comparing the efficacy of stimulants for ADHD in children and adolescents using meta-analysis. *European Child & Adolescent Psychiatry, 19,* 353–364.

Geller, D., Donnelly, C., Lopez, F., Rubin, R., Newcorn, J., Sutton, V., . . . Sumner, C. (2007). Atomoxetine treatment for pediatric patients with attention-deficit/hyperactivity disorder with comorbid anxiety disorder. *Journal of the American Academy of Child and Adolescent Psychiatry, 46,* 1119–1127.

Hanwella, R., Senanayake, M., & de Silva, V. (2011). Comparative efficacy and acceptability of methylphenidate and atomoxetine in treatment of attention deficit hyperactivity disorder in children and adolescents: A meta-analysis. *BMC Psychiatry, 11,* 176.

Hazell, P. L., Kohn, M. R., Dickson, R., Walton, R. J., Granger, R. E., & Wyk, G. W. (2011). Core ADHD symptom improvement with atomoxetine versus methylphenidate: A direct comparison meta-analysis. *Journal of Attention Disorders, 15,* 674–683.

Jain, R., Segal, S., Kollins, S. H., & Khayrallah, M. (2011). Clonidine extended-release tablets for pediatric patients with attention-deficit/hyperactivity disorder. *Journal of the American Academy of Child and Adolescent Psychiatry, 50,* 171–179.

Kattimani, S., & Mahadevan, S. (2011). Treating children with attention-deficit/hyperactivity disorder and comorbid epilepsy. *Annals of Indian Academy of Neurology, 14,* 9–11.

Klassen, A., Miller, A., Raina, P., Lee, S. K., & Olsen, L. (1999). Attention-deficit hyperactivity disorder in children and youth: A quantitative systematic review of the efficacy of different management strategies. *Canadian Journal of Psychiatry, 44,* 1007–1016.

Kollins, S. H., Jain, R., Brams, M., Segal, S., Findling, R. L., Wigal, S. B., & Khayrallah, M. (2011). Clonidine extended-release tablets as add-on therapy to psychostimulants in children and adolescents with ADHD. *Pediatrics, 127,* e1406–e1413.

Kratochvil, C. J., Wilens, T. E., Greenhill, L. L., Gao, H., Baker, K. D., Feldman, P. D., & Gelowitz, D. L. (2006). Effects of long-term atomoxetine treatment for young children with attention-deficit/hyperactivity disorder. *Journal of the American Academy of Child and Adolescent Psychiatry, 45,* 919–927.

Lawson, K. A., Johnsrud, M., Hodgkins, P., Sasane, R., & Crismon, M. L. (2012). Utilization patterns of stimulants in ADHD in the Medicaid population: A retrospective analysis of data from the Texas Medicaid program. *Clinical Therapeutics, 34,* 944–956, e944.

Majewicz-Hefley, A., & Carlson, J. S. (2007). A meta-analysis of combined treatments for children diagnosed with ADHD. *Journal of Attention Disorders, 10,* 239–250.

Mannuzza, S., Klein, R. G., Bessler, A., Malloy, P., & Hynes, M. E. (1997). Educational and occupational outcome of hyperactive boys grown up. *Journal of the American Academy of Child and Adolescent Psychiatry, 36,* 1222–1227.

Mannuzza, S., Klein, R. G., Bessler, A., Malloy, P., & LaPadula, M. (1998). Adult psychiatric status of hyperactive boys grown up. *American Journal of Psychiatry, 155,* 493–498.

Marcus, S. C., Wan, G. J., Kemner, J. E., & Olfson, M. (2005). Continuity of methylphenidate treatment for attention-deficit/hyperactivity disorder. *Archives of Pediatrics & Adolescent Medicine, 159,* 572–578.

Molina, B. S., Hinshaw, S. P., Swanson, J. M., Arnold, L. E., Vitiello, B., Jensen, P. S., . . . MTA Cooperative Group. (2009). The MTA at 8 years: Prospective follow-up of children treated for combined-type ADHD in a multisite study. *Journal of the American Academy of Child and Adolescent Psychiatry, 48*(5), 484–500.

The MTA Cooperative Group (MTA). (1999). A 14-month randomized clinical trial of treatment strategies for attention-deficit/hyperactivity disorder. The MTA Cooperative Group. Multimodal Treatment Study of Children with ADHD. *Archives of General Psychiatry, 56,* 1073–1086.

Nair, V., & Mahadevan, S. (2009). Randomised controlled study-efficacy of clonidine versus carbamazepine in children with ADHD. *Journal of Tropical Pediatrics, 55,* 116–121.

National Institute of Health and Clinical Excellence [NICE]. (2008). Attention deficit hyperactivity disorder diagnosis and management of ADHD in children, young people and adults Retrieved from http://www.nice.org.uk/nicemedia/live/12061/42059/42059.pdf

Palli, S. R., Kamble, P. S., Chen, H., & Aparasu, R. R. (2012). Persistence of stimulants in children and adolescents with attention-deficit/hyperactivity disorder. *Journal of Child and Adolescent Psychopharmacology, 22,* 139–148.

Peterson, K., McDonagh, M. S., & Fu, R. (2008). Comparative benefits and harms of competing medications for adults with attention-deficit hyperactivity disorder: A systematic review and indirect comparison meta-analysis. *Psychopharmacology, 197,* 1–11.

Pliszka, S. (2007). Practice parameter for the assessment and treatment of children and adolescents with attention-deficit/hyperactivity disorder. *Journal of the American Academy of Child and Adolescent Psychiatry, 46,* 894–921.

Polanczyk, G., de Lima, M. S., Horta, B. L., Biederman, J., & Rohde, L. A. (2007). The worldwide prevalence of ADHD: A systematic review and metaregression analysis. *American Journal of Psychiatry, 164,* 942–948.

Remschmidt, H. (2005). Global consensus on ADHD/HKD. *European Child & Adolescent Psychiatry, 14,* 127–137.

Ross, R. G. (2006). Psychotic and manic-like symptoms during stimulant treatment of attention deficit hyperactivity disorder. *The American Journal of Psychiatry, 163,* 1149–1152.

Sallee, F. R., McGough, J., Wigal, T., Donahue, J., Lyne, A., & Biederman, J. (2009). Guanfacine extended release in children and adolescents with attention-deficit/hyperactivity disorder: A placebo-controlled trial. *Journal of the American Academy of Child and Adolescent Psychiatry, 48,* 155–165.

Schachter, H. M., Pham, B., King, J., Langford, S., & Moher, D. (2001). How efficacious and safe is short-acting methylphenidate for the treatment of attention-deficit disorder in children and adolescents? A meta-analysis. *Canadian Medical Association Journal, 165,* 1475–1488.

Spencer, T., Biederman, J., Wilens, T., Harding, M., O'Donnell, D., & Griffin, S. (1996). Pharmacotherapy of attention-deficit hyperactivity disorder across the life cycle. *Journal of the American Academy of Child and Adolescent Psychiatry, 35,* 409–432.

Stein, M. A. (2008). Impairment associated with adult ADHD. *CNS Spectrums, 13*(8 Suppl. 12), 9–11.

Stiefel, G., & Besag, F. M. (2010). Cardiovascular effects of methylphenidate, amphetamines and atomoxetine in the treatment of attention-deficit hyperactivity disorder. *Drug Safety, 33,* 821–842.

Storebo, O. J., Skoog, M., Damm, D., Thomsen, P. H., Simonsen, E., & Gluud, C. (2011). Social skills training for attention deficit hyperactivity disorder (ADHD) in children aged 5 to 18 years. *Cochrane Database of Systematic Reviews, 12,* CD008223.

Taylor, E., Dopfner, M., Sergeant, J., Asherson, P., Banaschewski, T., Buitelaar, J., . . . Zuddas, A. (2004). European clinical guidelines for hyperkinetic disorder—first upgrade. *European Child & Adolescent Psychiatry, 13*(Suppl. 1), 17–30.

Van der Oord, S., Prins, P. J., Oosterlaan, J., & Emmelkamp, P. M. (2008). Efficacy of methylphenidate, psychosocial treatments and their combination in school-aged children with ADHD: A meta-analysis. *Clinical Psychology Review, 28,* 783–800.

Winterstein, A. G., Gerhard, T., Shuster, J., Zito, J., Johnson, M., Liu, H., & Saidi, A. (2008). Utilization of pharmacologic treatment in youths with attention deficit/hyperactivity disorder in Medicaid database. *Annals of Pharmacotherapy, 42,* 24–31.

World Health Organization (WHO). (1993). *The ICD-10 classification of mental and behavioral disorders: Diagnostic criteria for research.* Geneva: Author.

Zwi, M., Jones, H., Thorgaard, C., York, A., & Dennis, J. A. (2011). Parent training interventions for attention deficit hyperactivity disorder (ADHD) in children aged 5 to 18 years. *Cochrane Database of Systematic Reviews, 12,* CD003018.

Integrating Psychopharmacology and Psychotherapy in Insomnia

Karl Doghramji and Dimitri Markov

INTRODUCTION

Insomnia is the complaint of an inability to fall or stay asleep, or unrefreshing sleep. After pain, it represents the second most commonly expressed complaint in clinical settings (Mahowald, Kader, & Schenck, 1997). It is also one of the most commonly encountered and challenging complaints by psychiatric practice. Although a vast array of treatment modalities is available for this malady, individual treatments do not confer absolute benefit for insomnia in all patients. Treatment resistance is noted in more than one third of insomnia patients following the application of standard pharmacological therapies (Mini, Wang-Weigand, & Zhang, 2008). Additionally, insomnia represents a persistent symptom following the management of its comorbidities; for example, nearly half of responders in the pharmacological management of major depression in one study had persistent sleep disturbances (Nierenberg et al., 1999). The persistence of insomnia represents a treatment complication, as it introduces the possibility of polypharmacy and a wider array of side effects, enhances the risk of daytime cognitive and functional impairment, and is associated with a higher risk of relapse, especially in the context of mood disorders. Cognitive behavioral therapies (CBT) have long been known to be effective in the management of insomnia (Morin et al., 2006). This chapter will explore the role of integration of CBT and pharmacotherapy in optimizing the management of insomnia.

Prevalence and Impact

One third of the adult population experiences insomnia during the course of 1 year (Mellinger, Balter, & Uhlenhuth, 1985), with half experiencing the problem as severe, and 20.1% of adults are dissatisfied with their sleep or take medication for sleeping difficulties (Ohayon, 1996). The prevalence of insomnia is highest in women, especially during pregnancy and the peri- and postmenopausal years; the elderly; nontraditional occupational schedule laborers; members of the lower income groups; divorced, widowed, or single individuals; those who live in settings that are not conducive to sound sleep, such as noisy environments; and individuals who are affected by mental and physical conditions and who misuse recreational substances (Doghramji, Grewal, & Markov, 2009).

Insomnia is associated with significant impairments in daytime functioning. Compared to individuals without sleep difficulties, insomniacs report a greater rate of difficulties with coping, accomplishing tasks, impaired mood, breaches in interpersonal relationships, psychosocial upheaval, and cognitive deficits (Hauri, 1997a; Espie, Inglis, Harvey, & Tessier, 2000), and the severity of these quality-of-life impairments is directly related to the severity of the insomnia. Insomnia is also associated with an enhanced rate of work-related impairments and absenteeism (Kupperman et al., 1995) and a greater utilization of healthcare resources (Chevalier et al., 1999). Laboratory studies have shown that insomniacs display a higher rate of psychomotor performance deficits when responding to challenging cognitive tasks (Espie et al., 2000). There is also emerging evidence linking primary insomnia to cardiovascular abnormalities such as enhanced heart rate variability (Bonnet & Arand, 1988) and hypertension (Lanfranchi et al., 2009).

Insomnia also confers a greater risk for the development and intensification of a variety of medical and psychiatric comorbidities. For example, the persistence of insomnia is directly related to an increased risk for the development of new mood, anxiety, and substance use disorders (Ford & Kamerow, 1989; Weissman, Greenwald, Nino-Murcia, & Dement, 1997; Breslau, Roth, Rosenthal, & Andreski, 1996; Chang, Ford, Mead, Cooper-Patrick, & Klag, 1997). Experimentally induced sleep disruption and deprivation increases sensitivity to pain (Onen, Alloui, Gross, & Eschallier, 2000; Roehrs, Hyde, Blaisdell, Greenwald, & Roth, 2006). Persistent insomnia is also associated with a greater risk of the future development of cardiovascular abnormalities and even predicts mortality (Dew et al., 2003; Mallon, Broman, & Hetta, 2002). A significant body of evidence is emerging, therefore, to suggest that the relationship between insomnia and many of its medical and psychiatric comorbidities is a bidirectional one. Such considerations highlight the importance of effective management of insomnia in clinical settings.

Classification

The *Diagnostic and Statistical Manual of Mental Disorders* (DSM-IV-TR) (DSM, 2000) organizes insomnia into two major categories according to presumed etiology. These include (a) primary insomnia and (b) insomnia related to other mental and medical disorders, as well as insomnia that is substance induced. Regarding primary insomnia, the complaint must have a duration of at least 1 month and cause clinically significant distress or impairment in social, occupational, or other important areas of functioning. The DSM-IV-TR views insomnia, therefore, as a complaint that either stands alone, in which case it is presumed to represent an independent disorder or one that is secondary to other medical or psychiatric disorders. Inherent in this view is the notion of causality. Recently, however, a National Institutes of Health State of the Science Conference challenged the primary/secondary distinction, noting that the limited understanding of mechanistic pathways in insomnia precludes drawing firm conclusions about the nature of the associations between insomnia and comorbid conditions or the direction of causality (National Institutes of Health [NIH], 2005), and recommended the use of term "comorbid insomnia" for those instances in which insomnia occurs in the context of other medical and psychiatric disorders. This conceptualization, which has been widely accepted in the field of sleep medicine, further emphasizes the potential for the existence of insomnia as an autonomous disorder, either alone or in the context of other disorders, which may warrant independent clinical attention. This movement away from causal attributions is reflected in the proposed DSM-5 sleep–wake disorders nosology (American Psychiatric Association [APA], 2012), which eliminates the notion of "primary insomnia" in favor of "insomnia disorder" and replaces "sleep disorder related to another mental disorder" and "sleep disorder due to a general medical condition" with "insomnia disorder" with concurrent specification of clinically comorbid medical and psychiatric conditions.

The proposed DSM-5 nosology also changes the nature of the primary complaint from "a difficulty initiating or maintaining sleep, or nonrestorative sleep" to a complaint of "global sleep dissatisfaction." This complaint appears to be more strongly associated with daytime impairments than insomnia symptoms alone (Ohayon, 2002). It also adds a subcategory of "early morning awakening," which promises to improve specificity of symptoms (Morin, 2006), changes the minimum duration to 3 months, and adds a minimal insomnia frequency of 3 nights per week.

Pathophysiology

Although the pathophysiology of primary insomnia is poorly understood, a variety of aberrations have been noted. A basic knowledge of these changes is of relevance for readers of this chapter, since each set of changes is associated with a unique set of approaches to evaluation and management.

Neurophysiologic Hyperarousal

A fundamental neurophysiologic alteration in insomnia is *hyperarousal*, or an overly active arousal system, both during wakefulness and sleep. Insomniacs complain that their thought processes are overly active and that their minds do not "shut off" when they go to bed. They also have difficulty falling asleep during attempts at napping. These complaints have been objectively validated by neurophysiologic studies, which demonstrate increased sleep latencies at bedtime and a decreased ability to fall asleep, compared to normal sleepers, during daytime nap opportunities (Edinger, Means, Carney, & Krystal, 2008). Hyperarousal is also evident as a reduction in sleep-related low frequency slow wave activity and an increase in high frequency beta power (Merica, Blois, & Gaillard, 1998).

Increased cortisol and adrenocorticotropic hormone levels are noted in insomniacs before and during sleep (Vgontzas et al., 2001). Single-photon emission computed tomography (SPECT) and positron emission tomography (PET) scans reveal increased global glucose metabolic rates during both wakefulness and sleep compared with healthy control subjects, and the usual sleep-related decline in metabolism in brainstem arousal centers is attenuated (Nofzinger et al., 2004). Even peripheral physiology is affected as noted by an increase in heart rate, a decrease in heart beat-to-beat variability (Bonnet & Arand, 1988), and an increase in whole-body metabolic rate during sleep (Bonnet & Arand, 1997).

Circadian Disruption

Both delays and advances in sleep/wake cycling have been implicated in insomnia. These are associated with difficulties in falling asleep and early awakenings, respectively. In these disturbances, the circadian system is deranged, causing sleep/wakefulness, melatonin, cortisol, and presumably other endogenous rhythms to be either delayed or advanced in relationship to the environmental light/dark cycle. Recent findings of a genetic basis for these disorders in at least some individuals (a mutation in a human clock gene [Per2] was shown to produce advanced sleep phase syndrome, and a functional polymorphism in Per3 is associated with delayed sleep phase syndrome) further supports genetic models of insomnia (Hamet & Tremblay, 2006).

Psychological Upheaval

In recent history, the role of psychological processes in the genesis of insomnia was first highlighted by Sigmund Freud. Dreaming represented the product of conflictual, anxiety-producing, unconscious wishes, which were transformed from their raw forms into more acceptable, less troublesome dreams, through a series of mental processes. This transformation, in turn, was necessary for the preservation of sleep, and insomnia represented a failure of this dream work due to the intensity of the anxiety caused by the underlying conflicts (Freud, 1955).

Cognitive and behavioral disturbances have been the focus of more recent studies. Insomniacs are theorized to have a predisposition to heightened psychological arousal, supported by studies indicating they have difficulty relaxing; feel tense and anxious; and are overly preoccupied with a myriad of thoughts, worried, and depressed (Kales et al., 1984). Traumatic events have greater emotional impact, therefore, on such individuals, and more easily produce difficulty in relaxing and going to sleep. Once insomnia is produced, however, it is further aggravated and perpetuated by distorted cognitions and beliefs about sleep itself, including the belief that poor sleep is inevitable, that the lack of a full night of sleep will inevitably lead to disastrous health consequences, and that a minimum of 8 hours of sleep per day is critical to maintain health. This can induce further emotional and cognitive arousal. Such catastrophizing is encouraged by many nights of poor sleep, which can foment cognitive rumination and worry about not falling asleep and about the potential for disastrous next-day consequences of sleeplessness. Excessive cognitive monitoring of mental and body sensations, as well as external cues such as the bedroom clock and environmental noises at bedtime, can further perpetuate insomnia. Arousal at bedtime readily becomes a learned response, where repeated experiences of poor sleep promote an association between sleeplessness and both presleep activities and the sleep setting. Once these connections are established, the bedtime rituals and environment become contextual cues for arousal rather than for sleep (Yang, Spielman, & Glovinsky, 2006).

Evaluation and Management of Comorbidities

Insomniacs should receive a thorough evaluation prior to proceeding with treatment. An in-depth discussion of this area is beyond the scope of this chapter, and readers are referred to reviews, published elsewhere (Doghramji et al., 2009). Insomnia typically occurs in the context of one or more comorbidities (NIH, 2005). Despite a high prevalence of comorbid psychiatric disorders such as mood, anxiety, and substance use disorders (Ford & Kamerow, 1989), a significant proportion of insomniacs suffer from nonpsychiatric comorbidities. Therefore, even in the psychiatric setting, insomnia warrants a systematic and comprehensive evaluation, followed by treatment of associated comorbidities, prior to proceeding to direct management of insomnia itself. Unmanaged, or ineffectively managed, comorbidities may account for an important segment of refractory insomnia cases. For example, 39%–55% of patients suffering from sleep apnea syndrome (OSA) complain of insomnia (Luyster, Buysse, & Strollo 2010), and effective treatment of OSA can lead to an improvement in insomnia severity (Krakow et al., 2004). Likewise, up to 90% of restless legs syndrome (RLS) sufferers report insomnia (Montplaisir et al., 1997), which is mitigated by effective RLS management (Erichsen, Ferri, & Gozal, 2010).

When insomnia occurs in the context of psychiatric disorders, effective management of these disorders also, in general, results in a decrement in insomnia complaints (van Mill,

Hoogendijk, Vogelzangs, van Dyck, & Pennix, 2010). In the case of nonpharmcological treatments, cognitive behavioral therapy (CBT) can ameliorate insomnia when used for the treatment of generalized anxiety disorder (GAD) (Belanger, Morin, Langlois, & Ladouceur, 2004), and imagery rehearsal therapy can improve sleep continuity when used to treat the nightmares of patients with posttraumatic stress disorder (PTSD) (Krakow et al., 2001). Nonpharmacological treatments directed primarily at the mood disorder can also diminish sleep disturbances, yet their effects may be more modest than those of antidepressants.

Pharmacological therapies directed at comorbid psychiatric disorders can also diminish insomnia complaints, although their effects are complex, and often unpredictable. Many can exacerbate insomnia. Knowledge of receptor profiles for these agents may guide their use, and receptor systems and their potential effects on sleep continuity are listed in Table 9.1 (Espana & Scammell, 2004). Tables 9.2 and 9.3 summarize potential effects of antidepressants and antipsychotic agents on sleep continuity (Winokur, 2001; Krystal et al., 2008). Nevertheless, it is important to bear in mind that none of these agents, with the exception of low-dose doxepin, have been systematically explored with respect to sleep and wakefulness and in the context of insomnia, and none are indicated for its treatment by the U.S. Food and Drug Administration (FDA). Of patients treated with pharmacological agents for mood or anxiety disorders, 25% to 45% continue to complain of insomnia following remission (Nierenberg et al., 1999; van Mill et al., 2010), and the extent to which insomnia is due to the direct, iatrogenic, effects of these effects on sleep is unclear.

Table 9.1 Impact of receptor systems on sleep continuity.

	Increased Sleep Continuity	Decreased Sleep Continuity
Antihistaminic		5HT1A binding
5HT2 blockade		5HT2 binding
Alpha-1 norepinephrine blockade		Dopamine binding
		Norepinephrine binding

Table 9.2 Effects of antidepressants on sleep continuity.

Antidepressant	Receptor Profile	Impact on Sleep Continuity
MAOI	↑ 5HT1A, 5HT2; NE, and DA	↓
TCA	↑ 5HT1A, 5HT2, NE, DA (weak); ↓ HA, NE, Ach	→ To ↑
SSRI	↑ 5HT1A, 5HT2 Binding	→ To ↓
Venlafaxine	↑ 5HT1A, 5HT2; NE and DA (weak) Binding	↓
Bupropion	↑ NE, and DA	→ To ↓
Nefazodone	↓ 5HT2	↑
Trazodone	↓ HA, 5HT2, NE; weak ↑ 5HT1A, 5HT2	↑
Mirtazapine	↓ HA, 5HT2; ↑ NE, 5HT1A, 5HT2	↑

Table 9.3 Effects of antipsychotics on sleep continuity.

Antipsychotic	Shorten Sleep Latency	Decrease Awakenings and/or WASO
Clozapine	+	+++
Quetiapine	+++	+++
Ziprasidone	+	+++
Olanzapine	+	+++
Resperidone	+	++
Thiothixene	+++	+++
Haloperidol	+++	+++

WASO: Wake after sleep onset. 0, no effect; +, mild effect; + +, moderate effect; + + +, strong effect.

DIRECT MANAGEMENT OF INSOMNIA

Pharmacologic Agents

FDA-Approved Hypnotic Medications

These are summarized in Table 9.4 (Markov & Doghramji, 2010; Neubauer, 2012; Transcept Pharmaceutical, 2012). Some are effective for sleep initiation, some for sleep maintenance, and some for both. All should be administered at bedtime, yet zolpidem sublingual 3.5/1.75 mg, or zaleplon oral 5–10 mg can be administered following middle-of-the-night awakenings, but only if patients have the opportunity to be in bed for at least 4 hours after administration.

Adverse effects of the newer benzodiazepine receptor agonists (BzRAs) include daytime sedation and psychomotor and cognitive impairment. Hypnotics should be used with caution in individuals with respiratory depression (e.g., chronic obstructive pulmonary disease and OSA), in the elderly, in those with hepatic disease, those with multiple medical conditions, and those who are taking other medications that have CNS-depressant properties. Individuals who must awaken during the course of the drug's active period should not take these medications. All of the BzRAs are DEA Schedule IV agents and carry a risk of abuse liability (Doghramji & Doghramji, 2006). All of these agents are also implicated in causing abnormal nocturnal awakenings (sleep walking, sleep driving, sleep eating, etc.).

Ramelteon is a melatonin receptor (MT1 and MT2) agonist that is not addictive, nor related to the BzRAs. The most common adverse effects that are associated with ramelteon include somnolence, fatigue, and dizziness. It is not recommended for use with fluvoxamine due to a CYP 1A2 interaction. A mild elevation in prolactin levels has been noted in a small number of females, and a mild decrease in testosterone values has been noted in elderly males, yet the clinical relevance of these changes remains unclear. Ramelteon does not demonstrate respiratory depression in mild to moderate OSA or in mild to moderate COPD. It is DEA nonscheduled and does not carry the risk of abuse liability (Zammit et al., 2007).

Doxepin is a traditional tricyclic antidepressant at full doses, but at minimal doses (3–6 mg) is an antihistamine-based hypnotic agent. The most common adverse effects associated with low-dose doxepin are somnolence/sedation, nausea, and upper respiratory tract infection. At higher, antidepressant, doses, it is associated with anticholinergic side effects, including sedation, confusion, urinary retention, constipation, blurred vision,

Table 9.4 FDA-approved hypnotic agents.

Class	Hypnotic	Doses (mg)	Elimination Half-Life (hr)	Indications	DEA Class
Benzodiazepine receptor agonist (BzRA) benzodiazepines	Flurazepam	15, 30	48–120	"treatment of insomnia characterized by difficulty in falling asleep, frequent nocturnal awakenings, and/or early morning awakening"	IV
	Temazepam	7.5, 15, 22.5, 30	8–20	"short-term treatment of insomnia"	IV
	Triazolam	0.125, 0.25	2–4	"short-term treatment of insomnia"	IV
	Quazepam	7.5, 15	48–120	"treatment of insomnia characterized by difficulty in falling asleep, frequent nocturnal awakenings, and/or early morning awakenings"	IV
	Estazolam	1, 2	8–24	"short-term management of insomnia characterized by difficulty in falling asleep, frequent nocturnal awakenings, and/or early morning awakenings . . . administered at bedtime improved sleep induction and sleep maintenance"	IV
Benzodiazepine receptor agonist non-benzodiazepines	Zolpidem	5, 10	1.5–2.4	"short-term treatment of insomnia characterized by difficulties with sleep initiation"	IV
	Zaleplon	5, 10	1	"short-term treatment of insomnia . . . shown to decrease the time to sleep onset"	IV
	Eszopiclone	1, 2, 3	5–7	"treatment of insomnia . . . administered at bedtime decreased sleep latency and improved sleep maintenance"	IV
	Zolpidem ER	6.25, 12.5	2.8–2.9	"treatment of insomnia characterized by difficulties with sleep onset and/or sleep maintenance (as measured by wake time after sleep onset)"	IV
	Zolpidem Oral spray	5, 10	2.7	"short-term treatment of insomnia characterized by difficulties with sleep initiation"	IV
	Zolpidem Sublingual	5, 10	2.9	"short-term treatment of insomnia characterized by difficulties with sleep initiation"	IV
	Zolpidem Sublingual	Men 3.5, Women 1.75	2.5	"use as needed for the treatment of insomnia when a middle-of-the-night awakening is followed by difficulty returning to sleep. Limitation of use: Not indicated for the treatment of middle-of-the-night awakening when the patient has fewer than 4 hours of bedtime remaining before the planned time of waking"	IV
Melatonin receptor agonist	Ramelteon	8	1–2.6	"treatment of insomnia characterized by difficulty with sleep onset"	None
H-1 receptor antagonist	Doxepin	3, 6	15.3	"treatment of insomnia characterized by difficulties with sleep maintenance"	None

and dry mouth, and other effects such as hypotension and dose-dependent cardiotoxicity; nevertheless, these effects are not observed at these lower hypnotic doses. Doxepin is contraindicated in patients with severe urinary retention, narrow angle glaucoma, and who have used monoamine oxidase inhibitors (MAOIs) within the previous 2 weeks (Markov & Doghramji, 2010).

Tolerance, a decrement in clinical efficacy following repeated use, and rebound insomnia, an escalation of insomnia beyond baseline severity levels following abrupt discontinuation, can occur even after a few weeks of administration, especially with the traditional benzodiazepine hypnotics. It appears to be more pronounced following the administration of higher doses of hypnotics and of the older, benzodiazepine, agents that have a short elimination half-life, such as triazolam, than the longer-elimination half-life benzodiazepines and some of the newer nonbenzodiazpine BzRAs (Soldatos, Dikeos, & Whitehead, 1999). Eszopiclone (Krystal et al., 2003), zolpidem ER (Krystal et al., 2008), and ramelteon (Mayer et al., 2009) have been evaluated for up to 6 months in controlled studies, and have demonstrated a low proclivity for the production of these effects. Nevertheless, clinical wisdom suggests that all hypnotics should be utilized for short periods of time as much as possible. Patients utilizing these medications for longer periods of time should be evaluated periodically for tolerance and carefully monitored for withdrawal symptoms following abrupt discontinuation. The risk of rebound insomnia and withdrawal symptoms can be minimized by utilizing the lowest effective dose and by gradually tapering the dose over the course of a few nights.

Hypnotics carry the potential for severe allergic reactions and complex sleep-related behaviors, which include sleep driving. The latter may be associated with concomitant ingestion of alcohol and other sedating substances (Southworth, Kortepeter, & Hughes, 2008). It may be prudent, therefore, to advise patients to limit the use of such substances whenever possible.

Hypnotics should be utilized at reduced dosages in the elderly, and, whenever possible those with the shortest half-lives should be considered. The BzRAs should also not be offered to patients with a history of drug and alcohol dependence without close monitoring. The addition of alcohol and other sedating agents may lead to potentiation of sedative effects and decreased margin of safety.

FDA-Nonapproved Medications for Insomnia

These consist mainly of the sedating antidepressants and antipsychotic agents, typically utilized at low doses that are subtherapeutic from the standpoint of their intended applications. As noted above, the evidence supporting their use for insomnia is scant (National Institutes of Health, 2005). Trazodone and mirtazapine are the most commonly utilized agents; there are no published studies on the latter, and the former has received little scientific attention, in primary insomnia (James & Mendelson, 2004). Although trazodone does increase total sleep time in patients with major depressive disorder, there are virtually no dose-response data for trazodone vis-à-vis sleep and, similarly, no available data on tolerance to its possible hypnotic effects. Concerns have been raised regarding daytime somnolence, the significant dropout rates in clinical studies, and the induction of cardiac arrhythmias, primarily in patients with histories of cardiac disease, as well as the development of priapism. Sedating antipsychotic agents have also received little scientific attention for the management of insomnia, and their spectrum of potential side effects includes sedation, EPS, and metabolic disturbances; their use in primary insomnia cannot, therefore, be wholeheartedly supported except in certain circumstances (insomnia due to mania, schizophrenia, or treatment refractory insomnia, etc.).

Over-the-Counter (OTC) Agents

Those marketed for insomnia contain the antihistamines diphenhydramine or doxylamine. Although the evidence supporting their efficacy in insomnia is scant, antihistamines may produce mild to moderate sedation and may improve sleep latency and continuity for some individuals. However, tolerance to their sedating effects can develop rapidly (Richardson, Roehrs, Rosenthal, Koshorek, & Roth, 2002). They are also associated with morning grogginess, daytime sleepiness possibly leading to impairment of driving ability, delirium, urinary retention, constipation, dry mouth, blurry vision, and psychomotor impairment (Basu, Dodge, Stoehr, & Ganguli, 2003).

Although their use is not regulated by the FDA, dietary supplements and herbal remedies also enjoy extensive usage, owing to a variety of factors, including their widespread availability, lack of prescription requirements, relatively low cost, and the widespread belief that they are safe and have a relatively low abuse risk. These include, among others, valerian, kava-kava (Piper methysticum), melatonin, chamomilla, passiflora, avena sativa, and humulus lupulus. Most of these have not been well studied for safety and efficacy; melatonin, which has received the widest evaluations, may be effective in the treatment of delayed sleep phase disorder and shift work disorder, but does not appear to be consistently effective in treating most primary or comorbid sleep disorders with short-term use (Buscemi et al., 2004).

NONPHARMACOLOGIC METHODS

The various established options in this category, and levels of evidence supporting the use of each method, are listed in Table 9.5 (Morgenthaler et al., 2006). A majority of insomniacs respond to nonpharmacologic methods. When compared with pharmacologic methods, they are at least as efficacious, and have the advantage of longer duration of benefit, and less adverse effects (Morin, 2006).

Sleep hygiene education strives to rectify habits and behaviors that may be counterproductive to good sleep. By itself, sleep hygiene education is not likely to resolve insomnia, yet it is considered to be a necessary component of any nonpharmacological strategy, since poor sleep hygiene habits may impair the efficacy of other therapeutic techniques. Sleep hygiene recommendations are summarized in Table 9.6 (Hauri, 1997a).

Stimulus control therapy (SCT) addresses conditioned insomnia and strives to sever the association between bedroom cues and conditioned arousal that occurs with repeated wakefulness, to imprint bed as sleep stimulus, and to associate the bedroom environment with falling asleep (Yang et al., 2006). Specific instructions are listed in Table 9.7 (Yang et al., 2006).

Sleep restriction therapy strives to diminish sleep discontinuity, regardless of cause, by curtailing time spent in bed. This results in the buildup of some sleep debt, which, in turn, results in greater sleep continuity as long as naps are avoided. It also leads to enhanced sleep

Table 9.5 Psychological and behavioral therapies for insomnia.

Technique	Goal	Method
Sleep hygiene education	Promote habits that help sleep; eliminate habits that interfere with sleep	Promote habits that help sleep; eliminate habits that interfere with sleep
Stimulus control therapy	Strengthen bed and bedroom as sleep stimuli	If unable to fall asleep within 20 minutes, get out of bed and repeat as necessary
Restriction of time in bed (sleep restriction)	Improve sleep continuity by limiting time spent in bed	Decrease time in bed to equal time actually asleep and increase as sleep efficiency improves
Cognitive therapy	Dispel faulty beliefs that may perpetuate insomnia	Talk therapy to dispel unrealistic and exaggerated notions about sleep
Relaxation therapies	Reduce arousal and decrease anxiety	Biofeedback, progressive muscle relaxation
Paradoxical intention	Relieve performance anxiety	Patient is instructed to try to stay awake
Cognitive behavioral therapy	Address multiple dimensions of insomnia to enhance efficacy	Combines sleep restriction, stimulus control, and sleep hygiene education with cognitive therapy

Table 9.6 Elements of sleep hygiene education.

Do the following:	Avoid the following:
Awaken at the same time every morning	Napping, unless a shift worker
Increase exposure to bright light during the day	Alcohol
Establish a daily activity routine	Caffeine, nicotine, and other stimulants
Exercise regularly in the morning and/or afternoon	Exposure to bright light during the night
Set aside a worry time	Exercise within 3 hours of bedtime
Establish a comfortable sleep environment	Heavy meals or drinking within 3 hours of bedtime
Do something relaxing prior to bedtime	Noise
Try a warm bath	Excessive heat/cold in room
	Using your bed for things other than sleep (or sex)
	Watching the clock
	Trying to sleep

Table 9.7 Rules of stimulus control therapy.

- Go to bed only when sleepy
- Use bed for sleep and sex only; avoid watching television, reading, or eating in bed
- If not able to fall asleep in 15 minutes, then leave the bedroom as soon as start to feel anxious or irritable and go to another room. Do not watch the clock
- Return to bed only when sleepy
- Repeat above tactic as often as needed
- Regardless of total sleep time, always wake up at the same time
- Avoid daytime naps

efficiency, which, in turn, may result in the perception of improved sleep quality. Principles of this approach are summarized in Table 9.8.

Cognitive therapy attempts to correct the cognitive distortions, catastrophization, and pre-occupation with sleeplessness that accompany insomnia and ultimately contribute to poor

Table 9.8 Sleep restriction therapy.

- Determine average time spent asleep from 1- to 2-week sleep diary
- Set time in bed to equal time spent asleep, never less than 5 hours
- Determine mean sleep efficiency (time spent asleep ÷ time in bed × 100 = %) over 5-day period
- If efficiency ≥ 90%, increase time in bed by 15–20 minutes
- If efficiency < 85%, decrease time in bed by 15–20 minutes
- Regular wake time
- No napping

---

sleep. These are described earlier in this chapter. Insomniacs' dysfunctional beliefs and attitudes toward sleep are directly challenged, their unrealistic expectations about sleep are corrected by cognitive confrontation and education, and their perceptions of the consequences of insomnia are reappraised so that they become more realistic (Yang et al., 2006).

Relaxation therapy addresses emotional hyperarousal in insomnia by inducing a relaxed state, thus allowing sleep to occur. Progressive muscle relaxation, autogenic training, guided imagery, and biofeedback are among the many techniques which have been used to reduce arousal and induce relaxation. These are learned and practiced in the therapist's office, and thereafter utilized at bedtime (Yang et al., 2006).

Paradoxical intention addresses cognitive preoccupation with sleeplessness, which foments insomnia, by instructing patients to try to stay awake for as long as possible. Its effectiveness may be a result of redefining the task, thus removing the performance anxiety associated with the urgency of falling asleep (Ascher & Efran, 1978).

Cognitive behavioral therapy (CBT) combines various nonpharmacological strategies, as noted in Table 9.5. Unlike many forms of therapy, CBT for insomnia is structured, time limited, and focused on sleep-related issues. Data are lacking regarding the specific type of psychotherapy or combination of therapies that are optimal for a given patient; therefore, CBT attempts to address multiple dimensions of insomnia by combining these various strategies to enhance efficacy. In clinical settings, the types of strategies utilized may vary in relation to the nature of the insomnia. The combination of strategies utilized can also change over time, as the nature of the insomnia changes with treatment. Individual treatment sessions are typically conducted once per week over the course of 6 to 8 weeks. However, in clinical settings, the length of treatment and the number and frequency of visits may vary as a function of various factors such as the presence of comorbid conditions, the severity of the insomnia, the combined use of hypnotics, and the patient's motivation and ability to engage in therapy. The utility of CBT has been demonstrated mostly in primary insomnia, yet there is a growing body of literature that suggests that it can be useful in comorbid insomnias, including alcoholism, fibromyalgia, Alzheimer's disease, osteoarthritis, and COPD (Stepanski & Rybarczyk, 2006).

CBT has been shown to have consistent short-term (average 5 weeks) efficacy, and durability of benefit of up to 6 months following the termination of treatment (Belanger, Morin, Langlois, & Ladouceur, 2004). It is at least as effective as pharmacotherapy, and has superior long-term durability of benefit, possibly owing to its attempt to dissipate poor sleep habits, anticipatory anxiety, and misconceptions about sleep—factors that develop following the initiation of insomnia that serve to perpetuate it for long periods of time. It also enjoys greater patient acceptance than pharmacotherapy (Morin, Gaulier, Barry, & Kowatch, 1992). Its major drawbacks, relative to pharmacotherapy, lie in its greater reliance on patient initiative and motivation; greater patient participation in the treatment process; patients' ability to accept the notion of delayed gratification; greater inconvenience; greater time commitment; possibly greater cost; and limited availability of practitioners, in the form of trained therapists, who are capable of conducting treatment. Attempts have recently been made to address some of these drawbacks through the provision of treatment in groups, training primary care nurse practitioners and nurses in primary care settings to provide CBT, and even devising telephone, videotape, and Internet treatment modalities; a recent study demonstrated both short-term efficacy and long-term durability of benefit with Internet CBT (Ritterband et al., 2009). Attempts have also been made to provide CBT with an abbreviated number of sessions; a recent study demonstrated the efficacy of individualized behavioral instructions delivered in two intervention sessions and two telephone calls over the course of 4 weeks; improvements were maintained over 6 months (Buysse et al., 2011).

The adverse effects of CBT have not been systematically explored, although they seem to be few and minor. Limiting caffeine intake during sleep hygiene education can result in caffeine withdrawal symptoms such as headaches and malaise. Sleep restriction can trigger seizures and should be avoided in patients with a history of seizures, especially if they are not optimally controlled. Sleep restriction can also result in high levels of daytime sleepiness, which, in turn, can increase gait instability in the elderly and in those with preexisting disorders that interfere with balance, and can interfere with occupational or social functioning. Patients should be counseled to avoid driving if sleepy.

Circadian Rhythm Adjustment

When insomnia involves a circadian component, management of the sleep component of these conditions includes behavioral measures such as sleep schedule adjustment and proper sleep hygiene practices, timed bright light administration, melatonin, and hypnotic agents. Studies have shown that correction of the underlying sleep phase misalignment can result in improved sleep continuity, diminished sleep latency, and a lessening of insomnia severity (Sack, 2007a and Sack, 2007b). Although melatonin has not been widely accepted as a consistently effective treatment modality for undifferentiated insomnia complaints, it has been shown to be effective in advancing the sleep–wake rhythm and endogenous melatonin rhythm in delayed sleep phase disorder, leading to a decrease in sleep latency in that disorder (van Geijlswijk, Korzilius, & Smits 2010). It has also been shown to hold promise in the treatment of shift work disorder, where results have been inconsistent, with some studies revealing a shift in circadian phase in parallel with improved sleep quality and duration (Morgenthaler et al., 2007). A thorough review of circadian rhythm disorders associated with insomnia and their management is beyond the scope of this chapter, and readers are referred to other publications in this area (Morgenthaler et al., 2007).

INTEGRATING PHARMACOTHERAPY WITH CBT

CBT Versus Pharmacotherapy

From the discussion above, it is evident that both hypnotic agents and CBT offer important avenues for the treatment of insomnia. Short-term (6- to 8-week) treatment studies have generally shown them to be equally effective in addressing specific aspects of insomnia, such as sleep latency, number of awakenings, wake time after sleep onset, total sleep time, and sleep quality; CBT may, however, be more effective in reducing latency to sleep onset (Smith et al., 2002). The improvement sustained by medication tends to be rapid, yet this improvement is lost rapidly after drug discontinuation. On the other hand, benefit derived from CBT is slower, yet well sustained long after the discontinuation of treatment (Morin, Colecchi, Stone, Sood, & Brink, 1999; Morin et al., 2009; Sivertsen et al., 2006).

Despite the proven effectiveness of these two modalities, there are no studies providing guidance as to which therapeutic modality may be more appropriate to initiate for a given clinical situation. Below, therefore, are the authors' suggestions of some factors to consider in selecting the choice of therapy.

Factors Favoring the Initiation of Treatment With CBT or Pharmacotherapy

Some of these factors, with the corresponding optimal initial choice of treatment, are noted in Table 9.9. A careful clinical assessment of the patient's specific needs prior to the institution of treatment is essential in determining the optimal treatment options. The identification of psychological, cognitive, and behavioral factors that either caused, or continue to perpetuate, the insomnia favors the initiation of treatment with CBT. For example, patients who have poor sleep habits such as persistently adhering to irregular bedtimes and who consume caffeinated beverages close to bedtime may benefit from sleep hygiene education; patients who have unrealistic expectations regarding sleep needs or who focus on the catastrophic consequences of poor sleep may benefit from cognitive therapy; patients whose sense of anxiety and tension increases with the approach of bedtime may benefit from relaxation training techniques, and so forth. As noted above, CBT requires considerable patient participation in the treatment process and an ability to delay gratification, and the lack of these two essential ingredients favors the use of pharmacotherapy. In addition, the need for rapid symptomatic improvement, as in the case of a severely sleepy patient whose social and occupation

Table 9.9 Factors favoring the initiation of treatment with CBT or pharmacotherapy.

Factor	CBT	Pharmacotherapy
Identification of psychological, cognitive, or behavioral factors in the perpetuation of insomnia	√	
High capacity to delay gratification	√	
Motivation to be an active participant in the treatment process	√	
Need for rapid clinical improvement		√
Need for sustained clinical improvement	√	
History of, or present, substance use/abuse	√	
Multiple comorbid medical conditions (e.g., COPD, OSA)	√	
Need to minimize the metabolic burden of multiple medications	√	
History of sensitivity to medication side effects	√	
Limitation of available time on the part of patient or provider		√
Failure following multiple hypnotic trials	√	
Failure of CBT		√
Limitation of financial resources		√
Shortage of trained CBT therapists		√
Impaired ability to communicate		√

functioning is significantly impaired as a result of insomnia, pharmacotherapy may be more appropriate of an initial treatment option.

Combination Strategies

Studies examining the combination of pharmacologic agents and CBT in the initial management of primary insomnia are listed in Table 9.10. As is evident, there are only a handful of studies that have utilized diverse methodologies, and many are limited by the small numbers of subjects.

As noted above, available treatments for insomnia do not provide full remission in all patients. The most common rationale for utilizing a combined approach is to manage nonresponse or poor response on one form of therapy, or to strive to maximize response by initiating combined treatment. Therefore, medication management can be combined with CBT in a number of different scenarios: (a) pharmacotherapy and CBT can both be initiated at the same time; (b) pharmacotherapy can be initiated first; and (c) CBT can be initiated first. Studies in Table 9.10 collectively indicate there is a slight increase in short-term efficacy

Table 9.10 Studies examining the combination of pharmacologic agents and CBT in the initial management of primary insomnia.

Reference	Groups	Medication	Duration	Results
Milby et al., (1993)	CBT (2,5) + med, sham CBT	Triazolam	3 weeks	CBT + med > sham CBT
Hauri et al., (1997)	CBT (1,5), followed by CBT + med or waiting list	Triazolam	6 weeks	Acute: CBT=Med. 10-mo follow-up: CBT alone > med
Morin et al., (1999)	CBT (1,2,3,4), med, CBT + med, placebo	Temazepam	8 weeks	All treatments > placebo, trend for CBT + med > either treatment alone. Sustained benefit only for CBT 3, 12, and 24 mos. later
Rosen et al., (2000)	Med + CBT(5,8, or 1)	Estazolam	4 weeks	Improvement in all conditions
Jacobs et al., (2004)	CBT (1,2,3,4,5), med, CBT + med, placebo	Zolpidem	6 weeks	CBT and CBT + med > med and placebo. CBT ≥ CBT + med
Vallieres et al., (2005)	Med then Med + CBT; Med + CBT then Med; CBT	Zoplicone	Two treatments of 5 weeks each	Combined treatment followed by CBT only yielded best results
Wu et al., (2006)	CBT, med, CBT + med, placebo	Temazepam	8 weeks	All treatments > placebo, trend for CBT + med > either treatment alone. Sustained benefit only for CBT 3 and 8 mos. later
Morin et al., (2009)	CBT(1,2,3,4,5), CBT + Med	Zolpidem	6 weeks followed by 6 months	6 weeks: CBT + Med > CBT; 6 months: best long-term results with initial combination therapy followed by CBT alone

Key: 1. Sleep hygiene education; 2. Stimulus control therapy; 3. Restriction of time in bed (sleep restriction); 4. Cognitive therapy; 5. Relaxation therapies; 6. Paradoxical intention; 7. Cognitive behavioral therapy; 8. Guided imagery. Med: Medication; >: More efficacious.

when combined approaches are utilized relative to medication alone. Therefore, CBT may be utilized to augment medication efficacy in patients who are initiated on pharmacotherapy. However, combined approaches are not consistently superior to CBT alone, suggesting that the addition of medication to CBT may not necessarily be of added benefit. This is not totally surprising, inasmuch as patients who are offered pharmacotherapy may lose some of the motivation and emotional investment in CBT following the introduction of pharmacotherapy.

Regarding long-term efficacy, the available data suggest that, regardless of the combination strategy utilized, initial, and even continued, CBT appears to be critical in ensuring that benefits are sustained. Nevertheless, long-term results are difficult to interpret in regards to combination strategies, since some suggest that initial treatment with CBT alone may confer better long-term benefit than combination therapies. When various sequences were examined, the optimal sequence appeared to be when CBT is introduced early on in treatment, either before or concurrently with medication. In fact, initial or continued treatment with medications risks the possibility of diminishing long-term efficacy, possibly through decreasing initiative and effort on the part the patient, key ingredients in any CBT technique.

Continued treatment with CBT can also be of assistance in tapering and discontinuing hypnotic medications in long-term hypnotic users. In a clinical trial with two comparison groups, one group of patients with chronic insomnia and one group of patients with chronic insomnia and hypnotic abuse (using zolpidem in doses of 20 to 70 mg per night), Zavesicka, Brunovsky, Matousek, and Sos (2008) demonstrated that 8 weeks of CBT was highly effective in improving sleep efficiency in both groups. Further, this study found that in a group of hypnotic abusers, sleep efficiency improved significantly after a gradual discontinuation of the hypnotic in the course of CBT treatment (week 2 to 6 of 8-week protocol). This study is consistent with the findings of multiple other studies showing that providing CBT produces significantly better outcomes in sleep quality for patients who undergo gradual hypnotic discontinuation and for patients with secondary insomnia.

In carefully selected cases, combination therapies may also be useful in enhancing compliance to either treatment alone; CBT may serve as a method to address concerns and misconceptions regarding medications in a patient who has been recommended pharmacotherapy. Similarly, medication management may promote sleep in a patient recommended CBT, and whose frustration with slow progress threatens to lead to noncompliance. Clearly, these considerations need to be counterbalanced with the need to maintain motivation and emotional investment in patients undergoing CBT. No data are currently available regarding these uses.

CONCLUSIONS

Insomnia is a common and consequential complaint in psychiatric settings. Its management necessitates a systematic evaluation, followed by effective management of comorbidities. Direct management of insomnia can be effectively accomplished with an array of hypnotic agents or CBT. A careful examination of the patient's specific needs is important in determining which therapeutic modality may be optimal. In addition, combination strategies can be considered for patients in whom an initial strategy is not optimally effective.

REFERENCES

American Psychiatric Association. (2012). Sleep-wake disorders. *DSM-5: The Future of Psychiatric Diagnosis*. Retrieved from http://www.dsm5.org/proposedrevision/Pages/Sleep-WakeDisorders.aspx

Ascher, L. M., & Efran, J. S. (1978). Use of paradoxical intention in a behavioral program for sleep onset insomnia. *Journal of Consulting and Clinical Psychology, 46*, 547–550.

Basu, R., Dodge, H., Stoehr, G. P., & Ganguli, M. (2003). Sedative-hypnotic use of diphenhydramine in a rural, older adult, community-based cohort: Effects on cognition. *American Journal of Geriatric Psychiatry, 11,* 205–213.

Belanger, L., Morin, C. M., Langlois, F., & Ladouceur, R. (2004). Insomnia and generalized anxiety disorder. Effects of cognitive behavior therapy for GAD on insomnia symptoms. *Journal of Anxiety Disorders, 18,* 561–571.

Bonnet, M. H., & Arand, D. L. (1997). Physiological activation in patients with sleep state misperception. *Psychosomatic Medicine, 59,* 533–540.

Bonnet, M. H., & Arand, D. L. (1998). Heart rate variability in insomniacs and matched normal sleepers. *Psychosomatic Medicine, 60,* 610–615.

Breslau, N., Roth, T., Rosenthal, L., & Andreski, P. (1996). Sleep disturbance and psychiatric disorders: A longitudinal epidemiological study of young adults. *Biological Psychiatry, 39,* 411–418.

Buscemi, N., Vandermeer, B., Pandya, R., Hooton, N., Tjosvold, L., Hartling, L., et al. (2004). Melatonin for treatment of sleep disorders. *Evidence Report/Technology Assessment (Summary), 108,* 1–7.

Buysse, D. J., Germain, A., Moul, D. E., Franzen, P. L., Brar, L. K., Fletcher, M. E., et al. (2011). Efficacy of brief behavioral treatment for chronic insomnia in older adults. *Archives of Internal Medicine, 171,* 887–895.

Chang, P. P., Ford, D. E., Mead, L. A., Cooper-Patrick, L., & Klag, M. J. (1997). Insomnia in young men and subsequent depression. The Johns Hopkins precursors study. *American Journal of Epidemiology, 146,* 105–114.

Chevalier, H., Los, F., Boichut, D., Bianchi, M., Nutt, D. J., Hajak, G., et al. (1999). Evaluation of severe insomnia in the general population: Results of a European multinational survey. *Journal of Psychopharmacology, 13,* S21–S24.

Dew, M. A., Hoch, C. C., Buysse, D. J., Monk, T. H., Begley, A. E., Houck, P. R., et al. (2003). Healthy older adults' sleep predicts all-cause mortality at 4 to 19 years of follow-up. *Psychosomatic Medicine, 65,* 63–73.

Diagnostic and statistical manual of mental disorders. (2000). Arlington, VA: American Psychiatric Association.

Doghramji, K., & Doghramji, P. (2006). Clinical management of insomnia. West Islip, NY: Professional Communications, Inc.

Doghramji, K., Grewal, R., & Markov, D. (2009). Evaluation and management of insomnia in the psychiatric setting. *Focus: The Journal of Lifelong Learning in Psychiatry, 7,* 441–454.

Edinger, J. D., Means, M. K., Carney, C. E., & Krystal, A. D. (2008). Psychomotor performance deficits and their relation to prior nights' sleep among individuals with primary insomnia. *Sleep, 31,* 599–607.

Erichsen, D., Ferri, R., & Gozal, D. (2010). Ropinirole in restless legs syndrome and periodic limb movement disorder. *Journal of Therapeutics and Clinical Risk Management, 6,* 173–182.

Espana, R. A., & Scammell, T. E. (2004). Sleep neurobiology for the clinician. *Sleep, 27*(4), 811–820.

Espie, C. A., Inglis, S. J., Harvey, L., & Tessier, S. (2000). Insomniacs' attributions. Psychometric properties of the dysfunctional beliefs and attitudes about sleep scale and the sleep disturbance questionnaire. *Journal of Psychosomatic Research, 48,* 141–148.

Ford, D. E., & Kamerow, D. B. (1989). Epidemiologic study of sleep disturbances and psychiatric disorders: An opportunity for prevention? *Journal of the American Medical Association, 262,* 1479–1484.

Freud, S. (1955). *The interpretation of dreams.* London: Hogarth Press.

Hamet, P., & Tremblay, J. (2006). Genetics of the sleep-wake cycle and its disorders. *Metabolism, 55,* S7–12.

Hauri, P. J. (1997a). Cognitive deficits in insomnia patients. *Acta Neurologica Belgica, 97,* 113–117.

Hauri, P. J. (1997b). Can we mix behavioral therapy with hypnotics when treating insomniacs? *Sleep, 20,* 1111–1118.

Jacobs, G. D., Pace-Schott, E. F., Stickgold, R., & Otto, M. W. (2004). Cognitive behavior therapy and pharmacotherapy for insomnia: A randomized controlled trial and direct comparison. *Archives of Internal Medicine, 164,* 1888–1896.

James, S. P., & Mendelson, W. B. (2004). The use of trazodone as a hypnotic: A critical review. *Journal of Clinical Psychiatry, 65,* 752–755.

Kales, J. D., Kales, A., Bixler, E. O., Soldatos, C. R., Cadieux, R. J., Kashurba, G. J., & Vela-Bueno, A. (1984). Biopsychobehavioral correlates of insomnia, V: Clinical characteristics and behavioral correlates. *American Journal of Psychiatry, 141,* 1371–1376.

Krakow, B., Hollifield, M., Johnston, L., Koss, M., Schrader, R., Warner, T. D., et al. (2001). Imagery rehearsal therapy for chronic nightmares in sexual assault survivors with posttraumatic stress disorder: A randomized controlled trial. *Journal of the American Medical Association, 286,* 537–545.

Krakow, B., Melendrez, D., Lee, S. A., Warner, T. D., Clark, J. O., & Sklar, D. (2004). Refractory insomnia and sleep-disordered breathing: A pilot study. *Sleep & Breathing = Schlaf & Atmung, 8*(1), 15–29. doi:10.1007/s11325-004-0015-5

Krystal, A. D., Erman, M., Zammit, G. K., Soubrane, C., Roth, T., & ZOLONG Study Group. (2008). Long-term efficacy and safety of zolpidem extended-release 12.5 mg, administered 3 to 7 nights per week for 24 weeks, in patients with chronic primary insomnia: A 6-month, randomized, double-blind, placebo-controlled, parallel-group, multicenter study. *Sleep, 31,* 79–90.

Krystal, A. D., Walsh, J. K., Laska, E., Caron, J., Amato, D. A., Wessel, T. C., & Roth, T. (2003). Sustained efficacy of eszopiclone over 6 months of nightly treatment: Results of randomized, double-blind, placebo-controlled study in adults with chronic insomnia. *Sleep, 26,* 793–799.

Kuppermann, M., Lubeck, D. P., Mazonson, P. D., Patrick, D. L., Stewart, A. L., Buesching, D. P., & Fifer, S. K. (1995). Sleep problems and their correlates in a working population. *Journal of General Internal Medicine, 10,* 25–32.

Lanfranchi, P. A., Pennestri, M. H., Fradette, L., Dumont, M., Morin, C. M., & Montplaisir, J. (2009). Nighttime blood pressure in normotensive subjects with chronic insomnia: Implications for cardiovascular risk. *Sleep, 32,* 760–766.

Luyster, F. S., Buysse, D. J., & Strollo, P. J., Jr. (2010). Comorbid insomnia and obstructive sleep apnea: Challenges for clinical practice and research. *Journal of Clinical Sleep Medicine : JCSM : Official Publication of the American Academy of Sleep Medicine, 6*(2), 196–204.

Mahowald, M. W., Kader, G., & Schenck, C. H. (1997). Clinical categories of sleep disorders I. *Continuum, 3*, 35–65.

Mallon, L., Broman, J .E., & Hetta, J. (2002). Sleep complaints predict coronary artery disease mortality in males: A 12-year follow-up study of a middle-aged Swedish population. *Journal of Internal Medicine, 251*, 207–216.

Markov, D., & Doghramji, K. (2010). Doxepin for insomnia. *Current Psychiatry, 9*, 67–77.

Mayer, G., Wang-Weigand, S., Roth-Schechter, B., Lehmann, R., Staner, C., & Partinen, M. (2009). Efficacy and safety of 6-month nightly ramelteon administration in adults with chronic primary insomnia. *Sleep, 32*, 351–360.

Mellinger, G. D., Balter, M. B., & Uhlenhuth, E. H. (1985). Insomnia and its treatment. Prevalence and correlates. *Archives of General Psychiatry ,42*, 225–232.

Merica, H., Blois, R., & Gaillard, J. M. (1998). Spectral characteristics of sleep EEG in chronic insomnia. *European Journal of Neuroscience, 10*, 1826–1834.

Milby, J. B., Williams, V., Hall, J. N., Khuder, S., McGill, T., & Wooten, V. (1993). Effectiveness of combined triazolam-behavioral therapy for primary insomnia. *American Journal of Psychiatry, 150*, 1259–1260.

Mini, L., Wang-Weigand, S., & Zhang, J. (2008). Ramelteon 8 mg/d versus placebo in patients with chronic insomnia: Post hoc analysis of a 5-week trial using 50% or greater reduction in latency to persistent sleep as a measure of treatment effect. *Clinical Therapeutics, 30*, 1316–1323.

Montplaisir, J., Boucher, S., Poirier, G., Lavigne, G., Lapierre, O., & Lesperance, P. (1997). Clinical, polysomnographic, and genetic characteristics of restless legs syndrome: A study of 133 patients diagnosed with new standard criteria. *Movement Disorders: Official Journal of the Movement Disorder Society, 12*(1), 61–65. doi:10.1002/mds.870120111

Morgenthaler, T., Kramer, M., Alessi, C., Friedman, L., Boehlecke, B., Brown, T., et al. (2006). Practice parameters for the psychological and behavioral treatment of insomnia: An update. An American academy of sleep medicine report. *Sleep, 29*, 1415–1419.

Morgenthaler, T. I., Lee-Chiong, T., Alessi, C., Friedman, L., Aurora, R. N., Boehlecke, B., et al. (2007). Standards of Practice Committee of the American Academy of Sleep Medicine: Practice parameters for the clinical evaluation and treatment of circadian rhythm sleep disorders. An American academy of sleep medicine report. *Sleep, 30*(11), 1445–1459.

Morin, C. M. (2006). Combined therapeutics for insomnia: Should our first approach be behavioral or pharmacological? *Sleep Medicine, 7*(Suppl. 1), S15–S19.

Morin, C. M., Bootzin, R. R., Buysse, D. J., Edinger, J. D., Espie, C. A., & Lichstein, K. L. (2006). Psychological and behavioral treatment of insomnia: Update of the recent evidence (1998–2004). *Sleep, 29*,1398–1414.

Morin, C. M., Colecchi, C., Stone, J., Sood, R., & Brink, D. (1999). Behavioral and pharmacological therapies for late-life insomnia: A randomized controlled trial. *Journal of the American Medical Association, 281*, 991–999.

Morin, C. M., Gaulier, B., Barry, T., & Kowatch, R. A. (1992). Patients' acceptance of psychological and pharmacological therapies for insomnia. *Sleep, 15*, 302–305.

Morin, C. M., Vallieres, A., Guay, B., Ivers, H., Savard, J., Merette, C., et al. (2009). Cognitive behavioral therapy, singly and combined with medication, for persistent insomnia: A randomized controlled trial. *Journal of the American Medical Association, 301*, 2005–2015.

National Institutes of Health. (2005, June 13–25). National Institutes of Health State of the Science Conference statement on manifestations and management of chronic insomnia in adults. *Sleep, 28*, 1049–1057.

Neubauer, D. N. (2012). Pharmacotherapeutic approach to insomnia in adults. In T. J. Barkoukis, J. K. Matheson, R. Ferber, & K. Doghramji (Eds.), *Therapy in sleep medicine* (pp. 172–180). Philadelphia: Elsevier Saunders.

Nierenberg, A. A., Keefe, B. R., Leslie, V. C., Alpert, J. E., Pava, J. A., Worthington, J. J., III, et al. (1999). Residual symptoms in depressed patients who respond acutely to fluoxetine. *Journal of Clinical Psychiatry, 60*, 221–225.

Nofzinger, E. A., Buysse, D. J., Germain, A., Price, J. C., Miewald, J. M., & Kupfer, D. J. (2004). Functional neuroimaging evidence for hyperarousal in insomnia. *American Journal of Psychiatry, 161*, 2126–2128.

Ohayon, M. (1996). Epidemiological study on insomnia in the general population. *Sleep, 19*, S7–S15.

Ohayon, M. M. (2002). Epidemiology of insomnia: What we know and what we still need to learn. *Sleep Medicine Reviews, 6*, 97–111.

Onen, S. H., Alloui, A., Gross, A., & Eschallier, A. (2000). The effects of total sleep deprivation, selective sleep interruption and sleep recovery on pain tolerance thresholds in healthy subjects. *Journal of Sleep Research, 10*, 35–42.

Richardson, G. S., Roehrs, T. A., Rosenthal, L., Koshorek, G., & Roth, T. (2002). Tolerance to daytime sedative effects of H1 antihistamines. *Journal of Clinical Psychopharmacology, 22*, 511–515.

Ritterband, L. M., Thorndike, F. P., Gonder-Frederick, L. A., Magee, J. C., Bailey, E. T., Saylor, D.K., & Morin, C. M. (2009). Efficacy of an Internet-based behavioral intervention for adults with insomnia. *Archives of General Psychiatry, 66*, 692–698.

Roehrs, T., Hyde, M., Blaisdell, B., Greenwald, M., & Roth, T. (2006). Sleep loss and REM sleep loss are hyperalgesic. *Sleep, 29*, 145–151.

Rosen, R. C., Lewin, D. S., Goldberg, L., & Woolfolk, R. L. (2000). Psychophysiological insomnia: Combined effects of pharmacotherapy and relaxation-based treatments. *Sleep Medicine, 1*, 279–288.

Sack, R. L., Auckley, D., Auger, R. R., Carskadon, M. A., Wright, K. P., Jr, Vitiello, M. V., et al. (2007a). Circadian rhythm sleep disorders: Part I, basic principles, shift work and jet lag disorders. An American Academy of Sleep Medicine review. *Sleep, 30*(11), 1460–1483.

Sack, R. L., Auckley, D., Auger, R. R., Carskadon, M. A., Wright, K. P., Jr, Vitiello, M. V., et al. (2007b). Circadian rhythm sleep disorders: Part II, advanced sleep phase disorder, delayed sleep phase disorder, free-running disorder, and irregular sleep-wake rhythm. An American Academy of Sleep Medicine review. *Sleep, 30*(11), 1484–1501.

Sivertsen, B., Omvik, S., Pallesen, S., Bjorvatn, B., Havik, O. E., Kvale, G., et al. (2006). Cognitive behavioral therapy vs zopiclone for treatment of chronic primary insomnia in older adults: A randomized controlled trial. *Journal of the American Medical Association, 295*, 2851–2858.

Smith, M. T., Perlis, M. L., Park, A., Smith, M. S., Pennington, J., Giles, D. E., & Buysse, D. J. (2002). Comparative meta-analysis of pharmacotherapy and behavior therapy for persistent insomnia. *American Journal of Psychiatry, 159*, 5–11.

Soldatos, C. R., Dikeos, D. G., & Whitehead, A. (1999). Tolerance and rebound insomnia with rapidly eliminated hypnotics: A meta-analysis of sleep laboratory studies. *International Clinical Psychopharmacology, 14*, 287–303.

Southworth, M. R., Kortepeter, C., & Hughes, A. (2008). Nonbenzodiazepine hypnotic use and cases of "sleep driving." *Annals of Internal Medicine, 148*, 486–487.

Stepanski, E. J., & Rybarczyk, B. (2006). Emerging research on the treatment and etiology of secondary or comorbid insomnia. *Sleep Medicine Reviews, 10*, 7–18.

Transcept Pharmaceuticals I. (2012). Intermezzo—zolpidem tartrate tablet. http://app.purduepharma.com/xmlpublishing/pi.aspx?id=i

Vallieres, A., Morin, C. M., Guay, B. (2005). Sequential combinations of drug and cognitive behavioral therapy for chronic insomnia: An exploratory study. *Behaviour Research and Therapy, 43*, 1611–1630.

van Geijlswijk, I. M., Korzilius, H. P., & Smits, M. G. (2010). The use of exogenous melatonin in delayed sleep phase disorder: A meta-analysis. *Sleep, 33*(12), 1605–1614.

van Mill, J. G., Hoogendijk, W. J., Vogelzangs, N., van Dyck, R., & Penninx, B. W. (2010). Insomnia and sleep duration in a large cohort of patients with major depressive disorder and anxiety disorders. *Journal of Clinical Psychiatry, 71*, 239–246.

Vgontzas, A. N., Bixler, E. O., Lin, H. M., Prolo, P., Mastorakos, G., Vela-Bueno, A., et al. (2001). Chronic insomnia is associated with nyctohemeral activation of the hypothalamic-pituitary-adrenal axis: Clinical implications. *Journal of Clinical Endocrinology and Metabolism, 86*, 3787–3794.

Weissman, M. M., Greenwald, S., Nino-Murcia, G., & Dement, W. C. (1997). The morbidity of insomnia uncomplicated by psychiatric disorders. *General Hospital Psychiatry, 19*, 245–250.

Winokur, A., Gary, K. A., Rodner, S., Rae-Red, C., Fernando, A. T., & Szuba, M. P. (2001). Depression, sleep physiology, and antidepressant drugs. *Depression and Anxiety, 14*(1), 19–28.

Wu, R., Bao, J., Zhang, C., Deng, J., & Long, C. (2006). Comparison of sleep condition and sleep-related psychological activity after cognitive-behavior and pharmacological therapy for chronic insomnia. *Psychotherapy and Psychosomatics, 75*, 220–228.

Yang, C. M., Spielman, A. J., & Glovinsky, P. (2006). Nonpharmacologic strategies in the management of insomnia. *Psychiatric Clinics of North America, 29*, 895–919.

Zammit, G., Erman, M., Wang-Weigand, S., Sainati, S., Zhang, J., & Roth, T. (2007). Evaluation of the efficacy and safety of ramelteon in subjects with chronic insomnia. *Journal of Clinical Sleep Medicine, 3*, 495–504.

Zavesicka, L., Brunovsky, M., Matousek, M., & Sos, P. (2008). Discontinuation of hypnotics during cognitive behavioural therapy for insomnia. *BMC Psychiatry, 8*, 80.

10

Integrating Psychotherapy and Medication for Addicted Patients

Diane St. Fleur and Brian Johnson

INTRODUCTION, EPIDEMIOLOGY, AND CLASSIFICATION

Addiction is a complex neurological and psychological pathology, a difficult and deadly disease to treat. Forty-five million Americans are addicted to nicotine—22% of men and 17% of women. Twenty-two million Americans suffer from addiction to alcohol and illicit drugs (Okie, 2010). This number has been relatively stable with a slight positive trend.

Nicotine, alcohol, and marijuana are the three most common substances of abuse and have been for some time. Opioid medications have increased up to the fourth most commonly abused drug. However, the two most lethal drugs, nicotine and alcohol, are sold legally in the United States, and physicians are empowered to prescribe three classes of addictive drugs: opioids, benzodiazepines, and stimulants, making the induction of addiction a complex and multifactorial matter. Treatment, therefore, is often difficult and multimodal. There are patient, clinician, legal, corporate, and public health variables at play.

The definition of "addiction" (repeated harm from use) should guide the provision of treatment regardless of the source of addiction. Addiction is characterized by repeated harm and at the same time, strong urges to continue to use the drug. A denial system is required for victims of addictive illness to continue using the drug that is hurting them. A formal, DSM IV-TR diagnosis of addiction requires significant impairment from use of a drug and further delineates the diagnosis of abuse versus dependence with the latter containing more physiological signs and symptoms of addiction. After two decades of utilizing the DSM-IV as a diagnostic guide, the American Psychiatric Association (APA) DSM-5 Substance-Related Disorders Work Group has proposed significant shifts in the diagnostic categorizations of addiction (Peer et al., 2013). The authors found it prudent to highlight some of the general changes to assist readers in creating an up-to-date diagnostic framework as they utilize this text. As most fundamental changes, DSM-5 will:

1. replace the diagnoses of abuse and dependence with specifiers that exist along a continuum to reflect severity;
2. organize itself according to substance rather than diagnosis;
3. lower the diagnostic threshold making the syndrome easier to achieve.

A change in these diagnostic frameworks will likely have an impact on the epidemiology, individual illness behavior, biopsychosocial treatment approach, and research implications. The authors suspect that the changes in DSM-5 will allow the prevalence of substance use disorders (SUD) to modestly increase, thus increasing the need for credible and more widely available psychotherapy and pharmacotherapy treatments (Peer et al., 2013).

Fundamental Concepts of the Neurology and Psychology of Addiction

There are only about 20 chemicals known to humans that alter the drive system so as to create a new drive (Johnson, 2008). These substances (alcohol, nicotine, benzodiazepines, opioids, stimulants, marijuana, phencyclidine, etc.) all work by diverse mechanisms (Nestler, 2005), but with the same uniform end result. They cause sensitization of the ventral tegmental dopaminergic SEEKING system to the chemical (Berridge & Robinson, 1998). After sufficient exposure to the chemical, the person begins to want the drug, irrationally and insistently.

Initial actions of the drugs work as follows: Stimulants such as cocaine and methamphetamines increase dopamine barrages from the ventral tegmental area (VTA) directly to the nucleus accumbens shell by blocking the dopamine reuptake transporter protein (Niehause, Cruz-Bermudez, Kauer, 2009). Opioids act as a brake on an inhibitory system involving gabaergic interneurons that slow dopamine neurotransmission from the VTA to the nucleus accumbens shell (Nestler, 2005). Removing this inhibition from the VTA results in increased dopamine barrages to the nucleus accumbens shell. Cannabis's tetrahydrocannabinol lodges in endocannabinoid receptors in inhibitory gabaergic VTA interneurons, inhibiting this brake so that there is increased dopaminergic stimulation of the nucleus accumbens shell (Fattore, Fadda, Spano, Pistis, & Fratta, 2008). Nicotine has receptors on the VTA, and stimulates activating signaling from the amygdalae (Nestler, 2005). The mechanism for alcohol and benzodiazepines may be that in withdrawal from these gabaergic drugs, there is a lessening of gabaergic inhibition of the VTA, and dopamine neurotransmission is increased (Enoch, 2008). Despite this variability, the initial mechanism of physical addiction for every addictive drug is that dopamine neurotransmission from the VTA to the nucleus accumbens shell is altered. The pathway does not end with the nucleus accumbens shell. As seen in Fig. 10.1, there are limbic and frontal centers connected with this subcortical pathway. As the effects of stimulation in the subcortical pathway cause long-term potentiation of higher centers, and drugs are wanted, drug cues recognized at pathways involving amygdalar, hippocampal, and frontal activation provoke neural firing, and descending glutamatergic pathways increase craving by stimulating more dopamine release. The higher centers notice possible availability of drugs, and turn up craving.

However, the pathways in Fig. 10.1 allow for the concept that there are two mechanisms of induction of craving: the *upper* and the *downer* pathways. The upper pathway, activated by cocaine, methamphetamine, and nicotine, directly increases firing from the VTA to the NA. The downer pathway is less direct. The interneuron braking system is deactivated, leading to increased activation of VTA to NA dopamine. This would account for the fact that the *upper* drugs cause drug craving so commonly, and are harder to become abstinent from, while downer drugs such as cannabis, alcohol, opioids, or benzodiazepines provoke addiction with lower frequency. Patients routinely say that nicotine is harder to stop than alcohol or heroin. When drugs in the downer group are used for recreational or medical reasons, most users do

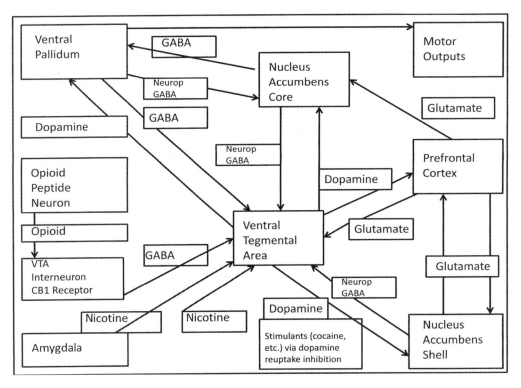

Figure 10.1 Craving/Dreaming Pathways: Neurop = neuropeptides, GABA = gamma amino butyric acid, CB = cannabinoid.

not become addicted. Fig. 10.1 shows the upper (right lower triangle) and downer (starting with the opioid peptide neuron) circuits.

Persons whose brains have been changed by addictive drugs via the mechanisms just noted must obtain the chemical or they are punished by ferocious displeasure if there is, "[a] resistance to the compulsion, a hold-up in the discharge reaction," or distinct withdrawal effects (Freud, 1920). By using drugs, individuals begin to "want" them for no reason other than that brain changes stipulate they are needed by associative learning. This might be construed as being unconscious or biological, that the brain is now becoming hardwired to obtain the substance even at deleterious costs. There are secondary changes in the brain as addiction progresses as well. Later brain changes involve routinization of drug SEEKING by reorganization of pathways (Koob & Volkow, 2010) involving the nucleus accumbens core (Kalivas & Volkow, 2005) and diminished prefrontal inhibition (Everitt & Robbins, 2005), especially if there are losses of brain tissue due to the various degrading effects of these drugs. The longer active addiction occurs, the harder it is to recover. Initiating brain changes with one drug results in faster adaptation with craving for a second addictive drug (Berridge & Robinson, 1998).

Initially, the drug recruits the SEEKING system so that the addicted person urgently wants the drug no matter what the consequences. Later on, a state emerges in which the addicted person relies on the drug of abuse to render him or herself free from the negative affective state that relentlessly endures when the drug is absent (Koob & Volkow, 2010). The unconscious compulsive behavior of seeking and consuming the substance(s) is an effort to mitigate this stressful, anxiety-provoking state, as well as a reflection of how the drug has altered the neurocircuitry involved.

The maladaptive changes are significantly driven by "opponent process" (a = change induced by the drug, b = compensatory brain adaptation), whereby the homeostatic nature of the hedonic system self-adjusts to changes induced by the drug (Koob & Volkow, 2010). Neural circuits are driven by a number of neurotransmitters that shift in accordance with the opponent process. Their main location is in the basal forebrain and mesocortical limbic system. The "b" process tends to outweigh the "a" process, resulting in accelerating dysphoria that is briefly relieved by additional drug administration. Drug addiction also entails altering of pathways such as the hypothalamus–pituitary axis, which increases baseline stress (Koob & Volkow, 2010).

PHARMACOLOGICAL TREATMENTS

Similar to the treatment of other psychiatric disorders, the field of addiction treatment is Balkanized even further at times, with more clinicians of varying credentials providing care. This more often than not creates a split model paradigm where prescribers do not provide psychotherapy and psychotherapists do not prescribe, or in some models suggest no prescribing occur at all (Miller & Dunlop, 2011). In a recent description of "the combined behavioral intervention," which is based on principles of motivational interviewing, cognitive behavioral therapy (CBT), and 12-step facilitation, leaders in the field asked the question, "What kinds of behavioral therapies should be offered in combination with medications to maximize treatment effects?" (Longabach, Zweben, Locastro, & Miller, 2005). The answer to date is not clearly known, but available data will be presented throughout this chapter.

Pharmacological treatments will be covered first, as a standalone treatment to provide a quick review. Coverage of psychosocial treatments will be discussed initially from a psychoanalytic perspective, but then broadened to include other approaches. Psychoanalysis has theoretical explanatory power, and yet continues to be the least supported by empirical studies. As with any psychotherapeutic approach, patient and clinician variables must be weighed before choosing an appropriate theoretical approach for each patient. In the conclusion, we will examine the limited literature on combining psychosocial and pharmacological treatments, as this is the true goal of this chapter.

Most authors and most approved pharmacologic indications suggest that medication management alone is not to be used as a definitive treatment for any addiction. Most regulatory studies contain at least supportive or motivational aspects in addition to taking a cessation-based medication. To be thorough, yet brief, Table 10.1 summarizes available medication treatments based upon the abused substance at hand. A discussion of treatment options is organized according to the overall effect of the drug: acting as a stimulant or depressant.

Cocaine and Amphetamines

Researchers have investigated several psychotropic agents as treatments to prevent relapse. Regarding anticonvulsant treatment, treatment arms may carry a higher retention rate than placebo, but a 2008 Cochrane review demonstrated that anticonvulsants are not efficacious and are often side-effect prone (Minozzi et al., 2008). The alcohol cessation drug disulfiram is not only pro-dopaminergic but also anti-noradrenergic, which theoretically may attenuate cocaine effects on addiction circuits. Despite these properties, data has not supported it as an efficacious treatment (Pani et al., 2010).

In light of the success of methadone maintenance treatment, researchers have trialed psychostimulants as cocaine agonist therapy as well. Conclusions were not significant, though

Table 10.1 Summary of pharmacotherapies of common addictive drugs.

Drug	Treatment	Dose (mg)	Efficacy	Side Effects
Alcohol	Disulfiram	250–1500 mg daily	None given to patient, good when administration observed	Garlic taste, Fatigue Monitor LFT
	Naltrexone	100 mg daily	Some decrease of craving and relapse	Nausea
	Topiramate	200 mg daily	Some decrease of craving and relapse	Fatigue, Confusion
	Acamprosate	666 mg three times per day	Little	Diarrhea Arrhythmia
Opioids	Methadone	60–200 mg daily	Decrease of crime, HIV, hepatitis C. Opioids and other drugs commonly used.	Sexual dysfunction Constipation Increased pain
	Buprenorphine	8–24 mg daily	Similar to methadone	Similar to methadone
	Naltrexone	50 mg by parenteral (PO) 384 mg intramuscularly (IM)		Nausea, Anhedonia
Nicotine	Varenicline	1 twice a day	1 year abstinence: 21% vs. 9% placebo	Depression, Nausea
	Bupropion	300–450 mg daily	1 year abstinence: 26% vs. 18% placebo	Anxiety, Dry mouth
	Nicotine	less than 23 mg	1 year abstinence: 18% vs. 12% placebo Source: meta-analysis	

trends for bupropion, d-amphetamine, and modafinil had the highest rates of abstinence (Castells et al., 2010).

Antidepressants have also been studied. A 2011 Cochrane review that analyzed 37 studies of 3,551 participants discovered mixed results. A greater number of treated individuals achieved abstinence as a trend only. The evidence most strongly supported tricyclic antidepressants (TCA) (Pani et al., 2010). Dopamine agonists were not efficacious (Amato et al., 2011).

Regarding amphetamines, a series of small studies have investigated agents with pro-dopaminergic properties ranging from stimulants, antidepressant, and anti-emetics with 5HT3 receptor properties. Since then, review studies have shown that tyrosine, anti-depressants such as mirtazapine, and anti-emetics such as ondansetron are not effective. D-amphetamine agonist treatment is supported by limited data only (Castells et al., 2010).

Nicotine

Bupropion, varenicline, and nicotine-replacement therapies (NRTs) are FDA-approved treatments for nicotine dependence. Varenicline is the most effective treatment, followed by bupropion and then NRTs (Wu, Wilson, Dimoulas, & Mills, 2006). These are some of the best-studied cessation medications, and again all utilized supportive psychotherapies integrated with the pharmacotherapy in their regulatory trials. Varenicline is a partial nicotinic agonist and has two- to threefold greater cessation rates than attempts of quitting without any pharmacologic treatment while undergoing supportive therapy (Cahill, Stead, & Lancaster, 2012). A 2012 systematic review found varenicline to be a superior treatment compared to NRTs and bupropion (Mills et al., 2012). Bupropion SR taken at 300 mg/day was also superior to placebo (Hays et al., 2001). There was brief cessation counseling at each visit. In an actual practice setting, bupropion had a 1-year cessation maintenance rate of 24% to 33%. In an open label trial (Swan et al., 2003), NRTs were shown to have superior efficacy compared to placebo. However, the effects were dependent on the duration and the level of support that was provided. NRTs were shown to be more effective with a combination of the standard dose patch and rapid delivery NRT such as nicotine chewing gum (Stead, Perera, Bullen, Mant, & Lancaster, 2008).

Alcohol

The Food and Drug Administration (FDA) has approved four pharmacological agents for the treatment of alcohol addiction. Acamprosate has demonstrated to be more efficacious than placebo in over two dozen double-blind RCTs. Acamprosate decreases alcohol consumption by its effect in the nucleus accumbens and ventral tegmental area via glycine- and nicotine-mediated receptors respectively (Chau, Hoifodt-Lido, Lof, Soderpakm, & Ericson, 2010). Acamprosate may also mitigate withdrawal symptoms by inhibiting glutamate receptors (Naassila, Hammoumi, Legrand, Durbin, & Daoust, 1998). Disulfiram may also enhance the efficacy of acamprosate when combined in a polypharmacy approach (Wilde & Wagstaff, 1997). Disulfiram monotherapy inhibits aldehyde dehydrogenase. A severe sick reaction occurs in the setting of any ingested or absorbed alcohol due to disulfiram-mediated increase in acetaldehyde levels. Disulfiram is effective for short-term abstinence, but its long-term efficacy is limited (Jorgensen, Pedresen, & Tonnesen, 2011). Naltrexone is an antagonist that competes with opioid agonists in the CNS. It promotes abstinence and decreases alcohol cravings and binge drinking. A double-blind placebo-controlled study of subjects in outpatient alcoholism treatment settings demonstrated that 54% of the placebo-treated subjects relapsed versus the 23% of the naltrexone-treated group (Volpicelli, Alterman, Hayashida, & O'Brien, 1992). Naltrexone's efficacy is often superior to acamprosate and disulfiram (Witkiewitz, Saville, & Hamreus, 2012). Topiramate, the fourth agent, may be neuroprotective by mitigating glutamate surges (Likhitsathian et al., 2012). Compared to naltrexone at 50 mg per day, studies have shown better efficacy for topiramate at a mean dose of 200 mg per day in a sample of 182 patients.

Opioids

Methadone- (MMT) and buprenorphine-maintenance treatment (BMT) are the gold standards for opioid use disorders. Although efficacious in terms of harm reduction, the individual is still addicted to opioids and using prescribed agonist agents in a harm-reduction model. Buprenorphine is a partial-opioid agonist with a lower abuse potential than methadone and generally has less severe side effects (Jasinski, 1997). There are mixed views about the difference of efficacy and safety profile of buprenorphine and methadone. A dosage of 8 mg daily of buprenorphine is as effective as 60 mg daily of methadone (Johnson, Jaffe, &

Fudala, 1992). Buprenorphine has been found to be more effective than off-label alpha ago-nists such as clonidine and lofexidine, which are often used in detoxification (Gowing, Ali, & White, 2009).

Cannabis

Currently, there is no clearly efficacious treatment for cannabis use disorders. Rimonabant, a cannabinoid receptor (CB1) antagonist and buspirone may aid treatment, but the data that supports this is inconclusive. The antidepressant mirtazapine has not been shown to be effec-tive in treating cannabis use disorders but may mitigate withdrawal symptoms (Benyamina, Lecacheux, Blecha, Reynaud, & Lukasiewez, 2008).

PSYCHOTHERAPY

In a meta-analysis of controlled trials of treatments for alcohol use disorders, Miller and Wilbourne (2002) ranked psychotherapy as number 44 of 46 listed interventions. They ex-plained, "Differentiation among various psychodynamic and other insight-oriented psycho-therapies appeared unnecessary in that none was found to affect drinking outcomes." (Miller and Wilbourne, 2002, p.268) Miller and Wilbourne's number one intervention was one or two visits for advice about drinking. The second most evidence-based therapy was motiva-tional enhancement.

Beginning this chapter's review of psychotherapy approaches are psychoanalytic and psy-chodynamic modalities. The hallmark of these stances is that the patient is the center of the initiative. Aspects of character, or how we habitually behave, are a part of implicit thinking. Patients can only modify behavior if it enters explicit thinking. Hence, the analytic therapist seeks to help the patient be consciously aware of how he or she is behaving in regards to ad-diction and why. In the next section, the authors propose to briefly review their approach within a psychoanalytic framework. This will be followed by a review of other psychotherapy modalities in order to have a theoretically balanced chapter.

Three Basic Views of Addiction From Psychoanalysis

I. *Neurobiology*—The concept of addiction being driven by the capture of the ventral tegmental dopaminergic SEEKING system as mentioned above. Exposure to addictive drugs changes the brain's activity. Not only do the drugs become urgently wanted, but also the conflict between the drive to obtain the drug and the dire consequences of using the drug generates a new set of unconscious defenses, the "denial system."

II. *Affect Intolerance*—Addiction has also been described as a manifestation of inability to tolerate affect or intense emotional states. Khantzian's (1985, 1999) "self medication hypothesis" states that addictive drugs ameliorate psychologically intolerable states. Khantzian (1999) also suggests that addiction has to do with the inability of an addict to internalize self-care from parents. The concept of affect intolerance has been further developed by Dodes (1990, 1996), describing addictive behaviors as unconscious expres-sions of rage in response to feeling helpless.

III. *Object/Transitional Object*—This view started with Winnicott's (1958) observation that the child becomes addicted to the transitional object. Kernberg (1975) described object-related dynamics of addiction, to replace a parental image in depression, an all-good mother in borderline personality, to refuel the grandiose self in narcissism. Wurmser (1974) described the terror of being separated and saw the intense shame and rage manifested in addictive behaviors as part of an attempt to maintain contact with objects. In his formulation, slavish submission to an unreasonable set of internal prohibitions alternates with unregulated rebellious addictive behaviors. Johnson's (1993) formulation of addiction as an object suggests that addictive behaviors generate a sense of being accompanied that is on a continuum of character types. Borderline patients have difficulty having steady nurturing relationships. Addicted patients use their addictive behaviors to replace unreliable parents during adolescence. Therefore, the addictive behaviors become a transitional object equivalent adopted during adolescence rather than the blanket/teddy adopted during separation–individuation. Narcissistic and antisocial individuals adopt a set of internalized fantasies that they rely on, fitting social norms such as being a famous athlete in narcissism or being asocial and individually determined in antisocial personality, such as, "It is OK to kill this person this time." Narcissistic and antisocial defenses can break down during adult life, resulting in new addictive behaviors. In this formulation, relatedness to the addictive behavior is protected by the denial system. Addicted persons who get sober are besieged by difficulty relating. This period may be resolved by improved ability to depend on humans. If this new skill is not acquired, the person reverts to active addiction. Addicted persons who get sober may also be tempted to use narcissistic defenses, which place them beyond help—doomed to return to the addictive behavior when the narcissistic defense fails.

Interpreting these analytical situations and unconscious forces may allow the following ameliorative process:

1. The aggressive drive for control of one's existence with integrity is nothing to be ashamed of.
2. The patient needs to struggle to be conscious of what he or she really wants, rather than settle for addictive responses.
3. Conflicts and vulnerabilities regarding self-assertion, and difficulty tolerating helplessness when necessary, have their origin in childhood experiences that need to be remembered and worked through in treatment.

These underlying ideas and theories behind these psychotherapeutic approaches may be psychological or biological or both in nature. Psychopharmacologists may want to consider these as common themes when engaging in medication management sessions where patients continue with repetitive patterns and behaviors that appear dynamic in nature and thwart medication compliance and adherence. In other words, having a psychological framework in which to address and manage the patient may improve rapport, compliance, and ideal outcomes in medication management.

A neuropsychoanalytic formulation of addiction would make integrative sense if the provider assumes that both pharmacotherapy and psychotherapy are biological processes (Solms & Turnbull, 2002). Using the above formulation that addictive drugs capture the SEEKING system, an updated and neuroscience-based equivalent of Freud's drive system, the authors formulate the mechanism of addiction as adding a new, artificial drive to the innate drives for food, water, sex, and relationships (Johnson, 2008). The experience of drives operating inside us can impel us to do things that we do not consciously "want" to do. This often leads to an interpretation by the analyst that certain behaviors are "intentional but not conscious." The reasons patients do things are often not apparent to them. Much of the work of psychoanalysis has to do with patients becoming conscious of their real motives, what are the true goals of their will (Wheelis, 1956).

Therapy modalities targeting automatic thoughts, response prevention, and motivational and statistical harm reduction seek abstinence through promoting new learning. Psychoanalytic oriented therapies seek abstinence through understanding psychic conflicts and therefore targeting the unconscious nidus of addiction. In this way, psychoanalytic approaches may actually map to the functional neuroanatomy of addiction and be best understood in parallel with the neurobiological mechanisms of addiction.

Dynamic deconstructive psychotherapy (DDP) is a neuropsychodynamically based treatment for co-occurring alcohol use disorders and borderline personality disorder. It is delivered as a weekly, manual-based treatment over a 12- to 18-month period. It is hypothesized to remedy three neurocognitive functions: *association*—the ability to identify, acknowledge, and sequence emotional experiences; *attribution*—the ability to form complex and integrated attributions of self and others; and *alterity*—the ability to form realistic and differentiated attributions of self and others. Outcomes over 30 months are shown in Fig. 10.2, compared to the best care available in the community, or optimized community care (OCC). OCC participants received more treatment than the DDP subjects, including individual psychotherapy, alcohol counseling, case management, and medication management. DDP participants (Fig. 10.2) displayed significant improvement in heavy drinking from baseline to 30 months, with an effect size of 1.77. (An effect size of 0.2 is regarded as small, 0.5 as medium, and 0.8 as large.) There was not a significant change from baseline

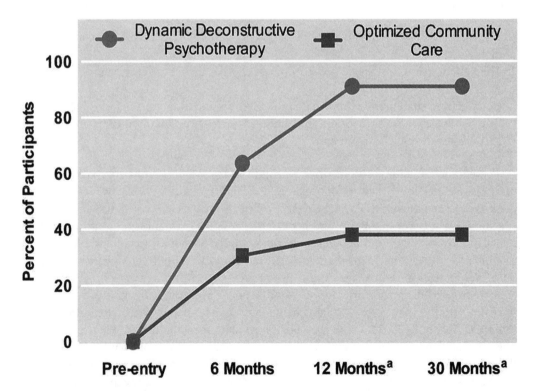

Figure 10.2 Cumulative response to DDP treatment as measured by the proportion of participants achieving at least 25% improvement in Borderline Improvement of Severity Over Time score; primary outcome measure.

for OCC subjects. Recreational drug use completely remitted by the end of DDP treatment, and remained in remission at 30 months (effect size 1.13). For OCC subjects, recreational drug use worsened. Five of 15 OCC subjects were using street opioids, cocaine, sedatives, amphetamines, and/or cannabis (Gregory, Delucia-Deranja, & Mogle, 2010). DDP allows for simultaneous medication management and was delivered by psychiatrists in this trial, and could be considered an integrated treatment. In the only other published randomized controlled study of treating these commonly comorbid disorders used dialectical behavioral therapy (DBT). There were no changes in symptoms 6 months after the end of treatment (Van den Bosch, Verheul, Schippers, & Van den Brink, 2002).

Certainly other psychotherapy approaches must be reviewed in regards to treating addiction and especially where integrated approaches converge. However, the reader will notice a difference in outcome reporting. A neuropsychoanalytic therapy such as DDP has as its goal fundamental character change, including the patients' orientation toward the use of drugs and alcohol. Therefore, reports of alcohol and drug use over time, such as 1-year abstinence rates, make sense. Behavioral therapies have as their goal harm reduction. Reports of continuous abstinence over time are often unusual. Outcomes tend to be reported as changes in overall use, such as percentage of drug-free days. The "evidence base" of these treatments is based on reduction of using days, harm reduction, rather than change in orientation toward use. This can make comparing studies difficult at times in regards to outcomes.

The underlying assumption of CBT of addiction is that learning processes play an important role in the development and continuation of addiction. Therefore, these same learning processes can help patients recover from their addictions (Carroll 1998). Adherence to the specific goals of treatment is measured as part of outcome studies. CBT of addiction is usually delivered as a time-limited intervention, 12–24 visits. Short treatments that seek to impart a particular set of patient-driven interventions are ideal for measuring outcomes.

The two main components of CBT are functional analysis and skills training. Functional analysis plays an important role in helping the patient understand high-risk situations that may provoke relapse to active addiction. These situations would include both internal emotional states as well as external drug cue-containing environments. Skills training includes both the unlearning of old habits associated with drug and alcohol use as well as learning or relearning healthier skills and habits. In addition to delivering specific skills, the therapist must attend to the therapeutic alliance, which is an essential base for skills delivery. Homework is often a part of this treatment. The patients are encouraged to think about the skills outside the treatment session, write down their application of the concepts delivered during the training sessions, and explain to the therapist how they applied the concepts when faced with real-life situations that demanded new skills.

Rawson et al. (2006) showed a reduction in 30-day use of cocaine or methamphetamine from 9 days/month to 4 days/month 1 year after a 16-week treatment for 45 subjects. As is typical of this kind of reporting, the clinical significance of reducing stimulant addiction from 9 to 4 days/month is unknown, but from a harm reduction point of view, more than 50% of use was averted.

A meta-analysis of 53 randomized trials of CBT conducted from 1982 to 2006 that included 23 alcohol studies, 11 stimulant studies, 11 polydrug studies, 6 marijuana studies, and 2 opioid studies showed a reduced use effect size at 1 year of 0.096 (Vocci & Montoya, 2009). While this finding was statistically significant due to a large pool of subjects, the clinical significance of this small effect size is questionable, and the meta-analysis appears to be quite diluted and not homogenous in nature. This systematic review of psychological treatments for stimulant misuse described the addition of contingency management—a behavioral approach that gives rewards for submitting drug-free urines—to a CBT variant, called Matrix therapy, as follows. "The Matrix as well as contingency management group had significantly more methamphetamine-free urine samples (P = 0.01) and a greater mean period of continuous abstinence (4.6 versus 2.8 weeks for treatment as usual, P = 0.02), demonstrating a clear treatment effect of add-on contingency management" (Rawson et al., 2006, p. 267).

Motivational Enhancement Therapy (MET)

Another widely utilized approach is motivational enhancement therapy (MET). Key intervention strategies for MET include open-ended questions, affirming clients, reflective listening (clarification), summarizing statements, eliciting change, talk, and empathy. MET uses as a framework a hierarchy of "states of change" that is navigated with addicted patients (Rollnick & Miller, 1995). These "states" are labeled precontemplation, contemplation, planning, action, and maintenance. In the precontemplation stage, individuals simply use their drug thoughtlessly, and have no interest in stopping. As they move through these stages, the individual thinks more and more realistically about having to stop their drug, how to stop, and what the requirements are to stay in sustained sobriety. These states are descriptive, and the underlying mechanisms of why one person would be in "precontemplation" and another in "action" are not discussed in the motivational interviewing literature. Describing the mechanisms of progression through these states requires this discussion of the intersection of psychodynamics and neurophysiology.

A Cochrane review (Smedslund et al., 2011) of 59 studies that included 13,342 participants in treatment for alcohol use disorders or drug use disorders found no effect at long-term follow-up. They found: "The evidence is mostly of low quality" and concluded that "[t]he results show that people who have received [motivational interviewing] (MI) have reduced their use of substances more than people who have not received any treatment. However, it seems that other active treatments, treatment as usual and being assessed and receiving feedback can be as effective as motivational interviewing" (Smedslund et al., 2011, p. 2) in certain patients. There was not enough data to conclude about the effects of MI on retention in treatment, readiness to change, or repeat convictions. Again, this analysis was conducted on a very heterogeneous population, making the outcomes published difficult to apply to specific patient populations.

Twelve-Step Facilitation (TSF)

TSF was originally created to be a control treatment against which to measure the outcomes of the "active" treatment, CBT and MET, in Project Match. Its manual features 12–15 structured psychotherapy sessions where the patient is encouraged to attend either Alcoholics Anonymous (AA) or Narcotics Anonymous (NA). It is a brief exposure to 12-step recovery without having to go to the meetings. An absolute need for abstinence and the need for others to participate in one's recovery are central tenets of this approach (Donovan & Floyd, 2008).

The Project Match trial found TSF similar in efficacy to CBT and MET. Since it had been set up as a control treatment, currently no independent outcome studies could be found that measured the effect of TSF.

Comparative Outcomes for Psychotherapy

To our knowledge, there has been only one randomized-controlled trial directly comparing outcomes of psychoanalytic therapy (PT) to CBT and none to MET. The comparison between PT and CBT for patients with cocaine dependence indicated no difference in outcomes between these two treatments (Crits-Christoph et al., 1999). Most reviews have reported that psychosocial treatments of addiction have relatively modest effects and that there are only minor differences between treatments. In his review, Woody (2003) described the overall effect size of addiction therapy as small to medium. A recent meta-analysis reached similar conclusions and reported an overall effect size of 0.45 (Dutra et al., 2008). In describing Project Match, which compared outcomes for CBT, MET, and TSF, Cutler and Fishbain (2005) found that only 3% of the drinking outcome at follow-up could be attributed to any specific treatment.

The UKATT study of alcohol treatment (UKATT Research Team, 2007) modeled on Project Match, followed a cohort of 742 clients with alcohol problems over 12 months. Treatment was randomized between social and behavioral network therapy (SBNT) and MET. Initial hypotheses were that clients with weak social networks would show better outcomes with SBNT and that the following four conditions would respond better to MET: low levels of readiness to change, severity of psychiatric morbidity, high anger index, and level of alcohol dependence. None of these hypotheses achieved statistical significance in this study. In their discussion, adding in the findings of Project Match, the Research Team concluded:

> The conditions in question here are that two large, rigorous, multi-center randomized controlled trials in two different health systems have failed to demonstrate any clinically meaningful increment to treatment effectiveness. It therefore seems warranted to consider the possibility that there were no substantial matching contingencies waiting to be discovered. . . . An explanation of this phenomenon is that "the technological model" of treatment in which specific theory-based treatment techniques are held to be responsible for effectiveness is invalid. Rather, all effective treatments share one or more non-specific ingredients that are able to facilitate the required change in behavior. A related idea is that any kind of credible treatment represents a culturally sanctioned opportunity that gives the client "permission" to change behavior; once an intentional decision to solve the alcohol problem has been made, a process of change is instigated that proceeds independently of any particular component of or theory of treatment. (UKATT, 2007, p. 234)

Outcomes for a Combined Behavioral Intervention—The COMBINE Study

The most rigorous outcome study in the addiction literature likely was the COMBINE study (Anton, O'Malley, & Cirauloda, 2006). Here, 1,383 alcohol-dependent individuals were randomized into nine groups: placebo and medical management; acamprosate and medical management; naltrexone and medical management; acamprosate, naltrexone, and medical management; placebo and the combined behavioral intervention (CBI); acamprosate and CBI; naltrexone and CBI; acamprosate, naltrexone, and CBI; and CBI alone. The CBI was designed by a team of experts who incorporated elements of the three psychotherapies described above, CBT, MET, and TSF. Potential subjects who were addicted to drugs other than alcohol, cannabis, or nicotine were excluded, and potential subjects who required medications for a comorbid psychiatric disorder were excluded. Albeit a larger study, it excluded key comorbidities, so application to the general population may be limited. The outcome of the COMBINE study for alcohol dependence showed that positive composite clinical outcomes at 1 year were observed in 38%–50% of patients, with the worst outcomes in patients who received medical management with placebo (no naltrexone or acamprosate) and better outcomes in those who received medical management plus either naltrexone or specialized alcohol counseling. Naltrexone use appeared to have the greatest impact upon sobriety when compared to psychotherapy, combined or otherwise. There was no apparent difference shown for any treatment during the 1-year follow-up, suggesting that combining psychotherapy with medication management had little benefit in this particular study.

Efficacy, Effectiveness, and a Critique of RCTs of Psychotherapy

Efficacy refers to a carefully demarcated treatment that employs a manual to which therapists are required to adhere. The manualized treatments are tested by randomized controlled trials (RCTs) either against an inert control, such as patients on a waiting list, or against other psychotherapies. These psychotherapies are tested under conditions that may not resemble real clinical practice (i.e., less comorbidity, less severity, less at-risk populations). In contrast, effectiveness studies measure outcomes for psychotherapies that have been conducted by practitioners in the real world, but the "evidence" of the impact of the treatment on the outcome is limited by a lack of homogeneity of the treatment delivery and the patient population, and a lack of randomization and controlled doses of treatment (Westen & Bradley, 2005; Ablon & Jones, 2002). According to Carroll (1998)

> A review of randomized-controlled trials (RCTs) suggests that, across substances of abuse but most strongly for tobacco, there is good evidence for the effectiveness of CBT compared with no-treatment controls. The most rigorous level of testing compared CBT with other active treatments (in effect asking the question "Is CBT more effective than other widely used treatments?" rather than, "Is CBT better than no treatment or minimal treatment?"). These comparisons have led to less consistent results; some studies indicate the superiority of CBT, while others have shown CBT as comparable to, but not more effective than, other approaches.

Of course, the randomized controlled study of DDP against optimized community treatment (OCC), described earlier in the chapter, would be a wonderful example of constructing an effective test of a newly designed neuropsychoanalytic treatment against what practitioners in the community are currently doing to help their patients. The DDP study is obviously limited by the fact that it was carried out in only one location, and contains only 15 DDP subjects and 15 OCC subjects.

In a review of the RCT approach, Morgenstern and McKay (2007) explained, "The review suggests weak support for the technology model of psychotherapy research. Lack of support is interpreted as indicating flaws in several model assumptions about how to conceptualize and measure patient responsivity and the interaction of non-specific and specific therapeutic factors." We have cited evidence that a listing of RCT "efficacious" treatments is likely to be flawed by virtue of an incorrect assumption that a psychotherapy such as MET is fundamentally different than PT. Ironically, some of the most stringent prospective studies have found little benefit to integrated, combined medication plus psychotherapy care. The authors have explained that this may be due optimistically to the idea that all psychotherapies utilize core skills and techniques regardless of dogma. Pessimistically, it may be that many interventions simply do not work, or do not work any better than other treatments.

Najavits and Weiss (1994) reviewed outcomes in addiction psychotherapy and found them much more related to the nature of the psychotherapists than the particular brand of treatment they offered. Skilled interpersonal functioning by the therapist was related to good outcomes. This is not surprising, given the evidence that the therapeutic alliance has been the most consistently reliable predictor of psychotherapy outcome (Horvath & Symonds, 1991). Najavits and Weiss (1994) suggested some research support relating good outcomes to the capacity to establish alliance, warmth and friendliness, affirmation, understanding, helping, protecting, and an absence of belittling and blaming. They also cited suggestions that the ability to be active; tolerate anger and control one's own anger; be flexible, patient, and advocating for involvement in AA; being charismatic, emotional, and inspiring; being conscious of avoiding power struggles, willing to confront denial, and enjoying working with addicted patients led to more positive outcomes. Many of these therapist traits could be considered universal, and the more that are applied in session, the greater likelihood of a response. These core skills are often involved in pharmacotherapy sessions, or should be reintroduced, to build rapport and to enhance compliance and outcomes. Clinicians who are aware of these skills sets could escalate them in medication management sessions and provide integrative treatment to the addictive patient in the office setting.

Similarities and Differences—Process Research

Psychotherapy process research attempts to break down different approaches into their technical components. It can be used in a comparative trial to assess whether the psychotherapy as delivered is really different from what it is being tested against. In an analysis of a RCT of psychotherapy for depression, Ablon and Jones (2002) found that the psychotherapy delivered as "interpersonal psychotherapy" contained more CBT interventions than interventions that were classified as unique to interpersonal psychotherapy.

There are a number of articles from psychoanalytically oriented writers discussing the similarities and differences with CBT approaches (Migone & Liotti, 1998; Williams, 1999; Milton, 2011). Perhaps the most valuable of these has been the study of how expert clinicians' prototypes of an ideal treatment correlate with outcome in psychodynamic and CBT. Eleven psychodynamic and ten cognitive behavioral internationally recognized therapists performed a Q-sort of their psychotherapeutic techniques. Through this procedure, the most common techniques could be identified in each approach. Two psychodynamic and one CBT of 30, 38, and 32 hours were then rated according to the same Q-sort of potential therapeutic interventions by independent raters. The findings indicated that the psychodynamic therapists applied a significant amount of cognitive behavioral strategies in addition to psychodynamic technique, whereas the cognitive behavioral therapists applied primarily cognitive-behavioral techniques, but also included occasional use of psychodynamic techniques. They concluded that cognitive behavioral techniques could be considered a subsample of the techniques used by the psychodynamic therapists (Ablon & Jones, 1998). Extrapolating to the psychopharmacologist providing a medication only framework, he or she may want to consider that they are *always providing psychotherapy*. Whether one was initially trained psychodynamically, cognitively, or interpersonally, the prescriber is likely utilizing overlapping skill sets. Regardless of taxonomy, the prescriber should be aware of these skill sets and actively use them in session when treating addicted patients. This is true integration of techniques if the psychopharmacologist keeps these skill sets in mind and has a long enough session to employ them.

In the above study, psychodynamic techniques, though infrequent, predicted positive outcome when employed in CBT approaches. Perhaps *integration* should include use of multiple psychotherapy skills and combining with medication management? Focusing on the impact of distorted cognitions was negatively correlated with outcome. Further, when therapists tried to correct problems in the therapeutic alliance by increasing their adherence to the techniques in the cognitive behavioral manual, it further strained the alliance, whereas use of psychodynamic interventions was correlated with positive outcome. The authors offered that the high degree of overlap in applied technique across different treatment models may explain why different forms of treatment in standard outcome studies demonstrate similar results (Ablon & Jones, 1998).

Addiction psychotherapy is more unitary than might be assumed by the existence of PT, CBT, MET, and TSF. The treatment approaches are so overlapping as to make siding with one or another approach adventitious. After a careful review, many differences appear to be the result of "branding" of therapies and use of different terms for the same ideas in one or another tradition. The reason for overlap is that they all exist to treat very difficult patients, and over time, individual practitioners have found some interventions that work better than others.

Psychotherapy of addiction is a wide-open field with no clear superiority of any one approach and where outcomes could doubtless be better. An ideal psychotherapy for addiction has yet to be described. PT, CBT, MET, and TSF are all valid approaches that find their uses according to the particular training of the therapist and the conditions under which the treatment is delivered. Addicted patients have a life-threatening illness that is ruled by unconscious factors. All psychotherapies aim to make patients more conscious of the choices that they are constantly making.

Ideally, therapists will vary their approach to make it specific for each patient. PT, MET, TSF, and CBT have strengths and weaknesses for addicted patients. The strength of PT (and also of MET) is that by putting the patient at the center of initiative, the patient can feel empowered, and the psychoanalytic therapist can monitor associations and use increasingly powerful interpretations, from clarification to transference interpretation, to help the patient be conscious, and therefore more likely to be in control, of decisions regarding drugs and alcohol. A study by Karno and Longabaugh (2005) has indicated that the outcome of alcoholic patients with moderate or high reactance is strongly and negatively related to the degree of therapist directiveness.

However, the CBT therapist's more structured and directive stance may be helpful for certain patients. Patients who use avoidance will often not bring up obvious relapse-oriented behaviors and may state, "I can't think of anything to say." Patients are sometimes screening their associations from the therapist because the first thing that comes to mind refers to their intention to drink/use. CBT might better unearth relapse-oriented behaviors and cravings by virtue of its more directive and systematic approach to screening for relapse tendencies. Psychopharmacologists all may have different approaches when prescribing. Some are more directive and forceful. Others offer a partnership and deliberation with their patients. The astute psychopharmacologist also should improve therapeutic skills to match the individual patient being seen at the time. Further process research is needed to better delineate these specific treatment interventions within therapeutic modalities that mediate the relationship between patient characteristics and outcome, so that treatment may be tailored to the individual needs of a particular patient.

The authors hope that this discussion of similarities and differences has made addiction practitioners more comfortable in using what they know without worrying that they are taking sides in some conflict about what is "right" in psychotherapy.

COMBINING PSYCHOTHERAPY AND MEDICATION

The final part of the above section suggests that clinicians who treat addiction might want to consider integrated psychotherapy approaches. This final section could ask, "Might there be a way to combine our psychotherapy approaches to addiction with our understanding of the neural mechanisms to other pharmacological somatic interventions?" There is a limited literature on this approach. Most studies start with a particular method, and add in a complementary treatment, such as adding psychotherapy to methadone maintenance, as will be described below. The single treatment that was specifically designed to incorporate both medication and psychotherapy from the beginning is behavioral couples therapy (BCT).

Behavioral Couples Therapy

Rather than have a single patient arrive for treatment, BCT is organized to have family members arrive together. The nonalcoholic partner is asked to give the alcoholic partner disulfiram as a part of the treatment. Medication administration occurs as part of a prescribed daily engagement where difficult topics can be broached, but expressions of love and appreciation are also required. Compared to couple education or interactional couples treatment, the effect size was 0.55 after the conclusion of treatment and 0.45 at 12-month follow-up. In a comparison of BCT with individual treatment of men with alcoholism, 50% of the subjects remained abstinent during treatment versus 30% receiving individual treatment. During the year of treatment, 8% of BCT subjects had drug-related arrests versus 28% of individually treated men, and 13% of BCT subjects required inpatient treatment versus 35% of individually treated men (Fals-Stewart, O'Farrell, & Birchler, 2004).

CBT and Disulfiram for Cocaine Dependence

Eighty-five percent of cocaine dependent persons were also alcohol dependent (Suh, Pettianati, Kampman, & O'Brien, 2006). A late pharmacodynamic discovery is that there is a second action of disulfiram: inhibition of dopamine beta hydroxylase. This is the enzyme that converts dopamine to norepinephrine. The apparent mechanism of action of disulfiram is to reduce norepinephrine-induced stress that leads to relapse (Gaval-Cruz & Weinshenker, 2009). Participants in a yearlong study of CBT and 250 mg of disulfiram daily were more reliably abstinent than subjects taking placebo and subjects treated with interpersonal psychotherapy and disulfiram (Carroll et al., 2004). Therefore, disulfiram has two advantages in treating patients with cocaine dependence. The patient is protected from starting with alcohol and progressing to cocaine use. Independently, the patient is protected from starting a relapse with cocaine.

Methadone Maintenance and Psychotherapy or Drug Counseling

Woody (2003) used the same general schema of psychoanalytic therapies, CBT, motivational interviewing, and drug counseling/TSF that was described in this review. He described the outcomes of each approach in the treatment of patients in methadone maintenance programs based at Yale University and the University of Pennsylvania (Penn). Subjects with low comorbidity improved with any treatment. The Penn study showed that subjects with high psychiatric comorbidity did better in terms of employment, legal, psychiatric, and drug use indices, as measured by the Addiction Severity Index. This finding was not replicated at Yale. Woody's explanation for the divergence of findings was that at Penn the psychotherapy offices were located within the methadone maintenance program, whereas the Yale psychotherapy offices required a short walk from the methadone program.

As the reader can see, there is much theory that can support the integration of psychotherapy plus pharmacotherapy for the treatment of addiction patients, but the amount of stringent research studies related to an integrated approach are few.

CONCLUSION

The neurobiology of addiction is much better understood in the 21st century than it was for much of the 20th century. Manipulating the brains of addicted patients with medications and combining reasonable psychotherapies that take advantage of medication interventions makes perfect sense. However, evidence-based treatments with this approach are just beginning to appear.

As described above, the technology of exactly how to document that one or another approach is more effective needs much development before any school of psychotherapy can declare victory over another. The methodology of Gregory et al. (2010) in showing the outcomes of dialectical deconstructive psychotherapy compared with optimized community care might be the most sophisticated attempt currently available, albeit on a small scale at present. As noted in the critique of Westen and Bradley (2005), clinicians need to know that one or another approach, *applied in the real world and compared against another commonly used approach using real world subjects and with carefully documented outcomes*, is shown to be psychotherapist friendly, and is more effective than another intervention for patients who are at risk of dying from addiction. The phenomenon of "branding," that academics borrow interventions and techniques from other therapies, but label them as if they were a unique invention, may be at times destructive toward the goal of identifying effective treatments.

Finally, the best approach probably resides in the person of the psychotherapist. This may be an underlying reason that TSF has such strong research support as a treatment. It is often carried out by recovering people who care deeply about their own experience, strength, and hope, and want to carry the message of recovery to patients with whom they identify. Alliance; warmth; friendliness; affirmation; understanding; helping; protecting; and being charismatic, inspiring, and emotional—all wrapped up with a sense of pleasure in being paid to do what comes as part of their spiritual recovery—means that practitioners of TSF may have a built-in advantage over other trained providers.

Hopefully, this review has been helpful to the reader. Pharmacology treatments have been reviewed. Psychotherapy treatments have been reviewed. Finally, where available, integrated treatments have been reviewed or at least theorized in regards to how the work to improve patient outcomes.

REFERENCES

Ablon, J. S., & Jones, E. E. (1998). How expert clinicians' prototypes of an ideal treatment correlate with outcome in psychodynamic and cognitive behavioral therapy. *Psychotherapy Research, 8*, 71–83.

Ablon, J. S., & Jones, E. E. (2002). Validity of controlled clinical trials of psychotherapy: Findings from the NIMH treatment of depression collaborative research program. *American Journal of Psychiatry, 159*, 775–783.

Alcaro, A., & Panksepp, J. (2011). The SEEKING mind: Primal neuroaffective substrates for appetitive incentive states and their pathological dynamics in addictions and depression. *Neuroscience Biobehavior Review, 35*, 1805–1820.

Amato, L., Minozzi, S., Pani, P. P., Solimini, R., Vecchi, S., Zuccaro, P., & Davoli, M. (2011). Dopamine agonists for the treatment of cocaine dependence. *Cochrane Database of Systematic Reviews, 12*(12), CD003352.

Anton, R. F., O'Malley, S. S., & Cirauloda, D. A. (2006). Combined pharmacotherapies and behavioral interventions for alcohol dependence. *Journal of the American Medical Association, 295*, 2003–2017.

Benyamina, A., Lecacheux, M., Blecha, L., Reynaud, M., & Lukasiewcz, M. (2008). Pharmacotherapy and psychotherapy in cannabis withdrawal and dependence. *Expert Review of Neurotherapeutics, 8*, 479–491.

Berridge, K. C., & Robinson, T. E. (1998). What is the role of dopamine in reward: Hedonic impact, reward learning, or incentive salience? *Brain Research Reviews, 28*, 309–369.

Cahill, K., Stead, L. F., & Lancaster, T. (2012). Nicotine receptor partial agonists for smoking cessation. *Cochrane Database of Systematic Reviews, 4*, CD006103.

Carroll, K. M. (1998). A cognitive behavioral approach: Treating cocaine addiction. *National Institute of Drug Abuse Publication, 98*, 4308.

Carroll, K. M., Fenton, L. R., Ball, S. A., Nich, C., Frankforter, T. L., Shi, J., & Rounsaville, B. J. (2004). Efficacy of disulfiram and cognitive behavior therapy in cocaine-dependent outpatients: A randomized placebo-controlled trial. *Archives of General Psychiatry, 61*, 264–272.

Castells, X., Casas, M., Perez-Mana, C., Roncero, C., Vidal, X., & Capella, D. (2010). Efficacy of psychostimulant drugs for cocaine dependence. *Cochrane Database of Systematic Reviews, 2*(2), CD007380.

Chau, P., Hoifodt-Lido, H., Lof, E., Soderpalm, B., & Ericson, M. (2010). Glycine receptors in the nucleus accumbens involved in the ethanol intake-reducing effect of acamprosate. *Alcoholism: Clinical and Experimental Research, 34*, 39–45.

Crits-Christoph, P., Siqueland, L., Blaine, J., Frank, A., Luborsky, L., Onken, L. S., et al. (1999). Psychosocial treatments for cocaine dependence: National Institute on Drug Abuse Collaborative Cocaine Treatment Study. *Archives of General Psychiatry, 56*, 493–502.

Cutler, R. B., & Fishbain, D. A. (2005). Are alcoholism treatments effective? The Project Match data. *BMC Public Health Journal, 5*, 75–87.

Dodes, L. M. (1990). Addiction, helplessness and narcissistic rage. *Psychoanalytic Quarterly, 59*, 398–419.

Dodes, L. M. (1996). Compulsion and addiction. *Journal of the American Psychoanalytic Association, 44*, 815–835.

Donovan, D. M., & Floyd, A. S. (2008). Facilitating involvement in twelve-step programs. *Recent Developments in Alcoholism, 18*, 303–320.

Dutra, L., Stathopoulou, G., Basden, S. L., Leyro, R. M., Powers, M. B., & Otto, M. W. (2008). A meta-analytic review of psychosocial interventions for substance use disorders. *American Journal of Psychiatry, 165*, 179–187.

Enoch, M. (2008). The role of GABA-A receptors in the development of alcoholism. *Biochemistry and Behavior, 90*, 95–104.

Everitt, B. J., & Robbins, T. W. (2005). Neural systems of reinforcement for drug addiction: From actions to habits to compulsion. *Nature Neuroscience, 8*, 1481–1489.

Fals-Stewart, W., O'Farrell, T. J., & Birchler, G. R. (2004, August). Behavioral couples therapy for substance abuse: Rationale, methods and findings. *Science and Practice Perspectives, 2*, 30–41.

Fattore, L., Fadda, P., Spano, M. S., Pistis, M., & Frattta, W. (2008). Neurobiological mechanisms of cannabinoid addiction. *Molecular and Cell Endocrinology, 286*, S97–S107.

Freud, S. (1920). Beyond the pleasure principle. *Standard Edition of the Complete Psychological Works of Sigmund Freud, 18*.

Gaval-Cruz, M., & Weinshenker, D. (2009). Mechanisms of disulfiram-induced cocaine abstinence. *Molecular Interventions, 9*, 175–187.

Gowing, L., Ali, R., & White, J. M. (2009). Buprenorphine for the management of opioid withdrawal. *Cochrane Database of Systematic Reviews, 3*(3), CD002025.

Gregory, R. J., DeLucia-Deranja, E., & Mogle, J. A. (2010). Dynamic deconstructive psychotherapy versus optimized community care for borderline personality disorder co-occurring with alcohol use disorders, a 30 month follow up. *Journal of Nervous and Mental Disease, 198*, 292–298.

Hays, J. T., Hurt, R. D., Rigotti, N. A., Niaura, R., Gonzales, D., Durcan, M. J., . . . White, J. D. (2001). Sustained-release bupropion for pharmacologic relapse prevention after smoking cessation. A randomized, controlled trial. *Annals of Internal Medicine, 135*, 423–433.

Hovarth, A. O., & Symonds, B. D. (1991). Relations between working alliance and outcome in psychotherapy: A meta-analysis. *Journal of Counseling Psychology, 38*, 139–149.

Jasinski, D. R. (1997). Human pharmacology of narcotic antagonists. *British Journal of Clinical Pharmacology, 7*, 287S–290S.

Johnson, B. (1993). A developmental model of addiction, and its relationship to the Twelve Step Program of Alcoholics Anonymous. *Journal of Substance Abuse Treatment, 10*, 23–32.

Johnson, B. (2008). Just what lies beyond the pleasure principle? *Neuropsychoanalysis, 10*, 201–212.

Johnson, R. E., Jaffe, J. H., & Fudala, P. J. (1992). A controlled trial of buprenorphine treatment for opioid dependence. *Journal of the American Medical Association, 267*, 2750–2755.

Jorgensen, C. H., Pedersen, B., & Tonnesen, H. (2011). The efficacy of disulfiram for the treatment of alcohol use disorder. *Alcoholism: Clinical and Experimental Research, 35*, 1749–1758.

Kalivas, P. W., & Volkow, N. D. (2005). The neural basis of addiction: A pathology of motivation and choice. *Journal of the American Psychiatric Association, 162*, 1403–1413.

Karno, M. P., & Longabaugh. R. (2005). Less directiveness by therapists improves drinking outcomes of reactant clients in alcoholism treatment. *Journal of Consulting and Clinical Psychology, 73,* 262–267.

Kernberg, O. (1975). *Borderline conditions and pathological narcissism.* New York: Aronson.

Khantzian, E. J. (1985). The self-medication hypothesis of addictive disorders: Focus on heroin and cocaine dependence. *American Journal of Psychiatry, 142,* 1259–1264.

Khantzian, E. J. (1999). *Treating addiction as a human process.* Northvale, NJ: Jason Aronson.

Koob, G. F., & Volkow, N. D. (2010). Neurocircuitry of addiction. *Neuropsychopharmacology, 35,* 217–238.

Koob,G., & Le Moal, M. (2001). Drug addiction, dysregulation of reward, and allostasis. *Neuropsychopharmacology, 2,* 97–129.

Likhitsathian, S., Saengcharnchai, P., Uttawichai, K., Yingwiwattanapong, J., Wittayanookulluk, A., & Srisurapanont, M. (2012). Cognitive changes in topiramate-treated patients with alcoholism: A 12-week prospective study in patients recently detoxified. *Psychiatry and Clinical Neuroscience, 66,* 235–241.

Longabaugh, R., Zweben, A., Locastro, J. S., & Miller, W. R. (2005, Supplement). Origins, issues and options in the development of the combined behavioral intervention. *Journal of Studies on Alcoholism, 15,* 179–187.

Migone, P., & Liotti, G. (1998). Psychoanalysis and cognitive-evolutionary psychology: An attempt at integration. *International Journal of Psychoanalysis, 79,* 1071–1095.

Miller, P., & Dunlop, A. (2011). Rhetoric, reality and research: What they mean for achieving the best possible treatment system for addiction-related problems. *International Journal of Drug Policy, 22,* 196–197.

Miller, R. W., & Wilbourne, P. C. (2002). Mesa grande: A methodological analysis of clinical trials of treatments for alcohol use disorders. *Addiction, 97,* 265–277.

Mills, E. J., Wu, P., Lockhart, I., Thorlund, K., Puhan, M., & Ebbert, J. O. (2012). Comparisons of high-dose and combination nicotine replacement therapy, varenicline, and bupropion for smoking cessation: A systematic review and multiple treatment meta-analysis. *Annals of Medicine, 44,* 588–597.

Milton, J. (2011). Psychoanalysis and cognitive behavioral therapy—rival paradigms or common ground? *International Journal of Psychoanalysis, 82,* 431–448.

Minozzi, S., Amato, L., Davoli, M., Farrell, M., Lima Reisser A. A., . . . Vecchi, S. (2008). Anticonvulsants for cocaine dependence. *Cochrane Database of Systematic Reviews, 2*(2), CD006754.

Morgenstern, J., & McKay, J. R. (2007). Rethinking the paradigms that inform behavioral treatment research for substance use disorders. *Addiction, 102,* 1377–1389.

Naassila, M., Hammoumi, S., Legrand, E., Durbin, P., & Daoust, M. (1998). Mechanism of action of acamprosate. Part I: Characterization of spermidine-sensitive acamprosate binding site in rat brain. *Alcoholism: Clinical and Experimental Research, 22,* 802–809.

Najavits, L. M., & Weiss, R. D. (1994). Variations in therapist effectiveness in the treatment of patients with substance use disorders: An empirical review. *Addiction, 89,* 679–688.

Nestler, E. J. (2005). Is there a common molecular pathway for addiction? *Nature Neuroscience, 8,* 1445–1449.

Niehaus, J. L., Cruz-Bermudez, N. D., & Kauer, J. A. (2009). Plasticity of addiction: A mesolimbic dopamine short-circuit? *American Journal of Addictions, 18,* 259–271.

Okie, S. (2010). A flood of opioids, a rising tide of deaths. *New England Journal of Medicine, 363,* 981–985.

Pani, P. P., Trogu, E., Vacca, R., Amato, L., Vecchi, S., & Davoli, M. (2010). Disulfiram for the treatment of cocaine dependence. *Cochrane Database of Systematic Reviews, 1*(1), CD007024.

Peer, K., Rennert, L., Lynch, K. G., Farrer, L., Gelernter, J., & Kranzler, H. R. (2013). Prevalence of DSM-IV and DSM-5 alcohol, cocaine, opioid, and cannabis use disorders in a largely substance dependent sample. *Drug and Alcohol Dependence, 127,* 215–219.

Rawson, R. A., McCann, M. J., Flammino, F., Shoptaw, S., Miotto, K., Reiber, C., & Ling, W. (2006). A comparison of contingency management and cognitive behavioral approaches for stimulant-dependent individuals. *Addiction, 101,* 267–274.

Rollnick, S., & Miller, W. R. (1995). What is motivational interviewing? *Behavioral and Cognitive Psychotherapy, 23,* 325–334.

Smedslund, G., Ber, R. C., Hammerstrom, K. T., Steiro, A., Leiknes, K. A., Dahl, H. M., & Karlsen, K. (2011). Motivational interviewing for substance abuse. *Cochrane Database of Systematic Reviews, 11,* CD008063.

Solms, M., & Turnbull, O. (2002). *The brain and the inner world: An introduction to the neuroscience of subjective experience.* New York: Other Press.

Stead, L. F., Perera, R., Bullen, C., Mant, D., & Lancaster, T. (2008). Nicotine replacement therapy for smoking cessation. *Cochrane Database of Systematic Reviews, 1*(1), CD000146.

Suh, J. J., Pettianati, H. M., Kampman, K. M., & O'Brien, C. P. (2006). The status of disulfiram a half century later. *Journal of Clinical Psychopharmacology, 26,* 290–302.

Swan, G. E., McAfee, T., Curry, S. J., Jack, L. M., Javitz, H., Dacey, S., & Bergman, K. (2003). Effectiveness of bupropion sustained release for smoking cessation in a health care setting: A randomized trial. *Archives of Internal Medicine, 163,* 2337–2344.

UKATT Research Team. (2007). UK Alcohol Treatment Trial: Client-treatment matching effects. *Addiction, 103,* 228–238.

Van den Bosch, L. M., Verheul, R., Schippers, G., & van den Brink, W. (2002). Dialectical behavioral therapy of borderline patients with and without substance use problems: Implementation and long-term effects. *Addictive Behavior, 27,* 911–923.

Vocci, F. J., & Montoya, I. D. (2009). Psychological treatments for stimulant misuse, comparing and contrasting those for amphetamine dependence and those for cocaine dependence. *Current Opinion in Psychiatry, 22,* 263–268.

Volpicelli, J. R., Alterman, A. I., Hayashida, M., & O'Brien, C. P. (1992). Naltrexone in the treatment of alcohol dependence. *Archives of General Psychiatry, 49,* 876–880.

Westen, D., & Bradley, R. (2005). Evidence-supported complexity: Rethinking evidence-based practice in psychotherapy. *Current Directions in Psychological Science, 14,* 266–271.

Wilde, M. I., & Wagstaff, A. J. (1997). Acamprosate. A review of its pharmacology and clinical potential in the management of alcohol dependence after detoxification. *Drugs, 53,* 1038–1053.

Wheelis, A. (1956). Will & psychoanalysis. *Journal of the American Psychoanalytic Association, 40,* 285–303.

Williams, P. (1999). Psychoanalysis and cognitive-evolutionary psychology: An attempt at integration" by Paolo Migone and Giovanni Liotti. *International Journal of Psychoanalysis, 80,* 415–423.

Winnicott, D. W. (1958). Transitional objects and transitional phenomena. In D. W. Winnicott, *Collected Papers.* New York: Basic Books.

Witkiewitz, K., Saville, K., & Hamreus, K. (2012). Acamprosate for treatment of alcohol dependence: Mechanisms, efficacy, and clinical utility. *Journal of Therapeutics and Clinical Risk Management, 8,* 45–53.

Woody, G. E. (2003). Research findings on psychotherapy of addictive disorders. *American Journal on Addiction, 12,* S19–S26.

Wu, P., Wilson, K., Dimoulas, P., & Mills, E. (2006). Effectiveness of smoking cessation therapies: A systematic review and meta-analysis. *BMC Public Health, 6,* 300.

Wurmser, L. (1974). Psychoanalytic considerations of the etiology of compulsive drug use. *Journal of the American Psychoanalytic Association, 22,* 820–843.

11

Integrating Pharmacotherapy and Psychotherapy in Perinatal Distress

Amy Wenzel

INTRODUCTION

Although the integration of pharmacotherapy and psychotherapy is important to achieve in the treatment of many, if not all, clinical presentations, it is particularly important to achieve in the treatment of perinatal distress. I define *perinatal distress* as the presence of clinically significant psychiatric symptoms of depression or anxiety in women who are pregnant or who are in the first year postpartum. The decision to medicate a perinatal woman is made with great care, as during pregnancy, medications cross the placenta and are absorbed by the fetus, and when postpartum women are breastfeeding, a portion of the medication can be measured in the breast milk. Thus, medicating a woman during pregnancy and lactation means that the prescriber is, to some degree, medicating the fetus or the infant. For this reason, many practitioners and patients, alike, unilaterally opt for psychotherapy rather than pharmacotherapy. That being said, there are numerous instances in which the medication of a pregnant or lactating woman is indicated on the basis of aspects of her clinical presentation. In other words, the decision not to medicate a perinatal woman is not so clear-cut and certainly not a rigid rule of thumb. Rather, prescribers consider a number of different variables in ultimately making a treatment recommendation.

The empirical literature on pharmacotherapy and psychotherapy for perinatal distress is largely separate from one another; as such, I summarize and evaluate these bodies of literature in a sequential manner in the first parts of this chapter. Specifically, I describe available data on the safety of two general classes of pharmacological interventions for the fetus and infant, as well as data on some specific medications within those classes. The few efficacy studies that have evaluated pharmacological treatments for perinatal distress are examined. In addition, I describe the literature that evaluates the efficacy of two evidence-based psychotherapies for perinatal distress, providing commentary on design limitations and clinical implications. However, what is most innovative is the consideration of the integration of the two approaches to psychiatric treatment. Thus, in the last major section of the chapter, I evaluate current practice guidelines that practitioners can consult as they weigh the advantages and disadvantages of various approaches to treatment and provide additional insight about other variables that have relevance for the integration of pharmacotherapy and psychotherapy for perinatal distress. I conclude the chapter with suggestions for future research.

PHARMACOTHERAPY FOR PERINATAL DISTRESS

The decision to medicate a pregnant or lactating woman is complex and must be made on the basis of a number of competing factors. As might be expected, one of the first factors that the prescriber considers is the risk of harm to the developing fetus or nursing infant due to exposure to the medication. Currently, the U.S. Federal Drug Administration (FDA) provides guidelines for prescribers by assigning all medications to one of five risk categories during pregnancy: (a) Category A indicates that well-designed research with humans has failed to demonstrate that there is risk to the fetus if the medication is taken during pregnancy; (b) Category B indicates that well-designed animal studies have failed to demonstrate that there is risk to the fetus if the medication is taken during pregnancy, but there are no well-designed studies in humans; (c) Category C indicates that animal studies have demonstrated that there *may* be adverse risk to the fetus if the medication is taken during pregnancy, but there are no well-designed studies in humans, and the benefit of taking the medication might outweigh the risk; (d) Category D indicates that there is evidence from research with humans that there is risk to the fetus if the medication is taken during pregnancy, but the benefit of taking the medication might outweigh the risk; and (e) Category X indicates that animal and/or human research has demonstrated that there is risk to the fetus if the medication is taken during pregnancy, and that the risk of taking the medication outweighs the benefits. Most of the medications that are commonly prescribed to treat depression and anxiety fall in Categories C and D.

There are a number of criticisms of these FDA guidelines. First and foremost, they pertain only to pregnancy and exclude lactation. Although a separate set of guidelines for the medication of lactating women has been developed by Dr. Thomas Hale, a renowned professor of pediatrics (Hale, 2012), having one set of guidelines that spans pregnancy through lactation using a similar format and similar criteria would achieve the greatest continuity of care. Second, the FDA guidelines imply that risk systematically increases from Category A to Category X, which is overly simplistic because (a) different categories rely more or less on data from animal studies rather than human studies; and (b) Categories C–X consider risk relative to benefit, rather than risk alone (FDA, 2009). In addition, the FDA guidelines are problematic because they (a) give the impression that all medications in the same category are associated with the same level of toxicity; (b) do not identify adverse effects that vary as a function of dose, duration, frequency of administration, or gestational time of exposure; and (c) consider only planned administration at the exclusion of inadvertent exposure (Public Affairs Committee of the Teratology Society, 2007; Wenzel & Stuart, 2011). As a result, clinical decisions about medicating pregnant women are often made on the basis of category designations alone, failing to consider the subtle nuances that could facilitate a more complete conceptualization of the degree to which pharmacotherapy is indicated for a perinatal woman.

In response to these limitations, the FDA has drafted a Proposed Rule that contains a new set of guidelines for labeling risk associated with medication use in both pregnant and lactating women (http://www.fda.gov/Drugs/DevelopmentApprovalProcess/DevelopmentResources/Labeling/ucm093310.htm). It eliminates Categories A–X altogether and instead contains concise descriptive summaries that pertain to the many dimensions described above that affect risk to the developing fetus and nursing infant. The pregnancy subsection contains (a) a risk summary that addresses risk for structural abnormalities, fetal and infant mortality, impaired physiologic function, and alternations to growth and that explicitly states whether the data are based on human or animal subjects; (b) clinical considerations for prescribing;

(c) predicted risks for inadvertent exposure before a woman knows she is pregnant; (d) factors influencing prescribing decisions, including pregnancy-related dosing adjustments, pregnancy-related adverse effects, interventions that may be needed, and risks to the woman and fetus; and (e) a detailed discussion of available data. The lactation subsection contains: (a) a risk summary that describes the effects of the drug on milk production, the degree to which the drug is present in human milk, and the effect of the drug on the nursing infant; (b) clinical considerations, such as ways to minimize exposure to the nursing infant (e.g., timing of medication ingestion); and (c) a detailed discussion of available data. At the time of the writing of this chapter, the Proposed Rule has not been adopted by the FDA in an official capacity, so the existing categories of pregnancy risk should be used, supplemented with Hale's (2012) guidelines for medication during lactation. However, the Proposed Rule is presented here because it will change the manner in which prescribers make decisions to medicate perinatal women in the future.

Although the consideration of risk to the developing fetus and nursing infant is essential in deciding whether to medicate a pregnant or lactating woman, other factors carry additional weight. For example, deciding *not* to medicate a pregnant or lactating woman may put the developing fetus or nursing infant at more risk than deciding to medicate because her psychiatric condition may be associated with adverse physiological and neurochemical sequelae and may affect her own self-care, prenatal care, and/or ability to care for the newborn (Goldstein & Sundell, 1999). Thus, prescribers are encouraged to take on a careful risk–benefit analysis that weighs potential risks to the developing fetus or nursing infant against the potential consequences of an unmedicated psychiatric disorder. Moreover, the mother's preferences should also be considered when making this decision, as ambivalence about taking medications while pregnant and lactating could lead to excessive guilt and rumination, exacerbating psychopathology, and could be associated with noncompliance. Finally, prescribers should factor in the woman's previous response to treatment, as treatments that have been successful in the past would be the logical first-line treatment to use during pregnancy and lactation when a timely response to treatment is of great importance (Ragan, Stowe, & Newport, 2005).

Although there are no expert guidelines for the treatment of anxiety disorders during pregnancy, there are well-established guidelines for the treatment of depression that are endorsed by the American Psychiatric Association and the American College of Obstetricians and Gynecologists during pregnancy (Yonkers et al., 2009). Because depression and anxiety are often treated with the same medications (e.g., selective serotonin reuptake inhibitors [SSRIs]), it is logical to consult these guidelines in the treatment of anxiety until more specific expert guidelines become available (Wenzel & Stuart, 2011). According to the expert guidelines for depression, psychotherapy is indicated for mild to moderate depression, and medications are indicated for moderate to severe depression (Yonkers et al., 2009). I say more about these guidelines later in the chapter where I consider variables that affect the integration of pharmacotherapy and psychotherapy.

When medications are used to treat perinatal women, prescribers must monitor their patients especially closely and adjust the dosage and timing of medication administration as a function of the woman's gestation or breastfeeding status. For example, pregnant women might need higher dosages because of an increase in total body water, which lowers drug serum concentrations (Bindorf & Sacks, 2008). Moreover, antidepressant serum levels decrease during pregnancy because of increases in plasma volume, enzyme activity, and renal clearance rates, and drug binding decreases during pregnancy because of lower levels of protein (Altshuler & Hendrick, 1996; Jeffries & Bochner, 1988). Experts have recommended

(a) that prescribers carefully monitor drug levels, side effects, therapeutic response, and toxicity throughout pregnancy because pregnant women's bodies are constantly changing; and (b) that the lowest dosage to achieve a therapeutic effect should be used (Bindorf & Sacks, 2008; Nonacs & Cohen, 1998). When lactating women are taking psychotropic medications, they are often encouraged to feed their infant immediately before taking the drug, when plasma concentrations are at their lowest (Eberhard-Gran, Eskild, & Opjordsmoen, 2006).

The discussion to this point in the chapter makes it clear the complexities that must be considered in making the decision to medicate perinatal women with depression and anxiety. Of utmost importance is that prescribers remain mindful of the current literature on the safety profiles and efficacy of the particular psychotropic medications that they prescribe. In the follow sections, I provide an overview of the empirical research that has examined the safety and efficacy of medications for perinatal distress.

Safety Data

Antidepressants. The most frequently prescribed medications to treat depression and anxiety are the serotonin reuptake inhibitors, which fall into two main classes: (a) selective serotonin reuptake inhibitors (SSRIs), and (b) serotonin–norepinephrine reuptake inhibitors (SNRIs). All of these medications fall either in the FDA's Category C, meaning that there may be risk to the fetus or infant, but no well-designed studies have confirmed this association, or Category D, meaning that well-designed studies have determined that their use during pregnancy is associated with risk to the fetus. Hale (2012) classified all of the SSRIs and SNRIs as either "safer" to take during pregnancy, meaning that limited studies have found no adverse effects in nursing infants exposed to the breast milk of a mother taking these medications, or as "moderately safe" for use while breastfeeding, meaning that the risk to the infant is likely to be minimal and nonthreatening, and that it is likely that effects will be seen only in small doses. However, these recommendations must be taken with caution, as the literature on the effects of antidepressants on nursing infants is based almost entirely on case studies or case series.

The vast majority of available research on the safety of these antidepressants is focused on the SSRIs. SSRI use during pregnancy is not associated with increased rates of miscarriage and organ malformation above and beyond the rates observed in the general population (Malm, Klukka, & Neuvonen, 2005; McElhatton et al., 1996; Wen et al., 2006), with the exception of cardiovascular malformations associated with paroxetine use (Cole, Ephross, Cosmatos, & Walker, 2007). One large study determined that SSRI use after 20 weeks gestation was associated with a sixfold increase in the rate of pulmonary hypertension of the newborn (PPHN; Chambers et al., 2006), though the absolute level of risk was quite low. Although a large database study found that SSRI use during pregnancy is associated with shorter gestations, longer hospital stays, lower birth weights, respiratory distress, jaundice, and feeding difficulties (Oberlander, Warburton, Misri, Aghajanian, & Hertzman, 2006), it is likely that these findings were statistically significant because of the size of the database, and many findings were rendered nonsignificant when severity of mothers' depression was controlled. Relative to infants whose mothers did not take SSRIs during pregnancy (i.e., non-exposed infants), infants whose mothers took SSRIs during pregnancy (i.e., exposed infants) demonstrated serotonergic overactivity characterized by tremor, restlessness, and increased muscle tone, but the symptoms declined over the first few days, and no differences were detected at the 2-week and 2-month follow-up visit (Laine, Hekkinen, Ekblad, & Kero, 2003). In a longer-term study, Misri et al. (2006) found that there were no differences in internalizing symptoms in 4-year-old children who had and had not been exposed to SSRIs in utero. With regard to lactation, SSRIs have low levels of excretion into breast milk and are associated with few and minor adverse infant outcomes (e.g., colic, gastrointestinal problems, sleep disturbance; Eberhard-Gran et al., 2006).

The body of literature examining the safety of specific antidepressant medications is growing rapidly. For example, prospective research has determined that fluoxetine use during pregnancy is associated with elevated rates of miscarriage, preterm labor, and admission to special-care nurseries (Chambers, Johnson, Dick, Felix, & Jones, 1996; see Levine, Oandasan, Primeau, & Berenson, 2003, for a review), although other studies have failed to replicate these findings, and women taking fluoxetine in these studies were characterized by elevated rates of other factors that put the fetus and infant at risk for these outcomes, such as smoking, alcohol use, and low weight gain (Goldstein & Sundell, 1999; Wenzel & Stuart, 2011). In contrast, there is no evidence for an association between fluoxetine use during pregnancy and major organ malformations (e.g., Nulman & Koren, 1996) or long-term cognitive, emotional, and behavioral problems (Nulman et al., 1997; Nulman et al., 2002). As mentioned previously, a large database study found that paroxetine use during the first trimester of pregnancy was associated with cardiovascular defects (Cole et al., 2007), which prompted the FDA to change paroxetine's label from Category C to Category D. However, this conclusion is not without controversy, as a subsequent meta-analysis found that elevated rates of cardiac defects were found in exposed infants of mothers who took other SSRIs during the first trimester of pregnancy (Bar-Oz et al., 2007), and results from another large database study suggest that rates of cardiac defects in infants exposed to paroxetine are well within the population incidence of approximately 1% (Einarson et al., 2008). There is less prospective research on other serotonin reuptake inhibitors, such as sertraline, citalopram, escitalopram, and venlafaxine, although the studies that have been published provide no evidence to conclude that these medications are associated with adverse infant outcomes (e.g., Ericson, Kallen, & Wilholm, 1999; Kulin et al., 1998; Malm et al., 2005). There is only one published case report, in the form of a letter to the editor, on duloxetine use during pregnancy, which described poor neonatal adaptation that commenced within hours after birth (Eyal & Yeager, 2008).

Benzodiazepines. Benzodiazepines are often prescribed for the treatment of anxiety disorders, and many prescribers also use them as adjuncts to antidepressants in the treatment of depression with anxious and agitated features. All of the benzodiazepines that are recommended for the treatment of anxiety disorders are in the FDA's Category D, meaning that well-designed studies have determined that their use during pregnancy is associated with risk to the fetus. For example, the risk of oral cleft in infants whose mothers took benzodiazepines during pregnancy is 0.6%, which is a tenfold increase over the 0.06% risk in the general population (Dolovich et al., 1998). Thus, it has been recommended that benzodiazepine use during the first trimester be avoided because that is the period of time in which major skeletal development occurs (Nonacs, Cohen, Viguera, & Mogielnicki, 2005). Exposure to benzodiazepines is also associated with withdrawal symptoms when the infant is born, such as mild sedation, hypotonia, reluctance to suck, apnea, cyanosis, and temperature dysregulation (March & Yonkers, 2001), although most experts view these symptoms as temporary and easily managed (Nonacs et al., 2005). Hale (2012) classified benzodiazepines as "moderately safe" for use while breastfeeding, meaning that the risk to the infant is likely to be minimal and nonthreatening, and that it is likely that effects will be seen only in small doses (March & Yonkers, 2001). However, as with the recommendations for antidepressants, these recommendations must be taken with caution because the literature on the effects of benzodiazepines on nursing infants is based almost entirely on case studies or case series.

The vast majority of the literature that documents the effects of specific benzodiazepine use in perinatal women consists of case studies. In one exception, two prospective studies of women who used alprazolam during the first trimester found no conclusive evidence for increased rates of congenital abnormalities and pregnancy loss (Schick-Boschetto & Zuber, 1992; St. Clair & Schirmer, 1992), although these findings contradict conclusions drawn from case studies (e.g., Barry & St. Clair, 1987). Case studies suggest that clonazepam use during pregnancy is associated with congenital abnormalities, toxicity, and withdrawal symptoms in infants, but the majority of women described in these studies were taking a combination of medications, making the unique effect of clonazepam unclear (Iqbal, Sobhan, & Ryals, 2002). Lorazepam is often viewed as good option for managing anxiety during pregnancy because it is relatively short acting, it does not easily cross the placenta, it metabolizes primarily to a pharmacologically inert substance (Iqbal et al., 2002), and it is easier to metabolize than other benzodiazepines because it requires hepatic glucuronidation and not hepatic oxidation (Elizebeth Goldman, personal communication, November 14, 2012). There is no evidence of neonatal toxicity associated with oral administration of lorazepam during pregnancy (Godet, Damato, & Daley, 1995). Perhaps the greatest amount of research on specific benzodiazepine use during pregnancy has focused on diazepam, although the vast majority of these reports were published 3–4 decades ago when diazepam was prescribed more frequently than it is today. These studies suggest that diazepam use during pregnancy is associated with cleft lip (e.g., Saxen & Saxen, 1975), low birth weight, small head circumference (Laegreid, Hagberg, & Lundberg, 1992), and a symptom profile similar to fetal alcohol syndrome (Laegreid, Olegard, Wahlstrijm, & Comradi, 1987), although it must be acknowledged that many studies have failed to identify these associations (e.g., Rosenberg et al., 1983).

Efficacy Data

There is a noticeable paucity of research on the efficacy of psychotropic medications for perinatal women. In fact, most of the efficacy data that have been conducted with general psychiatric samples does not necessarily apply to perinatal women, as perinatal women are often excluded from randomized controlled trials (RCTs) due, in part, to the safety concerns previously described.

The existing research on the efficacy of psychotropic medications for perinatal distress is focused specifically on the treatment of postpartum depression. Approximately 15 years ago, Applby, Warner, Whitton, and Faragher (1997) examined reduction in depressive symptoms in 87 postpartum women 6 to 8 weeks following childbirth, who were assigned to one of four treatment cells: fluoxetine or placebo and one or six sessions of "cognitive behavioural counseling." Although postpartum women in all cells reported a decrease in depressive symptoms, those receiving fluoxetine reported more benefit than those receiving placebo, and those receiving six counseling sessions reported more benefit than those receiving one session. However, there was no interaction between fluoxetine and counseling, leading the researchers to conclude that the combination of both treatment modalities is not needed, and that patients and their healthcare providers have a choice. Wisner et al. (2006) investigated the efficacy of an 8-week trial of sertraline versus nortriptyline (i.e., a tricyclic antidepressant) in 109 women whose depression began within 4 weeks postpartum[1] and found that use of both medications was associated with similar response and remission rates, times to response, improvements in psychosocial functioning, and side effect burdens (though the specific side effect profiles for each medication differed). Yonkers, Lin, Howell, Heath, and Cohen (2008) compared the efficacy of immediate-release paroxetine and placebo in 31 postpartum women with new-onset major depressive disorder. Although depressive symptoms declined similarly across the 8-week trial in both conditions, greater improvement in clinical severity was found in the paroxetine group, and 37% of women in the paroxetine group achieved remission, relative to 15% of women in the placebo group. Thus, the little data that exist suggest that fluoxetine, sertraline, paroxetine, and nortriptyline are viable medications for the treatment of postpartum depression. However, there are no data that speak to the efficacy of medications for depression during pregnancy, nor to the efficacy of these medications for other conditions such as anxiety disorders.

Summary

It is understandable that many women are reluctant to take psychotropic medications during pregnancy and lactation, as the fetus or infant will be exposed to these medications, there are some large prospective studies documenting adverse effects in the fetus or infant, and there are numerous case studies that describe an array of concerning clinical presentations in infants exposed to medications in utero soon after they are born. However, it is important to weigh these risks with observations that most perinatal complications documented in the literature seem to be short-lived and able to be managed (Nonacs et al., 2005; Wenzel & Stuart, 2011). Moreover, important methodological caveats must be considered when interpreting results from large studies that find an association between medication use and adverse fetal and infant effects. For example, most of these studies do not control for the effects of maternal psychopathology, and it could be that maternal psychopathology rather than medication use, per se, is associated with adverse fetal and infant outcomes (Nonacs et al., 2005; Yonkers et al., 2009). In addition, it is often the case that a significant finding detected in one study is not replicated in another study. Many of the significant findings use large databases of thousands of subjects, which makes it likely that small differences between exposed and unexposed infants will be statistically significant, even if their clinical meaningfulness is questionable. For example, one study found that SSRI use was associated with shorter gestational ages at birth, with those exposed infants being, on average, 38.5 weeks, and the unexposed infants being, on average, 39.4 weeks (Simon, Cunningham, & Davis, 2002). Both of these gestational ages are considered "full-term." Finally, most of the studies in this literature do not use blind raters to assess neonatal outcomes, so it is possible that findings are influenced by a priori study hypotheses (Nonacs et al., 2005).

My recommendation, then, is that prescribers carefully and collaboratively weigh the advantages and disadvantages of using psychotropic medication during pregnancy and lactation, taking care to acknowledge the risks associated with both medicating and not medicating the woman. Alternative treatments (e.g., an evidence-based psychotherapy) should be thoroughly described to the woman, and the availability of trained and competent providers should be investigated. Psychotherapeutic approaches for perinatal distress that have been evaluated in the empirical literature are described in the next section.

PSYCHOTHERAPY FOR PERINATAL DISTRESS

A much larger body of research has examined the efficacy of psychotherapy in women with perinatal distress, relative to the body of research that has examined the efficacy of pharmacotherapy. This is likely the case for two reasons. First, as stated previously, pregnant and lactating women have historically been excluded from RCTs examining the efficacy of pharmacotherapy for psychiatric disorders, so there was a pressing need to identify alternative treatments that were efficacious. Second, researchers in the related field of clinical psychology have long been interested in the phenomenology of perinatal distress, as the period surrounding childbirth represents an ideal set of circumstances in which to study diathesis–stress models of psychopathology. Indeed, during the 1970s and 1980s, several experimental psychopathologists examined the degree to which childbirth (i.e., a stressor) was associated with psychopathology in women who were viewed to be at risk (i.e., who had diatheses) (e.g., O'Hara, Rehm, & Campbell, 1982). A logical extension of this quasi-experimental research, then, was to develop efficacious interventions for women who were at risk for perinatal distress on the basis of these models. This section describes the two psychotherapeutic approaches that have been evaluated most often in the research literature: (a) interpersonal psychotherapy, and (b) cognitive behavioral psychotherapy.

Interpersonal Psychotherapy

Interpersonal psychotherapy (IPT) is a short-term, time-limited approach to psychotherapy that is rooted in psychodynamic theory but that focuses on interpersonal distress in the here and now (Weissman, Markowitz, & Klerman, 2000). Therapists work with their patients on current interpersonal distress in one or more of the following domains: (a) role transitions, (b) role disputes, and (c) unresolved grief (Stuart, 2012). Patients begin to understand their psychiatric distress in the context of their interpersonal relationships and make tangible gains in approaching their relationships with increased balance, formulating reasonable expectations for their relationships as well as for their own role in their relationships, and communicating effectively. Although a few small open trials and RCTs have demonstrated the efficacy of IPT for anxiety disorders (e.g., Lipsitz et al., 2006; Lipsitz et al., 2008; Robertson, Rushton, Batrim, Moore, & Morris, 2007), the majority of large RCTs have evaluated IPT for depression. Results from these trials indicate that the effect sizes for the efficacy of IPT relative to various control groups is in the moderate to large range (Cuipers et al., 2011; de Mello, Mari, Bacaltchuk, Verdeli, & Neugebauer, 2005).

IPT has been embraced wholeheartedly by the community of scholars who research treatments for perinatal distress, who reasoned that IPT would have particularly strong face validity for perinatal women who are facing the transition to parenthood, and hence, a major transition in their roles that has the potential to be associated with conflict in their close relationships. In a landmark study of a community sample of women with postpartum depression, O'Hara, Stuart, Gorman, and Wenzel (2000) found that IPT was associated with significantly greater reductions in interviewer-rated and self-reported symptoms of depression and significantly greater improvements in social functioning relative to a waiting list control condition. Spinelli and Endicott (2003) extended IPT for postpartum depression to antenatal depression and found that it was more efficacious than a parenting education program in reducing interviewer-reported and self-reported symptoms of depression. Moreover, IPT has been adapted into a culturally sensitive brief format for inner-city, low-income women, which includes a treatment engagement component and biweekly or monthly maintenance IPT in the first 6 months postpartum as needed (IPT-B; Grote, Bledsoe, Swartz, & Frank, 2004). Results from evaluations of this adaptation suggest that relative to usual care, IPT-B is associated with higher rates of attendance at an initial mental health appointment, higher rates of retention (Grote, Zuckoff, Swartz, Bledsoe, & Geibel, 2007), and reductions in self-reported depressive symptoms and rates of depression diagnoses (Grote et al., 2009). Although the efficacy of IPT has yet to be evaluated in perinatal samples with psychiatric disorders other than depression, Wenzel (2011) recommended that IPT can be considered as an evidence-based treatment for conditions for which it has been found to be efficacious in the larger literature when perinatal women (a) are nonresponsive to other treatments that have a larger empirical base; (b) have difficulty implementing or complying with aspects of other evidence-based treatments; (c) clearly have interpersonal issues associated with the onset, maintenance, and/or exacerbation of their psychiatric disorder; and/or (d) express a preference for this modality.

Cognitive Behavioral Therapy

Like IPT, cognitive behavioral therapy (CBT) is a short-term, time-limited approach to psychotherapy. In contrast to IPT, however, it is not limited to a focus on interpersonal relationships; rather, targets for treatment are any issues that are associated with emotional distress in the here and now. Although CBT is more of a family of psychotherapies than any one particular protocol in and of itself, the essential features of CBT are (a) a focus on cognitive case conceptualization, or the understanding of the individual clinical presentation in light of cognitive behavioral theory; (b) an organized session structure; (c) the application of cognitive change techniques to help patients achieve an accurate, helpful view of their life problems; and (d) the application of behavioral change techniques that are tailored to the particular clinical presentation (e.g., behavioral activation for depression, exposure for anxiety). While implementing these change techniques, the therapist attends to the therapeutic relationship and ensures that the therapeutic relationship serves as an additional agent of change (Wenzel, Brown, & Karlin, 2011). CBT has been evaluated relative to waiting list control conditions and supportive or educational psychotherapy placebo conditions in countless RCTs and is regarded as efficacious in the treatment of depression anxiety, eating disorders, and adjustment to many medical conditions, as well as an important adjunct in the treatment of bipolar disorder and even schizophrenia (Butler, Chapman, Forman, & Beck, 2006).

Unlike the body of literature on IPT for perinatal distress, the body of literature on CBT for perinatal distress lacks coherence. There have been no large-scale RCTs like that conducted by O'Hara et al. (2000) examining IPT for postpartum depression. Results from small outcome studies are decidedly mixed—one found that CBT is no more efficacious than routine care (Prendergast & Austin, 2000); another found that group-based psychoeducation that included cognitive behavioral techniques was more efficacious than routine care in reducing depressive symptoms, but not in improving self-reported social support, marital satisfaction, or coping (Honey, Bennett, & Morgan, 2002); and another found that CBT was equally as efficacious as nondirective group and individual counseling but more efficacious than routine care in reducing depressive and anxious symptoms in women with moderate to severe postpartum depression (Milgrom, Negri, Gemmill, McNeil, & Martin, 2005). Results from a large outcome study conducted in rural Pakistan indicated that home-based CBT administered by "community-based health workers" was associated with lower rates of major depression at 6 and 12 months postpartum, relative to home visits that contained no CBT (Rahman, Malik, Sikander, Roberts, & Creed, 2008). Studies examining CBT as an adjunct to medication have also yielded mixed results. Specifically, Applby et al.'s (1997) study yielded very large effect sizes for fluoxetine plus cognitive behavioural counseling (i.e., 3.871; Bledsoe & Grote, 2006).

In contrast, Misri, Reebye, Corral, and Milis (2004) found that the addition of CBT did not enhance the efficacy of paroxetine for postpartum depression and anxiety.

Many studies have examined CBT packages that target the prevention of postpartum depression, such that they are delivered to at-risk women during pregnancy or in the hospital immediately following childbirth. Although three of these studies indeed found that the CBT package reduced self-reported depression (Chabrol et al., 2002; Cho, Kwan, & Lee, 2008) or the incidence of a major depressive episode (Muñoz et al., 2007) in the postpartum period relative to usual care, others found no advantage of the CBT package over usual care (Austin et al., 2008; Hagan, Evans, & Pope, 2004; El-Mohandes et al., 2008; Le, Perry, & Stuart, 2011; Zayas, McKee, & Jankowski, 2004; see Nardi, Laurenzi, Di Nicoló, & Bellantuono, 2012, for a review).

How does one make sense of this confusing body of literature? Many of the methodological limitations characteristic of the general psychotherapy literature apply here, such as sample sizes that are too small to have adequate power to detect statistical significance for small effect sizes, samples that are so prescribed that their generalizability to the general postpartum population is questionable, and high attrition (cf. Nardi et al., 2012). Many of the participants in these studies were only mildly depressed and spontaneously remitted early in the course of treatment, regardless of whether they were receiving CBT or usual care. However, a more fundamental problem with this body of literature is that no "gold standard" CBT protocol for this population has been developed, evaluated, and disseminated. Rather, the CBT protocols evaluated in these studies were very different—some were loosely based on a number of CBT treatment manuals in an unspecified manner (e.g., Misri et al., 2004); others focused primarily on psychoeducation (e.g., Honey et al., 2002; Zayas et al., 2004); others focused primarily on behavioral skills and problem solving (e.g., Austin et al., 2008; Milgrom et al., 2005); and others incorporated a combination of cognitive, behavioral, and communication skills (e.g., Griffiths & Barker-Collo, 2008; Prendergast & Austin, 2001). A range of healthcare providers delivered the CBT intervention, such as psychologists (e.g., Austin et al., 2008; Griffiths & Barker-Collo, 2008; Misri et al., 2004), "senior therapists" (e.g., Milgrom et al., 2005), nurses (Griffiths & Barker-Collo, 2008; Prendergast & Austin, 2001), "health visitors" (e.g., Honey et al., 2002), and midwives (e.g., Austin et al., 2008; Hagan et al., 2004), and, in most cases, it was unclear whether these providers were trained to a specific criterion (e.g., the threshold for competence on the Cognitive Therapy Rating Scale [Young & Beck, 1980]) and participated in regular supervision in order to maintain therapist fidelity.

Complicating matters further is the fact that it is probably misleading to refer to some of these treatment packages as CBT per se. For example, Chabrol et al.'s (2002) prevention program consisted only of one session in the hospital soon after women gave birth. Moreover, women who met probable criteria for depression 4–6 weeks later had the opportunity to participate in an eight-visit home-based treatment program that incorporated supportive, educational, cognitive behavioral, and psychodynamic components, the latter of which focused on helping "the subject to acknowledge her ambivalence and link it with her personal history, in particular Oedipal and separation-individuation conflicts" (p. 1041). These psychodynamic components are unequivocally inconsistent with the manner in which cognitive behavioral therapists conceptualize their course of treatment and deliver therapy. Yet, this study is one of the primary ones that are often cited by other scholars to support their statement of CBT's efficacy for perinatal women. Moreover, Applby et al. (1997) described their cognitive behavioral counseling condition as one that was "designed to be delivered by non-specialists in mental health after brief training" and as having sessions that were "structured to offer reassurance and practical advice on four areas of concern to depressed mothers" (p. 933). Contemporary cognitive behavioral therapists view reassurance seeking and the direct provision of advice as, at best, peripheral in CBT, and at worst, contraindicated (Wenzel, 2013). Thus, it cannot be determined whether "CBT" is an efficacious treatment for perinatal distress because each CBT package that has been evaluated is a unique adaptation that may or may not incorporate the core components of CBT described at the beginning of this section. I propose a solution to the state of this literature in the final section of the chapter.

Summary

IPT is a psychotherapy that is unequivocally regarded as an evidence-based treatment for perinatal depression. IPT-B, in particular, has the potential to be an especially good match for low-income women who historically do not seek or remain in treatment in clinic settings because it includes a flexible administration of sessions and a treatment engagement component. There is a vast literature suggesting that CBT is an evidence-based treatment for depression, anxiety, and other psychiatric conditions, and there are few reasons to believe that it would be inappropriate for perinatal women. Although the state of the literature on CBT for perinatal distress is equivocal at best, it can be explained by methodological limitations (e.g., small sample sizes) and, in most cases, the absence of an established and theoretically coherent cognitive behavioral foundation from which the treatment can be adapted for this population.

Despite the fact that the psychotherapy literature is more developed for perinatal distress than it is for many other conditions, there remains a discrepancy between the treatments that have empirical support and the availability of these treatments in the community (Wenzel & Kleiman, in press). Healthcare professionals who make referrals to mental health providers who claim to have expertise in IPT or CBT would be wise to confirm these providers' training and credentials and ensure that they are practicing the protocols that have empirical support in the literature, rather than implementing isolated interpersonal, cognitive, and behavioral techniques in an eclectic or atheoretical manner. One source for finding mental health professionals who specialize in perinatal distress is through Postpartum Support Internship's "get help" page (http://www.postpartum.net/Get-Help.aspx). Here, the consumer can be connected to knowledgeable area coordinators representing many different countries, as well as states within the United States.

INTEGRATING PHARMACOTHERAPY AND PSYCHOTHERAPY FOR PERINATAL DISTRESS

It is reasonable that clinicians would make decisions about treating perinatal women in the basis of the guidelines endorsed by the American Psychiatric Association and the American College of Obstetricians and Gynecologists (Yonkers et al., 2009). A major strength of these guidelines is that they were developed by leading experts in the field on the basis of empirically derived data on the safety of psychotropic medications for pregnant women. However, I would caution clinicians against routinely making the decision to recommend pharmacotherapy for moderate to severe psychiatric symptoms without critical evaluation. These guidelines do not account for the fact that at least one type of evidence-based psychotherapy—CBT—has been demonstrated to be as efficacious as antidepressant medication for moderate to severe depression and to have longer-enduring effects than antidepressant medication

(DeRubeis et al., 2005; Hollon et al., 2005). Also important for this consideration is that most evidence suggests that CBT and IPT are equally as efficacious (Jakobsen, Hansen, Simonsen, Simonsen, & Gluud, 2012), and IPT is regarded as an appropriate treatment for moderate to severe distress as well (cf. Stuart, 2012). Thus, I contend that CBT and IPT are also reasonable options for perinatal women with moderate to severe distress, especially when these women are hesitant to take psychotropic medications. It would behoove clinicians in these instances to carefully monitor response to treatment; for example, if objective ratings of depressive and anxious symptoms are not decreasing across the course of several weeks of treatment, and these symptoms are associated with substantial interference with self-care or child-care, then medication augmentation would be in order.

Even when a provider and patient collaboratively make the decision that psychotropic medications should be used as to treat the woman's distress, I encourage providers to make a referral for evidence-based psychotherapy. I base this suggestion on the substantial body of research demonstrating that evidence-based psychotherapy with or without concurrent pharmacotherapy is associated with much lower rates of relapse than medication alone (e.g., Hollon et al., 2005; see Cuipers et al., 2001, and Gloaguen, Cottraux, Cucherat, & Blarkburn, 1998, for meta-analytic reviews). Even when a woman's episode of distress remits over the course of the first year postpartum, she will still be faced with several years of raising a young child and perhaps balancing work–home responsibilities, and she may very well plan for another pregnancy during those first few years. An active, problem-focused, evidence-based approach to psychotherapy can provide such a woman the tools for coping with the ongoing life stressors and challenges that she will invariably experience, thus preventing a future recurrence of perinatal distress.

Another point to keep in mind is that there is a dynamic interplay between pharmacotherapy and psychotherapy process and outcome. For example, pharmacotherapy often relieves patients of bothersome symptoms that have the potential to interfere with making good use of psychotherapy (e.g., fatigue, sleep disturbance); thus, resolution of these symptoms early in the course of intervention can help patients assume readiness for psychotherapy. Conversely, psychotherapy often helps patients to identify self-defeating attitudes and behaviors, and addressing these cognitive and behavioral patterns has the potential to increase medication compliance and attendance at visits with prescribers. Similarly, in some instances, perinatal women will have ongoing concerns about the use of psychotropic medications, and a psychotherapy session might very well be a place in which they have the opportunity to systematically evaluate the advantages and disadvantages of this treatment modality. Thus, pharmacotherapy and psychotherapy do not proceed in isolation from one another, and it is very likely that they will exert bidirectional influences on one another in terms of process (i.e., the mechanism by which each modality exerts its effects) as well as the content (i.e., the issues that are discussed at the time of the appointments).

The most direct way to facilitate a seamless interplay between pharmacotherapy and psychotherapy is though close collaboration between the prescriber and psychotherapist. Initial consultation with one another ensures that both healthcare professionals have a similar and complete conceptualization of the patient's clinical presentation. Ongoing communication allows each to be privy to the patient's attendance at the other's appointments, side effects, and any factors that enhance or interfere with treatment. Perhaps most importantly, ongoing communication ensures that both healthcare professionals are in agreement with the treatment plan and are proceeding with treatment in a manner that reinforces the treatment plan, rather than inadvertently thwarting it. For example, consider an anxious patient who relies on benzodiazepines prescribed on an as needed basis as a way for managing her anxiety during situations she would rather avoid. Many cognitive behavioral therapists regard benzodiazepine usage in this manner as a false safety signal that interferes with the ability to gain benefit from a corrective learning experience and, thus, as contraindicated (e.g., Abramowitz, Deacon, & Whiteside, 2011). Clear and consistent communication between providers can avoid these scenarios.

Although it is clear by this point in this chapter that I am a strong advocate for the delivery of evidence-based psychotherapy with or without concurrent pharmacotherapy for perinatal women, I must acknowledge the fact that it is difficult for many perinatal women to arrange for the logistics that will allow them to attend regular psychotherapy sessions. Perinatal women are exhausted; they are managing numerous medical appointments; and they are undergoing a major life transition that leaves many overwhelmed and unsure of themselves. Regular attendance at psychotherapy can often seem like too much to handle (Wenzel & Kleiman, 2014). Thus, prescribers should have access to other means for perinatal women to obtain some of the benefits that are typically gained from psychotherapy. For example, self-help books often describe many well-established strategies and tools for managing mood disturbance, and they provide a guided framework for readers to begin to implement those tools in their lives. I recently summarized and evaluated many self-help resources for perinatal women, and I provided tips for maximizing their usage (Wenzel, 2011). In addition, peer-run support groups are another option for perinatal women to obtain information and emotional support from others. Thus, prescribers may need to broaden their view of psychotherapeutic processes and benefits and consider other options to which perinatal women may be more amenable.

CONCLUSIONS AND FUTURE DIRECTIONS

Research on postpartum depression has surged over the past 20 years, and research on perinatal anxiety disorders is burgeoning. There is a large body of literature on the short-term effects of taking psychotropic medications on the fetus and infant, and evidence-based psychotherapies are being adapted for this population. Many researchers and clinicians, alike, have developed specialty areas in perinatal psychology, which have led to the creation of many treatment programs and resources to which perinatal women can turn when they need help.

Despite these scientific and clinical advances, much future research is needed to guide the optimal care of perinatal women. The literature on the efficacy of specific psychotropic medications for perinatal distress is small and is limited to postpartum depression. We clearly need more data on the efficacy of the full range of antidepressants and benzodiazepines for both depression and anxiety disorders during both pregnancy and the postpartum period. Moreover, the literature on the integrative treatment of pharmacotherapy and psychotherapy is just as limited, and at present, there is no evidence to suggest that combination treatment enhances outcome. However, the existing studies on combination treatment used small samples sizes and, at times, protocols for the psychotherapy condition that were not necessarily those that have been validated in the larger psychotherapy research literature, so the degree to which psychotherapy can enhance pharmacotherapy and vice versa is unknown. What is needed in addition to larger and more targeted efficacy studies is a set of empirically supported guidelines to facilitate the selection of specific treatments at various points during a woman's pregnancy and adjustment in the postpartum period.

In addition, a glaring omission from the literature on psychotherapy for perinatal distress is a large, well-designed study of CBT for postpartum depression. Unlike IPT experts, who carefully exported the original treatment (Klerman, Weissman, Rounasville, & Chevron, 1984) and evaluated modest adaptations for perinatal women before making more substantial modifications for particular subgroups of perinatal women (e.g., low-income, inner-city women) in a step-wise manner, researchers to date who have evaluated CBT for perinatal distress have developed diverse protocols that may or may not reflect the key components of CBT packages that have an evidence base in the larger psychotherapy literature. As a result, results from more studies than not suggest that CBT is no more efficacious than usual care. This pattern of results is at odds with the larger psychotherapy literature, which points to moderate to large effect sizes in favor of CBT when it is compared with usual care or a psychotherapy placebo (Butler et al., 2006). I strongly encourage CBT researchers to follow the model established by the IPT community, such that a well-established evidence-based protocol is evaluated in a large sample of perinatal women (such as that described in Beck, Rush, Shaw, & Emery, 1979; see Wenzel et al., 2011 for a "contemporary" version of CBT for depression), and then modifications be made systematically in response to the needs of subtypes of perinatal women. In addition to such a research program, I encourage both the IPT and CBT communities to conduct larger-scale RCTs to evaluate these psychotherapeutic approaches for perinatal anxiety disorders, as there is much evidence in the general psychotherapy literature that anxiety disorders respond to these treatments. A trend for such research in the CBT literature is beginning to emerge (Ayers, McKenzie-McHarg, & Eagle, 2007).

After systematically developing and evaluating the efficacy of these treatments in controlled settings, it will behoove researchers to evaluate the effectiveness of these protocols in "real-life" community settings. Much psychotherapy for perinatal distress is delivered by nurses, midwives, and other support professionals, oftentimes in women's homes. It will be important to demonstrate that evidence-based psychotherapies can be transported to these settings in a manner in which their integrity is maintained. Moreover, it is surprisingly difficult to find mental health professionals in the community who are trained to deliver evidence-based treatments like IPT and CBT, and it is even more difficult to find an IPT or CBT expert who also has expertise in perinatal psychology. The dissemination of the therapeutic approaches described in this chapter will be crucial in order to reach perinatal women in the community, as well as to facilitate the optimal integration of pharmacotherapy and psychotherapy for perinatal distress.

ACKNOWLEDGMENT

I wish to thank Elizabeth Goldman, MD, for her helpful comments on previous drafts of this manuscript and, more generally, for her collaboration in the integrative treatment of our shared perinatal patients.

NOTE

1   After recruitment for the study had commenced, the authors received additional funding to enroll women with chronic depression (i.e., depression that began before the index pregnancy).

REFERENCES

Abramowitz, J. S., Deacon, B. J., & Whiteside, S. P. H. (2011). *Exposure therapy for anxiety: Principles and practice.* New York: Guilford Press.

Altshuler, L. L., & Hendrick, V. (1996). Pregnancy and psychotropic medication: Changes in blood levels. *Journal of Clinical Psychopharmacology, 16,* 78–80.

Applby, L., Warner, R., Whitton, A., & Faragher, B. (1997). A controlled study of fluoxetine and cognitive-behavioural counselling in the treatment of postnatal depression. *British Medical Journal, 314,* 932–936.

Austin, M.-P., Frilingos, M., Lumley, J., Hadzi-Pavlovic, D., Roncolato, W., Acland, S., . . . Parker G. (2008). Brief antenatal cognitive behaviour therapy group intervention for the prevention of postnatal depression and anxiety: A randomized controlled trial. *Journal of Affective Disorders, 105,* 35–44.

Ayers, S., McKenzie-McHarg, K., & Eagle, A. (2007). Cognitive behaviour therapy for postnatal post-traumatic stress disorder: Case studies. *Journal of Psychosomatic Obstetrics & Gynecology, 28,* 177–184.

Bar-Oz, B., Einarson, T., Einarson, A., Boskovic, R., O'Brien, L., Malm, H., . . . Koren, G. (2007). Paroxetine and congenital malformations: Meta-analysis and consideration of potential confounding factor. *Clinical Therapeutics, 29,* 918–926.

Barry, W. S., & St. Clair, S. M. (1987). Exposure to benzodiazepines in utero. *Lancet, 1,* 1436–1437.

Beck, A. T., Rush, A. J., Shaw, B. F., & Emery, G. (1979). *Cognitive therapy of depression.* New York: Guilford Press.

Bindorf, C. A., & Sacks, A. C. (2008). To medicate or not: The dilemma of pregnancy and psychiatric illness. In S. D. Stone & A. E. Menken (Eds.), *Perinatal and postpartum mood disorders: Perspectives and treatment guide for the health care practitioner* (pp. 237–265). New York: Springer.

Bledsoe, S. E., & Grote, N. K. (2006). Treating depression during pregnancy and the postpartum: A preliminary meta-analysis. *Research on Social Work Practice, 16,* 109–120.

Butler, A. C., Chapman, J. E., Forman, E. M., & Beck, A. T. (2006). The empirical status of cognitive behavioral therapy: A review of meta-analyses. *Clinical Psychology Review, 26,* 17–31.

Chabrol, H., Teissedre, F., Saint-Jean, M., Teisseyre, N., Rogé, B., & Mullet, E. (2002). Prevention and treatment of postpartum depression: A controlled randomized study on women at risk. *Psychological Medicine, 32,* 1039–1047.

Chambers, C. D., Hernandez-Diaz, S., Van Marter, L. J., Werler, M. M., Louik, C., Jones, K. L., . . . Mitchell, A. A. (2006). Selective serotonin-reuptake inhibitors and risk of persistent pulmonary hypertension of the newborn. *The New England Journal of Medicine, 354,* 579–587.

Chambers, C., Johnson, K., Dick, L., Felix, R. J., & Jones, K. L. (1996). Birth outcomes in pregnant women taking fluoxetine. *The New England Journal of Medicine, 335,* 1010–1015.

Cho, H. J., Kwon, J. J., & Lee, J. J. (2008). Antenatal cognitive behavioral therapy for prevention of postpartum depression: A pilot study. *Yonsei Medical Journal, 49,* 553–562.

Cole, J. A., Ephoss, S. A., Cosmatos, I. S., & Walker, A. M. (2007). Paroxetine in the first trimester and the prevalence of congenital malformations. *Pharmacoepidemiology and Drug Safety, 16,* 1075–1085.

Cuipers, P., Geraedts, A. S., van Oppen, P., Andersson, G., Markowitz, J. C., & van Straten, A. (2011). Interpersonal psychotherapy for depression: A meta-analysis. *American Journal of Psychiatry, 168,* 581–592.

de Mello, M. F., Mari, J. J., Bacaltchuk, J., Verdeli, H., & Neugebauer, R. (2005). A systematic review of research findings on the efficacy of interpersonal therapy for depressive disorders. *European Archives of Psychiatry and Clinical Neuroscience, 255,* 75–82.

DeRubeis, R. J., Hollon, S. D., Amsterdam, J. D., Shelton, R. C., Young, P. R., . . . Gallop, R. (2005). Cognitive therapy vs. medications in the treatment of moderate to severe depression. *Archives of General Psychiatry, 62,* 409–416.

Dolovich, L. R., Addis, A., Vaillancourt, J. M., Power, J. D., Koren, G., & Einarson, T. R. (1998). Benzodiazepine use in pregnancy and major malformations or oral cleft: Meta-analysis of cohort and case-control studies. *British Medical Journal, 317,* 839–843.

Eberhard-Gran, M., Eskild, A., & Opjordsmoen, S. (2006). Use of psychotropic medications in treating mood disorders during lactation: Practical recommendation. *CNS Drugs, 20,* 187–198.

Einarson, A., Pistelli, A., DeSantis, M., Malm, H., Paulus, W. D., Panchaud, A., . . . Koren, G. (2008). Evaluation of the risk of congenital cardiovascular defects associated with the use of paroxetine during pregnancy. *American Journal of Psychiatry, 165,* 749–752.

El-Mohandes, A. A., Kiely, M., Joseph, J. G., Subramanian, S., Johnson, A. A., Blake, S. M., . . . El-Khorazaty, M. N. (2008). An intervention to improve postpartum outcomes in African-American mothers: A randomized controlled trial. *Obstetrics and Gynecology, 112,* 611–620.

Ericson, A., Kallen, B., & Wilholm, B. (1999). Delivery outcome after the use of antidepressants in early pregnancy. *European Journal of Clinical Pharmacology, 55,* 503–308.

Eyal, R., & Yeager, D. (2008). Poor neonatal adaptation after in utero exposure to duloxetine. *The American Journal of Psychiatry, 165,* 651.

Federal Drug Administration (FDA). (2009). *Summary of proposed rule on pregnancy and lactation labeling.* Retrieved from http://www.fda.gov/Drugs/DevelopmentApprovalProcess/DevelopmentResources/Labeling/ucm093310.htm

Gloaguen, C., Cottraux, J., Cucherat, M., & Blarkburn, I. (1998). A meta-analysis of the effects of cognitive behavioral therapy in depressed patients. *Journal of Affective Disorders, 49,* 69–72.

Godet, P. F., Damato, T., & Dalery, J. (1995). Benzodiazepines in pregnancy: Analysis of 187 exposed infants drawn from a population-based birth defects registry. *Reproductive Toxicology, 9,* 585.

Goldstein, D. J., & Sundell, K. (1999). A review of the safety of selective serotonin reuptake inhibitors. *Human Psychopharmacology, 14,* 319–324.

Griffiths, P., & Barker-Collo, S. (2008). Study of a group treatment program for postnatal adjustment difficulties. *Archives of Women's Mental Health, 11,* 33–41.

Grote, N. K., Bledsoe, S. E., Swartz, H. A., & Frank, E. (2004). Feasibility of providing culturally relevant, brief interpersonal psychotherapy for antenatal depression in an obstetrics clinic: A pilot study. *Research on Social Work Practice, 14,* 397–407.

Grote, N. K., Swartz, H. A., Geibel, S. L., Zuckoff, A., Houck, P. R., & Frank, E. (2009). A randomized controlled trial of culturally relevant, brief interpersonal psychotherapy for perinatal depression. *Psychiatric Services, 60,* 313–321.

Grote, N. K., Zuckoff, A., Swartz, H., Bledsoe, S. E., & Geibel, S. (2007). Engaging women who are depressed and economically disadvantaged in mental health treatment. *Social Work, 52,* 295–308.

Hagan, R., Evans, S. F., & Pope, S. (2004). Preventing postnatal depression in mothers of very preterm infants: A randomized controlled trial. *British Journal of Obstetrics and Gynaecology, 111,* 641–647.

Hale, T. W. (2012). *Medications and mother's milk* (15th ed.). Amarillo, TX: Hale Publishing.

Hollon, S. D., DeRubeis, R. J., Shelton, R. C., Amsterdam, J. D., Salomon, R. M., . . . Gallop, R. (2005). Prevention of relapse following cognitive therapy vs. medications in moderate to severe depression. *Archives of General Psychiatry, 62,* 417–422.

Honey, K. L., Bennett, P., & Morgan, M. (2002). A brief psycho-educational group intervention for postnatal depression. *British Journal of Clinical Psychology, 41,* 405–409.

Iqbal, M. M., Sobhan, T., & Ryals, T. (2002). Effects of commonly used benzodiazepines on the fetus, neonate, and the nursing infant. *Psychiatric Services, 53,* 39–49.

Jakobsen, J. C., Hansen, J. L. Simonsen, S., Simonsen, E., & Gluud, C. (2012). Effects of cognitive therapy *versus* interpersonal psychotherapy in patients with major depressive disorder: Systematic review of randomized clinical trials with meta-analyses and trial sequential analyses. *Psychological Medicine, 42,* 1343–1357.

Jeffries, W. S., & Bochner, F. (1988). The effect of pregnancy on drug pharmacokinetics. *Medical Journal of Australia, 149,* 675–677.

Klerman, G. L., Weissman, M. M., Rounasville, B. J., & Chevron, E. S. (1984). *Interpersonal psychotherapy for depression.* New York: Basic Books.

Kulin, N., Pastuszak, A., Sage, S., Shick-Boschetto, B., Spivey, G., Feldkamp, M., . . . Koren, G. (1998). Pregnancy outcome following maternal use of the new selective serotonin reuptake inhibitors: A prospective controlled multicenter study. *JAMA, 279,* 609–610.

Laegreid, L., Hagberg, G., & Lundberg, A. (1992). The effect of benzodiazepines on the fetus and the newborn. *Neuropediatrics, 23,* 18–23.

Laegreid, L., Olegard, R., Wahlstrijm, J., & Comradi, N. (1987). Abnormalities in children exposed to benzodiazepines in utero. *Lancet, 1,* 108–109.

Laine, K., Hekkinen, T., Ekblad, U., & Kero, P. (2003). Effects of exposure to selective serotonin reuptake inhibitors during pregnancy on serotonergic symptoms in newborns and cord blood monoamine and prolactin concentrations. *Archives of General Psychiatry, 60,* 720–726.

Le, H. N., Perry, D. F., & Stuart, E. A. (2011). Randomized controlled trial of a preventive intervention for perinatal depression in high-risk Latinas. *Journal of Consulting and Clinical Psychology, 79,* 135–141.

Levine, R. E., Oandasan, A. P., Primeau, L. A., & Berenson, A. B. (2003). Anxiety disorders during pregnancy and postpartum. *American Journal of Perinatology, 20,* 239–247.

Lipsitz, J. D., Gur, M., Miller, N. L., Forand, N., Vermes, D., & Fyer, A. J. (2006). An open pilot study of interpersonal psychotherapy for panic disorder (IPT-PD). *The Journal of Nervous and Mental Disease, 194,* 440–445.

Lipsitz, J. D., Gur, M., Vermes, D., Petkova, E., Cheng, J., Miller, N., . . . Fyer, A. J. (2008). A randomized trial of interpersonal therapy versus supportive therapy for social anxiety disorder. *Depression and Anxiety, 25,* 542–553.

Malm, J., Klukka, T., & Neuvonen, P. J. (2005). Risks associated with selective serotonin reuptake inhibitors in pregnancy. *Obstetrics and Gynecology, 106,* 1289–1296.

March, D., & Yonkers, K. A. (2001). Panic disorder. In K. A. Yonkers & B. B. Little (Eds.), *Management of psychiatric disorders in pregnancy* (pp. 134–148). London: Arnold.

McElhatton, P. R., Garbis, H. M., Elefant, E., Vial, T., Bellemin, B., Mastroiacovo, P., . . . Dal Verme, S. (1996). The outcome of pregnancy in 698 women exposed to therapeutic doses of antidepressants. A collaborative study of the European network of the teratology information services (ENTIS). *Reproductive Toxicology, 10,* 285–294.

Milgrom, J., Negri, L. M., Gemmill, A. W., McNeil, M., & Martin, P. R. (2005). A randomized controlled trial of psychological interventions for postnatal depression. *British Journal of Clinical Psychology, 44,* 529–542.

Misri, S., Reebye, P., Corral, M., & Milis, L. (2004). The use of paroxetine and cognitive behavioral therapy in postpartum depression and anxiety: A randomized controlled trial. *Journal of Clinical Psychiatry, 65,* 1236–1241.

Misri, S., Reebye, P., Kendrick, K., Carter, D., Ryan, D., Grunau, R. E., . . . Oberlander, T. F. (2006). Internalizing behaviors in 4-year-old children exposed in utero to psychotropic medications. *American Journal of Psychiatry, 163,* 1026–1032.

Muñoz, R. F., Le, H. N., Ghosh Ippen, C., Diaz, M. A., Urizar, G. G., Jr., & Soto, J. (2007). Prevention of postpartum depression in low-income women: Development of the Mamás y Bebés/Mothers and Babies Course. *Cognitive and Behavioral Practice, 14,* 70–83.

Nardi, B., Laurenzi, S., Di Nicoló, M., & Bellantuono, C. (2012). Is the cognitive behavioral therapy an effective intervention to prevent the postnatal depression? A critical review. *International Journal of Psychiatry in Medicine, 43,* 211–225.

Nonacs, R., & Cohen, L. S. (1998). Postpartum mood disorders: Diagnosis and treatment guidelines. *Journal of Clinical Psychiatry, 59*(Suppl. 2), 34–40.

Nonacs, R. M., Cohen, L. S., Viguera, A. C., & Mogielnicki, J. (2005). Diagnosis and treatment of mood and anxiety disorders in pregnancy. In L. S. Cohen & R. M. Nonacs (Eds.), *Mood and anxiety disorders during pregnancy and postpartum (Review of Psychiatry, Vol. 24, No. 4),* (pp. 17–51). Washington, DC: American Psychiatric Publishing.

Nulman, I., & Koren, G. (1996). The safety of fluoxetine during pregnancy and lactation. *Teratology, 53,* 304–308.

Nulman, I., Rovert, J., Stewart, D. E., Wolpin, J., Gardner, H. A., Theis, J. G. W., . . . Koren, G. (1997). Neurodevelopment of children exposed in utero to antidepressant drugs. *The New England Journal of Medicine, 159,* 1889–1895.

Nulman, I., Koren, G., Rovert, J., Barrerea, M., Pulver, A., Stewart, D. E., Wolpin, J., Pace-Asciak, P., Shuhaiber, S., Feldman, B., (2002). Child development following exposure to tricyclic antidepressant drugs. *American Journal of Psychiatry, 336,* 258–262.

Oberlander, T., Warburton, W., Misri, S., Aghajanian, J., & Hertzman, C. (2006). Neonatal outcomes after prenatal exposure to selective serotonin reuptake inhibitor antidepressants and maternal depression using population-based linked health data. *Archives of General Psychiatry, 63,* 898–906.

O'Hara, M. W., Rehm, L. P., & Campbell, S. B. (1982). Predicting depressive symptomatology: Cognitive behavioral models and postpartum depression. *Journal of Abnormal Psychology, 91,* 457–461.

O'Hara, M. W., Stuart, S., Gorman, L. L., & Wenzel, A. (2000). Efficacy of interpersonal psychotherapy for postpartum depression. *Archives of General Psychiatry, 57,* 1039–1045.

Prendergast, J., & Austin, M.-P. (2001). Early childhood nurse-delivered cognitive behavioural counselling for post-natal depression. *Australian Psychiatry, 9,* 255–259.

Public Affairs Committee of the Teratology Society. (2007). Teratology Public Affairs Committee Position Paper: Pregnancy labeling for prescription drugs: Ten years later. *Birth Defects Research (Part A), 79,* 627–630.

Rahman, A., Malik, A., Sikander, S., Roberts, C., & Creed, F. (2008). Cognitive behaviour therapy-based intervention by community health workers for mothers in depression and their infants in rural Pakistan: A cluster-randomised controlled trial. *The Lancet, 372,* 902–909.

Ragan, K., Stowe, Z. N., & Newport, D. J. (2005). Use of antidepressants and mood stabilizers in breast-feeding women. In L. S. Cohen & R. M. Nonacs (Eds.), *Mood and anxiety disorders during pregnancy and postpartum (Review of Psychiatry, Vol. 24, No. 4),* (pp. 105–144). Washington, DC: American Psychiatric Press.

Robertson, M., Rushton, P., Batrim, D., Moore, E., & Morris, P. (2007). Open trial of interpersonal psychotherapy for chronic posttraumatic stress disorder. *Australian Psychiatry, 15,* 375–379.

Rosenberg, L., Mitchell, A. A., Parsells, J. L., Pashayan, H., Louik, C., & Shapiro, S. (1983). Lack of relation of oral clefts to diazepam use during pregnancy. *The New England Journal of Medicine, 309,* 1282–1285.

Saxen, I., & Saxen, L. (1975). Association between maternal intake of diazepam and oral clefts. *Lancet, 2,* 498.

Schick-Boschetto, B., & Zuber, C. (1992). Alprazolam exposure during early human pregnancy. *Teratology, 45,* 360.

Simon, G., Cunningham, M., & Davis, R. (2002). Outcomes of prenatal antidepressant exposure. *The American Journal of Psychiatry, 159,* 2055–2061.

Spinelli, M. G., & Endicott, J. (2003). Controlled clinical trial of interpersonal psychotherapy versus parenting education program for depressed pregnant women. *American Journal of Psychiatry, 160,* 555–562.

St. Clair, S. M., & Schirmer, R. G. (1992). First trimester exposure to alprazolam. *Obstetrics and Gynecology, 80,* 843–846.

Stuart, S. (2012). Interpersonal psychotherapy for postpartum depression. *Clinical Psychology and Psychotherapy, 19,* 134–140.

Weissman, M. M., Markowitz, J. C., & Klerman, G. L. (2000). *Comprehensive guide to interpersonal psychotherapy.* New York: Basic Books.

Wen, S. W., Yang, Q., Garner, P., Fraser, W., Olatunboson, O., Nimrod, C., . . . Walker, M. (2006). Selective serotonin reuptake inhibitors and risk of adverse pregnancy outcome. *American Journal of Obstetrics & Gynecology, 194,* 961–966.

Wenzel, A. (2011). *Anxiety in childbearing women: Diagnosis and treatment.* Washington, DC: APA Books.

Wenzel, A. (2013). *Strategic decision making in cognitive behavioral therapy.* Washington, DC: APA Books.

Wenzel, A., Brown, G. K., & Karlin, B. E. (2011). *Cognitive behavioral therapy for depressed veterans and military servicemembers: Therapist manual.* Washington, DC: U.S. Department of Veterans Affairs.

Wenzel, A., & Kleiman, K. (2014). Clinician response. In L. R. Grossman & S. Walfish (Eds.), *Translating research into practice: A desk reference for practicing mental health professionals* (pp. 443–446). New York, NY: Springer.

Wenzel, A., & Stuart, S. (2011). Pharmacotherapy for perinatal anxiety disorders. In A. Wenzel (Ed.), *Anxiety in childbearing women: Diagnosis and treatment,* (pp.157–180). Washington, DC: APA Books.

Wisner, K. L., Hanusa, B. H., Perel, J. M., Peindl, K. S., Piontek, C. M., Sit, D. Y., . . . Moses-Kolko, E. L. (2006). Postpartum depression: A randomized trial of sertraline versus nortriptyline. *Journal of Clinical Psychophamacology, 26,* 353–360.

Yonkers, K. A., Lin, H., Howell, H. B., Heath, A. C., & Cohen, L. S. (2008). Pharmacologic treatment of postpartum women with new-onset major depressive disorder: A randomized controlled trial with paroxetine. *Journal of Clinical Psychiatry, 69,* 659–665.

Yonkers, K. A., Wisner, K. L., Stewart, D. E., Oberlander, T. F., Dell, D. L., Stotland, N., . . . Lockwood, C. (2009). The management of depression during pregnancy: A report from the American Psychiatric Association and the American College of Obstetricians and Gynecologists. *General Hospital Psychiatry, 31,* 403–413.

Young, J. E., & Beck, A. T. (1980). *Cognitive Therapy Scale rating manual.* Unpublished manuscript, University of Pennsylvania, Philadelphia, PA.

Zayas, L. H., McKee, M. D., & Jankowski, K. R. B. (2004). Adapting psychosocial intervention research to urban primary care environments: A case example. *Annals of Family Medicine, 2,* 504–508.

Integrating Psychotherapy and Psychopharmacology in Sexual Disorders

Mehmet Z. Sungur and Anıl Gündüz

INTRODUCTION

New Challenges in the Area of Sexual Disorders

A considerable amount of available information regarding sexual disorders (SD) has been challenged during the last few decades. SD have long been defined as persistent and recurrent difficulties that interfere with one or more stages (desire, arousal, and orgasm) of human sexual response cycle. Today, even this gross definition has been subject to criticisms. Clinicians and researchers no longer want to base definitions of SD on sexual response cycles defined initially by Masters & Johnson (1966) and modified later by Kaplan (1974), as these cycles follow a linear pattern and are not likely to be analogous in men and women.

All the DSM classifications until the present time based definitions of SD on expert opinions that were not supported by clinical or epidemiological data. Additionally, they included vague terms such as "satisfactory," "rapid," "short," "minimal," "recurrent," "persistent," etc., that were not possible to be quantified and relied on interpretations of clinicians (McMahon, 2008; Waldinger & Schweitzer, 2008). It is argued that diagnostic criteria of many SD are so imprecise that they hamper advancements in the field of sexual medicine (Segraves, Balon, & Clayton, 2007). Therefore, operational definitions based on data coming from controlled clinical trials are more welcome than those that are authority based. One concrete outcome of efforts to establish operational criteria was acceptance of one minute duration from penetration to ejaculation as a necessary construct to diagnose premature ejaculation (PE) (McMahon, 2008; Waldinger & Schweitzer, 2008). Therefore 1 minute duration is included in the new DSM-5 definition of early ejaculation (American Psychiatric Association, 2013).

Clinicians and researchers recently shifted their attention toward understanding the normative sexual functions. Increasing knowledge obtained about normal physiological processes encouraged researchers to challenge the available information regarding sexual pathology. This challenge has brought many unresolved and controversial issues into discussion, particularly regarding female sexual dysfunctions.

One of the basic challenges is about defining what makes a sexual problem become a dysfunction or disorder. Conditions such as delayed ejaculation, vaginismus, or erectile dysfunction (ED) may indeed be symptoms that represent various etiological categories or manifestations of other medical diseases such as diabetes mellitus, rather than disorders. They can also be variations along normal distributions, which represent transient alterations in normal sexual activities. They may emerge as consequences of relationship problems and/ or in response to the sexual problems of the presenting partner for adaptive purposes.

Lack of consensus in defining SD leads to problems in determining their prevalence. Different methodologies, different study populations, lack of clear description of research inclusion criteria, differences in study periods, and difference in data collection and measurement instruments all lead to problems and biases in comparative analysis. Epidemiological data is important for assessment of overall impact of a clinical condition on a given society. Standardized operational criteria and standard measurements are therefore essential to improve our knowledge on prevalence rates, which may be crucial in determining health policies regarding sexual issues.

Whether there should be a specific duration and severity criteria in order to diagnose SD is another challenge. Including a duration and frequency criteria may help to identify more homogeneous groups and help differentiate sexual dysfunctions from variations of normal sexual response. Epidemiological research indicates that the criterion specifying duration of ≥ 6 months, combined with the criterion of occurring on ≥ 75% of sexual encounters, serves to distinguish sexual dysfunctions from transient sexual problems (Segraves et al., 2007). Establishment of duration and severity criteria is necessary when comparing the efficacy of two different interventions (Oberg, Fugl-Meyer, & Fugl-Meyer, 2004; Segraves et al., 2007). Unfortunately, specific durations have not been part of diagnostic criteria for SD until DSM-5 (American Psychiatric Association, 2013). However, adding a standard (6 months) duration criteria for all SD as suggested for DSM-5 may cause delay in diagnosis of some sexual dysfunctions such as vaginismus (defined as genito-pelvic pain/penetration disorder in DSM-5), where a period of 6 months' duration may be an unnecessary waste of time during which the couple may or may not manage to stay together due to the emergent and culturally demanding nature of the problem.

Subtyping definitions based on etiology such as organic, psychological, or mixed is another challenging issue, as most of the time it becomes rather hard to make such distinctions, and they are not necessarily helpful. Therefore this subtying is deleted in DSM-5 (American Psychiatric Association, 2013).

Another very important challenge comes from increasing recognition that male and female sexuality could be quite different (Chivers & Bailey, 2005). Until DSM-5, different genders' sexual responses were assumed to be analogous. However, there is considerable data today to claim that sexual interest, motivation, arousal, and pleasure may be experienced differently in different genders. Therefore, definitions based on common sexual response cycles are nowadays challenged, leading to a major paradigm shift suggesting that male and female sexuality are different and therefore subject to be classified and managed differently. This paradigm shift is reflected in DSM-5 concluding gender specific classifications.

Another challenge is to include terms such as "interpersonal difficulties" or "partner distress" in the definition in order to fulfill the criteria of SD. Many clinicians today tend to avoid labeling people on the basis of their partner's distress while they are not themselves uncomfortable.

These challenges make it difficult to define, assess, and treat SD. Additionally, more meaningful questions are being asked today such as: "Which treatments are most effective? pharmacotherapy? sex therapy? couple therapy or combined?"; "Which treatment works better for whom?"; "What are the advantages and disadvantages of each approach?"; "What are the costs and benefits of different treatment modalities?"; "What kind of training should be given to professionals working in the area of sexual medicine?"; "Does effective training in assessment and treatment of sexual disorders result in improved patient outcome and thera-pist competence?"; "Must both partners be included in treatment in order to achieve better long-term success?"; "What are the success criteria?"; "Are there reliable measures to assess outcome and success?"; "Are subjective reports more reliable than measurement of objective genital responses, at least in women?"; "Who determines treatment success: the clinician, the patient or both?". Some of these challenging questions are raised as significant and criti-cal for research and clinical practice in the arena of sexual medicine (Leiblum, 2007). This chapter addresses some of these issues and summarizes pharmacological, psychological, and combined treatments of SD as defined in DSM-IV-TR, with recommendations for the future.

SEXUAL DYSFUNCTION IN MEN

Erectile Dysfunction (ED)

ED is defined in DSM-IV-TR (American Psychiatric Association, 2000) as persistent and re-petitive inability to achieve and/or maintain penile erection sufficiently for sexual activity. DSM-5 (American Psychiatric Association, 2013) added marked decrease in erectile rigidity that interferes with sexual activity criterion to this definition. It is considered as one of the most prevalent and severe sexual health problems in men aged 40–70 years. The Massachu-setts Male Aging Study (Feldman, Goldstein, Hatzichristou, Krane, & McKinlay, 1994) showed 52% overall prevalence of ED in men aged between 40 and 70. Of these 52% men, 9.6% had severe, 25.2% had moderate, and 17.2% had mild ED. Primary efficacy measures that are used to assess ED are International Index of Erectile Function (IIEF) and Sexual Encounter Profile questions 2 and 3 (SEP2 and SEP3). SEP comprises five questions, but the second and third questions are used widely for assessment. SEP2 ("Were you able to insert your penis into your partner's vagina?") and SEP3 ("Did your erection last long enough for you to have successful intercourse?") questions turned out to be the most rigorous and most frequently used efficacy measures in clinical ED trials. IIEF comprises 15 questions in five domains and IIEF Erectile Function (EF) domain is used as outcome measure for ED. EF domain scores between 6–10 indicates severe, 11–16 is moderate, 17–25 is mild ED, and 26–30 is normal EF.

Pharmacotherapy for ED

Phosphodiesterase type 5 inhibitors (5PDEI). According to literature, tadalafil, vardenafil, and sildenafil have similar efficacy results, but differences exist regarding side effects, onset, and duration of action. Recently established 5PDEI such as avanafil, udenafil, mirodenafil, and lodenafil are not investigated as thoroughly as the older ones, and therefore further ef-ficacy studies are needed to reach final conclusions. Table 12.1 shows comparison of efficacy and side effects of 5PDEI. A review (Morales, Casillas, & Turbi, 2011) of available literature showed that 52%–65% of patients preferred tadalafil, whereas 12%–20% preferred vardenafil, and 8%–30% preferred sildenafil. A partners' preference study showed 79% of partners felt more relaxed and enjoyed more natural or spontaneous sexual experiences with tadalafil over sildenafil (Conaglen & Conaglen, 2008).

　　Daily usage. A double-blind, randomized controlled trial (DBRCT) (Zumbe et al., 2008) compared 10 mg daily and 20 mg on-demand vardenafil. No significant differences were found between them in mild to moderate ED, and both were significantly superior to placebo. Another DBRCT (Zhao et al., 2011) of once daily dosing of 50 and 75 mg udenafil showed

Table 12.1 Comparison of efficacy and side effects of 5PDEI (studies which use the same primary efficacy measures are chosen for comparative reasons).

Drug	Sildenafil (S) (Goldstein et al., 1998) 12 weeks	Tadalafil (T) (Carson et al., 2004) 12 weeks	Vardenafil (V) (Hellstrom et al., 2002) 12 weeks	Udenafil (U) (Paick, Kim et al., 2008) 12 weeks	Mirodenafil (M) (Paick, Ahn et al., 2008) 12 weeks	Lodenafil Carbonate (L) (Glina et al., 2010) 4 Weeks	Avanafil (A) (Goldstein et al., 2012) 12 weeks
EF Domain scores	S: 22.1 P: 12.2	T: 23.2 P: 15.3	V: 21.4 P: 15.0	U: 24.2 P: 13.1	M: 25.6 ± 5.16 P: 17.0 ± 7.70	L: 20.6 ± 7.7 P: 13.9 ± 5.2	A: 22.2 P: 15.3
SEP2	S: 85% P: 50%	T: 80% P: 50%	V: 80.5% P: 51.7%	U: 92.4% P: 53.8%	M: 91.9% P: 60.6%	L: 80.8 ± 32.3% P: 52.1 ± 41.4%	A: 77% P: 54%
SEP3	S: 69% P: 22%	T: 68% P: 31%	V: 64.5% P: 32.2%	U: 75.70% P: 15.44%	M: 73.20% P: 26.77%	L: 66.0 ± 39.3% P: 29.7 ± 38.1%	A: 57% P: 27%
Side Effects	Headache, flushing, dyspepsia, nasal congestion, urinary tract infection, abnormal vision, dizziness	Headache, dyspepsia, back pain, myalgia, nasal congestion, flushing, pain in limb	Headache, rhinitis, flushing, dyspepsia, sinusitis, flu syndrome	Flushing, headache, nasal congestion, ocular hyperemia, chest discomfort	Facial flushing, headache, nausea, ocular hyperemia, dizziness, dyspepsia	Rhinitis, headache, flushing, dizziness, visual disorder	Headache, flushing, nasal congestion, nasopharyngitis, back pain

a significant increase in mean EF domain score over placebo, but 25 mg did not. Another DBRCT of tadalafil 2.5 and 5 mg (Rajfer et al., 2007) showed significant increase in all efficacy measures. An open label study (McMahon, 2004) of 10/20 mg daily tadalafil in patients who had failed to respond to on-demand 20 mg tadalafil found that daily tadalafil (10/20 mg) was effective in salvage of previous tadalafil nonresponders.

Onset of action and duration of effect. Superior response rates for vardenafil over placebo for SEP3 was found at 10 minutes, 11 to 25 minutes, and at 25 minutes, following 10 and 20 mg intake (Montorsi et al., 2004). In a DBRCT, the initial onset of action was 16 minutes for tadalafil 20 mg in a smaller proportion, whereas one third to one half of patients responded within 30 minutes (Rosen, Padma-Nathan et al., 2004). Successful intercourse was reported in 35% of patients within 14 minutes and in 51% of patients within 20 minutes following intake (Padma-Nathan, Stecher et al., 2003). Seventy-two percent of patients achieved successful intercourse within 15 minutes following rapid-acting avanafil intake (Goldstein et al., 2012). Duration of effect was reported to continue in some patients up to 12 hours for sildenafil (Moncada, Jara, Subira, Castano, & Hernandez, 2004), 36 hours for tadalafil (Young et al., 2005), 8 hours for vardenafil (Porst et al., 2006), 6 hours for avanafil (Goldstein et al., 2012), and 12 hours for udenafil (Park, Park, Park, Min, & Park, 2010), measured by SEP3.

Apomorphine Sublingual (ASL). Effects were seen within 15–20 minutes after 2–3 mg dosing. ASL showed significant improvement over placebo and was most effective in men with mild to moderate ED (Stief, Padley, Perdok, & Sleep, 2002). A comparison study of sildenafil and ASL (Eardley, Wright, MacDonagh, Hole, & Edwards, 2004) showed that sildenafil patients reported more successful intercourse attempts (75% versus 35%) and higher EF domain scores.

Bremelanotide. Efficacy and safety of bremelanotide has been reported in some clinical trials. A group of 25 men with moderate and severe ED, who did not adequately respond to sildenafil in 12 months prior, responded to intranasal bremelanotide in a DBRCT (Rosen, Diamond, Earle, Shadiack, & Molinoff, 2004).

Yohimbine and Trazodone. A meta-analysis (Ernst & Pittler, 1998) showed superiority of yohimbine over placebo. There are inconsistent results for trazodone, and subgroup analyses suggest that it is more effective in men with pyschogenic ED (Fink, MacDonald, Rutks, & Wilt, 2003).

Intracavernosal injections (ICI). After the discovery of 5PDEI, ICI became the second-line treatment and are still used in men who are unresponsive to and/or have contraindications for use of 5PDEI.

Alprostadil (PGE1). Erection occurs 5–15 minutes following ICI. In one crossover, randomized open-label study, intraurethral alprostadil (MUSE; Medicated Urethral System for Erection) plus constriction ring (if preferred) and intracavernosal alprostadil were compared. Intracavernosal alprostadil showed greater efficacy over intraurethral for SEP2 and EF domain scores. Use of constriction ring increased response to the treatment. Sixty-nine percent of patients and 63% of partners preferred intracavernosal alprostadil (Shabsigh et al., 2000).

Papaverine was the first ICI for treatment of ED. It has a longer half-life than other ICI which explains the higher incidence of priapism when compared to others.

Phentolamine (P) and Vasoactive Intestinal Polypeptide (VIP). In a DBRCT of intracavernosal VIP and P, 25 mcg VIP plus 1.0 mg P produced more erections suitable for vaginal penetration than 25 mcg VIP plus 2.0 mg P. They were both significantly more effective than placebo (Dinsmore et al., 1999).

Papaverine-Phentolamine-PgE1 (Alprostadil) combination, known as Trimix, is a combination of lower doses of these three agents that aims to reduce side effects and enhance efficacy. In a prospective, randomized, single-blind comparative study (Seyam, Mohamed, Akhras, & Rashwan, 2005), effects of lower doses of Trimix started as fast as high doses of PgE1. In total, 29% of patients reported better response to PGE1, 51% to Trimix, and 20% reported similar response to both agents. Incidence of priapism with Trimix was 5%, which was significantly higher than PgE1, and the duration of erection was significantly longer with Trimix (120 min).

One study (Giuliano, Montorsi, Mirone, Rossi, & Sweeney, 2000) showed that more than two-thirds of ED patients who were switched from ICI to sildenafil reported maintenance or increase in treatment satisfaction with sildenafil. Another study (Hatzichristou et al., 2000) showed that 64% of the patients switched to sildenafil preferred taking sildenafil by the end of 3 months. These studies indicate that even in patients where ICI are highly successful, satisfaction may be improved by switching to sildenafil.

Psychosocial Interventions for ED

The Cochrane review (Melnik, Soares, & Nasselo, 2007) evaluated the effectiveness of psychosocial interventions. It showed that group sex therapy (GST) was significantly more effective than waiting list (WL) at the end of treatment. Two RCTs (Munjack et al., 1984; Price, Reynolds, Cohen, Anderson, & Schochet, 1981) showed maintenance of efficacy at 6-month follow-up. A study comparing group therapy versus sildenafil (Melnik & Abdo, 2005) found significant difference favoring group therapy determined by mean IIEF scores in psychogenic ED. This study also showed a higher dropout rate for sildenafil group. An evaluation of sex therapy approaches (Mathews et al., 1976) compared modified M&J approach with systematic desensitization plus counseling and with self-help instructions with minimum therapist contact in couples with a range of sexual problems. Although differences in the three treatment groups were limited, consistent trends were found by the end of treatment and 4 months later, favoring the modified M&J approach. Everaerd & Dekker (1985) compared sex therapy with systematic desensitization. Both forms of treatment had only limited positive effects, and no difference was found between them either at the end of treatment or at 6-month follow-up. A study (van Lankveld, Leusink, van Diest, Gijs, & Slob, 2009) that compared Internet-based CBT (IBCBT) with WL showed that IBCBT was efficacious for male erectile disorder. Another study (McCabe, Price, Piterman, & Lording, 2008) on Internet-based psychological intervention showed that those who completed the program reported improved erectile functioning and also sexual relationship satisfaction and quality. Larger RCTs with longer follow-ups are needed to conclude the effectiveness of psychosocial interventions for ED.

Combined Treatments for ED

Although 5PDEI have been regarded as first-line treatments due to their proven efficacy and safety profiles, increasing evidence suggests that many men with ED discontinue treatment due to diminished or failed expectations, fear of side effects, partner concerns, and inefficient focus on special needs of presenting partners (Rosen et al., 2004). Combined approaches may be beneficial regardless of etiology when couples have relationship problems, when one of the partners has severe psychological problems, when there is only limited response to 5PDEI, when the female partner also suffers from a sexual dysfunction, and when long-term maintenance is needed. A holistic approach that addresses all of these issues may improve overall satisfaction with treatment (Perelman, 2005). A study (Melnik & Abdo, 2005) randomly assigned men with psychogenic ED to three groups—namely, psychotherapy only, sildenafil only, and combined. All groups demonstrated significant improvement in posttreatment IIEF scores compared to baseline at the end of 6 months. However, utilizing the criterion of normalization of IIEF scores, the combined and psychotherapy only groups demonstrated statistically significant improvement, whereas the sildenafil only group did not. Satisfaction with the treatment, confidence, and naturalness significantly increased in the combined and psychotherapy only group but not in the sildenafil only group (Melnik, Abdo, de Moraes, & Riera, 2012). There have been several other articles recommending combined approach for treatment of ED. One study (Turner et al., 1989) showed that pharmacologically induced erections were not effective in improving psychogenic ED when it was not accompanied by psychological counseling. A more recent study (Abdo, Afif-Abdo, Otani, & Machado, 2008), which aimed to evaluate quality of life in men with ED before and after three kinds of treatments (counseling, sildenafil, and sildenafil plus counseling), showed that all treatments were significantly efficient, but the best results were achieved with sildenafil plus counseling. Another recent study (Banner & Anderson, 2007) compared the effectiveness of an integrative treatment protocol (sildenafil plus cognitive-behavior sex therapy [CBST]) with that of sildenafil only for men with psychogenic ED. Results yielded higher rates of clinical success within the first 4 weeks of therapy in integrated treatment. Similar significant improvements in the IIEF domain scores were found in both groups at 8 weeks when CBST was added to the sildenafil only group by the end of 4 weeks. These studies all suggest that combined treatments for ED improve the outcome and treatment satisfaction and reduce dropout when compared to pharmacological treatment groups alone. More research is needed for addressing the costs and benefits of combined treatment conducted in larger groups.

Strengths and advantages of 5PDEI in treatment of ED. Introduction of 5PDEI has maximized therapeutic polarization of professionals from different disciplines. Following its introduction, the question of whether there is still a space or a need for sex therapy became the main question that uroandrologists often asked sex therapists. Despite this provocative polarizing effect, 5PDEI are generally welcomed by many professionals due to their strengths and advantages which could be listed as follows: (a) When sex therapy is not acceptable or proves to be ineffective, 5PDEI become the choice of treatment; (b) 5PDEI may be a better choice of treatment in men who do not have partners to conduct sexual assignments (c) Drug treatments generate more publicity and attract the attention of media more than psychotherapy and therefore increased media coverage may encourage "silent sufferers" to come forward to seek help, (d) 5PDEI are easy to administer drugs with good efficacy, safety, and tolerability profiles (e) 5PDEI are "erection-facilitating" rather than "erection-inducing" drugs and produce a sexual stimulation related to natural erectile response; (f) The availability of erection-facilitating drugs make treatment more accessible; and (g) 5PDEI treatment regardless of ED etiology have reduced the costly and potentially invasive differential diagnostic procedures.

Limitations and weaknesses of using 5PDEI as sole approach in ED. There are some reasons why giving a "quick fix" with a pharmacological agent may not always be the best treatment option for men suffering from ED. First of all, "quick fix" approaches that aim at rapid restoration of physiological functions focus on the organ (dysfunctional penis), sometimes at the expense of disregarding the men behind the organ. Many men using drugs and having firm erections report that their feeling of inadequacy is not resolved as they attribute the success to the drug rather than themselves. They worry about long-term consequences of developing tolerance and increasing costs. Others ruminate about not being able to achieve erections despite using the drug. These ruminative negative cognitions may explain why some men are unable to respond to 5PDEI as well as others do. On top of that, little attention has been given to the partners of men with ED who also have a high prevalence of sexual problems. Drug treatment is not likely to resolve partner problems. Most importantly, sexual problems are highly comorbid with couple problems, which may both be causes or consequences of sexual dysfunctions. However, regardless of their origin, these problems are not likely to respond to medications alone. Treatment modality must be made attractive for partners in order to sustain its long-term use. Despite the overall safety, tolerability, and efficacy of 5PDEI, increasing evidence suggests that a substantial proportion of men with ED discontinue treatment. A large-scale, multinational study including more than 25,000 men found that only 16% of men continued to use the medication given by their physicians (Rosen et al., 2004).

Premature Ejaculation (PE)

There is no consensus about the definition, classification, and prevalence of PE. The high prevalence (20%–30%) reported is probably due to the vague terminology used in its definition. One source of vagueness is the lack of operational definitions until DSM-5. DSM-IV-TR (American Psychiatric Association, 2000) defines PE as persistent or recurrent ejaculation with minimal sexual stimulation before, on, or shortly after penetration. It is only recently that Intravaginal Ejaculation Latency Time (IELT) of 1 minute (from penetration to ejaculation) has been defined (McMahon, 2008; Waldinger & Schweitzer, 2008) as an operational measure to replace vague terms such as "shortly after" in defining PE. This is also reflected in DSM-5 (American Psychiatric Association, 2013) as ejaculation occurring within approximately one minute of beginning sexual activity. Masturbation ELT, oral ELT, and anal ELT are also suggested to be used for research in heterosexual or homosexual men with and without partners (Althof et al., 2010).

Pharmacotherapy for PE

On-demand serotonergic antidepressants. Meta-analysis of on-demand treatments showed that the mean percentage of IELT increase was 263% for clomipramine (25–50 mg), 929% for paroxetine (20 mg), and 553% for sertaline (50–100 mg) over baseline. This suggests that interpretation of on-demand treatment data should be made more cautiously, as studies were conducted with different methodologies, different antidepressants (AD) with different doses, different baseline IELT values, and different assessment techniques (questionnaire versus stopwatch) (Waldinger et al., 2004).

Dapoxetine is a fast-acting SSRI with a short half-life. A meta-analysis of five DBRCT which included 6,000 men (McMahon et al., 2011) showed that in patients whose baseline IELT was ≤ 2 minutes, 30 and 60 mg of first-dose dapoxetine produced significant increase in mean average IELT over placebo. After first-dose dapoxetine, mean IELT increased to 2.3, 2.7, and 1.5 minutes respectively, with dapoxetine 30 mg, 60 mg, and placebo from baseline, which was 0.9 minutes. At 12 weeks, mean IELT increased to 3.1, 3.6, and 1.9 minutes by dapoxetine 30 mg, 60 mg, and placebo from baseline, which was 0.9 minutes. Similar IELT increases were found for patients whose average IELT was ≤ 0.5 minute and ≤ 1 minute with 30 and 60 mg when compared to placebo. The most frequently reported side effect was nausea.

Tramadol. A DBRCT (Bar-Or, Salottolo, Orlando, Winkler, & Tramadol ODT Study Group, 2012) of tramadol orally disintegrating tablet (ODT) showed that in the group with baseline IELT ≤ 1 minute, the mean IELT increased to 2.78 and 3.19 minutes for tramadol 62 and 89 mg, respectively, versus 1.91 minutes with placebo. The authors also reported that tramadol ODT appeared to provide similar mean percentage IELT increase with dapoxetine.

Daily use of SSRIs. In a meta-analysis of eight double-blind, stopwatch-used studies (Waldinger et al., 2004), the order of efficacy in increasing IELT was 783% for paroxetine, 360% for clomipramine, 313% for sertraline, 295% for fluoxetine, and 47% for placebo. Overall, clomipramine, sertraline, and fluoxetine had similar effects.

5PDEI. A DBRCT of vardenafil showed increase in IELT (from 0.6 to 4.5 minutes) and ejaculatory control (Aversa et al., 2009). Tadalafil increased IELT from baseline 49.26 seconds to 186.53 seconds, and this increase was found to be larger with tadalafil plus fluoxetine when compared to tadalafil alone in men with lifelong PE (Mattos et al., 2008). A DBRCT of sildenafil (McMahon et al., 2005) showed mean IELT increase to 2.60 minutes from baseline of 0.96 minutes versus placebo, but the increase did not reach statistical significance. However, patients who took sildenafil reported significant increase in ejaculatory control. One systematic review of 5PDEI (McMahon, McMahon, Leow, & Winestock, 2006) reported that there is limited but reasonably convincing evidence that 5PDEI (alone or combined with daily or OD SSRI drugs) have a role in the treatment of acquired PE when comorbid with ED. One possible mechanism of action may be improved EF with reduction in performance anxiety, reduction of the erectile refractory period, and opposition of sympathetic vasoconstriction.

Topical anesthetic agents. A review of placebo-controlled studies of topical SS cream and lidocaine-prilocaine cream and spray reported significant increase in IELT compared to baseline and placebo (Morales, Barada, & Wyllie, 2007).

Psychosocial and Combined Interventions for PE

More than 97% of treatment success rates were reported for treatment of PE by behavioral techniques (BT) such as "stop and start" (Semans, 1956) and "squeeze" (Masters & Johnson, 1970). Although subsequent clinicians and researchers could not achieve similar success rates, these techniques are still being successfully used in PE. Despite their efficacy, both BT and pharmacological agents present some drawbacks. AD medications may impair sexual desire and arousal, and once they are stopped PE returns. BT may interrupt sexual activity and distract the person's attention from engagement in sexual activity. A study (de Carufel & Trudel, 2006) evaluated the effects of a newly defined functional sexological treatment (FST) that aimed to teach men how to control arousal and delay ejaculation without interrupting sexual activity. The authors compared FST with BT and WL for 12 weeks in 36 couples. Similar treatment results were obtained by BT and FST, which were superior to WL. Three trials compared psychotherapy with pharmacotherapy. One of these trials (Yuan, Dai, Yang, Guao, & Liang, 2008) allocated 96 PE patients to either BT only, citalopram only, or a combination of citalopram and BT. All of the three groups showed significant increase in IELT. Citalopram only versus BT comparison favored citalopram only group, whereas a comparison between the combined approach versus citalopram only favored the combination group. Another study (Li, Zhu, Xu, Sun, & Wang, 2006) allocating 90 PE patients to either psychological intervention plus chlorpromazine or chlorpromazine only favored the combined approach. One-month follow-up also showed significantly higher efficacy rates for combined treatment. Another RCT (Abdel-Hamid, El Naggar, & El Gilany, 2001) with 31 primary PE patients showed that the median ejaculation latency time significantly increased from the pretreatment median of 1 minute to 4 minutes with clomipramine, 3 minutes with sertraline, 4 minutes with paroxetine, and 3 minutes with pause–squeeze technique. A more recent study (van Lankveld et al., 2009) compared IB-CBT with WL and found no difference between IBCBT and WL in the treatment of PE. Better research designs, addressing specific interactions between patient characteristics and treatment modalities and identifying the psychological characteristics of men who perceive themselves as having control over ejaculation despite short IELT time or who perceive themselves as suffering from PE while having long IELTs are issues that remain to be explored further.

Hypoactive Sexual Desire Disorder (HSDD)

DSM-IV-TR (American Psychiatric Association, 2000) defines HSDD as a persistent or recurrent deficiency or absence of sexual fantasies for sexual activity that causes marked distress or interpersonal difficulty. Motivations (reasons/incentives) for attempting to become sexually aroused are scarce or absent. The prevalence of low desire varies between 14% and 17% in men.

Pharmacotherapy for HSDD in Men

A meta-analysis of RCTs (Isidori et al., 2005) supported the notion that increased testosterone (T) levels improved sexual thoughts regardless of T levels, which may imply that effects of T are not related to a fixed range but to transient increase in circulating sex hormones. A DBRCT of bupropion slow release (BSR) (225–450 mg/day) (Crenshaw, Goldberg, & Stern, 1987) and a single-blind crossover study of BSR 150 and 300 mg/day (Modell, May, & Katholi, 2000) significantly improved sexual functioning compared to placebo. A DBRCT, crossover study of Melanotan II showed increase in sexual desire (Wessells et al., 2000).

Psychosocial Interventions for HSDD in Men

A survey (O'Carroll, 1991) searching for controlled psychotherapy trials in men with HSDD (from 1970 to 1989) found only two trials, but they did not include a homogenous sample. Heiman, Epps, and Ellis (1995) searched couples where HSDD was the presenting problem and found significant treatment gains with BT that maintained at follow-up. However De Amicis et al.'s study (De Amicis, Goldberg, LoPiccolo, Friedman, & Davies, 1985) did not demonstrate sustained success in HSDD. Van Lankveld et al. (2001) reported that men presenting with HSDD in couples who were randomized to a cognitive behavioral bibliotherapy that included psychoeducation, sensate focus exercises, and rational-emotive analyses showed significant improvement in sexual function over waiting list control group.

Methodological problems regarding outcome research on HSDD make results largely inconsistent and uninterpretable. Lack or loss of sexual desire in men is probably not a single disorder but rather a shared symptom that may represent a common expression or complaint emerging as a result of a wide variety of different etiologies.

SEXUAL DYSFUNCTION IN WOMEN

Although different studies with different measurement tools show a wide range of frequency (20% to 30%) for low sexual desire (LSD), a large prevalence study showed that LSD had the highest prevalence (38.7%), followed by low arousal (26.1%), and orgasmic difficulties (20.5%) (Shifren, Monz, Russo, Segreti, & Johannes, 2008).

Hypoactive Sexual Desire Disorder (HSDD)

DSM-IV-TR refers to HSDD as persistent or recurrently absent sexual thoughts, fantasies, and/or desire for sexual activity. It was later claimed that lack of spontaneous sexual fantasies and desire cannot be labeled as HSDD in every woman, as desire and fantasies may not be spontaneously present but can be triggered or activated as a response to internal sexual stimuli or nonsexual reasons (Basson, Wierman, van Lankveld, & Brotto, 2010). HSDD is one of the sexual disorders with the lowest treatment success rate. Better results may be expected when patients are highly motivated. No gold standard treatment has been established for female sexual disorders (FSD) including HSDD.

Pharmacotherapy for HSDD in Females

Hormonal treatment. There are no drugs currently approved in the United States for the treatment of HSDD, but a transdermal testosterone patch is approved in several European countries. Different types of androgens (testosterone, dihydrotestosterone, dehydroepiandrosterone, androstenedione, and androgenic dietary supplements) are available in different forms (pellets, injectables, formulated creams, patches) in treatment of HSDD.

   Testosterone (T) in treatment of HSDD is not new, but systematic studies have been conducted only recently. Although some authors report a beneficial effect of adding T to conventional postmenopausal hormone therapy (HT), convincing data is unavailable to conclude its long-term benefits. A Cochrane review showed that sexual function scores and number of satisfying experiences were improved by adding T to HT (Somboonporn, Davis, Seif, & Bell, 2005). Regarding its delivery, the transdermal form appears to be the preferred choice, as it produces high levels of testosterone with fewer side effects when compared with oral form. Two multicentered, DBRCT parallel group design studies (Buster et al., 2005; Simon et al., 2005) showed that 300 mcg/day transdermal testosterone patch (TTP) used for 6 months in surgically menopausal women with concomitant estrogen therapy was found to be effective in increasing sexual desire (Buster et al., 2005; Simon et al., 2005). The 967 subjects who completed these two studies and who volunteered to attend a consequent open-label study with 4-year follow-up were monitored for long-term safety of the TTP treatment. Patients received 300 mcg/day TTP during the 4-year follow-up. Although there was a high rate of withdrawal seen over the 4-year course, a high safety profile was found (Nachtigall et al., 2011). Current data does not support the use of testosterone in pre- and perimenopausal women, but there are some studies showing some benefit. In a DBRC crossover study of transdermal testosterone therapy (TTT) conducted in premenopausal women with low libido, TTT improved well-being, mood, and sexual function, including sexual interest, when compared to placebo (Goldstat, Briganti, Tran, Wolfe, & Davis, 2003). Finding the balance that improves libido without side effects should be the aim of T therapy.

   Dehydroepiandrosterone (DHEA) levels decrease with aging, and assumptions have been made that a decrease in DHEA and DHEA-S results in loss of libido and well-being. The effects of oral DHEA on the sexual function of women have been evaluated in a number of RCTs with inconsistent findings (Labrie et al., 2009; Lovas et al., 2003; Panjari et al., 2009).

DHEA should be used with caution, as there is not enough data to show favoring effects, dosage, and duration of DHEA usage for FSD to make specific recommendations.

Tibolone is a synthetic steroid with metabolites that are estrogenic, progestogenic, and androgenic. A DBRC crossover study of tibolone 2.5 mg/day showed significant increase in sexual desire, arousability, and frequency of sexual fantasies when compared to placebo (Laan, van Lunsen, & Everaerd, 2001). Another study that compared estrogens, estrogens plus androgens, and tibolone in postmenopausal women showed that androgen and tibolone users have higher increases in their sexual interest, orgasms, and sexual responsiveness (Castelo-Branco et al., 2000).

Nonhormonal Treatments

Apomorphine. A crossover DBRCT of daily apomorphine sublingual (ASL) (2 or 3 mg) used in 62 premenopausal women with low desire and arousal disorder showed that sexual desire and arousal were improved when compared to placebo (Caruso et al., 2004).

Flibanserin is a 5-HT1A agonist and a 5-HT2A antagonist. A Phase III flibanserine study (Derogatis et al., 2012) found it to be effective and well tolerated in the treatment of HSDD for premenopausal women. But the U.S. FDA Advisory Panel reported that its benefits did not outweigh the side effects.

Bupropion. A DBRCT dose-escalating study of bupropion sustained release (SR) for treatment of HSDD in premenopausal women showed that bupropion had prosexual effects, but increase in desire was not statistically significant (Segraves, Clayton, Croft, Wolf, & Warnock, 2004). Another DBRCT for efficacy and safety of bupropion SR 150 mg/daily in ovulating women showed that bupropion SR significantly improved HSDD at several endpoints (Safarinejad, Hosseini, Asgari, Dadkhah, & Taghva, 2010).

Bremelanotide (PT-141). A DBRCT in women with sexual arousal disorder showed that bremelanotide had positive effects on desire and arousal (Diamond et al., 2006).

To conclude, the etiology of HSDD is complex and includes hormone and neurotransmitter imbalance, as well as psychosocial factors. Androgens improve HSDD, but further research is needed to address whether there is a subgroup that would specifically benefit from its use in the long term.

Female Sexual Arousal Disorder (FSAD)

FSAD is defined in DSM-IV-TR (American Psychiatric Association, 2000) as persistent or recurrent inability to attain, or to maintain, an adequate lubrication-swelling response of sexual excitement, coupled with marked distress or interpersonal difficulty. Different types of FSAD have been described (Basson et al., 2003), such as subjective sexual arousal disorder, genital sexual arousal disorder, and combined genital and subjective arousal disorder. FSAD in daily practice is generally comorbid with desire and orgasmic disorders, and proposals have been made to merge desire and arousal problems into one and this proposal has been welcome in DSM-5 (American Psychiatric Association, 2013) as female sexual interest and arousal disorder (FSIAD).

Pharmacotherapy for FSAD

Pharmacologic treatments for FSAD can be hormonal and nonhormonal.

Hormonal Treatments

Estrogen. A Cochrane review showed that in women with vaginal atrophy, intravaginal estrogenic preparations had a positive effect on dryness and dyspareunia, regardless of how estrogens were applied (creams, tablets, vaginal ring, or pessaries) when compared to placebo (Suckling, Lethaby, & Kennedy, 2006).

Testosterone. Two multicentered, DBRCT parallel group design studies (Buster et al., 2005; Simon et al., 2005) showed that TTP 300 mcg/day given to treat low desire in surgically menopausal women who are on concomitant estrogen therapy also increased arousal when compared with placebo. Studies using vaginal photoplethysmograph or Doppler velocimeter following chronic T supplementation have not found significant changes in genital response (Myers, Dixen, Morrissette, Carmichael, & Davidson, 1990). Vaginal application of T in premenopausal women without sexual dysfunction did not show any increase in genital or subjective sexual response (Apperloo et al., 2006). However, an acute dose of T in sexually functional premenopausal women in a crossover DBRCT of SL testosterone undecanoate showed significant improvement in genital sexual arousal, and increased subjective reports of sexual sensations compared to placebo after 4.5 hours of the peak of testosterone concentrations. These women had repeated exposure to visual sexual stimuli after T administration (Tuiten et al., 2000). A study which measured only two time points to eliminate repeated exposure to erotic material found an increase in vasocongestion at 4.5 hours but not in subjective reports. Based on these findings, authors concluded that an acute dose of T resulted in delayed effect on genital but not on subjective sexual arousal (Tuiten et al., 2002).

Tibolone. A DBRCT crossover study of tibolone 2.5 mg/day resulted in significant increase in sexual desire, arousability, frequency of sexual fantasies, and vaginal lubrication compared to placebo. It also increased vaginal pulse amplitude (VPA) during erotic fantasy periods but not during erotic film stimulation (Laan et al., 2001). In two DBRCT, tibolone 2.5 mg showed greater increase in the domains of sexual desire, arousal, and satisfaction over transdermal estradiol (E2) plus norethisterone acetate (NETA) (Nijland et al., 2008) and 0.625 mg conjugated equine estrogen plus 2.5 mg medroxyprogesterone acetate (CEE/MPA) (Ziaei, Moghasemi, & Faghihzadeh, 2010). Tibolone was also superior to placebo in both trials.

Nonhormonal Treatments

Apomorphine. A crossover DBRCT of daily apomorphine SL in treatment of HSDD and FSAD in premenopausal women showed increased arousal when compared to placebo (Caruso et al., 2004). A similar study examining the 3 mg SL apomorphine showed improvements in subjective and objective sexual arousal (Bechara, Bertolino, Casabe, & Fredotovich, 2004).

Bremelanotide (PT-141). Two DBRCT in treatment of FSAD showed that bremelanotide had positive effect on desire and arousal (Diamond et al., 2006; Safarinejad, 2008).

5PDEI. In a review of 16 studies of 5PDEI (Chivers & Rosen, 2010), three main clinical implications were reported: (a) 5PDEI do not show significant treatment effect in the management of FSAD as they do in men. On the other hand, 5PDEI efficacy is well established in the management of drug-related sexual dysfunctions in women taking antidepressants (Nurnberg et al., 2008). (b) When combined with psychosexual interventions such as sex therapy, 5PDEI may become effective agents in improving sexual functioning by facilitating the development of concordance between subjective and genital responses in FSAD. Sex therapy interventions (Brotto, Basson, & Luria, 2008) may help resolve underlying discordance between psychological and physiological states of female arousal. (c) Women with genital arousal disorder may respond to 5PDEI, unlike women with subjective or combined subjective-genital arousal disorder, showing that the impact of drug treatment could be very different in different subgroups of women suffering from FSAD. This may be attributed to the fact that women may show discordance between physiological and subjective aspects of sexual response. If the underlying problem for a woman with FSAD is discordance between physical and subjective aspects of sexual arousal, adding a 5PDEI could be counterproductive, as such pharmaceuticals that augment genital responding may not result in greater concordance between subjective and physiological aspects of sexual arousal.

Basson and Brotto's (2003) study suggested that women who showed less genital response with sexual stimulation prior to drug treatment showed greater increases in sexual functioning with sildenafil treatment. However, sildenafil increased latency to orgasm, suggesting that in women who are already genitally responsive, the drug delayed orgasm.

Alprostadil trials conducted with different methodologies showed inconsistent findings ranging from no significant improvement over placebo (Padma-Nathan et al., 2003) to increased sexual functioning and satisfaction (Liao et al., 2008).

Psychosocial Interventions for Sexual Desire and Arousal Disorders in Females

Sexual desire disorders have one of the lowest treatment success rates amongst all sexual disorders. The complex etiology, high comorbidity with other SD, and relationship problems and inconsistent motivation to improve sexual relation with the present partner are some of the factors that explain low treatment response. Genital–nongenital sensate focus and masturbation training exercises including directed masturbation are the BT used. Cognitive approaches include restructuring of maladaptive cognitions about sexual activity, reducing performance anxiety, and improving capacity to focus on sexual content. Couple therapy approaches for establishing trust and intimacy and improving communication and cooperation skills may be very helpful in psychosocial treatment of desire and arousal disorders. When there is lack of emotional intimacy, it might be a better choice to start with relationship issues and then proceed to sex therapy. Every case should be thoroughly assessed for past history of traumatic experiences. Results of a controlled study of three behavioral group approaches (focusing on either their sexual dysfunction, their interpersonal problems, or a combination of both compared to waiting list) in treatment of sexually dysfunctional women without partners showed no clinically meaningful differences between the groups. However, all of the active treatments proved to be more effective than the waiting list (Stravynski et al., 2007). A comparative study using orgasm consistency training plus standard group intervention versus standard group intervention only showed that the combined group reported greater sexual arousal and sexual assertiveness at posttreatment and at 3-month and 6-month follow-up evaluations (Hurlbert, 1993). Twelve weeks of CBT for treatment of 74 couples (Trudel et al., 2001) where the presenting women were diagnosed as HSDD showed significant improvement in sexual satisfaction, arousal, pleasure, perceived self-esteem, and couple relationship when compared to the control group who did not receive any treatment. Another CBT approach conducted with 365 couples showed consistent improvement during 1-year follow up (Sarwer & Durlak, 1997). Some factors reported to be associated with better treatment outcome are overall quality of the couples' relationship, motivation of partners and especially that of men, degree of physical attraction between the partners, absence of major psychiatric disorders, and compliance with the homework assignments at early stages in therapy (Sungur, 1994). Methodological problems and lack of well-controlled studies limit the value of findings regarding sex therapy outcome studies in women with HSDD. There is clearly a need for further controlled efficacy trials. One important concern for the future is conducting treatment of desire and arousal disorder in women conjointly with their partner's sexual dysfunction. On top of that, desire and arousal problems are frequently seen as co-morbid with orgasmic problems. A more integrative treatment approach considering sexual responses of women as a whole (like FSIAD diagnosis in DSM-5) with a unique formulation of each individual case is more likely to succeed.

Female Orgasmic Disorder (FOD)

FOD is defined as a persistent or recurrent delay in, or absence of, orgasm following a normal sexual excitement phase (American Psychiatric Association, 2000). It may emerge due to a wide variety of reasons, including general relationship issues. Although there are no approved specific medications to treat FOD, there are some promising pharmacological agents and strategies. In a review (West, Vinikoor, & Zolnoun, 2004), the rates of anorgasmia, orgasmic difficulty, or orgasmic disorders ranged between 20% and 50%.

Pharmacological Treatment for FOD

Nonhormonal Treatments

Bupropion. A single-blind sequential treatment of placebo and bupropion-SR 150–300 mg/day showed significant improvement in overall satisfaction, whereas only 150 mg/day showed satisfaction with intensity of orgasm relative to baseline (Modell et al., 2000).

Sildenafil. Two DBRCT showed significant increase in orgasm over placebo (Caruso, Intelisano, Farina, Di Mari, & Agnello, 2003; Cavalcanti et al., 2008), whereas another two (Basson & Brotto, 2003; Kaplan et al., 1999) showed nonsignificant minimal increase over placebo.

Hormonal Treatments

Data are limited on the effects of treatments with estrogens, testosterone, and DHEA. The effect of androgen replacement therapies for improving orgasmic functioning in women with hormonal deficiencies is hard to interpret, as the majority of the studies have recruited women with HSDD, and their orgasmic capacities were not initially assessed.

Testosterone. In postmenopausal women with HSDD, use of testosterone improved orgasm domains in multiple assessment scales in some RCTs (Buster et al., 2005; Simon et al., 2005). However, in a DBRC progressive cohort study, effects of additional methyltestosterone to combined hormone therapy (estrogens and progestogens) did not show additional benefits (Penteado et al., 2008). A crossover designed RCT of testosterone cream in premenopausal women with low libido showed significant benefits of the cream beyond placebo for improving orgasm (Goldstat et al., 2003).

Tibolone administered to menopausal women has shown to improve sexual functioning, including orgasm, compared with placebo (Castelo-Branco et al., 2000; Kamenov, Todorova, & Christov, 2007), although results of another study did not support this finding (Kokcu, Cetinkaya, Yanik, Alper, & Malatyalioglu, 2000).

DHEA treatment in postmenopausal women with low libido did not show any significant difference in improving sexual dysfunction including orgasm (Panjari et al., 2009). However, there are studies that showed improvement in orgasms in postmenopausal women when different application sites were selected (Labrie et al., 2009; Munarriz et al., 2002).

It may be concluded that improvement in orgasm cannot be assessed in isolation from increased sexual desire and arousal. Further studies need to be conducted with women who suffer exclusively from FOD to assess drug-specific effects.

FOD due to medication side effects. A meta-analysis showed that agomelatine, amineptine, bupropion, moclobemide, mirtazapine, and nefazodone did not show any difference with placebo in causing orgasmic dysfunction, and these medications may be the choice of treatment in SSRI-induced FOD (Serretti & Chiesa, 2009). In cases where FOD is a result of medication side effect, clinicians may decide to wait and see if there is any spontaneous remission, reduce the dose, change the medication and give brief drug holidays, and/or add an antidote.

Psychosocial Interventions for Treatment of FOD

Woman experiencing acquired FOD due to sexual anxiety may benefit from systematic desensitization and sensate focus exercises (Sotile & Kilmann, 1978). Directed masturbation (DM) is the most frequently used technique in women who have lifelong primary anorgasmia with reported success rates of 80%–90% (LoPiccolo & Stock, 1986; Riley & Riley, 1978), whereas the same rate for secondary anorgasmia ranges from 10% to 75% (Fichten, Libman, & Brender, 1986). Another study showed the effectiveness of a technique called "coital alignment" for women with secondary anorgasmia. In this study (Hurlbert & Apt, 1995), 37% of women on coital alignment technique and 18% of women on DM technique reported ≥ 50% improvement in orgasmic ability during intercourse. Some women who learn to achieve orgasm with DM transfer this skill successfully to their sexual activity with their partners, whereas others who experience orgasm exclusively with masturbation need additional stimulation techniques during their sexual interaction. In summary, there is evidence that CBT is effective, especially with primary orgasmic disorders. Although a systems approach that emphasizes mutual responsibilities has been applied more to treatment of sexual interest and arousal disorders (Verhulst & Heiman, 1988), it may be interpreted as a potentially valuable approach that needs to be tested in FOD as well. Long-lasting debates and discussions are still made as to whether orgasm is essential for sexual satisfaction and if inability to orgasm during intercourse may always be considered as pathological. It is important to keep in mind that as clinicians, our treatment targets are mainly determined by our clients' demands and the fact that each woman is unique in her sensual and sexual responses and preferences.

Vaginismus

Vaginismus appears in 15%–17% of women demanding help (Spector & Carey, 1990). This is much less than 52% to 73% of all female referrals made to sexual dysfunction treatment centers in some more traditional collective cultures (Sungur, 2013). Although there is little agreement regarding definition and phenomenology of vaginismus, its psychosocial treatment is generally considered to be successful. Vaginismus is defined as genito-pelvic pain penetration disorder in DSM-5 (American Psychiatric Association, 2013).

Psychosocial Interventions for Vaginismus

Unfortunately, the focus of treatment has long been the management of symptoms and therefore fixing the vaginal spasm has been the major priority. A RCT showed modest improvement rates in reduction of fear of pain when treatment was given in a group format (Bergeron et al., 2001). CBT focusing on reduction of fear of penetration and avoidance behavior showed significant benefits in achieving full vaginal penetration (Hawton & Catalan, 1990). Another more recent study showed similar efficacy of CBT when compared with waiting list (ter Kuile et al., 2007). Two RCT (Schnyder, Schnyder-Luthi, Ballinari, & Blaser, 1998; ter Kuile et al., 2009) showed that therapist-aided exposure was more effective than self-exposure. A high success rate of 90% was reported in these studies, which were comparable with effect sizes in uncontrolled outcome studies. However, some precautions need to be considered during treatment of vaginismus. Conceptualizations based on penile-vaginal penetration or interference with coitus are not likely to be beneficial, as they are only based on the penetrative aspect of sexual relationship. Definitions focused on muscle spasms and treatments based on reducing the contractions bring the increasing risk of irrelevant treatments such as hymenectomy, local injections of botilinum toxin, local anaesthetics, and other peculiar so-called treatments, which are often conducted in traditional cultures (Sungur, 2013).

WHEN AND WHAT KIND OF APPROACH FOR TREATMENT OF SD

Psychosocial approaches seem to be the reasonable choice of treatment for those who do not and who cannot take drugs, who have not found drugs effective, who have partners with sexual problems, and who have relationship problems. Choice of treatment inevitably relies on the background training of the clinician. The aim today must be to move away from unidimensional technician type of therapist to the multiskilled clinician who is able to tackle not only sexual problems but also couple and individual problems. This is a necessity, as sexual behaviors cannot be considered in isolation from other psychological, health, couple, or family issues (Sungur, 1998). A skillful integration of sex and couple therapy techniques may help clients to take additional benefits in sexual dysfunctions, whereas sex therapy alone is not very effective unless general relationship issues are also handled. Combining psychosocial approaches with medical treatments for gaining additional benefits is rapidly gaining more interest and attention amongst professionals working in the field of SD. To date, there is neither a consensus nor an evidence-based accepted model for conducting combination treatment. It is not yet known whether a sequential or a concurrent combination model works better. Combining disorder-focused psychotherapy with medical interventions is likely to improve outcome and reduce treatment blocks. In the future, it is expected that new treatment paradigms will emerge, and combined treatments will be the standard care for treatment of male and female SD.

FUTURE DIRECTIONS, RECOMMENDATIONS, AND CONCERNS

One basic direction that can be predicted for the future is the development of new drugs that will be used particularly in the area of FSD. Improved understanding of sexual physiology in women is likely to continue. No doubt, there is still room for improvement of pharmacotherapy used in the area of male SD and especially in the treatment of PE and HSDD. The search for effective and safe new drugs will hopefully result in new solutions for the needs of elderly people. Closer liaison and collaboration is required between sex therapists and healthcare providers in other disciplines, leading to access to the benefits of a multidisciplinary type of approach (Sungur, 1997). Additionally, there is need for more effective treatment approaches for people who have physical and mental disabilities. In order to prevent the area of sex from being over medicalized, further RCT conducted with bigger populations are required to evaluate the efficacy of psychosocial treatments. Most of the studies concerning effectiveness of psychotherapy are not controlled, and are conducted with small groups. Overemphasis on biological causes for SD, the tendency to find simple (quick fix) solutions for complex problems, and the strong influence of the drug industry are some risk factors that might lead to further medicalization in the area of sexual medicine.

No doubt a high prevalence of SD and an increasing demand for sexual help makes easy "access" a necessity, especially for those who do not have access to face-to-face treatment (Leiblum, 2007). Delivery systems of professional help are likely to expand to include long-distance counseling or treatment via Internet. The future of sex therapy will depend on which people practice this kind of approach and how it is practiced. Effective and ethical ways to function as a sex therapist wait to be redefined and reevaluated. Training and supervising mental health professionals working in the area of SD is another necessity. Establishing effective ways of helping gay, lesbian, bisexual, and transgender individuals (LGBT) is another important challenge for the future. A culturally sensitive approach is another issue in treatment, as cultural case formulations and conceptualizations provide clinicians with further tools for better understanding the unique character of each individual case (Sungur, 2013).

Modern sex therapy is far more than simple application of specific techniques developed for treatment of specific sexual dysfunctions. How the therapy should be best tailored to the particular needs of each person or couple is a significant question to be considered during treatment (Sungur, 1998). Sex therapy is obviously an ambiguous term. Binik and Meana's article (2009) points to this vagueness and criticizes sex therapy in a very informative, acknowledging, and thought-provoking manner. The future of sex therapy relies on how sex therapists are defined and what they do. Therapists from around the world are expected to describe operationally what they do with clients. Additionally, one of the main requirements for the evolution of psychotherapy from art to clinical science is to establish a common psychotherapy language. The absence of a common language for psychotherapy procedures leads different therapists to use different terms to describe the same procedure and/or the same term to describe different procedures. This often confuses professionals and patients. A shared language would reduce confusion and speed psychotherapy's evolution into a science. Some other significant questions that need to be answered to improve sex therapy can be listed as follows: What kind of background is necessary in order to conduct sex therapy both ethically and effectively? Should sex therapists be professionals working in the area of mental health, or can they also be nonprofessionals who have access to effective training? What are the essential components of effective sex therapy training? Does effective sex therapy training result in improved therapist competence and patient outcome? More research should be conducted regarding predictors of short- and long-term outcome in sex therapy.

REFERENCES

Abdel-Hamid, I. A., El Naggar, E. A., & El Gilany, A. H. (2001). Assessment of as needed use of pharmacotherapy and the pause-squeeze technique in premature ejaculation. *International Journal of Impotence Research, 13,* 41–45.

Abdo, C. H., Afif-Abdo, J., Otani, F., & Machado, A. C. (2008). Sexual satisfaction among patients with erectile dysfunction treated with counseling, sildenafil, or both. *The Journal of Sexual Medicine, 5,* 1720–1726.

Althof, S. E., Abdo, C. H., Dean, J., Hackett, G., McCabe, M., McMahon, C. G., . . . International Society for Sexual Medicine. (2010). International society for sexual medicine's guidelines for the diagnosis and treatment of premature ejaculation. *The Journal of Sexual Medicine, 7*, 2947–2969.

Apperloo, M., Midden, M., van der Stege, J., Wouda, J., Hoek, A., & Weijmar Schultz, W. (2006). Vaginal application of testosterone: A study on pharmacokinetics and the sexual response in healthy volunteers. *The Journal of Sexual Medicine, 3*, 541–549.

American Psychiatric Association. (2000). *Diagnostic and statistical manual of mental disorders* (4th ed., text rev.). Washington, DC: Author.

American Psychiatric Association. (2013). *Diagnostic and statistical manual of mental disorders* (5th ed.) Washington, DC.

Aversa, A., Pili, M., Francomano, D., Bruzziches, R., Spera, E., La Pera, G., & Spera, G. (2009). Effects of vardenafil administration on intravaginal ejaculatory latency time in men with lifelong premature ejaculation. *International Journal of Impotence Research, 21*, 221–227.

Banner, L. L., & Anderson, R. U. (2007). Integrated sildenafil and cognitive-behavior sex therapy for psychogenic erectile dysfunction: A pilot study. *The Journal of Sexual Medicine, 4*, 1117–1125.

Bar-Or, D., Salottolo, K. M., Orlando, A., Winkler, J. V., & Tramadol ODT Study Group. (2012). A randomized double-blind, placebo-controlled multicenter study to evaluate the efficacy and safety of two doses of the tramadol orally disintegrating tablet for the treatment of premature ejaculation within less than 2 minutes. *European Urology, 61*, 736–743.

Basson, R., & Brotto, L. A. (2003). Sexual psychophysiology and effects of sildenafil citrate in oestrogenised women with acquired genital arousal disorder and impaired orgasm: A randomised controlled trial. *BJOG: An International Journal of Obstetrics and Gynaecology, 110*, 1014–1024.

Basson, R., Leiblum, S., Brotto, L., Derogatis, L., Fourcroy, J., Fugl-Meyer, K., . . . Schultz, W. W. (2003). Definitions of women's sexual dysfunction reconsidered: Advocating expansion and revision. *Journal of Psychosomatic Obstetrics and Gynaecology, 24*, 221–229.

Basson, R., Wierman, M. E., van Lankveld, J., & Brotto, L. (2010). Summary of the recommendations on sexual dysfunctions in women. *The Journal of Sexual Medicine, 7*, 314–326.

Bechara, A., Bertolino, M. V., Casabe, A., & Fredotovich, N. (2004). A double-blind randomized placebo control study comparing the objective and subjective changes in female sexual response using sublingual apomorphine. *The Journal of Sexual Medicine, 1*, 209–214.

Bergeron, S., Binik, Y. M., Khalife, S., Pagidas, K., Glazer, H. I., Meana, M., & Amsel, R. (2001). A randomized comparison of group cognitive behavioral therapy, surface electromyographic biofeedback, and vestibulectomy in the treatment of dyspareunia resulting from vulvar vestibulitis. *Pain, 91*, 297–306.

Binik, Y. M., & Meana, M. (2009). The future of sex therapy: Specialization or marginalization? *Archives of Sexual Behavior, 38*, 1016–1027.

Brotto, L. A., Basson, R., & Luria, M. (2008). A mindfulness-based group psychoeducational intervention targeting sexual arousal disorder in women. *The Journal of Sexual Medicine, 5*, 1646–1659.

Buster, J. E., Kingsberg, S. A., Aguirre, O., Brown, C., Breaux, J. G., Buch, A., . . . Casson, P. (2005). Testosterone patch for low sexual desire in surgically menopausal women: A randomized trial. *Obstetrics and Gynecology, 105*, 944–952.

Carson, C. C., Rajfer, J., Eardley, I., Carrier, S., Denne, J. S., Walker, D. J., . . . Cordell, W. H. (2004). The efficacy and safety of tadalafil: An update. *BJU International, 93*, 1276–1281.

Caruso, S., Agnello, C., Intelisano, G., Farina, M., Di Mari, L., & Cianci, A. (2004). Placebo-controlled study on efficacy and safety of daily apomorphine SL intake in premenopausal women affected by hypoactive sexual desire disorder and sexual arousal disorder. *Urology, 63*, 955–959.

Caruso, S., Intelisano, G., Farina, M., Di Mari, L., & Agnello, C. (2003). The function of sildenafil on female sexual pathways: A double-blind, cross-over, placebo-controlled study. *European Journal of Obstetrics, Gynecology, and Reproductive Biology, 110*, 201–206.

Castelo-Branco, C., Vicente, J. J., Figueras, F., Sanjuan, A., Martinez de Osaba, M. J., Casals, E., . . . Vanrell, J. A. (2000). Comparative effects of estrogens plus androgens and tibolone on bone, lipid pattern and sexuality in postmenopausal women. *Maturitas, 34*, 161–168.

Cavalcanti, A. L., Bagnoli, V. R., Fonseca, A. M., Pastore, R. A., Cardoso, E. B., Paixao, J. S., . . . Baracat, E. C. (2008). Effect of sildenafil on clitoral blood flow and sexual response in postmenopausal women with orgasmic dysfunction. *International Journal of Gynaecology and Obstetrics: The Official Organ of the International Federation of Gynaecology and Obstetrics, 102*, 115–119.

Chivers, M. L., & Bailey, J. M. (2005). A sex difference in features that elicit genital response. *Biological Psychology, 70*, 115–120.

Chivers, M. L., & Rosen, R. C. (2010). Phosphodiesterase type 5 inhibitors and female sexual response: Faulty protocols or paradigms? *The Journal of Sexual Medicine, 7*, 858–872.

Conaglen, H. M., & Conaglen, J. V. (2008). Investigating women's preference for sildenafil or tadalafil use by their partners with erectile dysfunction: The partners' preference study. *The Journal of Sexual Medicine, 5*, 1198–1207.

Crenshaw, T. L., Goldberg, J. P., & Stern, W. C. (1987). Pharmacologic modification of psychosexual dysfunction. *Journal of Sex & Marital Therapy, 13*, 239–252.

De Amicis, L. A., Goldberg, D. C., LoPiccolo, J., Friedman, J., & Davies, L. (1985). Clinical follow-up of couples treated for sexual dysfunction. *Archives of Sexual Behavior, 14*, 467–489.

de Carufel, F., & Trudel, G. (2006). Effects of a new functional-sexological treatment for premature ejaculation. *Journal of Sex & Marital Therapy, 32,* 97–114.

Derogatis, L. R., Komer, L., Katz, M., Moreau, M., Kimura, T., Garcia, M., Jr., . . . VIOLET Trial Investigators. (2012). Treatment of hypoactive sexual desire disorder in premenopausal women: Efficacy of flibanserin in the VIOLET study. *The Journal of Sexual Medicine, 9,* 1074–1085.

Diamond, L. E., Earle, D. C., Heiman, J. R., Rosen, R. C., Perelman, M. A., & Harning, R. (2006). An effect on the subjective sexual response in premenopausal women with sexual arousal disorder by bremelanotide (PT-141), a melanocortin receptor agonist. *The Journal of Sexual Medicine, 3,* 628–638.

Dinsmore, W. W., Gingell, C., Hackett, G., Kell, P., Savage, D., Oakes, R., & Frentz, G. D. (1999). Treating men with predominantly nonpsychogenic erectile dysfunction with intracavernosal vasoactive intestinal polypeptide and phentolamine mesylate in a novel auto-injector system: A multicentre double-blind placebo-controlled study. *BJU International, 83,* 274–279.

Eardley, I., Wright, P., MacDonagh, R., Hole, J., & Edwards, A. (2004). An open-label, randomized, flexible-dose, crossover study to assess the comparative efficacy and safety of sildenafil citrate and apomorphine hydrochloride in men with erectile dysfunction. *BJU International, 93,* 1271–1275.

Ernst, E., & Pittler, M. H. (1998). Yohimbine for erectile dysfunction: A systematic review and meta-analysis of randomized clinical trials. *The Journal of Urology, 159,* 433–436.

Everaerd, W., & Dekker, J. (1985). Treatment of male sexual dysfunction: Sex therapy compared with systematic desensitization and rational emotive therapy. *Behaviour Research and Therapy, 23,* 13–25.

Feldman, H. A., Goldstein, I., Hatzichristou, D. G., Krane, R. J., & McKinlay, J. B. (1994). Impotence and its medical and psychosocial correlates: Results of the Massachusetts Male Aging Study. *The Journal of Urology, 151,* 54–61.

Fichten, C. S., Libman, E., & Brender, W. (1986). Measurement of therapy outcome and maintenance of gains in the behavioral treatment of secondary orgasmic dysfunction. *Journal of Sex & Marital Therapy, 12,* 22–34.

Fink, H. A., MacDonald, R., Rutks, I. R., & Wilt, T. J. (2003). Trazodone for erectile dysfunction: A systematic review and meta-analysis. *BJU International, 92,* 441–446.

Giuliano, F., Montorsi, F., Mirone, V., Rossi, D., & Sweeney, M. (2000). Switching from intracavernous prostaglandin E1 injections to oral sildenafil citrate in patients with erectile dysfunction: Results of a multicenter European study. The Sildenafil Multicenter Study Group. *The Journal of Urology, 164,* 708–711.

Glina, S., Fonseca, G. N., Bertero, E. B., Damiao, R., Rocha, L. C., Jardim, C. R., . . . Pagani, E. (2010). Efficacy and tolerability of lodenafil carbonate for oral therapy of erectile dysfunction: A phase III clinical trial. *The Journal of Sexual Medicine, 7*(5), 1928–1936.

Goldstat, R., Briganti, E., Tran, J., Wolfe, R., & Davis, S. R. (2003). Transdermal testosterone therapy improves well-being, mood, and sexual function in premenopausal women. *Menopause (New York, N.Y.), 10*(5), 390–398.

Goldstein, I., Lue, T. F., Padma-Nathan, H., Rosen, R. C., Steers, W. D., & Wicker, P. A. (1998). Oral sildenafil in the treatment of erectile dysfunction. Sildenafil Study Group. *The New England Journal of Medicine, 338,* 1397–1404.

Goldstein, I., McCullough, A. R., Jones, L. A., Hellstrom, W. J., Bowden, C. H., Didonato, K., . . . Day, W. W. (2012). A randomized, double-blind, placebo-controlled evaluation of the safety and efficacy of avanafil in subjects with erectile dysfunction. *The Journal of Sexual Medicine, 9,* 1122–1133.

Hatzichristou, D. G., Apostolidis, A., Tzortzis, V., Ioannides, E., Yannakoyorgos, K., & Kalinderis, A. (2000). Sildenafil versus intracavernous injection therapy: Efficacy and preference in patients on intracavernous injection for more than 1 year. *The Journal of Urology, 164,* 1197–1200.

Hawton, K., & Catalan, J. (1990). Sex therapy for vaginismus: Characteristics of couples and treatment outcome. *Sexual and Marital Therapy, 5,* 39–48.

Heiman J. R., Epps P. H., & Ellis B. (1995). Treating sexual desire disorders in couples. In N. S. Jacobson, A. S. Gurman, (Ed.) *Clinical handbook of couple therapy* (pp. 471–495). New York: The Guilford Press.

Hellstrom, W. J., Gittelman, M., Karlin, G., Segerson, T., Thibonnier, M., Taylor, T., & Padma-Nathan, H. (2002). Vardenafil for treatment of men with erectile dysfunction: Efficacy and safety in a randomized, double-blind, placebo-controlled trial. *Journal of Andrology, 23,* 763–771.

Hurlbert, D. F. (1993). A comparative study using orgasm consistency training in the treatment of women reporting hypoactive sexual desire. *Journal of Sex & Marital Therapy, 19,* 41–55.

Hurlbert, D. F., & Apt, C. (1995). The coital alignment technique and directed masturbation: A comparative study on female orgasm. *Journal of Sex & Marital Therapy, 21,* 21–29.

Isidori, A. M., Giannetta, E., Gianfrilli, D., Greco, E. A., Bonifacio, V., Aversa, A., . . . Lenzi, A. (2005). Effects of testosterone on sexual function in men: Results of a meta-analysis. *Clinical Endocrinology, 63,* 381–394.

Kaplan, H. S. (1974). *The new sex therapy.* New York: Brunner/Mazel.

Kaplan, S. A., Reis, R. B., Kohn, I. J., Ikeguchi, E. F., Laor, E., Te, A. E., & Martins, A. C. (1999). Safety and efficacy of sildenafil in postmenopausal women with sexual dysfunction. *Urology, 53,* 481–486.

Kamenov, Z. A., Todorova, M. K., & Christov, V. G. (2007). Effect of tibolone on sexual function in late postmenopausal women. *Folia Medica, 49,* 41–48.

Kokcu, A., Cetinkaya, M. B., Yanik, F., Alper, T., & Malatyalioglu, E. (2000). The comparison of effects of tibolone and conjugated estrogen-medroxyprogesterone acetate therapy on sexual performance in postmenopausal women. *Maturitas, 36*(1), 75–80.

Laan, E., van Lunsen, R. H., & Everaerd, W. (2001). The effects of tibolone on vaginal blood flow, sexual desire and arousability in postmenopausal women. *Climacteric: The Journal of the International Menopause Society, 4*, 28–41.

Labrie, F., Archer, D., Bouchard, C., Fortier, M., Cusan, L., Gomez, J. L., . . . Balser, J. (2009). Effect of intravaginal dehydroepiandrosterone (prasterone) on libido and sexual dysfunction in postmenopausal women. *Menopause (New York, N.Y.), 16*, 923–931.

Leiblum, S. R. (2007). Sex therapy today. In S.R. Leiblum (Ed.), *Principles and practice of sex therapy* (4th ed., pp. 3–22). New York: The Guilford Press.

Li, P., Zhu, G. S., Xu, P., Sun, L. H., & Wang, P. (2006). Interventional effect of behaviour psychotherapy on patients with premature ejaculation. *Zhonghua Nan Ke Xue, 12*, 717–719.

Liao, Q., Zhang, M., Geng, L., Wang, X., Song, X., Xia, P., . . . Liu, V. (2008). Efficacy and safety of alprostadil cream for the treatment of female sexual arousal disorder: A double-blind, placebo-controlled study in Chinese population. *The Journal of Sexual Medicine, 5*, 1923–1931.

LoPiccolo, J., & Stock, W. E. (1986). Treatment of sexual dysfunction. *Journal of Consulting and Clinical Psychology, 54*, 158–167.

Lovas, K., Gebre-Medhin, G., Trovik, T. S., Fougner, K. J., Uhlving, S., Nedrebo, B. G., . . . Husebye, E. S. (2003). Replacement of dehydroepiandrosterone in adrenal failure: No benefit for subjective health status and sexuality in a 9-month, randomized, parallel group clinical trial. *The Journal of Clinical Endocrinology and Metabolism, 88*, 1112–1118.

Masters, W. H., & Johnson, V. E. (1966). *Human sexual response.* Toronto; New York: Bantam Books.

Masters, W. H. & Johnson, V. E. (1970). *Human sexual inadequacy.* Toronto; New York: Bantam Books.

Mathews, A., Bancroft, J., Whitehead, A., Hackmann, A., Julier, D., Bancroft, J., . . . Shaw, P. (1976). The behavioural treatment of sexual inadequacy: A comparative study. *Behaviour Research and Therapy, 14*, 427–436.

Mattos, R. M., Marmo Lucon, A., & Srougi, M. (2008). Tadalafil and fluoxetine in premature ejaculation: Prospective, randomized, double-blind, placebo-controlled study. *Urologia Internationalis, 80*, 162–165.

McCabe, M. P., Price, E., Piterman, L., & Lording, D. (2008). Evaluation of an Internet-based psychological intervention for the treatment of erectile dysfunction. *International Journal of Impotence Research, 20*(3), 324–330.

McMahon, C. (2004). Efficacy and safety of daily tadalafil in men with erectile dysfunction previously unresponsive to on-demand tadalafil. *The Journal of Sexual Medicine, 1*, 292–300.

McMahon, C. G. (2008). The DSM-IV-TR definition of premature ejaculation and its impact upon the results of epidemiological studies. *European Urology, 53*, 887–889.

McMahon, C. G., Althof, S. E., Kaufman, J. M., Buvat, J., Levine, S. B., Aquilina, J. W., . . . Porst, H. (2011). Efficacy and safety of dapoxetine for the treatment of premature ejaculation: Integrated analysis of results from five phase 3 trials. *The Journal of Sexual Medicine, 8*, 524–539.

McMahon, C. G., McMahon, C. N., Leow, L. J., & Winestock, C. G. (2006). Efficacy of type-5 phosphodiesterase inhibitors in the drug treatment of premature ejaculation: A systematic review. *BJU International, 98*, 259–272.

McMahon, C. G., Stuckey, B. G., Andersen, M., Purvis, K., Koppiker, N., Haughie, S., & Boolell, M. (2005). Efficacy of sildenafil citrate (Viagra) in men with premature ejaculation. *The Journal of Sexual Medicine, 2*, 368–375.

Melnik, T., & Abdo, C. H. (2005). Psychogenic erectile dysfunction: Comparative study of three therapeutic approaches. *Journal of Sex & Marital Therapy, 31*, 243–255.

Melnik, T., Abdo, C. H., de Moraes, J. F., & Riera, R. (2012). Satisfaction with the treatment, confidence and "naturalness" in engaging in sexual activity in men with psychogenic erectile dysfunction: Preliminary results of a randomized controlled trial of three therapeutic approaches. *BJU International, 109*, 1213–1219.

Melnik, T., Soares, B. G., & Nasselo, A. G. (2007). Psychosocial interventions for erectile dysfunction. *Cochrane Database of Systematic Reviews (Online), 3*(3), CD004825.

Modell, J. G., May, R. S., & Katholi, C. R. (2000). Effect of bupropion-SR on orgasmic dysfunction in nondepressed subjects: A pilot study. *Journal of Sex & Marital Therapy, 26*, 231–240.

Moncada, I., Jara, J., Subira, D., Castano, I., & Hernandez, C. (2004). Efficacy of sildenafil citrate at 12 hours after dosing: Re-exploring the therapeutic window. *European Urology, 46*, 357–360; discussion 360–361.

Montorsi, F., Padma-Nathan, H., Buvat, J., Schwaibold, H., Beneke, M., Ulbrich, E., . . . ardenafil Study Group. (2004). Earliest time to onset of action leading to successful intercourse with vardenafil determined in an at-home setting: A randomized, double-blind, placebo-controlled trial. *The Journal of Sexual Medicine, 1*, 168–178.

Morales, A., Barada, J., & Wyllie, M. G. (2007). A review of the current status of topical treatments for premature ejaculation. *BJU International, 100*, 493–501.

Morales, A. M., Casillas, M., & Turbi, C. (2011). Patients' preference in the treatment of erectile dysfunction: A critical review of the literature. *International Journal of Impotence Research, 23*, 1–8.

Munarriz, R., Talakoub, L., Flaherty, E., Gioia, M., Hoag, L., Kim, N. N., . . . Spark, R. (2002). Androgen replacement therapy with dehydroepiandrosterone for androgen insufficiency and female sexual dysfunction: Androgen and questionnaire results. *Journal of Sex & Marital Therapy, 28*(Suppl. 1), 165–173.

Munjack, D. J., Schlaks, A., Sanchez, V. C., Usigli, R., Zulueta, A., & Leonard, M. (1984). Rational-emotive therapy in the treatment of erectile failure: An initial study. *Journal of Sex & Marital Therapy, 10,* 170–175.

Myers, L. S., Dixen, J., Morrissette, D., Carmichael, M., & Davidson, J. M. (1990). Effects of estrogen, androgen, and progestin on sexual psychophysiology and behavior in postmenopausal women. *The Journal of Clinical Endocrinology and Metabolism, 70,* 1124–1131.

Nachtigall, L., Casson, P., Lucas, J., Schofield, V., Melson, C., & Simon, J. A. (2011). Safety and tolerability of testosterone patch therapy for up to 4 years in surgically menopausal women receiving oral or transdermal oestrogen. *Gynecological Endocrinology: The Official Journal of the International Society of Gynecological Endocrinology, 27,* 39–48.

Nurnberg, H. G., Hensley, P. L., Heiman, J. R., Croft, H. A., Debattista, C., & Paine, S. (2008). Sildenafil treatment of women with antidepressant-associated sexual dysfunction: A randomized controlled trial. *JAMA: The Journal of the American Medical Association, 300*(4), 395–404.

Oberg, K., Fugl-Meyer, A. R., & Fugl-Meyer, K. S. (2004). On categorization and quantification of women's sexual dysfunctions: An epidemiological approach. *International Journal of Impotence Research, 16,* 261–269.

O'Carroll, R. (1991). Sexual desire disorders: A review of controlled treatment studies. *Journal of Sex Research, 28*(4), 607–624.

Padma-Nathan, H., Brown, C., Fendl, J., Salem, S., Yeager, J., & Harningr, R. (2003). Efficacy and safety of topical alprostadil cream for the treatment of female sexual arousal disorder (FSAD): A double-blind, multicenter, randomized, and placebo-controlled clinical trial. *Journal of Sex & Marital Therapy, 29,* 329–344.

Padma-Nathan, H., Stecher, V. J., Sweeney, M., Orazem, J., Tseng, L. J., & Deriesthal, H. (2003). Minimal time to successful intercourse after sildenafil citrate: Results of a randomized, double-blind, placebo-controlled trial. *Urology, 62,* 400–403.

Paick, J. S., Ahn, T. Y., Choi, H. K., Chung, W. S., Kim, J. J., Kim, S. C., . . . Jung, H. G. (2008). Efficacy and safety of mirodenafil, a new oral phosphodiesterase type 5 inhibitor, for treatment of erectile dysfunction. *The Journal of Sexual Medicine, 5,* 2672–2680.

Paick, J. S., Kim, S. W., Yang, D. Y., Kim, J. J., Lee, S. W., Ahn, T. Y., . . . Kim, S. C. (2008). The efficacy and safety of udenafil, a new selective phosphodiesterase type 5 inhibitor, in patients with erectile dysfunction. *The Journal of Sexual Medicine, 5,* 946–953.

Panjari, M., Bell, R. J., Jane, F., Wolfe, R., Adams, J., Morrow, C., & Davis, S. R. (2009). A randomized trial of oral DHEA treatment for sexual function, well-being, and menopausal symptoms in postmenopausal women with low libido. *The Journal of Sexual Medicine, 6,* 2579–2590.

Park, H. J., Park, J. K., Park, K., Min, K., & Park, N. C. (2010). Efficacy of udenafil for the treatment of erectile dysfunction up to 12 hours after dosing: A randomized placebo-controlled trial. *The Journal of Sexual Medicine, 7,* 2209–2216.

Penteado, S. R., Fonseca, A. M., Bagnoli, V. R., Abdo, C. H., Junior, J. M., & Baracat, E. C. (2008). Effects of the addition of methyltestosterone to combined hormone therapy with estrogens and progestogens on sexual energy and on orgasm in postmenopausal women. *Climacteric: The Journal of the International Menopause Society, 11,* 17–25.

Perelman, M. A. (2005). Psychosocial evaluation and combination treatment of men with erectile dysfunction. *The Urologic Clinics of North America, 32*(4), 431–445, vi.

Porst, H., Sharlip, I. D., Hatzichristou, D., Rubio-Aurioles, E., Gittelman, M., Stancil, B. N., . . . Vardenafil Study Group. (2006). Extended duration of efficacy of vardenafil when taken 8 hours before intercourse: A randomized, double-blind, placebo-controlled study. *European Urology, 50,* 1086–1094; discussion 1094–1095.

Price, S. C., Reynolds, B. S., Cohen, B. D., Anderson, A. J., & Schochet, B. V. (1981). Group treatment of erectile by dysfunction for men without partners: A controlled evaluation. *Archives of Sexual Behavior, 10,* 253–268.

Rajfer, J., Aliotta, P. J., Steidle, C. P., Fitch, W. P., III, Zhao, Y., & Yu, A. (2007). Tadalafil dosed once a day in men with erectile dysfunction: A randomized, double-blind, placebo-controlled study in the US. *International Journal of Impotence Research, 19,* 95–103.

Riley, A. J., & Riley, E. J. (1978). A controlled study to evaluate directed masturbation in the management of primary orgasmic failure in women. *The British Journal of Psychiatry: The Journal of Mental Science, 133,* 404–409.

Rosen, R. C., Diamond, L. E., Earle, D. C., Shadiack, A. M., & Molinoff, P. B. (2004). Evaluation of the safety, pharmacokinetics and pharmacodynamic effects of subcutaneously administered PT-141, a melanocortin receptor agonist, in healthy male subjects and in patients with an inadequate response to Viagra. *International Journal of Impotence Research, 16,* 135–142.

Rosen, R. C., Fisher, W. A., Eardley, I., Niederberger, C., Nadel, A., Sand, M., & Men's Attitudes to Life Events and Sexuality (MALES) Study. (2004). The multinational men's attitudes to life events and sexuality (MALES) study: I. Prevalence of erectile dysfunction and related health concerns in the general population. *Current Medical Research and Opinion, 20,* 607–617.

Rosen, R. C., Padma-Nathan, H., Shabsigh, R., Saikali, K., Watkins, V., & Pullman, W. (2004). Determining the earliest time within 30 minutes to erectogenic effect after tadalafil 10 and 20 mg: A multicenter, randomized, double-blind, placebo-controlled, at-home study. *The Journal of Sexual Medicine, 1,* 193–200.

Safarinejad, M. R. (2008). Evaluation of the safety and efficacy of bremelanotide, a melanocortin receptor agonist, in female subjects with arousal disorder: A double-blind placebo-controlled, fixed dose, randomized study. *The Journal of Sexual Medicine, 5,* 887–897.

Safarinejad, M. R., Hosseini, S. Y., Asgari, M. A., Dadkhah, F., & Taghva, A. (2010). A randomized, double-blind, placebo-controlled study of the efficacy and safety of bupropion for treating hypoactive sexual desire disorder in ovulating women. *BJU International, 106,* 832–839.

Sarwer, D. B., & Durlak, J. A. (1997). A field trial of the effectiveness of behavioral treatment for sexual dysfunctions. *Journal of Sex & Marital Therapy, 23,* 87–97.

Schnyder, U., Schnyder-Luthi, C., Ballinari, P., & Blaser, A. (1998). Therapy for vaginismus: In vivo versus in vitro desensitization. *Canadian Journal of Psychiatry (Revue Canadienne De Psychiatrie), 43,* 941–944.

Segraves, R., Balon, R., & Clayton, A. (2007). Proposal for changes in diagnostic criteria for sexual dysfunctions. *The Journal of Sexual Medicine, 4,* 567–580.

Segraves, R. T., Clayton, A., Croft, H., Wolf, A., & Warnock, J. (2004). Bupropion sustained release for the treatment of hypoactive sexual desire disorder in premenopausal women. *Journal of Clinical Psychopharmacology, 24,* 339–342.

Semans, J. H. (1956). Premature ejaculation: A new approach. *Southern Medical Journal, 49,* 353–358.

Serretti, A., & Chiesa, A. (2009). Treatment-emergent sexual dysfunction related to antidepressants: A meta-analysis. *Journal of Clinical Psychopharmacology, 29,* 259–266.

Seyam, R., Mohamed, K., Akhras, A. A., & Rashwan, H. (2005). A prospective randomized study to optimize the dosage of trimix ingredients and compare its efficacy and safety with prostaglandin E1. *International Journal of Impotence Research, 17,* 346–353.

Shabsigh, R., Padma-Nathan, H., Gittleman, M., McMurray, J., Kaufman, J., & Goldstein, I. (2000). Intracavernous alprostadil alfadex is more efficacious, better tolerated, and preferred over intraurethral alprostadil plus optional actis: A comparative, randomized, crossover, multicenter study. *Urology, 55,* 109–113.

Shifren, J. L., Monz, B. U., Russo, P. A., Segreti, A., & Johannes, C. B. (2008). Sexual problems and distress in United States women: Prevalence and correlates. *Obstetrics and Gynecology, 112,* 970–978.

Simon, J., Braunstein, G., Nachtigall, L., Utian, W., Katz, M., Miller, S., . . . Davis, S. (2005). Testosterone patch increases sexual activity and desire in surgically menopausal women with hypoactive sexual desire disorder. *The Journal of Clinical Endocrinology and Metabolism, 90,* 5226–5233.

Somboonporn, W., Davis, S., Seif, M. W., & Bell, R. (2005). Testosterone for peri- and postmenopausal women. *Cochrane Database of Systematic Reviews (Online), 4*(4), CD004509.

Sotile, W. M., & Kilmann, P. R. (1978). Effects of group systematic desensitization on female orgasmic dysfunction. *Archives of Sexual Behavior, 7,* 477–491.

Spector, I. P., & Carey, M. P. (1990). Incidence and prevalence of the sexual dysfunctions: A critical review of the empirical literature. *Archives of Sexual Behavior, 19,* 389–408.

Stief, C., Padley, R. J., Perdok, R. J., & Sleep, D. J. (2002). Cross-study review of the clinical efficacy of apomorphine SL 2 and 3 mg: Pooled data from three placebo-controlled, fixed-dose crossover studies. *European Urology Supplements, 1,* 12–20.

Stravynski, A., Gaudette, G., Lesage, A., Arbel, N., Bounader, J., Lachance, L., . . . Sidoun, P. (2007). The treatment of sexually dysfunctional women without partners: A controlled study of three behavioural group approaches. *Clinical Psychology & Psychotherapy, 14,* 211–220.

Suckling, J., Lethaby, A., & Kennedy, R. (2006). Local oestrogen for vaginal atrophy in postmenopausal women. *Cochrane Database of Systematic Reviews (Online), 4*(4), CD001500.

Sungur, M. (1994). Evaluation of couples referred to a sexual dysfunction unit and prognostic factors in sexual and marital therapy. *Sexual and Marital Therapy, 9,* 251–265.

Sungur, M. Z. (1997). Sexual dysfunctions and infertility. *Sexual and Martial Therapy, 12,* 181–182.

Sungur, M. Z. (1998). Difficulties encountered during the assessment and treatment of sexual dysfunction–a Turkish perspective. *Sexual and Marital Therapy, 13,* 71–81.

Sungur, M. (2013). The role of cultural factors in the course and treatment of sexual problems. In K. S. Hall & C. A. Graham (Eds.), *The cultural context of sexual pleasure and problems* (1st ed., pp. 308–332). New York: Routledge.

ter Kuile, M. M., Bulte, I., Weijenborg, P. T., Beekman, A., Melles, R., & Onghena, P. (2009). Therapist-aided exposure for women with lifelong vaginismus: A replicated single-case design. *Journal of Consulting and Clinical Psychology, 77,* 149–159.

ter Kuile, M. M., van Lankveld, J. J., de Groot, E., Melles, R., Neffs, J., & Zandbergen, M. (2007). Cognitive behavioral therapy for women with lifelong vaginismus: Process and prognostic factors. *Behaviour Research and Therapy, 45,* 359–373.

Turner, L. A., Althof, S. E., Levine, S. B., Risen, C. B., Bodner, D. R., Kursh, E. D., & Resnick, M. I. (1989). Self-injection of papaverine and phentolamine in the treatment of psychogenic impotence. *Journal of Sex & Marital Therapy, 15,* 163–176.

Trudel, G., Marchand, A., Ravart, M., Aubin, S., Turgeon, L., & Fortier, P. (2001). The effect of a cognitive behavioral group treatment program on hypoactive sexual desire in women. *Sexual and Relationship Therapy, 16,* 145–164.

Tuiten, A., Van Honk, J., Koppeschaar, H., Bernaards, C., Thijssen, J., & Verbaten, R. (2000). Time course of effects of testosterone administration on sexual arousal in women. *Archives of General Psychiatry, 57,* 149–153; discussion 155–156.

Tuiten, A., van Honk, J., Verbaten, R., Laan, E., Everaerd, W., & Stam, H. (2002). Can sublingual testosterone increase subjective and physiological measures of laboratory-induced sexual arousal? *Archives of General Psychiatry, 59,* 465–466.

van Lankveld, J. D. M., Everaerd, W., & Grotjohann, Y. (2001). Cognitive behavioral bibliotherapy for sexual dysfunctions in heterosexual couples: A randomized waiting-list controlled clinical trial in the Netherlands. *Journal of Sex Research, 38,* 51–67.

van Lankveld, J. J., Leusink, P., van Diest, S., Gijs, L., & Slob, A. K. (2009). Internet-based brief sex therapy for heterosexual men with sexual dysfunctions: A randomized controlled pilot trial. *The Journal of Sexual Medicine, 6,* 2224–2236.

Verhulst, J., & Heiman, J. R. (1988). A systems perspective on sexual desire. In Sexual Desire Disorders. S. R. Leiblum & R. C. Rosen (Ed.), (pp. 243–267). New York: Guilford Press.

Waldinger, M. D., & Schweitzer, D. H. (2008). The use of old and recent DSM definitions of premature ejaculation in observational studies: A contribution to the present debate for a new classification of PE in the DSM-V. *The Journal of Sexual Medicine, 5,* 1079–1087.

Waldinger, M. D., Zwinderman, A. H., Schweitzer, D. H., & Olivier, B. (2004). Relevance of methodological design for the interpretation of efficacy of drug treatment of premature ejaculation: A systematic review and meta-analysis. *International Journal of Impotence Research, 16,* 369–381.

Wessells, H., Gralnek, D., Dorr, R., Hruby, V. J., Hadley, M. E., & Levine, N. (2000). Effect of an alpha-melanocyte stimulating hormone analog on penile erection and sexual desire in men with organic erectile dysfunction. *Urology, 56,* 641–646.

West, S. L., Vinikoor, L. C., & Zolnoun, D. (2004). A systematic review of the literature on female sexual dysfunction prevalence and predictors. *Annual Review of Sex Research, 15,* 40–172.

Young, J. M., Feldman, R. A., Auerbach, S. M., Kaufman, J. M., Garcia, C. S., Shen, W., . . . Ahuja S. (2005). Tadalafil improved erectile function at twenty-four and thirty-six hours after dosing in men with erectile dysfunction: US trial. *Journal of Andrology, 26,* 310–318.

Yuan, P., Dai, J., Yang, Y., Guao, J., & Liang, R. (2008). A comparative study on treatment for premature ejaculation: Citalopram used in combination with behavioral therapy versus either citalopram or behavioral therapy alone. *Chinese Journal of Andrology, 22,* 35–38.

Zhao, C., Kim, S. W., Yang, D. Y., Kim, J. J., Park, N. C., Lee, S. W., . . . Park, J. K. (2011). Efficacy and safety of once-daily dosing of udenafil in the treatment of erectile dysfunction: Results of a multicenter, randomized, double-blind, placebo-controlled trial. *European Urology, 60,* 380–387.

Ziaei, S., Moghasemi, M., & Faghihzadeh, S. (2010). Comparative effects of conventional hormone replacement therapy and tibolone on climacteric symptoms and sexual dysfunction in postmenopausal women. *Climacteric: The Journal of the International Menopause Society, 13,* 147–156.

Zumbe, J., Porst, H., Sommer, F., Grohmann, W., Beneke, M., & Ulbrich, E. (2008). Comparable efficacy of once-daily versus on-demand vardenafil in men with mild-to-moderate erectile dysfunction: Findings of the RESTORE study. *European Urology, 54,* 204–210.

13

Integrating Psychopharmacology and Computer-Based Psychotherapy

John Greist

INTRODUCTION

It is obvious that both medications and psychotherapies work for many psychiatric disorders. Both modalities produce changes in neurotransmitters, neuromodulators, brain structures, and functioning. Despite treatment decision trees so plentiful it is difficult to see the forest, it remains difficult to predict for whom either modality or their combination will work best or be most acceptable. We remain guided largely by empirical trials with each patient, evaluating patient preference, risk/benefit ratio, past response, availability, and cost. Consideration of combination and augmentation therapies begins with this background of justifiable humility. Substitution of computer-based psychotherapies for human psychotherapists adds another variable in treatment decision making. This chapter addresses many of the issues regarding the development, evaluation, and implementation of computer-based psychotherapies and their combination with medications. We begin by considering medication combinations with psychotherapies provided by clinicians.

While it is logical that combining individually effective treatments should produce additive or synergistic effects, this logic does not always hold. But one example is the combination of potent serotonin reuptake inhibitors (SRIs) and cognitive-behavior therapy (CBT) for OCD. In children (March et al. 2004) and adults (Foa et al., 2005), SRIs are more efficacious than placebo, CBT more than twice as efficacious as SRIs by Yale–Brown Obsessive Compulsive Scale score reductions, and combined treatment surpasses CBT alone mainly in side effects (Figure 13.1).

Still, knowing that cohort results include individual patient results both better and worse than study means, continued trials of combinations are clearly warranted.

One interesting difference in both these OCD trials was significantly greater effect size for CBT at the Penn site with children than at Duke, and with a trend favoring Penn in the adult trial compared with Columbia. Conversely, Penn efficacy with SRIs lagged behind the other institution in both trials. As there was only a single baseline difference among many comparisons in the study populations in the adult trial and none in the pediatric trial, it seems probable that variables in psychotherapy and pharmacotherapy practice may explain these efficacy differences. Even at sites where intensive training and supervision of treatment are employed, standardization of psychotherapies remains a challenge. Disseminating faithful

Adult[1] and Pediatric[2] OCD Efficacy of SRIs and CBT Alone and in Combination – NIMH Grants

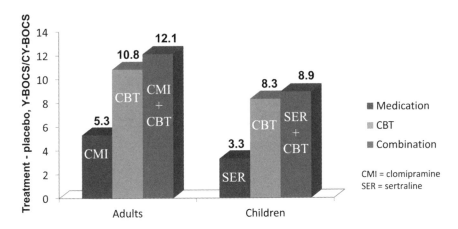

1. Foa et al. (2005) *American Journal of Psychiatry, 162*(1), 151-161.
2. March et al. (2004). *JAMA, 292*(16), 1969-1976.

Figure 13.1 Adult and pediatric OCD efficacy of SRIs and CBT alone and in combination.

facsimiles of RCT manual-based psychotherapies into routine care settings is even more diffi-cult. The fact that medication efficacy varied by institution bespeaks the difficulty of training clinicians and patients to employ even standardized medications systematically.

A similar efficacy result favoring CBT was found for chronic panic disorder with agora-phobia in a study completed in the United Kingdom and Canada 20 years ago (Marks et al., 1993). After 8 weeks in the randomized treatment trial,

> all four treatment groups (alprazolam and exposure [combined treatment]); or alprazolam and relaxation [a psychological placebo]; or placebo and exposure; or placebo and relaxation [double placebo], improved well on panic throughout. On non-panic measures, by the end of treatment, both alprazolam and exposure were effective, but exposure had twice the effect size of alpra-zolam. (Marks et al., 1993, p. 776)

After drug taper from 8 to 16 weeks and follow-up to week 43,

> gains after alprazolam were lost, while gains after exposure were maintained. Combining alpra-zolam with exposure marginally enhanced gains during treatment, but impaired improvement thereafter. . . . By the end of treatment, though gains on alprazolam were largely as in previous studies, on phobias and disability they were half those with exposure. Relapse was usual after alprazolam was stopped, whereas gains persisted to six-month follow-up after exposure ceased. Panic improved as much with placebo as with alprazolam or exposure. (Marks et al., 1993, p. 776)

PTSD paints a similar picture with guidelines from seven organizations on three conti-nents all strongly supporting "trauma-focused" psychotherapy, while most, but not all, rec-ognized "some benefit" from pharmacotherapy (Forbes et al., 2010).

In contrast, except in exceptional cases, few would think of treating schizophrenia or bipolar disorder with psychotherapy alone. Equally unthinkable would be providing medications for these disorders without at least supportive psychotherapy. But here the weight of efficacy evidence rests firmly with pharmacotherapy over psychotherapy.

A brief history and rationale for use of computer-based psychotherapies will be followed by a briefer review of the current status of combination therapy with medications and computer-based psychotherapies—necessarily briefer as few studies have been done.

Brief History of Computer-Based Therapies

When Warner Slack conducted the first patient–computer interviews (Slack et al., 1966), he rapidly recognized that the medium was capable of giving information to patients, as well as gathering information from them. Spontaneous responses during interviews indicated candor and transference unusual in doctor–patient interactions (e.g., "That's dumb. You already asked that question.").

The possibility of rough modeling of a psychotherapeutic relationship was also apparent in Joseph Weizenbaum's natural language parsing *Eliza* program that affected Rogerian therapy well enough that credible exchanges might continue for a few minutes (Weizenbaum, 1966). Ken Colby's simulation of the paranoid position passed the Turing test, as psychotherapists couldn't discern whether typed responses to their typed queries were generated by a person or a computer (Colby, 1972).

By the time Paulette Selmi submitted her doctoral dissertation "Computer-Assisted Cognitive-Behavior Therapy in the Treatment Of Depression" in 1983, the efficacy of CBT for depression was well described (Beck et al., 1979), although not accepted by many dynamic psychotherapists. Results of Selmi's RCT of 6-week acute treatment RCT with 2-month follow-up of computer-based cognitive-behavior therapy (CCBT) versus clinician CBT with wait list control waited 7 years before publication in the *American Journal of Psychiatry*, despite large effect sizes on all measures (e.g., 1.37 for Beck Depression Inventory) including small number needed to treat (1.59), where efficacy was indistinguishable from human CBT (Selmi, et al., 1990) (Figure 13.2.).

BT STEPS, a computer-based CBT for OCD developed in the mid-1990s, is familiar to the chapter author (Greist et al., 2002). The original BT STEPS combined a telephone-based interactive voice response (IVR) program with a text that patients used without therapist assistance to understand and implement exposure and ritual prevention (E&RP) treatment for their OCD. BT STEPS benefit was equal to that obtained from 12 hours of office-based therapy by experienced therapists plus homework for the 65% of BT STEPS patients who did at least one E&RP session guided by the computer (completer analysis) (Figure 13.3.).

In the intent-to-treat analysis, while clinician CBT had a larger effect size (1.22) than BT STEPS (0.84), both of which were larger than the relaxation control (0.35), there was no difference in reduction of hours per day obsessing and ritualizing for the therapies (3.36 and 3.44 hours, respectively), and both were larger than the relaxation control group (0.66 hours/ day) (Figure 13.4).

Consistent with the results above from Foa et al. (2005) and March et al. (2004) and relevant to our consideration of combining psychotherapy and medication, there was no difference in benefit for patients continuing SRIs (49%) and those who were not treated with SRIs.

The clear dose-response relationship seen in the BT STEPS RCT (Figure 13.5) was confirmed in a subsequent study of BT STEPS in a clinical care setting, which showed the value

Mean Beck Depression Inventory Scores
Computer vs. Therapist vs. Wait List

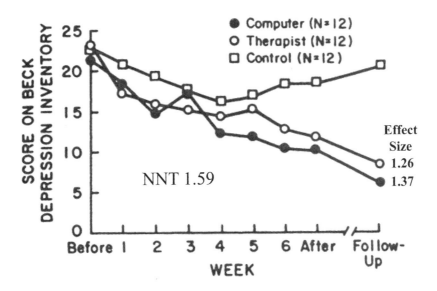

Selmi P.M, et al. (1990). *American Journal of Psychiatry, 147*, 1434-1439.

Figure 13.2 Change in Beck Depression Inventory scores with computer versus therapist CBT and wait control.

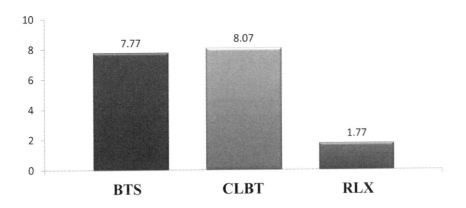

Greist et al. (2002). *Journal of Clinical Psychiatry, 63*, 138-145.

Figure 13.3 Completer analysis mean improvement in total Y-BOCS.

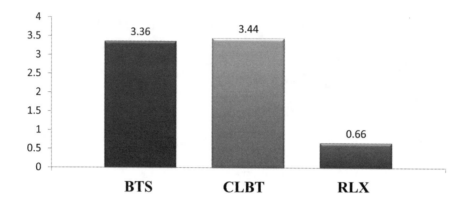

Greist et al. (2002). *Journal of Clinical Psychiatry, 63*, 138-145.

Figure 13.4 Mean reduction in rituals and obsessions hours/day.

Large Dose-Response Benefit

Y-BOCS Δ by # of BT STEPS E & RP Sessions

# Sessions	Y-BOCS Δ	p vs 0 Sessions
0	1.4	
1	6.2	.017
2-20	8.7	.001
>20	12.7	.003

Greist et al. (2002). *Journal of Clinical Psychiatry, 63*, 138-145.

Figure 13.5 Dose-response relationship between exposure and ritual prevention sessions with BT STEPS and reduction in Y-BOCS score.

of brief telephone coaching (Marks et al., 2003) to increase adherence and effect size (1.4) to a level comparable to clinician administered CBT.

Fear Fighter, (Hayward et al., 2007, p. 409), a CCBT program, has been used in rural areas where "[m]ajor improvements were obtained, with several large effect sizes, which remained at follow-up. It was concluded that computer-guided CBT can play a useful part in delivering CBT services in rural areas; and that self-help CBT may be the only treatment option available to some sufferers." Fear Fighter has been approved by the National Institute on Clinical Excellence (NICE) for use in the U.K. National Health Service.

Drug abuse/dependence is still another arena where positive results have been few and small with medications and psychotherapies. Against this difficult background, researchers at Yale reported a paradigm-shifting approach that closes the gap to cost effective real-world delivery of an efficacious CCBT program for substance dependence (Carroll et al., 2008). (Description of the Carroll et al. program is adapted from an editorial in the *American Journal of Psychiatry* by Greist, 2008.) Cleverly called CBT4CBT (computer-based training for cognitive behavioral therapy), this information age web-based program penetrates previously impregnable barriers to care delivery. Well-matched patients in a randomized controlled trial assigned to CBT4CBT plus treatment as usual had half as many positive urine specimens (2.2 versus 4.3 specimens, F = 6.18, p = 0.02, effect size d = 0.59) and longer urine-confirmed abstinence (22 versus 17 days, which while not statistically significantly longer, demonstrated a moderate effect size [d = 0.45]). Benefit persisted at 6-month follow up (Carroll et al., 2009).

How representative of the real world were the setting and patients in the study? A community-based outpatient substance abuse treatment program in Bridgeport, Connecticut, was the setting. Randomization worked, and treatment groups were balanced with regard to primary substance used, gender, and ethnicity. The population average age was 42 years, with a mean of 17 years of use of their primary substance of abuse. Fifty-eight percent were male, 46% African American, 34% European American, 12% Latin American, and 6% Native American. Twenty-two percent were married or in a stable relationship, 77% were unemployed, 37% on probation or parole, 27% sought treatment under duress from the criminal justice system, and 3 were arrested after randomization before participation in any treatment. Cocaine was the main drug problem for 59%, alcohol for 18%, opioids for 16%, and marijuana for 7%, while 80% used more than one drug. This was not a carriage trade setting or treatment population.

In 2007, a thorough review of computer-based psychotherapies (Marks et al., 2007) identified 97 computer therapy programs that had been tested in 175 studies including 103 randomized controlled trials of a wide range of psychiatric disorders, often with documented benefit.

By 2010, evidence supporting the benefit of CCBT was even stronger (Andrews et al., 2010). In 22 studies comparing CCBT with a control group for depression and panic, social anxiety, and generalized anxiety disorders, the effect size was 0.88 (NNT = 2.15), with improvement maintained for a median of 26 weeks. Five studies compared CCBT with face-to-face CBT, and both treatments were equally beneficial.

COMBINED/AUGMENTATION THERAPY

Thoughtful clinicians have speculated for decades about the possible additive or synergistic benefit of combining medications and psychotherapies. Two RCTs of CBT augmentation of SRI therapy for OCD support the value of the combination.

The first RCT added eighteen 45-minute clinician-administered CBT sessions plus homework to medication over 6 months, compared with four 30-minute pharmacotherapy sessions without CBT. Drug-only completer patients worsened, while CBT patients improved (+3.9 versus –3.9 change on Y-BOCS scores, respectively [p < 0.001]). Drug-only patients who received later CBT for 6 months also improved, though not significantly (Y-BOCS change –2.7 for completers) (Tenneij et al., 2005).

The second RCT compared addition of clinician-administered CBT or stress management training (SMT), a credible psychosocial control, to a mean of 64 weeks of SRI treatment. Each psychotherapy treatment provided two introductory planning sessions followed by 15 therapy sessions. CBT was significantly more efficacious than SMT (Y-BOCS score decreases of 11.2 and 3.6 points, respectively [p < 0.001; effect size = 1.31]; Simpson et al., 2008) (Figure 13.6).

Pharmacotherapy may also augment psychotherapy. d-cycloserine was shown to increase response to CBT in OCD (Wilhelm et al., 2008) (Figure 13.7), though the benefit may be more a speeding than augmentation of CBT's benefits (Chasson et al., 2010).

Accepting that some combinations of pharmacotherapy and psychotherapy have additive and possibly synergistic effects, what rationales support the use of CCBTs? Advantages of employing CCBT in clinical care are many. CCBT can help overcome the paucity of effective psychotherapists in both numbers and distribution. In our mind's eye, the ideal therapy might involve years with Freud. Poke-in-the-eye reality provides many patients with 15 minutes of Warholian fame with primary care clinicians hard-pressed by ever-growing nonclinical demands that distract from patient care. Even after CBT for OCD in adults and children has been proven more than twice as beneficial as FDA-approved pharmacotherapies (Foa et al., 2005; March et al., 2004), and is the preferred treatment of patients seeking care in a New York

CBT vs. SMT Augmentation in Resistant OCD

After a mean of *64 weeks* on adequate dose SRI

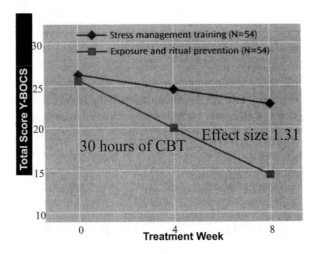

Simpson et al. (2008). *American Journal of Psychiatry, 163,* 6621-6630.

Figure 13.6 Effect of CBT and SMT as augmentation of SRI treatment.

D-Cycloserine* (n=13) vs. Placebo (n=13) in CBT for OCD

100 mg 1 hour before 10 twice weekly sessions

Enhances
short-term
learning and
memory

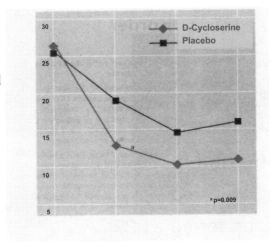

And treats
comorbid
TB!

Wilhelm et al. AJP. 2008;165:335-341

Figure 13.7 D-Cycleserine versus placebo in CBT for OCD.

City OCD treatment center (Patel & Simpson, 2010) (Figure 13.8), CBT for OCD remains rarely available. Only 5 of 40 mental health clinicians attending the 2012 26th Annual Door County Summer Institute Update on Pharmacotherapeutic Advances in the Treatment of Mood and Anxiety Disorders indicated they have referral access to high-quality CBT (J.G., personal communication, August 31, 2012).

Computer therapies offer truly standardized, measurement- and evidence-based care coupled with customization rivaling that of expert clinicians. Always available, computer therapies are most often used outside clinic office hours when therapists prefer not to work, but when patients find convenient. Web-based and IVR systems that provide access to programs via computers and smartphones don't require travel to a clinic and are often more comfortable for sensitive subjects, both topics and people, and lead to greater candor than face-to-face communications (Greist et al., 1973; Locke et al., 1992).

The study of computer therapies is easier than the study of therapies delivered by clinicians because of their perfectly standardized presentation of therapy components and the ease of applying component dismantling and addition protocols with large numbers of study participants. Proven improvements can be immediately available to subsequent users, a matter far different from effective continuing education of therapists. Delivered cost of CCBT can be substantially lower than for human therapists. The cost of developing CCBTs is a fraction of the cost of development of a new medication. A role for computer therapy in stepped care is a logical extender of the scarce resource of skilled human therapists, including assurance of programmed ego-free acknowledgement when CCBT isn't helping.

The advantages of computer therapy identified for clinical care apply to studies of CCBT in combination or augmentation with pharmacotherapies. Limitations of CCBT include the obvious: No therapy works for everyone, although CCBT programs should and usually do measure patient status and can refer patients elsewhere according to specified criteria. Early

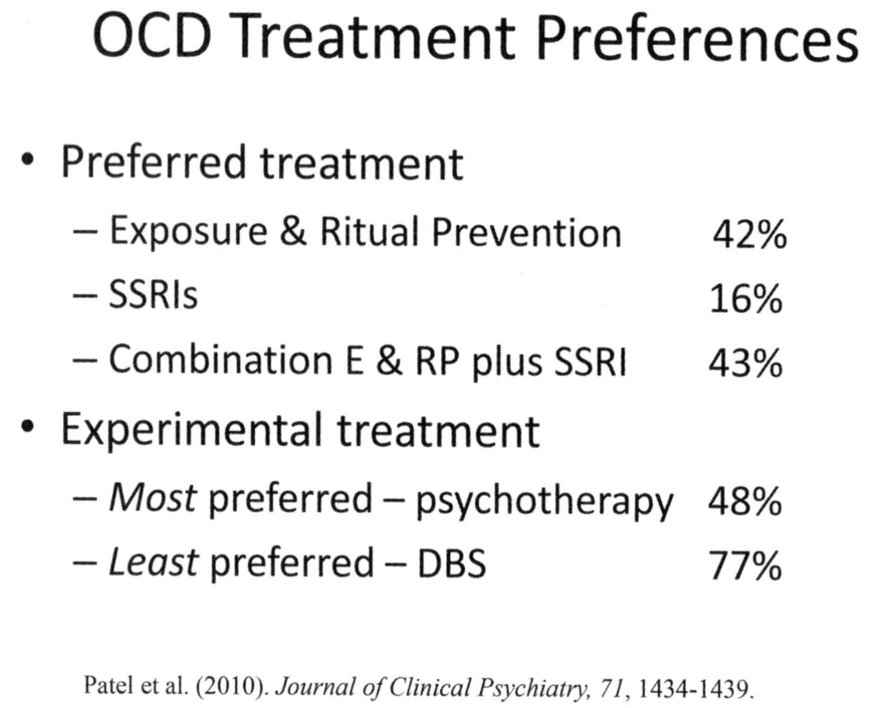

OCD Treatment Preferences

- Preferred treatment
  - Exposure & Ritual Prevention   42%
  - SSRIs   16%
  - Combination E & RP plus SSRI   43%
- Experimental treatment
  - *Most* preferred – psychotherapy   48%
  - *Least* preferred – DBS   77%

Patel et al. (2010). *Journal of Clinical Psychiatry, 71*, 1434-1439.

Figure 13.8 OCD treatment preferences.

stage programs won't best the best clinicians on their best days, though they can be improved through research and will at least provide a standardized level of care to every user. By analogy, there was a pair of quite famous six-game human-computer chess matches played between the IBM supercomputer Deep Blue and the World Chess Champion Garry Kasparov. The first match in 1996 Kasparov won 4–2, losing one game, drawing two, and winning three. A rematch, played in 1997, was won by Deep Blue 3 1/2–2 1/2.

Resistance to CCBT occurs on several levels. There is a general expectation that things on the web are free—or should be. Funding of development, evaluation, and delivery of CCBT may come from for-profit, not-for-profit, or government sources, with payment for use from equally varied sources. The cost of developing and evaluating a new CCBT is a fraction of the cost of a new medication.

The psychotherapy guild worries that its privileges and priorities, including income, are threatened by CCBT. To some degree, these concerns are correct. But as Warner Slack (1966) often observed in a jocular vein from the outset of direct patient–computer interactions, any doctor who can be replaced by a computer should be replaced by a computer. The benefit of coaching by individuals without clinical skills and with the goal not to do therapy but to increase adherence to effective programs has not been adequately studied, though its promise is real. The combination of computing programs and professionals across many professions complements, supplements, and augments what unaided professionals can provide. Computer programs safely land planes in poor visibility where humans cannot. Auto analyzers have essentially supplanted laboratory technicians. Specialization—in this instance, computers doing what computers do best and pharmacotherapists what they do best—optimizes functioning and patient outcomes.

It is hard for those in the pharmaceutical industry to shift to a view of itself as a healthcare industry, much as buggy whip manufacturers had difficulty shifting from their perspective, tradition, and product line at the birth of the automobile industry. There is potential for the pharmaceutical industry to develop a new CCBT product line that is efficacious, less expensive to develop than medications, protected not by patents but by continuous improvement based on data gathered through use, and easily and inexpensively disseminated as an integral part of stepped care.

Another obstacle to implementation of CCBT lies within the healthcare system itself. Even among well-intentioned practitioners, changes in practice patterns require adaptations that can be challenging. Electronic medical records provide obvious advantages and are being adopted widely and rapidly, though the learning curve in using them is steep and difficult enough that some practitioners retire when required to use a new electronic medical record system. CCBT is another computer system with marked advantages that requires changes in practice patterns—often simply remembering to utilize CCBT when patients would otherwise have no CBT available.

All of these resistances will abate and be swept away in the cross currents of need for equitable access to stepped and standardized evidence- and measurement-based care, limited human therapy capacity, Moore's law (Moore, 1965), improving CCBT quality, and increasing healthcare costs. To date, the manifest poor business skills of clinician developers have yet to overcome the obstacles to implementation, showing that clinician developers went to the wrong graduate school to do business.

One may speculate that the adoption of CCBT, with its *evolved endogenous pharmacotherapy* will occur at a pace quicker than the implementation of biomarkers in the pursuit of personalized medicine. Clinicians would rather have something that works well that's not well understood than understanding why something doesn't work.

We end where we began: Establishment of the value of combinations of effective medications and psychotherapies for medical disorders rests, as always, on careful research to identify strengths and weaknesses of each proposed combination. CCBTs standardize psychotherapies, reducing variability in this research, and have many other attributes that support prophecies of successful combinations with medications.

REFERENCES

Andrews, G., Cuijpers, P., Craske, M. G., McEvoy, P., & Titov N. (2010). Computer therapy for the anxiety and depressive disorders is effective, acceptable and practical health care: A meta-analysis. *PLoS One, 13*;5(10), e13196.

Beck, A. T., Rush, A. J., Shaw, B. F., Emery, G. (1979). *Cognitive therapy of depression.* New York: Guilford.

Carroll, K. M., Ball, S. A., Martino, S., Nich, C., Babuscio, T. A., Nuro, K. F., . . . Rounsaville, B. J. (2008). Computer-assisted delivery of cognitive behavioral therapy for addiction: A randomized trial of CBT4CBT. *American Journal of Psychiatry, 165,* 881–888.

Carroll, K. M., Ball, S. A., Martino, S., Nich, C., Babuscio, T. A., & Rounsaville, B. J. (2009). Enduring effects of a computer-assisted training program for cognitive behavioral therapy: A 6-month follow-up of CBT4CBT. *Drug and Alcohol Dependence, 100,* 178–181.

Chasson, G. S., Buhlmann, U., Tolin, D. F., Rao, S. R., Reese, H. E., Rowley, T., . . . Wilhelm, S. (2010). Need for speed: Evaluating slopes of OCD recovery in behavior therapy enhanced with d-cycloserine. *Behaviour and Research Therapy, 48,* 675–679.

Colby, K. M. (1972). Turing-like indistinguishability tests for the validation of a computer simulation of paranoid processes. *Artificial Intelligence, 3,* 199–221.

Foa, E. B., Liebowitz, M. R., Kozak, M. J., Davies, S., Campeas, R., Franklin, M. E., . . . Tu, X. (2005). Randomized, placebo-controlled trial of exposure and ritual prevention, clomipramine, and their combination in the treatment of obsessive-compulsive disorder. *American Journal of Psychiatry, 162,* 151–161.

Forbes, D., Creamer, M., Bisson, J. I., Cohen, J. A., Crow, B. E., Foa, E. B., . . . Ursano, R. J. (2010). A guide to guidelines for the treatment of PTSD and related conditions. *Journal of Traumatic Stress, 23,* 537–552.

Greist, J. H. (2008). A promising debut for computerized psychotherapies. *American Journal of Psychiatry, 165,* 793–795.

Greist, J. H., Gustafson, D. H., Stauss, F. F., Rowse, G. L., Laughren, T. P., & Chiles, J. A. (1973). A computer interview for suicide-risk prediction. *American Journal of Psychiatry, 130,* 1327–1332.

Greist, J. H., Marks, I. M., Baer, L., Kobak, K. A., Wenzel, K. W., Hirsch, M. J., . . . Clary, C. M. (2002). Behavior therapy for obsessive-compulsive disorder guided by a computer or by a clinician compared with relaxation as a control. *Journal of Clinical Psychiatry, 63,* 138–145.

Hayward, L., MacGregor, A. D., Peck, D. F., & Wilkes, P. (2007). The feasibility and effectiveness of computer-guided CBT (FearFighter) in a rural area. *Behavioural and Cognitive Psychotherapy, 35,* 409–419.

Locke, S. E., Kowaloff, H. B., Hoff, R. G., Safran, C., Popovsky, M. A., Cotton, D. J., . . . Slack, W. V. (1992). Computer-based interview for screening blood donors for risk of HIV transmission. *Journal of the American Medical Association, 268,* 1301–1305.

March, J. S., Foa, E., Gammon, P., Chrisman, A., Curry, J., Fitzgerald, D., . . . Tu, X. (2004). Cognitive behavior therapy, sertraline, and their combination for children and adolescents with obsessive-compulsive disorder: The pediatric OCD treatment study (POTS) randomized controlled trial. *JAMA, 292,* 1969–1976.

Marks, I. M., Cavanaugh, K., & Gega, L. (2007). *Hands-on help: Computer-aided psychotherapy.* Maudsley Monographs 49. A. S. David (Ed.). New York: Psychology Press.

Marks, I. M., Swinson, R. P., Baolu, M., Kuch, K., Noshirvani, H., O'Sullivan, G., . . . Sengun, S. (1993). Alprazolam and exposure alone and combined in panic disorder with agoraphobia. A controlled study in London and Toronto. *British Journal of Psychiatry, 162,* 776–787.

Moore, G. E. (1965). Cramming more components onto integrated circuits. *Electronics, 38,* 114.

Patel, S. R., & Simpson, H. B. (2010). Patient preferences for obsessive-compulsive disorder treatment. *Journal of Clinical Psychiatry, 71,* 1434–1439.

Selmi, P. M., Klein, M. H., Greist, J. H., Sorrell, S. P., & Erdman, H. P. (1990). Computer-administered cognitive behavioral therapy for depression. *American Journal of Psychiatry, 147,* 51–56.

Simpson, H. B., Foa, E. B., Liebowitz, M. R., Ledley, D. R., Huppert, J. D., Cahill, S., . . . Petkova, E. (2008). A randomized, controlled trial of cognitive behavioral therapy for augmenting pharmacotherapy in obsessive-compulsive disorder. *American Journal of Psychiatry, 165,* 621–630.

Slack, W. V, Hicks, G. P., Reed, C. E., Van Cura, L. J. (1966). A computer-based medical-history system. *New England Journal of Medicine, 274,* 194–198.

Tenneij, N. H., van Megen, H. J., Denys, D. A., & Westenberg, H. G. (2005). Behavior therapy augments response of patients with obsessive-compulsive disorder responding to drug treatment. *Journal of Clinical Psychiatry, 66,* 1169–1175.

Weizenbaum, J. (1966). ELIZA—a computer program for the study of natural language communication between man and machine. *Communications of the ACM, 9,* 36–45.

Wilhelm, S., Buhlmann, U., Tolin, D. F., Meunier, S. A., Pearlson, G. D., Reese, H. E., . . . Rauch, S. L. (2008). Augmentation of behavior therapy with d-cycloserine for obsessive-compulsive disorder. *American Journal of Psychiatry, 165,* 335–341.

14

A Delicate Balance
The Contribution of Psychosocial Factors to Biological Treatments of Mental Disorders

Roger P. Greenberg and Mantosh J. Dewan

INTRODUCTION

The following is a brief description of an actual case seen by one of us (RG) in his psychotherapy practice. The patient is a middle-aged man who was referred by his psychiatrist after a number of months of treatment on antidepressants. The patient, who had suffered with bouts of depression for most of his adult life, received some benefit from the initial course of medication treatment, but both he and his psychiatrist felt he might experience even more gains from the addition of psychotherapy treatment. The suspicion proved to be accurate. The patient was very responsive to talk therapy. Within a matter of a few months, several historical and interpersonal elements contributing to the patient's dysphoria were identified and discussed. Ways in which the patient distorted present experiences based on his past were uncovered, and the patient began to make changes in how he responded to others, how he dealt with important decisions, and how he assessed his perception of himself. His confidence improved, and symptoms of depression evaporated. Ultimately, positive feelings and a continued sense of stability led the patient—with the concurrence of his psychiatrist—to the decision to taper and eventually discontinue taking antidepressants. The positive outcome continued over the ensuing months.

However, one day the patient returned for a psychotherapy session and raised an issue that concerned him. He stated that his wife noticed that the bottle of antidepressant pills in the medicine chest had not been moved in some time and correctly concluded that her husband was no longer taking the medication. She had a very biological view of depression and was quite anxious that her husband would become depressed again if he was not continuing on the drug to "repair his body chemistry." The patient tried in vain to convince his wife that he was feeling fine, that stability without medication had now been in place for a long time, that he had a new outlook and tools for dealing with stressful events, and that he had discussed the situation with his mental health providers. Nonetheless, he was unable to allay her fears about the possible reappearance of depression. Therefore, the patient asked if he could bring his wife in for a joint session to discuss the issue.

When the wife came in with her husband, she expressed her anxiety about his not continuing to take pills. Her husband stated he had no objection to the pills and had experienced no side effects from them, but he thought they were now unnecessary. The wife was then asked if she would feel better and more relaxed if the patient was continuing to take pills. She said she would, and as a result, the husband agreed to begin taking pills again for a period of time if it would help his wife to feel calmer. This was envisioned to be a kind of anti-anxiety medication relief by proxy. He took the pills; she experienced the benefit. That plan was put into effect and lasted for a few months until the wife felt less anxious, more reassured, and open to his discontinuing the medication. He did so and has remained free of depression for a few years.

This case illustrates the role that expectations and beliefs can play in dealing with mental disorders. It also raises questions about the arbitrary distinctions sometimes made between biological and psychosocial treatments and aspects of human emotions. It is impressive how difficult it has been for investigators to arrive at a frame of reference that permits a clear distinction between the effects of "active psychotropic drugs" and the supposedly chemically inert "placebos." (For a lengthy discussion of this topic see Fisher & Greenberg, 1997.) At base, the presumed separation primarily results from the idea that active drug effects occur as a result of definable biochemical processes, while the placebo acts through psychological mechanisms. In truth, it can be argued that all effects occur in tissue, and neither effect is more biologically real than the other. Thus, a response to a psychotropic medication, a placebo, or psychotherapy can all be viewed as biological. Consider, for instance, the research suggesting that placebo effects are physiologically mediated by changes in endorphin levels (Evans, 1985); or the demonstration that placebo analgesia of pain is mediated by an endogenous opiate-related mechanism (Sauro & Greenberg, 2005); or the finding that successful psychotherapy treatment of obsessive-compulsive symptoms produces brain imagery changes that parallel those produced by drug therapy (Baxter et al., 1992); or that a common pattern of brain scan changes was identified in depressed patients who responded to treatment with either placebo or antidepressants (Mayberg et al., 2002).

This chapter is aimed at looking at what we now know in order to integrate psychosocial issues with medication management and make practical use of research findings for improving the process and outcome of treatment.

THE IMPACT OF PSYCHOSOCIAL FACTORS ON MEDICATION AND MEDICAL TREATMENTS

Typically it is assumed that medication treatments for mental disorders are powered by the chemical composition of the drugs with little to no effect resulting from psychosocial elements such as the nature of the drug setting, patient expectations, the attitude of the prescriber, or the quality of the doctor–patient relationship. Yet repeatedly, such psychosocial variables have turned out to play a significant part in whether the patient will achieve a satisfactory result (Dewan, Steenbarger, & Greenberg, 2008; Fisher & Greenberg, 1989; Fisher & Greenberg, 1997; Greenberg & Goldman, 2009; Kradin, 2008). In fact, evidence suggests that the majority of benefits provided by a variety of medical procedures and medications may be attributed to psychosocial or placebo effects. For example, placebos have been shown to account for more than 75% of the efficacy of antidepressants (Khan, Warner, & Brown, 2000; Kirsch, Moore, Scoboria, & Nicholls, 2002). Comparable results appeared in an even more recent meta-analytic study focused on all the drug trial data submitted to the Food and Drug Administration (FDA) on the newest class of antidepressants, the serotonin reuptake inhibitors (SSRIs) (Kirsch et al., 2008). Here analyses, based on both the published and unpublished data, showed that although on average all groups improved with treatment, there was virtually no difference between patients treated with placebos and those receiving the new generation drugs.

Such findings indicating the importance of psychosocial variables affecting medical outcomes are not restricted to psychiatric drug studies. Interesting and unexpected results are also obtained in reports on sham surgery, which put patients through a surgical experience without providing any surgical interventions considered to be specific to the condition being treated. Surprisingly, sham surgeries for osteoarthritis of the knee proved to be just as effective in reducing knee pain as the formerly accepted arthroscopic knee surgery had been (Moseley et al., 2002), and a double-blind sham surgery for stem-cell replacement in Parkinson's disease patients resulted in strong and enduring positive outcomes (McRae et al., 2004).

USEFUL FINDINGS FROM DEPRESSION TREATMENT RESEARCH

Evidence has emerged from studies on the effectiveness of antidepressants indicating that the same medications prescribed at the same dosages by different practitioners can produce significantly different results (Greenberg & Fisher, 1989; Greenberg & Fisher, 1997). An early example of this type of finding was presented by Greenblatt, Grosser, and Wechsler (1964). They published a multicenter study where improvement rates were compared for the same three antidepressant drugs using the same criteria for selection of depressed patients at three different hospitals. The rank order of treatment effectiveness among the hospitals was virtually the same no matter which treatment was used. One hospital consistently produced the best results, and another produced the worst. For instance, a comparison of the use of one of the antidepressants showed it was effective 67% of the time at the most effective hospital and only 31% of the time at the least effective medical center. Obviously, something other than the chemical composition of the medications was at play in the different settings.

Similarly, there is variability in drug effectiveness when prescribed by different clinicians. A good illustration of this occurs in the well-known National Institute of Mental Health (NIMH) Treatment of Depression Collaborative Research Program (TDCRP) (Elkin et al., 1989). Undoubtedly this was one of the largest, most publicized, and most ambitious studies of mental health treatments. It compared the treatment outcomes for 239 depressed patients seen at three different sites. Patients were randomly assigned to four different treatment conditions: cognitive-behavior therapy; interpersonal psychotherapy; imipramine plus clinical management; and a pill placebo plus clinical management control condition. Analyzing study results became a very complex task partly due to the number of different outcome measures and the many ways the patient sample could be configured. As Greenberg and Fisher (1997) indicated, some of the findings had a "now you see it, now you don't" quality because of the myriad ways the patient samples and the measures could be construed. Yet, one of the overarching conclusions was that each of the treatment conditions (including placebo) led to positive outcomes, and all were roughly equivalent in providing benefits for patients. Later analyses, juggling the data in new ways, went on to suggest the debated possibility of some of the treatments doing better with the more severely depressed patients.

For the purposes of this chapter, though, perhaps the findings of greatest interest appeared later on when looking at which factors led to the most reduction in patient depression. It turned out that the nature of the doctor–patient relationship or the level of therapeutic alliance (broadly defined as the collaborative bond between patient and clinician) exerted a strong and "very large effect" on outcome (Krupnick et al., 1996). In fact, to the astonishment of the researchers, the relationship ratings were as important for antidepressant outcome as they were for the outcome with psychotherapies or placebo. Improvement was significantly less related to the type of treatment received than to the quality of the relationship with their doctor that the patients experienced. This result is in accord with the Thase and Kupfer (1996) observation that 80% to 90% of the variability in outcome in treating most cases of depression can be accounted for by "nonspecific factors" such as clinical support.

Of special note, two studies by Blatt and his colleagues (Blatt, Sanislow, Zuroff, & Pilkonis, 1996; Blatt, Zuroff, Quinlan, & Pilkonis, 1996) explored the question of who were the most effective clinicians in the NIMH study, and what characteristics did they possess? They came to the conclusion that certain qualities were more common among the most successful practitioners whether they were providing psychotherapy or drug treatments. The more the clinicians were seen as empathic, caring, open, and sincere, the better their outcome ratings became. Relatedly, a cluster of characteristics described the most effective practitioners in the project. Again, it did not matter whether the treatments were psychotherapy or drugs. The most successful were those doctors who had a psychological rather than a biological orientation to the treatment of depression, those who in their regular clinical practices placed less emphasis on medication, and those who expected the outpatient treatment of depression would last for a longer period of time than did the less effective clinicians.

The idea that clinicians need to be especially sensitive, flexible, and tuned in to their impact on their relationship with patients is in keeping with modern research findings (Baldwin, Wampold, & Imel, 2007). In addition, providers who are able to adjust their interactions after obtaining feedback from patients about how the treatment is going obtain better outcomes (Lambert et al., 2003). It is also important for clinicians to promote an active collaboration in the treatment process. Patients who passively sit back, waiting for the drugs to provide the cure, are not likely to do as well as those who are led to be actively engaged in the process.

THE PROBLEM OF PATIENT TREATMENT ADHERENCE, PREMATURE TERMINATION, OR DROPOUT

Perhaps one of the most important psychosocial factors affecting whether treatment with drugs and/or psychotherapy will be beneficial is the patient's decision about whether to follow through on what is prescribed. For psychotherapy, this issue is often labeled premature termination or dropout, while drug providers describe the problem as treatment adherence. In either case, it is clear that benefits are limited when patients do not comply with the treatments offered by their providers.

For psychotherapy, a comprehensive meta-analysis of 669 studies involving more than 83,000 patients revealed the issue of patients dropping out of therapy has continued for many decades (Swift & Greenberg, 2012). Although premature termination is occurring at a lower rate than was estimated 20 years ago (Wierzbicki & Pekarik, 1993), it remains a significant problem with one out of every five patients dropping out of psychotherapy treatment. The rate of discontinuation was found to be higher when patients were being treated for a personality disorder diagnosis (such as borderline personality), eating disorders, or when there was no one specific disorder identified. Of note, there was no difference in dropout rates due to which model of psychotherapy was employed. However, more experienced providers had lower dropout rates than those in training and those with less experience (Swift & Greenberg, 2012).

The problem is, if anything, even more pronounced in studies of medication where reviews have shown treatment nonadherence results often ranging from 30% to 60%, with the rate typically estimated at about 50% (Meichenbaum & Turk, 1987). Additionally, it has been found that patients with psychiatric disorders may have lower levels of compliance with drug regimens than do those with physical disorders (Cramer & Rosenheck, 1998). Patients receiving antipsychotics are of particular concern since their rate of medication compliance appears to be even more reduced than those obtained by patients with other mental disorder diagnoses (Ascher-Svanum, Zhu, Faries, Furiak, & Montgomery, 2009). Meichenbaum & Turk (1987) report a dropout rate as high as 75% for schizophrenic patients.

The realization that noncompliance or dropout is so prevalent in mental health cases has led some to conclude that medical and psychiatric training should devote more time to dealing with the psychosocial issue of how to manage the doctor–patient relationship. Thus, Mintz (2005) has emphasized that it is important for psychiatry trainees to learn that it is "crucial" to develop an understanding of intrapsychic and interpersonal dynamics, even for those focusing exclusively on delivering somatic treatments. For instance, it is imperative to recognize that offering—or not offering—medications may have profound meaning to the patient. To illustrate, the patient might interpret the physician's message to mean, "She is a caring doctor who wants to use these medications to make me feel better quickly" or "He must think I am very seriously ill and does not think I can get better on my own with only the help of psychotherapy." Also, specific medications can have an idiosyncratic meaning. For example, "He said this medication is more likely to help me because it helped my mother but, God, I'd rather die than be like my mother!"

Chaplin and his colleagues (Chaplin, Lilliott, Quirk, & Seale, 2007) point to the need for consulting psychiatrists to master "negotiating styles" when prescribing antipsychotic medications. They advocate for careful listening, developing strong interpersonal skills, and becoming sensitive to differentiating when situations may require directive or nondirective interaction styles.

PRACTICE RECOMMENDATIONS FOR REDUCING DROPOUT

Attempts have been made to come up with clinical recommendations to reduce the likelihood of patients discontinuing treatment prematurely. For example, Swift, Greenberg, Whipple, & Kominiak (2012) detailed a number of practice strategies, based on the empirical literature, for dealing with the dropout problem. Though they emphasized findings derived from the psychotherapy literature, the suggestions can be applied to medication or combination approaches as well.

The first suggestion has to do with paying special attention to patient preferences. This may involve an assessment of patients' values, desires, or wants regarding the type of treatment that is to be implemented. Included could be a discussion of thoughts about medications, psychotherapy, or their combination, as well as the type of clinician the patient would most like working with, and the roles of the patient and the provider in working together. In fact, the American Psychological Association (APA Presidential Task Force on Evidence-Based Practice, 2006) has recommended that patient preferences be integrated into treatment planning and decision making as an important component of evidence-based practice. Research supports this idea. A meta-analysis of 18 studies demonstrated that patients whose preferences were taken into account were about half as likely to drop out of treatment no matter what their diagnosis or expressed type of treatment preference (drugs, psychotherapy, or combination) (Swift, Callahan, & Vollmer, 2011). Discussing preference does not mean that the practitioner automatically accedes to the patient's initial choice. Often patients are not aware of what the range of options might be for their particular situation. Instead, it can become an opportunity for the clinician to share information about what is known about a disorder and the best ways to deal with the problem. The end result would then be a collaborative decision about which approach might be most useful.

A second suggestion put forth by Swift, Greenberg, and their colleagues (2012) for reducing patient dropout has to do with educating patients about what to expect regarding treatment duration and patterns of change. As documented by Swift, Callahan, and Vollmer (2011), patients often hold incorrect or unrealistic expectations about what will happen in their treatment, how long it will take, what kinds of side effects may appear, and what kinds of benefits will result from therapy. Frequently, there may be a mismatch between what the clinician expects based on experience and reading the literature and unrealistic patient beliefs fed by advertisements, commercials, and an understandable desire for fast, almost magical solutions. Frank discussion may help patients to adjust their beliefs and stay with treatment as its course unfolds over ups and downs and a duration that may exceed initial expectations.

Another important suggestion for reducing the likelihood of premature patient termination has to do with helping patients strengthen hope about a positive outcome with treatment (Swift & Greenberg, 2012; Greenberg, Constantino, & Bruce, 2006). Belief in treatment is an important factor in motivating patient desire to continue. In fact, positive expectations for recovery have been viewed as explaining as much as 15% of the variability in therapy success (Norcross & Lambert, 2011). Frank and Frank's classic discussion of the nature of persuasion and healing in treatment (Frank & Frank, 1991) leads to the idea that hope can be aroused by the ways in which practitioners present themselves and their proposed interventions. Patients are more likely to have faith in a treatment that is presented by an individual who appears professional, shows expert knowledge about the agreed upon treatment approach, and presents a logical, credible explanation for how improvement will come about. The provider's confidence that treatment is apt to work is also helpful in instilling positive expectations (Constantino, Glass, Arnkoff, Ametrano, & Smith, 2011).

An additional research-driven suggestion for reducing premature termination comes from using periodic feedback from patients to monitor the course of treatment. A number of formal rating systems to evaluate patient progress have been proposed (Lambert, Hansen, & Finch, 2001; Miller, Duncan, Sorrell, & Brown, 2005). These systems clue providers in on whether treatment is moving in a positive or negative direction, allowing for a mid-course discussion and correction.

A review of studies examining the effects of patient feedback to clinicians about progress revealed significant favorable effects for patients whose doctors requested and received regular feedback about their progress (Lambert & Shimokawa, 2011). Patients who provided feedback to their doctors evidenced significantly better posttreatment outcomes, were more likely to show reliable gains in therapy, and were less likely to end treatment with a poor outcome.

Perhaps the most important element for achieving a successful treatment result lies in the creation of a collaborative treatment alliance. The treatment relationship and the role it plays in outcome is likely the most studied psychosocial factor in the research literature. It is often thought of as the main variable that underlies the discovery that different approaches (both biological and psychotherapeutic) can result in equally positive outcomes (Greenberg, 2012). The most widely accepted definition of the working alliance was presented by Bordin (1979). His definition indicated that the alliance is composed of an agreement between patient and clinician on the goals and tasks of therapy and the bond that exists between them.

The alliance construct has been found to be related to treatment outcome (Horvath, Del Re, Fluckiger, & Symonds, 2011), and, as would be expected, a meta-analysis of relevant studies has demonstrated that the strength of the alliance is positively related to lowering the probability of patient dropout (Sharf, Primavera, & Diener, 2010).

Given the research evidence, it follows that facilitating a positive treatment alliance would both lower dropout and increase benefits for those treated with medications, psychotherapy, or some combination of the two. It is especially important that efforts to strengthen the relationship occur early in treatment when the connections are first forming and the risk for nonadherence is highest. How might this be done? First, efforts need to be made in creating an agreement on the tasks and goals of the treatment. This can come from promoting patient discussion about their thoughts and preferences regarding treatment type, their concerns regarding collaboration, and routine feedback from patients about how they think the treatment is going (Tryon & Winograd, 2011). Obviously, benefits will also accrue from perceiving the clinician as empathic, warm, and nonjudgmental.

THE "DIFFICULT-TO-TREAT" PATIENT

Elsewhere, Dewan and Pies (2001) have addressed the generic factors that lead to psychiatric patients being labeled "difficult to treat." These include patient factors (inability to form a therapeutic alliance, nonadherence, severity of illness) and treatment provider factors (unempathic, cold, judgmental, and lacking in skill or knowledge). Even when all parties are well intentioned and have a good working alliance, studies indicate that many patients will be "difficult to treat." For example, a large prospective investigation of 3,671 patients titled the Sequenced Treatment Alternatives to Relieve Depression (STAR*D) revealed how difficult it is to treat depression with medications alone in the real world (Fava et al., 2003; Rush et al., 2004; Rush et al., 2006). The project demonstrated that even when using adequate antidepressant dosages and treatment durations and allowing medications to be switched or augmented over a series of four different treatment steps, the majority of patients did not achieve remission. Adding cognitive-behavior therapy as an option did not produce any better results. Similar disappointing results with antipsychotic medications were revealed in the so-called "Catie" study of schizophrenia treatment (Clinical Antipsychotic Trials of Intervention Effectiveness) (Lieberman et al., 2005). Here, both new and older antipsychotic medications were found to be comparably effective but were associated with high rates of discontinuation as a result of intolerable side effects or lack of adequate symptom control.

When confronted with a patient who is not doing well, it is important to take a step back. Was the diagnosis right? Is there an additional condition that was missed (e.g., 15% of severely depressed patients have psychotic symptoms and need an antipsychotic medication added to their antidepressant for an optimal response)? Was the dose and duration of the medication trials adequate? Was the psychotherapy they received disorder specific? For instance, a patient with OCD is much more likely to benefit from exposure and response prevention behavior therapy than from supportive therapy. It should be noted that just as psychosocial factors improve the effectiveness of medications, at times the use of medication allows for successful psychotherapeutic intervention. A psychotic patient needs to respond adequately to medication before family therapy or cognitive behavioral therapy can be usefully attempted. Similarly, some patients with OCD need to have their symptoms reduced by medications before they can face the increased anxiety of behavior therapy.

COMBINING MEDICATIONS AND PSYCHOTHERAPY

It has been well documented that some disorders require a combination of medications and psychotherapy for optimal outcomes (Dewan & Pies, 2001). While antipsychotics are a first-line remedy for the treatment of schizophrenia, one or more psychotherapeutic interventions are also helpful. These include family therapy, personal therapy, and cognitive behavioral therapy (Hogarty, Greenwald et al., 1997; Hogarty, Kornblith et al., 1997; Sadock, Sadock, & Ruiz, 2009). Similarly, for patients with bipolar disorder, it is necessary to combine a mood stabilizing medication with some form of psychotherapy, such as psychoeducational therapies aimed at illness management, cognitive behavioral approaches, interpersonal and social rhythms therapy, and family-focused therapy (Sadock et al., 2009). Even disorders that are treated primarily with psychotherapy frequently benefit from adding medication at some point in the course of treatment. For instance, patients suffering from borderline personality disorder may be primarily treated with long-term psychotherapy. However, they will at times suffer severe regressions and micro-psychotic episodes, which may respond to brief periods of low-dose antipsychotics. Similarly, they may lapse into persistent depression that responds to the addition of antidepressants (American Psychiatric Association, 2010).

Greenberg and Goldman (2009) have presented a review of the benefits that might be obtained from combining or not combining medications with psychotherapy for depression. They note that since each of the types of treatment (biological or psychological) has received empirical support, it could be logically theorized that the combination might routinely be more powerful than either treatment delivered alone. They cite several studies that do not support this speculation. However, the evidence does indicate that in the case of difficult-to-treat depressed patients, those whose depressions are more severe, the combination is preferable. Evidence for this occurs in a study by de Maat and colleagues (2007). Their meta-analysis of seven studies of 903 patients showed that combined treatments were more effective than psychotherapy alone, but *only* in patients with relatively severe, repetitive, chronic episodes of depression. Similar results were also reported by Friedman et al. (2004), who demonstrated across 17 studies that adding psychotherapy to antidepressants turned out to be most useful when patients were suffering with chronic or severe depressions. Comparable sentiments were expressed by Jindal and Thase (2003), who noted that there is little scientific reason to combine treatments in the usual care of milder or less severe depressions. Their recommendation for most cases was to rely on patient preferences and treatment availability. Greenberg and Goldman (2009) document in their review that psychotherapy might be considered as the initial treatment to be tried for most cases of depression because it is less likely to lead to relapse when terminated, produces fewer side effects, and appears to be the treatment that more patients would opt for if given the choice.

Patients whose primary treatment is medication (e.g., patients with schizophrenia) may also get a disorder-specific psychotherapy when available or receive supportive therapy for illness management, increased adherence, or decreasing the potential for suicide. Patients whose primary treatment is psychotherapy will often get medications targeted to specific symptoms (e.g., anxiety, depression or micro-psychotic episodes). It can be safely concluded then that a large percentage of patients will receive combined treatment.

SPLIT VERSUS COLLABORATIVE CARE

As noted above, there is increasing data to support the common wisdom that "difficult-to-treat" patients do better on a combination of psychotherapy and medication. Both these modalities can be provided as integrated treatment by a psychiatrist, which is time efficient and cost effective. Or, as often the case, care is "split" between a psychologist or social worker therapist and a prescribing psychiatrist, which allows for a greater range of expertise. When the patient, therapist, and prescriber are on the same page and working well together, "split" treatment is effective "collaborative" treatment. However, "split" treatment has the potential for the patient splitting the therapist–prescriber dyad and for mis- or noncommunication between the treatment providers, neither of whom gets reimbursed for the time it takes for regular collaboration (Dewan, 2012). Studies (Avena & Kalman, 2010; Kalman, Kalman, & Granet, 2012) show that, in fact, collaboration usually does not occur; this may contribute to some patients continuing to be "difficult to treat."

CONCLUSION

In order to best serve our patients, we need to employ one or several treatments from amongst all the evidence-based, specific treatments available for a particular condition. For optimal effectiveness of medication alone, psychotherapy alone, or combined modalities, treatment must be delivered by a caring, empathic, nonjudgmental treatment provider who is sensitive to the contribution of psychosocial factors and who works at informing the patient of all treatment options while establishing a robust, collaborative, working alliance. Next, patients do best with evidence-based, disorder-specific treatments; often a combination of two or more biological and psychotherapeutic modalities is useful for obtaining maximum benefit. If this combined approach is provided by two treatment providers—as is so often the case—a concerted effort must be made to prevent "split" treatment and to form a collaborative alliance that respects and maximizes the expertise of both treatment providers to the benefit of their common patient. When done well, this collaboration increases the chances of a good outcome and often makes working with even difficult-to-treat patients both manageable and rewarding.

REFERENCES

American Psychiatric Association. (2010). *APA practice guidelines for the treatment of patients with major depressive disorder* (3rd ed.). Arlington, VA: Author.

APA Presidential Task Force on Evidence-Based Practice. (2006). Evidence-based practice in psychology. *American Psychologist, 61,* 271–285.

Ascher-Svanum, H., Zhu, B., Faries, D. E., Furiak, N. M., & Montgomery, W. (2009). Medication adherence levels and differential use of mental-health services in the treatment of schizophrenia. *BMC Research Notes, 2,* 6.

Avena, J., & Kalman, T. (2010). Do psychotherapists speak to psychopharmacologists? A survey of practicing clinicians. *Journal of the American Academy of Psychoanalysis and Dynamic Psychiatry, 38,* 675–683.

Baldwin, S. A., Wampold, B. E., & Imel, Z. E. (2007). Untangling the alliance-outcome correlation: Exploring the relative importance of therapist and patient variability in the alliance. *Journal of Consulting and Clinical Psychology, 75,* 842–852.

Baxter, L. R., Jr., Schwartz, J. M., Bergman, K. S., Szuba, M. P., Guze, B. H., Mazziotta, J. C., et al. (1992). Caudate glucose metabolic rate changes with both drug and behavior therapy for obsessive-compulsive disorder. *Archives of General Psychiatry, 49,* 681–689.

Blatt, S. J., Sanislow, C. A., III, Zuroff, D. C., & Pilkonis, P. A. (1996). Characteristics of effective therapists: Further analyses of data from the National Institute of Mental Health Treatment of Depression Collaborative Research Program. *Journal of Consulting and Clinical Psychology, 64,* 1276–1284.

Blatt, S. J., Zuroff, D. C., Quinlan, D. M., & Pilkonis, P. (1996). Interpersonal factors in brief treatment of depression: Further analyses of the NIMH treatment of depression collaborative research program. *Journal of Consulting and Clinical Psychology, 64,* 162–171.

Bordin, E. S. (1979). The generalizability of the psychoanalytic concept of the working alliance. *Psychotherapy: Theory, Research, and Practice, 16,* 252–260.

Chaplin, R., Lilliott, P., Quirk, A., & Seale, C. (2007). Negotiating styles adopted by consultant psychiatrists when prescribing antipsychotics. *Advances in Psychiatric Treatment, 13,* 43–50.

Constantino, M. J., Glass, C. R., Arnkoff, D. B., Ametrano, R. M., & Smith, J. Z. (2011). Expectations. In J. C. Norcross (Ed.), *Psychotherapy relationships that work* (2nd ed., pp. 354–376). New York: Oxford University Press.

Cramer, J. A., & Rosenheck, R. (1998). Compliance with medication regimens for mental and physical disorders. *Psychiatry Services (Washington, D.C.), 49,* 196–201.

de Maat, S., Dekker, J., Schoevers, R., & DeJonghe, F. (2007). Relative efficacy of psychotherapy and pharmacotherapy in the treatment of depression. A meta-analysis. *European Psychiatry, 22,* 1–8.

Dewan, M. J. (2012). Combined brief therapy and medications. In M. J. Dewan, B. N. Steenbarger, & R. P. Greenberg (Eds.), *The art and science of brief psychotherapies: An illustrated guide* (2nd ed., pp. 279–286). Arlington, VA: American Psychiatric Publishing.

Dewan, M. J., & Pies, R. (Eds.). (2001). *The difficult to treat psychiatric patient.* Washington, DC: American Psychiatric Press.

Dewan, M. J., Steenbarger, B. N., & Greenberg, R. P. (2008). Brief psychotherapies. In R. E. Hales, S. C. Yudofsky, & G. O. Gabbard (Eds.), *The American Psychiatric Publishing textbook of psychiatry* (5th ed., pp. 1155–1170). Washington, DC: American Psychiatric Publishing.

Elkin, I., Shea, M. T., Watkins, J. T., Imber, S. D., Sotsky, S. M., Collins, J. F., et al. (1989). National Institute of Mental Health Treatment of Depression Collaborative Research Program. General effectiveness of treatments. *Archives of General Psychiatry, 46,* 971–982.

Evans, F. J. (1985). Expectancy, therapeutic instructions, and the placebo response. In L. White, B. Tursky, & G. E. Schwartz (Eds.), *Placebo: Theory, research and mechanisms* (pp. 215–234). New York: Guilford Press.

Fava, M., Rush, A. J., Trivedi, M. H., Nierenberg, A. A., Thase, M. E., Sackeim, H. A., et al. (2003). Background and rationale for the sequenced treatment alternatives to relieve depression (STAR*D) study. *Special Issue: Drug Therapy: Predictors of Response, 26,* 457–494.

Fisher, S., & Greenberg, R. P. (Eds.). (1989). *The limits of biological treatments for psychological distress: Comparisons with psychotherapy and placebo.* Hillsdale, NJ: Lawrence Erlbaum Associates, Inc.

Fisher, S., & Greenberg, R. P. (Eds.). (1997). *From placebo to panacea: Putting psychiatric drugs to the test.* New York: John Wiley & Sons, Inc.

Frank, J. D., & Frank, J. B. (1991). *Persuasion and healing: A comparative study of psychotherapy* (3rd ed.). Baltimore, MD: Johns Hopkins University Press.

Friedman, M. A., Detweiler-Bedell, J. B., Leventhal, H. E., Horne, R., Keitner, G. I., & Miler, I. W. (2004). Combined psychotherapy and pharmacotherapy for the treatment of major depressive disorder. *Clinical Psychology: Science and Practice, 11,* 47–68.

Greenberg, R. P. (2012). Essential ingredients for successful psychotherapy: Effect of common factors. In M. J. Dewan, B. N. Steenbarger, & R. P. Greenberg (Eds.), *The art and science of brief psychotherapies* (2nd ed., pp. 15–25). Washington, DC: American Psychiatric Press.

Greenberg, R. P., Constantino, M. J., & Bruce, N. (2006). Are patient expectations still relevant for psychotherapy process and outcome? *Clinical Psychology Review, 26,* 657–678.

Greenberg, R. P., & Fisher, S. (1989). Examining antidepressant effectiveness: Findings, ambiguities and some vexing puzzles. In S. Fisher & R. P. Greenberg (Eds.), *The limits of biological treatments for psychological distress: Comparisons with psychotherapy and placebo* (pp. 1–37). Hillsdale, NJ: Lawrence Erlbaum Associates, Inc.

Greenberg, R. P., & Fisher, S. (1997). Mood-mending medicines probing drug, psychotherapy, and placebo solutions. In S. Fisher & R. P. Greenberg (Eds.), *From placebo to panacea: Putting psychiatric drugs to the test* (pp. 115–172). New York: John Wiley & Sons, Inc.

Greenberg, R. P., & Goldman, E. D. (2009). Antidepressants, psychotherapy or their combination: Weighing options for depression treatments. *Journal of Contemporary Psychotherapy, 39,* 83–91.

Greenblatt, M., Grosser, G. H., & Wechsler, H. (1964). Differential response of hospitalized depressed patients to somatic therapy. *American Journal of Psychiatry, 120,* 935–943.

Hogarty, G. E., Greenwald, D., Ulrich, R. F., Kornblith, S. J., DiBarry, A. L., Cooley, S., et al. (1997). Three-year trials of personal therapy among schizophrenic patients living with or independent of family, II: Effects on adjustment of patients. *The American Journal of Psychiatry, 154,* 1514–1524.

Hogarty, G. E., Kornblith, S. J., Greenwald, D., DiBarry, A. L., Cooley, S., Ulrich, R. F., et al. (1997). Three-year trials of personal therapy among schizophrenic patients living with or independent of family, I: Description of study and effects on relapse rates. *The American Journal of Psychiatry, 154,* 1504–1513.

Horvath, A. O., Del Re, A. C., Fluckiger, C., & Symonds, D. (2011). Alliance in individual psychotherapy. *Psychotherapy (Chicago, Ill.), 48,* 9–16.

Jindal, R. D., & Thase, M. E. (2003). Integrating psychotherapy and pharmacotherapy to improve outcomes among patients with mood disorders. *Psychiatric Services, 54,* 1484–1490.

Kalman, T., Kalman, V., & Granet, R. (2012). Do psychopharmacologists speak to psychotherapists? A survey of practicing clinicians. *Psychodynamic Psychiatry, 40,* 275.

Khan, A., Warner, H. A., & Brown, W. A. (2000). Symptom reduction and suicide risk in patients treated with placebo in antidepressant clinical trials: An analysis of the food and drug administration database. *Archives of General Psychiatry, 57,* 311–317.

Kirsch, I., Deacon, B. J., Huedo-Medina, T. B., Scoboria, A., Moore, T. J., & Johnson, B. T. (2008). Initial severity and anti-depressant benefits: A meta-analysis of data submitted to the Food and Drug Administration. *PLoS Medicine/Public Library of Science, 5,* 260–268.

Kirsch, I., Moore, T. J., Scoboria, A., & Nicholls, S. S. (2002). The emperor's new drugs: An analysis of antidepressant medication data submitted to the U.S. Food and Drug Administration. *Prevention and Treatment, 5,* 1.

Kradin, R. (2008). *The placebo response and the power of unconscious healing.* New York: Routledge.

Krupnick, J. L., Sotsky, S. M., Simmens, S., Moyer, J., Elkin, I., Watkins, J., et al. (1996). The role of the therapeutic alliance in psychotherapy and pharmacotherapy outcome: Findings in the National Institute of Mental Health Treatment of Depression Collaborative Research Program. *Journal of Consulting & Clinical Psychology, 64,* 532–539.

Lambert, M. J., Hansen, N. B., & Finch, A. E. (2001). Patient-focused research: Using patient outcome data to enhance treatment effects. *Journal of Consulting and Clinical Psychology, 69,* 159–172.

Lambert, M. J., & Shimokawa, K. (2011). Collecting client feedback. In J. C. Norcross (Ed.), *Psychotherapy relationships that work* (2nd ed., pp. 203–223). New York: Oxford University Press.

Lambert, M. J., Whipple, J. L., Hawkins, E. J., Vermeersch, D. A., Nielsen, S. L., & Smart, D. W. (2003). Is it time for clinicians to routinely track patient outcome? A meta-analysis. *Clinical Psychology: Science and Practice, 10,* 288–301.

Lieberman, J. A., Stroup, T. S., McEvoy, J. P., Swartz, M. S., Rosenheck, R. A., Perkins, D. O., et al. (2005). Effectiveness of antipsychotic drugs in patients with chronic schizophrenia. *New England Journal of Medicine, 353,* 1209–1223.

Mayberg, H. S., Silva, J. A., Brannan, S. K., Tekell, J. L., Mahurin, R. K., McGinnis, S., et al. (2002). The functional neuroanatomy of the placebo effect. *The American Journal of Psychiatry, 159,* 728–737.

McRae, C., Cherin, E., Yamazaki, T. G., Diem, G., Vo, A. H., Russell, D., et al. (2004). Effects of perceived treatment on quality of life and medical outcomes in a double-blind placebo surgery trial. *Archives of General Psychiatry, 61,* 412–420.

Meichenbaum, D., & Turk, D. C. (1987). *Facilitating treatment adherence: A practitioner's guidebook.* New York: Plenum.

Miller, S. D., Duncan, B. L., Sorrell, R., & Brown, G. S. (2005). The partners for change outcome management system. *Journal of Clinical Psychology, 61,* 199–208.

Mintz, D. L. (2005). Teaching the prescriber's role: The psychology of psychopharmacology. *Academic Psychiatry: The Journal of the American Association of Directors of Psychiatric Residency Training and the Association for Academic Psychiatry, 29,* 187–194.

Moseley, J. B., O'Malley, K., Petersen, N. J., Menke, T. J., Brody, B. A., Kuykendall, D. H., et al. (2002). A controlled trial of arthroscopic surgery for osteoarthritis of the knee. *The New England Journal of Medicine, 347,* 81–88.

Norcross, J. C., & Lambert, M. J. (2011). Evidence-based therapy relationships. In J. C. Norcross (Ed.), *Psychotherapy relationships that work* (2nd ed., pp. 3–21). New York: Oxford University Press.

Rush, A. J., Fava, M., Wisniewski, S. R., Lavori, P. W., Trivedi, M. H., Sackeim, H. A., et al. (2004). Sequenced treatment alternatives to relieve depression (STAR*D): Rationale and design. *Controlled Clinical Trials, 25,* 119–142.

Rush, A. J., Trivedi, M. H., Wisniewski, S. R., Nierenberg, A. A., Stewart, J. W., Warden, D., et al. (2006). Acute and longer-term outcomes in depressed outpatients requiring one or several treatment steps: A STAR*D report. *American Journal of Psychiatry, 163,* 1905–1917.

Sadock, B., Sadock, V., & Ruiz, P. (2009). *Kaplan and Sadock's comprehensive textbook of psychiatry* (9th ed.). Baltimore: Williams & Wilkins.

Sauro, M. D. & Greenberg, R. P. (2005). Endogenous opiates and the placebo effect; A meta-analytic review. *Journal of Psychosomatic Research, 58,* 115–120.

Sharf, J., Primavera, L. H., & Diener, M. J. (2010). Dropout and therapeutic alliance: A meta-analysis of adult individual psychotherapy. *Psychotherapy (Chicago, Ill.), 47,* 637–645.

Swift, J. K., Callahan, J. L., & Vollmer, B. M. (2011). Preferences. *Journal of Clinical Psychology, 67,* 155–165.

Swift, J. K., & Greenberg, R. P. (2012). Premature discontinuation in adult psychotherapy: A meta-analysis. *Journal of Consulting and Clinical Psychology, 80,* 547–599.

Swift, J. K., Greenberg, R. P., Whipple, J., & Kominiak, N. (2012). Practice recommendations for reducing premature termination in therapy. *Professional Psychology: Research and Practice, 43,* 379–387.

Thase, M. E., & Kupfer, D. J. (1996). Recent developments in the pharmacotherapy of mood disorders. *Journal of Consulting and Clinical Psychology, 64,* 646–659.

Tryon, G. S., & Winograd, G. (2011). Goal consensus and collaboration. In J. C. Norcross (Ed.), *Psychotherapy relationships that work* (2nd ed., pp. 153–167). New York: Oxford University Press.

Wierzbicki, M., & Pekarik, G. (1993). A meta-analysis of psychotherapy dropout. *Professional Psychology: Research and Practice, 24,* 190–195.

Index

Note: Page numbers in *italics* indicate figures and tables.